GOVERNMENT AND POLITICS
IN SOUTH ASIA

SEVENTH EDITION

GOVERNMENT *and* POLITICS *in* SOUTH ASIA

Robert C. Oberst

Yogendra K. Malik

Charles H. Kennedy

Ashok Kapur

Mahendra Lawoti

Syedur Rahman

Ahrar Ahmad

WESTVIEW
PRESS

A Member of the Perseus Books Group

Westview Press was founded in 1975 in Boulder, Colorado, by notable publisher and intellectual Fred Praeger. Westview Press continues to publish scholarly titles and high-
quality undergraduate- and graduate-level textbooks in core social science disciplines.
With books developed, written, and edited with the needs of serious nonfiction readers,
professors, and students in mind, Westview Press honors its long history of publishing
books that matter.

Copyright © 2014 by Westview Press
Published by Westview Press,
A Member of the Perseus Books Group

Parts of this publication were originally published in East-West Center *Policy Studies* 43,
titled "Looking Back, Looking Forward: Centralization, Multiple Conflicts, and Democratic State Building in Nepal," and also in *Contentious Politics and Democratization in
Nepal* (Sage, 2007), edited by Mahendra Lawoti.

Every effort has been made to secure required permissions for all text, images, maps, and
other art reprinted in this volume.

Westview Press books are available at special discounts for bulk purchases in the United
States by corporations, institutions, and other organizations. For more information, please
contact the Special Markets Department at the Perseus Books Group, 2300 Chestnut
Street, Suite 200, Philadelphia, PA 19103, or call (800) 810-4145, ext. 5000, or e-mail
special.markets@perseusbooks.com.

Designed by Linda Mark

A CIP catalog record for the print version of this book is available from the Library of
Congress
PB ISBN: 978-0-8133-4879-7
EBOOK ISBN: 978-0-8133-4880-3

10 9 8 7 6 5 4 3 2 1

As in the past editions, this book is dedicated to our wives:

Usha Malik

Patricia A. Poe (Kennedy)

Kathy Shellogg (Oberst)

Deepika Kapur

Tannaz Khosrowshahi (Rahman)

Geeta G. Lawoti

Hasina Ahmad

CONTENTS

LIST OF TABLES
AND ILLUSTRATIONS

ix

MAPS

FIGURES

PREFACE TO THE SEVENTH EDITION

The seventh edition of this book marks its continued transformation since it was first published in 1987. We continue to mourn the loss of our colleague and friend Craig Baxter, who died on February 7, 2008. Without Craig this book would never have been published. His tireless effort and determination ensured that the first and later editions went to press. We have missed him dearly.

As in the sixth edition, we continue with the chapters on Nepal. Finally, the primary authorship of the Bangladesh chapters is a collaborative effort by Syedur Rahman and Ahrar Ahmad, and the Indian chapters are a collaborative effort by Ashok Kapur and Yogendra Malik.

With these changes the book continues its second generation of authors. Twenty years ago, none of us ever expected the book to last as long as it has. The original four authors believed there was a need for a book that examined all of South Asia rather than just India. Our original optimism has been reinforced by the support for the book over the first six editions. The South Asia we wrote about in 1987 no longer exists. It has been transformed by the changes sweeping across Asia. We have tried to keep up with those changes.

We wish to thank especially those at Westview Press. While we have worked with many at Westview Press over the years, we wish to thank Toby Wahl, who worked with us on this edition.

Our thanks and appreciation for the patience and encouragement of our wives is shown in the dedication of this work to them.

Robert C. Oberst
Yogendra K. Malik
Charles H. Kennedy
Ashok Kapur

Mahendra Lawoti
Syedur Rahman
Ahrar Ahmad

1

Introduction

To most people in North America, the Indian subcontinent is an exotic land of maharajas and sadhus. It holds a special place as part of the distant Orient. However, while our stereotypes continue to dominate the way we view the subcontinent, India and its neighbors have increasingly begun to play a major role in international affairs and the international economy and are thus an important subject for study and better understanding.

The subcontinent's population makes it significant. First, with a population of over 1.6 billion, or nearly one-quarter of the people on earth, the Indian subcontinent cannot be ignored.[1] Second, its role in the world economy is of increasing consequence, particularly as regards the growth of the information technology industry and the subcontinent's role in manufacturing and exports. Culturally, Bollywood movies have an international audience, and the South Asian diaspora has developed a footprint in North America's economic, political, and social life. Finally, the region has become important to North American strategic interests. The events of 9/11 thrust the region into the awareness of every citizen of North America and Europe. Pakistan's remote hill territories are hiding places for US enemies; for the people of South Asia, they are a breeding ground for terrorism.

The following chapters describe the countries of South Asia and examine the reason for their successes and failures. Each of these nations is struggling to create a stable political environment that will allow for rapid economic growth and the resolution of its most serious problems.

South Asia is home to one of the world's oldest civilizations. The Harappan (or Indus Valley) civilization was one of the world's earliest cultures. Existing more than 3,500 years ago, it was a marvel among the societies of that era and laid the groundwork for the civilization that would become India. The region's geography would protect the subcontinent for nearly 2,000 years. The land routes to the west required travel across the Hindu Kush range of mountains or across the great desert of Balochistan. To the north lay the natural wall of the Himalayas, and to the east, the narrow ranges and jungles of Burma. The seas to the south provided the easiest access and would become the preferred route of invasion for waves of Europeans.

Although Alexander the Great came to Pakistan in the fourth century BC, the first permanent colonies were created by the Portuguese, followed by the Dutch, French, and British. Among them, the British would prevail and rule India for over two hundred years.

Before the Europeans, sporadic streams of invaders had come and conquered for a brief time. The residents of the subcontinent would absorb some elements of their cultures with each wave. The first Muslim invaders came in the eighth century; the Mughal Empire, established in 1504, created some of the world's most important architectural treasures, including the Taj Mahal. The Mughals would also leave a remarkable administrative legacy, which the British eventually would adopt.

When compared with other former European colonies, the subcontinent stands out as a refuge for democratic and stable political development. Although some of the countries of the region are struggling with democracy, democratic values have taken hold in most of them. Each of these countries is also evolving as a major source of scientific research and development. India and Pakistan have both exploded nuclear bombs, while their scientists have flocked to richer Western nations. The rise of information technology has opened up South Asia as no other event could have. Today, it is a center of software development and a manufacturing hub for Western companies in India.

The 2001 terrorist attacks on the World Trade Center and Pentagon forced the Western nations to focus on Afghanistan and Pakistan. The spread of a more militant version of Islam than that known in South Asia for nearly a millennium has begun to split and transform the region's 400 million Muslims. It has also generated increased concern and scrutiny among military planners in the United States and Western Europe.

Each of the South Asian states faces five critical areas of political development: nation building, state building, participation, economy building, and distribution of wealth and social benefits. Although India, Pakistan, and Sri Lanka inherited fairly effective state apparatuses, they are facing different challenges.

Following this chapter's introductory discussion of the political heritage of the British era, Parts I through V examine the five largest countries of the region: India, Pakistan, Bangladesh, Sri Lanka, and Nepal. Part VI addresses the interrelationships among the states in the region and their roles in the international system and ties the themes of the book to a discussion of the political development of the region as a whole.

European and British Expansion

The South Asian political systems and societies of the twenty-first century owe much to the influence of British colonial rule. While colonialism destroyed the right of the people to govern themselves and placed an alien ruler, located 5,000 miles away, in charge of their destinies, it did leave some positive and lasting effects.

While other former colonies in Asia and Africa have struggled in their efforts to create democratic governments, the South Asian nation-states have been much more successful. Although we discuss the countries of the subcontinent separately, it is important to understand their common historical experience and the influence of British colonialism. The British did not rule the region as a single colony. The countries of India, Pakistan, and Bangladesh were part of the British colony of India, while Sri Lanka was a separate Crown colony, and Nepal was never a formal colony but rather a protectorate under British control. While we discuss them individually, their common British experience has helped to shape the success these nations have experienced in nation building. Although the British influence has been important in shaping the independent nations of the region, however, the experience was not all positive. The success of the people of the subcontinent in taking advantage of the positive contributions of the British and overcoming the negative influences is a testament to the resiliency of South Asian culture and its people.[2]

It is easy to forget that the British were not the first Europeans to arrive on the subcontinent. Vasco da Gama visited on his voyage of discovery around the Cape of Good Hope in Africa in 1498. He left a few Portuguese representatives behind to set up a trading post. In 1503, the Portuguese would set up the first European outpost in South Asia at Cochin, in what is now the South Indian state of Kerala. The Portuguese would spend the next century expanding their control of South Asia along India's western coast and in Sri Lanka. For the next 150 years the trading language of the region would be Portuguese. In 1600, Queen Elizabeth I presented a charter forming the British East India Company, with the British arriving at Surat (in present-day Gujarat) in 1612. The British would slowly establish their control of India in the face of the Portuguese who were already there and the Mughal Empire, ruled from Delhi, which challenged their ability to control the region. The Dutch East India Company, formed in 1602, also coveted the riches of South Asia and began to establish trading outposts along the coast of India and in Sri Lanka. In 1608, it would establish its headquarters on the Coromondal coast near Madras. After a series of failed attempts, the French established their first factory in India in 1668 at Surat.[3]

The British East India Company would be given a monopoly over all British trade with India. As the company expanded, it was forced to undertake more administrative and government functions, including maintaining an army for protection. The company would create the city of Calcutta in East India and establish its headquarters there until the British government dissolved the company and took over direct rule of India in 1862.

The first European efforts to establish economic and political control over South Asia encountered one major obstacle: the Mughal Empire. The Mughals were western and central Asians who had conquered India in 1526 and established a remarkable record of architectural, artistic, educational, and political accomplishments during their rule. The Mughals did not rule all of India, since several southern Hindu kingdoms resisted conquest. They did, however, rule from the Khyber Pass to Bengal across the north and as far south as the Deccan Plateau. The Mughals were the last of a series of Muslim dynasties that ruled India from the eleventh century onward.

Mughal rule was marked by great decentralization. The Mughals allowed a number of Hindu kingdoms to exist autonomously as long as they pledged to support the Mughal leadership. The first Europeans arrived as the Mughal Empire was founded (1526) and began establishing outposts as the empire peaked in its power and influence in the seventeenth century under the leadership of Jahangir and Shah Jahan. The overthrow of Shah Jahan by his son in 1657 marked the beginning of the decline of the empire. The decline would be hastened by the Europeans, especially the British, who would make alliances with Hindu kings seeking more autonomy from the Mughal leadership. The Mughal Empire would decline in power after 1750. The last emperor was exiled to Burma in 1858 after participating in the 1857 Sepoy Mutiny against the British.

In the last years of the empire, the British and the Europeans controlled the coastal areas of the country, gradually leaving the Mughals with control of only the Gangetic Plain (modern-day Uttar Pradesh) and finally the city of Delhi. After the collapse of the Mughals, the British maintained most of the Mughal administration and gradually imposed their rule. Their piecemeal approach resulted in two forms of control over the subcontinent. Some of the territory acquired by the British East India Company was ruled directly by the British governor-general and described as British India. It comprised 60 percent of the territory of India and two-thirds of the population.

The other territories were obtained through agreements with local rulers. These areas are usually called princely states. At the time of independence in 1947, there were more than five hundred of them. The British negotiated a separate agreement with each princely state, although they usually granted them autonomy while maintaining control over their foreign affairs, defense, and other matters.

The Mutiny and Its Aftermath

A defining moment of British rule was the 1857 Indian or Sepoy Mutiny (which many Indian nationalists refer to as the first war of independence). The causes of the uprising are too complex to discuss in detail here; broadly speaking, it resulted from the British East India Company's arrogance in its dealings with the princely states and the Indian people. The revolt was a carefully coordinated uprising led by the sepoys, who were the foot soldiers of the British East India Company's army in India. Initially the Indians captured many important urban centers of British rule and killed many British people living in the country. Ultimately the British forces would regain control of the country, and British rule would continue.

In the end, the British East India Company was dissolved on September 1, 1858, and the British Crown assumed control of India. The British government recognized the need to be more responsive to the Indian population and began a series of reforms to avoid future rebellions.

The Indian Councils Act of 1861, passed by the British Parliament, created the Legislative Council, which would advise the Executive Council (cabinet of the viceroy). It included a number of appointed, nonofficial members, who could be Indians. While the Legislative Council did not provide effective representation to the Indian people, it was a beginning that would lead to greater demands for more representation.

The Indian National Congress was founded in 1885 and became an outspoken representative of the Indian people and an important force for greater Indian representation in the colonial government. Later, in 1906, the Muslim League was founded, and the two organizations worked to pressure the British to provide more representation.

In 1906, Viceroy Lord Minto endorsed a plan that would become the Government of India Act of 1909. The act, more commonly called the Morley-Minto reforms, allowed for elected representatives to the Legislative Council. It also allowed one Indian to be named to the Executive Council. However, its significance was the provision for twenty-seven elected Indian members and five appointed Indian members of the Legislative Council, in addition to the thirty-six appointed members who were almost all British. This provision provided for nearly equal representation for Indian and British members on the legislative body.

The other unique feature of the Morley-Minto reforms was the creation of separate representation for religious groups. Each seat on the council was assigned to one of the major religious groups in India (Hindus, Sikhs, and Muslims), and only the members of that group could vote for the seat. The seats were apportioned roughly on the basis of the population; thus, most went to Hindus.

The Indian National Congress opposed separate electorates for religious groups when they were first demanded in 1906. However, in 1916 both the Congress and the Muslim League held their annual meetings in Lucknow, India, at the same time. During the meetings the two groups signed an agreement (the Lucknow Agreement) in which the Congress accepted the demand for separate Muslim and Sikh representation on the Legislative Council. The agreement was negotiated by two of the most important figures during the colonial era and the march to Indian independence. The Muslim League was represented by Muhammed Ali Jinnah (1876–1948), the primary architect of the pact; among the Indian National Congress negotiators was Motilal Nehru (1861–1931), who would become president of the Congress in 1919. His son, Jawaharlal Nehru (1889–1964), granddaughter, Indira Gandhi (1917–1984), and great-grandson, Rajiv Gandhi (1944–1991), would all serve as prime ministers of independent India. Both the League and the Congress believed the British were about to grant further reforms.

While Lord Morley stated that the British had no intention of granting self-government to India, the British secretary of state for India, Edwin Montagu, told the British Parliament in 1917 that the policy of the British government was to gradually develop self-government. In consultation Viceroy Lord Chelmsford and Montagu would present what would become the Government of India Act of 1919. More commonly called the Montagu-Chelmsford reforms, the act would increase Indian representation on the Legislative Council to a majority. It would also create a bicameral system, with a Council of State with 60 members and a Central Legislative Assembly with 145 members; 32 of the 60 Council of State members would be elected Indians, and 97 of the 145 Central Legislative Assembly members would be elected Indians. The Executive Council of the viceroy would now have four British and three Indian members. While the act expanded the powers of the Executive and Legislative Councils, ultimate power rested in the hands of the British viceroy, who could declare any act to be of paramount importance and override their decisions.

Administratively, the British had divided India into provinces and princely states.[4] The Montagu-Chelmsford reforms created councils at the provincial level. Control over nation-building departments, including agriculture, public works, health, and education, was left with the provincial legislatures. Finance, revenue, and security remained directly under the control of the British governor. This system, called dyarchy, or dual rule, would allow a substantial amount of self-rule for the Indians—much more than the British had granted to any of its other colonies.

The Indian National Congress rejected the Montagu-Chelmsford reforms because they did not go far enough in moving India toward self-government. This rejection led to a split within the Congress movement. Mohandas Karamchand Gandhi (1869–1948), who had begun a mass movement of nonviolent resistance against the British, wanted more power granted to the Indians. His movement had broadened the Congress from its original roots of elitist British-educated intellectuals. The early leaders of the movement came from the country's British-speaking elite, who, for the most part, supported cooperation with the British. Led by Motilal Nehru, this wing of the Congress would contest the Legislative Council elections and become the largest bloc in the council. Both groups were severely affected by the Amritsar massacre of April 13, 1919, when British troops opened fire on unarmed peaceful demonstrators, killing 379 and wounding 1,200. The event galvanized both wings of the party and convinced many that independence was the only option for India.

The Montagu-Chelmsford reforms called for a review of the act to determine its effectiveness, which would lead to even greater dissatisfaction. A commission was created in 1927 to evaluate the movement toward self-government by the Montagu-Chelmsford reforms but failed to include an Indian member. In anger, the Indian National Congress prepared a constitution for India. The British rejected the constitutional proposal, and the Indian National Congress, at its 1929 annual meeting, demanded complete independence from Britain.

To slow the growing dissatisfaction with their rule, the British held a round-table conference in London in 1930. These efforts failed as differences between the Muslims and Hindus emerged, preventing the two groups from presenting a united front. The Indian nationalist leadership was beginning to sense that British rule in India was destined to end and increased its pressure on the British.

The British tried one more time to offer reforms leading to self-government. The Government of India Act of 1935 was an effort to create dyarchy at the national level and thus give the Indians more power and influence. The act also sought to make India into a federal system by giving some autonomy to the provincial (state) governments. However, the act was not implemented at the national level, and the federal provisions were blocked by the leaders of the princely states, who saw the reforms as eroding their limited autonomy.

British efforts for reform were stalled with the advent of World War II. The British restricted freedoms for the Indians and incurred the wrath of the Indian National Congress leadership. The viceroy unilaterally declared India at war without consulting the provincial or princely leaders. The Congress boycotted the government, while one nationalist, Subhas Chandra Bose, formed the Indian National Army and fought with the Japanese in Burma to over-throw the British. In response, the British jailed most of the Congress leader-ship for the duration of the war.[5]

During the war, opposition to the conflict would weaken the Indian National Congress and its influence with the British. Meanwhile, the Muslim League would pledge its full support to the British war effort and gain influence with the British.

Independence and Partition

At the end of World War II, the British were ready to give India its independence. They also appeared to support a united India. A British cabinet mission was sent to India in 1946 and proposed a loose federation for independent India. Under the proposal, the provinces would hold the most power, while the central government would be limited to defense, foreign affairs, currency, taxation, and communication. They also proposed that the provinces could come together into three regional groups, one of which would comprise the Punjab, Sindh, the North-West Frontier Province, and Balochistan. These provinces roughly correspond to modern-day Pakistan and would have been a Muslim-majority region. A second group would include Bengal and Assam in India's east and would also be a Muslim-majority group. The rest of India would comprise the third group and would have a Hindu majority. The plan was accepted by the Muslim League but rejected by the Congress. As a result, the proposal was abandoned.

Support for the creation of Hindu and Muslim states gained strength after the 1946 cabinet mission collapsed. The Congress reluctantly agreed to the partition, while the Muslim League actively advocated for it. Lord Mountbatten arrived in India in 1947 as the new viceroy and on June 3, 1947, announced his partition plan. The Indian provinces were divided on the basis of their religious makeup, with two noncontiguous sections, one in the west and the other in the east, together designated as Muslim Pakistan. The other provinces would become Hindu India. The 565 princely states were given the choice of which country to join. Seventy-two days later, India was divided, and on August 15, 1947, both countries were granted independence from Great Britain.[6]

The partition became one of the greatest man-made tragedies in history. Fifteen million people would be displaced and forced to flee to lands where they had never lived. Hundreds of thousands would die in the violence that each side would exact against the other. The wounds caused by the division have taken many decades to heal. More importantly, as the following chapters show, the trauma from the partition has helped define the challenges faced by its three resultant states: modern India, Pakistan, and Bangladesh. All three countries have sought to define their national identities and to overcome the anger and resentment left by the partition.

The Crown Colony of Ceylon

Ceylon (now Sri Lanka) was governed separately by the British. After the Portuguese arrived in 1505, they were forced out by the Dutch, and in 1802 the British established Ceylon as a Crown colony. Initially, the British controlled the coastal areas only. The Sri Lankan kingdom of Kandy continued to exist in the central hill country of the island and resisted efforts by each of the colonial powers to conquer it until the British finally succeeded in 1818.

Ceylon adapted more quickly to Western education and the British system of administration. As a result, the British were more willing to let the local population join the civil service of the colony. In addition, an Executive Council and a Legislative Council were created in 1833 as a result of a British-created reform commission, the Colebrooke Commission. In the 1920s, the legislative council was given a Sri Lankan majority, and both councils were given more power over finances than the Indian Legislative Council. Self-rule in Ceylon advanced more rapidly than it did in India. In 1931, a state council elected by the people took over much of the power of government. Although the governor still retained control, Ceylon was, for all practical purposes, self-governing.

As in India, a cabinet commission was sent to discuss independence in 1945. A constitution was modeled on the British Westminster system of government, and on February 4, 1948, Ceylon became an independent member of the British Commonwealth. Independence was achieved without the violence or conflict that accompanied Indian independence.

Nepal

Nepal's history during the British era differed from that of the other countries of the region. The Himalayas formed a barrier that blocked British expansion into the Himalayan countries (Tibet, Sikkim, Nepal, and Bhutan). However, the mountains did not completely eliminate British influence.

Nepal's modern era began with the conquest of the country under the king of Gurkha, Prithvi Narayan Shah, who captured the Kathmandu Valley in 1768 and established the Shah dynasty. Before the defeat of the kingdom of the Kathmandu Valley, his opponents had sought and received the assistance of the British East India Company. On his way to victory, Prithvi Narayan defeated the British in 1767.

The Nepalese went to war with the British from 1814 to 1816 over the strip of lowland at the foot of the Himalayas, the Terai region. Although the Nepalese inflicted large losses on the British, they were forced to cede large segments of the Terai to the British and to allow a British representative to be housed in Kathmandu. This increased British influence over Nepal but did not lead to British colonization of the country. In 1923, the British signed an agreement with the Nepalese accepting their independence.

The modern political systems of South Asia are a product of their past along with the events since the British left. The following chapters describe and analyze these events and reasons behind the current political affairs in the region.

SUGGESTED READINGS

Useful overviews of Indian history include Percival Spear, *A History of India,* Vol. 2, rev. ed. (London: Penguin Books, 1978), and Stanley Wolpert, *A New History of India,* 6th ed. (New York: Oxford University Press, 2000). For nearly encyclopedic coverage of the British period, see the venerable *Oxford History of India,* 4th ed. (New York: Oxford University Press, 1981); this is an update of the original work by Vincent A. Smith.

For information on Ceylon (Sri Lanka), see W. Howard Wriggins, *Ceylon: Dilemmas of a New Nation* (Princeton, NJ: Princeton University Press, 1960). For Nepal, see Leo E. Rose and John T. Scholz, *Nepal: Profile of a Himalayan Kingdom* (Boulder, CO: Westview Press, 1980).

For further discussions of specific topics in this and other chapters in this book, see Maureen L. P. Patterson, *South Asian Civilizations: A Bibliographic Synthesis* (Chicago: University of Chicago Press, 1981), which can be supplemented by the annual *Bibliography of Asian Studies,* published by the Association for Asian Studies, now online (www.asian-studies.org/aboutbas .htm).

NOTES

1. Data in this section is taken from World Bank, *The Complete World Development Report, 1978–2010* (New York: Oxford, 2010), and World Bank, *World Development Report 2012* (New York: Oxford, 2012).

2. For an insider's account, see Maurice Zinkin and Taya Zinkin, *Britain and India* (Baltimore: Johns Hopkins University Press, 1964). Maurice Zinkin served in India as a member of the famed Indian Civil Service.

3. The term "factory" referred to a place where traders and merchants gathered to carry on business in a foreign country.

4. The territorial divisions of British India were termed "provinces." The term is still used in Pakistan and was used in India until the 1950 constitution was enacted. Since then, in India, the major divisions have been termed "states."

5. See S. Bose, *His Majesty's Opponent: Subhas Chandra Bose and India's Struggle Against Empire* (Cambridge, MA: Harvard University Press, 2011).

6. See Larry Collins and Dominique Lapierre, *Freedom at Midnight* (New York: Avon Books, 1975); Alex von Tunzelmann, *Indian Summer: The Secret History of the End of an Empire* (Toronto: McClelland & Stewart Ltd., 2007).

PART I

INDIA

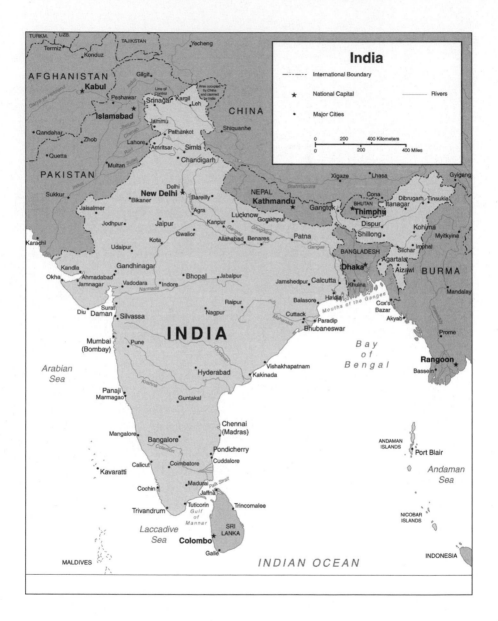

2

Political Culture and Heritage: A Changing Political Culture

India's difficulties in nation building, economic development, and political stability have been strongly influenced by a host of complex factors, most prominently its geographical setting, its sociocultural history, and a pattern of continuous external interventions. India is the largest state on the South Asian subcontinent. One-third the size of the United States—about 1,266,595 square miles—it is a country of great distances. From the Himalayas in the north to the Indian Ocean in the south, the distance is 2,000 miles, and it is some 1,700 miles from the western border with Pakistan to the eastern border with Burma. These distances and elevational changes mean that India has a wide variety of climates and landscapes, from snow-covered mountains and lush green forests to dry brown plains and sandy deserts.

Geographically, India is divided into three main regions, each with its own culture, traditions, and history. The various subregions add to the country's diversity of lifestyles and traditions. The first region consists of the vast plains of northern India, irrigated by the Ganges River and its tributaries. Originating in the Himalayas, the sacred Ganges runs more than 1,500 miles through several Indian states until it reaches the Bay of Bengal. The silt deposited by the river enriches the soil of the vast northern plains, where agriculture is the main livelihood of the people. In the Ganges Valley, the Hindu civilization flourished in ancient times.

The second region, the Deccan Plateau, is separated from the north by the Vindhya Mountains and from the coastal areas by the Eastern and Western Ghats, which form a kind of mountain wall. Although rich in mineral resources, the plateau receives little rainfall; hence it is not heavily populated, in contrast to the other regions of India. In this region the people and the cultures of north and south intermingle.

The third region, farther south, near the port city of Chennai (formerly Madras), is the ancient land of the Tamils and the heartland of the Dravidian people. This southern peninsula has been free of any extended domination by invaders and has preserved the ancient traditions of Hinduism.

India's society is basically agrarian. Rapid strides in industrialization since 1947, when India became independent, have reduced the percentage of workers who make their living from agriculture to 51.1 percent, and agriculture now only contributes 16 percent of India's gross domestic product.[1] However, India is still an agricultural nation. The fortunes of Indian farmers, who live in thousands of tiny villages, depend on the erratic monsoon, which can cause disastrous floods or droughts. Although, with recent improvements in irrigation, varieties of seeds, and petroleum-based fertilizers, the government has succeeded in increasing the country's agricultural output, the majority of Indian farmers remain untouched by these developments. Efforts by India's political elites to raise the standard of living of the country's more than 1 billion people and to bring them into the modern age are complicated by sociocultural practices, rural poverty, and economic policies that favor industrialization, the middle class, economic growth, and rigid labor laws. The 2004 and 2009 national general elections indicated a commitment to develop the countryside and build infrastructure to help economic growth and the rural poor, but implementation of these goals has been uneven.

Sociocultural Plurality: Historical Roots

Historians often divide Indian history into three distinct periods: Hindu, Muslim, and British. Each period left its impact on the cultural and sociopolitical structure of the country, leading to a composite culture enriched by these diverse sources.

Ancient Hindu Heritage

The origins of Hindu India can be traced back to the highly developed Indus Valley civilization of Harappa and Mohenjodaro, which thrived from 2000 to 1500 BC. It is now believed to be the source of many elements of Indian society and Hinduism. Archeological evidence discovered in the Indus Valley since the 1970s has challenged an earlier theory of Indian development that attributed Hinduism and Indian culture to the Aryans, who migrated to India from central Asia around 1500 BC, entering India through Afghanistan and the Hindu Kush mountains.

While the theory of the Aryan invasion attributes much of Indian culture and development to the Aryans, the archeological evidence from the Indus Valley has revealed that many of the contributions originally attributed to the Aryans existed before they arrived. In any case, the Sanskrit language developed. Philologists subsequently discovered Sanskrit to be Indo-European, or similar to the languages spoken by the people who settled in Iran and various parts of Europe. The languages spoken in present-day North India and in the western states of Maharashtra and Gujarat (along with the Sinhala language of Sri Lanka) belong to this Indo-European family of languages.

The development of Hinduism took centuries; the religion is evolutionary in nature and reflects a great deal of local and regional variation. Around 1200 BC the followers of Hinduism started composing hymns that were collected into the Vedas, the early Hindu scriptures. The Vedas are the "oldest known literature in any Indo-European language."[2] Later, in the post-Vedic period, the early Indians began discussing fundamental philosophical questions and speculating about the nature of the universe and the meaning of human life. These discussions have been summed up in the Darshanas, the literature that sets forth the intellectual heritage of Hindus.

Although there is no one source of Hindu religious thought, the two great epics composed in Sanskrit, the Ramayana and the Mahabharata, have profoundly influenced the religious, cultural, and literary worlds of the Hindus. These two epics describe the period between 1000 and 700 BC, and their heroes and heroines have been the subjects of writings in all Indian languages, including the languages of South India. Even today the stories in these two epics are told in Hindu families.

During the Vedic period a complex social structure developed. It is based on the caste system, in which the priests (Brahmins) and the warriors (Kshatriyas) occupied the highest positions, the traders (Vaishyas) the middle, and the menials (Sudras) the lowest. Despite repeated attacks on the caste system by subsequent reform-oriented social and religious movements, it still exists in India and has a strong impact on the sociopolitical behavior of Hindus.

Although ancient Hinduism was not egalitarian—it asserted that different classes were needed to perform different social functions—it nevertheless emphasized kindliness and tolerance of other human beings. The ethics of Hinduism required ritualistic sacrifices but also emphasized such personal virtues as honesty, hospitality, and "piety, in the sense of such religious acts as worship, pilgrimage, and the feeding of cows and brahmans."[3]

The most important challenge to the teachings of Hinduism and its hierarchical social order in ancient India came from Buddhism and Jainism, which were founded at almost the same time by two princes born into Kshatriya families. In the late sixth and early fifth centuries BC, Gautama Buddha (563–483 BC) turned ascetic, propounded his teachings, and established a new order of followers. These followers emphasized truthfulness, nonviolence, eschewal of hatred, purity of heart, and love for fellow human beings, irrespective of caste or class considerations. Vardhaman Mahavir (599–527 BC), the founder of Jainism, was equally emphatic regarding personal virtues as opposed to the ritualistic sacrifices practiced by Hindu Brahmins, but Mahavir placed far greater emphasis on self-discipline and nonviolence than the Buddha had done. Buddhists and Jains survive today as small religious minorities in India.

The cultural heritage of Hindus was also influenced by pre-Islamic Persia and especially by ancient Greece. Even before Alexander the Great invaded India in 326 BC, it was in touch with Greece through Persia. Many scholars find close parallels between early Greek and Indian schools of philosophy. After the Greek invasion, several Greek imperial outposts were set up in India; many were eventually absorbed into the cultural groups of North India.

Although various Hindu kingdoms were founded from time to time in both the north and the south, they never established control over the entire subcontinent of India. Most of these kingdoms were regional in nature, and their founders were unable to build a type of government that could survive the demise of the ruling dynasty.

There was a limited discussion of theoretical principles and practices in Hindu India. Kautilya's *Arthastra* is a well-known treatise on statecraft, but ancient India followed certain political principles of governance:

The king was not above the law (*dharma*); he was expected to interpret it, enforce it, and follow it and to administer his kingdom.
There was a system to raise revenue.
The village was a democratic, self-governing entity in what was called the *panchayat* system.[4]

Evidence suggests the existence of both monarchical and republican forms of government. In some cases monarchs were advised by a council of ministers; in others they were absolute rulers. In essence the Hindu system was authoritarian and feudalistic in structure. Even in republics the power belonged to the elders of the tribes or to the leaders of the guilds and community groups rather than to the ordinary citizens. In any case, the Hindus, who had made rich contributions to the development of civilization in India, largely failed to display a constructive ability to build stable and lasting political institutions.[5]

By the end of the tenth century AD, Hindu civilization had lost its dynamism and creativity. Hindu society had become stagnant and rigid. The rulers of the various Hindu kingdoms displayed no sense of nationalism or patriotism and were unable to withstand the onslaught of hardy Muslim invaders from the northwest.

Muslim Heritage

The advent of Islam in India proved a different story. Broadly speaking, the interaction between Muslims and Hindus in India followed three patterns. The first was terrorism: Muslim invaders came to plunder and slaughter the native population, leaving in their wake a trail of death and destruction. Mahmud of Ghazni, a Turk by descent, typifies this early aspect of India's contact with Islam. In AD 1000, he repeatedly invaded India in order to plunder the wealth of its towns and cities, particularly the fabulous offerings of gold and cash stored in Hindu temples. A devout Muslim, Mahmud concentrated his destructive tactics on nonbelievers. His example was later followed by Tamerlane, Nadir Shah of Persia, and Ahmad Shah Abdali of Afghanistan, although they were less religiously motivated than Mahmud and discriminated little between Muslim and Hindu gentry while looting. Most of these invaders went back to their native lands and did not settle in India.

The second pattern of Muslim invasion was characterized by conquest, settlement, and founding of kingdoms in parts of West and North India. This pattern is evident, for example, in the Arab conquest of Sindh in 712 by Muhammad bin Qasim, who founded an Arab kingdom and forced the Hindus to convert to Islam. This pattern of conquest was followed from the twelfth to the sixteenth centuries until the establishment of the Mughal Empire. During this period, divided Hindu kingdoms fell, one after another, to the Muslim invaders of Turkish, Persian, and Afghan origin. Although the Muslims left a majority of the resident Hindu population alone, some were subjected to humiliation and discrimination and occasionally to torture and forcible conversion to Islam. Many of these Muslim kingdoms were short-lived and ruled by transient dynasties, and most of them were unstable. The early Muslim rulers failed to build an efficient system of administration, and the organizational abilities they displayed were no better than those of their Hindu predecessors.

The founding of the Mughal Empire in the sixteenth century represented the third pattern of interactions. Not only did the Mughal rulers conquer most of India, but they also established a stable and centralized administration directed from Lahore, Agra, and Delhi. The founder of the Mughal Empire was Babur, who conquered Delhi in 1526. But it was Babur's grandson, Akbar, who during his long rule (1556–1605) laid the foundation of the Mughal Empire in North India. During his reign and those of his three successors, India achieved political stability unmatched in the history of India.

The Mughals were not only the new rulers but also the newest settlers in India. In the process they actively integrated the Hindus into both the civil and military administrations. In addition, they tried to reach across the religious divide to create a more coherent society by making matrimonial alliances with the Hindu princely houses of Rajasthan. Many of the Mughals, especially Akbar (who was highly rationalist in his orientation), were opposed to the orthodox and dogmatic Islamic traditions. They tried to create a composite Indian culture, incorporating both Hindu and Muslim values. But Islam, unlike many other religious movements of the past, was a young, vibrant, and aggressive religious force that could not be absorbed by Hinduism.[6]

Some progress was made during this period in uniting Hindus and Muslims in a composite culture. A powerful part of the Bhakti (devotional) movement criticized the orthodoxies of both Hindu Brahmins and Muslim ulema (religious scholars). Nanak, Kabir, and many other saint-poets emphasized a devotee's personal relationship with his god and tried to synthesize the teachings of Islam and Hinduism. Among the Muslims, similar efforts were made by the Sufis, who were influenced by Hindu mysticism.[7] As a result, many places of worship were established and frequented by both Muslims and Hindus. Yet, despite these efforts, the fundamental division and a sense of latent hostility persisted between Hindus and Muslims throughout India. No religious or social movement was able to bridge the deep gulf between the two communities.

The Mughal Empire brought progress in other areas, however. In addition to building forts and beautiful palaces and mausoleums, the Persian-speaking Mughal rulers spoke Urdu, a language rich in literary traditions and written in Persian script. It was spoken by cultivated people in and around Delhi, the principal seat of the Mughal Empire. But even though both Hindus and Muslims contributed to the development of Urdu literature, a majority of Hindus considered Urdu and its literature to be symbols of Muslim culture.

In contemporary India Hindu nationalists regard the Muslim period of Indian history as one of alien rule and subjugation. For them the desecration of Hindu temples and the slaughter of innocent followers of Hinduism are too painful to be forgotten, and the defeats of Hindu kings at the hands of Muslim invaders are shameful episodes of Indian history. The religious tolerance of Akbar, they assert, was only an exception, for his successors gave up this policy. Instead, following Islamic orthodoxy, they prohibited interreligious marriages, pulled down Hindu temples, and even imposed *jizya* (poll tax) on Hindus. Hindu nationalists today have disowned Urdu language and literature and instead consider Hindi to be the language of North India.

In contrast, secularist Hindus and nationalist Indian Muslims emphasize the positive side of the Muslim rule in India. They look upon the Mughal Empire, with its architectural achievements and Urdu literary traditions, as an important part of India's cultural heritage. For example, Jawaharlal Nehru, a leader of the freedom movement and the first prime minister of India, displayed a high regard for the Muslim contributions to Indian civilization. Nevertheless, the two contradictory attitudes toward the Muslim period persist in the contemporary politics of India.

British Rule and Contact with the West

The era of British supremacy, the third period of Indian history, was firmly established in 1858, when the queen-in-council took over direct administration of India from the British East India Company. British rule brought India face-to-face with a dynamic, creative, and vibrant culture. The British displayed far better administrative and organizational skills than did any of the earlier ruling classes of India. Not only did they establish control over the country and achieve territorial integration, but they also founded a centralized administration that could not be challenged easily.

The territorial integration of the country was strengthened by the building of an extensive network of highways, railroads, and post and telegraph systems. Such a system not only enabled the British to exploit India as a vast market for the sale of its manufactured goods but also gave the Indians a mobility within their own country that they had never before experienced. Trade between different parts of India expanded rapidly, and by the time the British left, India had developed a national economy that strengthened the unity among its different regions.

The efficient administrative machinery built by the British and the merit-based system of recruitment to the bureaucracy they introduced are two of the important traditions the Indians inherited from this period. The foundation of this system of administration at the district level had been laid earlier by the Mughals, who appointed local and provincial administrators to act as agents of the central government. But the British introduced a high degree of uniformity in both the civil and the judicial administrations; in addition, the administrative system possessed objectivity and impersonality, qualities not found in the previous system of administration. Such a system established rule of law, respect for personal liberty, and the equality of all persons of Indian origin, regardless of religion. Administratively, India became one—an achievement unparalleled in the political history of India.

The Western system of education brought a slow though radical transformation of the value structure and behavior patterns of Indian intellectuals. The new system of civil and judicial administration made acquiring English language and education a valuable avenue for achieving political influence, economic power, and social mobility. Thus it came as no surprise when thousands of Indians started flocking to the newly established institutions of higher learning that provided instruction in English. This system of education produced a new class of professionals and enlarged the size of the urban middle class; it also exposed Indian elites to the constitutional liberalism and democratic socialism propounded by English utilitarians and Fabian socialists. The democratic ideals of liberty, equality, and social justice gradually took root among the members of the intellectual establishment of the country. In short, the knowledge of English brought the upper classes of India into contact with the West, injecting a new dynamism into an ancient civilization.

The British impact, however, was not uniform throughout India. Princely India, with a few notable exceptions, remained feudal and isolated, and many regions of the country were slow to respond to the new ideas and values. In some parts of the subcontinent, the feudal order was dismantled, but in other areas it survived.

In the nation-building and modernization process, the unevenness of the British impact created problems for the elites in the postindependence period. The pace of modernization and development of a national identity has been faster in those communities that had a higher exposure to the West.

Quest for National Identity: The Cultural Revival and the Nationalist Movement

One of the most remarkable developments of the British period of Indian history was the growth of Indian nationalism. Many Indian leaders had received their training in England and understood the importance of liberal values. Their negative view of British racialism and domination, however, led them to mobilize the people against British colonial rule.

The English system of education and contact with the West brought the Indian elites in touch with nationalism as an ideological force at a time when it was at its zenith in Europe. Moreover, the English language provided communication links among the urban elites, who originated from different provinces and therefore spoke different native languages. Members of this elite class rose above the ascriptive and primordial ties characteristic of traditional India and propagated a national vision of India.

Nationalism as a movement was preceded by cultural revivalism and a social-reform movement. Contact with the West through the British forced Indians, especially Hindus, to examine critically the structure of Hindu society. Through this process of self-examination, Hindu elites became painfully aware of the deficiencies of Hindu society, which was permeated with social customs that could not be justified on rational or even religious grounds. The elites saw Hindu society as dominated by superstitions, idolatry, magical myths, and many reprehensible social customs. If Hinduism was to save itself from the onslaught of Western culture and proselytizing Christian missions supported by the British Empire, it needed not only to rid itself of social evils but also to reorganize its structure on a more rational basis. Consequently, an upsurge of social-reform movements occurred in different parts of the country. Some reformers sought a synthesis of Hinduism, Western liberalism, and select principles of Christianity, while others emphasized the glories of Hindu India and hoped to restore to it the essential Vedic values they felt had been lost in the course of Hindu subjugation during Muslim rule. Raja Ram Mohan Roy (1774–1833), a Bengali thinker and reformer, exemplified the first group of reformers. A learned person who had studied the scriptures of Christianity, Islam, and Hinduism and knew many languages, including Sanskrit, Arabic, English, Hebrew, and Persian, he was deeply influenced by the rationalist philosophies of the West. He strongly disapproved of idol worship, the caste system, the inferior status of women, untouchability, and other social evils of Hinduism. In order to propagate his reformist views, he founded the Brahmo Samaj, an organization that contributed a great deal to social reform and to the stimulation of cultural and intellectual activities in Bengal and several other parts of India.

The second type of social-reform movement, seeking social reforms coupled with Hindu revivalism, was reflected in the writings and activities of Swami Dayanand (1824–1883), a Gujarati Brahmin who sought to legitimize the reform of Hindu society on the basis of a reinterpretation of the Vedas. These ancient Hindu scriptures, Dayanand felt, not only contained sacred knowledge but were the source of all philosophical and scientific thought as well. He glorified the Hindu past and sought to purify contemporary Hinduism by getting rid of the caste system, untouchability, idol worship, and other superstitions. Such evil social practices, he stressed, were introduced into Hinduism by selfish Brahmins, who used them to perpetuate their dominance of Hindu society. In his quest to create a sense of pride among Hindus, he virulently attacked both Islam and Christianity. Dayanand was a staunch nationalist who thought social reform should precede *swarajya* (self-rule).

The Arya Samaj, a social-reform movement founded by Dayanand in 1875, became closely associated with educational activities, especially with the spread of English education through the Dayanand Anglo-Vedic (DAV) College movement in northwestern India. In subsequent years many leaders of the Arya Samaj movement joined hands with the proponents of Hindu nationalism.

In South India, the Theosophical Society became instrumental in both cultural revival and social reform among Hindus. The society worked to establish the superiority of Hindu philosophy over Western philosophy. Annie Besant (1847–1933), an Englishwoman deeply influenced by Hindu philosophy, became a major spokesperson for the society; she helped popularize its teachings and create a high degree of cultural pride among middle-class Hindus of South India.

But another group of reformers consisted of intellectuals and professionals who were deeply influenced by the rationalist thinking of the West. Although committed to preserving the basic institutions of Hindu society and its value system, they believed that it needed reform and reorganization in order to face the challenge of modern times. They held that patience, endurance, and understanding were needed to accomplish such changes, not a frontal assault on the traditional Hindu leadership. They sought these gradual changes by founding educational institutions, cultural organizations, research foundations, scientific and religious study groups, reading rooms, libraries, and so on. Justice M. G. Ranade (1842–1901) in Maharashtra and Debendranath Tagore (1817–1905) in Bengal represented this more secular route to social reform among Hindus.

Originally, contact with the West had created a sense of cultural inferiority among the English-educated Hindus. Swami Vivekanand (1863–1902) and his associates sought to counter this image by comparing Hinduism and Western culture. A powerful speaker and charismatic personality, Vivekanand called on Hindus to take pride in their spiritual heritage and attacked Western culture as inferior. For him, "the backbone, the foundation and the bedrock of India's national life was India's spiritual genius," which the West did not possess.[8]

The overall consequence was an unprecedented cultural revival among Hindus. Interest in classical Sanskrit writings and Hindu art and philosophy was stimulated by an outpouring of European scholarship in praise of India's cultural heritage. It was not surprising, therefore, that the glorification of Indian history became a staple of writings in various regional languages of India. In addition, literary elites and political leaders used Hindu religious symbols to arouse patriotism. They identified Indian nationalism with Hinduism and deified the motherland. Recollection of the glories of the past was essential to the creation of a sense of national respect and a new national identity.

But in this process of cultural revival and resurgence of Hindu nationalism, Muslims were left out. Initially, the Indian Muslims reacted to British rule by withdrawing into the shell of their own community and isolating themselves from the new ideas that British rule generated in Indian society. Sir Syed Ahmad Khan (1817–1898) brought the Muslims into the modern world by establishing in 1875 the Mohammadan Anglo-Oriental College at Aligarh (now known as Aligarh Muslim University). Syed Ahmad Khan strongly emphasized revival of Muslims' pride in their heritage, preservation of the Muslim subnational identity, and reconciliation of Muslim interests with British rule in India. Aligarh produced the main elements of the Western-educated Muslim intelligentsia, who became the vanguard of Muslim separatism in Indian politics.

In a politically and administratively united India, the cultural revitalization movement, as in other parts of South Asia, especially in Sri Lanka, led to the rise of a well-organized nationalist movement. The impetus for the organization of a national association that would speak on behalf of all Indians was provided, ironically, by the racially motivated policies of the British government, which discriminated against Indians in their own land. Even though, for instance, recruitment of Indians into the Indian Civil Service (ICS), the most prestigious bureaucratic organization in British India, was promised as early as 1858, all efforts were made to block the Indians' entry into such services. When an Indian such as Surendranath Banerjea (1848–1926) was successful in entering the ICS, he was dismissed on flimsy grounds. Indians faced further humiliation when Englishmen living in India were successful in withdrawing the Ilbert Bill of 1883, which had permitted the trial of a European in a court presided over by an Indian judge. Events such as this forced Indians to seek a national forum not only to articulate their demands and to protest against this discrimination but also to consolidate their ranks to force the British Government of India's attention to their needs. The result was the establishment of the Indian National Congress in 1885.

From its very inception, the Indian National Congress became intertwined with the nationalist movement in the country. This movement underwent several phases, however, and revealed considerable tension among its various leaders and factions with respect to both the ultimate goals of the movement and the methods to achieve them. Fortunately for India, its struggle for freedom was spread over a long period; the leaders of the movement were thus permitted the opportunity to debate openly the kind of society and polity to build once India achieved independence. By contrast, the Pakistan movement was not only single-issue oriented but dominated by a single powerful leader, Muhammad Ali Jinnah, who displayed little tolerance for dissent within his ranks. Not surprisingly, then, the Indian political elites at the time of India's independence were much better prepared to tackle the issues of institution building and economic development than were the leaders of Pakistan.

The first phase of the nationalist movement was dominated by the well-to-do segment of Indian society. The leaders representing this segment were steeped in British traditions and education and depended on the British sense of justice; they sought to ameliorate the conditions of Indians through an appeal to the British sense of fairness. Their main objective was to seek greater representation of educated Indians in the civil services and to introduce representative institutions at the provincial and local levels. They did not entertain the hope of complete independence from British rule; rather, they believed that continued association with the British Empire was in the interests of Indians. Surendranath Banerjea, who was twice elected president of the Indian National Congress, asserted that English civilization was the "noblest the world has ever seen, a civilization fraught with unspeakable blessings to the people of India."[9] These nationalists took pride in their citizenship in the British Empire and sought to propagate values of British liberalism throughout the country. During this period such men as Justice M. G. Ranade (1842–1901), Dadabhai Nauroji (1825–1917), and Pherozshah Mehta (1845–1915), all products of the British system of education, led the Indian National Congress and pressured the British government to address the problems. The British tried to defuse this pressure by passing the Government of India Act of 1909, which expanded political participation and electoral representation at both the provincial and central government levels. Representatives to the provincial legislative councils were to be elected by voters holding property or having high educational qualifications. This measure also introduced separate representation for Muslims, who were to elect their representatives from within their own community.

In the second nationalist phase, starting in 1905, the struggle for control of the Indian National Congress was divided between the moderates, led by Gopal Krishna Gokhale (1866–1915), and the extremists, led by Bal Gangadhar Tilak (1856–1920). These two leaders, both Maharashtrian Brahmins, differed not only in personality and ideological orientation but also in their approach to achieving self-rule for the country. Gokhale was a disciple of Ranade, a moderate, and even though he was much more vocal in his criticism of British government than Ranade, he believed in constitutional methods. He did not hesitate to work with British rulers, and he tried to represent Indians in the Imperial Legislative Council, where he was a member.

Bal Gangadhar Tilak and his extremist associates, on the other hand, did not trust the British government. Tilak was a Hindu nationalist and an ardent believer in the superiority of Hindu culture over Western culture. In his opposition to the moderates, Tilak was supported by Lala Lajpat Rai of the Punjab and Bipan Chandra Pal and Aurobindo Ghose of Bengal, militant extremists who provided philosophical justification for the use of violence against the alien rulers of India. Unlike the moderates, the extremists asserted that political freedom could be won only by waging war against the enemy. Whereas the moderates believed that they would be able to achieve self-government with the blessings of British rulers, the extremist Tilak declared, "Swaraj [self-rule] is my birthright and I will have it." Also, unlike Gokhale and his associates, the extremists openly used Hindu religious symbols and traditions to stimulate nationalist sentiments among the masses. They never stopped attacking the moderates for their subservience to Western culture.

In 1907 the extremists lost out to Gokhale and his moderate associates in their struggle to control the Congress organization. But British suppression, Tilak's confinement in Mandalay, the arrests of Pal and Ghose, and the political exile of Lala Lajpat Rai turned the extremists into popular heroes. By 1915, the two factions had reconciled, and Tilak and his associates once again became active within the Congress Party. The united nationalist leadership of the Indian National Congress demanded, and was promised by the British, a large measure of self-government at the end of World War I.

This second nationalist phase also witnessed the rise of self-assertiveness among the minorities. The emergence of the Hindu-dominated Indian National Congress onto center stage in Indian politics and the fear that Hindus would become the rulers of the country owing to their overwhelming majority in the population spurred the Muslims into political activity, resulting in the organization of the All-India Muslim League in 1906. The Muslims demanded separate representation and allied themselves with the British, seeking their favor and protection against what the Muslims perceived as the aggressiveness of the Hindu-dominated Indian National Congress. Given the pluralistic structure of Indian society, the rise of such particularistic movements was not surprising. However, the leaders of the nationalist movement underestimated the strength of these subcultural and regional movements in perceiving the problem of national integration to be primarily a political one.

The end of World War I brought about a radical transformation in the political expectations and aspirations of Indians. The British government responded by enacting the Government of India Act of 1919. This act introduced partial responsible government in the provinces; increased the number of elected representatives in the Central Legislative Assembly; gave separate representation to the Sikhs, the Europeans settled in India, and the Anglo-Indians (Eurasians); and extended voting rights to almost 10 percent of the adult population of the country. Even though these steps provided opportunities for Indians to learn about parliamentary government, to organize voters for electoral purposes, and to gain experience in self-government, they did not satisfy the political aspirations of the nationalist leaders. Their alienation from the British rulers in India increased due to continuation of the repressive policies that the government had adopted during the war. The British government still possessed enormous powers to restrict civil liberties, imprison politically active

Indians, and declare martial law. Increased protests against such repressive measures after World War I resulted in a declaration of martial law and the Amritsar tragedy. This brutal action shocked the Indian nationalists, but the House of Lords, ignoring Indian sentiments, passed a resolution in 1920 in appreciation of General Reginald Dyer's services to the empire.

The conflict between the Indian extremists and the British left the moderates outside the mainstream of the nationalist movement. As the extremist faction led by Tilak took over the Congress organization in 1917, the moderates withdrew from the party and founded their own organization, the Indian Liberal Federation. Tilak then became the undisputed leader of the nationalists. After Tilak's death in 1920, the leadership passed into the hands of Mohandas Karamchand Gandhi (1869–1948), who rejected both the moderates' gradualist approach to political reforms and the extremists' philosophical justification of violence. His nonviolent approach, using mass mobilization and peaceful defiance of British authority, radicalized Indian politics far beyond the expectations of Tilak's followers.

During his twenty years in South Africa practicing law among Indian settlers, Gandhi developed his concept of *satyagraha* (loosely translated as "soul force") and the technique of civil disobedience. On his return to India, before he plunged into Indian politics, Gandhi traveled widely throughout the country, observing the culture, traditions, and living conditions of the people. He felt the leaders of the nationalist movement were out of touch with the people who lived in India's many villages. He realized that in order to win freedom from Britain, the nationalist movement required a mass base; it needed to involve the people living in the countryside. Accordingly, Gandhi not only established his headquarters in rural India but also sent the nationalist leaders and party workers to live in the villages, to undertake social services, and to lead simple and austere lives. He enforced strict discipline, emphasized nonviolence, and demanded sacrifices from his followers. This pacifist approach, austere and rigorous life, and complete identification with the common man earned Gandhi the saintly title of Mahatma (great soul).

Gandhi called for peaceful breaching of unjust laws; protesting through strikes, fasts, and noncooperation with the authorities; and boycotting not only imported goods but also British educational institutions. But he insisted on peaceful defiance of authority, seeking arrest by breaking laws. Soon, thanks to his charismatic personality and simple and saintly lifestyle, Gandhi had built a formidable nationwide following for both himself and the Indian National Congress. Under his leadership the elitist nationalist movement became a mass movement. Although the top leaders of the Congress organization were still English-educated, upper-class Indians, they were nevertheless able to identify with the plight of the common man. In addition, the second tier of leadership at the provincial and local levels was more attuned to the sensitivities of the masses than any other group in the country. A well-organized vernacular press and an articulate vernacular-speaking intelligentsia established strong links between these national leaders at the center of Indian politics and the mass of Indians living on the periphery.

Thus began the third phase of the nationalist movement, in which the nationalist leadership, with an expanded mass base, started to press for complete independence. During its Lahore session in 1929, the Indian National Congress, no longer willing to accept dominion status and membership in the British Commonwealth of Nations, adopted a resolution demanding complete independence for India. During this phase of the nationalistic movement, Gandhi launched several mass drives: the noncooperation movement of 1921, the breaking of salt laws (the Salt March) in 1930, and the civil disobedience of 1933. Each of these movements succeeded in enhancing mass political consciousness and demonstrated Gandhi's ability to mobilize the country, and many young and leftist leaders criticized their sudden suspension. The British government responded to them by passing the Government of India Act of 1935, which established complete provincial autonomy and proposed partial responsible government at the center. These concessions were no doubt a substantial improvement on the institutional setup created by the Government of India Act of 1919, but they were too little and too late. The nationalist movement had planted deep roots in Indian soil, and Gandhi's Indian National Congress had captured the imagination of the masses. The popularity of the Congress became evident when, in the elections of 1937, it won the majority of legislative seats in six provinces; it had become the single largest party and formed the government in eight of eleven provinces in British rule. For the next twenty-eight months (1937–1939), when the party's leadership ran the provincial governments, it not only gained administrative experience but also made substantial progress in social and economic programs for the masses.

It should be noted, however, that while the Indian National Congress represented the nationalist aspirations of a majority of Indians, several smaller movements represented the aspirations of religious and regional minorities that could not be absorbed by the nationalist group led by Mahatma Gandhi. The Muslim League, for example, under the able leadership of Muhammad Ali Jinnah, became a powerful rival of the Indian National Congress, claiming to be the sole representative of the Indian Muslims. Similarly, in Kashmir, the National Conference, under the dynamic leadership of Sheikh Muhammad Abdullah, and in the Punjab, the Akali Dal, led by Master Tara Singh, represented the Kashmiri Muslims and the Punjabi Sikhs, respectively. During the 1940s the subnationalist movements gained momentum and became a major challenge to the nationalist goals of the leaders of the Indian National Congress.

The final phase of the nationalist movement (1940–1947) was dominated by the Congress leaders' two concerns: complete independence from British rule and preservation of the territorial unity of India through accommodation of the aspirations of these subnationalist movements, especially the leaders of the Muslim League.

By 1942 it had become evident to the leaders of the Indian National Congress that the British government was in no mood to meet its demands for independence despite the Congress' offer to support the British war efforts against Japan and Germany. In August 1942, therefore, Mahatma Gandhi planned to launch a massive "Quit India" movement. But before the leaders could organize it, the British government arrested many of the leaders of the Indian National Congress, including Gandhi. The British were always baffled by the success of Gandhi's methods of nonviolence and uncertain as to how to deal with them. However, a preemptive strike by the government in August 1942 saved it from the unpleasant task of brutalizing Gandhi's nonviolent soldiers. Despite some disruption of the administration, order was restored in a short time.

While the Congress leaders were in jail, the leaders of such subnationalist parties as the Muslim League and the Akali Party of the Sikhs were able to consolidate their positions within their respective communities. Toward the end of World War II, it became evident to the British government that it would not be able to keep India under control and would have to reach an agreement with the nationalist leaders. Hence, in 1944 Gandhi and many of his associates were released.

Once out of jail, the nationalist leaders confronted not only the prospect of independence but also the possibility that the country might become divided on a religious basis. In 1940 the Muslim League had demanded the creation of a Muslim-majority state out of British India consisting of provinces in which the Muslims formed a majority. The Sikhs, for their part, sought the creation of a Sikh homeland in Punjab, where the Sikh religion had originated. The leaders of the Indian National Congress were ill prepared to face the challenges of rival nationalist groups based on religion; their nationalist ideology, in fact, sought to downgrade the importance of religious divisions within the Indian population.

During the 1945–1946 elections, the Muslim League emerged as the representative body of the Muslims of India, capturing 446 of 496 provincial seats in the Muslim-majority provinces of the country. In addition, the Muslim League launched a massive campaign to press its demand for the division of the country. This action resulted in widespread Hindu-Muslim rioting; indeed, there emerged a real threat of civil war in India. Ultimately, the Congress leaders agreed in 1947 to a division of the country on the basis of religion. The demand for Pakistan was conceded, Punjab and Bengal were divided, Muslim-majority areas went to Pakistan, and the rest became parts of India. Such religious and ethnic minorities as the Sikhs were not able at the time to manage sovereign states for themselves. On August 15, 1947, India became independent from Britain. However, the division of the country was accompanied by massive Hindu-Muslim rioting and migration in which an estimated half million Hindus, Muslims, and Sikhs perished.

Quest for Institution Building and Modernization: The Development of New Goals

Even before independence, Indian elites frequently discussed questions regarding the future setup of an independent India. The dominant sector of the Indian National Congress, the modernists, agreed on the form of government they wanted. Their experience with representative government during British rule and their observation of the parliamentary system in the United Kingdom fixed their choice on the Westminster model of government.

The elites were convinced that if people could participate in the political process on a secular basis, national unity would be consolidated, and the national identity that the cultural revival and nationalist movement had nourished would be strengthened. The establishment of a liberal democracy in India thus became the modernists' new goal. Freedom of speech and expression was also to become an essential attribute. Conscious of the social and economic disparities in Indian society, the leaders believed that the ideals of democratic socialism would help them achieve some degree of social and economic equality in the society, with the state actively helping the poor, the backward, and the helpless. In subsequent chapters we assess their success or failure in fulfilling these ideals.

With independence, India needed modernization and economic development. The nationalist leaders inherited from the British rulers a primarily agricultural economy; an overwhelming majority (80 percent) of the population depended on the land to earn a living. Furthermore, Indian agriculture was one of the most inefficient and backward systems in the world. Indians were hardly able to feed themselves. The land was tormented by frequent droughts, famines, floods, and pestilence. Most of the industries the British had set up were established merely to meet consumers' need for cotton textiles, tea, sugar, and jute. Despite India's possession of certain strategic raw materials, such as iron ore, coal, mica, bauxite, magnesite, chromite, titanium, and refractory materials, the country lacked a significant capital goods industry. It was heavily dependent on Great Britain and other industrialized countries of the West for its machinery and engineering goods.

The elites differed as to the approach they should undertake to raise the living standards of the people. There were two main viewpoints—one advocated by Gandhi and his followers, the other by a more modernist and secular-minded group. Gandhi's approach was the product of his moral and religious orientations. He strongly disapproved of the profit motive, favored strict limits on private property, and opposed the tyranny of machines and the ruthless competition of a market economy. He also favored the development of agricultural and consumers' cooperatives. According to Gandhi, India needed to maintain its agricultural, rural-based economy, while redeveloping and expanding its traditional cottage and small-scale industries, which would once again make the village society self-sufficient. His vision of India also recognized the need for low consumption of resources and development of indigenous technologies suitable for the local environment and culture. Gandhi's strategy of economic development would have resulted in a higher investment of resources in rural India. Such a vision of India, however, was incompatible with the quest to develop a modern industrial state.

Jawaharlal Nehru and his modernist associates, influenced by socialist thought, disagreed with the Gandhian approach to the economic development of India. Nehru looked to science and technology and investment in capital goods industries as the key elements in the transformation of the character of Indian society. These modernists attributed underdevelopment of societies such as that of India to the insufficiency of technological development. They believed centralized planning, increased output of technically skilled labor, and importation of technical know-how would ultimately make India a technologically self-sufficient country. In such a system the state would play a key role; it would set the development priorities. Although no wholesale takeover of industries and businesses would occur, and although private initiative and investment would be allowed, the private sector of the economy was to be subservient to public needs, which the government alone was capable of defining.

Of these two ideological approaches to India's economic and industrial development, the political elites preferred Nehru's to Gandhi's. As a result, the new goal became the development of an extensive scientific and technological infrastructure based on the model of advanced industrialized societies.

In sum, India's sociocultural background, history, and geographic and demographic diversity made the task of nation building and modernization extremely difficult for its leaders. Reflecting the religious division of the country, India's political leaders—in contrast to those of Pakistan—refused to adopt the religion of the majority as the state religion. Instead, they opted to build a modern nation-state on the twin principles of democracy and socialism. The development of Indian socialism during the Nehru years (1947–1964) and thereafter produced a pattern of extensive state intervention in India's economic life and a system of bureaucratic and political controls that impeded private-sector development and India's participation in the global economy. India took the path of economic reforms in the early 1990s, a decade after China did, and resistance to reforms by Indian leftists inhibited the process. This shows the role of ideology in India's economic-development policies since 1947.

Social Structure and Political Culture

The stability of a political system depends on the support it enjoys from its citizens. In a society divided by religion, language, region, and competing economic, social, and political interests and demands, pressure from below continuously affects the political behavior of Indian leaders and the government. A description of India's social structure and the nature of its political culture can help us understand the conditions under which the country operates.

India is an ancient civilization but a new nation in the making; the values and attitudes of its citizens, the nature of its political culture, and its political processes are influenced by both its traditional past and its contemporary experiences.

Through a complex network of primary and secondary structures, the people of India have successfully transmitted several key elements of their cultural and political structure from generation to generation. It is through this process of socialization that India has developed its distinct political culture.

The Dominant Cultural Pattern: The Hindu Worldview

Despite the confluence of the various cultures that have affected the Indian people, the Hindu worldview constitutes the dominant cultural force in the society. The religious teachings of Hinduism and its belief system deeply influence the social behavior and political attitudes of its followers.

Hindus have often been described as otherworldly and fatalistic, because Hinduism teaches that an individual is bound by the cycle of birth and death. Karma (one's actions in life) determines the nature of one's next life. In order to escape the earthly cycles of birth and death, an individual needs salvation through an ultimate union of his soul (*atman*) with the Supreme Reality (*parmatman*).

Even though acquisition of material wealth and a desire for enjoyment and reproduction are important for human survival, spiritual salvation through this union of the soul with the Supreme Reality is superior to all other life goals.

TABLE 2.1 Religious Distribution of the Population of India (2001 Census)

Religion	Total	Percentage
Hindus	827,578,868	80.5
Muslims	138,188,244	13.4
Christians	24,080,016	2.3
Sikhs	19,215,730	1.9
Buddhists	7,955,207	0.8
Jains	4,225,053	0.4
Others	6,367,214	0.7

Source: Census of India, 2001, "Religious Composition," www.censusindia.gov.in/Census_Data_2011 /India_at_glance/religion.aspx (retrieved February 26, 2008).

NOTE: The Census of India, 2011, has not at time of writing (November 2012) released data about Indian religions. For general information about the 2011 census, see http://censusindia.gov.in.

Therefore, to Hindus the quest for political power and secular activities ought to be secondary to spiritual affairs. In actual life, however, there is a considerable gap between religious prescriptions and an individual's behavior. Thus, despite their emphasis on spiritual values, Hindus continue to pursue vigorously material goals in their lives.

Hinduism, however, is known for its flexibility. Because there is no organized church or clerical authority among the Hindus as there is among the Christians, there is no uniform enforcement of the rules among Hindus. God may be perceived and worshiped in many ways. Not only may individuals choose different paths to reach the Supreme Reality, but they are also free to worship deities of their own choosing. Hindus are therefore divided into numerous sects, each with its own deity, temples, and rituals. This kind of flexibility is nowhere more evident than in the villages of India, where the majority of Indians live. Their belief system enables Hindus to live side by side with the followers of such other religions as Buddhism, Jainism, and Christianity, often without friction. (For distribution of population by religion, see Table 2.1.) Peaceful coexistence between Hindus and Muslims, however, has been difficult to achieve.

The Caste System

India's traditional social order divides Hindus into a hierarchical structure consisting of four classifications, or *varna*: the Brahmins (priests and custodians of sacred knowledge), Kshatriyas (warriors and rulers), Vaishyas (traders), and Sudras (manual laborers and menial workers). In this order the Brahmins occupy the top position and the Sudras the lowest. In the past a person born into a particular caste rarely had an opportunity to change status within the society, regardless of his or her talents or achievements. In rural India the system created a highly segregated residential pattern in which the Sudras lived on the outskirts of the villages and towns, away from the high-caste neighborhoods. Some sections of Sudras were treated as "untouchable" by the members of the upper castes because their hereditary occupations (such as scavenging and leather working) were considered unclean. Even after the legal abolition of untouchability in postindependence India, it is still recognized and prevalent in many sections of Hindu society, especially in rural India. Although in theory Hinduism may be one of the most tolerant and flexible religions in the world, in its social order it displays a high degree of rigidity. Still, India's Dalits (formerly "untouchables") have gained political power and social mobility in significant ways. Dalits have served as chief ministers and federal government ministers and as a major-political-party president, a president of India, and a chief justice of the Supreme Court. They are influential now in university administrations. India's caste system is not static. It is a dynamic force in Indian politics and society.[10]

The Hindu caste system does not adhere to this simple fourfold division. The four *varna* are actually formal names for an organizational structure consisting of 3,000 castes into which the present Hindu society is divided. In rural India, where the caste system is most pervasive, a close interrelationship exists among social status, economic power, and occupational divisions. In the thousands of villages, the landowners traditionally make up the upper castes—the Kshatriyas and the Brahmins. In South India the situation is different in that non-Brahmins constitute the landowning castes. Money lending, banking, and trading are done mostly by the Banias, a term used almost interchangeably with Vaishyas. Landholding and well-to-do castes are traditionally expected to look after the well-being of the members of lower castes, who in turn perform services for the upper castes. In this kind of *jajmani* (superordinate-subordinate) relationship, both the upper and lower castes have rights and obligations vis-à-vis each other. Both the caste obligations and occupational differentiations have religious sanctions. In this way each caste group is obligated to fulfill its role in the society, whatever its status and the nature of the work it is obliged to perform.

The status, functions, and organizations of the castes (*jatis*) vary considerably from one region of the country to another. Many of the castes are confined to a subregion of the country and others to a locality or village. Yet, despite these variations, the caste system is deeply embedded in the subconscious of the individual Hindu. Indeed, caste affiliations influence and often determine the social and political behavior of all citizens.

Organization of the members of a caste to protect and promote their common sociopolitical interests has been a frequent phenomenon. Caste group activity has long been in evidence, even since before the introduction of representative institutions in India. Since independence in 1947, some castes have become highly politicized. Whether the castes infiltrate the parties or the parties use existing caste associations to mobilize voters is debatable, but there is little doubt that candidates for public office, regardless of their ideological orientations and party affiliations, are attuned to the sensitivities of caste groups. It is not surprising, therefore, that in the selection of candidates for political offices, the parties are deeply influenced by the caste composition of the population of an electoral district.

In recent years electoral politics has enhanced caste consciousness among the voters and led to the formation of political parties that represent a group of castes with common interests. Such particularistic parties have come to play an important role both in state and national politics.

Castes and subcastes are important instruments of political socialization. In the formation of the political attitudes of young adults and children, the caste affiliation plays an important role. Empirical evidence suggests that persons originating from the upper castes (Brahmins and Kshatriyas) have a higher sense of personal efficacy and interpersonal trust; they also seem to have a stronger commitment to the operation of democracy than do the members of the Jats (an agriculturist subcaste) and the low castes. There is a clear tendency on the part of children and young adults to identify themselves with the national political leaders originating from their own caste rather than with those from other castes. Mahatma Gandhi, for instance, is a political hero more favored by the members of his own caste, the Vaishya, than, say, by the Jats.

Family and Kinship

Indians' sociopolitical and economic behavior is likely to be influenced not only by caste but by family and kinship group. The basic unit of Hindu society in particular, and of religious communities of India in general, is not the individual but the extended or joint family, which may consist of three generations living under the same roof.

Minority Religions and Subgroup Identities

Although Hinduism is the religion of the majority of Indians, important religious minorities, such as Muslims and Sikhs, have been able to preserve their group identities.

Religion and aspects of cultural life, such as language, art, literature, and social institutions, become intertwined and lead to the development of powerful group identities that often inhibit the development of a cohesive national political community.

Ideology of Nationalism: Various Versions

There are two dominant versions of the pan-Indian ideology of nationalism: Indian nationalism and Hindu nationalism. Indian nationalism is a vital element of the ideology on which the Indian state was founded. Basically liberal and humanitarian, it recognizes the pluralistic nature of the society and rejects the idea of homogenizing the society by eliminating religious and cultural diversities. Its founders recognized that individuals in India belong to a variety of communities based on caste, religion, occupation, region, and a host of other factors. They were, furthermore, aware that such communities enjoyed a great degree of autonomy. The founders held that even though a majority of the country's population was Hindu, the Hindus have a tradition of tolerance and the capacity to absorb the ideas, values, and norms of behavior of other groups. Hindu religious traditions not only allow a wide range of sectarian diversity but also teach respect for all religions. These traditions enabled such minority religions as Islam and Christianity and such cultures as Greek, Turkish, Iranian, and others to contribute to the development of the composite culture of the country.

Because it was deeply influenced by European liberal-rationalist thought, Indian nationalism was committed to the reform and rationalization of the structure and organization of the society. It held that the state authority could be used to reform a traditional society. Middle-class elites, exponents of Indian nationalism, were wedded to the ideals of modern science, industrialization of the country, distributive justice, protection of the rights and cultures of ethnic and religious minorities, and development of a secular democratic polity based on the British system of parliamentary government.

Starting in the 1980s, however, many of the vital elements of Indian nationalism, developed and nurtured both before and after India's independence, came to be challenged by Hindu nationalists on both practical and intellectual bases. Although Hindu nationalism originated in the Hindu cultural revival movement of the nineteenth century and developed as a reaction against Indian nationalism, only in the recent past has it emerged as a major ideological force in the politics of the country. Hindu nationalists advocate a single, homogeneous national identity for the whole country, rejecting the idea that India is a multicultural and multinational state. To them, the term "Hindu" has a geocultural, not a religious, connotation. For Hindu nationalists the political-territorial concept of nationalism without its Hindu cultural content, as advocated by Nehru and his associates, is incapable of maintaining the unity of the country. For them the secular concept of Indian national identity, based on an alien ideology of socialism, is limited to the state and lacks those psychic elements that bind the people as a nation. They argue that common economic interests do not give birth to a nation; people's love for their land is based on common traditions and culture. For the Hindu nationalists, Bharat, or India, is not only their motherland; it is also their holy land. They believe that all Indians, irrespective of their religion, should take pride in India's ancient cultural heritage.

Hindu nationalists are also influenced by British ideologies that emphasize equality before the law, a uniform civil code, democracy, universal suffrage, and the system of representative government. Contrary to Indian nationalists, Hindu nationalists are opposed to providing special rights or protections for minorities. Hindu nationalism has been blamed in the Hindu-Muslim killings (e.g., Gujrat, 2002), but in some instances, such as the Mumbai railway blasts (2006) and the terrorist attack in 2008 in Mumbai, the two communities have helped each other.

New Status Symbols and the Role of Political Power in Social Mobility

Despite the persistence of traditional values, caste stratification, and belief in the superiority of the sacred over the secular, new secular values and status symbols are becoming increasingly important. The criterion for measuring a person's success has become the amount of money that person has rather than his or her social origin. Higher social origin may help in establishing contacts for material advancement, but social origin alone does not always guarantee higher status and success. Persons of lower social origin who are successful in accumulating wealth may actually be able to earn the respect of their fellow citizens now that social origin is somewhat less significant.

The ongoing industrial and agricultural revolutions and the introduction of the electoral process based on universal suffrage have increased the opportunities for social and economic mobility as well as political participation. Education, knowledge of the English language, political power, material wealth, and higher social status have become interdependent. Higher education, as in other modern societies, is considered a primary means of achieving upward social mobility. In India an understanding of English and proficiency in writing and speaking it give a person a head start. Although many people might criticize a westernized Indian, in urban areas they can hardly disguise their eagerness to accept him as their role model. If they cannot adopt his values and lifestyle in their own lives, they would like their children to emulate him. Moreover, the image of such an Indian as an ideal to emulate has been reinforced by television, movies, magazines, and newspapers. Both the politically influential and the nouveaux rich send their children to the exclusive private schools that provide education in English.

With the diversification of political activity in India, the competition for elective positions has increased immensely. Naturally this process has enhanced the demand for people who are politically ambitious and who possess organizational abilities. The older generation of leaders who commanded authority because of their age and contributions to the independence movement has almost disappeared, and now there is demand for a new political leader who is willing to use all means to acquire power.

The postindependence period has also witnessed the emergence of a middle class. It includes members of the business community, the managerial-political elites, and the powerful, wealthy, and influential farmers of the countryside. In urban areas, the members of this class have embraced the materialism and consumerism of Western societies and are comfortable with the challenges and opportunities presented by advancement in a globalizing world economy. This growing middle class provides political support for political parties at the national and regional levels. They participate in the development of political, commercial, and social linkages within India. As a result of India's economic boom since the 1990s, India's middle class has grown. Estimates of the size of India's middle class vary; McKinsey and Company puts it at 50 million people, reaching 600 million by 2030; Deutsche Research estimates it to be 300 million.[11]

India's Planning Commission's estimates show a decline in poverty in India: 27.5 percent of the population was below the poverty line in 2004–2005, compared with 51.3 percent in 1977–1978 and 36 percent in 1993–1994.[12]

Despite India's impressive overall growth rate since the 1990s, the level of growth and development varies among Indian states. Gujrat, Haryana, and Delhi, for instance, enjoy higher rates than Bihar, Uttar Pradesh, and Orissa.

Changes in India's Political Culture

Given the enormous complexity of India's sociocultural structure and a power-hungry and competitive system of politics among political parties, it is not surprising that Indian political values and norms of behavior often give contradictory signals. There is considerable intermingling of modern and traditional values. For example, one may find hero worship verging on idolatry along with an expression of strong democratic impulses, supersensitive nationalism along with strong parochialism, egalitarianism along with the existence of a hierarchical social order, a high degree of tolerance and passivity along with occasional outbursts of violence, and so on. These contradictory tendencies may be attributed to the vast size of the country and its diversity, as well as to the uneven levels of exposure to modern values in the different segments of the population.

The introduction of democratic institutions in India, as is well known, was not the result of an internal groundswell. The ordinary person in India has little awareness of the advantages of a democracy. It was the Western-educated and Anglicized elites who deliberately chose democracy over other forms of government. John Osgood Field puts it well: "Indians struggled against Englishmen for the right to run a British system in India."[13] The political elites believed that through the introduction of universal suffrage and the mass political participation that would follow, a traditional society based on an ascriptive oligarchic structure would transform itself into an egalitarian and open society. In addition, the spread of mass media and industrialization would help to internalize democratic values and lead to the development of an egalitarian political culture. To an extent these values are becoming increasingly integrated into the personality structure of the newer generations of Indians. However, values of caste, ethnicity, and minority politics exist as well. Says Mark Tully, "India has shown that democracy alone is not enough—nor, incidentally, is economic growth. What are required are politics and a political system which are relevant for India's past traditions and present circumstances."[14]

The frequent elections held at the state and national levels on the basis of adult franchise have broken the traditional isolation in which most of the villagers of India formerly lived. Many of the groups in the village society have developed political awareness and are learning to use their political power, and the members of the so-called backward (lower) castes and former untouchables (now called Dalits) are becoming increasingly restive and challenging the domination of the landowning upper castes. Consequently, electoral participation and voter turnout are impressive. India's Election Commission has a reputation of conducting free and fair elections.

Even though the degree of politicization is higher in urban than in rural areas, issue awareness among the rural poor has increased. Average citizens, though often illiterate and relatively ill informed, are not ignorant. In fact, they tend to display sound common sense in politics. They may or may not always be aware of the national issues involved in the elections, but pocketbook issues have a strong impact on their voting behavior. Moreover, they have penalized politicians and the parties for their high-handedness and insensitivity toward the people in national and state elections.

Despite the divisions within Indian society, Indians on the whole display a positive attitude toward the system and its accomplishments. They express pride in the creation and operation of its democratic political institutions; indeed, India's achievements in her external affairs and the growth of her soft power are symbols of political pride. India's technological, scientific, and industrial achievements in nuclear science, space, information technology, manufacturing, and military capability evoke positive responses among the elite and nonelite segments of the population. There is growing confidence among Indians about the country's future and individual well-being as a result of several developments: impressive economic gains, assertiveness in the military and nuclear spheres, the growth of power-projection capabilities in space and at sea, growing strategic partnerships with traditional players (Russia, United Kingdom, France, and Germany) and with nontraditional partners (United States, Israel, Japan, and Australia), an ability to manage relations with traditional rivals (Pakistan and China), and the lingering problem of foreign-aided and homegrown terrorism in Kashmir and other parts of India. Following the growth of global terrorism after September 2001, the value of India as a stabilizing element in the region became apparent to international observers.[15]

Traditionally, Indians have emphasized consensus, conciliation, compromise, and accommodation. In particular, community and caste leaders have widely used conflict management through consensus or arbitration. Gandhi employed this method to resolve intraparty disputes as well as a variety of conflicts arising in national politics. Most successful Indian leaders have been conciliators and consensus builders who were able to balance conflicting political interests based on religious, linguistic, and cultural diversities. It is widely believed that India's unity and integrity have been preserved primarily through the practice of the politics of consensus and conciliation as opposed to the politics of confrontation and partisan divisions.

Another dominant trait of Indian political culture, shaped by its religious traditions and literature, as well as by the behavior of such political leaders as Mahatma Gandhi and his followers, is a negative attitude toward the assumption of dictatorial powers (as in the case of Indira Gandhi during the Emergency in 1975) and toward abuse of power by elected leaders and public servants. Indian civil society groups have grown in numbers and involvement with a variety of social, environmental, legal, and political questions. Indian ethics emphasize self-negation—that is, renunciation of desire for power, money, and status. According to the ancient Hindu ordering of personal virtues, *satogun* (purity of heart and absence of desire for power and wealth) ranks higher than *rajogun* (the desire to acquire power or wealth); a *sanyasi* (a person who has renounced such desires and devotes himself entirely to social service) is superior to a king. Indians therefore tend to revere those who seek to influence politics and public policy without seeking political power. Hence, India has witnessed the introduction of what W. H. Morris-Jones has called the "language of saintly politics," a kind of politics that "is important as a language of comment rather than of description of practical behavior."[16] It sets very high standards of public behavior, with the Mahatma as the role model.

However, starting with the Nehru years (1947–1964), while Indian practitioners have talked in Gandhian terms, in reality traditional Indian utopian and moral principles, including Gandhian ones, have been marginalized, if not rendered irrelevant, in Indian political behavior. Change in Indian politics and policy making reflects the primacy of entrenched government rules and regulations, ad hocism, consensus building, and satisfactory official behavior as a basis of governance. As politics has become an important avenue of social mobility, and political ambition is playing an increasingly important role in the acquisition of political power, Indian politics has become what could be termed "amoral politics." This brand of politics is characterized by a decline of the political values associated with democratic institutions and political leaders during the early stages of independent India. For example, both the elected officials and the people know that the high-sounding moral phrases of politics serve rhetorical purposes only; they are not likely to be put into practice. In addition, the giving and accepting of bribes is a normal practice in political life; elected officials frequently seek and receive monetary rewards for the services they render, and persons hoping to acquire elective positions frequently purchase votes and distribute gifts to uneducated voters on or before polling days. Indeed, there is the widespread belief in India that with money and political influence, rules can be bent, and laws can be broken. Many politicians and their children are in league with black marketeers or other criminal elements, yet are rarely penalized for their transgressions. Such politicians are considered to be free looters interested only in plunder and power. Many in India look on the power-hungry professional politicians as a new breed of pundits, careerists, and dream merchants who have fooled many people often in the name of democracy and public service, but whose motive is self-aggrandizement more than public welfare. Moreover, corruption and the flow of black money (undeclared income) are widespread among Indian political parties, businesses, and official circles. In this respect the politicians and political representatives in India are not much different from those characteristic of the early stages of political development in many Western societies. Indeed, the politics based on representation rather than coercion tend in general to develop patron-client relationships rooted in amoral politics. As James Scott has noted, "Self-interest thus provides the necessary political cement when neither a traditional governing elite nor a ruling group based upon ideological or class interest is available."[17]

SUGGESTED READINGS

Basham, A. L., ed. *A Cultural History of India.* Oxford: Clarendon, 1975.

Brass, Paul. *Language, Religion, and Politics in North India.* London: Cambridge University Press, 1974.

————, ed. *Routledge Handbook of South Asian Politics*. London: Routledge, 2010.

Brown, D. Mackenzie. *The Nationalist Movement: Indian Political Thought from Ranade to Bhave*. Berkeley: University of California Press, 1965.

Dalrymple, William. *White Mughals*. London: Penguin Books, 2002.

de Bary, William T., ed. *Sources of Indian Tradition*. Vol. 1. New York: Columbia University Press, 1958.

Hardy, P. *The Muslims of British India*. Cambridge: Cambridge University Press, 1972.

Kohli, Atul, ed. *India's Democracy: An Analysis of Changing State-Society Relations*. Princeton, NJ: Princeton University Press, 1988.

Menon, V. P. *The Transfer of Power in India*. Princeton, NJ: Princeton University Press, 1957.

Moore, R. J. *Escape from Empire: The Attlee Government and the Indian Problem*. Oxford: Clarendon, 1980.

Muller, F. Max. *India: What Can It Teach Us?* New Delhi: Rupa Paperback, 2002.

Nandy, Ashis. *At the Edge of Psychology: Essays in Politics and Culture*. New Delhi: Oxford University Press, 1980.

————. "The Political Culture of the Indian State." *Daedalus* (fall 1989): 1–21.

Northrop, F. S. C. *The Meeting of East and West*. New York: Macmillan, Co., 1946, chs. 9 and 11.

Philips, C. H., ed. *Politics and Society in India*. New York: Praeger, 1962.

Radhakrishnan, S. *The Hindu View of Life*. New York: Macmillan, 1962.

Rudolph, Susanne H. "Consensus and Conflict in Indian Politics." *World Politics* (April 1981): 385–399.

Spear, Percival, ed. *A History of India*. Vol. 2. Rev. ed. London: Penguin Books, 1978.

————. *The Oxford History of India*. 3rd ed. London: Oxford University Press, 1967.

Srinivas, M. N. *Caste in Modern India and Other Essays*. Bombay: Asia Publishing House, 1962.

Upadhyaya, Prakash Chandra. "The Politics of Indian Secularism." *Modern Asian Studies* 26, no. 4 (1992): 816–853.

Varshney, Ashutosh. "Contested Meanings: India's National Identity, Hindu Nationalism, and the Politics of Anxiety." *Daedalus* (summer 1993): 227–261.

Weiner, Myron. "India: Two Political Cultures." In *Political Culture and Political Development*, edited by Lucian W. Pye and Sidney Verba, 199–244. Princeton, NJ: Princeton University Press, 1965.

Wolpert, Stanley. *India*. Upd. ed. Berkeley: University of California Press, 1999.

Zinkin, Maurice, and Taya Zinkin. *Britain and India*. Baltimore: Johns Hopkins University Press, 1964.

NOTES

1. Agricultural workforce from World Bank, "Development Indicators," http://data.worldbank.org/indicator/SL.AGR.EMPL.ZS/countries/IN?display=default. GDP data from Ministry of Finance, Government of India, "Economic Survey 2011–12," http://indiabudget.nic.in/survey.asp.

2. Percival Griffiths, *The British Impact on India* (London: Archon, 1953), 22; F. Max Muller, *India: What Can It Teach Us?* (New Delhi: Rupa Paperback, 2002).

3. A. L. Basham, *The Wonder That Was India* (New York: Grove, 1954), 341.

4. Arthur Lall, *The Emergence of Modern India* (New York: Columbia University Press, 1981), 12–13; E. B. Havell, *The History of Aryan Rule in India* (London: A. Harrap, 1918), xiii.

5. Griffiths, *British Impact*, 26. William Dalrymple, *White Mughals* (London: Penguin Books, 2002), Part 3, 110–156, explains wars, alliances, and intrigue among fueding Hindu and Muslim kingdoms in the Deccan and the role of East India Company and its French rivals, which led to instability.

6. Bamber Gascoigne, *The Great Moghuls*, rev. ed. (London: Robinson, 1998).

7. H. G. Rawlinson, *India: A Short Cultural History* (New York: Praeger, 1968), 245.

8. Dennis Dalton, "The Concept of Politics and Power in India: Ideological Traditions," in *The States of South Asia: The Problem of National Integration,* ed. J. R. Wilson and Dennis Dalton (London: C. Hunt, 1982), 177.

9. D. Mackenzie Brown, *The Nationalist Movement: Indian Political Thought from Ranade to Bhave* (Berkeley: University of California Press, 1965), 15.

10. With respect to representation in legislative bodies, the legal term for "untouchables" is "Scheduled Castes"; the unassimilated tribals are called "Scheduled Tribes." For significant changes in Dalits' political standing, see Christopher Jaffrelot, *Reservations and the Dalits at the Crossroads,* Center for the Advanced Study of India, University of Pennsylvania, May 8, 2007, http://casi.ssc.upenn.edu/iit/cjaffrelot. For a nuanced view of Indian caste politics—its negative and positive aspects—see Mark Tully, *Non-stop India* (New Delhi: Allen Lane/Penguin Books, 2011), 27–54.

11. Diana Farrell and Eric Beinhocker, "Next Big Spenders: India's Middle Class," Mckinsey Global Institute, May 19, 2007, http://www.mckinsey.com/Insights/MGI/In_the_news/Next _big_spenders_Indian_middle_class.

12. Ministry of Finance, Government of India, *Economic Survey 2011–2012*, http://indiabudget .nic.in/es2011–12/echap-13.pdf, 307.

13. John Osgood Field, *Consolidating Democracy: Politicization and Participation in India* (New Delhi: Manohar, 1980), 347.

14. Mark Tully, *No Full Stops in India* (New York: Penguin Books, 1991), 11.

15. Note, for example, the significant changes in US attitudes about India's economic, military, and politicosocial importance among the executive branch, congressional leaders, and the business community.

16. W. H. Morris-Jones, *The Government and Politics of India* (Garden City, NY: Doubleday, 1967), 47.

17. James C. Scott, "Corruption, Machine Politics, and Political Change," *American Political Science Review* (December 1969): 1151.

3

State Institutions and Changing Political Dynamics

Amajor problem facing the leaders of third world countries is creating stable political institutions capable of governing effectively, accomplishing sociopolitical changes peacefully, and providing smooth transitions of power. Events preceding Indian independence and the widespread religious rioting that accompanied the partition of the country had convinced the leaders of the Indian National Congress, who inherited power from the British government, that India needed a powerful, effective set of political institutions at the national level to provide stability in a vast land. Sardar Vallabhbhai Patel, deputy prime minister and home minister, summed up their position when he said that "the first requirement of any progressive country is internal and external security. It is impossible to make progress unless you first restore order in the country."[1] India's scorecard shows smooth transitions of power and peaceful power sharing, but there remain internal and external security problems.

The assembly that deliberated the institutional structure for the new nation and undertook the task of framing a new constitution was created by the British government. An overwhelming majority of its members were elected indirectly by the legislative bodies existing in the provinces of British India. Although elections to the provincial legislative bodies, before the creation of a Constituent Assembly, were not held on the basis of universal suffrage, as many as 46 million voters participated in the 1946 elections. The Constituent Assembly convened in December 1946 was thus a representative body of Indians. Its

43

membership, dominated by the Indian National Congress, consisted of intellectuals, lawyers, constitutional experts, and administrators, as well as ideologues. In short, it was a representative body from which emanated the different shades of opinion to be found in the India of the 1940s. Three years of discussion, debate, and deliberation on the draft of the constitution were required before it was adopted in November 1949. The new constitution, which came into effect on January 26, 1950, when India became a republic, is a lengthy, complex document. It is based on Western legal tradition and liberal democratic principles. Our discussion below shows that since independence, the balance of power has shifted among India's state organizations, political parties, and political institutions, such as the judiciary, the parliament, state governments, and national and regional political parties; however, the constitution continues to function as the framework for India's state apparatus.[2]

The Theory of India's Constitution

The Indian constitution represents a triumph of the modernists over the neotraditionalist elements. It represents the viewpoint of the nationalist leaders who envisioned India as a modern nation-state. Such leaders drew freely from the US and British constitutional systems and were deeply influenced by the experience of the liberal democratic societies of Canada and Western Europe. They also drew heavily from the Government of India Act of 1935.

The neotraditionalists, represented by hardcore followers of Mohandas Gandhi, pressed for the creation of a highly decentralized, partyless system of government based on the village *panchayats* (councils). Not seeing much wisdom in building a modern state system based on a Western model, they had suggested that the village, in which direct election would prevail, should constitute the core of the system. The rest of the political institutions would be elected indirectly. The neotraditionalists, however, lost out to the modernists.

During the colonial period, Indian leaders, while waging a war against the arbitrary exercise of power by British rulers, had learned to value civil liberties. The incorporation of a detailed list of fundamental rights into the constitution reflected their determination to safeguard the civil rights and individual freedoms of the common people. This list includes the rights to equality, to freedom of religion, to constitutional remedies, and to freedom from exploitation. The list also includes certain cultural and educational rights.

The constitution, with its impressive list of rights, seeks to alter the traditional Indian system of social stratification based on birth and occupation. Its various articles abolish untouchability, provide equal opportunity for jobs, and ensure equality of individuals in the eyes of the law. Recognizing that a democratic polity cannot operate without freedoms, its articles provide such basic rights as freedom of speech and expression, freedom to form associations, freedom of movement, and freedom to assemble peacefully without arms. The division of the country on the basis of religion had created a sense of insecurity among the minorities, especially the Muslims. To assuage their fears and guarantee their security, the constitution provides for freedom of religion and worship and prohibits discrimination in administrative, political, and social life on the basis of caste, creed, sex, or social origin.

All of these rights are protected by the courts, and judicial procedures are provided to ensure their enforcement. The Indian judiciary, especially the Supreme Court, has been active in protecting the basic rights of citizens.

These rights are not absolute or unlimited, however. The framers of the constitution were also concerned about India's unity and territorial integrity. Many subcontinental empires had been broken up in the past as a result of the divisive forces existing within India, most recently exemplified by the creation of Pakistan. Thus the framers incorporated emergency provisions into the constitution to safeguard national unity. In an emergency caused by foreign aggression or internal civil disorder, civil rights can be suspended. Through such laws as the Preventive Detention Act (1950), the Defense of Internal Security of India Act (1971), the Maintenance of Internal Security Act (1971), and other measures, great authority has been placed in the hands of government. Under these acts the government can limit personal freedom and arrest people without specifying the charges. Such limitations have often been criticized by advocates of civil liberty.

The Directive Principles of State Policy, another distinguishing feature of the Indian constitutional system, is a statement of principles, goals, and ideals to be pursued by the state and the national governments in their policy formulations. The declaration was borrowed from the constitution of the Irish Republic. These principles direct the state to provide satisfactory means for people to earn their living, to obtain proper distribution of material resources of the community, to protect children and youth against exploitation, to promote the interest of the weaker sections of society, and to ban alcohol and cow slaughter. As they have no force of law, they cannot be enforced by the courts.

For purposes of amendment, the constitution has been divided into three sections. The section dealing with such important matters as the creation of new states out of existing states and the creation and abolition of the second chambers of state legislatures can be amended by a simple parliamentary majority. A second section dealing primarily with fundamental rights can be amended by a two-thirds majority vote in parliament. Amendment of the last section of the constitution, which deals with the fundamentals of government, such as the offices of the president and prime minister and the powers of the Supreme Court, requires not only a two-thirds majority of parliament but also ratification by a majority of the state legislative assemblies.

The President, Vice President, Prime Minister, and Cabinet

The government in India is headed by the president, the executive by the prime minister, and the judiciary by the Supreme Court; the parliament is entrusted with the exercise of legislative power (see Figure 3.1). India has adopted the British system of parliamentary democracy. The president in India, like the queen in the United Kingdom, is a ceremonial chief of state. The executive powers lie with the prime minister, who heads the government. The Indian prime minister, unlike the US president, does not have a fixed term of office but can be removed from office by the lower house of parliament by a vote of no confidence.

The President

The president is the chief of state rather than the head of government. He or she is elected for a term of five years, with no restrictions on reelection (although no president of India has ever been elected for a third consecutive term). The president is chosen by an electoral college consisting of all elected members of the legislative assemblies existing in each of India's twenty-eight states, along with the elected members of the two chambers of the Indian parliament. A single transferable ballot is used, and the members of the electoral college are allowed to give their first and second preferences. If no candidate wins a clear majority of the votes, the second-preference votes cast for the

FIGURE 3.1. **Organization of the Central Government of India**

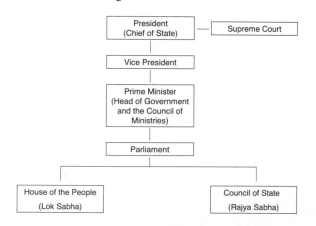

candidate with the lowest number of votes are transferred to other candidates. Such vote transferences continue until one candidate secures an absolute majority of votes and is declared the president of the country. This process of election, while complex, gives substantial voice to the states in choosing who will serve as chief of state. As the presidential election is conducted by an electoral college, there is no popular participation, and the event does not generate national excitement. A president may be removed by a process of impeachment conducted in the parliament.

Although vested with many executive powers, in actual practice the president of India acts only on the advice of the prime minister and the cabinet. During periods of national crisis—for instance, in the event of an attack by a foreign power, internal insurrection, or acute financial crisis—the president may declare a state of emergency. In such situations, the powers of the national government are enormously enlarged. Fundamental rights and freedoms may be suspended, and the country may be brought under a kind of authoritarian rule. The president also may declare a state of emergency in a particular state where the constitutional machinery has failed and take over its administration for a limited period. However, the exercise of such drastic powers by the president is subject to control by both the cabinet and the parliament.

The president of India has powers normally exercised by ceremonial chiefs of state in other countries, such as the right to address the joint sessions of parliament, to sign bills with a limited veto, to appoint the justices of the Supreme Court and other high public officials, to receive ambassadors from other countries, and to grant pardons. He or she also serves as the head of the nation's armed forces. All of these powers are exercised only at the advice of the prime minister, however.

A majority of the twelve persons who have been elected president were drawn from active politics. Their backgrounds have been diverse (see Table 3.1). Rajendra Prasad, the first president of India and a stalwart of the freedom movement, held the position from 1952 to 1962. A person with strong views on sociopolitical issues and a strong base in the conservative sector of the Congress Party, he had constant political differences with Jawaharlal Nehru, the first prime minister of the country, although these differences were rarely made public. Nehru, however, treated him as the constitutional head of state.

Prasad was succeeded by Sarvapalli Radhakrishnan (1962–1967), an academician and philosopher of international stature. Although Radhakrishnan had no independent power base in national politics, he did not hesitate to express his disagreement with Nehru's policies. Both Prasad and Radhakrishnan were elected as the nominees of the Congress Party, but they were able to rise above party politics and met frequently with the leaders of the opposition parties.

TABLE 3.1 Presidents of India

Year of Election	Name of President	Religion	Party	Region/State	Native Language
1952	Rajendra Prasad	Hindu	Congress	North (Bihar)	Hindi
1957	Rajendra Prasad	Hindu	Congress	North (Bihar)	Hindi
1962	Sarvapalli Radhakrishnan	Hindu	Congress	South (Tamil Nadu)	Tamil
1967	Zakir Hussain (died in office)	Muslim	Congress	North (Uttar Pradesh)	Urdu/ Hindi
1969	V. V. Giri	Hindu	Independent (supported by Indira Gandhi)	South (Andhra Pradesh)	Kannada
1974	Fakhruddin Ali Ahmed (died in office)	Muslim	Congress (I)	Northeast (Assam)	Assamese/ Urdu
1977	Neelam Sanjiva Reddy	Hindu	Janata	South (Andhra Pradesh)	Telugu
1982	Giani Zail Singh	Sikh	Congress (I)	Northwest (Punjab)	Punjabi
1987	R. Venkataraman	Hindu	Congress (I)	South (Tamil Nadu)	Tamil
1992	Shankar Dayal Sharma	Hindu	Congress (I)	Central India	Hindi
1997	K. R. Narayanan	Hindu	Independent	South (Kerala)	Malayalam
2002	A. P. J. Abdul Kalam	Muslim	Independent (supported by BJP)	South (Tamil Nadu)	Tamil
2007	Pratibha Patil	Hindu	Congress (I)	Central (Maharashtra)	Marathi
2012	Pranab Mukherjee	Hindu	Congress (I)	West Bengal	Bengali

In 1967 Zakir Hussain, another academician, a Muslim, and a favorite of Prime Minister Indira Gandhi, was elected to the presidency as a nominee of the Congress Party. With Hussain's election the presidency became more partisan than it had been in previous years. In 1969 Hussain died of a heart attack. Indira Gandhi then supported V. V. Giri, an independent trade union leader, in opposition to the official Congress Party candidate, Neelam Sanjiva Reddy. (Reddy was a nominee of the syndicate, an informal body of party bosses.) Giri was elected, defeating the official Congress Party nominee. Even though Giri rarely showed any partisanship and always acted on the advice of the prime minister, he never saw himself as Indira Gandhi's protégé. Hence, in later presidential elections Gandhi became very careful in selecting candidates and sought to elevate to the office only persons who would not defy her or show even nominal independence.

When Giri's term expired in 1974, Fakhruddin Ali Ahmed, a cabinet member and staunch supporter of Indira Gandhi, was elected. It was Ahmed who signed the 1975 declaration of emergency proposed by Indira Gandhi that resulted in the suspension of democracy and established, for a time, what amounted to an authoritarian system in India. Indira Gandhi's manipulation of the presidency made it evident that the occupant of this high office could play a key role in the operation of the country's institutional structure, as in the selection of the prime minister and the declaration of a state of emergency. This implication was further reinforced by the actions of Neelam Sanjiva Reddy, who was elected president in 1977 after Ahmed died and the Janata Party captured power by defeating the Congress Party at the polls. Even though Reddy was a member of the Janata Party, he was elected as a consensus candidate. During his term (1977–1982), he played a controversial role in the selection of the prime minister, especially when the Janata Party lost its majority and no party had an absolute majority in parliament. Generally outspoken on public issues, he did not hesitate to criticize a prime minister when he felt it was needed.

In 1982, when Reddy's term expired, Indira Gandhi, who had won the parliamentary election in 1980, successfully installed Giani Zail Singh, a Sikh, as the seventh president of India, instead of asking Reddy to seek a second term. As Zail Singh had neither the educational background nor the intellectual stature of his predecessors, the country's establishment did not acclaim his elevation to the presidency. He was viewed as an unabashed Indira loyalist who would faithfully carry out her bidding to prove his loyalty. Zail Singh remained loyal to Indira and later helped in the smooth succession of Rajiv Gandhi to the position of prime minister after his mother's assassination. Nevertheless, Zail Singh brought his high office close to the people. He was termed "the people's president" because he was one of the country's most accessible presidents.

R. Venkataraman, a senior statesman and experienced administrator elected in 1987, proved to be more impartial and nonpartisan than his immediate predecessor. Shankar Dayal Sharma, the highly respected elder statesman who succeeded him in 1992, followed the traditions set by Venkataraman. In 1997, while celebrating fifty years of independence, Indian political parties elected former diplomat K. R. Narayanan to the presidency, marking the first time a Dalit (former untouchable) had been elected to the office. Dr. A. P. J. Abdul Kalam became the eleventh president of India on July 25, 2002, having been nominated by the rightist, Hindu-oriented Bharatiya Janata Party (BJP) prime minister Atal Bihari Vajpayee. Kalam is a distinguished scientist of Muslim faith, the first Indian president with a string of achievements in the development of India's space and missile programs. He is committed to using science and technology for India's development and transforming India into a developed nation by 2020. His choice was a signal event in Indian politics because he was chosen for his distinguished record in the defense sector and his literary pursuits rather than for personal loyalty to the ruling party or the Nehru-Gandhi dynasty.

In 2007, Pratibha Patil was elected president. As the first woman to hold the office, she has an impressive party resume. She was a Congress Party member of parliament (MP), the first woman governor of Rajasthan, and a protégé of Sonia Gandhi, the Congress Party president. Her predecessors were involved in government formation when a clear majority did not exist in the parliament and in providing advice to the government. Like President Zail Singh, Indira Gandhi's nominee, President Patel has functioned as a rubber stamp of the Singh government.

In 2012 Pranab Mukherjee assumed the presidency. He has been a senior government minister holding all major portfolios, such as finance, defense, and external affairs, and has a reputation as a problem solver in a coalition government. A protégé of P. V. Narasimha Rao, Indira Gandhi, and Sonia Gandhi, he was sidelined by Rajiv Gandhi, who saw him as a threat to his leadership. Mukherjee has extensive international experience as a member of the boards at the International Monetary Fund and the World Bank. He has a leftist electoral base in West Bengal, but his policies show a pro-US orientation because he facilitated the United States–India Nuclear Accord despite leftist objections and he supports defense procurements from the United States.

The Vice President

India's vice presidency is not very different from its counterpart in the United States. Though elected by the two chambers of parliament in a joint session rather than by an electoral college, the vice president performs some of the same functions as a US vice president. In addition to presiding over the sessions of the Council of State, the upper house of Indian parliament, the vice president succeeds the president in the event of the latter's resignation, death, or incapacity. Unlike the US vice president, however, the Indian vice president does not complete his predecessor's term. He acts as president only until a new president is elected—an event that must take place within six months. Under normal circumstances, the vice president is elected for a term of five years. Some vice presidents (such as Radhakrishnan, Zakir Hussain, and Giri) have subsequently been elevated to the office of the presidency. The president and vice president are traditionally expected to come from different regions of the country.

The Prime Minister and the Cabinet

The real executive of the country comprises the prime minister and the cabinet. The personality of the prime minister determines the nature of the authority that he or she is likely to exercise. Such prime ministers as Lal Bahadur Shastri and Morarji Desai served as firsts among equals, but this was not the case with Jawaharlal Nehru and his daughter, Indira Gandhi. Longtime domination of government by charismatic and powerful personalities such as Nehru, Indira Gandhi, and Vajpayee, and particularly the centralization of political power by Gandhi in her office, has rendered the Indian executive a prime ministerial rather than a cabinet government. However, Manmohan Singh (2004–present) is widely perceived and criticized as a weak leader who lacks the political capacity to develop major economic reforms and depends for his policies on Sonia Gandhi, Congress Party president and the real power center in the ruling coalition. Under his tenure the authority of the prime minister, the cabinet, and the parliament has diminished. Thus far, India has a unique record as a successful electoral democracy with smooth transfers of power and absence of fear of a military coup. However, the experience of the Manmohan Singh–Sonia Gandhi pattern of governance raises a question: Is the Indian government an instrument of meaningful economic and social change, as was expected by India's nationalist and democratic movement, or is it now a revolving door for power-hungry politicians who displace current office holders for personal gain?

The prime minister is selected by the president of India. In reality, the president invites the leader of the majority party in parliament to form the council of ministers. Usually major political parties go to the parliamentary polls with a clear choice of leaders. For the most part, the voters know who is likely to be the prime minister if a particular party wins a majority in the lower house of parliament. Until 2004 the Congress Party had faced parliamentary elections with a known leader as its head—a strategy that has often given voters the opportunity to elect the prime minister of the country. In the 1984 and 1989 parliamentary elections, for instance, the Congress (I) Party (i.e., the Indira Congress, originally dominated by Indira Gandhi) went to the polls with Rajiv Gandhi as its leader. In the 1996 elections the Bharatiya Janata Party (BJP) followed the same process with Atal Bihari Vajpayee as its leader and projected him as the future prime minister of the country in case the party won a majority in parliament. However, the 2004 and 2009 general elections broke this pattern. Sonia Gandhi led the Congress Party to power but declined to become the prime minister and instead choose Manmohan Singh for the post. The latter did not have a seat in the Lok Sabha; nor did he seek election in the lower house. This was a break from convention in India and in Western parliamentary democracies.

The president can exercise some discretion in the selection of the prime minister when no party commands a clear majority in the lower house of parliament. When a party leader has clear majority support in the lower house of parliament, the president has no choice but to call on him to form the council of ministers.

In general, the prime minister determines the composition of the council of ministers as well as its inner core, the cabinet. Members of the cabinet occupy the highest position within the council of ministers and meet regularly under the chairmanship of the prime minister. The prime minister also distributes the portfolios. However, the character of India's prime ministerial and cabinet system has changed since 2004. The United Progressive Alliance (UPA-1, 2004–2009, and UPA-2, 2009–present) is a coalition of minority parties. Sonia Gandhi, the head of the Congress Party and the senior coalition partner in both UPA-1 and UPA-2, is the real source of power and decision making. A coalition cabinet reflects a need to accommodate coalition members' demands for ministerial berths and policy changes—and Sonia Gandhi's interests. Dr. Singh is not the apex of political power and authority as Nehru, Indira Gandhi, and Atal Bihari Vajpayee were. The system now, since 2004, is a two-headed system, which has degraded the process of national decision making and policy development. Three cases illustrate the problem: (1) The government announced changes in foreign retail investments. Following criticism in parliament and complaints from several state governments about the lack of consultation and arrogance by the Congress minority government, the decision was quickly reversed. (2) The government banned cotton exports, a major economic policy issue, but the national agricultural minister complained that he had not been consulted. The ban was reversed. (3) The government, in a major 2008 decision, issued second-generation (2G) mobile licenses. This led to charges of corruption, and the minister responsible is facing an inquiry and has been jailed. The Indian Supreme Court revoked 122 licenses, calling the spectrum sale "arbitrary and unconstitutional."[3]

Ever present in the cabinet have been organizations and committees, formal and informal, that serve as the prime minister's inner core of advisers. According to Michael Brecher, in the early period of Nehru's prime ministership, major policy decisions were made by an informal supercabinet consisting of Nehru and Patel, the two stalwarts of the freedom movement. Such decisions were subsequently submitted to the regular cabinet for approval.[4] After Patel's death in 1950, an informal kitchen cabinet consisting of Maulana Abdul Kalam Azad and Rafi Ahmad Kidwai, later joined by Govind Ballabh Pant, became Nehru's main advisory body. Since Nehru's time the cabinet has always contained many subcommittees consisting of important cabinet members. Indira Gandhi, for example, chaired the Political Affairs Committee, a small subcommittee consisting of senior members of the cabinet that came to be known as a cabinet within a cabinet. However, the Nehru–Indira Gandhi system of cabinet consultation has broken down since 2004.

TABLE 3.2 Prime Ministers of India

Prime Minister	Party Affiliation	Year of Birth	Year of Death	Leadership Dates	Caste/Subcaste (Religion)	Language/Region
Jawaharlal Nehru	Congress	1889	1964	Aug. 1947–May 1964	Brahmin (Hindu)	Hindi, North (UP)
Lal Bahadur Shastri	Congress	1904	1966	Jun. 1964–Jan. 1966	Kayastha (Hindu)	Hindi, North (UP)
Indira Gandhi	Congress	1917	1984	Jan. 1966–Mar. 1977	Brahmin (Hindu)	Hindi, North (UP)
Morarji Desai	Janata	1896	1995	Mar. 1977–Jul. 1979	Brahmin (Hindu)	Gujarati, West (Gujarat)
Charan Singh	Janata (Secular)	1902	1987	Jul. 1979–Jan. 1980	Jat (Hindu)	Hindi, North (UP)
Indira Gandhi	Congress (I)	1917	1984	Jan. 1980–Oct. 1984	Brahmin (Hindu)	Hindi, North (UP)
Rajiv Gandhi	Congress (I)	1944	1991	Oct. 1984–Dec. 1989	Parsi-Brahmin (Hindu)	Hindi, North (UP)
V. P. Singh	Janata Dal	1931	2008	Dec. 1989–Nov. 1990	Rajput (Hindu)	Hindi, North (UP)
Chandra Shekhar	Janata Dal (Secular)	1927	2007	Nov. 1990–Jun. 1991	Rajput (Hindu)	Hindi, North (UP)
P. V. Narasimha Rao	Congress (IP)	1921	2004	Jun. 1991–May 1996	Brahmin (Hindu)	Telugu, South (AP)
Atal Bihari Vajpayee	BJP	1926		May 1996–Jun. 1996	Brahmin (Hindu)	Hindi, central India
H. D. Deve Gowda	Janata Dal	1934		Jun. 1996–Apr. 1997	Backward caste (Hindu)	Kannada, South
Inder Kumar Gujral	Janata Dal	1920	2012	Apr. 1997–Apr. 1998	Khatri (Hindu)	Punjabi/Urdu, Northwest (Punjab)
Atal Bihari Vajpayee	BJP	1924		Apr. 1998–May 2004	Brahmin (Hindu)	Hindi, central India
Manmohan Singh	Congress	1932		May 2004–present	Sikh	Punjabi, Punjab

A majority of Indian prime ministers have come from the Hindi-speaking states of North India. There has been no prime minister from the Scheduled Castes, consisting of former untouchables, now known as Dalits (see Table 3.2).

Influential Prime Ministers

Jawaharlal Nehru: Charismatic, Modernist, and Flawed

Whereas Gandhi is called the father of the Indian nation, Nehru (1889–1964) should be credited with building India's modern political institutions and laying the foundations of its economic and foreign policies. In 1947, Nehru became independent India's first prime minister, and he held this position and dominated the Indian political scene until his death on May 24, 1964.

Nehru's commitment to democratic institutions and norms of behavior, his unbounded faith in science, technology, and the industrialization of the country, his emphasis on planned economic development in India, and his concern for the poor, the downtrodden, and the minorities all deeply influenced political developments in India. He valued individual freedom and believed that only in a democratic system can individuals realize their full potential. Although the introduction of a parliamentary system in India based on the British model may be attributed to the collective efforts of Western-educated elites, it was Nehru, as the first prime minister and most powerful leader of the country, who put it into practice.

Not only did he adhere to the practice of holding elections for parliament on the basis of universal suffrage, an unusual practice in a third world country, but he also respected the autonomy of the Election Commission and never intervened in its affairs.

Continuing a pre-independence practice, he held regular elections of party officials at all levels and thus maintained intraparty democracy. On occasion Nehru was unwilling to tolerate dissent within the Congress Party, as in 1951, when he forced Purushottam Das Tandon out of the party presidency because of the latter's commitment to Hindu chauvinistic ideology. But he respected the popular electoral verdict, even when it favored his ideological opponents. Nehru, like Gandhi, adhered to constitutional procedures and norms of behavior.

Nehru also permitted the democratic process to operate in the states. He was willing to accommodate the Congress Party chief ministers, even when they disagreed with him. He rarely intervened in their affairs as long as they broadly followed the party platform. And he was willing to accommodate the demands of the regional leaders, even if they did not belong to his party.

In addition, Nehru withstood pressure from the right wing of the Congress Party, which, after the creation of Pakistan, was less willing to treat Indian

Muslims as equals of the Hindu majority. This right-wing faction wanted to modify Nehru's vision of a secular state in favor of Hindus. Ultimately, however, Nehru prevailed, granting Muslims and other minorities equal rights in the constitution of India. Nehru, like Mohandas Gandhi, had a national support base. He never appealed to regional or religious sentiments to keep himself in power. In addition to his authority based on the constitution, which Muhammad Ali Jinnah's successors in Pakistan lacked, Nehru had charisma and soon became a folk hero. He enjoyed the support of the masses, but he also had a very large following among intellectuals, especially among the English-educated, westernized, and leftist intelligentsia, whose members were committed to his ideas of religious tolerance and secular political culture.

As a modernist, Nehru considered science-based technology the key to the future prosperity and transformation of Indian society. He thus initiated policies that resulted in the establishment of a score of scientific institutions in India. For him, the industrialization of the country and scientific and technological development were interrelated goals for achieving the economic independence of the country—hence his great emphasis on planned economic development. Although Nehru's ideals were remarkable, his economic and diplomatic record in hindsight shows many failures. Since the early 1990s, his successors began to dismantle his ideology and policy of socialist planning by accepting economic and market-oriented reforms.

Indira Gandhi: Dynamic, Divisive, and Authoritarian
The period of Indira Gandhi's dominance in Indian politics, from 1966 to 1984, put enormous strain on the country's political institutions as well as on the informal rules used to settle conflicts among elites. Unlike her father, Jawaharlal Nehru, Indira Gandhi (1917–1984) had little regard for established procedure and norms of democratic politics. In 1966 she was brought to power as the prime minister by the party bosses; by 1969 she had become embroiled in a power struggle with the same group of leaders. This power struggle evolved into a conflict between the Young Turks, represented by Indira Gandhi, and the older, conservative party bosses, represented by the syndicate. She split the Congress Party in 1969. Gandhi's progressive image resulted from the introduction of her mildly radical program of nationalization of banks, abolition of privy purses (pensions) for the rulers of the former native states, liberal loan terms for the poor sector of the society, and strong denouncement of the monopoly of business and industrial establishments in India. This progressive strategy paid her rich dividends. She earned the support of most of the intellectual establishment in India, particularly the leftists and Marxists. She was quite successful in projecting the image of a dynamic leader seeking the establishment

of an egalitarian social order. These progressive projects also helped her to ward off any threat to her authority from the communist or socialist parties, which claimed to be champions of the poor. Having conducted herself as an accomplished politician, she surprised nobody when she won a massive majority in the 1971 parliamentary elections.

Riding on the wave of popularity generated by India's victory in the war with Pakistan over the issue of the creation of the independent nation of Bangladesh, she carried her Congress Party to victory in the 1972 state elections. With these electoral victories, she became not only the dominant force within the Congress Party but also the undisputed leader of the country.

Indira Gandhi's departure from the established constitutional practices that had been in operation since independence came as a shock, however. One of the most dramatic developments in the postindependence period was her declaration of national emergency, based on a provision included in the constitution of India for cases in which internal insurrection or external aggression threatens the country's security. Only twice previously had such an emergency been declared, and for external reasons: once in 1962, when India and the People's Republic of China fought a brief war over a border dispute, and again in 1971, when the Indo-Pakistani War broke out over the liberation of Bangladesh. In 1975, however, India witnessed widespread discontent over the failure of Indira Gandhi's economic policies. She was unable to reduce unemployment, control inflation, or cut widespread corruption. The opposition leaders organized mass rallies and protest marches, some demanding the resignation of the state governments led by her party.

Ultimately, a crucial court decision against her led to the declaration of internal emergency. On June 12, 1975, on the basis of an election petition, a judge of the High Court in Allahabad convicted Gandhi of breach of election laws. She lost her seat in parliament and was barred from holding elective office for six years. As the violations were based on minor technicalities of the law, however, she appealed the conviction to the Supreme Court of India, which reversed the decision of the lower court and allowed her to stay in power. But the lower court's verdict had undermined the legitimacy of her office. When the opposition leaders demanded her resignation, she feared both loss of her office and widespread disruption and nationwide protests. The declaration of emergency on June 26, 1975, enabled her to arrest all her political opponents, including Jaya Prakash Narayan, a venerable Gandhian leader; Morarji Desai, a former deputy prime minister; Charan Singh, a prominent opposition leader; and thousands of other opposition leaders and party workers.

Indira Gandhi made the decision to declare an emergency with the support of her family and some of her close associates rather than in consultation with the cabinet as required by constitutional law. The declaration has been criticized as a violation of both the spirit of the constitution and the democratic policies in practice since independence. Here a major policy decision showed the influence of Indira Gandhi, her son Sanjay Gandhi (an unelected insider), and a few advisors. This episode revealed that decision-making power had shifted to the prime minister's household—a pattern consolidated by Rajiv Gandhi and Sonia Gandhi.

The eighteen-month period of emergency was the first authoritarian rule experienced by India since the country had attained independence. Indira Gandhi enforced rigid press censorship. Numerous organizations were banned. Furthermore, paramilitary and police organization became arbitrary, creating an atmosphere of widespread oppression and fear. Gandhi also successfully amended the constitution to free the prime minister from judicial control. In the future, electoral disputes involving such high public officials as the president, vice president, and prime minister would not be referred to the courts. She also postponed a parliamentary election.

During this period her son, Sanjay, became a center of extra-constitutional authority. Although not a member of the government, he launched his Five Point Program, which included, among other projects, forced sterilization—a stipulation limiting families to only two children. His arbitrary and arrogant exercise of political power created widespread discontent and alienation, even among the members of the Congress Party and India's widely respected bureaucrats. He arbitrarily transferred many civil servants and even dismissed chief ministers of the states who opposed his policies.

In short, Indira Gandhi not only differed from her predecessors in her style of leadership but also drastically changed even the substance of Indian politics. She sought to exercise state power on a personal level, sometimes disregarding constitutional norms and practices—as when she groomed her son Sanjay to be her successor. In March 1977 she called parliamentary elections to legitimize her authority and the constitutional changes made during the period of emergency, but she miscalculated. Her party lost the election, and she could not even get herself elected to parliament. Such a humiliating defeat for Nehru's daughter demonstrated that India's illiterate voters had come to value the rules and procedures of a democratic polity. They resented the arbitrary exercise of political power by men such as Sanjay and the members of India's police administration. They also resented the loss of links with the administration that they had enjoyed earlier through their representatives. Indira Gandhi was brought back into power in the 1980 elections when her opponents could not manage their differences with each other. She was assassinated on October 31, 1984.

Indira Gandhi's dedication to a strong and united India was never questioned, but her leadership style left a bitter legacy. She undermined the democratic fabric of India by encouraging the rise of her son, Sanjay Gandhi, as an extra-constitutional center of power and influence in Indian politics and policy making. The Indira Gandhi era set in motion the theory that the Nehru-Gandhi dynasty was critical to India's destiny and that Indian secularism was tied to rule by the Nehru dynasty and the Congress Party. Sonia Gandhi, currently the leader of the Congress Party, is the guardian of this view.

Rajiv Gandhi: Dynastic Rule with Limited Competence

Rajiv Gandhi (1944–1991) became the seventh prime minister of India following his mother, Indira Gandhi's assassination on October 31, 1984. His elevation to the position of prime minister followed the established procedure of succession, and his appointment to this position by the president of India was subsequently confirmed by his unanimous election as party leader by 497 Congress (I) members of parliament. Nevertheless, Rajiv was the first person to become prime minister of this vast land without having held any ministerial position at either the national or state level. He was elevated to the high office of prime minister over the protests of numerous senior cabinet members and party men, many of whom had far more administrative and political experience than Rajiv, whose political experience was limited to two years of organizational work within the Congress (I). A former airline pilot, he was brought into politics by his mother after the accidental death on June 23, 1980, of his younger brother, Sanjay. In 1981 he was elected to the lower house of parliament in a special election to fill the vacancy caused by Sanjay's death. Rajiv entered politics reluctantly, his main incentive being to help his mother, who had ceased to trust almost everybody except the members of her immediate family. He worked in his mother's shadow until he became prime minister.

The Congress (I) members certainly made some cold calculations when they elected Rajiv as leader of the party. None of the members of Indira Gandhi's cabinet were leaders of national standing. They would have been little help to the party in winning the forthcoming parliamentary elections. However, as a grandson of Jawaharlal Nehru and heir to the Nehru dynasty, Rajiv had national recognition. In addition, the sympathy generated by the brutal assassination of Indira Gandhi ultimately helped the party, led by Rajiv, to win the parliamentary elections of 1984.

At the outset of his administration in 1984, the people of India had high expectations of Nehru's grandson. Unlike many of the old guard of Indian politics, Rajiv was blessed with a clean public image, potential for a new style of management, and a pragmatic approach to politics. Very shortly these high hopes were dashed as Rajiv developed an imperial and arrogant style of governance, becoming inaccessible not only to the people but also to high government and party officials.

Rajiv reshuffled his cabinet twenty-seven times during his five-year term of office, and between 1985 and 1989 he changed Congress (I) Party chief ministers in the states twenty times. In addition he surrounded himself with a small number of advisers, primarily civil servants, media experts, and foreign-trained technocrats with no roots in traditional Indian society.

Following the pattern set by his mother, he tended to centralize power in the prime minister's office and household. Although Rajiv liberalized the economy, the benefits of growth were unevenly distributed. The tendency toward arrogance and corruption and the unequal distribution of new wealth led to public disenchantment with Rajiv, resulting in his electoral defeat in 1989.

In March 1991, after two governments fell in quick succession, general elections were called. In the ensuing elections, Rajiv and his party seemed to have a slight edge over the opposition parties. However, Rajiv's political career was tragically cut short on May 21, 1991, when he was assassinated during an election rally by a member of the Sri Lankan Tamil Tigers. His death temporarily ended the hold of the Nehru-Gandhi dynasty on both the Congress (I) Party and the national government.

Indira Gandhi's tenure marked the start of dynastic rule in Indian politics, but she was known for her ability to outmaneuver Congress Party bosses, cut Indian princes down to size, nationalize Indian banks, and engineer the Bangladesh War (1971) and the breakup of Pakistan against the fierce opposition of President Richard Nixon, his adviser Henry Kissinger, and China's leaders. India's economy lacked luster, and Indian politics were polarized, but her ability to manipulate her opponents and the bureaucracy to protect her position showed her understanding of the weakness of her political opponents and the usefulness of skilled administrators. Indira Gandhi's rule laid the foundation for the Indira–Rajiv–Sonia Gandhi dynasty. It showed that personalities mattered more than ideologies, and personal power was more important than development of policies for the public good. Her tendency to destabilize state governments that opposed her and the failure to conduct elections for Congress Party officeholders prevented the rise of strong leaders with grassroots support. Ironically, the Indira–Sanjay–Rajiv–Sonia Gandhi habit of intervention against state governments gave regional political parties the impetus to develop grassroots support and to make states' power the basis for balancing the power and interests of the center with those of the state governments.

Indira Gandhi's activism was partly self-serving and partly served Indian interests. Rajiv Gandhi's tenure revealed activism in the form of ill-conceived measures. Three examples suffice: (1) he wanted to develop a nondiscrimina-tory nuclear nonproliferation treaty—a nonstarter; (2) he wanted to discuss nu-clear disarmament with China, only to be reminded by Beijing that he did not have nuclear arms and there was nothing to discuss; and (3) he sent the Indian army as peacekeepers to Sri Lanka, and the mission ended in failure. His death in 1991 at the hands of a Sri Lankan Tamil suicide bomber ended his career prematurely and appeared to end the Nehru family dynasty, until the rise of Sonia Gandhi.

Atal Bihari Vajpayee

Atal Bihari Vajpayee (1924–present), one of the best-known national leaders of the BJP, was the first genuine non–Congress Party prime minister of the coun-try. A powerful orator, a versatile and enduring politician, and a charismatic personality, Vajpayee convinced his reluctant party members in the Mumbai session of the BJP to accept his Gandhian socialism and humanistic liberalism as the new political creed of the party in order to broaden its base.

A founding member of the Bharatiya Jana Sangh, the right-wing Hindu na-tionalist party, he never gave the impression of being a spokesman for Hindu fundamentalism or chauvinism, despite his long association with the Rashtriya Swayamsevak Sangh (RSS), a militant, right-wing social and political organiza-tion. Vajpayee was president of the Jana Sangh from 1968 to 1973; earlier he had held the position of general secretary. From 1957 to 1977 he was also leader of the Jana Sangh parliamentary party.

Born into a Brahmin family from Gwalior (Madhya Pradesh), Vajpayee was educated at the Victoria (now Laxmibai) College of Gwalior and Dayanand Anglo-Vedic (DAV) College of Kanpur, where he earned a master of arts de-gree. He started his political career as a journalist and edited various Hindi-language magazines and newspapers, all of them associated with Hindu nationalist organizations.

Vajpayee was first elected to the Lok Sabha, the lower house of the Indian parliament. A skilled parliamentarian gifted with a sense of humor, a rare qual-ity for an Indian politician, Vajpayee has earned the respect of his colleagues in both his own party and the opposition. During his term as Janat Party govern-ment minister for external affairs, he displayed his flexibility, diplomatic so-phistication, and administrative abilities.

Vajpayee's ideological liberalism, political flexibility, and use of diplomatic skills at home and abroad enabled him to head a multiparty National Demo-cratic Alliance (NDA) government and move India forward on economic and strategic fronts. In 1998 the Vajpayee-led BJP government, in defiance of in-ternational opinion, conducted nuclear tests and embarked on the development of nuclear weapons. In 2000, under his leadership, the NDA government was able to repair the diplomatic damage by reaching understandings with the United States and other major powers. The United States and India became strategic partners, leading to significant land, sea, and air cooperation between Indian and American military services, as well as increased economic interactions. On the domestic front his government could also claim credit for introducing the second generation of economic reforms, notably relating to opening up the insurance sector and telecommunications industry to private investment and to disinvestment of public-sector undertakings. Furthermore, it created the three new states of Uttarachal, Jharkhand, and Chattisgarh.

Vajpayee, however, still faced the challenge of removing the feeling of insecurity that often haunts the Christian and Muslim minorities of the country and meeting the demands of various ethnicities and nationalities in Jammu and Kashmir and northeastern India.

Though short-lived, the Vajpayee era introduced major changes in Indian diplomatic and strategic affairs, external relationships, and the approach to internal secessionist movements. The 1998 nuclear tests were justified by the Sino-Pakistani nuclear threats to India, a stance that highlighted the role of nuclear weaponry in India's China and Pakistan policies and in international conference diplomacy relating to Nuclear Nonproliferation Treaty (NPT) and Comprehensive Nuclear-Test Ban Treaty (CTBT) issues. By adopting a nuclear weapons policy, India was freed from the ambivalence on the nuclear question that had been the basis of its nuclear policy since the Nehru days. In 2001–2002, Pakistan was threatened by Indian war mobilization, and at the same time a peace process was initiated. Strategic dialogues were opened up with traditional (Russia, France, and United Kingdom) and nontraditional (United States, Japan, Australia, and Germany) partners.

A Look East policy was highlighted to build commercial and strategic ties between India and Southeast Asian countries that were uncomfortable with China's looming presence and sought external balances. Nehru and his successors had ignored the region, while the Vajpayee government projected the South China Sea as India's new frontier and engaged in naval cooperation with the United States and its allies in the region. The region thus became a front of engagement between Indian and Chinese interests. Finally, processes for political dialogue with Kashmiri separatists and insurgents in India's northeast were established. The new approaches have been resilient and survived the defeat of the BJP at national polls in 2004. Observers believe that BJP overconfidence in its "India Shining" slogan and concern about BJP's secularism led to its defeat and the Congress Party's appeal on the grounds that it was the voice of secularism and India's rural poor.

Manmohan Singh

The selection of the first Sikh prime minister of India could not have come in a more unusual manner. In 2004 Sonia Gandhi's skilled electioneering brought the Congress Party back into power as the head of a minority coalition. Sonia chose not to become prime minister. Instead, she decided to concentrate on party work and behind-the-scenes supervision of the Manmohan Singh government and on grooming her son and daughter for public office. Her son is an MP, and her daughter is a party organizer. Rahul Gandhi, however, failed badly in the Congress Party's bid to win power in the Uttar Pradesh (UP) state elections in 2012. His prospects for becoming prime minister have dimmed as he is not seen as the vote catcher his mother was in the 2004 and 2009 general elections.

Sonia's decision to forgo the prime ministership apparently reflected the controversy in India about her Italian birth. She named Dr. Manmohan Singh to assume the responsibility. Singh was educated at Cambridge and Oxford Universities, held important economic appointments in India, and was acclaimed as an author and architect of the first phase of Indian economic reforms that started in 1991. He has maintained the post-Nehruvian framework of India's external policies that Vajpayee initiated, and with the help of P. Chidambaran, his Harvard-trained finance minister, the minority Congress Party government has deepened India's economic reforms and ties with the West, China, and Russia, as well as with Asian neighbors. The landmark United States–India nuclear deal took shape under Singh's lead, as did the buildup of defense ties with Russia and the United States. Singh's prime ministership is a novelty in Indian politics because he is an unelected leader; he sits in India's upper house as a nominated member. India has two coleaders (with Sonia Gandhi as the Congress Party leader, whose agenda at times differs from that of the government). His term as prime minister has been marked by corruption scandals, poor management of coalition partners, and a lack of leadership in economic and foreign policy making.

Parliament and the Legislation

The Indian parliament, entrusted with the power to legislate, consists of two houses, the Lok Sabha (House of the People) and the Rajya Sabha (Council of State). The first is the lower house and the second the upper house of India's national legislature.

The Lok Sabha consists of 552 members elected from state and union territories on the basis of population. In addition, two members are appointed to represent the Anglo-Indian (Eurasian) community. Each state is divided into several electoral districts, and each MP represents around 1.5 million people. India has universal adult suffrage, with all citizens age eighteen and older eligible to vote. Turn out in elections is high, between 50 and 65 percent of voters. There has been a constant increase in voter participation over the years. The qualifying age for seeking election to the Lok Sabha is twenty-five. Elections are conducted by an autonomous agency, the Election Commission, headed by a chief election commissioner, who is assisted by two other members. The members of the Election Commission and its chief enjoy status and power equivalent to that of Supreme Court judges. They are not subject to political pressure and governmental interference.

The upper house (Rajya Sabha) has 250 members: 238 are elected by state legislators, and 12 are nominated by the president. Members serve six-year terms, with one-third retiring or being reelected after two years. Occasionally the Rajya Sabha has blocked legislation passed by the lower house, and it has an equal say in the presidential election.

In the post-Nehru era, India's parliament has lost its appeal as a forum for national debate and policy influence. There are a number of reasons behind this disturbing trend: (1) When parliamentarians are motivated by the allure of office and benefits, they are beholden to party leaders who provide tickets and funds to win election campaigns. This results in clientelism and cronyism. (2) With the rise of two national parties and several regional parties, it is easy to make parliament a forum for noisy debate and ideological posturing rather than reasoned evidence- and ideology-driven policy development. (3) With coalition politics and the lack of a majority mandate for any political party, parliament has become an arena to form and apply the unit veto system in the context of a two-coalition era, shifting between the BJP-led coalition (1998–2004) and the Congress Party–led coalition (2004–present). (4) Several parliamentarians have been charged with corruption and criminal offences. Some are in jail, but India's political culture now tolerates their presence in the public policy-making sphere. As a result, accountability in India's political system exists to the extent that Indian voters oust incompetent and corrupt incumbents and not as a result of parliamentary actions.[5]

Of the two houses of parliament, the Lok Sabha is far more powerful than the Rajya Sabha. The Lok Sabha has effective control over both ordinary legislation and money bills. If a deadlock develops between the two houses over an ordinary bill, a joint session of the two chambers is convened, and a decision is made by a majority vote. Money bills can be initiated only in the Lok Sabha. The Rajya Sabha may scrutinize such bills, but it has no power to veto them. Similarly, the Lok Sabha exercises ultimate control over the prime minister and the council of ministers, as only the Lok Sabha can pass a vote of no confidence.

The Rajya Sabha plays a role secondary to that of the Lok Sabha in that it has no control over the executive branch. Nevertheless, during a state of emergency, if the Lok Sabha is under suspension, the Rajya Sabha can become a forum for the voicing of public concerns and thus serve as a check on any arbitrary exercise of power by the executive.

Supreme Court: The Guardian of the Constitution and Law

The Supreme Court is India's highest judicial tribunal. It consists of a chief justice and associate justices who are appointed by the president in consultation with the judges of the High Courts and the prime minister. India has a unified judicial system. There are no separate state supreme courts. Each state has a High Court subordinate to the Supreme Court, and at the national level, the Supreme Court sits at the head of an integrated judiciary. The Supreme Court has original as well as appellate jurisdiction. Following the practice existing in most federations, the original jurisdiction of the Supreme Court covers disputes arising between the national and state governments, as well as cases involving two or more states. In significant civil and criminal cases, the Supreme Court serves as the final court of appeal.

Like the Supreme Court of the United States, India's Supreme Court enjoys the right of judicial review, even though its rights are not as extensive as those of its US counterpart. The Indian Supreme Court has been the primary protector of civil liberties and fundamental rights, especially the right to private property. There has been constant conflict between the Supreme Court's right of judicial review and the parliament's claim to legislative sovereignty. The Supreme Court has denied parliament the absolute right to amend the constitution in a way that limits citizens' fundamental rights and civil liberties, particularly where the arbitrary takeover of private property is involved. The Congress Party–dominated and Indira Gandhi–led parliament in 1976 passed the Forty-Second Amendment, which asserted parliament's ultimate power to amend the constitution. Gandhi also tried to pack and politicize the Court. A balance between the Supreme Court's power of judicial review and parliamentary authority was restored during the rule of the Janata Party government (1977–1979) through the provision of the Forty-Fourth Amendment, which partially modified the absolute power granted to parliament under the Forty-Second Amendment.[6]

Since the 1990s the judges of the Supreme Court have assumed an activist role. Through public-interest litigation, filed by private citizens and civil liberties organizations, judges have tried to establish the principle of accountability for persons holding high public office, including the prime minister, members of the cabinet, and state chief ministers.

The year 2006 was became a landmark in Indian justice, with politicians, who had hitherto avoided conviction and jail time, being held accountable for misconduct. For the first time, a serving minister, an ally of the ruling Congress Party, received life imprisonment for murder. An MP was later sent to jail for manslaughter. That almost 25 percent of Indian MPs have been charged with murder, extortion, or rape signals the increasing prevalence of crime in Indian politics.[7] During 2011–2012, the Supreme Court was also active in pursuing corruptions cases involving UPA-2 (2009–present) ministers, two of whom have been charged and jailed pending investigation. Faced with the failure of the Manmohan Singh government to check and punish corruption in his government, the Supreme Court has assumed this role and, as noted earlier, revoked 122 2G licenses awarded by the UPA-2 government, calling the awards arbitrary and unconstitutional. Here the Supreme Court has emerged as the guardian of public interest and public policy, whereas the executive and legislative branches of the Indian government (2004–present) have failed to provide checks and balances in policy making and governance practices.

Nonetheless politicians still enjoy a privileged status even in prison. They are housed in VIP quarters and can exercise influence from behind bars.[8]

Role of the State Governments

The Indian constitution provides for a federal system of government, with a division of powers between the national and the state governments. Despite the existence of a powerful central government, the state governments have control over such important subjects as public order, police, administration of justice, agriculture, water supply and irrigation, education, public health, land rights, industries, and mineral development. They have the right to levy taxes to raise revenue for their administrations and to determine policies related to land use and land distribution as well as agricultural and industrial development within their states. In short, by capturing political power at the state level, a party or group of political leaders can exercise control over the distribution of vital goods and services within its area. Because state government is an important source of patronage, there is intense competition among elites to capture elective positions at the state level.

Several important implications are related to the operation of India's federal system. This system provides institutional structures that grant self-government to its diverse people. It also provides the means to satisfy the political ambitions of regional elites and regional parties. State-level politics serves as a training ground for the politicians who may subsequently assume important roles in national politics. Many of India's able administrators and some of its prime ministers have held important elective positions at the state level before becoming prominent in national politics. Such former prime ministers as Lal Bahadur Shastri, Morarji Desai, Charan Singh, and V. P. Singh were initially elected to state legislative bodies and served in the state cabinets or as state chief ministers. Today, powerful state leaders include Mamta Bannerjee (All-India Trinamool Congress) in West Bengal; Mulayam Singh Yadav and his son, Akhilesh Singh (Samajwadi Party) in Uttar Pradesh; Nitish Kumar (BJP) in Bihar; Narendra Modi (BJP) in Gujrat; Jayaram Jayalalitha (All-India Anna Dravida Munnetra Kazhagam) in Tamil Nadu; Naveen Patnaik (Biju Janata Dal) in Orissa; Farooq Abdullah and his son, Omar (Jammu and Kashmir National Front) in Jammu and Kashmir; and Mayawati (Bahujan Samaj Party) in UP. The emergence of female leaders with strong political followings, as well as administrative and organizational experience, is noteworthy, as is the growth of non-Congress and non-BJP parties at the state level.

There are considerable differences in attitude, orientation, and behavior between the national political leaders and the state-level politicians. Politicians at the state or regional level have close ties with caste and community leaders. Often they become intertwined with powerful local interests that are eager to maintain the status quo. The state political leaders keep themselves in power by appealing to the primordial loyalties of caste, ethnicity, and religion and to issues concerning women, tribal and landless peoples, the environment, economic policy, rural development, mining and industrial development, and development issues that entail socioeconomic reforms. Many of them use their positions to benefit the members of their kinship group or community.

In theory, national leaders, on the other hand, seek to build national cohesion by playing down the traditional divisions existing within the society. Nehru (1947–1964) clearly represented this approach. However, the national and provincial (state) categories no longer appear relevant in Indian politics, particularly since 2004. With the breakdown of the Congress Party's dominance in post-Nehru India, the rise of the BJP as a national party that nonetheless could not gain majority status in the center, and the fragmentation of Indian politics, the pattern of coalition politics—led by the BJP (1999–2004) and the Congress Party (2004–present)—requires coalition building with the support of regional, state-based parties. Table 3.3 shows the election results at the state level. As a result state interests that reflect the ambitions of state leaders, the strength of their base of local and provincial support, and their skill in exploiting the compulsions of the national party to stay in power have gained seats for state leaders at the high table of the center's politics and policy-making

TABLE 3.3 Election Results in India by State: Number of Seats Won by Largest Party or Coalition, 2008–2012

State	Date of Most Recent Election	Seats Won by Largest Party/Coalition	Seats Won by Second-Largest Party/Coalition	Seats Won by Third-Largest Party/Coalition
Andhra Pradesh	2009	157 (INC)	106 (TDP/TRS/Left)	18 (PRP)
Arunachal Pradesh	2009	42 (INC)	5 (AITC)	13 (others)
Assam	2011	78 (INC)	10 (AGP/Left)	2 (independent)
Bihar	2010	206 (NDA)	22(RJD)	4 (INC)
Chattisgarh	2008	50 (BJP)	37 (INC)	2 (BSP)
Delhi	2008	43 (INC)	23 (BJP)	4 (others)
Goa	2012	21 (BJP)	9 (INC)	10 (others)
Gujarat	2007	117 (BJP)	59 (INC)	3 (NCP)
Haryana	2009	40 (INC)	32 (INLD)	18 (others)
Himachal Pradesh	2007	41 (BJP)	23 (INC)	1 (BSP)
Jammu and Kashmir	2008	28 (JKNC)	17 (INC)	21 (PDP)
Jharkhand	2009	25 (INC)	20 (BJP)	36 (others)
Karnataka	2008	110 (BJP)	80 (INC)	28 (JD[S])
Kerala	2011	45 (CPI[M])	38 (INC)	57 (others)
Madhya Pradesh	2008	143 (BJP)	71 (INC)	7 (BSP)
Maharashtra	2009	144 (NCP/INC)	91 (BJP/SHS)	37 (others)
Manipur	2012	42 (INC)	7 (TMC)	11 (others)
Meghalaya	2008	25 (INC)	15 (NCP)	11 (UDP)
Mizoram	2008	32 (INC)	3 (MNF)	4 (others)
Nagaland	2008	26 (NPF)	23 (INC)	2 (BJP); 2 (NCP)
Orissa	2009	103 (BJD)	27 (INC)	6 (BJP)
Pondicherry	2011	15 (AINRC)	7 (INC)	8 (others)
Punjab	2012	68 (SAD/BJP)	46 (INC)	3 (others)
Rajasthan	2008	96 (INC)	78 (BJP)	6 (BSP)
Sikkim	2009	32 (SDF)	—	—
Tamil Nadu	2011	150 (AIADMK)	29 (DMDK or DMK)	19 (CPI[M]/CPI); 13 (others)
Tripura	2008	45 (CPI[M])	10 (INC)	5 (others)
Uttarakhand	2012	32 (INC)	31 (BJP)	7 (others)
Uttar Pradesh	2012	224 (SP)	80 (BSP)	47 (BJP)
West Bengal	2011	226 (AITC/INC)	40 (CPI[M])	28 (others)

AGP—Asom Gana Parishad; AIADMK—All-India Dravida Munnetra Kazhagam; AINRC—All-India NR Congress; AITC—All-India Trinamool Congress; BJD—Biju Janata Dal; BJP—Bharatiya Janata Party; BSP—Bahujan Samaj Party; CPI—Communist Party of India; CPI(M)-led alliance; CPI(M)—Communist Party of India (Marxist); DMK—Dravida Munnetra Kazhagam; INC—Indian National Congress; INLD—Indian National Lok Dal; JD(S)—Janata Dal (Secular); JKNC—Jammu and Kashmir National Conference; MNF—Mizo National Front; NCP—Nationalist Congress Party; NPF—Nagaland People's Front; PDP—People's Democratic Party; SAD—Shiromani Akali Dal; SDF—Sikkim Democratic Front; SHS—Shiv Sena; SP—Samajwadi Party; TDP—Telugu Desam Party; TMC—Trinamool Congress; TRS—Telangana Rashtra Samithi

Sources: Election Commission of India; Wikipedia, "State Assembly Elections in India," for 2008, 2009, 2010, 2011, and 2012.

FIGURE 3.2 Dynamics of State-Center Parties at 2009 Elections

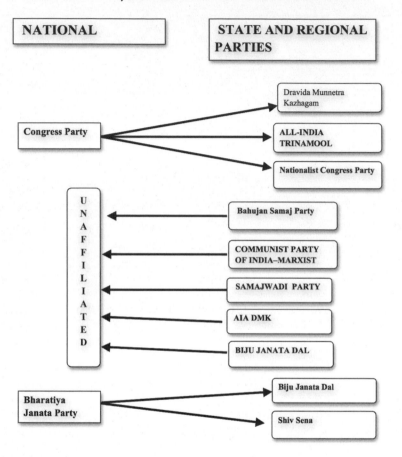

activity. As elections are the only way to legitimize the quest for power, Indian politicians are continuously positioning and repositioning themselves for the next election. Figure 3.2 shows the new pattern and framework of post-Nehru politics. The existence of a horizontal ideological cleavage between BJP and Congress Party leaders and the need for and availability of state leaders as coalition partners have widened the space for top-down (center-to-state) and down-top (state-to-center) coalition building. However, coalitions are fragile, while coalition building is a constant activity. Both are driven by a quest for power rather than the firm ideological convictions of the players.

There are twenty-eight states in India. Figure 3.3 presents the organization of each of the state governments.

FIGURE 3.3 Organization of the State Governments of India

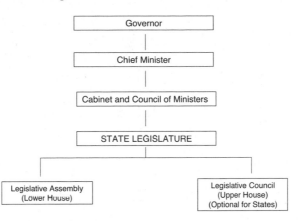

Governor

The governor is appointed by the president for a term of five years and holds office for as long as he or she enjoys the president's confidence. The governor is a representative of the national government in the state and exercises more powers in the state than the president does at the national level. Although the governor was intended to be the constitutional figure in the governmental setup of a state and to act in nonpartisan ways, the office has become politicized in recent years. Many governors have become embroiled in state politics, especially in those states in which non–Congress Party governments have been in power. The governor invites the leader of the majority party in a state legislative assembly to form the government and to assume the office of chief minister. In the event that no party has a majority in the assembly, the governor becomes actively involved in the formation of a state government. The governor also has the power to dismiss a popularly elected state government. He or she can recommend instituting the "president's rule" in a state, enabling the national government to take over the administration of a state temporarily. These practices go against both the principles of a federation and the spirit of representative government and are controversial.

The chief minister, the cabinet, and the council of ministers are vested with the exercise of executive power in a state. The institutional setup at the state level is normally under the control of the chief minister, who is the most powerful person in state politics. The chief minister also commands a majority in the state legislative assembly, determines the size of his or her council of ministers, distributes portfolios among these ministers, and presides over the meeting of his or her cabinet. During Nehru's prime ministership many state chief ministers became powerful regional leaders with considerable influence in national politics. W. H. Morris-Jones has described this stage of the operation of the Indian polity as a "bargaining federalism." In such a federation, he points out, "neither centre nor states can impose decisions on others." Instead, "hard competitive bargaining" takes place in such federally instituted agencies as the Finance Commission and Planning Commission.[9] Chief ministers played a crucial role in the bargaining process until Indira Gandhi, after her 1972 landslide victory, undercut the power of most of the Congress Party chief ministers. However, with the rise once again of many regional parties, the office of state chief minister has emerged as an independent and autonomous center of power. This pattern of state-center dynamics is now an important trend in Indian politics.

The state legislatures are particularly important to state politics. Some of these legislatures are bicameral, consisting of a legislative assembly (lower house) and a legislative council (upper house); many, however, have only the assembly. The legislative assembly (Vidhan Sabha) has the right to legislate on all state subjects. It also controls the chief minister and the council of ministers, who can be dismissed by the adoption of a vote of no confidence. The state assemblies are elected on the basis of universal adult suffrage. Inasmuch as the elections of state assemblies have generally been separated from parliamentary elections, elections for the Vidhan Sabha are dominated by local and state issues.

The legislative councils are elected in part directly and in part indirectly, and some of the members are appointed by the governors on the advice of the chief ministers. The legislative council (Vidhan Parishad) plays a role secondary to that of the legislative assembly. The state legislative bodies work under almost the same rules of procedure as those followed in the national parliament.

The elections for the state legislative bodies are contested vigorously. It is through their representatives in the state legislative assembly that ordinary people are able to make political statements. For most Indian voters the state administration is their first and most important avenue for redressing grievances.

The members of the legislative assembly (MLAs) are generally less interested in legislative business or policy formulation than in securing benefits for their constituents or serving as power brokers between the bureaucrats and powerful interests in their constituencies. The services of an MLA are in great demand. Ordinary citizens seek the help of MLAs to intercede with the administration on their behalf. Their easy accessibility makes them an invaluable link between the people, the administration, and the state government.

Local Governments: The Roots of India's Democracy

India's thousands of villages, towns, and cities are home to a host of self-governing institutions. Local self-government in urban areas was, of course, introduced by the British government, which, through several acts, established various types of local bodies, town committees, municipalities, and municipal corporations, all endowed with different levels of autonomy and financial power. Whereas corporations exist in the metropolitan areas or large cities, area committees with only limited powers are present in small towns.

Although its powers are limited, the city government is the only representative body that exists in a city. The members of a municipal committee, or a municipal corporation, and its presiding officials are included among the politically influential members of the community. They develop vital links with the MLAs, especially if they belong to the same party. Through various channels they are able to influence the allocation of resources at the state capital.

In rural areas the self-governing institutions are known as the *panchayats* (village councils), *panchayat samithis* (associations of village councils), and *zila parishads* (district councils), existing at the village and district levels, respectively. Like the city councils, these rural self-governing institutions are elected on the basis of universal adult suffrage. The *zila parishads* are the highest self-governing institutions in rural India. Over the years the powers, functions, financial resources, and role in developmental activities of these institutions have varied greatly.

Local politicians who are elected to these self-governing institutions are able to build links with community organizations on the basis of ascriptive and kinship ties, as well as with state-level politicians who belong to various political parties. Through this kind of informal network of power and influence, local politicians and political notables mobilize the voters for the political leaders and also distribute patronage among their clients and supporters. This kind of institutional network, existing as it does at the different levels of Indian society, has integrated diverse elements of the population into a working political order.

Tendency Toward Increased Centralization in the Indian Political System

The framers of the Indian constitution created a powerful center, believing that this would help in maintaining the unity of the country. Nevertheless, in view of India's cultural diversity, they preferred a federal over a unitary system of government. Since the adoption of the constitution, however, for various reasons, certain important changes have occurred, resulting in greater centralization of political power than the framers of the constitution had envisioned.

Although no constitutional change took place in India's federal system, Indira Gandhi frequently resorted to its subversion. She made dubious use of some of the constitutional means to undermine the federal structure, especially the authority of the opposition-run state governments.

The office of the state governor is a carryover from the days of the Raj. It was left in the postindependence constitutional structure, perhaps with the understanding that the state governor would perform only ceremonial functions and would not play any political role. In recent years, however, the office of the governor has become increasingly politicized. Both the Congress Party and the Janata Party (later Janata Dal) governments have appointed their party men as state governors. After her 1980 return to power, Indira Gandhi frequently appointed discredited state politicians and her loyalists as governors of the opposition-run state governments. She also transferred those governors of the states who refused to carry out her instructions. The governor of Jammu and Kashmir, B. K. Nehru, an able administrator and former member of the Indian Civil Service (ICS), refused to dismiss Farooq Abdullah's government in Kashmir, as demanded by the Congress (I) supporters of Gandhi, on the grounds that such a move would not be in the national interest. He was replaced soon afterward by Jagmohan, a Gandhi loyalist. Jagmohan carried out Indira Gandhi's instructions and dismissed Abdullah's government, disregarding established constitutional practices.

Nehru was extremely reluctant to impose president's rule (basically a takeover of the state administration by the national government) in the states. In 1949 he is reported to have observed that "so far as I am concerned, I do not propose, nor intend, nor look forward to, nor expect governments falling apart except through a democratic process."[10] The evidence suggests that he never started or encouraged any efforts to topple the opposition-run state government. Under Indira Gandhi, however, the toppling of state governments by encouraging defection from the ranks of the opposition parties became a standard practice.

The national government has far greater financial resources at its disposal than the states have. In fact, through grants-in-aid, budgetary provisions, and financial institutions, the center has been making inroads into many of the subjects allocated to the state governments.[11] Such encroachments by the national government on states' rights and responsibilities have strained center-state relations considerably.

Center-state relations and the extent of state autonomy are issues likely to be debated in the coming years. Pressure is likely to increase for greater state autonomy. For many years the chief ministers from several states have asked for greater legislative and administrative autonomy and insisted on a new definition of center-state relations.

Three shades of opinion reflect the position of different groups on the nature of the Indian federation. One group, led by the Sikh party, the Akali Dal of the Punjab, has demanded the transfer of all powers to the states, with the exception of defense, foreign affairs, communications, railways, and currency. Such a demand does not have countrywide support, however. Another group, led by moderate regional leaders, hopes to maintain a distance from the political control of New Delhi and seeks a reassertion of the spirit of federalism as embodied in the constitution. The third group, led by M. Karunanidhi of Tamil Nadu and Jyoti Basu of West Bengal, has sought an extensive revision of center-state relations in light of political experience gained over the sixty-odd years that the Indian constitution has been in effect. All groups, no doubt, seek the revisions within the framework of the Indian constitution. A one-man commission headed by a retired Supreme Court justice, Ranjit Singh Sarkaria, was appointed in March 1983 to look into the issue. In particular, the commission was authorized to examine the center-state relationship and to make recommendations to meet the new demands coming from the non–Congress Party–run state governments. The commission submitted its report in 1988. The government did not implement its recommendations.

Political leaders in India, such as the Sri Lankan elites, have been successful in building and operating an effective and complex institutional structure. Unlike the systems in neighboring Pakistan and Bangladesh, that in India provides its citizens with ample opportunities to become involved in the political process. Indeed, the citizens of India have frequently used the constitutional process to change the government. The federal system of government, furthermore, provides enough opportunities to state and local politicians to protect their regional interests and to preserve their subnational identities. Even though occasional tensions arise between the national and state governments, the political institutions overall have shown considerable flexibility in defusing them without leading to any breakdown of the system.

The Executive and the Bureaucracy:
Policy Formulation and Implementation

Along with political institutions and political parties, the Indian bureaucracy is an important element, in part because it helps to ensure stability and administrative continuity. The bureaucracy of India consists of tenured civil servants who remain in their administrative posts even when the political bosses lose their elective positions. In addition, they must observe certain rules and procedures that are essential to the orderly conduct of administration.

Like other South Asian states, India inherited well-developed traditions of administration from the British Raj. But unlike in Pakistan and Bangladesh, where civil servants and members of the armed forces have in the past taken over the government, in India elected politicians have remained the top decision makers.

Although it is a legacy from the British, the Indian bureaucracy under British rule served primarily as a regulatory agency whose primary responsibility was to raise revenue and maintain law and order so as to serve the interests of the colonial rulers. Its functions remained limited even when the British government adopted certain benevolent policies directed toward expansion of educational and other public service–related activities. The British did not use the government and bureaucracy as agents of India's economic and social development. After independence, however, the government became actively involved in shaping the social and economic life of the country.

During the Nehru years (1947–1964), India was committed to an economic structure based on state socialism, self-reliance, and a highly state-regulated economy. Following adoption of economic reforms in the early 1990s, the political-administrative leadership is engaged in deregulating the economy, making it more responsive to market forces and more open to direct foreign investment than it was in the past. Elected representatives, in order to ensure social justice, also make decisions on social policy, such as the introduction of a quota system in the recruitment of civil servants, reservation of seats in educational institutions for members of the backward castes, and adequate representation of women in parliament and state legislative bodies.

Accordingly, the members of parliament and the council of ministers have set development goals. These individuals are not experts, however; it is the bureaucrats who make recommendations for the introduction of appropriate legislation to help achieve those goals.

Under these conditions the responsibilities of the bureaucracy have increased enormously. The actions of civil servants are expected to reflect the aspirations of elected representatives, and the bureaucrats themselves are expected to mobilize human and material resources to help modernize the society. As a consequence of the growth of governmental activities and the increasing complexity of public policy making and management, the bureaucracy has emerged as the major locus of political power in the central and state governments.

Despite their key administrative positions, however, the bureaucrats are no longer the masters they were during the British period. The real power lies with the ministers, who often remind the members of the bureaucracy that they are public servants.

Organization and Tradition of Indian Bureaucracy

Broadly speaking, the civil services in India can be grouped into three major categories: all-India services, central (union) services, and state civil services.

1. The top echelon of all-India services consists of the Indian Administrative Service (IAS) and the Indian Police Service (IPS), both of which have their roots in the British period of Indian history. The IAS is the successor to the British-designed elite Indian Civil Service, which is frequently referred to as being "heaven born" because of the high prestige and status bestowed on it by the society and the ruling classes. Contemporary members of the IAS claim to have inherited the traditions of their predecessor. The IPS and other all-India services originating during the British period also carry the glamour inherited from that period. In a country in which the unemployment rate is very high even among university graduates, a government job not only provides security and health benefits but also pays well and offers a good retirement package. Entry into all-India service jobs is all the more desirable because they command a high status among government jobs.

2. The ICS ruled India for a century and, assisted by the IPS, provided the well-known "steel frame" that enabled the British to govern India so effectively for such a long period. Both the ICS and the IPS were originally staffed by the British, although considerable Indianization of these services had occurred even before India achieved independence. Because of the services' close association with British rule, many Indian nationalists sought their abolition after independence. Sardar Patel, however, defended the services and very wisely perceived them as institutions of enormous value for the effective administration of a country as vast as India.

3. The members of the IAS, the elite component of the bureaucratic system in the country, see themselves as the guardians of the interests, unity, and territorial integrity of the country. They claim to stand above the linguistic and communal cleavages in Indian society. In this respect they are the representatives of what Myron Weiner called the "elite political culture" of the country.[12] The members of both the IAS and the IPS are very conscious of their high status within Indian society, and the traditions have fostered an esprit de corps among them.

4. The central services include such divisions as the Indian Revenue Service, the Postal Service, the Indian Audit and Account Service,

the Indian Railways Account Service, and the Indian Customs and
Excise Service.

5. Finally, there are the cadres of civil services created by the states,
   which perform similar functions at the state level. The national IAS
   and the IPS, however, occupy positions of power and status; the state
   bureaucracies are assigned mostly to subordinate positions.

Recruitment and Training of Bureaucrats

Recruitment to the services is based on merit, and there is considerable objectivity in the selection process. The Union Public Service Commission, an
autonomous body, is entrusted with the job of holding examinations for the
applicants seeking entry into the top echelon of Indian bureaucracy. The examinations, with slight variations for each service, emphasize the applicant's
proficiency in English and background in humanities and social sciences. Personality tests, through extensive interviewing conducted by the members of
the Union Public Service Commission, constitute a vital part of the selection
process. No candidate is allowed to join the services without being inter-
viewed. The recruits are fairly young (twenty-one to twenty-four years old),
and only college graduates are allowed to take the test. Every year thousands
of college graduates from all parts of the country compete for the two hundred or so positions to be filled.

The young recruits are first given one year of extensive training in the National Academy of Administration, located in the hill town of Mussoorie.
The new entrants study economics, public administration and government
organization, the constitution of India, and Indian criminal law, among other
subjects. In recent years the Indian Institute of Public Administration in
New Delhi has begun to offer short courses and seminars designed to expose
senior members of the IAS to the newest methods of management and empirical research. However, on-the-job training is still considered the highest
priority.

Each state in India designs its own rules and procedures for the recruitment
of state-level bureaucrats; most are modeled on the procedures established at
the national level. All states maintain their own public service commissions and
use objective criteria to fill positions in the civil services.

The members of both the IAS and the state civil services are trained as generalists on the basis of British traditions.[13] As generalists they are expected to be
equipped with the knowledge, skills, values, and attitudes to make policy recommendations not only in the area of administration but also in scientific,
technical, and educational matters as well. Upward career mobility, enhanced

status, and increased financial rewards are dependent on their performance as well as their obedience and loyalty to their immediate superiors.

Administrative Responsibilities and Upward Mobility

Upon completion of his or her training, an IAS or IPS officer is assigned to a state cadre. According to established practice, no more than 50 percent of recruits to India's elite services will serve in the states of their origin. These officers, then, are recruited and trained on the national level, and a substantial number of them will serve outside of their own states. Through this process they develop a national orientation and become instruments of national integration. The uniformity of values and training of these civil servants is unmatched by any other organization except the armed forces.

New IAS officers usually start their careers at the district level (for administrative purposes, each of India's states is divided into several districts). IAS officers are put in charge of district administration with the title of collector, district officer, or deputy commissioner. During the British period such officers were given almost full responsibility for the administration of the district; in fact, they were chief magistrates. Not only were they responsible for maintaining law and order, inasmuch as they had control over the police, but they also supervised the administration of local self-government, public health, education, agriculture, irrigation, and other activities.

In the postindependence period, IAS officers have also been assigned duties related to the economic and industrial development of the district. Each officer is assisted by several junior officers who belong to the state civil service cadre. During this field assignment, an IAS officer's administrative abilities are tested with respect to generalism.

In the state secretariat, situated in the state capital, the members of the IAS hold important positions. As secretaries of the departments, they assist state ministers in the performance of their functions. In addition, they make recommendations leading to the formulation of department policies. The highest position an IAS officer can hold in the state is that of chief secretary. A chief secretary is responsible for the coordination of the many departments. He may also influence the postings of younger and junior IAS officers to different positions.

In India the states are required to contribute officers to the central secretariat, which stands at the apex of the national bureaucratic structure. At this level the final policy decisions are made. Positions in the central secretariat carry a great deal of prestige and are therefore desirable to the members of the IAS. Each state prepares a list of those IAS officers it is willing to spare, from which the central government can make its selection. Most of these officers go on deputation to New Delhi, some for a specific number of years, others on a permanent basis. In the central secretariat they start as undersecretaries or deputy secretaries, become joint secretaries, move on to the senior positions of additional secretaries, and then finally become the secretaries of departments. Most serve as the chief administrative aides of the ministers. The brightest and best officers are placed in the prime minister's secretariat or in such key ministries as home, defense, finance, foreign affairs, industries, and commerce. Frequently a state and the central government will compete with each other over the services of intelligent and talented administrators.

The national and state governments have set up several corporations that engage in economic and business activities. The managing heads, who require specialized training, are normally recruited from the private sector. Occasionally, however, an IAS officer is put in charge of such a corporation. In that case he or she will be required to make business decisions and to act as an executive rather than as an administrator.

Social Origins and Value Orientations

As a result of their key position within the state machinery, the members of India's elite services have attracted recruitment from educated families. Because of a quota system, almost 35 percent of the new entrants to the IAS since independence have been members of the low or backward castes; consequently the social base of recruitment reflects the privileged position of Indian Dalits. Members of the business community are less represented than recruits from civil service and professional backgrounds, and outside the middle class, farmers and agricultural laborers are grossly underrepresented in all services, even more so than artisans and industrial workers. Just as the IAS is dominated by the middle class, there are members of the landowning class belonging to the Jat subcaste in the Indian Police Service.

During British rule, the Indian Civil Service was often criticized as being India's new caste system, created to maintain the elitist nature of the colonial system of administration. Today, it is not uncommon to hear the IAS referred to as the continuation of the ICS under a new name. Despite the elitist nature of Indian bureaucracy, however, it would be hard to deny that its highly intelligent and skilled members are committed to the goals of modernization and industrialization of the country.

The Bureaucracy and the Changing Political Culture

The bureaucracy in India has been under pressure from various directions. The introduction of representative government has generated tension between elected representatives and the bureaucrats. These strains result from the differences between the cultures to which the groups belong. Unlike the career of a member of the administrative services, that of an elective representative depends on his ability to respond to the needs of his constituents. He is guided by what has been termed political rather than administrative rationality. Unlike the administrator, the politician has no tenure; reelection depends on the results he obtains for the voters. Hence the more services he is able to provide the electorate, the better are his chances for reelection. Bureaucrats, on the other hand, as they are not dependent on voters, are more concerned with rules, regulations, and procedures. The contrast creates tensions between the results-oriented politician and the rule-bound civil servant.

Until 1947 bureaucrats were unaccustomed to taking orders from elected representatives. Now the situation is dramatically different. Civil servants face far greater pressure at the state and local levels than at the national level. Before independence, for instance, a district officer was not subject to any local control, and his administrative powers were almost unrestrained. Now a local MLA represents a major restraint on the district officer's administrative authority. An influential MLA of the ruling party frequently intervenes in the administration on behalf of his supporters and allies. And an MLA's easy access to the state chief minister makes him a powerful person in a district and often forces the district officials to yield to pressure. Despite the tenured position and protection enjoyed under the civil service regulations, however, the district officer and his associates can be transferred to undesirable locations or to a position without much power and glamour if they refuse to cooperate with an influential MLA.

The tension between administrators and elected representatives has been aggravated by the growing role of the state in the expansion of social services and the economic and agricultural development of the country. The government has set up numerous elective bodies at the village, town, city, and state levels so that the popular representatives can become involved in the process of economic development. Under these conditions, the cooperation between elective representatives and civil servants becomes important in the mobilization of the masses necessary to achieve the goals set by the planners.

In the post-Nehru era civil servants and the central secretariat have been constantly subjected to political pressure. Both the Congress (I) and opposition party ministers have tried to politicize the bureaucracy, for instance, by rewarding the more pliant and politically loyal bureaucrats with promotion and choice appointments. Of course, such efforts undermine the traditional nonpartisan and independent nature of the IAS.

The bureaucrats of India also feel threatened by the rise of a new class of technocrats. The government's economic and industrial development goals require the services of a host of engineers, scientists, economists, agricultural experts, planners, and other specialists, and the government has accordingly hired thousands of technocrats. These experts not only demand equal status with the administrators but also seek to share power with them. As a result, the new class of technocrats has further undercut the powers of the Indian civil bureaucracy.

Bureaucratic Corruption

While corruption among bureaucrats and members of the law enforcement agencies occurred even during the British period, it was never as widespread as it is today. Traditionally, status within the society was assigned on an ascriptive basis, social mobility was limited, and social stratification was rigid. Even though these ascriptive principles persist, money and material wealth are now becoming the basis on which one can achieve higher status. The far greater social acceptance of corruption today than in previous periods can be attributed to the decline in the Indian value system.

At the same time, wide disparities have developed since independence in the incomes of bureaucrats, business people, and manufacturers. A sheltered market and growing middle-class demand for consumer goods account for the tremendous rise in income for business people and manufacturers of consumer goods. By contrast, the pay scales of top-level bureaucrats have not increased correspondingly; indeed, today bureaucrats are paid far less than their counterparts in private industry and business. Moreover, the often excessive and vulgar displays of wealth on the part of business people may account in part for civil servants' vulnerability to accepting bribes.

The chances for bureaucratic corruption are further aggravated by the multiplicity of rules and regulations dealing with economic and industrial expansion and the granting of government approval for projects.[14] Alleged widespread corruption in the civil services has engendered a cynical attitude about the integrity and honesty of the bureaucrats.[15]

Conclusion

The evolution of India's political life since 1947 demonstrates the durability of two constant elements: (1) There is a strong constitutional framework in which the center and the states formed the core of a federal system; this system and its constitutional base has endured, and it has not been threatened by a military coup or by refusal of a political leader to accept the results of an election. (2) With widespread criticism of the performance of leaders and governments, the Indian voters have enthusiastically embraced their voting rights and the chance to turf out governments that fail to satisfy public expectations.

At the same time, four variables have emerged to give India's political life a complicated, vibrant, and evolving future: First, the end of Congress Party dominance of national and state politics, the hallmark of the Nehru era, weakened the preeminent position of the center in India's political and economic life and increased the political space for regional parties and state governments. Second, Indira Gandhi, the Congress Party (I), and Indira's sons Sanjay and Rajiv broke Nehru's political rules. Nehru was a true democrat because he did not interfere with state governments and state elections. He believed in peaceful change and respected election results. Indira Gandhi believed that state opposition was directed against her, her party, and India, because she falsely conflated India with Indira and Indira with India. Her use of president's rule to dismiss elected state governments broke Nehru's political convention of respect for elected state leaders and for states' rights in the federation. The post-Nehru era under Indira Gandhi was divisive inasmuch as it undermined Indian federal principles and Nehru's practices. It paved the way for the rise of the BJP in national and state politics and for the rise of regional leaders and parties that could not abide Gandhi's dictates.

Third, the emergence of the BJP and the decline of the Congress Party's domination of Indian political life after Nehru marked the growth of transactional politics among ambitious political leaders at the national and state levels; as none of them could lead with a majority, all needed allies, which required deal making based on personal ambition, power distribution, and in some cases ideological convictions.

Fourth, the end of Congress Party dominance converged with the fragmentation of Nehruvian statist economic planning and socialism. Economic reforms (1991–present) unleashed Indian and global market forces and the formation of commercial-political linkages at the national and state levels and created the cocoon of a political-bureaucratic-commercial nexus. But this is not the story of a banana republic. When this cocoon bumps against Indian constitutional principles and public expectations about good and effective governance, the debate about the public good comes into focus through India's electoral democracy, judicial interventions, media exposure of scandals, and mass public movements.

SUGGESTED READINGS

Baxi, Upendra, and Bhikhu Parekh. *Crisis and Change in Contemporary India.* New Delhi: Sage, 1995.

Bayley, David H. *The Police and Political Development in India.* Princeton, NJ: Princeton University Press, 1969.

Bhambhri, C. P. *Bureaucracy and Politics in India.* Delhi: Vikas, 1971.

Braibanti, Ralph, ed. *Asian Bureaucratic Systems Emergent from the British Imperial Tradition.* Durham, NC: Duke University Press, 1966.

Brass, Paul, ed. *Routledge Handbook of South Asian Politics.* New York: Routledge, 2010.

Chanda, Asok. *Federalism in India.* London: Allen and Unwin, 1965.

Heginbothan, Stanley. *Cultures in Conflict: The Four Faces of Indian Bureaucracy.* Berkeley: University of California Press, 1975.

Jayal, Niraja Gopal, Amit Prakash, and Pradeep K. Sharma, eds. *Local Governance in India: Decentralization and Beyond.* New York: Oxford, 2007.

Khosla, Madhav. *The Indian Constitution: Oxford India Short Introductions.* New Delhi: Oxford, 2012.

Maheshwari, S. R. *Local Government in India.* New Delhi: Orient Longman, 1971.

———. *State Government in India.* Delhi: Macmillan, 1979.

Malik, Yogendra K. "Political Finance in India." *Political Quarterly* (January 1989): 75–94.

Manor, James, ed. *Nehru to the Nineties: The Changing Office of Prime Minister in India.* Vancouver: University of British Columbia Press, 1994.

Mishra, B. B. *The Government and Bureaucracy in India.* New Delhi: Oxford University Press, 1986.

Morris-Jones, W. H. *Parliament in India.* Philadelphia: University of Pennsylvania Press, 1957.

———. *The Government and Politics of India.* Garden City, NY: Doubleday, 1967.

Palmier, L. *The Control of Bureaucratic Corruption.* Delhi: Allied, 1985.

Tully, Mark. *No Full Stops in India.* New York: Penguin Books, 1991.

———. *Non-stop India.* New Delhi: Allen Lane/Penguin Books, 2011.

Weidner, Edward W., ed. *Development Administration in India.* Durham, NC: Duke University Press, 1970.

NOTES

1. Quoted in Granville Austin, *The Indian Constitution: Cornerstone of a Nation* (London: Oxford University Press, 1966), 45.

2. See Constitution of India, updated up to 97th Amendment Act, 2011. The database is owned, maintained, and updated by Legislative Department, India's Ministry of Law and Justice.

3. See "Backlash Grows over Reform of Indian Retail," *Financial Times*, November 27, 2011. K. Subramanian, "From Policy Paralysis to Policy Paroxysm," Chennai Centre for China Studies, C35 Paper No. 949, March 13, 2012. "India's Bumble Bee Defies Gravity," *Financial Times*, February 15, 2012.

4. Michael Brecher, *Nehru: A Political Biography* (London: Oxford University Press, 1959), 395.

5. Stanley Kochanek, "Corruption and Criminalization of Politics in South Asia," in *Routledge Handbook of South Asian Politics*, ed. Paul R. Brass (London: Routledge, 2010), 364–381.

6. Lloyd I. Rudolph and Susanne H. Rudolph, "Judicial Review versus Parliamentary Sovereignty: The Struggle over Stateness in India," *Journal of Commonwealth and Comparative Politics* (November 1981): 231–255.

7. Samuel Paul and M. Vivekananda, "Knowing Our Legislators," India Together, October 2004, http://www.indiatogether.org/2004/oct/gov-knowmps.htm.

8. Sanjoy Majumder, "Watershed Year for Indian Law," BBC News, January 5, 2007, http://news.bbc.co.uk/2/hi/south_asia/6224701.stm.

9. W. H. Morris-Jones, *The Government and Politics of India,* 3rd ed. (London: Hutchinson University Library, 1971), 152.

10. Quoted in Henry C. Hart, "Indira Gandhi: Determined Not to Be Hurt," in *Indira Gandhi's India: A Political System Reappraised,* ed. Henry C. Hart (Boulder, CO: Westview Press, 1976), 256.

11. K. K. George and I. S. Gulati, "Central Inroads into State Subjects: An Analysis of Economic Services," *Economic and Political Weekly,* April 6, 1985, 592–602.

12. Myron Weiner, "India: Two Political Cultures," in *Political Culture and Political Development,* ed. Lucian W. Pye and Sidney Verba (Princeton, NJ: Princeton University Press, 1965), 199–244.

13. Asok Chanda, *Indian Administration* (London: George Allen & Unwin, 1967), 97–134; Richard P. Taub, *Bureaucrats Under Stress* (Berkeley: University of California Press, 1969), 191.

14. Surjit Singh, "Political and Bureaucratic Corruption in India," *Journal of Government and Political Studies* (September–March 1978–1979): 65.

15. Samuel J. Eldersveld, V. Jagannadham, and A. P. Barnabas, *The Citizens and the Administrator in a Developing Democracy* (Glenview, IL: Scott, Foresman, 1968), 29.

4

Shifting Perspectives About Political Parties and Political Leaders

Characteristics of the Indian Party System and Its Context

The Indian National Congress dominated the political scene of pre-independence India, even though some parties and political factions were present in colonial India. As an umbrella organization leading the freedom movement, it attracted persons of diverse ideological persuasions and varying political goals who were willing to work toward achieving independence for the country. Whereas the Muslim League in Pakistan disintegrated soon after the creation of a Muslim-majority state, in India the Congress not only survived but was converted from a loosely organized freedom movement into a cadre-based mass party. In 1948, at the urging of Sardar Vallabhbhai Patel, the Congress Working Committee (the party's top executive organization) passed a resolution banning factions with their own constitution or organizational structure, which had previously been allowed to operate within the Indian National Congress. This action led to the exit of various factions, which then converted themselves into new political parties. When the Congress became the ruling party of India, for many dissidents the only course left open was to form opposition parties.

India's party system has evolved with the Congress Party at the center of the system and a changing balance of power between centralism versus regionalism and nationalism versus communalism and caste-ism. Sugata Bose and Ayesha Jalal argue that the Congress Party claimed independence as a victory of centralism and nationalism. Furthermore, in Jawaharlal Nehru's time decision-making power shifted from the parliament to the executive branch, and a partnership between the Congress Party, the bureaucracy, and the police emerged to form a nexus of bureaucratic authoritarianism, state consolidation, and one-party (Congress) rule legitimized by free and fair elections. The challenge of regionalism occurred from 1967 onward, along with the rise of the Maoist Naxalites, a movement of poor peasants and militant students, as argued by Bose and Jalal.[1]

Our view of the dialectic between centralism and regionalism and between nationalism and communalism/caste-ism dates the origins of the changing narrative to as early as 1952, with it gaining traction from 1957 onward. The story begins in the south, in Andhra Pradesh and Kerala, and in the east in Orissa, then spreads to the north and west in the regional politics of Uttar Pradesh, Bengal, Punjab, Gujrat, and Maharashtra. Ramachandra Guha notes that the early debate was not between socialism and free enterprise. In 1938 the Congress Party set up India's Planning Committee (not the same as Planning Commission elsewhere), whose principle was "service before profit." The private sector accepted central planning. Rather, the debate started in 1952 between the right-wing Jan Sangh, precursor to the Bharatiya Janata Party (BJP), and the Nehruvian socialists. Other elements in the debate were the quest for Naga independence in the northeast, the Jharkhand movement in the early 1950s, and the issue of caste and regional politics.[2]

In sum, during the Nehru era (1952–1959), Nehru's government faced a number of ideological challenges from Indian communists and the right-wing Jana Sangh, the extreme rightist Rashtriya Swayamsevak Sangh (RSS), and later the Swatantra Party, as well as from regional groupings in Bombay (now Mumbai), Kerala's elected communist government, the tribals in Nagaland and Jharkhand, the Sikhs in Punjab, and later the landless peasants and militant students in Bengal. Political movements in India's vast regions challenged India's centralism under Nehru and the Congress Party. These challenges involved a mix of peaceful ideological controversies, identity politics, and militancy at the street level in a quest for social and economic justice. Regional nationalism was challenging and redefining Indian nationalism and centralism even before Indian politics became mixed in Hindu-Muslim controversies in the 1990s and early 2000s. Outwardly, India was strong centrally, with a Congress Party–directed federal structure and a party and a state apparatus that dominated India's political and economic life. Inwardly, however, the Nehru approach was fraying as a result of controversies between Nehru's government and the regional challengers, as well as the reorientation of Congress Party politics under Indira Gandhi.[3]

The Socioeconomic Background of Party Leaders

The first generation of Indian leaders originated in the politically conscious stratum of Indian society and shared the experience of the freedom movement. Most of them were members of the upper or upper-middle classes. Most were educated in the West or in schools in India that followed a Western curriculum. This was true for the leadership of both the Congress and the parties of the ideological Left and Right. Lately the Dalits and Scheduled Castes have emerged as political players and secured social and educational reforms and better employment opportunities.

Reliance on Powerful Personalities

Although the parties have built organizational structures, they rely heavily on charismatic and powerful personalities or community and religious leaders. But this tradition has its disadvantages. For example, a party that depends on one leader tends to disappear with his or her demise. In addition, influential persons sometimes change parties in search of power and position and bring their followers into the party of their choice. Domination of parties by small oligarchies is common. In the parties that capture power at the national or state level, parliamentary wings under these strong leaders become dominant, and organizational or mass wings are relegated to a secondary position, used primarily for the mobilization of the voters. For years India's Congress Party was the dominant party and was identified with the independence movement, nationalism, and governance. As a result of manipulation of the party by Indira Gandhi, her sons Sanjay and Rajiv, and her daughter-in-law Sonia Gandhi, the party lost its moral and political status and reputation as a progressive builder of party norms and national policies.

Factions Within the Parties

All political parties tend to be factionalized. In noncommunist parties, the faction leaders tend to be community, caste, or religious leaders who have skillfully built patron-client relationships among the members of different castes or communities. Such factional leaders vie among themselves for political influence within the party and the government, entering into political alliances with one another in order to keep their political rivals out of power. Most of these factional alliances are not ideological; they also tend to shift and keep the parties in a state of flux. In rural areas, moreover, traditional hostilities based on caste and kinship are transformed into factional fights that lead to inter- and intraparty power struggles. In order to maintain unity, party leaders must constantly try to balance the interests of different factions.

In the communist or socialist parties, on the other hand, ideological considerations frequently lead to faction formation, although personality, caste, and regional affiliations can also play divisive roles. Political parties have also created various auxiliary organizations in an effort to mobilize different sectors of the society. More specifically, most of the prominent parties have organized youth wings, student unions, women's organizations, and peasant and labor groups. In addition, parties with the necessary strength and resources hold camps, seminars, and conferences for the different wings of the party.

The Use of Nonparliamentary Means to Power

Although electioneering and campaigning in an effort to capture a maximum number of seats in public offices are said to be the main functions of the parties, very few parties are able to make a respectable showing using only these legitimate methods. As a result, political parties of all ideological persuasions frequently try to exploit political or social discontent to their advantage. They do not hesitate to use such nonparliamentary means as civil disobedience, mass demonstrations, strikes, and protest rallies to embarrass the party or group in power. Sometimes the use of these tactics leads to violence.

The use of mob violence, however, has an unfortunate association with the methods of the Congress Party. As W. R. Crocker points out,

> [Nehru] must take his share of the blame too for a spirit of violence which the Independence movement brought into Indian life. The Independence movement was dedicated to the purpose of breaking the British Government in India by all means possible (though Gandhi would have added, not quite convincingly, "by all means short of terrorism"). . . . The Nationalist agitators called in the mob to sabotage the British Government; but in doing that they risked destroying the principle of government itself, the principle of authority.[4]

The growth of Naxalite *gherao* and illegal strikes became widespread in Bengal and other areas. In the 1980s they represented the mob mentality that India's independence leaders had encouraged. The BJP government was tarnished by its tolerance of mob violence in Gujrat between Hindus and Muslims in 2002, when Muslims burned a train carrying Hindu pilgrims, and Muslims suffered mob violence. A Congress government was also associated with killings of innocent Sikhs in 1984 as a result of Indira Gandhi's assassination. So tolerance of mob violence has emerged as a subrosa aspect of Indian party politics and society.

A Multiparty System

Since the disintegration of the consensus-based Congress system in 1967, the Indian parties have comprised a multiparty system. The Congress Party itself is a coalition of diverse interests, factions, groups, and individuals. It has rarely captured more than 50 percent of the vote, with the remainder being won by the opposition parties and independents. At the state level, the dominance of the Congress Party is frequently contested by regional and local parties.

Indian parties are divided into four major groups. First, all-India political parties have been officially defined as those national parties with broad-based national support that win a minimum of 4 percent of the votes or more than 3 percent of the seats in at least four state legislative assemblies. Also considered all-India political parties are those able to win 4 percent of the votes or 4 percent of the seats in the Lok Sabha. These parties present national platforms and emphasize national issues in parliamentary elections.

Currently, the following parties are classified as all-India parties: the Congress (I), the Bharatiya Janata Party, the Rashtriya Janata Dal, the Communist Party of India (CPI), the Communist Party of India (Marxist) (CPI[M]), the Bahujan Samaj Party (BSP), and the Nationalist Congress Party. These parties draw support from different segments of the society and put up their candidates across state lines.

The second group consists of regional parties that clearly represent subregional nationalism based on the common languages, culture, and history of a region. Given the pluralist nature of Indian society, the rise of such parties is not surprising. These parties try to aggregate regional interests and mobilize the caste and religious affiliations of their members. Their power base and voting strength are confined to a particular geographic area. The following are the best-known regional parties: the Dravida Munnetra Kazhagam (DMK) and the All-India Anna DMK (AIADMK) of Tamil Nadu, the Telugu Desam Party (TDP) of Andhra Pradesh, the National Conference of Jammu and Kashmir, Asom Gana Parishad (AGP) of Assam, the Samajwadi Party in Uttar Pradesh, and the Akali Party in Punjab.

The third group includes those parties and organizations that are exclusive in their membership; that is, they accept as members only members of a particular religious or ethnic community. They seek to protect and promote the interests of that community alone, are basically nonaggregative, and generally mobilize their supporters by appealing to their particularist sentiments. The following parties fall into this category: the Shiromani Akali Dal of the Punjab, the Muslim League in Kerala, and the Shiv Sena in Mumbai.

The fourth group of parties consists of those organized around powerful persons or local and state issues. Such parties may appear for a short period and then disappear completely or merge with other parties. There are currently several such parties existing in various states.

The Congress System and the Congress (I)

The Congress system emerged after India attained independence. From 1947 until it broke down in 1967, this system was at the center of Indian politics, spanning three distinct stages in the country's postindependence development. The first phase (1947–1967) was the period of the Congress system; the second (1967–1977) was characterized by the decline and disintegration of the Congress system and the consolidation of power by a small oligarchy; and the third and current phase (from 1977–present) witnessed the development of a new system, which, because of its domination by Indira Gandhi, became known as the Indira Congress, or Congress (I). The third phase is now entrenched. It highlights a political culture that openly flaunts the dominance of a single Congress Party leader who controls the power of patronage, the party's treasury, and the power to nominate loyalists to ministerial and party posts and election as members of parliament (MPs). Indira Gandhi started this system, and Sanjay and Rajiv Gandhi built on it; Sonia Gandhi inherited it and used her popularity to continue it.

Rajni Kothari, who developed the model of the Congress system, asserts that the Congress Party, based on a broad consensus, was able to accommodate diverse interests and factions within its fold. These factions competed with each other but usually reached compromises that avoided any breakdown of the system. The opposition parties worked outside the system and used the factional leaders of the Congress Party to influence its policy decisions. These parties acted as pressure groups and frequently created informal alliances with the factional leaders of the ruling party. The Congress system showed remarkable flexibility and accommodation in withstanding pressure from within its own ranks as well as from the opposition groups. Often the programs, policies, and even personnel of the opposition parties were absorbed by the Congress system, leading to the strengthening of the one-party system in India. This system operated during Nehru's leadership of the Congress Party.[5]

The second phase in its development started with the critical elections of 1967, when the Congress Party lost its predominant position at both the state and national levels. The social and political mobilization resulting from two decades of independence had increased subgroup awareness in Indian society. Many new groups were brought into politics, and there was increased polarization among different castes, communities, and religious minorities. In addition, several dissi-dent groups became active, leading to increased competition at the state level for power and prestige within the Congress Party. When the party became incapable of satisfying their aspirations, factional leaders sought to form alliances with the leaders of the opposition parties, contributing to the disintegration of local and state Congress Party organizations. As Nehru's authority in national and interna-tional affairs diminished in the latter part of his tenure, the growing power and policy vacuum in Indian politics and government presented opportunities for others to occupy the space at times by co-opting Nehru to their agenda(s). Nehru's indecisiveness, his political loneliness or aloofness from a coterie of peers, and the burden of governing a complex society helped others to influence his de-cisions and thinking.

At the national level, the death of Nehru and the rise of Kamaraj Nadar as the president of the organizational wing of the party led to the weakening of its parliamentary wing. The renewed conflict between the two sides was ultimately settled by the 1969 split within the party. Indira Gandhi, the leader of the par-liamentary wing and the prime minister of the country, defied and defeated the party bosses by successfully supporting the election of V. V. Giri to the presi-dency. She thus became the dominant force within the party. No longer based on broad consensus, the Congress Party became dependent on the charismatic personality and populist policies of Indira Gandhi for electoral victories. Party and Indian norms suffered when Indira and her supporters propagated the view that Indira was India (and vice versa). As the cult of personality grew, party norms suffered, and the system of checks and balances in a constitutional gov-ernment—involving all branches of the Indian government and various seg-ments of attentive Indian publics outside the government—broke down.

The parliamentary victories in the 1971 elections and the subsequent party sweep of the state legislative assembly elections in 1972 not only made Indira Gandhi the party's undisputed leader but also transformed its nature. The new members recruited into the parliament and state legislative assemblies were not always part of the local party organizations and often lacked an independent power base. Moreover, the autonomy of the state party units was subverted by Indira Gandhi's policy of creating divisions between the organizational and leg-islative wings of the party.

Indira Gandhi intervened in state elections and was known for dismissing state governments she did not like. This was not Nehru's approach. She adopted a divide-and-rule approach to state politics and was reinforced in this attitude by Sanjay Gandhi's determination to teach opponents a lesson. Her de-claration of national emergency and the suspension of fundamental rights in 1975 reflected Sanjay Gandhi's influence and the rise of an extra-constitutional power center in the prime minister's household. As a result Indian politics acquired a dual character. While elections were free and fair under supervision of the Indian Election Commission and international observers, the decision-making process in the political and policy spheres had a secretive and manipulative character. In general, the central leadership became highly oligarchic and autocratic. But in 1975, unable to contain the unrest caused by economic and social discontent and challenged by the opposition leaders and total collapse of the party organizations in various states, Indira Gandhi declared a state of emergency and suspended democratic activities. With this period of emergency ended the second phase of the Congress Party's history.

The third phase commenced after Indira Gandhi's defeat in the 1977 election, which was held after the termination of her emergency rule. In this election for the Lok Sabha, the Congress won 34.5 percent of the votes and 153 seats, in contrast to the 43.6 percent of the votes and 352 seats it had won in the 1971 elections. Indira Gandhi even lost her own seat in parliament. This defeat resulted in another split within the party. Many of the old and experienced leaders left the party, blaming Gandhi for its humiliating defeat in the elections. As a result, the new Congress (I) Party emerged and became completely identified with her personality. Many of the party's top decision-making agencies, such as the Congress Working Committee and the All-India Congress Committee, lost their powers. Similarly, state party organizations were brought under her direct control, as was the presidency of the Congress Party, since she handpicked the top functionaries. She built a pyramid-like organization run by her or her henchmen.[6] When the 1980 elections were held after the collapse of the Janata Party government, the Congress (I), led by Indira Gandhi, returned to power by winning a massive majority. Assisted by her son Sanjay, she selected only persons of proven loyalty to the Nehru-Gandhi family to run for parliament. She especially sought to reward political cronies who had stood by her during the period in which she had been out of power; administrative experience and parliamentary skill did not matter. In the 1980 Lok Sabha elections, the Congress (I) captured 43 percent of the vote and won 351 of 539 seats.[7] In June of the same year, Gandhi called elections for state legislatures, and the Congress (I) captured power in fifteen of twenty-two states.

The return of the Congress (I) to power in 1980 was attributed to the failure and eventual disintegration of the Janata Party coalition that had captured power in 1977. In the 1980 elections the opposition leaders who had become discredited failed either to put up a joint front against the Congress or to build electoral alliances to give it a tough fight. Starting in 1971 a dramatic change in the composition of the Congress Party elites had taken place. In that year a large number of political careerists and opportunists joined the party. In 1980, in addition to these elements, many persons of dubious character and even criminal background entered into the Congress Party.[8] Under Indira's leadership the party simply became an instrument of personal power. She also sought to use the organization for dynastic succession. First, she groomed Sanjay, her younger son, to take over the leadership of the party; then, after his accidental death in June 1980, she brought in her elder son, Rajiv.[9] In the 1984 parliamentary elections, after the assassination of Indira Gandhi, the Congress (I) won with a record-setting vote, capturing around 50 percent of the popular vote and 396 Lok Sabha seats—a feat unmatched in the history of free India. The relentless campaign mounted soon after Rajiv's mother's assassination brought him a great many sympathy votes. His victory was made easier by a fragmented opposition led by old-guard politicians who had failed to establish their credibility with the masses.

The key issue in the 1984 election was the threat to national unity. Events in the Punjab and a separatist movement led by Sikh extremists were alarming enough to persuade the people to vote for the Congress (I), a party with a national image. The Congress (I) under the leadership of Rajiv Gandhi swept all the states in the country except Andhra Pradesh, Jammu and Kashmir, and Sikkim.

In the 1989 parliamentary elections, however, the Congress (I) was able to capture only 193 of 525 seats, losing power at the center. The party was routed in the densely populated Hindi-speaking states of North India. In the 1991 May–June parliamentary elections, after the assassination of Rajiv Gandhi, the Congress (I) was able to improve its position when it won 226 seats. Its new leader, P. V. Narasimha Rao, became prime minister with the support of some regional and minor parties and independent members of the Lok Sabha. In 1992 it further increased its strength when it won twelve of thirteen seats from the state of Punjab. In the 1990 elections for the state legislative bodies, once again the Congress (I) suffered humiliating defeat at the hands of the Janata Dal and BJP and lost power in important states like Madhya Pradesh, Bihar, Rajasthan, Gujarat, Orissa, Himachal Pradesh, and Uttar Pradesh.

The constitution of the Congress Party provides for an elaborate organization headed by a president, assisted by the Congress Working Committee (the executive of the party), and supplemented by the All-India Congress Committee (AICC), the deliberative branch of the party. Its central office in New Delhi supervises the work of the Pradesh (state) Congress committees as well as other subordinate organizations. However, when she had control of the party, Indira Gandhi stifled intraparty democracy and did not hold party elections after 1972. Under the leadership of Rao, who became the party president after the May 1991 assassination of Rajiv Gandhi, efforts were made to revitalize the party organization. In 1992 Rao held party elections, which, though not flawless, introduced a considerable degree of democracy into the internal functioning of the party.

During the period of Nehru-Gandhi family domination of the Congress, the party was committed to democratic socialism and planned economic development. It gave the dominant role to the state in running such key industries as steel, heavy chemicals, and fertilizers. However, in the 1992 session of the AICC held at Tirupati, the party accepted the Rao government's private enterprise–oriented policies of economic liberalization. While paying lip service to the Nehru legacy of democratic socialism and planned economic development, it stressed efficiency and productivity, even at the cost of privatizing public-sector industries. This was a turning point that set in motion a series of economic reforms in India.[10]

In the 1996 elections for the Lok Sabha, with the party bereft of charisma and vision and plagued by charges of widespread corruption, the Congress (I) suffered its worst defeat ever and lost power. Consequently, Rao had to quit as both president of the organizational wing and leader of the party in the parliament. Subsequently the party went through several leadership changes without much electoral success, until 1998 when it installed Sonia Gandhi, the widow of Rajiv and heir to the Nehru-Gandhi dynasty, as president of the Congress Party. Initially, Sonia helped the party win elections in such states as Rajasthan, Madhya Pradesh, Karnataka, and Delhi. Nonetheless, in the 1999 national elections the Congress suffered the worst defeat in its history despite vigorous campaigning by Sonia Gandhi. Sonia, on the other hand, was elected for the first time to the lower house of the Indian parliament and became the leader of the opposition.

The stunning 1999 defeat served as a lesson for Sonia, who began to rebuild the party. In 2004, in the middle of a strong economic boom, she led the Congress Party into national elections that almost all analysts believed would return the BJP to power. However, the Congress targeted the rural population and inhabitants of the regional cities, constituencies that the economic boom of the BJP years had largely bypassed, benefiting instead larger urban areas such as Mumbai and Delhi. The Congress's appeal received very strong support and returned the party to power in a coalition government.

The Congress Party and its allies won the largest number of seats in parliament, 221 to the BJP's and its allies' 186 seats. Because the Congress and their allies did not win a majority, they formed a minority coalition with smaller independent parties. Table 4.1 shows the overall picture of party performance and alliances from 2009 to the present.

The 2004 election solidified the new nature of national party politics in India. The Congress Party's decline as a national party has left the country with coalitions that form over local issues and stay together as long as the local, smaller parties

TABLE 4.1 2009 Lok Sabha Election Results and Pattern of Party Coalitions

Alliances	Party	Seats Won	Change	Popular Vote	Vote Percentage	Swing (%)
United Progressive	Indian National Congress	206	+ 61	119,110,776	28.55	+2.02
	All-India Trinamool Congress	19	+ 17	13,355,986	3.20	+1.13
Seats: 262	Dravida Munnetra Kazhagam	18	+ 2	7,625,397	1.83	+0.02
Seat change: +80	Nationalist Congress Party	9		8,521,349	2.04	+0.24
Popular vote: 153,482,356	National Conference	3	+1	498,374	0.55	+0.42
	Jharkhand Mukti Morcha	2	–3	1,665,173	0.40	–0.07
Popular vote percentage: 37.22%	Indian Union Muslim League	2	+1	877,503	0.21	+0.01
	Viduthalai Chiruthaigal Katchi	1	+1	735,847	0.18	+0.18
Swing: +3.96%	Kerala Congress (Mani)	1	+1	404,962	0.10	+0.05
	All-India Majlis-e-Itrehadul Muslimeen	1	—	308,061	0.07	–0.04
National Democratic Alliance	Republican Party of India (Athvale)	—	–1	378,928	0.09	—
	Bharatiya Janata Party	116	–22	78,435,538	18.80	–3.36
Seats: 159	Janata Dal United	20	+12	6,331,079	1.52	–0.83
Seat change: –17	Shiv Sena	11	–1	6,454,850	1.55	–0.26
Popular vote: 102,689,312	Rashtriya Lok Dal	5	+2	1,821,054	0.44	–0.19
	Shiromani Akali Dal	4	–4	4,004,789	0.96	+0.06
Popular vote percentage: 24.63%	Telangana Rashtra Samithi	2	–3	2,582,326	0.62	–0.01
	Asom Gana Parishad	1	–1	1,773,103	0.43	–0.10
Swing: –4.88%	Indian National Lok Dal	—	—	1,286,573	0.31	–0.19
Third Front	Communist Party of India–Marxist	16	–27	22,219,111	5.33	–0.33
Seats: 79	Communist Party of India	4	–6	5,951,888	1.43	+0.02
Seat change: –30	Revolutionary Socialist Party	2	+1	1,572,650	0	
Popular vote: 88,174,229	All-India Forward Bloc	2	–1	1,345,803	0.32	–0.03
	Bahujan Samaj Party	21	+2	25,728,889	6.17	+0.84
Popular vote percentage: 21.25%	Biju Janata Dal	14	+3	6,612,552	1.59	+0.29
Swing: –1.06%	All-India Anna Dravida Munnetra Kazhagam	9	+9	6,953,591	1.67	–0.52

	Seats	Seat change	Popular vote	%	Swing
Fourth Front					
Seats: 27					
Popular vote: 21,456,117					
Janata Dal (Secular)	3	–1	3,434,082	0.82	–0.65
Marumalarchi Dravida Munnetra Kazhagam	1	–3	1,112,908	0.27	–0.16
Popular vote percentage: 5.12%					
Haryana Janhit Congress	1	+1	816,395	0.20	+0.20
Pattali Makkal Katchi	—	–6	1,944,619	0.47	–0.09
Samajwadi Party	23	–13	14,284,638	3.42	–0.90
Swing: –2.30%					
Rashtriya Janata Dal	4	–20	5,279,059	1.27	–1.14
Lok Janshakti Party	—	–4	1,892,420	0.45	–0.26
Other parties and independents					
Seats: 16					
Assam United Democratic Front	1	+1	2,184,556	0.52	+0.52
Seat change: +9					
Popular vote: 27,146,939					
Jharkhand Vikas Morcha (Prajatantrik)	1	+1	963,274	0.23	+0.23
Nagaland People's Front	1		832,224	0.20	+0.20
Bodoland People's Front	1	+1	656,430	0.16	+0.16
Popular vote percentage: 6.51%					
Swabhimani Paksha	1	+1	481,025	0.12	+0.12
Bahujan Vikas Aaghadi	1	+1	223,234	0.05	+0.05
Sikkim Democratic Front	1	—	59,351	0.04	—
Swing: +2.04%					
Independents	9	+4	21,646,845	5.19	+0.94
Total:					
364 political parties	543		417,156,494		

Sources: Election Commission of India (http://eci.nic.in/eci_main/archiveofge2009/Stats/VOLI/12_PerformanceOfNationalParties.pdf; http://eci.nic.in/eci_main/archiveofge2009/Stats/VOLI/13_PerformanceOfStateParty.pdf; http://eci.nic.in/eci_main/archiveofge2009/Stats/VOLI/14_PerformanceOfRegistered_UnRecognisedParties.pdf); IBN Live (http://ibnlive.in.com/politics/loksabhafinal/plist.php); Business Standard (http://www.business-standard.com/india/news/more-congress-less-upa/358357).

gain their objectives from the coalition. At the moment, it appears unlikely that either the Congress Party or the BJP will emerge as a truly national majority party. The Congress Party victory was slim, and the party needs to solidify its base of strength before the next national elections. Between 2008 and 2012 the Congress-led coalition government was implicated in major scandals related to its granting of 2G telecom licenses (2008), awarding of contracts for the Commonwealth Games (2010), and deciding to privatize the coal industry (2011–2012). These scandals came to light as a result of official audits by India's auditor-general and media disclosures. As a result the Congress Party's record of governance was badly tarnished and evoked much derisive commentary. The corruption scandals also helped to confirm the gradual decline of national parties in India.

Non-Congress Parties: Janata Dal and the National Front— Ad Hoc Coalitions of Factional Leaders

Non-Congress centrist parties constitute an important segment of India's polarized multiparty system. This segment is of growing importance in India's political development. This constellation consists of influential caste and community leaders seeking to dislodge India's entrenched political elite. Many of these groups—for example, the Jats, the peasant proprietors of western Uttar Pradesh, the Yadavs, the Kurmis, and the members of other backward castes (OBCs) of Hindus, the Scheduled Castes and Tribes, and Muslim minorities— were recently mobilized. Their common disenchantment and disillusionment with the Congress (I) and the BJP tend to override the disparity in their interests. Their supporters are the rural poor as well as people with education and administrative experience.

It is very difficult, if not impossible, to create class consciousness among groups divided by status and other conflicts of interest. For instance, there is intense competition among the Jats, Yadavs, Kurmis, and other members of OBCs for status in the highly stratified Hindu social structure. On the other hand, in rural India, members of the Scheduled Castes and Tribes are frequently victims of violence perpetrated by the Yadavs or the Jats. There is also frequent hostility between Muslims and Jats or Yadavs, who are Hindus, on the basis of religion. Such internal tensions and contradictions lead to the formation of unstable political alliances.

Cultural Disparity of the Factions

The leaders of these parties are people with dramatically different social and cultural backgrounds. For example, there was little commonality between Raj Narain and Jagjivan Ram or between Charan Singh and Morarji Desai, all leaders of the non-Congress centrist Janata Party founded in 1977. Whereas Raj Narain represented the disruptive and anarchic traditions cultivated by Ram Manohar Lohia, Jagjivan Ram, an able administrator and shrewd politician, was a leader of the Scheduled Caste establishment, deeply entrenched in the ruling circles of the Congress (I). Similarly, Charan Singh, a representative of the affluent peasant proprietors and a strong supporter of agrarian interests, was an opportunist, whereas his rival, Morarji Desai, a Gujarati Brahmin and favorite of Indian industrialists and businessmen, was a stickler for principles. Such contradictions in the backgrounds of the actors, together with significant differences in their attitudes and orientations, all fueled by their political ambitions, often created friction among coalition partners, finally leading to disintegration of the coalitions. Such a pattern of behavior was repeated in 1989 when V. P. Singh forged an alliance of factions led by Devi Lal, Ajit Singh, Mulayam Singh Yadav, Chandra Shekhar, Arun Nehru, and others. They represented different interests, sociocultural backgrounds, and policy orientations and were motivated by conflicting political ambitions.

Many of these factional leaders demand absolute loyalty from their followers, equating political dissent with personal betrayal. They seek constant recognition of their status and authority from political rivals. Because of this concern with power and status, they sometimes pursue strategies to undermine each other's positions within the party or government rather than focusing on conducting the business of the government or building the organizational structure of the party.

In earlier years, most of the centrist parties depended on the notables of caste and community groups for mobilization of voters. With the decline in status of such notables, many leaders of these factions now turn to local thugs and musclemen belonging to a particular caste or community to help them win elections. These characteristics of the centrist parties have contributed to the growing perception of corruption and criminal behavior in the party system.

After the sweeping electoral victories of the Congress (I) in 1971 relegated the centrist parties to the margins of Indian politics, many of them underwent further mergers and name changes in their quest for continuing relevance. They began resorting to agitation, protest movements, and demonstrations for political survival and as a means of maintaining public visibility. By 1975 the centrist parties, first led by Morarji Desai, had brought down the corrupt Congress (I) government in Gujarat. Subsequently, under the leadership of Jaya Prakash Narayan, a massive agitation to bring down the central government forced Indira Gandhi to declare a national emergency and arrest most of the leaders of the opposition. The Janata Party, which came into existence in 1977 with the merger of the centrists, socialists, and various other groups, was primarily a collection of former members of the Congress Party united in a desire to dislodge the Indira Gandhi–dominated Congress Party from power. The only non-Congress group to join the new party was the right-wing Hindu nationalist Jana Sangh. In 1977, the Janata Party succeeded in capturing power nationally in 1977 and winning several state governments, especially in North India. However, lacking a common program, a grassroots organization, and any sense of unity, this coalition of diverse factional leaders could not survive for long. The leaders of the new party became engaged in an intense power struggle, which led to numerous fissures and the fall of its government in 1979.

Unable to devise a common electoral strategy or to plan a meaningful seat adjustment among themselves, the leaders of the centrist parties failed to deny massive majorities to the Congress (I) in both the 1980 and the 1984 elections. But in 1989 these factional leaders were once again brought together in the form of the Janata Dal by V. P. Singh and his associates, who either had resigned or been expelled from the Congress (I). As the prospects for an electoral victory looked promising, it was not surprising to see these factional leaders subordinate their personal ambitions to dislodge the Congress (I) from power. After entering into electoral alliances and seat adjustments with such right-wing political parties as the Bharatiya Janata Party and others, in the 1989 Lok Sabha elections the Janata Dal emerged as the second-largest party in parliament with 143 seats.

At the national level a loose confederation of national and regional parties founded in 1988 by the late N. T. Rama Rao, with V. P. Singh as its convener, became the center of the new coalition government, with the Janata Dal as its anchor. Under the leadership of V. P. Singh, the Janata Dal/National Front, with the support of the communists and right-wing BJP, was able to form a government. Subsequently, in the 1990 assembly elections held in ten states, the Janata Dal managed to capture power in three critical states, Bihar, Gujarat, and Orissa, having earlier won election in Uttar Pradesh, India's most populous state.

The Janata Dal, as expected, undermined the Congress Party support base built by Indira Gandhi, especially in Uttar Pradesh and Bihar. It attracted the votes of well-to-do peasant proprietors such as the Jats, who traditionally voted for the Lok Dal, and also received the votes of Muslims, Scheduled Castes, and backward castes such as the Yadavs and Kurmis. However, state and local party units rarely depended on the national leadership or its organization because they were controlled primarily by the state party bosses. Since the Janata Dal had no grassroots organization and was based on a precarious and unstable alliance of disparate factions at the national level, the survival of not only the government but even the party itself was doubtful.

In its public policies and programs, the Janata Dal occupied a centrist position, placing greater emphasis on rural development, decentralization of power both in the economy and in politics, restoration of civil liberties, and accommodation of the demands of India's various religious and linguistic minorities. In foreign policy, it sought understanding and accommodation with India's neighbors rather than confrontation. However, the centrist parties have declined in recent years as regional parties have increased in influence.

The Party of the Right: Bharatiya Janata Party

The Bharatiya Janata Party, a proponent of right-wing Hindu nationalism, suddenly emerged as the second-largest party in the Lok Sabha by winning unexpected electoral victories in 1991 and again in 1996–1997 and 1999. It virtually eliminated the Congress Party in the Hindi-speaking states of North India. The BJP poses a major challenge to secularist political ideology and to the Congress and other centrist parties that have ruled India since independence in 1947. For the last twenty years, the BJP has remained the only national challenger to Congress dominance.

The BJP Nationalist Ideology

The BJP represents an important version of nationalism in India that originated in the nineteenth century but was rendered peripheral when the Indian nationalist movement of Gandhi and Nehru dominated Indian politics. The basic premise of the BJP's ideology is that India's national identity is rooted in Hindu culture for the obvious reason that Hindus comprise the majority in the country and nations are built on the basis of common culture and historic traditions. The BJP maintains that genuine Indian nationhood should incorporate the Hindu heritage along with the traditions, practices, and beliefs that flow through the ancient history of the country. It holds that the groups that make up a nation come together for a purpose represented by a community of projects, desires, and historic undertakings. Such essentials for nation building are provided by a culture based on a people's shared experience. According to this view, minorities must reconcile themselves to the political reality of Hinduism and its social values, as well as its centrality in the formation of India's national identity. By thus appealing to the majority community's religious and cultural sentiments and distaste for minority Muslim politics, which the Congress leaders had favored, the leadership of the BJP sought to build and consolidate its base of support. It was perceived to hold an anti-Muslim bias, but our discussion can be broadened. Was the BJP advocacy a plea to recognize the political vitality of Hinduism and its relevance to Indian politics, or was it only a rigid anti-Muslim position?

Repudiation of Centralized, State-Controlled Economic Planning

The BJP repudiates not only the secular version of Indian nationalism as propagated by Nehru and the Congress Party and support of special Muslim rights but also the concept of centralized and state-directed economic planning and socialism in favor of free enterprise and a market economy. Earlier it had advocated drastic liberalization of the economy, lifting of state control, abolition of the system of permits and licenses, and turning over most public-sector enterprises to private business. Adoption of many of the BJP's economic policy pronouncements by the Rao government forced the BJP leadership to modify some of its earlier economic positions. At one point it was protectionist and opposed the entry of multinationals in Indian markets, except in the area of high technology. This attitude changed after 1997 when the centrist government of Atal Bihari Vajpayee, in opposition to the extreme rightist RSS leaders and extremist Indian leftists, cautiously embraced globalization, favored a tilt toward the United States in economic and strategic affairs, and pushed selective economic reforms in India. The BJP, like the Congress Party, seeks rapid industrialization of the country and India's emergence as a major economic and military power in the world.

Despite advocating economic decentralization and greater state autonomy, the BJP is unwilling to accommodate the demands of religious and ethnic minorities for political and economic rewards based on their minority status. In its foreign and security policies the BJP adopted a more aggressive nationalist and militant posture than the Congress or other centrist parties. The BJP government under Vajpayee had an anti-Nehruvian orientation and adopted a set of economic, diplomatic, and military policies at odds with the Nehruvian paradigm of socialism, nonalignment with a pro-Soviet tilt, and peace diplomacy. The BJP's policies enabled India to join the global economic and strategic mainstream by tilting toward the United States and Israel, by balancing and broadening India's search for relations with traditional and nontraditional partners, and by adopting coercive diplomacy as a method of action with Pakistan.

The BJP inherited the traditions and ideology of the Jana Sangh, founded in 1951 by Dr. Shyama Prasad Mookerjee (1901–1953). In 1977 it merged into the Janata Party. The party came into existence in its present form in 1980, under the leadership of Atal Bihari Vajpayee, a former president of the Jana Sangh. To join the mainstream of Indian politics and expand its popularity, the party adopted Gandhian socialism as its political ideology. In 1986, failing in its efforts to expand its electoral base and shunned by the centrist parties, the party, under the leadership of Lal Krishna Advani, adopted Hindutva, militant Hindu nationalism, in place of Gandhian socialism as its political ideology. However, while in power from 1997 to 2004, the BJP faced internal controversies. Vajpayee represented the pragmatic side of the BJP in economic and strategic affairs, while his deputy, Lal Krishna Advani, expressed the ideological view of Hindutva and was associated with events like the mob attack in the demolition of the old Muslim Babri Masjid in 1992.

Changing Strategies: Electoral Alliances and Religious Symbols for Voter Mobilization

BJP leader Lal Krishna Advani cleverly used religious symbols to mobilize the masses by exploiting Hindu resentment against the Protection of [Muslim] Rights on Divorce passed by the Rajiv Gandhi government. In its pursuit of political power, the BJP leadership adopted a strategy of making electoral deals with the centrist parties. Thus in 1989, to avoid multiple contests and to split the votes of the opposition parties, the party under Advani's leadership made an electoral agreement with the Janata Dal not to oppose each other for the same seats, and the BJP captured eighty-six seats in the Lok Sabha, emerging as the third-largest party in parliament. In contrast, in 1984 it had won only two seats.

In the 2009 Lok Sabha elections, the BJP continued to form alliances with other parties and to utilize religious symbols. While the Congress Party coalition won the election, the BJP's National Democratic Alliance (NDA) coalition won 159 seats with 43 of them won by their coalition partners.

The Inability of the Party to Demonstrate Administrative Responsibility

Throughout its history, the BJP has failed to demonstrate responsible leadership after winning elections. The BJP had an opportunity to act as a responsible political party and to demonstrate its administrative capabilities in the states under its rule. Large states like Uttar Pradesh, Madhya Pradesh, and Rajasthan faced many developmental problems. They were plagued by poverty rooted in an economy based on backward agricultural practices and sluggish industrialization. People were looking for a clean government with a capacity to uplift the sagging morale of the bureaucracy and to rein in disorderly behavior by the police establishment.

The December 1992 destruction of the Babri Masjid mosque by Hindu militants and the inability of the BJP government in Uttar Pradesh to protect the lives and property of the minority community raised serious concerns about the responsible behavior of its leadership. The result was the dismissal of the BJP-led state governments and imposition of president's rule by the central government.

In the 1993 elections in the key states of Uttar Pradesh, Rajasthan, Madhya Pradesh, Himachal Pradesh, and Delhi, the BJP captured only Rajasthan and Delhi, losing control of other states. The BJP was able to maintain its popular support (it actually increased its share of votes in Uttar Pradesh, Delhi, and Madhya Pradesh and lost marginally in Rajasthan), but its capacity to win seats declined. In most cases, this was because of the consolidation of Hindu backward castes and the Dalits with the Muslims, which tilted the balance against the BJP. An aggregate analysis of votes polled by parties in all five states (Uttar Pradesh, Madhya Pradesh, Himachal Pradesh, Rajasthan, and Delhi) shows that the BJP secured 36.2 percent against 26.2 percent, 9.1 percent, and 16.6 percent, respectively, by the Congress, the Janata Dal, and the combined Socialist Party–Bahujan Samaj Party.[11]

The BJP has gradually been extending its support in the south, especially in Karnataka, where it improved its yield from five seats in 1989 to eighty-four in the 2004 state legislative assembly elections, where it was able to form a coalition government. The dramatic electoral victories that the BJP scored over its main opponents, the Congress and the Janata Dal, in the two western states of Gujarat and Maharashtra established it as a major contender for power at the national level. While in Maharashtra the BJP formed the government with Shiv Sena as its senior partner, in Gujarat it formed the government on its own. In the May–June 1996 elections to the Lok Sabha, the BJP emerged as the largest single party, with 162 seats, leaving the Congress behind with only 141 seats. Supported by some of the regional parties as well as ideological allies, with a total of 192 seats in the Lok Sabha, and led by a moderate and well-known national leader, Atal Bihari Vajpayee, the BJP staked its claim to form the government at the national level. However, it was unable to win support from other parties and failed in its efforts to come to power at the center.

The rise of the BJP was halted by the 2004 general elections. Overwhelming defeat led the party to reassess its electoral strategy. Many within the party felt that the leadership, assuming victory, failed to campaign adequately. This criticism included a belief that it had relied too heavily on television and cell phone campaign ads. In any case, the party has attempted to reestablish its electoral majority since the 2004 loss.

The party has continued to succeed in elections to the state legislative assemblies and rebuilt much of its electoral base. However, at the national level, the Congress was reelected to power in 2009 and can rule until 2014. The BJP's aging leadership may no longer be in a position to lead the country unless the party can cultivate a new generation of younger leaders.

National Democratic Alliance

Since the late 1980s, both of the national parties, the Congress and the BJP, have been unable to win absolute majorities and thus form a government on their own. The importance of the regional and minor parties has thus increased. Their support is essential to achieving a stable government at the national level. Atal Bihari Vajpayee and his associates in the BJP were quick to understand the imperatives of coalition politics. Therefore, in the 1999 elections, Vajpayee actively sought an electoral and political alliance with important regional parties. The result was the formation of the National Democratic Alliance, consisting of such parties as the DMK of Tamil Nadu, Telugu Desam of Andhra Pradesh, Janata Dal United, Akali Dal of Punjab, Shiv Sena of Maharashtra, the Manipur State Congress Party, the Trinmool Congress of West Bengal, the Biju Janata Dal of Orrisa and Jammu, the Kashmir National Conference, and various others. Led by the BJP, with mutual seat adjustment, the NDA contested elections on a common political platform. Such an electoral strategy paid rich electoral dividends and gave the regional parties a stake in national politics; it also forced the BJP to dilute its ideology of militant Hindu nationalism. With the support of important constituents of the NDA, the BJP has been able to keep the Congress Party, its main rival, out of power at the national level.

Limitations of BJP Ideological and Electoral Strategies

Between 1997 and 2004 the BJP emerged as an alternative to Congress Party rule. But despite its extensive cadre-based organization and links with the RSS, and despite its good record in the economic and strategic spheres during its tenure as a minority government, its RSS links and ideology and events in Babri Masjid (1992) and Gujrat (2002) generated a belief among the Indian public that the BJP was antisecular and anti-Muslim. This view, together with the party's overconfidence in 2004, led to its defeat in the polls and the replacement of the BJP minority government with a Congress Party minority government (2004–present). This result showed that neither party had the trust of a majority of voters.

After its unexpected electoral defeat in 2004, the BJP lost its sense of direction. Supported by poll numbers before the election, the BJP had felt confident that a booming economy, elevation of India as a major global player and power, stability despite a coalition government during its five-year rule, and an improved relationship with Pakistan before the election would lead to the party's return to power. Overconfidence, growing inequality despite a booming economy, and disenchantment among its core extremist Hindu base due to adoption of a more moderate attitude are some explanations given for the loss. Afterward, some sections of the party began to question its more moderate policies and called for a return to its previous exclusionary posture.

In its attempts to gain direction, the party has changed leadership several times. Venkaiah Naidu quit, and Lal Krishna Advani became the president of the party again in 2004 but had to resign in 2005 after a furor broke out within the party over a remark he made while visiting Pakistan that the country's founder, Muhammad Ali Jinnah, was secular. Rajnath Singh, former union minister and Uttar Pradesh chief minister, became president of the party in January 2006. In 2007, the BJP declared Lal Krishna Advani its prime ministerial candidate, perhaps laying the groundwork for the 2009 general elections. The party also set a quota of 33 percent female members to attract women to join its organizations.

The BJP's performance in state elections has been mixed since 2004. It regained power in Uttarakhand and Himachal Pradesh from the Congress while retaining Gujarat in 2007. It also formed coalition governments in Punjab and Karnataka. However, the party faced a major electoral setback in Uttar Pradesh, the most populous state. Likewise, several prominent leaders, like Uma Bharati and Madan Lal Khurana, left the party to form their own political fronts. It gained Kerala with Catholic support in the 2012 state elections and supported the Akali Dal in Punjab. (See Table 3.3 for its performance in state assembly elections.)

The alliance that would form a government at the center after the next general elections would depend on the type of alliance the BJP and Congress alliances formed as both received nearly equal percentages of the vote. In 2004, the Congress-led alliance won 219 seats with 34.51 percent of the vote, while the BJP-led alliance won 185 seats with 34.83 percent. In the 2009 general elections, the Congress-led alliance won 262 seats with 37.22 percent of the vote, while the BJP-led alliance won 159 seats and 24.63 percent. Thus BJP's path to power in the center may depend on whether it is able to form a winning coalition while retaining the support of its core, which was not happy with the party's moderate posture in forming alliances with regional and other parties. On the other hand, with the consolidation of their power, improved administrative capacity, and vote-catching skills, regional parties in Uttar Pradesh, West Bengal, Bihar, Andhra Pradesh, and Tamil Nadu pose a major challenge to the Congress Party and BJP in the foreseeable future.

Despite its organizational efficiency, the party is plagued by factional divisions and ideological conflicts. Anecdotal evidence indicates that factionalism is rampant in many state units of the BJP, especially in Madhya Pradesh, Maharashtra, Rajasthan, and Delhi. Following the Congress Party model of organization, the

BJP's central leadership is unwilling to grant autonomy to the state party units. Given the complex variations existing in the regional subcultures, the central leadership of the BJP cannot impose its will on the state party organizations with any greater hope of success than the centrist parties have realized since the 1970s.

The questionable practices of the Congress and other centrist parties have also left their impact on the BJP. For instance, the BJP has within its roster of MPs and members of the legislative assemblies persons with alleged criminal backgrounds, some even charged with serious crimes. In addition, the BJP's associations with the Bajrang Dal, representing the lumpen elements of Hindu militants, and the Vishwa Hindu Parishad, the Hindu revivalist organization, along with its tendency to take to the streets to settle political scores with the ruling party, do not enhance its image as a responsible political party ready to rule a country as vast as India.

Bahujan Samaj Party: Dalits as a Swing Element

Caste-based politics has been embedded in the Indian political process since independence. Although earlier caste-based political parties, such as the Republican Party organized by Dr. B. R. Ambedkar, were not successful in electoral politics, this was largely because the Congress Party was able to win Scheduled Caste votes and to co-opt many of their Scheduled Caste leaders within its ranks. The leadership of the Congress (I) appeared unable to bring about significant improvement in the lot of the lower castes and the Scheduled Castes, who during the past sixty-odd years have nevertheless produced a middle class of their own. It is thus not surprising that starting in the 1980s leaders of the Scheduled Castes decided to create a party of their own in order to become active players in state and national politics.

In 1984 the Bahujan Samaj Party was launched by Kanshi Ram, a Sikh Chamar leader from Punjab. With the decline of the Congress Party and the continuing inability of the upper-caste leadership of the major political parties to satisfy the rising expectations of the educated middle class of the Scheduled Castes, the BSP sought to challenge their political domination and electoral exploitation of the lower castes. The BSP entered the electoral arena in 1985, when it competed in the special election to fill vacancies in the legislative assemblies. However, only in the 1989 Lok Sabha elections did the BSP make earnest efforts in the states of Uttar Pradesh, Punjab, and Madhya Pradesh. Although the party did not win any seats in Madhya Pradesh, polling only 4.3 percent of the votes, it won two seats in Uttar Pradesh with 9 percent and one seat in Punjab with 8.6 percent. In addition to selecting the Scheduled Caste candidate, it also put up candidates from among both Muslims and the backward castes. From then on, the BSP became a political force to reckon with in these states and began to expand its base in other states as well.

Meanwhile, a short spell of power in Uttar Pradesh (June–October 1995), with outside support from the BJP, played an instrumental role in softening the BSP attitude toward the upper castes. In the 1996 Lok Sabha elections, the BSP included some upper-caste candidates in its electoral list. This strategy improved its electoral performance; it was able to win eleven seats (six from Uttar Pradesh, three from Punjab, and two from Madhya Pradesh) in the Lok Sabha. The party made especially impressive gains in Uttar Pradesh, improving its popular vote tally from 9.9 percent in the 1989 elections to 20 percent in 1996. In the October 1996 legislative assembly elections in Uttar Pradesh, the Congress (I) was forced to enter into electoral alliance with the BSP as a junior partner; the BSP captured sixty-seven seats, and the Congress was able to win only thirty-three seats. The BSP won a majority in the 2007 state legislative elections with 206 out of 402 seats, but it lost the state assembly elections to the Samajwadi Party in 2012. In short the Dalit vote is important but no longer belongs solely to the BSP.

The Communist Party of India

The communist movement in India has undergone various strategic and ideological transformations. It has always been plagued with factional conflicts and has experienced several splits. The Communist Party of India, which held its first all-India session in 1927, faced serious problems in its effort to create a suitable balance between the political realities of India and the foreign policy goals of the Soviet Union. Its leadership's ideological subservience to Moscow frequently led it into conflicts with the nationalist aspirations of the people of India. Thus, in 1942, when the Indian National Congress under the leadership of Mahatma Gandhi launched the Quit India movement and sought freedom from British rule in exchange for India's support for British war efforts, the CPI decided to join with the British government and denounced Gandhi's movement. Britain and the Soviet Union had formed a common front against Nazi Germany, so the communists supported the "people's war," while ignoring the dominant Indian nationalist aspirations. Similarly, in 1947 they supported the Muslim League on the issue of Pakistan and thus alienated the majority of Indians, who opposed the division of the country on a religious basis.

After independence in 1947, the CPI followed the Stalinist line by denouncing Congress Party leaders as slaves of imperialist interests. Under the leftist leadership of B. T. Ranadive, the CPI launched a terrorist movement and incited peasant uprisings, which were suppressed by the national government. But with the new political leadership in the Soviet Union and the ongoing process of de-Stalinization under Nikita Khrushchev, the Soviets decided to befriend the Nehru government. This change in Soviet foreign policy forced the CPI to alter its course. Thus, in 1958 it adopted the Amritsar resolution pledging to seek power and social change through parliamentary means. The dominant faction within the party supported Nehru's progressive policies, especially his foreign policy.

During the 1969 split in the Congress Party, and later during the national emergency, the CPI consistently supported Indira Gandhi and her government. Only after the 1977 defeat did it try to chart an independent course. The more radical Marxists in India view the CPI as primarily a revisionist party that has lost its revolutionary direction. The CPI has pockets of support in different parts of the country, primarily Andhra Pradesh, Bihar, eastern Uttar Pradesh, Kerala, and West Bengal. In the 1989 national elections the CPI captured twelve seats, twice the number it won in 1984. Again in 2004, the party retained its level of support by winning ten seats. It supported the Congress minority coalition in United Progressive Alliance (UPA)–1 (2004) from outside, but split with the Congress government on the United States–India Nuclear Agreement in 2008. In the 2009 general elections the Communist Party of India (Marxist) (CPI–M) won sixteen seats, and CPI won four seats; these results indicated an erosion of these parties' electoral position.

India's Communists

India's communists did not play a role in India's independence movement alongside Mahatma Gandhi and Nehru, but a prominent Indian leftist, Krishna Menon, a friend of Nehru, played an important role in shaping British attitudes toward India's independence. Nehru was the idol of left-wing Congress Party members during the 1930s and 1940s.[12] Indian leftists, trained in British Fabian politics, gained a voice in Indian national politics and administration with Nehru's patronage.

Nehru's belief in democratic socialism and a socialist economy in India, together with his tilt toward Moscow in foreign and military affairs, strengthened the Nehru-leftist connections at the intellectual and policy levels.

However, Indian communists followed two different trajectories than Nehru's leftist fellow travellers. The history of Indian communism reveals one trajectory that sought political power by parliamentary means and a second that advocated armed struggle to secure land and educational reforms. The second path has a pronounced Maoist orientation, although in its origin the Indian communist movement was aligned with Moscow and, along with Moscow, sought radical changes in Indian economic and political life. The adoption of the parliamentary road was associated with Moscow's acceptance of Nehru's nonalignment policy. The Communist Party of India, originally known as the CPI, adopted the peaceful path in the mid-1950s. It functioned as a peaceful parliamentary opposition. It had distinguished parliamentarians such as Hiren Mukherjee and A. K. Gopalan and came to power in Kerala through elections. But ideologically, as a party in power in Kerala, it was at odds with the Congress. It faced opposition from the feudal landlords regarding land reforms and from the Catholics on education reforms. The Congress relied on the landlords. In 1957 Indira Gandhi encouraged anticommunist agitation against the elected communist government, and her father, the prime minister, dismissed the communist government in 1959. Clearly the agendas of the Indian communists and the Congress Party were at odds on India's domestic affairs.

The division between the parliamentary road to power and armed struggle has dominated communist politics and the Indian social and political landscape.

In 1964, the Communist Party of India (Marxist) was formed to develop a people's democracy, but here the method of radical change was still meant to be peaceful. The radicals, however, sought changes by armed struggle. In 1967 the Naxalbari uprising occurred in Bengal, and Radio Peking joined the fray, urging a revolutionary armed struggle. This revealed a connection between China's opposition to the Nehru government and the USSR; it also injected Maoism into the peaceful path–armed struggle divide in the Indian communist movement. In 1969, CPI(M) became CPI (Marxist Leninist) (CPI[ML]), an embodiment of a new belief in armed struggle and guerrilla warfare in India.

CPI(ML) cadres believed that the Indian state was run by the rich landlords and bureaucratic capitalists and that the answer was to spread peasant revolts. These took shape in Andhra Pradesh, Orissa, Bihar, West Bengal, and parts of Uttar Pradesh and Punjab, then spread into Madhya Pradesh and Maharashtra. The movement attracted urban youth and intellectuals and tapped into antiwar sentiment in the West. In 2004 the CPI (Maoist) was formed as an offshoot of CPI(ML). It now has a network in 160 districts in India, in about ten states, covering about one-eighth of India's landmass. Today, tribals, women, and landless peasants are involved in the armed struggle.[13]

Regional Parties with a National Presence

As the Congress Party has declined nationally, regional parties have become more important and are crucial partners in winning national coalitions. The rise of such parties has further strengthened the multiparty nature of Indian politics.

The Dravida Munnetra Kazhagam and the All-India Anna DMK (AIADMK) represent the cultural nationalism of the people of Tamil Nadu, who speak the Tamil language and take pride in their Dravidian (South Indian) heritage. The Dravidian cultural revival movement and the DMK are closely intertwined.[14] C. N. Annadurai, the charismatic leader of the DMK, transformed this sociocultural revival movement into a political party. Initially the party sought creation of a sovereign state in the south; later on, however, it gave up its separatist demand. Now the DMK seeks only greater state autonomy and an end to the domination of the south by the Hindi-speaking north.

In the 1967 election, the DMK defeated the Congress Party at the polls and became the ruling party in Madras, a state that the DMK renamed Tamil Nadu (meaning "a country of Tamils"). After the death of Annadurai in 1969, a power struggle developed between M. Karunanidhi and M. G. Ramchandran (known by his initials, MGR), leading to MGR's forming the AIADMK in 1972. Soon thereafter the AIADMK came to dominate the state's politics; its success in the 1977 elections resulted in MGR's assumption of the chief ministership. It won a majority in the 2012 state elections and has expanded its presence in Kerala, Karnataka, Pondicherry, and Andhra Pradesh.

AIADMK, under MGR and, after his death, under his successor, Jayaram Jayalalitha, became closely allied with the Congress (I) in national politics. Since 1967 Tamil Nadu has been ruled by either AIADMK or DMK, to the exclusion of the Congress (I). In the 1996 state elections, the DMK, led by M. Karunanidhi, defeated Jayalalitha and her AIADMK. In the 2004 parliamentary elections, the DMK allied itself with the Congress Party and won each of the sixteen seats it contested, while the BJP-allied AIADMK lost every one of the thirty-three seats it contested.

The Telugu Desam Party (TDP) is a comparatively new political party that in 1982 gained dominance in Andhra Pradesh's politics under the leadership of the late N. T. Rama Rao, a former matinee idol (just as M. G. Ramchandran had been in Tamil Nadu). The party originated in reaction to Indira Gandhi's frequent imposition of unpopular Congress Party chief ministers on the people of Andhra Pradesh. Most of these chief ministers did not last very long, and the faction-ridden state Congress Party failed to deliver on its promises. Rama Rao had only to appeal to the subnational pride of the Telugu people; the TDP denounced New Delhi's domination of the state's politics and in 1983 won an impressive majority in the state election, defeating the Congress Party. It is the second-largest party in the Lok Sabha and gained a majority in state elections in 2009.

Since its formation, the TDP has faced various challenges from the Congress Party. In both the 1984 parliamentary elections and the March 1985 state elections, however, it routed the Congress (I) at the polls: for the Lok Sabha, it won 28 of 49 seats, and in the state elections, it won 202 of 287 seats. In the 1989 parliamentary and state elections, the TDP suffered a humiliating defeat at the hands of the Congress (I), losing control of the state government.

In the 1993 Andhra Pradesh Legislative Assembly elections, however, the TDP defeated the Congress (I) and returned to power in the state. After Rama Rao's death, his son-in-law, Chandrababu Naidu became the chairman of the National Front. After the decline of the National Front and subsequent disintegration of the non-Congress Third Front, the TDP, led by Naidu, became allied with the BJP. In the 1999 parliamentary elections, the party was able to win twenty-nine of the thirty-four Lok Sabha seats it contested, but in 2004 it won only five seats. In the 2009 elections, the TDP and allies gained 106 seats.

The Jammu and Kashmir National Conference was founded in 1939 by Sheikh Muhammad Abdullah, a Kashmiri freedom fighter. His efforts resulted in the development of Kashmiri self-respect and a strong sense of subnational identity. The National Conference under his leadership was able to secure for Jammu and Kashmir a special status in the Indian union not given to any other Indian state.

After Sheikh Abdullah's death in 1982, however, the party became divided into two factions—one led by the sheikh's son, Dr. Farooq Abdullah, and the other by the sheikh's son-in-law, G. M. Shah. Abdullah's government, which won a clear majority in the 1982 state election, was dismissed through Congress (I) manipulation. In its place Indira Gandhi installed a government led by G. M. Shah's faction of the National Conference, which was supported by the Congress (I) members. In the 1984 elections, however, the Farooq-led National Conference once again swept the parliamentary election in Kashmir Valley.

In January 1990, when Jagmohan was appointed governor of the state, Dr. Abdullah and his ministry resigned, protesting the failure of V. P. Singh's government to consult them before his appointment. In July 1990 the state of Jammu and Kashmir was placed under president's rule: faced with insurgency, the state was deprived of the democratic process by the central government. Political activity came to a virtual halt, and the National Conference wandered in a political wilderness. Only with the restoration of the democratic process in 1996 did the National Conference become active again in state politics.

Elections for the state legislative assembly were held in September 1996 in Jammu and Kashmir. While the All-Party Hurriyat Conference, a conglomerate of parties seeking secession from India, boycotted the elections, eight major parties of the state, along with several independent candidates, participated; 505 candidates vied for eighty-seven seats. The Jammu and Kashmir National

Conference, which had earlier stayed away from the Lok Sabha elections, won a majority of the seats. Farooq Abdullah, the leader of the National Conference, became the chief minister (1981–2002), followed by his son Omar Abdullah (2002–2009). With Congress Party support, it remains the ruling party (2009–present) in the state.

India has produced several dynamic female state-level leaders who now have a national presence. Mamata Banerjee is head of the ruling party in West Bengal, the All-India Trinamool Congress (2011–present). She is a politician, legislator, former bureaucrat, writer, and the first female chief minister of West Bengal. She first jointed the Congress Party and held cabinet-level posts between 1999 and 2004 in railways, and coal and mines, as well as without portfolio. In the late 1990s, she lost confidence in the Congress because of corruption in the party, and she opposed the West Bengal communists who ruled the state from 1977 to 2011. She formed her party All-India Trinamool Congress in 1997, and she won a massive majority of the seats in the state assembly elections. Banerjee is a human rights activist and champions women's and children's rights. She successfully opposed forcible acquisition of land to build the proposed Tata car factory, and her actions give her a strong popular base. She was a coalition partner of UPA-2 and left the coalition in 2012, citing policy differences. In 2012 this party was the second-largest member of the UPA-2 Congress-led coalition and the sixth-largest party in the Lok Sabha.[15]

The Bahujan Samaj Party, led by Mayawati (no last name is used), represents the Dalits; the party name means "people in majority." Formed in 1984 by Kanshi Ram, it follows the philosophy of B. R. Ambedhar, the architect of India's constitution. Mayawati became the leader in 2003. Her power base is the Dalits in Uttar Pradesh, and the Bahujan Samaj became the fourth-largest party in the Lok Sabha in the 2009 elections. She lost power to the Samajwadi Party in the 2012 state assembly elections due to voter anger at growing corruption in her government and the use of funds to build memorials to Dalit leaders, including herself. The BSP, however, remains a factor in state and national politics because it represents the Dalit vote.

In addition to the major parties, there are such minor regional parties as Jharkhand Mukti Morcha in Bihar; Sikkim Sangram Parishad (SSP), led by N. B. Bhandari; and Asom Gana Parishad, led by Prafulla Mahanta, in Assam.

Communal or Sectarian Parties

Of all the sectarian and communal parties in India in the postindependence period, the most successful in promoting the cause of a particular religious community has been the Shiromani Akali Dal. A militant political organization with religious appeal, the Akali Dal claims to be the exclusive representative of the Sikhs, who constitute a majority in the state of Punjab. The Akali Dal is closely associated with the educational, cultural, and religious life of the Sikhs. For example, it has a monopoly over the Shiromani Gurudwara Prabhandak Committee (SGPC), which not only exercises control over the Sikh temples but also possesses huge revenues from the offerings made by Sikh devotees. Through its skillful use of SGPC funds, the Akali Dal manages several Sikh educational, cultural, and religious institutions. Thus the Sikh denominational schools, colleges, and other societies not only employ Sikh intellectuals and party workers but also try to create a distinct subnational identity among the Sikhs.[16]

From time to time the Akali Dal has been in power in the Punjab, but it is able to maintain itself in power only in coalition with other parties. Such coalitions are usually unstable, and the Akali Dal governments collapsed frequently. Akalis have therefore often resorted to agitation in seeking to achieve their political goals. In 1982 the Akalis launched a mass agitation against the national government, seeking, along with certain religious concessions, greater autonomy for the Sikh-dominated state of Punjab. When the party lost control of the agitation to religious fundamentalists and Sikh extremists, a bloody confrontation with the national government resulted. In 1985 the majority faction of the Akali Dal, led by Harcharan Singh Longowal, reached an agreement with the national government and terminated its agitation. Subsequently it won elections in the state and was brought back to power in the Punjab.

Summing Up

The emergence of vibrant regional parties in India points to the creation of a political and ideological bandwidth that challenges the position of the two national parties—the Congress Party and the BJP—as well as the position of the Nehru-Gandhi dynasty. Writing in 1984 Salman Rushdie notes,

> The facts indicate that family rule has not left Indian democracy in particularly good shape. The drawing of all power to the Centre has created deep and sometimes violently expressed, resentments in the states; the replacement of Nehru's more idealistic vision by his descendants' politics of power-at-any-cost has resulted in a sharp lowering of the standards of public life; and the creation, in Delhi, of a sort of royal court, a ruling elite of intimates of the family, unelected and unanswerable to anyone but the prime minister, has further damaged the structure of Indian democracy. It is beginning to look just possible—is it not?— that the interests of "the world's largest democracy" and those of its ruling family might not be quite the same.[17]

In 1967, Neville Maxwell, a longtime *London Times* correspondent, predicted the collapse of Indian democracy and the onset of military rule.[18] He was wrong on both points. Instead, the development of party politics in the states and at the center demonstrates the commitment to democracy, India's voters' mistrust of majority Congress Party or BJP rule, and an implicit rejection of the Nehru-Gandhi dynasty.

SUGGESTED READINGS

Barnett, Marguerite Ross. *The Politics of Cultural Nationalism in South India.* Princeton, NJ: Princeton University Press, 1976.

Baxter, Craig. *The Jana Sangh: A Biography of an Indian Political Party.* Philadelphia: University of Pennsylvania Press, 1969.

Dasgupta, B. *The Naxalite Movement.* Bombay: Allied, 1974.

Erdman, Howard. *The Swatantra Party and Indian Conservatism.* Cambridge: Cambridge University Press, 1967.

Fickett, Lewis P., Jr. *The Major Socialist Parties of India: A Study in Leftist Fragmentation.* Syracuse, NY: Maxwell School, Syracuse University, 1970.

Graham, B. D. *Hindu Nationalism and Indian Politics: The Origins and the Development of the Bharatiya Jan Sangh.* Cambridge: Cambridge University Press, 1990.

Hardgrave, Robert L., Jr. *The Dravidian Movement.* Bombay: Popular Prakash, 1965.

Hartmann, Horst. *Political Parties in India.* New Delhi: Meenakshi Prakash, 1982.

Kochanek, Stanley A. *The Congress Party of India: The Dynamics of One-Party Democracy.* Princeton, NJ: Princeton University Press, 1968.

Ludden, David. ed. *Making India Hindu: Religion, Community, and the Politics of Democracy in India.* Delhi: Oxford University Press, 1996.

Malik, Yogendra K., and V. B. Singh. *Hindu Nationalists in India: The Rise of the Bharatiya Janata Party.* Boulder, CO: Westview Press, 1994.

Naik, J. A. *The Opposition in India and the Future of Democracy.* New Delhi: S. Chand, 1983.

Nayar, Baldev Raj. *Minority Politics in the Punjab.* Princeton, NJ: Princeton University Press, 1966.

Sen Gupta, Bhabani. *Communism in Indian Politics.* New York: Columbia University Press, 1972.

Weiner, Myron. *Party Politics in India: The Development of a Multi-party System.* Princeton, NJ: Princeton University Press, 1957.

NOTES

1. Sugata Bose and Ayesha Jalal, *Modern South Asia*, 2nd ed. (London: Routledge, 2003), 167–176.

2. Ramachandra Guha, *India After Gandhi* (New York: Harper Collins, 2007), 203–209, 212–212, 231, 267–283, 288–305. See also C. von Fürer-Haimendorf, "Caste and Politics in South Asia," 52–70, F. A. Bailey, "Politics and Society in Contemporary Orissa," 97–114, and W. H. Morris-Jones, "India's Political Idiom," 133–154, all chapters in *Politics and Society in India*, ed. C. H. Philips (New York: Praeger, 1962).

3. Guha, *India After Gandhi,* 433–434, shows the differences in the aims and methods of Nehru and Indira Gandhi. Indira Gandhi was less cosmopolitan in her worldviews, more manipulative of the political system to serve her political ends, and more heavily reliant on an inner core of Kashmiri advisers.

4. W. R. Crocker, *Nehru* (London: George Allen and Unwin, 1967), 166–167.

5. W. H. Morris-Jones, "Parliament and Dominant Party: Indian Experience," *Parliamentary Affairs* (summer 1964): 296–307; Gopal Krishna, "One Party Dominance: Development and Trends," in *Party System and Election Studies*, ed. Rajni Kothari et al. Centre for the Study of Development Societies, Occasional Papers 1 (Bombay: Allied, 1967), 19–98. Rajni Kolkari, "The 'Congress System' in India," *Asian Survey* (December 1964): 1161–1173.

6. Stanley A. Kochanek, "Mrs. Gandhi's Pyramid: The New Congress," in *Indira Gandhi's India: A Political System Reappraised,* ed. Henry C. Hart (Boulder, CO: Westview Press, 1967), 93–124.

7. Richard Sisson and William Vanderbock, "Mapping the Indian Electorate: Trends in Party Support in Seven National Elections," *Asian Survey* (October 1983): 1142; Javeed Alam, "The Vote for Political Stability and the Implications: An Analysis of 1980 Election Results," *Political Science Review* 21, no. 4 (1983): 313.

8. Paul R. Brass, "National Power and Local Politics in India: A Twenty-Year Perspective," *Modern Asian Studies* 18, no. 1 (1984): 89–118; James Manor, "Anomie in Indian Politics: Origins and Potential Impact," *Economic and Political Weekly,* May 21, 1983, 225–234.

9. Robert L. Hardgrave Jr., "India on the Eve of Elections: Congress and the Opposition," *Pacific Affairs* (fall 1984): 404–428.

10. See Stuart Corbridge, "The Political Economy of Development in India Since Independence," Ch. 21, and Jan Breman, "The Political Economy of Agrarian Change in India," Ch. 22, in *Routledge Handbook of South Asian Politics*, ed. Paul R. Brass (London: Routledge, 2010).

11. Yogendra K. Malik and V. B. Singh, *Hindu Nationalists in India: The Rise of the Bharatiya Janata Party* (Boulder, CO: Westview Press, 1994), 211.

12. Percival Spear ed., *A History of India,* rev. ed. (London: Penguin Books, 1978), 2:245.

13. This section draws on Sumanta Banerjee, "Radical and Violent Political Movements," in *Routledge Handbook of South Asian Politics*, ed. Paul R. Brass (London: Routledge, 2010), 384–391.

14. Marguerite Ross Barnett, *The Politics of Cultural Nationalism in South India* (Princeton, NJ: Princeton University Press, 1976).

15. *Encyclopaedia Britanica*, 2012, web, March 26, 2012.

16. Baldev Raj Nayar, *Minority Politics in the Punjab* (Princeton, NJ: Princeton University Press, 1966); Paul R. Brass, "Ethnic Cleavages and the Punjab Party System, 1952–1972," in *Electoral Politics in the Indian States,* ed. Myron Weiner and John Osgood Field (New Delhi: Manohar, 1974), 4:7–61.

17. See Salman Rushdie's introduction in Tariq Ali, *The Nehrus and the Gandhis: An Indian Dynasty* (London: Chatto & Windus, 1985), xii.

18. Cited in Guha, *India After Gandhi,* 417–418.

5

Groups and Multiple Demands on the System

The manner in which India's independence was achieved has shaped the role of competing groups in India's democratic and developmental system. Maurice Zinkin outlines the British idea as follows: "The old British idea expressed to perfection in the Government of India Act, 1935, had been that independence came only when a country was fully ready, by the agreement of all major interests, and with full protection for every minority. *The new pattern* established in 1947 was that a country could get its independence as soon as its *political classes wanted it*, and that it would be *granted on whatever terms those political classes could be pushed into accepting*."[1] In the Britain–Congress Party–Muslim League political triangle, the political classes got what they wanted in 1947 after Britain wanted a graceful exit from India. Jawaharlal Nehru and Mohammed Ali Jinnah wanted independence and power. After 1947, however, the process of pushing others into accepting the new terms and benefits intensified.

The Indian idea before 1947 had relied on mass-based political agitation and the use of British liberal democratic principles to seek independence. After 1947 the new pattern recognized the virtues of democracy and party politics, as well as the need for a developmental model to deal with India's massive economic and social problems. However, these ideals and their rhetoric had a parallel reality: India's new rulers had limited administrative experience; their policy actions revealed their reliance on foreign experiences (e.g., British liberal political values, communist socialism) and their vulnerability to foreign advice and interventions in foreign and military affairs. The British India experience was a point of opposition against foreign rule, and yet British India itself was a point of attraction as a model democracy. India's constitution reflects this duality. It produced a conception of the rights of the Indian people in the new India, a novelty since Indians had lacked such recognition by their rulers, be they Mughal emperors, native princes, the East India Company, or the British government. This was a step forward in the evolution of Indian political and social thought that nonetheless created a framework for competitive group activities.

The formation of interest groups and multiple demands after 1947 is an evolutionary story driven by multiple catalysts. The first catalyst lies in the general governmental context: the Nehru government (1947–1960s) held the commanding heights of Indian politics, economy, and diplomacy, but it became a system of groups' demands, eroding the authority of the Congress Party governments at the center and state levels, and new political players emerged. The winning tactic of changing policies and politics is an old one: gains in India— as in the British India–Nehru–Jinnah case—are granted on whatever terms the political classes can be pushed into accepting. Indian interest groups understand this political culture and the mode of change in the country's internal arrangements. The constitution provides the legal framework to organize India's political, economic, and social life; however, the catalysts that favor interest group activity reflect a different set of calculations. The groups need first to create opportunities for group activity and then to use that activism to push their demands.

The second catalyst is that the quest for political power by leaders stimulates the development of a field of power politics among competing leaders and political parties at the national, regional, and local (municipal and village) levels. The political needs of aspiring leaders require mobilization of voters and resources to win elections. This engenders an environment for developing patron-client, transactional relationships that require continuous bargaining. This in turn creates opportunities for expression of group demands, which evolve constantly.

The third catalyst is that growing economic inequality within India, along with tangible signs of internal economic growth, generates a push toward upward social and economic mobility of the middle and poor classes. This social catalyst converges with the popular rhetoric of politicians about eradicating poverty. This element has created opportunities for caste- and class-based activities at the regional and national levels. Such activities touch policies relating to education, representation in the administration, rural health, women's rights, the environment, and the uplift of the underprivileged sections of society.

The fourth catalyst is that the search for profit by the business community since 1947 reflects the long history of dynamic Indian capitalism (from the 1400s), while governmental interventions in economic affairs distorted the development of private Indian capitalism. This was a game changer. Indian capitalism was wrecked by British India, as Karl Marx's *On Colonialism* demonstrates empirically.[2] It was also distorted by Nehruvian socialism when the state held the commanding heights of the national economy and produced a corrupt License Raj that led to anemic economic growth and the start of crony capitalism after 1947. With economic reforms, starting in the 1990s, business groups gained opportunities for private-sector advancement. The quest to expand businesses within India and India's position in the global economy were powerful drivers to make India a viable developmental model.

The fourth catalyst stimulated the rise of the fifth catalyst. With growing business and state intervention to promote economic activity, environmentalists and civil society advocates urged attention to the negative impacts of economic development on the environment and sought to develop policies to ensure economic and social justice for the poor.[3]

Finally, India's military fights with Pakistan and China and strategic concerns about her interests in the Indian Ocean area have become a catalyst for the rise of a powerful national security constituency in India, a departure from the Nehruvian-Gandhian belief in peaceful changes in the world environment.

In sum, with growing political, social, economic, and military polarities within India and in her external strategic neighborhood, the opportunities to articulate demands in the Indian system have grown since 1947, along with the capacities and skills of influential players.

The segmented nature of Indian society and politics has stimulated diverse group activity. Before India came under British control, traditional and ascriptive ties based on kinship and community provided avenues for people to organize to protect their common interests. With the advent of British rule, competition for jobs and the need to obtain economic and business concessions encouraged Indians to organize themselves. The subsequent introduction of representative institutions and electoral politics after independence provided the incentive to politically ambitious people to organize all kinds of groups and associations.[4]

The British Raj was replaced by the Nehru–Congress Party–Indian bureaucracy raj. India's new political rulers became the objects of group demands in the highly politicized and bureaucratic environment of independent India. After 1947 India was new in the sense that a new political class had come into power and the foreign ruler had been expelled. With the establishment of a new political elite came a new style and rhetoric that emphasized nationalism and modernity, nation building and populism, and a new foreign and military policy. In the peace-oriented frame of reference, the group demands of the Indian armed forces were marginalized, and the demands of political and business groups, such as Indian leftists, trade unions, and the Birla businesses, were highlighted, along with a buildup of state planning groups that expressed the political values of Nehruvian socialist economy. The new Indian political orientation of socialism and democracy built a superstructure of more bureaucratic and political controls on top of the structure of the British-origin Indian government. The new government of India adopted en masse the rules, procedures, laws, and governmental organizations of British India.

Group Activity

Group demands in India should be examined in light of the following observations. First, as Zinkin points out, demands are granted on terms that the political classes can be pushed into accepting. Second, Gunnar Myrdal, the Swedish economist and author of the famous report on the Asian drama, notes,

> And so the South Asian planners remain in their paradoxical position: on a general and non-committal level they freely and almost passionately proclaim the need for radical social and economic change, whereas in planning their policies they tread most warily in order not to disrupt the traditional social order. And when they do legislate radical institutional reforms—for instance in taxation or in regard to property rights in the villages—they permit the laws to contain loopholes of all sorts and even let them remain unenforced. This contradiction is intellectualized in two opposing views, simultaneously held, on what planning for development really requires in the way of social change. On the one hand, it is propounded that social change must be radical and go very deep. On the other hand, it is stressed that it must proceed with the utmost caution, upsetting the inherited traditional social setting as little as possible.[5]

Third, and finally, Robert Hardgrave and Stanley Kochanek argue that Indian democracy "confronts an indeterminate political future" and the "Indian masses are an awakening force that has yet to find coherence and direction."[6]

The implication of each view is different. Zinkin shows how demands are granted (i.e., there is a push and pull involved in the dynamics between groups and the holders of political power). Myrdal's assessment, made over forty years ago, is still accurate. It implies that there is a gap between declared ideals and realized achievements; he is right to point to the paradox between the proclaimed need for radical economic and social change, which is embedded in the

Indian constitution and leadership declarations, and the actual policy-making process, which is cautious and respects Indian traditions. While Myrdal is impatient and frustrated with the slow pace of change, Hardgrave and Kochanek are pessimistic about the prospect of gaining coherence and direction in Indian politics and policies.

Our view is that Indian group demands follow the Zinkin approach, and the process is consistent with the Indian paradox outlined by Myrdal. Group activities articulate demands; thereafter, a push-and-pull process politicizes and activates the issues, and the process of engagement between the groups and the government slowly produces economic and social reforms in India. One must be mindful of two characteristics of Indian politics and governments: (1) The Indian government at the central and state levels is the successor to the British colonial government. Undoubtedly, the social and economic agenda of the Indian government seeks radical reforms, but the demands for reform are processed or filtered through the mechanics of the British-Indian administrative structure and the new post-1947 political system. (2) Group activities seek to push the envelope of the political space between Myrdal's paradox (i.e., seeking radical social and economic reforms at the declaratory level and proceeding with caution, mindful of Indian traditions and the use of consensus in decision making). Below, we give examples to show how the envelope has been pushed, albeit slowly, to give Indian policies coherence and direction; this is contrary to the pessimism of Hardgrave and Kochanek. Continuous pulls and pushes between the government and the groups is hence a continuous characteristic of the Indian method of decision making and has given limited direction and coherence to India's policies.

Indian groups' activities revolve around core issue areas, which are reflected in the catalysts. The champions of economic, political, and social change are entrenched and institutionalized and have a voice in the national and international discourse. The key constituents now in the game are listed below.

Subgovernmental Units. The complex postindependence institutional network created by the new constitution of India provided a new focus for interest groups. Multiple power centers have emerged since 1947. The village councils, municipal governments, district administrations, state legislative bodies, council of ministers, and a host of bureaucratic organizations and administrative agencies have become subject to various kinds of pressure, intensifying group activity.

Religious Groups. The competition for power and influence among rival groups is both a divisive and an integrative process. On the one hand, the activities of religious minorities, such as Muslims, Sikhs, and Christians, evoke protest from the members of the majority religion and tend to aggravate intercommunal tension and reinforce religious divisions. On the other hand, many nontraditional economic groups, such as the Chamber of Commerce and Industry, the trade unions, and the peasants' and farmers' organizations, tend to play an integrative role. These groups draw their membership from people of all segments of Indian society engaged in the same trade.

Policy Groups. After independence, interest groups in India did not enjoy much autonomy. Interest in linguistic and ethnic rights, the rights of the underprivileged, civil society development, child labor reforms, disarmament, environmental protection, and women's rights emerged later. These issues are given voice now in national debates, but their effect on policy making varies. With growing opportunities to develop India's federal system, economy, and radical social agenda, the opportunities for group activities have increased. Group activity is a response to either governmental initiatives or to local/provincial issue-oriented demands by groups that produce a governmental response. The push-pull process is a constant in Indian politics, and change is usually not linear. Here are some examples of major issues and initiatives that fit into Myrdal's assessment cited earlier:

1. Prior to 1947 the Congress Party sought to redraw state boundaries along linguistic lines, but its leaders, Nehru and Sardar Vallabhbhai Patel, were cautious about the need for states' unity, security, and economic integrity. In 1953 the States Reorganization Commission was set up for this task. It viewed language as an important criterion but also assessed the economic and geographical realities of the proposed state. It reported in 1955; a bill was passed in 1956 and amended several times thereafter. The issues are not totally resolved, as new states have been formed and new group demands based on local/regional, language, social, and political conditions for more states persist.[7] In sum, there has been movement toward new state formation as well as ambivalence about the importance of linguistics compared to geographical and economic considerations in new state formation. The debate on the issues continues to this day.

2. Another major issue involves the empowerment of India's socially and economically underprivileged groups. In 1979, the Janata Party government established the Mandal Commission. In 1980 the commission supported an affirmative action policy giving members of the Scheduled Castes and Tribes and other backward classes (OBCs) exclusive access to government jobs and places in universities, recommending an increase in their quotas in both universities and jobs from 27 to 49.5 percent. The recommendation to reserve positions for OBCs in government jobs was implemented in 1993. The reserva-

tions policy in educational institutes was implemented in 2008. This process made caste politics a part of the Indian political mainstream. The advocacy of former untouchables now had official sanction. This advocacy to remove past injustices also had its critics. It was seen as a form of discrimination, and with separate quotas for religious minorities, it was thought to dilute secularism; it was also seen to dilute the merit principle in university admissions, and talk to extend the reservations policy to the private sector was thought to deter foreign investment in India's economy. The debate continues.[8]

Other group demands have been rejected or resisted. Demands by the Bharatiya Janata Party (BJP) to remove Jammu and Kashmir's special status in the Indian constitution have not been accepted. The demand by regional states to adjust center-state relations led to the establishment of the Sarkaria Commission in 1983. Its final report was 1,600 pages long, with 247 recommendations; none of them were implemented.

India has many voices on a long list of social, economic, and political issues, but the mainstream movers of group interests and activities are as follows.

Business

Business and commercial classes long had a poor image in Indian society. In the Hindu social system, the trading and commercial classes represented by the Vaishya caste occupy a lower status than the Brahmins, the carriers of sacred knowledge, and the Kshatriyas, the administrators and warriors. The Banias and Marwaris, leading members of India's trading community, also had a poor image. British administrators shared a similarly jaundiced view of the commercial classes and often distanced themselves from the "box wallahs." Moreover, as Stanley Kochanek has pointed out, modern political ideologies such as Marxism and Gandhism, to which many Indian leaders subscribe, depict businesspeople as exploiters.[9]

In the late 1980s this situation began to change. A new breed of enterprising businesspeople with considerable business and political sophistication arose, and the political parties, in order to meet the escalating cost of electioneering, became dependent on business donations. These developments have given the world of business a new respectability and political clout. They have also contributed to India's growing problem with corruption.[10]

The introduction of economic liberalization by the Rao government in 1991 led to a dramatic change in the environment surrounding business organizations. Party leaders and government ministers now seek to address their audiences, assuring them of their cooperation in the economic growth of the country. Leading businessmen are often included in government delegations visiting foreign countries looking for direct foreign investment.

Students

Students constitute one of the most politicized segments of Indian society. The political development of the student community is attributed partly to the freedom movement and partly to the behavior of political leaders in the postindependence period. Before India achieved its independence, the leaders of the Indian National Congress frequently called on students to give up their studies to participate in the civil disobedience movement. Since independence, leaders and political parties have vied with each other both to capture the student unions existing on the campuses of more than 105 universities and thousands of colleges and to recruit student leaders into political parties. Many students are ready to use even minor grievances as reasons to stage protests, strikes, and demonstrations against unresponsive school administrations.

Only a small minority of the more than 500,000 university graduates each year obtains gainful employment. With few or no job possibilities, many ambitious students look to parties and political leaders to advance their careers. For this reason, student politics in India merits attention.[11] Students are also an influential pressure group in universities and Indian politics. With the introduction of admissions quotas for Dalits, there is increasing polarization between Dalit and non-Dalit students.

The government's decision to allow 50 percent reservations in university admissions (including all professional schools) and jobs emerged as a new and powerful issue in India's political system. It was seen as undermining the merit basis of university recruitment, a principle that enabled top Indian academic institutions and graduates to gain worldwide recognition. Indian political parties have viewed the issue in political and electoral terms and deem it politically incorrect to criticize the new policy. Despite criticism that the government's policy undermines the merit principle in university admissions and recruitment in professional programs such as medicine, the trend toward promoting the underprivileged sectors of Indian society is entrenched.

The Military

India's military establishment is not politicized as in Pakistan and Bangladesh. It is subordinate to and controlled by the country's civilian rulers. This is not to say that India's military establishment is devoid of influence, however. The rise of a national security state in India has facilitated the enormous growth of influence of the Indian armed forces in policy making, in shaping the limits of policy action by Indian politicians and bureaucrats (e.g., in Kashmir and on the

India-China border), and in resource allocations by government to all branches of the armed forces.

The position of the military in India today has changed radically since the Nehru-Menon days (1950–1962). Nehru relied on diplomacy to promote Indian interests, and the Indian armed forces were starved of funds in the belief that no power would dare attack India. If it were attacked, other powers were expected to come to India's rescue. Krishna Menon felt that Pakistan, not China, was India's main enemy. As a result of the Nehru-Gandhi-Menon faith in pacifism and disarmament, the development of conventional and nuclear military capabilities was ignored.

At present India maintains one of the largest armies in the world, with over 1.3 million people in uniform.[12] It is a well-disciplined and thoroughly professional body. Since 1962 the Indian defense ministry has been headed by politicians with national stature and distinguished administrative abilities who have advanced the needs of India's military establishment. Now the chiefs of staff of the three armed forces have been granted a voice in defense-policy formulation and easy access to the higher echelons of political decision-making agencies. India also has a growing and modern air force and navy equipped with modern weapons. The modernization of India's navy is noteworthy because it was historically the poor cousin of the Indian army in resource allocation. Today, however, it must deal with challenges that emerge from growing Chinese and Pakistani navies with a focus on the Persian Gulf, the Bay of Bengal, and the sea lanes between the South China Sea and the Indian Ocean. The coast guard is responsible for monitoring drug trade and illegal infiltration from hostile neighbors into India's vast and generally unpoliced coastline. With growing competition for energy resources in African, Persian Gulf, Middle Eastern, and Indian Ocean areas, the role of the Indian navy is likely to grow in importance.

Three other defense-oriented constituencies form a wide and deep foundation of India's national security structure: (1) The Department of Atomic Energy (DAE) was established in 1947 to promote peaceful uses of atomic energy. With India's formal declaration of its nuclear weapon status in 1998, the DAE's facilities have become a key part of India's nuclear deterrent. (2) With the growth of India's short-range and long-range missile capabilities, India's defense research and space organization now have a military and a civilian rationale. Space is India's new frontier, and the growth of its capacities reveals the marriage between space technology, military power-projection capacity, and civil applications of such technology.[13] (3) Finally, the proliferation of India's paramilitary forces under the ministries of defense and home affairs shows the importance of managing long and porous borders and signal the threat of internal insurgencies.

The Intelligentsia

India possesses a well-established, articulate intelligentsia. India's technocrats include engineers, doctors, agronomists, scientists, and computer engineers. This group provides highly skilled technical services, but its political influence was limited in the past. Now Indians with science and engineering backgrounds have entered different branches of the central and state governments, and with an official platform, they are able to influence policy making and implementation. Indians with legal and financial credentials (e.g., Arun Shourie, lawyer, BJP; P. Chidambaran and Manmohan Singh, economists, finance and prime minister, respectively, Congress Party) have also joined political parties; as ministers, they are now decision makers. So the rise of the knowledge sector of Indian society and its participation in political and government activity have broken the stranglehold over Indian politics by the nontechnical but professional politician who dominated Indian political life from the 1930s to the turn of the century. As India's problems with agriculture, water, electricity, and the environment loom large, the role of scientific experts in each area is bound to grow. The strength of India's technically qualified manpower is estimated to be over 2.5 million, the third largest in the world.[14] More than 2,000 research units employ thousands of scientists and researchers.

India's national newspapers, such as the *Times of India, Indian Express, Hindustan Times, Statesman,* and *Hindu,* are known for their high standards. In recent years such English periodicals as *Sunday, Frontline,* and *India Today* have also emerged as major sources of information. The investigative news reporting in *India Today,* in particular, has earned widespread acclaim. Many young reporters and journalists have successfully exposed scandals involving politicians and public officials. India's business press has emerged quickly and professionally. Papers like *Economic Times* and *Business Standard* offer timely reporting of market trends and developments and policy analysis relating to India. With growing acceptance of capitalism by India's middle class, the role of India's business press is likely to grow.

The vernacular intellectual establishment occupies a less prestigious position than its English counterpart, but it has a larger readership. Although their impact at the national level is limited, vernacular-speaking intellectuals exercise considerable influence in the state capitals. And even though writings in regional languages (with few exceptions) have yet to develop the national press tradition of cogent analysis of political and economic issues, the regional press has frequently demonstrated the courage to withstand heavy political pressure. Often they provide a better measure of Indian public opinion in contrast to the expression of elite opinion—by the elites for the elites—in the English language medium.

Caste and Religious Groups

Indian groups organized on the basis of social origin may be referred to as community associations. These groups date back to nineteenth-century British India and are now mainstream participants in Indian party politics at the center and state levels. Moreover, with intermarriage and migration of individual caste members, caste characteristics have evolved and diluted into "intermediate castes."

In contrast to caste associations, India's various religious groups tend to organize on an all-India basis.

Hindu Groups. Many Hindus have grievances to voice. In the first place, they have long felt that even though Hindus constitute an overwhelming majority in the country, politicians have ignored their interests. Some Hindus blame the Congress Party's leadership for the division of their motherland by the creation of the Muslim state of Pakistan on India's western border. In addition, some Hindus object to their treatment by Muslims: they point out that in neighboring Pakistan the majority's religion, Islam, has become the state religion, and the Hindus have been driven out. In Bangladesh, another neighboring country in which Muslims are a majority, Hindus have little representation and feel that they are treated as second-class citizens. The ruling political elite of India, they assert, have put the interests of religious minorities before those of the majority in order to win elections.

There are several Hindu sectarian organizations. The most active and articulate is the Rashtriya Swayamsevak Sangh (RSS), which provides an important channel for the expression of militant Hindu nationalism. The RSS was founded in 1925 by a Maharashtrian Brahmin, Keshav Baliram Hedgewar, in Nagpur, where it still maintains its headquarters. Slowly and steadily it established its branches in all parts of India, although its largest following is in the Hindi-speaking heartland of North India.

The RSS has built an effective paramilitary organization and possesses a large, active, and well-disciplined membership. Although it claims to be a cultural rather than a political organization, the RSS became a major force behind the Jana Sangh, a militant Hindu nationalist party. Since 1979, with the formation of the Bharatiya Janata Party, the RSS seems to have achieved a degree of autonomy, and it supports the parties and candidates that it believes are committed to Hindu interests. It has maintained a militant anti-Muslim posture, and its workers are frequently blamed for inciting anti-Muslim rioting in urban areas.[15]

Muslim Groups. The creation of a Muslim-majority state out of British India against the strong opposition of the Hindu majority left India's more than 100 million Muslims in a state of confusion. A large number of the educated, well-to-do, and politically conscious Muslims went to Pakistan, leaving millions of their coreligionists behind without leaders or a well-knit political organization. For the most part these groups protect their interests by supporting the Congress Party and state-level parties that seek their electoral support and help their interests.

SUGGESTED READINGS

Andersen, Walter K., and Shridhar D. Damle. *The Brotherhood in Saffron: The Rashtriya Swayamsevak Sangh and Hindu Revivalism.* Boulder, CO: Westview Press, 1977.

CIA. "South Asia: India." CIA World Fact Book. https://www.cia.gov/library/publications /the-world-factbook/geos/in.html.

Cohen, Stephen P. *The Indian Army: Its Contribution to the Development of a Nation.* 2nd ed. New York: Oxford University Press, 1991.

Erdman, Howard L. *Political Attitudes of Indian Industry.* London: Athlove, 1971.

Giri, V. V. *Labor Problems in Indian Industry.* 3rd ed. New York: Asia Publishing House, 1972.

Jaffrelot, Christophe. *Religion, Caste and Politics in India.* New York: Columbia University Press, 2011.

Kapur, Ashok, *Pokhran and Beyond.* 2nd ed. New Delhi: Oxford India Paperbacks, 2003.

Kochanek, Stanley A. *Business and Politics in India.* Berkeley: University of California Press, 1974.

NOTES

1. Maurice Zinkin and Taya Zinkin, *Britain and India* (Baltimore: Johns Hopkins University Press, 1964), 103; my emphasis.

2. Karl Marx and Frederick Engels, *On Colonialism,* 4th enl. ed. (Moscow: Progress Publishers, 1968); see his articles on British India and opium trade from British India to China.

3. See Stuart Corbridge, "The Political Economy of Development in India Since Independence," Ch. 21, and Jan Bremen, "The Political Economy of Agrarian Change in India," Ch. 22, in *Routledge Handbook of South Asian Politics,* ed. Paul R. Brass (London: Routledge, 2010). Mark Tully, *Non-stop India* (New Delhi: Allen Lane/Penguin, 2011), Ch. 8, for a general picture of India's developmental policies.

4. Anil Seal, "Imperialism and Nationalism in India," in *Locality, Province, and Nation: Essays on Indian Politics, 1870 to 1940,* ed. John Gallagher, Gordon Johnson, and Anil Seal (London: Cambridge University Press, 1973), 21.

5. Gunnar Myrdal, *An Approach to the Asian Drama* (New York: Vintage Books, 1970), 117.

6. Robert L. Hardgrave Jr. and Stanley Kochanek, *India: Government and Politics in a Developing Nation,* 5th ed. (New York: Harcourt Brace Jovanovich, 1993), 1.

7. "Linguistic States of India," Indian Child, http://www.indianchild.com/linguistic _states_india.htm; "India Linguistic States," Photius Coutsoukis, http://www.photius.com /countries/india/society/india_society_linguistic_states.html; R. Upadhyay, "Creation of New States," South Asia Analysis Group, paper no. 142, September 3, 2000.

8. For details, see "Mandal Commission," Wikipedia, http://en.wikipedia.org/wiki/Mandal _Commission.

9. Stanley A. Kochanek, "The Federation of Indian Chambers of Commerce and Industry and Indian Politics," *Asian Survey* (September 1971): 866–885; Stanley A. Kochanek, *Business and Politics in India* (Berkeley: University of California Press, 1974).

10. Tully, *Non-stop India*, 168, notes the allegation that "business is responsible for much of the political and bureaucratic corruption that plagues the country."

11. Lloyd I. Rudolph, Susanne H. Rudolph, and Karuna Ahmed, "Student Politics and National Politics in India," in *The Context of Education in Indian Development,* ed. Joseph Di Bona (Durham, NC: Program in Comparative Studies on Southern Asia, 1974), 206.

12. International Institute for Strategic Studies (London), *Annual Military Balance and Strategic Survey for Military Data and Assessments.*

13. Ashok Kapur, *Pokhran and Beyond*, 2nd ed. (New Delhi: Oxford India Paperbacks, 2003).

14. Government of India, *Sixth Five-Year Plan* (Delhi: Government of India Press, 1981), 318.

15. Craig Baxter's *The Jana Sangh: A Biography of an Indian Political Party* (Philadelphia: University of Pennsylvania Press, 1969) is a pioneering study.

6

Conflict Management

The ongoing process of sociopolitical and economic change in India and the increased competition for scarce resources and political power are placing enormous pressure on the political system. The central government is being pressured to effectively redistribute political and economic power among emerging regions in India and to strengthen the Indian union with a strong national political center that projects pan-Indian values and policies for the common good. At the same time, it is expected to lay the foundation for strength in world affairs. Regionalism expresses issues of identity and language, regional economic grievances, and quests for power by local elites. The fear that strong regional power centers may dilute the strength of a center needed to hold India together is balanced by the view that satisfying regional ambitions may reduce the cost of managing regional agitations and insurgencies and enhance both the process of developing the culture and means to advance peaceful economic, political, and social change. The relationship between India's central government and its regional authorities is not a zero-sum game. At the same time, the success of the Indian political experiment is not guaranteed because excessive regionalism or localism could lead to a reversion to the pre–British India system as a sum of small and large principalities and kingdoms and states engaged in war, intrigue, and coalition building against rivals. The worst-case scenario is based on the premise that political disunity among Indian peoples is the dominant theme in pre-1947 Indian history and politics. If the space for divisive tendencies grows, and that for unifying tendencies decreases as a result of minority governments and coalition governments at the center, India's experiment to secure major change in its institutions and values could be undermined. Moreover, increased mass expectations as well as enhanced sectarian and caste/class consciousness are placing stresses and strains on the society that hitherto have not been experienced. The following sections describe the main areas of concern.

The Government of India has a poor record of conflict management, while the number of issues requiring resolution has grown and the fault lines have deepened. Still, India has managed to muddle through and to land on her feet. The Indian union has been under pressure from the outset. Jammu and Kashmir became a disputed territory in 1947–1948 and a military battleground for secession in the 1980s. In the 1980s the Sikhs sought an independent homeland in the strategic Punjab. The Nagas in India's strategic northeast sought independence in the late 1940s and gained Chinese and British material and moral support. Telengana in Andhra Pradesh (South India) was a center of communist-led insurgency in 1948. These revolts were managed by military (fighting involving police and military action), political (political dialogue with secessionist movements), and diplomatic (attempts to neutralize third-party interference) means. The political means sought conflict resolution within the framework of the Indian constitution. However, the process was slow and tortured because issues involved consideration of social and economic justice, self-determination, and secession, and psychological grievances were often attached to tangible issues.

The agenda for conflict management has grown in importance precisely when the authority of the central government has declined, even as the military and police capacity of the Indian state has increased since 1947. Several reasons explain the slow process of conflict management and resolution: (1) The number of players—the central and state governments, the militant movements, and their external supporters—has proliferated over time. (2) India lacks a proactive political-resolution culture, and often a conflict has to come to a boil before the government reacts to the problem. (3) India's intelligence machinery is weak; it reacts after an event rather than anticipating its likelihood. (4) Indian politicians are more preoccupied with their own power than with policy development. (5) Despite the existence of a free press, government actions are clouded by secrecy, and public opinion is not an effective check on governmental activity. These reasons indicate that Indians are at war with themselves and do not trust each other to settle issues in a cooperative way.

What fault lines are embedded in the structure of India's state and society and in her economic and political history and culture? What is the government's record of addressing the major polarities? Here are the current issues and current scholarship concerning them. As Sumanta Banerjee points out, social conflicts in India date back to colonial times:

> The violent forms that radical movements are assuming in parts of South Asia today have a long tradition stretching back to the unresolved conflicts that were

left behind in the wake of the transfer of power by the British colonial rulers to the nationalist leaders in the late 1940s. Since then, during the last half century or so, discord between the landless and the landed gentry, contention for power among different ethnic communities, and hostility between religious majority and minority groups, among other divisive matters, have off and on reached flashpoints in the postcolonial states. The governments of these South Asian states have been incapable of disentangling the roots of these conflicts which they inherited from the pre-independence era, and have failed to resolve them through a democratic process.[1]

Landless People versus Landed Gentry

This is a fault line because the interests of the landowner and the tiller are not aligned. The landowner has the rights, underwritten by British India and later by various governments in India, even though the Indian constitution speaks of social justice for the underprivileged members of Indian society. The peasants, including the landless poor, constitute almost 80 percent of the population. The peasant voter is now a member of the attentive public and an active member of a caste community. As a politically conscious voter, he or she seeks upward mobility. Likewise, the political parties seek peasants' votes in their quest for electoral victory and political power.

This fault line stimulated the rise of antifeudal struggles under India's communist leaders.[2] The issues then, as now, concerned social and economic exploitation of the poor. Telengana, then a part of the Nizam's princely state, saw the rise of peasant guerillas and armed struggle under communist guidance after 1946. The Nizam's rule ended in 1948, when India took over the Nizam's kingdom, but communist insurgency lasted until 1951, when the Communist Party of India sought the parliamentary road to power. The Indian communist–led insurgency had paralleled the militancy of Soviet communism (1940s–1951), but when Stalin shifted toward peaceful coexistence, Soviet and Indian communist leaders abandoned armed struggle, which had an immediate effect on Indian politics. While Indian communists had shifted tactics by the mid-1950s, the fault line between rich landlord and poor peasant has persisted in Indian society from the pre-1947 period to the present. Three reasons explain this: (1) In the state planning process, the Indian Congress Party and the Government of India thought of land reform, but there was no provision to give land to the landless.[3] (2) Indian communists, seeking the parliamentary road to power from the mid-1940s onward, gained power in Kerala, but they ran into opposition from local feudal elements when they tried land reform and from the Catholic Church when they tried education reform. A coalition of landlords, the church, and the

Congress Party brought down an elected communist government in Kerala, a move engineered by Indira Gandhi and Jawaharlal Nehru from 1957 to 1959. (3) Later, in 1967, the peasants in Naxalbari, West Bengal, rose up against the government headed by the Communist Party of India (Marxist) (1967–2007). The Naxalbari uprising showed the polarity between the CPI(M) government's adoption of the parliamentary road to power and the lack of land reforms.[4] For example, while in power the CPI(M) sought to acquire land to build a Tata car factory, but this move was opposed by the landless and led to the downfall of the communists in the 2007 state assembly elections. The point is that neither the Congress Party nor Indian leftists have so far found a policy to deal with the landless question and have instead cooperated with local feudal elements and corporate capitalists in their quest for power through elections.

Indian Marxists versus Indian Maoists

In adopting the parliamentary road to power, Indian Marxists abandoned their commitment to armed struggle. However, following the split between Indian Marxists and Maoists, the latter adopted the Chinese model to end feudalism. They seek land redistribution among the landless and want to set up a parallel administration to punish oppressive landlords. The Sino-Soviet split was reflected in the split in Indian communism, which led to the formation of a triangular relationship, with the Congress Party and Indian Marxists aligned against the Maoists. This polarity reinforced the struggle between the landless and the feudal elements, and it continues to be a feature of India's politics and social contradictions.[5]

Ethnic and Religious Conflict

India has eight major religions, twenty-two official languages, and about 1,652 dialects. (See Table 6.1.) With a complicated mix of ethnic and religious groupings, it is not a melting pot like America. Even though Hindus are in the majority, India is neither a Hindu state nor a Hindu nation. India's national census—the last one was carried out in 2011—does not recognize racial or ethnic groups in India, but anthropologists distinguish between North Indian (Indo-European) and South Indian (Dravidian) languages. India has many languages: Hindi, Assamese, Bengali, Gujrati, Kannada, Malayalam, Marathi, Tamil, Telugu, Punjabi, Urdu, and other dialects. In a population of over 1 billion people, about 422 million speak Hindi,[6] and 83 million speak Bengali. Ethnicity is shaped in part by the individual's identification with linguistic and local or regional culture and not simply by religion. About 43 percent of Hindus speak Hindi, but others speak Assamese, Bengali, Gujrati, Punjabi, and South Indian languages. About 45 percent of Muslims in India speak Urdu, while others speak the other languages. One-third of Indian Christians speak Malayalam, one-sixth use Tamil, and the rest use other languages. This variety of religions, languages, and ethnicities make India a social mosaic.

S. D. Muni has listed several features of ethnic diversity in India. First, there is no general pattern of dominance–subordination among ethnic groups. Second, groups have distinct cultural characteristics, but these do not coincide with state boundaries even after Indian states were formed on linguistic lines. For example, Bengali migration into Assam since the 1970s (from West Bengal,

TABLE 6.1. Official (Scheduled) Languages as of 2011

Language	In Millions, 2001 Census	State(s)
Hindi	422	Andaman and Nicobar Islands, Arunachal Pradesh, Bihar, Chandigarh, Chattisgarh, Delhi, Haryana, Himachal Pradesh, Jharkhand, Madhya Pradesh, Rajasthan, Uttar Pradesh and Uttarakhand
Bengali	83	West Bengal, Tripura, Andaman and Nicobar Islands
Telugu	74	Andhra Pradesh, Pondicherry, Andaman and Nicobar Islands
Marathi	72	Maharashtra, Goa, Dadar and Napar Haveli, Daman and Diu, Madhya Pradesh
Tamil	61	Tamil Nadu, Andaman and Nicobar Islands, Pondicherry
Urdu	52	Jammu and Kashmir, Andhra Pradesh, Delhi, Bihar, Uttar Pradesh and Uttarakhand
Gujrati	46	Gujrat, Dadra and Nagar Haveli, Daman and Diu
Kannada	38	Karnataka
Malayalam	33	Kerala, Andaman and Nicobar Islands, Pondicherry, Lakshandeep
Oriya	33	Orissa
Punjabi	29	Chandigarh, Delhi, Haryana, Punjab
Assamese	13	Assam, Arunachal Pradesh
Maithili	12	Bihar, Jharkhand, West Bengal
Santhali	6	Jharkhand, Assam, Bihar, Orissa, Tripura, West Bengal
Kashmiri	5	Jammu and Kashmir
Nepali	3	Sikkim, West Bengal
Sindhi	3	Gujarat
Konkani	2	Goa, Karnataka, Kerala
Dogri	2	Jammu, Himachal Pradesh, Punjab
Manipuri	1	Manipur, Assam, Tripura
Bodo	1	Assam
Sanskrit	<1	

Sources: Census of India, "Scheduled Languages in Descending Order of Speaker's Strength—2001," http://censusindia.gov.in/Census_Data_2001/Census_Data_Online/Language/Statement4.htm.

NOTE: 2011 census data about languages has not been released at time of writing.

which is legal, and from East Pakistan before 1971 and Bangladesh after 1971, which is illegal) has created tension between Bengali and Assamese ethnic communities. Third, says Muni, "vested political interests" have stimulated the growth of ethnic subnationalism because it is or was not a popular grassroots phenomenon. Here, the conduct of political parties in search of electoral support and ethnic voters' banks can stimulate interethnic tensions. It is widely believed that the Congress Party in India promotes Muslim minority rights to gain the Muslim vote, and it has tolerated or encouraged illegal Bengali migration into Assam to develop electoral support. But if party politics is seen to encourage communalism in India, policies that facilitate economic development of underdeveloped regions such as India's northeast, efforts to strengthen state-center relations, and federalism and democracy can reduce interethnic tensions just as poor economic-development policies can increase them. Both tendencies have been in play in India's political and ethnic activities. Fourth, Muni notes that ethnic and religious conflicts have ebbed and flowed. The Ayodhya controversy over the demolition of the Babri Masjid mosque (1990–1991) has faded in Hindu-Muslim memory, as has the clamor for a Sikh homeland and an independent Kashmir (1980s). So ethnic and religious conflict does not follow a linear pattern.[7] The studies show that the role of political parties in fanning communalism in India should be recognized. Says Ashutosh Varshney, "Parties have not hesitated to fan communal flames for electoral gains. The most recent example was the openly communal campaigning by the Congress in the violence-torn Assam elections. This new mode of realpolitik has been adopted by the new provincial and local leaders of post parties."[8]

While the headlines highlight Hindu-Muslim conflicts in Kashmir, Ayodhya, and Gujrat, the three conflict zones deserve attention: (1) India's northeastern region, (2) Jammu and Kashmir, and (3) India's eastern and central region, where Naxalite-Maoist insurgency is ongoing. The case of Assam, in the northeast, illustrates that the problem in Assam involves Assamese and Bengalis (Hindus and Muslims) and is not a straightforward Hindu-Muslim question. According to Varshney's data, Assam has the highest rate of population growth for the last century, which started with British efforts to promote migration of tea plantation workers into Assam. It now has two sources of migration: West Bengali migrants (legal) and Bangladeshis who cross the porous border (illegal). With the rise of Assam's middle class, a tussle has emerged against Bengali dominance. From 1961 to 1971, the number of Bengali speakers increased, and 1.2 million migrants were added to Assam's population of 14.6 million in 1971. The number of registered voters also increased from 6.5 million in 1972 to 8.7 million in 1979. This pattern has stimulated protest and animosity among Assam's middle class and students. The growth of antimigrant and anti-Muslim sentiment in Assam's politics is thus an issue of ethnicity and territoriality rather than simple religion.

The situation in Assam represents a case study involving a volatile mix of ethnicity, religion, party politics, legal and illegal migration, economic issues, and state-level territoriality. The second zone of conflict, Jammu and Kashmir, is well known but differs significantly from the Assam case. Jammu and Kashmir has a special constitutional status. Jammu and Kashmir is for state citizens only, and migration into the state is not allowed; the Hindu-Muslim conflict there has an overlay of the India-Pakistan conflict respecting Kashmir. The situation has stabilized as secessionists have been curbed by Indian military action against terrorists, a peace process between the central government and various Kashmiri groups has taken hold, and the holding of free and fair elections when certified by foreign observers has provided a democratic outlet for Kashmiri demands. Here the parameters of the conflict are well defined and indicate an example of conflict management. Similarly, the Sikh-Hindu conflict and the Khalistan movement have been contained by coercive and political means.

The third conflict zone involves Maoist and Naxalite-inspired tribals and landless people in eastern and central India in a belt that extends from Orissa to Andhra Pradesh and involves Jharkhand and Chattisgarh. Here, as in Assam, the conflict is growing, and conflict management is not easy because the issues involve the rights of tribal people and the need to balance economic development and mining by state and corporate authorities with the rights of the people and environmental security. Leftist ideology also plays a role because Indian Maoists gain their inspiration from the theory of armed struggle and see their and India's salvation in revolution; this conflict is against the Indian state as well as Indian party politics and democratic norms. It has also gained the moral and material support of China, which has been active since the 1950s in the insurgency by the Nagas under Phizo and in the last decade in the politics of Nepal.

The number of fatalities in Indian conflicts reveals the history of ethnic and religious conflicts, but from this data one cannot predict future trends. According to the Uppsala Conflict Data Program, which is recognized by the United Nations, the insurgency in Northeast India has claimed 25,000 lives, the Naxalite-Maoist insurgency had about 11,500 fatalities, and Jammu and Kashmir had about 68,000 lives lost.[9] Currently the situation is stable in Jammu and Kashmir and in Punjab, but conflicts continue in the other areas. As such, the record of conflict management in India is a mixed one.

The Hindu-Muslim Divide

The theory of divide and rule was applied to India by the British India government, and this theory became the basis for partition as well as communalism in India. The British government established separate electorates for Hindu and Muslim voters on the theory that the two comprised different nations. Partition in 1947 validated this view and the communal division of India. This polarity is a legacy of pre-1947 India and has resulted in many communal riots.[10]

Furthermore, externally directed Islamist terrorism has grown in Kashmir, Afghanistan, Pakistan, and other parts of India and the subcontinent since the 1980s. However, in response two Muslim approaches to political action have emerged. The first emphasizes, citing Indian/Hindu oppression of Muslims in Kashmir and religious rioting in Gujrat, the importance of jihad to liberate the Muslims in India. This plays on fear of a numerical Hindu majority by a numerical Muslim minority. (An extreme version of this approach suggests the existence of a Hindu–Christian–American Jewish conspiracy against the Muslims.) In the second approach, Indian Muslims consider the Indian theory of secularism and Indian constitutional arrangements to be entrenched in India's political system and society (especially in the media, national party politics, and judiciary), and they have been able to use the legal, political, and social opportunities to survive and to prosper in India. Millions of Muslims voted with their feet after partition by refusing to leave India for Pakistan. In this view, more needs to be done to enhance the political, economic, and social mobility of Indian Muslims by improving their access to educational opportunities and employment in the government and private sectors.

In postindependence India, Muslims have freely participated in the political process of the country. They have used their votes as leverage for political bargaining in seeking accommodation for themselves. The fear of majority Hindu domination persists even though Hindus have never functioned as a political majority or as rulers in either Indian history or post-1947 politics. Caste, ethnicity, regionalism, right-wing and left-wing ideologies, and attitudes favoring nonviolent versus armed struggle have prevented the possible rise of monolithic Hindu-majority rule in India. The development of Hindu-Muslim political integration is problematic, first, because Muslim (and many other) voters see themselves as a swing element in party politics and elections, and, second, with the robust growth of Islamist, Hindu, and leftist extremism and insurgencies (e.g., movements in Telengana, Kashmir, Uttarakhand, Gorkhaland, Northeast Indian states, and central India since 1947), strong polarities exist between extremists (seeking violent change) and moderates (seeking peaceful change). In other words, Indian moderates are under pressure from the extremists, and advocates of peaceful change are under pressure from advocates of revolution through violent change.

Communal violence springs not only from religious conflict but from political and sociological problems as well. Gangs of unemployed, rootless, and alienated youths often roam the streets of towns and cities that have experienced an influx of migrants from outside their areas who have no neighborhood ties and are seen as intruders. Frequently formed along religious or caste lines, these gangs are on the lookout for opportunities to indulge in violence. They often enjoy the protection of local party bosses or communal leaders, who use them for political purposes. With weak government administrations at the central and state levels, poor intelligence, and growing corruption, criminal elements have gained opportunities in India's political system, and criminal-state and criminal-communal nexuses have emerged. Also, external forces have stimulated political violence in India. Pakistan's Inter-Services Intelligence is widely believed to have intervened in Kashmir, Punjab, and East India in order to provide opposition to Indian government rule in these areas. India has large and porous borders with Pakistan, Nepal, Bangladesh, China, Myanmar, and Sri Lanka, and transnational ethnic ties, along with concerted foreign intervention, facilitate militancy in India.

Sikhs

Another example of the assertion of religious identity is in the rise of Sikh fundamentalism. Sikhism, born out of a fusion of Hinduism and Islam, is a young and vibrant religion. Guru Nanak Dev (1469–1539), who founded Sikhism, advocated monotheism and opposed Hindus' idolatry and caste system. He was followed by nine gurus (teachers). Guru Gobind Singh (1666–1708), the tenth guru, gave the Sikhs a distinct organization and turned them into militant fighters against the Muslim rulers. The Sikhs believe in one sacred book, the Adi Granth, a collection of hymns written mainly by Nanak, Kabir, and Hindu and Muslim saints. The caste system is still prevalent among them despite its denunciation by the Sikh gurus. An overwhelming majority of the followers of Sikhism converted from Hinduism. Sikhs and Hindus intermarried and celebrated each other's religious festivals. But the early part of the twentieth century witnessed the rise of numerous Sikh sectarian organizations that emphasized the distinct Sikh identity. Claiming Punjabi as their religious language and looking upon the northwestern Indian state of Punjab as their homeland, the Sikhs have developed a very strong subnational identity.

In 1982 the members of the Akali Dal, a moderate Sikh political party, launched a peaceful agitation in which they demanded certain religious concessions. They also wanted greater political autonomy for the Sikh-majority state of Punjab than had been granted by the constitution of India. Soon, however, the militant Sikhs, led by a fundamentalist preacher, Sant Jarnail Singh Bhindranwale (1947–1984), resorted to terrorism and converted the Golden Temple, the holiest shrine of the Sikhs, into an armed fortress. In June 1984 Prime Minister Indira Gandhi sent the army to flush the terrorists out of the temple. The result was considerable loss of life; in addition to the large number of terrorists killed, many innocent pilgrims were fatally trapped in the temple. The Sikhs as a community felt humiliated and angered. They became alienated from the national government, and some even sought the establishment of an independent and sovereign Sikh state called Khalistan. The subsequent assassination of Indira Gandhi by two Sikh bodyguards, on October 31, 1984, resulted in widespread Hindu retaliation against the Sikhs.

Punjab emerged as a major center of Hindu-Sikh and Sikh–Congress Party polarity in the 1980s. Following a bitter campaign, the Khalistan movement was crushed by coercive state action and by a campaign to rebuild Punjab's political and economic institutions and processes. Here, Sikh grievances and Pakistani intervention communalized the state, but again the moderate-extremist polarity among the Sikhs was settled in favor of the moderates as of 2006. Punjab's political space revealed a pattern of stability if the Sikh political class was given power, and furthermore, Punjab politicians showed the maturity to share power with the Bharatiya Janata Party (BJP). The pattern of Akali-BJP coalition politics was repeated in state elections in 2007 and again in 2012, when this coalition defeated the incumbent Congress Party government and formed a new government. Here Sikh ethnicity and coalition politics, Punjab's regionalism, and BJP alliance politics combined to create a winning coalition in a key Indian border state that adjoins Pakistan and Kashmir.

Criminalization of Indian Politics

The introduction of criminal elements into politics has paralleled the rise of a new breed of politicians who find enormous opportunities for social mobility, economic power, and political influence in Indian politics and society. Because politicians depend on politics for their social status as well as their income, in urban areas many are willing to form alliances with criminals, smugglers, and other antisocial elements, as well as with the police establishment, to stay in power. According to the BBC, in 1996 India's Election Commission alleged that over seventy parliamentarians and more than one hundred elected members of state assemblies had a "criminal background." Further, a large number of scams since 2005 have involved the government and billions of rupees.[11]

Modes of Conflict Management and Resolution

The government authorities have adopted a mix of methods to deal with the polarities: (1) Armed confrontation has been used against insurgents and separatists in India's northeast, Kashmir, Punjab, Andhra Pradesh, and central India, combined with negotiations to address separatist issues. While civil society groups have criticized the Indian authorities for excessive use of force and breach of human rights, Indian laws justify the use of force to maintain law and order to defeat antinational activities. (2) At the same time, negotiations correspond to the Indian norm that peaceful social, economic, and political change is necessary to deal with pressing internal socioeconomic problems. The problem of the landless people and tribal rights in mineral-rich areas of central India (e.g., Jharkhand and Andhra Pradesh) is an intractable one because incremental rural development, road building, improved intelligence activity, and paramilitary policing—seventy-one battalions now fight the insurgents, up from thirty-seven in 2009—are offset by the growing criminalization of Indian political parties, including the leftists, who appear to be attracted to extortion and women.[12] Mark Tully makes the point that India has the constitutional provisions and political institutions in place, but the records of the various governments show that the system is not delivering the socioeconomic justice and peaceful change expected by the independence movement and its leaders. (3) Political parties' coalitions must maneuver and form temporary alignments to gain power, and to do so they have to meet the socioeconomic-sociopolitical demands and ease the tensions of their voting publics. Though practical, this approach to conflict management is not stable and creates space for criminal gangs in India's political and economic activity. This method has reduced poverty, created income distribution, and improved governance and justice in select parts of India, but the record is spotty. It is not a trend; nor has it altered the growing problem of poor governance and corruption. Tully's interviews with people associated with Indian businesses, community organizations, and political groups reveal that the private sector of India is a "partner in corruption," and the License Raj set up by Nehru served the interests of the politicians and bureaucrats who issued the licenses and the business community that paid for them.[13]

All three methods of conflict management are in play in India, but none appears likely to achieve conflict resolution on a continuous and stable basis in the foreseeable future.

SUGGESTED READINGS

Akbar, M. J. *India: The Siege Within.* New York: Viking Penguin, 1985.

Basu, Amrita, and Srirupa Roy, eds. *Violence and Democracy in India.* Calcutta: Seagull Books, 2007.

Bonner, Arthur, et al. *Democracy in India: A Hollow Shell.* Washington, DC: American University Press, 1994.

Das, Veena, ed. *Mirrors of Violence: Communities, Riots, and Survivors in South Asia.* Delhi: Oxford University Press, 1990.

Galanter, Marc. *Competing Equalities: Law and Backward Classes in India.* Delhi: Oxford University Press, 1984.

Nussbaum, Martha. *The Clash Within: Democracy, Religion, Violence and India's Future.* Cambridge, MA: Harvard University, 2009.

Rajgopal, P. R. *Communal Violence in India.* New Delhi: Uppal, 1987.

Wright, Theodore P., Jr. "The Indian State and Its Muslim Minority: From Dependency to Self-Reliance?" In *India: Fifty Years of Democracy and Development,* edited by Yogendra K. Malik and Ashok Kapur, 313–340. New Delhi: Ashish, 1997.

Zakaria, Rafique. *Widening Divide: An Insight into Hindu-Muslim Relations.* New Delhi: Viking, 1995.

Zelliot, Eleanor. "Fifty Years of Dalit Politics." In *India: Fifty Years of Democracy and Development,* edited by Yogendra K. Malik and Ashok Kapur, 285–311. New Delhi: Ashish, 1997.

NOTES

1. 1 Sumanta Banerjee, "Radical and Violent Political Movements," in *Routledge Handbook of South Asian Politics,* ed. Paul R. Brass (London: Routledge, 2010), 382.

2. For the relationship between feudal forces (upper-caste landlords, religious groups) and the antifeudal communists in post-1947 India, see Banerjee, "Radical and Violent Political Movements," 382–383.

3. Ramachandra Guha, *India After Gandhi* (New York: Harper Collins, 2007), 212–213 and 321–322, explains the role of the Planning Committee (1938–). This pre-1947 approach outlined Congress thinking and framework, but it ignored the issue of the landless Indians before and after 1947.

4. See Banerjee, "Radical and Violent Political Movements," 384–385.

5. Banerjee, "Radical and Violent Political Movements," 385. Mark Tully, "Red India," Ch. 1 in *Non-stop India* (New Delhi: Allen Lane/Penguin, 2011); "India's Maoists: Blood in the Corridor," *The Economist,* March 31, 2012, 50–51.

6. Based on the 2001 census.

7. S. D. Muni, "Ethnic Conflict, Federalism, and Democracy in India," United Nations University, http://archive.unu.edu/unupress/unubooks/uu12ee/uu12eeOi.htm.

8. Varshney Ashutosh, "Ethnic and Religious Conflicts in India," *Cultural Survival,* February 11, 2010, http://www.culturalsurvival.org/ourpublications/csq/article/ethnic-and-religious-conflicts-india. I have freely used Varshney's data regarding Assam.

9. Uppsala Conflict Data Program (UCDP), "Charts & Graphs," http://www.pcr.uu.se/research/ucdp/charts_and_graphs. UCDP does not provide data about Punjab-Khalistan–related violence.

10. See Guha, *India After Gandhi,* 431, regarding communal riots in the late 1960s.

11. Seema Chishti, "India's Love Affair with 'Tainted' Politicians," BBC News, August 2, 2004, news.bbc.co.uk/2/hi/south_asia352771 (accessed November 3, 2012).

12. Tully, *Non-stop India,* 14.

13. Tully, *Non-stop India,* xiii, xix.

7

Modernization and Development with Indian Characteristics

Since the end of World War II, South Asian societies have sought modernization and development. Modernization refers to the assertion of norms that are secular rather than sacred, rational rather than mythical, universal rather than parochial, and achievement oriented rather than ascriptive.[1] In a modern society, then, the individual, no longer just a member of the parochial world, is inducted into the larger world of state and international society. However, even as India borrowed foreign economic thinking and constitutional principles for national development, the dynamics of center-state party politics, the politics and slow pace of economic reforms since 2009, and the problems of the Indian poor—one in three poor people in the world are Indians—have impeded an even development of India. Furthermore, without basic education, jobs, water, electricity, and land ownership, modernity does not exist for the majority of poor in India, while religion and caste-based kinship remain important. As Mark Tully notes, democracy and economic growth are not enough for many Indians; past traditions are important as psychological anchors and sources of stability and dignity.[2]

To bring about a transformation, Indian elites chose a path of political moderation, economic socialism, and bureaucratic controls over India's political and economic life. India's approach to development and modernization issues was, and remains, state centric, although limited economic reforms since 1991 have fostered significant economic growth of the private sector. The original development philosophy, conceived in the late 1930s and officially adopted in the constitution and in the government's policy after 1947, had the following characteristics:

- In 1938, the National Planning Committee (NPC) was set up to propose a policy for India's economic development,
- Its approach was based on state intervention and centralized planning in all major sectors (i.e., the commanding heights of the economy), and the principle was service before profit. In 1944 Indian industrialists agreed with the approach and advocated an enlargement of the state's role. India's constitution went on to emphasize that state controls were meant to serve the common good. India's five-year plans were based on these aims.

The emphasis was, first, on building the industrial infrastructure and, second, on agriculture, but for the landless and the poor (about 80 percent of the population), poverty reduction remained a neglected topic in policy development.[3]

With the Congress Party's dominance of Indian politics during the Nehru years (1947–1964), Indian officials and Congress Party leaders managed the formation of the five-year plans as per their philosophy. Jawaharlal Nehru and his personally appointed high officials were the referees of economic and social policy making. With the rise of the Bharatiya Janata Party (BJP) and regional political parties, however, diffusion of power into non-Congress hands eroded the Congress Party's dominance. Without a national referee like Nehru, competing ideological, political, social, and economic agendas proliferated. Two results followed: (1) The non-Congress parties, along with Indian groups, sought self-help and coalition building to promote their interests. (2) Without a national referee, Indian groups' development policies lacked uniformity and a consensus to distribute economic gains and resources to build national capacities for development. This is evident in India's poor infrastructure (e.g., roads, ports), poor irrigation facilities, and poor environmental record.

Self-help had several significant manifestations:

1. The rise of the Dalits as a political and economic class tells a story. Kanshi Ram, a Dalit, started to promote the Dalit cause in 1971. Another Dalit, Dr. B. R. Ambedkar, chaired the assembly to write the Indian constitution. Jagjivan Ram, a veteran Congress Party leader (1950s–1980s), protected Dalit interests in the Congress Party. Thereafter, the Dalits sought two ways to gain power: one was to gain a foothold in administrative posts as clerks and magistrates and in the Indian Administrative Service and Indian Foreign Service; the other was to gain political power first and then to move into administration. The Dalits comprise about 15 percent of the population.

By 1995, 2 million Dalits held government jobs and were lawyers, teachers, and administrators.[4]

2. With economic reforms in 1991 came the rise of the private sector and the growing middle class. A pattern of coalition politics between the rich in India and political parties in search of money (and votes) emerged with two results: the rise of crony capitalism and corruption.

3. Development activities to uplift the rural poor suffered except in the context of vote getting.

These self-help activities explain the growth of multiple voices in the national political, economic, and social discourse, but thus far the trend is not to form a casteless and classless society or to put service above profit.

India's record of modernization has been mixed at best.

Six decades of democracy in India have enhanced the capacity of the political system to survive, but internal pressures have increased over time. Frequent outbreaks of communal rioting, violent expressions of linguistic nationalism, and territorial claims made by regional elites against one another amply demonstrate the strength of primordial loyalties and the continuing conflict between the traditional and modern elements in Indian society. Demographic change in India's northeastern states stems from higher Muslim birthrates and mass migration of Bangladeshi Muslims into the northeastern areas. This increases the prospect of Islamization of India's northeast. Increased militancy in the Jammu and Kashmir region is associated with the rise of Taliban presence in Pakistan and Afghanistan. The growth of armed insurgencies in Bihar, Northeast India, Chattisgarh, Jharkhand, Orissa, and Andhra Pradesh are signs of growing radicalism in India. This is not to imply a breakup of India or the failure of India's tradition of political compromise, but it suggests that the vitality of Indian democratic elections does not guarantee a rosy future for the Indian union. Also, increased corruption scandals and stalled economic reforms have tarnished the reputation and performance of the current Congress Party government.

Will the Indian government reform itself? What are the likely sources of change? Several new developments show an inclination by institutions other than the prime minister's office, government ministries, or the parliament to act against corruption and bad governance. In 2012 India's central bank issued a sharp critique of the Indian government's economic mismanagement. Policy uncertainties have led to a 35 percent reduction in foreign direct investment in India, and high debt levels reveal the danger of negative action by the rating agencies and a slower growth rate. The auditor-general continues to uncover scams; the latest, in 2012, showed that Indian politicians had secured land at cheap rates for trusts linked to them and their relatives. India's judiciary has been active in prosecuting such cases precisely when the executive branch and parliament have failed as guardians and promoters of the public good. Such scams reveal a contrast between China and India in terms of corruption. In the former, graft is offset by high growth and continuous state investment into China's economic and social development. In India there is graft and a stifling bureaucracy.

The Hollowing of the Congress Party System and the Rise of Corrective Measures

Indian politics underwent a dramatic change with Indira Gandhi's rise to a dominant position in national politics. Gandhi transformed the Congress Party beyond recognition. She stripped such party agencies as the Congress Working Committee, the parliamentary board, and the All-India Congress Committee of their power, rendering them nonentities. She reduced the state party organizations to the extent that they no longer played an independent role in the regions they were supposed to represent. In addition, she tried to subvert federalism in India by undermining the authority of state governments.

Indira Gandhi demanded personal, not institutional, loyalty. As a result, there was considerable politicization of the Indian civil services, once famed for their professional independence and integrity. She created a personality cult and the Indira-centric Congress Party and governmental system. This approach continued with Rajiv Gandhi after he succeeded his mother as prime minister. Following the 2004 and the 2009 general elections, which brought the Congress Party back into power, Sonia Gandhi, as party chief, stayed outside government but continues to dominate the members of parliament, who are beholden to her for support and resources for fighting election campaigns. She also exercises enormous influence over her appointee, Prime Minster Manmohan Singh, who has never won an election and therefore lacks political legitimacy and a political base of his own. Without Sonia Gandhi's leadership, the Congress Party would be a hollow shell because the party lacks a pool of strong, independent leaders. Sonia Gandhi and Manmohan Singh have projected Sonia's son, Rahul Gandhi, as the next generation's party leader. These actions continue India's pattern of dynastic rule, which is now at the core of Congress Party culture. Independent commentators, however, question whether the interests of the dynasty are aligned with the interests of Indian democracy.[5]

Despite the Gandhis' efforts to manipulate the country's political institutions to achieve their personal and partisan goals, the constitutional system has remained intact. Political institutions have already started to reassert themselves. India's civil service still attracts highly qualified, intelligent, and talented young persons from all parts of the country, and the bureaucracy still possesses the organizational structure to reassert its autonomy. Despite the asymmetry in the distribution of political power in favor of the Gandhi family, checks and balances exist in the Indian political system as a result of work by the judiciary, the media, the BJP and other opposition parties, regional state administrations and parties, civil society groups, and occasionally the president, who maintains the right to refer decisions for review and is not always a rubber stamp.

The peaceful transition of power not only from one leader to another but from one political party to another has tested the stability and strength of India's system. Even after the assassination of two powerful leaders, Prime Minister Indira Gandhi in 1984 and candidate Rajiv Gandhi in 1991, a smooth transition ensued without any constitutional crisis. Rajiv Gandhi's murder was even more remarkable in that it occurred three weeks before the end of national elections. The Congress Party was able to select a new leader and easily form the new government. This orderly transfer of power may be partly explained by the institutional framework created by India's political system, but the informal rules and procedures developed by the leaders to resolve succession struggles and intraelite conflicts are another important factor.

Finally, the operation of an independent judiciary headed by the Supreme Court of India, the administrative workings at the district, local, and village levels, and the operation of several autonomous commissions and agencies also point to the strength of India's institutional structure.

India's planned economic development has been directed toward (1) achieving a high economic growth rate, (2) building the country's industrial and technological self-reliance, (3) creating full employment, and (4) achieving social justice by removing gross social inequalities. These aims are constants in India's political history, and different political parties in the left-centrist-right political and ideological spectrum in India are in consensus about their importance. Controversies, however, have existed about policies and methods to secure these aims. Nehru's Congress Party relied on socialist policies, economic nationalism, autarchy, limited dependence on economic links with Western powers, and an abiding suspicion of Western economic colonialism following India's independence. Hence economic planning had a strong bias toward state regulations and public-sector enterprises, checks on private-sector development, and creation of a vast bureaucracy to exercise the controls and direct economic activity. Since the economic culture was statist and socialist, market principles and globalization imperatives took a backseat to Nehruvian prescriptions. The first crack in this approach occurred in 1981 when Prime Minister P. V. Narasimha Rao shifted toward partial economic reforms. He recognized that India was lagging behind China, a socialist country that had accepted capitalist principles as the basis of its development, while India, a liberal democracy, remained tied to the principles of a socialist economy. Nonetheless, contention between the capitalist and socialist modes of production persisted. With the acceptance of free market–private sector–globalization imperatives, the contention between economic nationalists and economic rationalists was joined, irrevocably so. Under the BJP, the reform process was pushed further, and India became part of the global economic mainstream. The BJP's acceptance of the necessity and value of strong United States–India, India–West, and India–Israel strategic and economic partnerships increased the political space of private-sector voices in India and the West. The Manmohan Singh government (2004–present) strengthened the process and the space for reformers, despite resistance from their leftist coalition partner. Still, minority governments—those of the BJP and the Congress—have been weak and hence dependent on negotiating the common ground in the area of economic reforms. Due to a rising trend of weak, minority government leaders, the debate between economic nationalists and economic rationalists is likely to continue with a reactive, zigzagging approach to economic reforms.

Though impressive, India's rapid economic growth since the 1990s is not continuous and stable.[6] Even though India's economy has at times been estimated to rank among the largest in the world and has a rapidly growing middle class compared to the economies of the People's Republic of China and Southeast Asian nations such as South Korea, Taiwan, Singapore, and Indonesia, India's economic performance has been uneven. In 1990 India's gross domestic product (GDP) grew at a poor 1.2 percent, and India faced a serious economic crisis and an acute shortage of foreign exchange because of mismanagement of the national economy. In comparison, the economies of China and the Southeast Asian nations had a healthy growth rate with robust foreign exchange reserves. India's economic performance from the 1950s through the 1980s was anemic, with food shortages and dependence on foreign aid, but it is not relevant since the 1990s. India has poverty but no famine or food shortage. It has strong foreign exchange reserves. In 2006 its GDP grew by 9.2 percent—a one-year performance that equaled India's total economy thirty-five years ago. In 2006–2007 foreign direct investment in India grew by 44 percent ($16 billion, up from $2.2 billion in 2003–2004). India also has a pool of 500 million young, well-trained people who can engage the world and mobilize India. But by 2012, 35 percent of foreign investment had left India.

India still puts significant limits on foreign investments and ownership rules. Ironically, China shed its fixation against capitalism and developed massive economic links and leverage with the United States and Europe. India's pro-China leftists, who have partnered with the ruling Congress Party coalition, however, still have an ideological fixation against Indo-US economic ties, which are a major engine of India's economic growth and international trade. Here domestic politics, weak minority coalition governance, and the theory of state controls and bureaucratic rule trumps economic rationality in the Indian and global marketplace and the social and economic needs of India's poor. Furthermore, despite significant growth in India's middle class, almost 30 percent of Indians live below the poverty line, despite a slight reduction in that population pool.

By the early 1990s, India's ruling elites became aware of the limitations of the state-controlled economic-development strategy and were willing to undertake piecemeal economic reforms. To its credit, the Rao government in 1991 introduced economic reforms and freed the Indian economy from excessive state regulation. By the end of 1996, India's economy had achieved a 6.5 percent growth rate. India also became an attractive market for direct foreign investment despite significant government limits. Economic liberalization resulted in a steady increase in direct foreign investment "from a paltry $30 million in 1990 to around $5 billion by the second quarter of 1995." India's foreign exchange reserve also grew from $1 billion in 1991 to $35 billion in October 2000. Many blue-chip corporations—Procter & Gamble, General Motors, General Electric, Siemens, Enron, Volkswagen, Daimler-Benz, and others—have established new plants or expanded existing operations. Still, India remains a story of uneven development in which politics trumps economic policy making that should be based on service and profit; instead, there is often a greater emphasis on profit and personal aggrandizement through corruption than on services for the poor.

SUGGESTED READINGS

Barddhan, Pranab. *The Political Economy of Development in India*. New York: Basil Blackwell, 1984.

Brass, Paul. *The New Cambridge History of India: The Politics of India Since Independence*. Cambridge: Cambridge University Press, 1990.

Frankel, Francine R. *India's Political Economy, 1947–1977*. Princeton, NJ: Princeton University Press, 1978.

Ghate, Cheten. *The Oxford Handbook of the Indian Economy*. New York: Oxford University, 2012.

Mellor, John W., ed. *India: A Rising Middle Power*. Boulder, CO: Westview Press, 1979.

Nayar, Baldev Raj. *India's Mixed Economy: The Role of Ideology and Interests in Its Development*. Bombay: Popular Prakashan, 1989.

———. *India's Quest for Technological Independence*. Vols. 1–2. New Delhi: Lancers, 1983.

Rosen, George. *Industrial Change in India, 1970–2000*. Riverdale, MD: Riverdale Co. Pub., 1988.

Rudolph, Lloyd, and Susanne H. Rudolph. *In Pursuit of Lakshmi: The Political Economy of the Indian State*. Chicago: University of Chicago Press, 1987.

Wilson, A. Jayaratnan, and Dennis Dalton, eds. *The States of South Asia: Problems of National Integration*. London: Hunt, 1982.

NOTES

1. Lloyd I. Rudolph and Susanne H. Rudolph, *The Modernity of Traditions* (Chicago: University of Chicago Press, 1967), 3.

2. Mark Tully, *No Full Stops in India* (New York: Penguin Books, 1991), 11.

3. Ramachandra Guha, *India After Gandhi* (New York: Harper Collins, 2007), 212–232.

4. Guha, *India After Gandhi,* 604–606.

5. Tariq Ali, *The Nehrus and the Gandhis: An Indian Dynasty*, with an introduction by Salman Rushdie (London: Chatto & Windus, 1985).

6. John Adams, "Reforming India's Economy in an Era of Global Change," *Current History* (April 1996): 151, explains the first phase of reforms. Vijay Joshi and I. M. D. Little, *India's Economic Reforms, 1991–2001* (Oxford: Oxford University Press, 1996), Ch. 7. Also Jagdish Bhagwati, *India in Transition: Freeing the Economy* (Oxford: Oxford University Press, 1993), Chs. 1 3. These works reflect pre 2004 assessments.

PART II

PAKISTAN

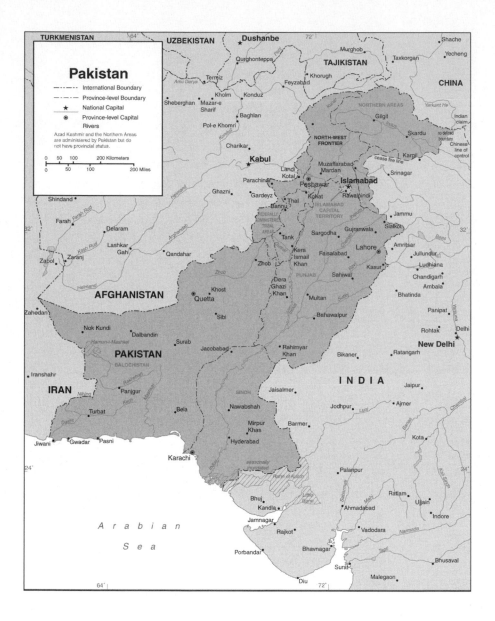

8

Political Culture and Heritage

Dominant Political Values and Beliefs

Pakistan came into existence as the fulfillment of a dream to create a Muslim homeland in South Asia. Consequently, Pakistan's dominant political values and beliefs have revolved around alternative interpretations of the meaning of "Muslim nationalism," which advocates understand as the ideal for pursuing a stable democratic polity that represents the people who reside within Pakistan's territorial confines. In this context Muslim nationalism is indistinguishable from Pakistani nationalism, which in turn is functionally equivalent to the expression of other state nationalisms in South Asia (e.g., Indian nationalism). To so-called Islamists, on the other hand, Muslim nationalism has a different meaning. Islamists favor the expansion of Islamic law in various spheres of Pakistani national life—with regard to punishments and the style of dispensing justice or as the source of legal provisions, the method of training judges, and the final arbiter of legislation. They may also favor the expansion of Islamic practices, such as abolition of financial interest (*riba*), prohibition of alcohol, gender segregation, Islamic taxation, and so forth. Finally, they may favor severing ties with Western society and culture. The basic thrust of such Islamist thought is not conservative in the sense of preserving institutions; rather, it is activist. The goal is to restructure Pakistan in greater accordance with perceptions of what an Islamic state should be. Conversely, "nationalists" restrict the role of Islam in a Muslim state. They may oppose the expansion of Islamic law and the enforcement of Islamic practices and favor development along the secularist lines of the West.

Pakistan's founders were ambivalent with respect to the meaning of Pakistani nationalism. For instance, renowned Pakistani poet and philosopher Muhammad Iqbal (1876–1938) made an important early proposal for a separate state based on the principle of Muslim nationalism. In December 1930 he stated, "I would like to see the Punjab, North-West Frontier Province, Sind and Balochistan amalgamated into a single state. Self-government within the British Empire, or without the British Empire, the formation of a consolidated North-West Indian state appears to me to be the final destiny of the Muslims of at least North-West India."[1] Another founding father of the state, Chaudhury Rehmat Ali (1897–1951), is credited with having coined the name "Pakistan" as an acronym created from the names of the territories proposed for inclusion in the new state: Punjab, Afghania (North-West Frontier Province), Kashmir, Iran, Sindh, Tukharistan, Afghanistan, and Balochistan.[2] As Pakistan also literally translates to "land of the pure," the acronym was doubly meaningful.

Despite yearnings for a separate Muslim state, however, mainstream Muslim opinion, represented by the Muslim League and its leader, Muhammad Ali Jinnah (1876–1948), pursued a policy of cooperation with the Congress Party and favored a loose federal relationship among provinces within a united India once independence from Britain was achieved. By 1937, however, Jinnah and the Muslim League had a change of heart. Two explanations are usually given for this volte-face: (1) Jinnah and his colleagues were growing increasingly impatient with the Congress Party's insistence on a strong central government wholly independent from Britain (prospectively dominated by Hindus) at the expense of minority community (i.e., Muslim) interests. This development, the Muslim League argued, ran counter to the intent of the Government of India Act of 1935. Therefore, the demand for a separate state was portrayed essentially as a defensive strategy to preserve the rights of minority Muslims. (2) In 1937 the Muslim League, running on the platform of an undivided India in the elections to the provincial assemblies sanctioned by the Government of India Act of 1935, was handed an unexpected and overwhelming defeat. Of the 489 Muslim seats, the Muslim League won only 104.[3] This rebuff at the polls forced the Muslim League to change tactics. The strategy eventually adopted was to invoke the specter of Hindu domination in an undivided India by stressing the theme of "Islam in danger" and the consequent solution of a separate Muslim state.

Accordingly, the Muslim League adopted a resolution at its annual meeting on March 23, 1940, the so-called Lahore Resolution, calling for the creation of a separate Muslim state. The substantive passage reads, "Geographically contiguous units of British India are to be demarcated into regions which should be so constituted, with such territorial adjustments as may be necessary, that the areas in which the Muslims are numerically in a majority as in the North-

Western and Eastern zones of India should be grouped to constitute *Independent States* in which the constituent units shall be autonomous and sovereign."[4]

After the Lahore Resolution was presented, sentiment for a divided India grew rapidly. The popularity of the Muslim League and Jinnah soared now that they represented an easily identifiable platform, and the time of partition neared.[5]

Ethnic Makeup and Social Divisions

Since the separation of Bangladesh in 1971, truncated Pakistan has contained five major politically significant ethnic groups or nations: Punjabis, Sindhis, Pakhtuns (Pathans), muhajirs (the Indian Muslims who opted for Pakistan during partition; the term has been extended to their descendants as well), and the Baloch. Each nation is defined by an admixture of linguistic and regional attributes. Generally speaking, the Punjabis are centered in Punjab, and their ostensible mother language is Punjabi; the Sindhis are domiciled in Sindh and speak Sindhi; the Pakhtuns live in the Khyber-Pakhtunkhwa (KP), formerly known as the North-West Frontier Province (NWFP), and speak Pushto; the muhajirs live in the urban areas of Pakistan (particularly Karachi and Hyderabad) and are usually native speakers of Urdu; and the Baloch live in Balochistan and speak Balochi or Brohi. Also, since 2010 the Siraiki-speaking inhabitants of the southern districts of Punjab province have more insistently demanded recognition as politically significant within Pakistan and advocated for the creation of a separate (from Punjab) province.

There is significant slippage in these definitions of ethnic identity, however. Pakistan's ethnic composition has been deeply affected by external and internal migration. Most obvious is the case of the muhajirs, who settled for the most part in Karachi and other urban areas of Sindh. Furthermore, since partition around 4 million international migrants, primarily from India and East Pakistan (later Bangladesh), have settled in Pakistan. Not included in the above are approximately 2.8 million temporary migrants or refugees from Afghanistan (as of 2013). Most such individuals speak Pushto and are close ethnic relatives of the Pakhtuns. Accordingly, most have taken up residence in border communities or refugee camps in the KP, Balochistan, and the Federally Administered Tribal Areas (FATA).[6]

In addition to such international migration, significant inter- and intraprovincial migration has taken place. Two patterns are noteworthy. One has been the phenomenon of rural-to-urban migration, spurred by brighter employment prospects in the cities. The urban population of Pakistan has grown by around 21 million since the last official Pakistan census was reported (48 percent), while the overall population of the state has grown by around 44.3

million, from 132.4 million in 1998 to 176.7 million in 2012.[7] A second phenomenon beginning as early as the 1950s, also largely fueled by employment
prospects, has been the interprovincial shifting of Punjabis and Pakhtuns
throughout the state. This has had two major consequences. First, the major
urban areas of Pakistan (Karachi, Lahore, and Rawalpindi/Islamabad) have become more ethnically diverse, and the indigenous populations of the smaller
provinces, particularly Balochistan and Sindh, have become threatened by the
prospect of outside domination. For instance, Quetta, the capital of Balochistan, has more Pakhtun and Punjabi residents than local Baloch, and Sindhis
constitute less than 10 percent of the inhabitants of the four districts of Karachi
(Sindh's largest city).[8]

Pakistan has a national language, Urdu, and a majority of the population can
speak or at least understand it. Less than 5 percent of the population can speak
or understand English; yet it has remained the predominant language of higher
education, the courts, and government since independence. Although numerous attempts have been made to enhance the significance of Urdu in the national life of Pakistan, along with parallel attempts to limit the importance of
English, such efforts have been blunted from two directions. Some have argued,
on the one hand, that increasing the use of Urdu would detract from the importance of provincial languages, particularly Sindhi and Pushto. Many others
argue, on the other hand, that discarding English would limit the international
employment and educational prospects of Pakistanis and that such a policy
would favor native speakers of Urdu and closely related Punjabi at the expense
of other linguistic communities. Underlying the debate regarding the enhance-
ment of Urdu in Pakistan is the fact that Urdu, though the official language of
the state, is the primary language of a small minority of the population. The
1998 census disclosed that Urdu was "usually spoken" by only 7.8 percent of
the households in Pakistan (mostly muhajirs and primarily in Karachi and Is-

TABLE 8.1 Major Mother Language by Province/Region, 1998 (percentage)

	Urdu	Punjabi	Pashto	Sindhi	Balochi	Siraiki
Punjab	4.5	75.2	1.1	0.1	0.7	17.4
Islamabad	10.1	71.7	9.5	.6	—	1.1
NWFP	0.8	1.0	73.9	—	—	3.9
FATA	0.2	0.2	99.1	—	—	—
Rural Sindh	1.6	2.7	0.6	92.0	1.5	0.3
Urban Sindh	41.5	11.5	8.0	25.8	2.7	1.7
Balochistan	1.6	2.9	23.0	6.8	58.6	2.6
Pakistan	7.8	45.4	13.0	14.6	3.5	5.5

Compiled by Charles H. Kennedy from Government of Pakistan, *Population Census Organisation*, 1998.
Provincial Census Reports (various dates, 2000–2002).

lamabad), far less than the percentage for Punjabi and around half those for Pashto and Sindhi (see Table 8.1). A further complicating factor is that such linguistic diversity is not related exclusively to provincial domicile. For instance, only 75 percent of those domiciled in Punjab speak Punjabi in their homes, 74 percent of those domiciled in the North-West Frontier Province speak Pushto, 59 percent of Balochistan-domiciled people speak either Balochi or Brohi, and 60 percent of those domiciled in Sindh speak Sindhi.[9]

Religious Factors

Islamic identity is at the core of Pakistani beliefs and values. Islam, one of the world's great religious traditions, is based on the teachings and life experiences of the Prophet Muhammad. The basic teachings of Islam were revealed to Muhammad through divine inspiration and are found in the Quran. The life experiences of the Prophet (Sunnah) were compiled by his early followers and are codified in the books of traditions (Hadith). The Quran and the Sunnah are inseparably linked components of the corpus of Islam. Islam is both a religious doctrine and a code of social and political organization. Accordingly, there is no contradiction involved in seeking an Islamic solution to the secular ills of society. This fact is crucial to understanding Pakistan's development. As already noted, in many ways Pakistan's existence is predicated on Islam. In addition, its population is composed overwhelmingly of Muslims, who were found to constitute over 97 percent of the total population in the 1998 census.[10] Given this confluence of factors, Pakistan has possessed a so-called Islamic mandate—a basis for the creation of an Islamic state. Islamists in Pakistan give this mandate great emphasis, although it is contested, at times bitterly, by others.

After partition Pakistan took nine years to adopt its first constitution. One major reason for the delay was contention over prospective Islamic provisions in the document. The first task of the Constituent Assembly was to define the basic directive principles of the new state, and in March 1949 the fruit of this exercise, the Objectives Resolution, was passed. It contained the following provisions dealing with Islam:

> The Government of Pakistan will be a state . . .
>
> Wherein the principles of democracy, freedom, equality, tolerance and social justice, as enunciated by Islam, shall be fully observed; Wherein the Muslims of Pakistan shall be enabled individually and collectively to order their lives in accordance with the teachings and requirements of Islam, as set out in the Holy Quran and Sunnah; Wherein adequate provision shall be made for the minorities freely to profess and practice their religion and develop their culture."[11]

These provisions have remained virtually unchanged in the otherwise fluid environment of constitutional law that has characterized Pakistan's statehood. Indeed, in 1985 the Objectives Resolution was incorporated into Pakistan's constitution. However, the new state ran into difficulty when it attempted to frame the basic principles to be implemented by the Constituent Assembly, and the Basic Principles Committee took nearly three years to complete its report. Regarding Islam, it recommended—at the urging of the ulema (religious scholars)—that the constitution establish a Board of Ulema consisting of not more than five persons "well-versed in Islamic law" to review all provisions passed by the national legislature. If this board deemed unanimously that any pending legislation was "repugnant to the Holy Quran or Sunnah," the legislation would be referred back to the legislature for amendments. Excluded from the purview of such a board would be all fiscal legislation.[12] This recommendation received a cold response when it was released to the general public, and the final *Basic Principles Report* eventually adopted by the Constituent Assembly in 1955 contained no mention of the board.[13]

Nor were provisions for the establishment of such an institution included in the final draft of the 1956 constitution. In its place the president was empowered to appoint a committee that would look into the question of "bringing existing law into conformity with the Holy Quran and Sunnah." Other Islamic provisions of the 1956 constitution were similarly without teeth. The preamble adopted the vague wording of the Objectives Resolution. The Directive Principles of State Policy provided that the "state shall endeavor . . . to make the teaching of the Holy Quran compulsory for Muslims; to promote the unity and observance of Islamic moral standards; and to secure the proper organization of *zakat* (charitable tax), *wakfs* (religious endowments), and mosques." The state was also to "endeavor" to "prevent prostitution, gambling, the taking of injurious drugs, and . . . the consumption of alcoholic liquor other than for medicinal . . . purposes." The preamble also called upon the state to "eliminate *riba* as soon as possible."[14] One outcome of the nine-year process of constitution formation in Pakistan, then, was a dilution of the Islamist position. Pakistan was created to be an Islamic state or perhaps a state for Muslims, but the constitutional mechanisms to implement such visions were intentionally weak, vague, or ill defined.

The 1956 constitution was short-lived, abrogated two and a half years after its adoption as a consequence of the military coup that brought General Muhammad Ayub Khan (1907–1974) to power in 1958. During the discussion preceding the adoption of the 1962 constitution, the status of Islam in Pakistan was again debated, and once again the nationalists prevailed. And when it came time to write the 1973 constitution (the 1962 constitution was suspended in 1969 and abrogated in 1972), the outcome was similar. Each of Pakistan's constitutions has defined Pakistan as an "Islamic state" but left determining what that meant in terms of law or practice for later.

General Muhammad Zia-ul-Haq (1924–1988) assumed power after a military coup in July 1977. Eighteen months later he announced a series of reforms termed *nizam-i-Mustafa* (rule of the Prophet), proclaimed to bring all laws into conformity with Islamic tenets and values. The main thrust of such reforms was directed at legal and economic institutions and practices in the state.

Most importantly, Zia created two new courts and assigned them extensive jurisdiction to examine existing laws in light of the injunctions of Islam. The most active of these has been the Federal Shariat Court (FSC), which, since 1979, has addressed hundreds of Shariat petitions (petitions challenging the validity of laws on the basis of Islam) and completed a monumental review of all civil and criminal laws in Pakistan, testing for repugnancy to Islam. Indeed, the FSC has assumed many of the functions envisaged by the Basic Principles Committee for the Board of Ulema. Appeals from the FSC are heard by Zia's second creation, the Shariat Appellate Bench (SAB) of the Supreme Court.

Since the early 1990s, the pace of such legal change has slowed, and the role played by the FSC and SAB has been reduced. But the cumulative effect of the earlier hectic legal activity has been significant. Findings by the FSC and SAB have prompted the rewriting of numerous provisions pertaining to criminal law, land transfer, financial transactions, laws of bodily hurt, standards of evidence, and inheritance.[15]

Numerous groups in Pakistan have voiced opposition to the Islamization process, including women's organizations and the Pakistan People's Party (PPP). Indeed, Prime Minister Benazir Bhutto (1953–2007) promised to dismantle Zia's Islamic policies, claiming that Zia's *nizam-i-Mustafa* was barbaric, reactionary, undemocratic, and discriminatory toward women. But she was unable or unwilling to deliver on her promise during either of her tenures as prime minister (1988–1990, 1993–1996). Conversely, her main political rival, Mian Nawaz Sharif (b. 1949), pressed for the passage of a Shariat bill during his first administration in 1991.[16] Its passage, however, raised more questions than it answered. Islamists argued that the bill was too weak; nationalists, that it usurped Pakistan's democratic constitutional structure. Nawaz addressed these concerns during his second administration, and in August 1998 he proposed the introduction of a constitutional amendment (Fifteenth Amendment) that would guarantee the supremacy of the Quran and Sunnah over other provisions of the constitution.[17] The Fifteenth Amendment failed to gain passage, however, during the remainder of his regime, which ended abruptly when General Parvez Musharraf (b. 1943) led a military coup that dislodged his government in October 1998. During the subsequent decade, Musharraf (as president), championing the image of "enlightened moderation," gradually rolled back the Islamist project: the Fifteenth Amendment was abandoned, Islamist judicial activism was discouraged and weakened, and Zia's much maligned *hudood* ordinances were rescinded through the passage of the Protection of Women Act in 2006. In late 2010 the FSC found that the rescinding of the latter act was beyond the purview of the National Assembly as its passage was extra-constitutional.[18] The court's finding is currently (February 2013) under appeal before the SAB. Regardless of the final decision of the Supreme Court, determining what form Islam should take in the Islamic state of Pakistan is likely to remain problematic and contested for the foreseeable future. Indeed, the turmoil that has gripped Pakistan since mid-2007 is inextricably associated with the still unresolved issue of Pakistan's Islamic identity.

Geographical and Social Factors

Pakistan possesses one of the most varied geographical settings in the world. Sindh, the southernmost province of the state, boasts the fine white-sand beaches of the Arabian Sea and Karachi, a large natural port and the largest city in the country. Inland Sindh is a semidesert region whose population is clustered along the winding banks of the Indus River. Balochistan, Pakistan's largest province, presents a startlingly forbidding landscape. Eastern Balochistan is dominated by the Sindhi Desert, and the western part of the province is composed of surrealistic mountains. Except for the area surrounding Quetta, Balochistan is sparsely settled. Punjab, fed by five major rivers (the Indus and its four tributaries, the Jhelum, Chenab, Ravi, and Sutlej), is the breadbasket of Pakistan and its most densely populated province. Depending on the availability of water, Punjabi topography varies from the semiarid regions in the south to the lush, irrigated plains near Lahore and the foothills surrounding Islamabad and Rawalpindi. Khyber-Pakhtunkhwa presents the most varied landscape of all. In the south the province is indistinguishable from the plains of Sindh or Balochistan, and in the west the mountains, particularly in the Khyber Pass region, are reminiscent of Balochistan's mountains. In the north, however, the KP features breathtaking scenery that, depending on rainfall and local ecology, varies from arid, forbidding wastelands to deciduous Alpine slopes to lush, river-fed valleys. Gilgit-Baltistan (formerly the Northern Areas) and Azad Kashmir possess some of the highest mountains in the world, including the legendary Karakoram 2 (K2). The region also defines the ostensible site of the mythical kingdom of Shangri-la.

The average quality of life of Pakistanis has improved significantly during the past thirty years. Using the four indicators that constitute the basis for the

United Nations Development Programme's (UNDP) Human Development Index (HDI) since 1980 (1980–2011), Pakistan's mean life expectancy has risen 7.5 years from 57.9 to 65.4; the expected mean years of schooling (for those under twenty-five) has risen 1.2 years from 5.7 to 6.9; the mean years of schooling for adults (older than twenty-five) has risen 3.1 years from 1.8 to 4.9; and Pakistan's gross national income per capita in real terms has more than doubled from $1,228 to $2,550. In comparison with the other major states of South Asia, however, Pakistan's performance has lagged. In 2011 Pakistan ranked 145th of the 187 states in the combined HDI, a rank similar to those of India (134) and Bangladesh (146). But thirty years earlier Pakistan was far ahead of both the latter states on all four UNDP indicators of quality of life.[19]

The limitations preventing more rapid improvement of the quality of life in Pakistan are demographic and political. Demographically, Pakistan suffers the effects of rapid population growth, the highest rate of increase of all the South Asian states at around 2 percent per year. Pakistan's current population (2011) is estimated to be 176.4 million; by 2025 its population will likely exceed 220 million. Given current trends, it is estimated that Pakistan's population will stabilize around 400 million, at which point Pakistan will be the third most populous state in the world, trailing only China and India. Such rapid growth exerts extreme pressure on social services (e.g., health, education, transportation); it also swells the ranks of the underemployed labor force. Politically, Pakistan has been, and continues to be, deeply affected by the two Afghanistan wars and its continuing enmity with India. Indisputably Pakistan faces one of the most difficult security environments in the world. It has also suffered the consequences of largely ineffective civilian governments and long periods of military rule.

Many daunting challenges continue to face Pakistan. The next chapter outlines Pakistan's numerous attempts to structure political institutions to meet such challenges.

SUGGESTED READINGS

Hayat, Sikandar. *Aspects of the Pakistan Movement.* Lahore: Progressive, 1991.

Jalal, Ayesha. *The Sole Spokesman: Jinnah, the Muslim League, and the Dream of Pakistan.* New York: Cambridge University Press, 1985.

Kugleman, Michael, and Robert Hathaway, eds. *Reaping the Dividend: Overcoming Pakistan's Demographic Challenges.* Washington, DC: Woodrow Wilson International Center for Scholars, 2011.

Malik, Ifttikhar H. *State and Civil Society in Pakistan: Politics of Authority, Ideology and Ethnicity.* New York: Macmillan, 1997.

Rehman, Tariq. *Language and Politics in Pakistan.* Karachi: Oxford University Press, 1996.

Talbot, Ian. *Pakistan: A Modern History.* London: Hurst, 1998.

Wolpert, Stanley. *Jinnah of Pakistan.* New York: Oxford University Press, 1984.

Ziring, Lawrence. *Pakistan in the Twentieth Century: A Political History.* Karachi: Oxford University Press, 1997.

NOTES

1. Khalid bin Sayeed, *Pakistan: The Formative Phase, 1857–1948* (Karachi: Oxford University Press, 1968), 103–104.

2. Sayeed, *Pakistan*, 104.

3. Sayeed, *Pakistan*, 83. Also see Stanley Wolpert, *Jinnah of Pakistan* (New York: Oxford University Press, 1984).

4. Quoted in Muhammed A. Quddus, *Pakistan: A Case Study of a Plural Society* (Columbia, MO: South Asia Books, 1982), 24.

5. See David Gilmartin, *Empire and Islam: Punjab and the Making of Pakistan* (Berkeley: University of California Press, 1988).

6. UNHCR, *2013 UNHCR Country Operations Profile (2013)*, unhcr.org/pages/49e487016 .html (accessed February 14, 2013). Around 1 million of these are not officially registered with the United Nations.

7. Pakistan conducted a national census in 2011 (it had been delayed three years from its scheduled date in 2008), but the results of the census are not likely to be released until at least mid-2013. The last official reported census was released in 2000 (conducted in 1998). As no official figures exist for the 2011 census, estimates of Pakistan's current population vary widely. The figures referenced here are from the United Nations, Department of Economic and Social Affairs, "World Urbanization Prospects, the 2011 Revisions," http://esa.un.org/unpd/wup /index.htm, and "World Population Prospects, the 2010 Revisions," http://esa.un.org/wpp (both accessed on October 28, 2012).

8. Calculated by the author from relevant census data. Government of Pakistan, Population Census Organization, "1998—Census Data [2000]," http://www.census.gov.pk/datacensus.php. Provincial and district census reports were also consulted.

9. For details on language origins and the politics of language movements, see Tariq Rahman, *Language and Politics in Pakistan* (Karachi: Oxford University Press, 1996).

10. Hindus constitute around 1.5 percent of the population and reside primarily in Sindh province; Christians constitute around 1 percent and reside primarily in Punjab province.

11. Adapted from Government of Pakistan (GOP), Ministry of Justice and Parliamentary Affairs, *The Constitution of the Islamic Republic of Pakistan as Amended up to March 2011* (Lahore: Manzoor Book House, 2011), Article 2(a).

12. GOP, *Report of the Basic Principles Committee* (Karachi: GOP Press, 1952), Ch. 3, nos. 3–8.

13. GOP, *Report of the Basic Principles Committee As Adopted by the Constituent Assembly of Pakistan on the 21st September 1954* (Karachi: GOP Press, 1954). A detailed account of the formation of the 1956 constitution is found in Herbert Feldman, *A Constitution for Pakistan* (Karachi: Oxford University Press, 1956); Leonard Binder, *Religion and Politics in Pakistan* (Berkeley: University of California Press, 1961).

14. The Constitution of the Islamic Republic of Pakistan (1956), Articles 25, 28, 29, and 198.

15. For details, see Charles H. Kennedy, "Repugnancy to Islam—Who Decides? Islam and Legal Reform in Pakistan," *International and Comparative Law Quarterly* (October 1992): 769–787; Charles H. Kennedy, "Islamization and Legal Reform in Pakistan, 1979–1989," *Pacific Affairs* (spring 1990): 62–77.

16. Enforcement of Shariah Act, 1991 (Act of 1991), *PLD* 1991, Central Statutes 373. For discussion, see Kennedy, "Repugnancy to Islam," 60–64.

17. Constitution (Fifteenth Amendment) Bill, 1998 (August 28, 1998). Text found at Pakistani.org/Pakistan/constitution/amendments/15amendment.html.

18. *Abdur Raazaq Aamir v. Federal Government, PLD* 2011 FSC 1.

19. Derived by the author from UNDP, *Human Development Report: 2011 Pakistan* (2012), undp.org.pk/2011 and hdr.undp.org/en/statistics (accessed February 14, 2013).

9

Constitutional Structure

Pakistan's record as an independent nation-state is not a happy one. The litany of failures includes the inability to compose a constitution until nine years after independence; the abrogation of that constitution and two others during the next twenty years; four military coups; three wars with India, one of them a clear defeat for Pakistan; the failure to resolve the Kashmir dispute; the inability to form stable democratic institutions; the failure either to sustain economic development or to effect meaningful redistribution of wealth to the impoverished masses; the loss of a majority of the population when the state of Bangladesh was formed; the inability to silence regional and sectarian disputes; the inability to deal effectively with domestic and international terrorism; and, finally, the inability to sustain a clear concept of and direction for Pakistan's nationalism.

Constitutional government in Pakistan has been more sham than substance. Pakistan has had five constitutions in its brief history: one inherited at independence (the Government of India Act of 1935, as modified by the India Independence Act of 1947), and four indigenous creations in 1956, 1962, 1972, and 1973. Pakistan has also been governed at times without the benefit of a written constitution (1958–1962, 1969–1971), under a suspended constitution (1977–1985), and under a "modified" though "restored" constitution (1985–1997)—the latter having been wholly altered by the passage of the Thirteenth Amendment (1977–1999). Between 1999 and 2010 the state was dominated by the military under various legal devices, including two Provisional Constitution Orders (PCOs) in 1999 and 2007, a Legal Framework Order, and a significantly modified constitution revised by the Seventeenth Amendment. During the latter part of this period (2008–2010), Pakistan was led by a weak civilian administration increasingly controlled by the decisions of the Supreme

Court of Pakistan. Since April 2010, following passage of the Eighteenth Amendment, Pakistan has restored a civilian-led prime ministerial system but has significantly weakened the authority of the central government. Ideally, a constitution provides the framework for a government's intentions; it describes structural arrangements, allocates functional powers, and establishes limits to political authority. But constitutions, however artfully drafted, cannot fully overcome the machinations of military and civilian politicians. Pakistan is a case in point. This chapter outlines the characteristics of Pakistan's thirteen constitutional phases since independence.

Phase One: 1947–1956

At partition in 1947, Pakistan was declared a free, sovereign dominion to be governed until a constitution could be formulated by the Constituent Assembly (CA) acting under the Government of India Act of 1935, as amended by the Indian Independence Act. Until the new constitution could be drafted, the CA doubled as a National Assembly, and in this role it was empowered to enact legislation. Therefore, the combination of prepartition enactments and CA legislation constituted the effective law of the state. The duties of the governor-general, however, were ambiguous. At the core of the ambiguity were two questions: whether the CA could pass laws without the consent of the governor-general, and whether the governor-general had the legal authority to disband the CA. This ambiguity remained unchallenged until 1954.

The task of constitution making facing the CA proved so difficult that Governor-General Ghulam Muhammad (1895–1956) tested the aforementioned constitutional ambiguity by disbanding the CA on October 24, 1954. He argued that since the CA was unable to produce a constitution, it was prolonging its existence at the expense of the nation. The Supreme Court of Pakistan upheld Ghulam Muhammad's action in 1955, arguing that the governor-general had the power not only to disband the CA but also to veto any legislation passed by it. Therefore, when the second Constituent Assembly was convened, it could do little more than follow the framework established by the governor-general. Instead of a decentralized, legislature-dominated system, a form of presidential government emerged. The viceregal tradition of a strong executive set apart from and superior to other political machinery had been reestablished.

Phase Two: 1956–1958

Pakistan's first indigenous constitution was promulgated on March 23, 1956. It established Pakistan as an Islamic republic and replaced the governor-general with a president. The constitution was described as "federal in form and parliamentary in composition," but objective circumstances in the state made both claims dubious. First, as a means of muting the question of representation for East Pakistan, Iskander Mirza (1899–1969), the new governor-general, amalgamated the provinces of West Pakistan into one unit in October 1955. This arrangement, which persisted until 1970, negated any federal solution to Pakistan's problems of regionalism. With only two units in the federation, and with one holding effective control, the possibility of meaningful federalism was nil. Second, by 1956, the prospects for parliamentary democracy had become bleak. The Muslim League, the only party of national unity, was in disarray. It commanded almost no support in East Pakistan, and its platform was virtually nonexistent. The only other significant party was the Awami League (its strength limited to East Pakistan), a party that ultimately repented its decision to support the 1956 constitution. Such party weakness led to extreme governmental instability. From August 1955 to October 1958, Pakistan had four separate governments. Under such circumstances, it is no wonder that the promised general elections to the National Assembly were never held, and that President Iskander Mirza (governor-general, 1955–1956; president, 1956–1958) was encouraged to suspend political activity, disband the legislative assembly, and declare martial law, thus abrogating the constitution less than three years after its promulgation.

Phase Three: 1958–1969

Pakistan was governed under martial law, without the benefit of a written constitution, from 1958 to 1962. General Muhammad Ayub Khan (1967–1974), commander in chief of the army since 1951, staged a military coup in association with Iskander Mirza, but then forced Mirza out of the presidency and assumed the post himself in October 1958. From Ayub's vantage point as a soldier, the politicians had brought Pakistan to the brink of collapse. He believed that a centralized government with strong leadership was required. These views were embodied in the institutions he created (discussed later) as well as in Pakistan's second indigenous constitution, the latter largely a creation of Ayub.

Ayub's constitution, promulgated on March 1, 1962, established a presidential form of government. Pakistan's president (Ayub) was to be both head of state and head of government. Essential decisions were to flow to and from his office, implemented by powerful civilian bureaucrats (members of the executive). The constitution also established the Basic Democrats (elected local officials) as an electoral college to select the president and members of the National Assembly and provincial legislatures. The 1962 constitution created a National

Assembly, but its powers were weak; it was designed more to legitimize the decisions made by the executive than to act as an independent lawmaking body.

Phase Four: 1969–1971

Ayub resigned in March 1969. General Agha Muhammad Yahya Khan (1917–1980), his successor, suspended the 1962 constitution, ended the electoral role of the Basic Democrats, and reestablished martial law. Yahya also held national elections in December 1970. But the results of these elections proved unacceptable to Pakistan's ruling elite, and martial law, now termed "emergency rule," remained in force. Eventually General Yahya sent additional troops to East Pakistan, thereby precipitating the civil war and the dismemberment of the state.

Phase Five: 1971–1977

After the civil war, Pakistan's military was in shambles and saw no choice but to hand over authority to the most successful candidate in West Pakistan in the 1970 election, Zulfiqar Ali Bhutto (1928–1979). Bhutto governed until 1973 under military-sponsored emergency legislation; indeed, Bhutto was originally installed as civilian chief martial law administrator and president.

Within four months Bhutto had lifted martial law and in April 1972 institutionalized his regime in the context of an interim constitution. Under the terms of this document, Bhutto as president was granted broad powers reminiscent of the powers granted viceroys under the British Raj. For instance, provincial governors were appointed by the president and solely responsible to him, and the powers of the National Assembly were left weak and ineffective.

Once secure in office, Bhutto presided over the drafting of Pakistan's fourth constitution, which was promulgated on April 10, 1973. Unlike the interim constitution, the 1973 constitution called for the establishment of a parliamentary system. The prime minister (a post Bhutto assumed after resigning as president) would be the effective head of government, with the president consigned to the role of a figurehead. Although the 1973 constitution established that the prime minister was to be elected by a majority of the National Assembly, many restrictions were placed on this provision. For instance, votes of no confidence could not be passed unless the assembly had already named the prospective successor to the prime minister, and for a no-confidence vote to be accepted, a majority of the prime minister's party had to cast votes of no confidence. Functionally, the power granted Bhutto under the 1973 constitution was as broad as that delegated to Ayub under the 1962 constitution. Again, the vice-regal tradition of Pakistani politics had prevailed.

Phase Six: 1977–1985

Bhutto was removed from office after mass disturbances led by the Pakistan National Alliance and alleged voting irregularities presaged a military coup on July 5, 1977. The successor regime under Muhammad Zia-ul-Haq (1924–1988), however, chose not to abrogate the 1973 constitution. Rather, Zia's government suspended the operation of the constitution and governed directly through the promulgation of martial law regulations. Such regulations were defined by the courts as functionally equivalent to constitutional precepts. Between 1977 and 1981, Pakistan did not have legislative institutions. In 1981, Zia appointed the Majlis-i-Shura (Federal Council), but its functions were wholly advisory to the chief martial law administrator. In December 1984 Zia was elected by referendum to the position of president. Nonpartisan elections (political parties were not allowed to compete, although members of the defunct parties could do so as individuals) were held in February 1985 to choose members of the newly established national and provincial assemblies.

Phase Seven: 1985–1988

Before the newly elected assemblies could meet, President Zia announced long-expected modifications in Pakistan's constitution. Accordingly, on March 2, 1985, Zia promulgated the Revival of the Constitution of 1973 Order. This document ushered in the seventh phase of Pakistan's checkered constitutional history. Although nominally a revival of the 1973 constitution, the presidential order fundamentally altered the terms of that constitution. Most importantly, the revival order dramatically increased the powers of the president. First, it reversed the lines of functional authority between the prime minister and the president. The president was given the power to appoint and dismiss the prime minister, and the prime minister's role was defined as largely advisory to the president. Second, it gave the president authority to appoint and dismiss the governors of the provinces and the federal ministers. Third, the president was given the functional authority to dissolve the National Assembly and the provincial assemblies.

In November 1985 the National Assembly passed the Constitution (Eighth Amendment) Act, which further legitimized Zia's constitutional order. Indeed, the Eighth Amendment protected actions taken during Zia's martial law regime with a retrospective constitutional justification. Article 270(A)(2) states,

> All orders made, proceedings taken and acts done, by any authority or by any
> person, which were made, taken or done, or purported to have been made, taken

or done, between the fifth day of July 1977, and the date on which this Article comes in force, in exercise of the powers derived from any Proclamation, President's Orders, Ordinances, Martial Law Regulations, Martial Law Orders, Enactments, notifications, rules, orders, or bylaws, or in execution of or in compliance with any order made or sentence passed by any authority in the exercise or purported exercise of powers as aforesaid, shall, notwithstanding any judgment of any Court, be deemed to be and always to have been validly made, taken or done and shall not be called in question in any Court on any ground whatsoever.[1]

In short, the revival order, coupled with the Eighth Amendment, substantially modified the 1973 constitution by concentrating predominant political authority in the hands of the president.

Despite such constitutional safeguards, the government under Prime Minister Muhammad Khan Junejo (1932–1993) proved too independent for President Zia's liking, and on May 29, 1988, Zia dissolved the National Assembly and the provincial assemblies and promised to hold new elections by November. Before such elections could be held, however, Zia was assassinated on August 17. His sudden death left Pakistan without a president, prime minister, National Assembly, chief ministers, or provincial assemblies. The chairman of the senate (not dissolved by Zia's order), Ghulam Ishaq Khan (1915–2006), became interim president. Under Ghulam Ishaq, elections were held in November 1988, resulting in Benazir Bhutto's emergence as prime minister. In December Ghulam Ishaq was elected to a five-year term in office as president.

Phase Eight: 1988–1997

The election of Benazir Bhutto did not in itself change Zia's constitutional system. Although Benazir campaigned on a platform calling for the restoration of the 1973 constitution, her electoral mandate was too narrow to engineer the two-thirds majority necessary to amend the constitution or to rescind the Eighth Amendment.

Moreover, Ghulam Ishaq Khan pursued policies that jealously safeguarded the powers of the presidency. For instance, on August 27, 1990, the president, exercising his powers under Article 58(2)(b) of the constitution, dismissed Benazir Bhutto's government and called for new elections to be held under the caretaker administration of Ghulam Mustapha Jatoi (1931–2009). Pakistan's four provincial governments were also dismissed. The superior courts upheld the actions of the president, and elections were held, resulting in the victory of the Islami Jamhoori Ittehad (IJI, Islamic Democratic Alliance) and Mian Nawaz Sharif (b. 1949).[2]

Relations between President Ghulam Ishaq Khan and Prime Minister Nawaz Sharif soured over the next three years, and on April 17, 1993, the president dismissed Nawaz Sharif's government. This time, however, in a landmark decision, the Supreme Court accepted the ousted prime minister's appeal and ordered that his government be restored.[3] The court reasoned that the president's power to dissolve governments was limited to cases in which there were compelling reasons to dismiss a standing government. That is, it drew a distinction between the 1990 and 1993 dissolutions. The 1990 dissolution was a proper exercise of presidential authority because it had been prompted by the extra-constitutional actions of Benazir Bhutto's government, whereas the 1993 dissolution had been prompted solely by a personal rift between the prime minister and the president. The Nawaz Sharif case established the important principle that the president's power was limited by the Supreme Court. This was a profound departure from the president-dominated system envisioned by President Zia and marked a new phase in Pakistan's confusing constitutional history.[4]

The remedy afforded to the Nawaz Sharif government proved short-lived. Barely three months after the restoration of his government, the military establishment, concerned with the deteriorating order in the state, brokered (some say forced) the resignation of both Ghulam Ishaq Khan and Nawaz Sharif. An interim government was established, and general elections held in December returned Benazir Bhutto to power. Shortly thereafter Farooq Leghari (b. 1940), a Pakistan People's Party (PPP) loyalist, was elected as president.

Although relations between Benazir Bhutto and the new president were cooperative at first, they deteriorated in 1996, particularly after the death of Mir Murtaza Bhutto (1954–1996) in September. In a widely publicized speech, Benazir charged that Leghari was behind the plot to "murder" her brother. In fact, there was no evidence linking Leghari with the death. Reluctantly, Leghari moved on Benazir's government, dissolving the National Assembly on November.[5] Again, such actions were challenged before the Supreme Court, but the Court, citing numerous examples of misrule by the Benazir government, upheld the actions of the president.[6] Elections were held in February 1997, and Nawaz Sharif and his faction of the Pakistan Muslim League(PML[N]) routed the PPP.

Phase eight, then, can be characterized as a period of checks and balances, of competing institutional authority. The prime minister effectively ran the government, while the president retained the ultimate power to dissolve the national and provincial assemblies. But such presidential authority was circumscribed by the superior judiciary, which could reverse the actions of the president and restore the assemblies. However ingenious or democratic this system was, it proved untidy. Between 1988 and 1997, Pakistan had eight prime ministers and four presidents.

Phase Nine: 1997–1999

Nawaz Sharif and the Pakistan Muslim League had received a convincing majority of seats in the 1997 election, far more than the two-thirds necessary to revise the constitution. This he did in a rapid and forceful manner. In April he orchestrated the unanimous passage of the Thirteenth Amendment, repealing Articles 58(2)(b) and 112(2)(b) of the constitution, which had respectively empowered the president to suspend the National Assembly and the governors (appointed by the president) to suspend the provincial assemblies. These articles had served as the basis of presidential control of the government. Obviously the passage of the Thirteenth Amendment was an attack on the authority of the president, but it was also a frontal assault on the authority of the superior judiciary. Before the introduction of the Thirteenth Amendment (from 1988–1997), the Supreme Court had served (for all intents and purposes) as the power broker between the president and the prime minister.

In one stroke the passage of the Thirteenth Amendment undid years of work by the superior judiciary. If this wasn't enough, Nawaz Sharif further signaled his intention to consolidate power by pushing through the Fourteenth Amendment to the constitution in July. This amendment prohibited "floor crossing" (changing party affiliation or voting against party policy) by members of Pakistan's parliament. Combined, the two amendments left the office of prime minister (read: Nawaz Sharif) functionally insulated from any challenges. The president had been reduced to a figurehead, the Fourteenth Amendment had left the opposition powerless to introduce a vote of no confidence, and the Supreme Court had been stripped of its powers to referee the succession process.

The superior judiciary was obliged to strike back and found its vehicle in writ petitions filed before the Supreme Court that challenged provisions of the Fourteenth Amendment. Accordingly, on October 29, 1997, a three-judge bench of the Supreme Court, headed by Chief Justice Sajjad Ali Shah (b. 1933), admitted a petition challenging the amendment and suspended its operation while the case was under review.[7] Nawaz Sharif, angered by the Supreme Court's action, issued an intemperate public diatribe against the Court and its chief justice. On November 2, Sajjad Ali Shah responded in kind by citing Nawaz Sharif for contempt of court.

Earlier, two other judges of the Supreme Court (Sharif appointees) had issued an order declaring that the original appointment (by Benazir Bhutto) of

Sajjad Ali Shah as chief justice was illegal as, at his time of appointment to the position, Justice Shah was not the senior-most jurist on the bench.[8] Upon learning of this order, Sajjad Ali Shah issued his own order (November 26) directing that no more cases be sent to the two offending judges. The next day the two latter justices, joined by one of their colleagues, issued a counterorder contending that Sajjad Ali Shah was not competent to hold the post of chief justice and that, consequently, any orders he made in that capacity were null and void. Before these warring judicial orders could be resolved, a mob (encouraged, if not directed, by Nawaz Sharif and the leadership of the PML[N]) occupied the Supreme Court building, disrupting the first day of the contempt hearing of the prime minister. The hearing was postponed.

Subsequently, the full bench of the Supreme Court (December 23) passed an order declaring that the original appointment of Sajjad Ali Shah was illegal and unconstitutional. Justice Ajmal Mian (b. 1934), as the most senior judge, was duly sworn in as the new chief justice.[9]

During the factional wrangling, Sajjad Ali Shah had issued an order suspending the Thirteenth Amendment, undoubtedly with the support of President Leghari. There was considerable speculation at the time that a constitutional crisis was imminent and that the military would be obliged to intervene in order to reestablish the pre–Thirteenth Amendment system, that is, to reintroduce Article 58(2)(b). However, the military chose not to intervene.[10] Left hanging, President Leghari resigned and was replaced in December by Nawaz Sharif's choice, Rafiq Ahmed Tarar (b. 1929). With Sajjad Ali Shah out of the picture, the Ajmal Mian–led Supreme Court dismissed the contempt charges against the prime minister and rejected petitions challenging the constitutionality of the Fourteenth Amendment.

When the dust had finally settled by the end of 1997, Nawaz Sharif stood triumphant. The Thirteenth and Fourteenth amendments were law and had withstood legal challenge; the Supreme Court (without Sajjad Ali Shah) was behaving itself; Farooq Leghari had been replaced by the more Nawaz-friendly Rafiq Tarar; and the military had decided, at least for the time being, to stay in the barracks. But it wouldn't remain there for long.

Phase Ten: 1999–2000

General Parvez Musharraf (b. 1943), chief of army staff (COAS), seized power on October 12, 1999, in a bloodless coup after Nawaz Sharif dismissed the COAS while Musharraf was abroad in Sri Lanka. The prime minister then allegedly attempted to prevent General Musharraf's return to Pakistan by ordering the hijacking of his airplane on its return flight from Colombo. The coup was undoubtedly motivated as well by Nawaz Sharif's earlier authoritarian actions, as detailed above. In any case, General Musharraf (now the self-styled chief executive) moved quickly to legitimize his takeover by promulgating the Provisional Constitution Order of 1999. Curiously, it neither suspends the constitution nor limits the power of the judiciary except insofar as the constitution or courts may intrude on the actions of the chief executive (read: Parvez Musharraf):

> Notwithstanding the abeyance of the provisions of the constitution of the Islamic Republic of Pakistan, hereinafter referred to as the constitution, Pakistan shall, subject to this Order and any other Orders made by the Chief Executive, be governed, as nearly as may be, in accordance with the constitution.
>
> Subject as aforesaid, all courts in existence immediately before the commencement of the Order, shall continue to function and to exercise their respective powers and jurisdiction provided that the Supreme Court or High Courts and any other court shall not have the powers to make any order against the Chief Executive or any other person exercising powers or jurisdiction under his authority.

The PCO also directs that "no judgment, decree writ, order or process whatsoever shall be made or issued by any court or tribunal against the Chief Executive or any authority designated by the Chief Executive."[11]

To remove any possible remaining loopholes in this order, the military regime deemed it expedient for members of the superior judiciary to take a fresh oath of office under the terms of the PCO. Accordingly, on January 28, 2000, the jurists were required to take an oath promising to uphold the PCO. Such jurists had previously taken an oath promising to "uphold the constitution."[12] Six justices of the Supreme Court, including the chief justice, refused to take the oath and hence stood retired; nine High Court judges also refused to take the oath.[13]

The chief executive also employed the Anti-Terrorism Courts (ironically introduced and championed by Nawaz Sharif) to try those accused of hijacking the airplane carrying Musharraf to Karachi. In April 2000 a Karachi-based Anti-Terrorism Court convicted Nawaz Sharif of hijacking and ordered him imprisoned for life. In December 2000 Nawaz Sharif and his family members were allowed to leave the country for Saudi Arabia. The military's actions, including the coup, the issuance of the PCO, the dissolution of the national and provincial assemblies, and the introduction of the new oath for the superior judiciary, were validated by the Supreme Court decision in the *Zafar Ali Shah* case handed down in May 2000. However, the Court ordered that the national and provincial assemblies be reconstituted and that fresh elections to such institutions be held no later than three years from the date of the coup, October 12, 2002.[14]

Phase Eleven: 2000–2007

Perhaps Chief Executive Musharraf actually intended, as he had often promised, to hold elections as soon as practicable and return the military to the barracks. But such plans were dashed following the events of September 11, 2001, and the subsequent targeting of Afghanistan and al-Qaeda by the US-led coalition. Pakistan was obliged to become a key US ally in the global war against terrorism, with Musharraf and the Pakistani military the key players in the alliance. It was hardly time to place global security in the hands of weak, corrupt, and discredited civilian leaders. But Musharraf faced four obstacles to the continuation of his regime: (1) he had to assume the presidency, (2) he had to significantly revise the constitution in order to remove Nawaz Sharif's amendments, (3) he had to hold and win elections by October 12, 2002, and (4) he had to get the newly constituted National Assembly to validate his reengineering of Pakistan's political and constitutional structure.

Musharraf proved adept at such tasks.

First, on May 1, 2002, borrowing from the playbook of his military predecessors (Ayub and Zia), he held a referendum. The chief executive asked the voters to elect him for a five-year term as president in order to consolidate his "reforms and reconstruction of institutions of state for the establishment of genuine and sustainable democracy . . . and to combat extremism and sectarianism."[15] It was reported that 97.5 percent of Pakistan's electorate voted yes.[16]

Second, Musharraf directed the National Reconstruction Bureau to craft a package of constitutional revisions and publish them online for public discussion in June 2002. Such suggested revisions were far-reaching and became the basis of the Legal Framework Order (LFO) promulgated by President Musharraf on August 22, 2002.[17] Among its many provisions, the LFO legitimized Musharraf's five-year term as president; altered the electoral system to disfavor candidates from the opposition and conversely to favor candidates supporting Musharraf and the Pakistan Muslim League (Quaid-i-Azam), or PML(Q); abrogated the Thirteenth and Fourteenth Amendments (restoring the power of the president to dissolve the national and provincial assemblies); and validated all laws and actions taken by Musharraf since he assumed power.

Third, elections were held on schedule under the terms of the LFO. Not surprisingly, given the electoral reforms and the absence of the two main opposition candidates (both in exile), the PML(Q) was able to win a plurality of seats, and Mir Zafarullah Khan Jamali (b. 1944) was asked to form a government.

Fourth, the newly elected National Assembly eventually agreed to validate Musharraf's new constitutional system—for a price. In exchange for support of the LFO, which was presented to parliament as the Seventeenth Amendment, the loyal opposition insisted that Musharraf relinquish his position as COAS by the end of December 2004.[18] On the basis of this deal, the Seventeenth Amendment was passed on December 30, 2003, and on January 1, 2004, the elected assemblies provided Musharraf with a vote of confidence, confirming his continuation as president. Reluctant to keep his promise to relinquish his position as COAS, in October 2004 Musharraf cobbled together a majority to gain passage of the President to Hold Another Office Act in the National Assembly. Although this bought him time, it did not obviate the objection that Musharraf's continuation as COAS (the so-called uniform issue) ran afoul of Article 63 of the constitution, which mandates that no one can hold at any one time more than one "properly paid position in the service of Pakistan."[19]

Nonetheless, Musharraf, subsequent to the passage of the Seventeenth Amendment, established a new constitutional order—a system with a strong president, a weak and generally ineffective, if occasionally raucous, National Assembly, and a relatively effective, if depoliticized, government. In Musharraf's system, there was little scope for politicians. Indeed, in 2004 he arranged the selection of a new prime minister, replacing Muhammad Jamali with economist-technocrat and former executive of Citibank Shaukat Aziz (b. 1949), who had served as Pakistan's finance minister since 1999.

But in 2007 Musharraf's carefully crafted system unraveled. Before embarking on a campaign to seek a second five-year term as president, he decided to take preemptive action against the "unreliable" chief justice of the Supreme Court, Iftikhar Muhammad Chaudhry (b. 1948), by suspending him on March 9. Justice Chaudhry contested his suspension (a superior court judge cannot be suspended without cause) and filed a petition to the Supreme Court challenging Musharraf's actions. His refusal to resign, typified by his supporters as "heroic," galvanized the support of many who objected to Musharraf's system and took to the streets. Playing a prominent role in the street demonstrations were lawyers and opposition political party workers of the Pakistan People's Party and the Pakistan Muslim League (Nawaz), or PML(N). On May 12, Justice Chaudhry, at the invitation of the Karachi Bar Association, visited Karachi. But before he could reach the venue for a scheduled rally, his motorcade and supporters were attacked, ostensibly by party workers of the Muttahida Qaumi Mahaz (MQM, United National Movement, long-term rivals of the PPP). When the dust settled, 42 people were dead, and over 150 had been injured. The Sindh government, allied with Musharraf, was generally blamed for providing inadequate security.[20] Ten weeks later, on July 20, a full bench of the

Supreme Court ruled that Musharraf's suspension of Chaudhry was illegal and reinstated him as chief justice. Chastened by the Supreme Court, Musharraf sought another remedy to his dilemma. On October 5, he promulgated the National Reconciliation Ordinance (NRO). Among other things the NRO withdrew and terminated all pending legal proceedings related to financial improprieties initiated before October 12, 1999. Benazir Bhutto, who had been forced into exile in 1998 to avoid prosecution on numerous charges of corruption and impropriety allegedly committed during her two terms as prime minister, was thus cleared to return to Pakistan without risk of going to jail. On October 6, one day after the NRO was promulgated, President Musharraf was reelected by the members of the National Assembly, senate, and provincial assemblies by a narrow vote of 55 percent. The PPP (Benazir's party), unlike other opposition parties, did not boycott the polls but rather contested the election by putting up Makhdoom Amin Fahim (b. 1939) as a candidate. Therefore, the PPP's actions had the effect of legitimizing the election. It was generally assumed that Benazir and Musharraf had struck a deal, which some claimed had been brokered by US officials.

Unfortunately for him, Musharraf's woes were not over. The Supreme Court, emboldened and perhaps angered by the attempt to suspend the chief justice, began to hear arguments challenging the legality of Musharraf's election on various grounds, including the uniform issue. Before they could issue their findings, which many thought would go against Musharraf, the latter struck by declaring a state of emergency and issuing a new Provisional Constitution Order on November 3, thus ending the eleventh phase of Pakistan's constitutional history.

Phase Twelve: 2007–2010

Musharraf's actions were a first in Pakistan's quite turbulent and creative constitutional history. In effect the suspension of the constitution was a military coup by a standing COAS against the president, where the COAS and the president were one and the same person. That is, Musharraf dismissed his own government and replaced it with his own government. Although Musharraf legitimized his actions as based on a breakdown of law and order "posing a grave threat to the life and property of the citizens of Pakistan," the real target of the coup was Pakistan's superior judiciary, which was, according to Musharraf, "working at cross purposes with the executive and legislature in the fight against terrorism and extremism."[21] The remedy proposed to correct this deficiency was to require all superior court judges to take a fresh oath of office under the terms of the 2007 PCO in order to continue to hold their seats;

otherwise they would stand retired. The PCO in turn suspended numerous fundamental rights and mandated that the superior courts had no power to "make any order against the President or Prime Minister or any person exercising powers or jurisdiction under their authority." For good measure the PCO also mandated that no court could challenge the validity of the PCO.[22]

Sixty-three superior court judges ultimately refused or were not invited to take the new oath under the terms of the PCO, including Chief Justice Iftikhar Chaudhry and all but four of the standing judges of the Supreme Court. Subsequently, Justice Abdul Hameed Dogar (b. 1944), the most senior judge taking the fresh oath, was sworn in as the new chief justice. The government moved rapidly to fill the vacancies in the Supreme Court and the High Courts, detaining some justices who had refused to take the fresh oath, including former chief justice Chaudhry.[23] The government also cracked down on prominent members of the legal community, most notably Aitzaz Ahsan (b. 1945), and imposed draconian restrictions on the press.

On November 13 the newly constituted Supreme Court issued an order dismissing the challenges to Musharraf's election as president, which paved the way for President Musharraf to dismiss the National Assembly (having completed its five-year term) and name a caretaker cabinet headed by the chair of the Senate, Muhammad Mian Soomro (b. 1950). The Supreme Court's order also paved the way for Musharraf to finally resolve the uniform issue by stepping down as COAS on November 28 and naming General Ashfaq Parvez Kayani (b. 1952) the new COAS, which in turn enabled Musharraf to announce that elections to the new national and provincial assemblies would be held on January 8, 2008. Finally, on December 15 Musharraf revoked the emergency and repealed the PCO, mandating that the current justices of the superior courts (those who had taken an oath under the PCO) would now take oaths under the restored constitution.[24]

As 2007 was coming to an end, Musharraf had weathered a constitutional storm. He had arranged to be elected for a second five-year term as president, he had defused the judicial crisis by changing the composition of the superior courts, and he had finessed the uniform issue. Following the December 10 announcement that the PML(N) would contest the general elections, thus joining the PPP, he effectively ended the political boycott of the elections and emasculated the opposition to his regime and the 2007 PCO. Then, on December 27, following a campaign rally in Rawalpindi, Benazir Bhutto was assassinated.

Benazir's death deeply challenged Musharraf's carefully orchestrated plans to extend his tenure as president. First, the elections had to be postponed ultimately until February 18, 2008. Second, Musharraf and his administration were blamed directly or indirectly for Benazir's death. Some prominent members of the PPP charged that Pakistan's military intelligence, the Inter-Services Intelligence (ISI), was responsible for the murder and called for a UN-led investigation into Benazir's death; others blamed Musharraf's regime for not providing adequate security for her campaign motorcade. Third, the alleged deal between Benazir and Musharraf became null and void. Following Benazir's death, the PPP (ostensibly following the wishes of Benazir) named her son, Bilawal Bhutto Zardari (b. 1988), and her widowed husband, Asif Ali Zardari (b. 1954), as cochairs of the party. Neither had made a deal with Musharraf, and Asif Zardari and the PPP proved quite adept at pushing the advantage afforded by a sympathy vote for the party's fallen martyr. Fourth, Nawaz Sharif, making the most of the changed circumstances and skillfully championing the cause of the retired superior court judges, led a resurgent PML(N) in the general election campaign.

The combination proved a perfect storm for Musharraf. In the 2008 general election (see Chapter 10), the PPP won a plurality of seats, Musharraf's PML(Q) suffered significant losses, and in March the PPP was able to put together a government headed by long-term PPP leader Syed Yousaf Raza Gilani (b. 1952). Divided along partisan lines, the opposition and government could agree on little except two things: (1) Musharraf should leave office, and (2) the superior judges who had been forced out by the 2007 PCO should be reinstated. The latter dovetailed neatly with the former. The judges issue was proof of Musharraf's authoritarian past and challenged the legitimacy of his government. Accordingly, politicians from both sides of the aisle joined together with lawyers and civil society groups, which had coalesced originally around the dismissal of Chief Justice Chaudhry and now called for the resignation of Musharraf and the restoration of the judges. As spring moved into summer, Musharraf became increasingly isolated and under siege. On August 7, 2008, proceedings were initiated in the National Assembly to impeach Musharraf. On August 18 he resigned. It is widely believed that the military encouraged his resignation. On September 6, parliament elected Asif Ali Zardari, PPP cochairman and Benazir Bhutto's widower, president.

Although much of the support for Musharraf's resignation came from those who had demanded that the superior court judges be restored to office, President Zardari was loath to take that step. He had reason to delay. A restored Supreme Court would likely find the NRO (Musharraf's ordinance granting immunity to the Bhuttos) to be extra-constitutional. Ultimately, that could mean that Zardari would either have to leave the country or go to jail. He also faced significant challenges from the political opposition, particularly Nawaz Sharif and the PML(N), champions of the defrocked justices. In any case, Zardari decided to drop the reinstatement of judges from the PPP agenda, reneging on the party's implicit deal with the PML(N).

As Zardari delayed, the Movement for the Restoration of the Judges (aka the Lawyers' Movement) continued to grow, and with party workers of the PML(N) and PPP now factionalized along partisan lines, respectively for and against its goals, the movement turned increasingly violent. With the active involvement of Nawaz Sharif, the defrocked judges, PML(N) workers, and various civil society groups, the movement planned a "Long March" from Lahore to Islamabad to press its agenda. With carnage likely, President Zardari relented. On March 16, 2009, he restored the justices to their former positions, leaving their seniority intact. He also left in place the judges who had taken an oath under the 2007 PCO, thus expanding the size of the superior courts, through a rider attached to a finance act that had passed parliament.

The restored Supreme Court, with Chief Justice Iftikhar Chaudhry back in control, moved quickly. The Court employed a broad interpretation of Article 184(3) of the constitution, which gives the Court standing to hear cases and issue orders if it deems that a "question of public importance with reference to the enforcement of any of the Fundamental Rights" has been violated to justify a very activist agenda.[25] On May 26 the Court reversed a decision of the Dogar Court, which had disqualified the Sharif brothers from holding public office[26]; on July 17, the Court nullified Nawaz Sharif's conviction in the hijacking case; and on July 31, in the *Sindh High Court Bar Association* case, the Court declared the 2007 PCO wholly null and void.[27] The latter decision had the effect of reversing the appointments of the new superior court judges who had taken their oath under the terms of the PCO. Finally, on December 16, the Court nullified the National Order Reconciliation[28]; the latter decision served to reopen the legal proceedings against Asif Ali Zardari and other prominent PPP politicians and supporters.

The Chaudhry Court has also employed Article 184(3) to greatly expand the scope of the Human Rights Cell of the Supreme Court. The latter organization, established by Chief Justice Chaudhry in 2007, provides the Court with the institutional capacity to hear cases brought to it by individuals on matters of "public importance"; it also allows the Court to seek information on cases publicized in Pakistan's very active media.[29]

Phase Thirteen: 2010–

Zardari's regime was a strange constitutional hybrid. His claim to power was almost wholly based on the fact that he had been married to Benazir Bhutto before her untimely death, and he became president nearly six months after Yousaf Raza Gilani had established a working PPP-led government as prime minister. However, despite his inexperience, Zardari had inherited the most powerful position in the state, the presidency, from Musharraf, who had created a presidential-dominant system to enhance and insulate his power. Moreover, during his first months in office his legitimacy was challenged by the Supreme Court as well as by the strident opposition in the parliament.

Finessing this awkward situation, a grand compromise was reached between the PPP and the PML(N), which led to the drafting and eventual passage of the Eighteenth Amendment on April 8, 2010. This amendment wholly changed the constitutional structure of the state. Among other things, it (1) eliminated the power of the president to dissolve the national assembly; (2) provided that only chief ministers (elected by the provincial assemblies), not governors (appointed by the president), could dissolve their respective provincial governments; and (3) established provisions that made the president's and the governors' decisions advisory to the prime minister and chief ministers. Together these three changes functionally reduced the roles of president and governor to head of state and province, respectively, while the prime minister, at the center, and the chief ministers, in the provinces, became the respective heads of their governments. That is, it fully restored a parliamentary form of government, replacing the presidential system.[30]

But the reforms introduced by the Eighteenth Amendment went even further by devolving significant and unprecedented authority from the center to the provinces. Before the amendment, Pakistan's federal and provincial powers were governed by a federal legislative list (a list of powers exclusively reserved for the federal government) and a concurrent legislative list (a list of powers with shared jurisdiction between the federal and provincial governments).[31] In the case of a disagreement between the respective governments, the position of the federal government would prevail. That is, Pakistan had a weak federal system (similar to that of India), a pattern inherited from the British colonial system. The Eighteenth Amendment omitted the concurrent list, thus transferring the forty seven items on the list from dual authority to sole provincial authority. Among the most notable subjects transferred to sole provincial authority were criminal law; criminal procedure; civil procedure; family law (marriage, inheritance, etc.); preventive detention; environmental pollution and ecology; welfare of labor; trade unions; newspapers and print media; tourism; curricula and standards of education; Islamic education; legal, medical, and other professions; and jurisdiction and powers of all courts except the Supreme Court and Federal Shariat Court.

The Eighteenth Amendment also claimed authority at the federal and provincial levels for the establishment of judicial commissions that would recommend nominations to the courts, which would be confirmed by a parliamentary committee. That is, parliament would effectively hold a veto power over appointments to the superior judiciary. The Supreme Court accepted challenges to this provision of the Eighteenth Amendment, declaring the amendment extra-constitutional, and suggested a reform that significantly limited parliamentary authority in the appointment of judges, effectively transferring such authority to the judges of the respective courts themselves.[32] In response parliament passed the Nineteenth Amendment on December 20, 2010, which wholly adopted the Court's "suggestion."[33]

The Supreme Court has continued to flex its muscles since this latter victory. Subsequent to the nullification of the NRO in 2009, the Court has doggedly pursued the quest to reopen the corruption trial of President Zardari in Switzerland (the Swiss Bank case). In this regard the Court directed that Prime Minister Gilani write a letter to Swiss authorities requesting them to reopen the case. Gilani consistently refused to comply with the Court's directive, asserting that the president, while in office, enjoyed immunity from prosecution. Ultimately, on April 19, 2012, the Court found Gilani to be in contempt and demanded his resignation. Gilani eventually complied with the Court order and resigned on June 19, 2012. Subsequently, the PPP-led government nominated Raja Parvaiz Ashraf (b. 1950) for the post of prime minister, and he assumed office after his election by the National Assembly on June 22. Since then the Supreme Court has continued to press the new prime minister on the Swiss Bank case, aggressively pursued various allegations that Ashraf has engaged in widespread corruption, and accordingly called for his resignation or removal from office. As of February 2013, Ashraf and the PPP have fended off these attacks through various legal stratagems that have served to delay the implementation of the Court's designs. Ostensibly, the government wants to buy time. The stakes are high—the term of the National Assembly ends in March, President Zardari's term of office expires in September, and Chief Justice Iftikhar Chaudhry reaches retirement age in December.

As the dust continues to settle after the extraordinary activism of the restored Supreme Court, the forced resignation of President Musharraf, the monumental passage of the Eighteenth and Nineteenth amendments, and the forced resignation of Prime Minister Gilani, Pakistan's constitutional system, in its thirteenth incarnation, has been transformed from a presidential-dominant system with a strong center and relatively weak provincial authority to a parliamentary system with a relatively weak center and a significant devolution of power to the provinces.

SUGGESTED READINGS

Kennedy, Charles H., and Cynthia Botteron, eds. *Pakistan: 2005*. Karachi: Oxford University Press, 2006.

Khan, Hamid. *Constitutional and Political History of Pakistan.* 2nd ed. Karachi: Oxford University Press, 2009.

Newberg, Paula. *Judging the State: Courts and Constitutional Politics in Pakistan.* New York: Cambridge University Press, 1995.

Shafqat, Saeed, ed. *New Perspectives on Pakistan.* Karachi: Oxford University Press, 2007.

NOTES

1. Act VIII of 1985, Constitution (Eighth Amendment) Act, 1985–1986, *PLD,* Central Statutes, 6.

2. The president's dissolution was upheld by *Ahmad Tariq Rahim v. Federation of Pakistan, PLD* 1991 Lahore 78; *Ahmad Tariq Rahim v. Federation of Pakistan, PLD* 1992 SC 646.

3. *Mian Nawaz Sharif v. President of Pakistan, PLD* SC 473.

4. For a detailed discussion, see Charles H. Kennedy, "Presidential–Prime Ministerial Relations: The Role of the Superior Courts," in *Pakistan: 1995,* ed. Charles H. Kennedy and Rasul B. Rais (Boulder, CO: Westview Press, 1995), 17–30.

5. Ironically, Benazir Bhutto's husband, Asif Ali Zardari (b. 1954), was implicated in Murtaza Bhutto's murder. He was indicted for this crime in July 1997. This charge was finally dropped in March 2008.

6. *Benazir Bhutto v. President of Pakistan, PLD* 1998 SC 388.

7. *Dastoor v. Federation of Pakistan, PLD* 1998 SC 1263. Also see S. M. Zafar, "Constitutional Developments in Pakistan, 1997–99," in *Pakistan: 2000,* ed. Charles H. Kennedy and Craig Baxter (Lanham, MD: Lexington, 2000), 1–23.

8. As per the Supreme Court's dicta in *Jehad Trust v. Federation of Pakistan, PLD* 1996 SC 324.

9. For additional details, see Zafar, "Constitutional Developments in Pakistan, 1997–99."

10. COAS General Jehangir Karamat, after failing to establish a National Security Council against the objections of Nawaz Sharif (an institution designed to institutionalize the power of the military), had resigned on October 6. That is, the military had already decided not to intervene prior to the Supreme Court crisis.

11. Provisional Constitution Order no. 1 of 1999, *PLD* 1999, Central Statutes 446.

12. Oath of Office (Judges) Order, 1999 (Order no. 10 of 1999), *PLD* 2000, Central Statutes, 38.

13. Those on the Supreme Court refusing to take the oath were Chief Justice Saeeduzaman Siddiqui and Justices Mamoon Kazi, Khalilur Rehman Khan, Nasir Aslam Zahid, Wajihuddin Ahmad, and Kamal Mansur Alam. Justice Irshad Hasan Khan became the new chief justice.

14. *Zafar Ali Shah v. Parvez Musharraf, PLD* 2000 SC 869.

15. International Crisis Group, "Pakistan: Transition to Democracy?" *ICG Asia Report 40* (Islamabad: ICG, 2002), 3.

16. Ayub's (1960) referendum garnered only 95.6 percent affirmation; Zia's (1984) referendum drew 97.7 percent support. See Charles H. Kennedy, "A User's Guide to Guided Democracy: Musharraf and the Pakistani Military Governance Paradigm," in *Pakistan: 2005,* ed. Charles H. Kennedy and Cynthia Botteron (Karachi: Oxford University Press, 2006), 120–157.

17. Government of Pakistan, Chief Executive Secretariat, National Reconstruction Bureau, *Conceptual Framework of Proposals on the Government of Pakistan on the Establishment of Sustainable Democracy,* June 26, 2002. The text of the Legal Framework Order, 2002, is found at Pakistani.org/Pakistan/constitution/Musharraf_const._revival/lfo.html.

18. "Text of the 17th Amendment Bill," *Daily Times* (Lahore), December 30, 2003, http://www.dailytimes.com.pk/default.asp?page=story_30–12–2003_pg7_38.

19. For details, see Charles H. Kennedy, "Pakistan 2005: Running Very Fast to Stay in the Same Place," *Asian Survey* (January 2005): 105–111.

20. Massoud Ansari, "The Day Karachi Bled," *Newsline,* June 12, 2007, http://www
.newslinemagazine.com/2007/06/the-day-karachi-bled.

21. Provisional Constitution Order no. 1, 2007. Text found at pakistanpolicy.com/2007/11
/03/Musharraf-declares-state-of-emergency.

22. The text of the Provisional Constitution Order is found in *Dawn,* November 4, 2007,
dawn.com. The fundamental rights suspended by the PCO related to security of persons (Article
9), safeguard as to arrest and detention (Article 10), freedom of movement (Article 15), freedom
of assembly (Article 16), freedom of association (Article 17), freedom of speech (Article 19), and
equality of citizens (Article 25).

23. Fifteen justices on a bench of nineteen did not take a fresh oath in the Supreme Court.
The four justices who took the fresh oath were Abdul Hameed Dogar, Muhammad Nawaz
Abbasi, Faqir Muhammad Khokhar, and M. Javed Buttar. In the Lahore High Court thirteen
of thirty-one; in the Sindh High Court twenty-three of twenty-seven; and in the Peshawar
High Court five of thirteen did not take the fresh oath. All five of the justices of the Balochistan
High Court took the fresh oath.

24. "Revocation of Proclamation of Emergency Order, 2007," Pakistan.org/constitution.

25. The fundamental rights consist of Articles 8–28 of the Constitution. They have a broad
compass similar to the Indian constitution.

26. *Federation of Pakistan v. Nawaz Sharif, PLD* 2009 SC 644.

27. *Sindh High Court Bar Association v. Federation of Pakistan, PLD* 2009 SC 789.

28. *Mubashir Hassan v. Federation of Pakistan, PLD* 2010 SC 1; *Mubashir Hassan v. Federation of Pakistan, PLD* 2010 SC 265.

29. During Iftikhar Chaudhry's tenure as chief justice, the HRC has heard over 10,000 cases
covering a remarkable range of subjects. Through the operation of the HRC, the Court has assumed the role of a powerful federal ombudsman, identifying and helping to right the wrongs of
individuals caught up in the injustices of the system. However, the Court lacks the resources to
effectively implement or enforce its numerous directives and orders to recalcitrant military and
civilian leaders. See Charles H. Kennedy, "The Judicialization of Politics in Pakistan," in *The Judicialization of Politics in Asia,* ed. Bjoern Dressel (New York: Routledge, 2012), 139–160.

30. The full text of the Eighteenth Amendment Bill is found on the website of Pakistan's Ministry of Information and Broadcasting at http://www.infopak.gov.pk/Constitution/Full%20text
%20of%2018th%20Amendment%20Bill.pdf. Its incorporation into the Constitution is found
in *The Constitution of the Islamic Republic of Pakistan as Amended to 2011* (Lahore: Manzoor Law
Book House, 2011).

31. These lists are found in Schedule 4 of the Constitution.

32. *Nadeem Ahmed v. Federation of Pakistan, PLD* 2010 SC 1165.

33. The full text of the Nineteenth Amendment is found in *The News* (December 21, 2010),
www.thenews.com.pk/Todaysprintdetail.aspx/ID=21434&Cat=2. It is incorporated into the
Constitution in *The Constitution of the Islamic Republic of Pakistan as Amended to 2011.*

10

Political Parties and Political Leaders

Political Parties

Political parties have not worked very well in Pakistan—though not for want of trying. Literally hundreds of political parties have existed during Pakistan's brief history, but with a few short-lived exceptions, they have been ineffective in performing the functions usually associated with such institutions—interest articulation, interest aggregation, and policy formulation. Of course, other institutions have taken up the slack. The policy process in Pakistan has typically bypassed political parties, with effective power going to unelected advisers of heads of government, civil and military bureaucrats, and the superior courts.

There are four explanations for such ineffectiveness. The first is personalism. Pakistan's political parties have served as the vehicles of their respective founders and then disintegrated on the founder's death. For instance, the Muslim League dispersed into warring factions after its leader and motive force, Muhammad Ali Jinnah, died in 1948, and it disintegrated after Liaquat Ali Khan's (1895–1951) assassination three years later. The Pakistan People's Party (PPP) survived the death of its founder, Zulfiqar Ali Bhutto, but only through the transfer of authority to his daughter, Benazir Bhutto. Similarly, the latter's assassination in December 2007 resulted in the unlikely transfer of party leadership to her nineteen-year-old son, Bilawal Bhutto Zardari (b. 1988), and her controversial husband, Asif Ali Zardari, bypassing more experienced and qualified members of the party. Currently Asif Ali Zardari is president of the state, and Bilawal is the party chairman.

TABLE 10.1 General Election Results, National Assembly, 2002, Number of Seats Won

Party	Punjab	Sindh	NWFP	Balochistan	FATA	Total
PML(Q)	68	4	4	2		78
PML(N)	14			1		15
PPP(P)	36	27				63
MMA	4	6	29	6		45
MQM		13				13
NA	7	5		1		13
Others	6	5	2	3		16
Independents	15	1		1	12	29
Total Seats	148	61	35	14	12	272

Key: PML(Q)—Pakistan Muslim League (Quaid-i-Azam); PML(N)—Pakistan Muslim League (Nawaz); PPP(P)—Pakistan People's Party (Parliamentarians); MMA—Muttahida Majlis-i-Amal; MQM—Muttahida Qaumi Mahaz; NA—National Alliance; others—eleven other parties won at least won seat; independents—FATA's elections are nonpartisan.

Additionally, as mandated by the Legal Framework Order (2002), 60 National Assembly seats were reserved for women and 10 for minorities, which were allotted to the parties following the election. The PML(Q) was allotted 26 reserved seats (22 women, 4 minorities); the PML(N) 4 (3 women, 1 minority); the PPP(P) 17 (15 women, 2 minorities); the MMA 14 (12 women, 2 minorities); the MQM 4 (3 women, 1 minority); the NA 3 (3 women); and two minor parties, the Pakistan Muslim League (Functional) and the Pakistan Muslim League (Junejo), were allotted 1 women's seat each.

Source: Derived from Mohammad Waseem, *Democratization in Pakistan: A Study of the 2002 Elections* (Karachi: Oxford University Press, 2006), 164, 167.

Second, political parties in Pakistan typically derive most of their support from a specific region of the state. For instance, in the 2002 and 2008 general elections (see Tables 10.1 to 10.4)[1] the Pakistan Muslim League (Quaid-i-Azam), or PML(Q), and the PML (Nawaz), or PML(N), derived most of their support from the Punjab; the constituent parties of the Muttahida Majlis-i-Amal (MMA, United Action Council) from their respective bases of support; and the Muttahida Qaumi Mahaz (MQM) from Sindh (and then almost entirely from Karachi and Hyderabad). The only major party with significant strength in more than one province is the PPP, with support in both Sindh and the Punjab, although the core of its support remains centered in Sindh. This is not a new phenomenon; regionalism has dominated party politics in Pakistan since independence.

A third explanation for the ineffectiveness of political parties in Pakistan is factionalism. This factor is primarily attributable to the operation of kinship (*biradari*) politics. In Pakistan politics is often viewed as a struggle between competing kinship groups for scarce resources and for prestige and honor. Political parties, then, become loose confederations of kinship groups, and political leaders are typically prominent members of important families. Loyalty to

TABLE 10.2 General Election, Provincial Assemblies, 2002, Number of Seats Won

Party	Punjab	Sindh	NWFP	Balochistan
PML(Q)	131	11	6	11
PML(N)	38		4	
PPP(P)	63	51	8	2
MMA	9	8	48	13
MQM		32		
NA	12	12		5
ANP			8	
BNM				5
JWP				3
PKMAP				4
PPP (S)			9	
PML(J)	3			
PML(F)		10		
Others	3	1	1	3
Independents	38	5	15	7
Total Seats	297	130	99	33

Key: See Table 10.1; additionally ANP—Awami National Party; BNM—Balochistan National Movement; JWP—Jamhoori Watan Party; PKMAP—Pakhtun Khwa Milli Awami Party; PPP(S)—Pakistan People's Party (Sherpao); PML(J)—Pakistan Muslim League (Junejo); PML(F)—Pakistan Muslim League (Functional).

Source: Mohammad Waseem, *Democratization in Pakistan: A Study of the 2002 Elections* (Karachi: Oxford University Press, 2006), 171.

such parties, therefore, is generated by neither doctrinal nor ideological allegiance to a program but rather by individuals within the party. When personal considerations or rivalries intervene (and they often do), leaders typically abandon the party and take their followers with them.

Finally, party politics in Pakistan has been subject to a history of repression. Authoritarian civilian regimes (in which curbs are placed on political activities) and direct military government (in which political parties are typically banned) have been the rule and not the exception in Pakistan's political process.

Muslim League

The Muslim League was the only major political party in existence in Pakistan at independence, and it possessed all of the advantages a party could wish for. Nearly every Muslim in Pakistan claimed allegiance to the party (sixty-two of seventy-six members of the First Constituent Assembly were members of the Muslim League; most of the others were Hindus). The party was associated with the dynamic and exceedingly popular Muhammad Ali Jinnah, who was the governor-general and presided over the Constituent Assembly. Finally, the

Muslim League had few institutional rivals. Yet less than ten years later, the party had disintegrated into numerous warring factions. Why? First, the two individuals most closely associated with the party, Jinnah and Liaquat, died shortly after independence. With the death of these party stalwarts went the image of the Muslim League as the party of all of Pakistan. Second, the Muslim League never developed a coherent ideology. The party had been formed to secure the independence of the Muslim state from British India. After independence, however, its task was much less clear. These difficulties were compounded by the party's continued attempts to be a party of national unity (a vestige of Jinnah's influence), integrating diverse shades of opinion under its mantle. Such attempts rendered the remnants of the Muslim League's platform vague and platitudinous. Third, the constitutional impasse, peculiar to the formation of the new state and caused by the unresolved issues of political representation and the status of Islam, proved to be beyond the organizational capabilities of the party.

Accordingly, in 1954 the Muslim League was routed in the East Pakistan provincial election, winning only 10 of 309 seats, and in 1955 it lost its majority in the West Pakistan Legislative Assembly to the landlord-dominated, Punjab-centered Republican Party.[2] Between 1955 and 1958, the fortunes of the party continued to decline. In 1957 the Muslim League lost control of the national government, and in 1958 General Muhammad Ayub Khan staged a bloodless military coup. Since 1958 the Muslim League has remained defunct, although several parties have borrowed its name, including, most prominently, the political parties associated with Parvez Musharraf and Nawaz Sharif.

Pakistan Muslim League (Nawaz)

The PML(N) is a lineal descendant of the Islami Jamhoori Ittehad (IJI, Islamic Democratic Alliance), a composite party formed in 1988 to contest the general elections. Originally the IJI consisted of nine parties, but two parties predominated: the Pakistan Muslim League (Forward Bloc) and the Jamaat-i-Islami (JI, Association of Islam). The former was a faction of the PML that remained loyal to General Muhammad Zia-ul-Haq after he dissolved the National Assembly on May 29, 1988. The JI severed its official ties with the IJI in 1991. Under the leadership of Mian Nawaz Sharif, the IJI won 32 percent of the votes in the 1988 National Assembly election; more significantly, it won a plurality of seats in the Punjab Provincial Assembly and accordingly formed the government. From his position as chief minister of Punjab, Nawaz Sharif and his IJI emerged as the main opposition to Benazir Bhutto's government. On November 1, 1989, Sharif led a no-confidence motion against Benazir's government in the National Assembly. It failed by only twelve votes. Nine months later, on August 2, 1990, the IJI accomplished this goal when President Ghulam Ishaq Khan dismissed Benazir's government and named Ghulam Mustapha Jatoi as caretaker prime minister pending elections announced for October. The 1990 elections resulted in a sweeping victory for the IJI, which won 105 seats in the National Assembly, and Nawaz Sharif became prime minister.

The IJI disintegrated in 1992 as both the JI and the MQM deserted the coalition. Weakened, Nawaz Sharif's government was dismissed by President Ghulam Ishaq Khan in April 1993, but it was later restored by the Supreme Court.[3] The damage had been done, however, and Nawaz Sharif was obliged to hold general elections in November. This time the election was close; the PPP emerged as the winner with eighty-six seats to the PML(N)'s seventy-three and was able to form the government. However, the PPP received fewer popular votes than the PML(N). After another round of presidential dissolutions of assemblies and early general elections, the PML(N) won a resounding victory in February 1997, capturing 134 seats in the National Assembly compared to the PPP's eighteen. This overwhelming majority allowed Nawaz Sharif and the PML(N) to restructure Pakistan's constitution. Nawaz's government was removed by a military coup in October 1999. Following the coup, Nawaz fled to Saudi Arabia to avoid imprisonment in Pakistan. With its leader exiled, the PML(N) contested the 2002 election but won only fifteen seats in the National Assembly elections. In November 2007 Nawaz was allowed to return to Pakistan (following a decision by the Supreme Court) in order to lead his party in the prospective 2008 elections, although he was still banned from contesting the election himself. In the general elections, the PML(N) made a very strong showing, winning the second-largest number of seats in the National Assembly and commanding a plurality in the Punjab Provincial Assembly. At the national level, the PML(N) joined the coalition government in March, and the PML(N) was able to form the Punjab government in April. (See Tables 10.3 and 10.4.)

Pakistan Muslim League (Quaid-i-Azam)

The Pakistan Muslim League (Quaid-i-Azam) began as a faction of the PML(N) when several prominent members of the National Assembly (MNAs), including Mian Muhammad Azhar, Syeda Abida Hussain, and Syed Fakr Imam, broke from the leadership of Nawaz Sharif following the 1997 election. In 1999 the faction threw its support behind Parvez Musharraf, earning the pejorative nickname "king's party." In 2001 the faction formally organized and contested the 2002 elections. It gained a plurality of seats in the National

TABLE 10.3 General Election Results, National Assembly, 2008, Number of Seats Won

Party	Punjab	Sindh	NWFP	Balochistan	FATA	Total
PML(Q)	28	5	6	3		42
PML(N)	61		4	1		66
PPP(P)	45	29	10	4		88
MMA			3	2		5
MQM		19				19
ANP			10			10
Others	1	5	1	3		10
Independents	15	3	1	1	12	32
Total Seats	150	61	35	14	12	272

Key: PML(Q)—Pakistan Muslim League (Quaid-i-Azam); PML(N)—Pakistan Muslim League (Nawaz); PPP(P)—Pakistan People's Party (Parliamentarians); MMA—Muttahida Majlis-i-Amal; MQM—Muttahida Qaumi Mahaz; ANP—Awami National Party; others – four other parties won at least one seat; independents—FATA's elections are nonpartisan. Punjab includes two Islamabad seats, both won by the PML(N).

Additionally, as mandated by the Legal Framework Order (2002), 60 National Assembly seats were reserved for women and 10 for minorities, which were allotted to the parties following the election. The PML(Q) was allotted 13 reserved seats (11 women, 2 minorities); the PML(N) 19 (16 women, 3 minorities); the PPP(P) 25 (22 women, 3 minorities); the MMA 2 (2 women); the MQM 6 (5 women, 1 minority); the ANP 4 (3 women, 1 minority); and the Pakistan Muslim League (Functional) was allotted 1 women's seat.

Source: Derived from Raja Asghar, "PPP-PML-N In Sight of Magical Number," *Dawn*, February 20, 2008, and "Pakistan Election 2007-8," www.elections.com.pk. (accessed February 28, 2008).

Assembly and the Punjab Provincial Assembly and formed coalition governments in each. Accordingly, the PML(Q) headed three governments between 2002 and November 2007, led respectively by Zafarullah Khan Jamali, Chaudhury Shujaat Hussain, and Shaukat Aziz. The PML(Q) is a centrist party that favors the policies followed by Musharraf to combat terrorism and extremism and devolution and to provide continuing support for US policies in the region. The PML(Q) was routed in the 2008 elections, winning only forty-two seats in the National Assembly.

Pakistan People's Party

The Pakistan People's Party was largely the creation of one man, Zulfiqar Ali Bhutto. As such, the party was as enigmatic, complex, and full of contradictions as the man himself. On one hand, the party represented a left-leaning populist movement: Bhutto espoused the cause of Islamic socialism, which attempted to blend the spirit of Islam with socialism. The resulting policies included land re-

TABLE 10.4 General Election, Provincial Assemblies, 2008, Number of Seats Won

Party	Punjab	Sindh	NWFP	Balochistan
PML(Q)	66	9	6	17
PML(N)	101		5	
PPP(P)	78	65	17	7
MMA	2		9	6
MQM		38		
PML(F)	3	7		
ANP		2	31	2
BNP				5
PPP(S)			5	
NPP		3		1
PML(Z)				1
Independents	35	1	18	12
Not finalized*	12	5	8	
Total seats	297	130	99	51

Key: See Table 10.1; additionally ANP—Awami National Party; BNP—Balochistan Nationalist Party; PML(F)—Pakistan Muslim League (Functional); PPP(S)—Pakistan People's Party (Sherpao); NPP—National People's Party; PML(Z)—Pakistan Muslim League (Zia-ul-Haq).

*As of April 1, 2008.

Source: Derived from "Pakistan Elections 2007-8," www.elections.com.pk (accessed April 1, 2008).

form to favor the peasants, the nationalization of industry to limit the power of the industrialists, and administrative reforms to curb the power of the unelected bureaucratic elite. Indeed, in its early days the PPP counted many leftist intellectuals among its members. On the other hand, the PPP was built on the foundations of the old ruling class of Pakistan (the landed gentry), and Bhutto's political style was reminiscent of *biradari* factionalism, replete with personal vendettas and periodic purges of PPP members. Moreover, as many analysts of PPP policies have argued, the outcomes of the reforms contemplated by the party fell far short of its ambitious platform.

The PPP came to power by capturing a majority of the West Pakistan seats in the 1970 election; it won with an even greater margin in 1977. However, the nine-party alliance that formed to contest the 1977 election, the Pakistan National Alliance, claimed the election had been rigged. Civil unrest ensued during the spring and early summer, and General Zia staged a coup in July. Bhutto was eventually imprisoned on the charge of complicity in the attempted murder of a political rival (Ahmad Raza Kasuri), whose father was mistakenly murdered instead. After a lengthy trial he was hanged on April 4, 1979.

Zia banned the PPP, along with other parties, in 1979, but after party restrictions were lifted in early 1986, the party reemerged as a potent political force under the dynamic leadership of Benazir Bhutto, Zulfiqar's daughter. Although the PPP secured a plurality in the National Assembly elections of 1988, the party's mandate was much narrower than it had been during the elder Bhutto's regime. The PPP entered into a coalition with the MQM and several independent MNAs to form the government in December 1988. Benazir's government was dismissed in 1990 and lost the ensuing general election to the PML(N). The PPP and Benazir returned to power in 1993, but her government was dismissed again in 1996. The resultant 1997 election was a disaster for the PPP. It won only eighteen seats in the National Assembly—all from Sindh province. Moreover, the party was shaken by charges of corruption and criminality. Numerous indictments were issued against both Benazir Bhutto and her husband, Asif Ali Zardari, charging them with, inter alia, corruption and financial impropriety. Zardari was also indicted for complicity in the 1996 murder of Murtaza Bhutto (Benazir's brother).[4] Convicted in absentia for misappropriation of funds in 1998 and facing a five-year jail sentence, Benazir went into self-imposed exile, dividing her time between Dubai and England. In her absence her party, now called the Pakistan People's Party (Parliamentarians), did remarkably well in the 2002 elections. In October 2007, President Musharraf promulgated the National Reconciliation Ordinance (NRO), which vacated her conviction and allowed her to return to Pakistan. While campaigning for her party in Rawalpindi, she was assassinated on December 27, leaving the party in the shaky hands of her teenage son, Bilawal, and her widower, Asif Ali Zardari.

Nonetheless, the PPP did very well in the 2008 general elections, winning a plurality in the National Assembly and becoming the largest component of the coalition government. Accordingly, a Punjabi member of the PPP, Yousaf Raza Gilani (b. 1952), was selected as prime minister in March. Following the resignation of Musharraf in 2008, Asif Ali Zardari was elected president.

Islamist Parties: The Jamaat-i-Islami and the Jamiat Ulema Islam

Islamist parties have been the most ideologically consistent parties in Pakistan, and the largest and most articulate of these has been the Jamaat-i-Islami, or Association of Islam. The JI was founded in 1941 in Lahore by Maulana Maududi (1903–1974). Its general aim, shared by all Islamist parties in Pakistan, has been to promote Islamic policies, practices, and politicians. Moreover, the JI has opposed westernization by campaigning, for example, against capitalism, socialism, and party-based representative government. It has also opposed the adoption of corrupt Western social practices such as bank interest, birth control, relaxed sexual mores, and Western-style feminism. In the place of Western institutions and practices, it foresees the adoption of a state ruled by Sharia (Islamic law). In such a state a pious emir (nonhereditary king) will rule with the consent of learned Islamic legal scholars (i.e., ulema). Members of the JI have been prominent in Pakistan's politics since independence. The JI was the dominant voice for ulema interests in the debates preceding the adoption of Pakistan's first constitution and was active in the anti-Ahmadiyya communal disturbances of 1953. The JI also led the opposition to the Family Law Ordinance (1961) and participated in opposition politics from 1950 to 1977 and during Benazir Bhutto's two governments. The JI is organized around party cells in universities, and membership in the party is based solely on selection by the leadership. Consequently, most of its members are university educated, although socially they represent the urban lower middle class. Despite its ideological prominence, the JI has generally enjoyed only limited electoral success in Pakistan.[5]

The Jamiat Ulema Islam (JUI, Association of Ulema) is a Deobandi party that derives its support almost exclusively from Pakhtuns in the North-West Frontier Province (NWFP) and Balochistan. It was founded by Mufti Mahmood (1919–1980). His son, Fazl Rahman, now leads the dominant faction of the current JUI, the JUI(F); a consummate politician, Rahman has been allied in one capacity or another with every government in Pakistan since Zia's military coup. A much smaller faction of the party, the JUI(S), is led by Sami-ul-Haq. Like the JI, the JUI advocates Islamist issues, but its particular interest is Afghanistan. The JUI was closely affiliated with the Taliban, and in recent years it has criticized the US-led occupation of the state. Also like the JI, the JUI has enjoyed little electoral success in Pakistan.

In the 2002 elections, six Islamist parties united under the rubric of the Muttahida Majlis-i-Amal to contest the elections.[6] Partially owing to the weakness of the PML(N), Legal Framework Order–inspired electoral rules that favored candidates of the Islamist parties, and seat-distribution agreements between the various Islamist parties, the MMA emerged as the third-largest party in the National Assembly and gained a plurality of seats in the NWFP and Balochistan provincial assemblies.[7] Subsequently, the MMA alliance disintegrated over the issue of whether to boycott the 2008 elections, with the JUI(F) deciding to contest the elections and the other five members of the MMA deciding to boycott. Largely as a consequence of this disunity, the MMA suffered a devastating setback in the 2008 elections, winning only five seats in the National Assembly (it had won forty-five in 2002).[8]

Regional Parties

As previously noted, national parties in Pakistan have derived the bulk of their support from particular regions of the state, but their platforms have typically attempted to attract all of Pakistan's voters. The two most successful Pakistani parties—the Muslim League (with strongholds in West Pakistan, particularly Punjab and Sindh) and the PPP (Sindh and Punjab)—were no exceptions to this rule; neither were the Islamist parties: JUI (Khyber-Pakhtunkhwa [formerly NWFP] and Balochistan) and JI (urban Sindh and Punjab). However, numerous other parties have focused their appeal on regional autonomy. The National Awami Party (NAP) and its successors, the National Democratic Party (NDP), and the Awami National Party (ANP) have derived the bulk of their strength from Pakhtun voters in Khyber-Pakhtunkhwa and Balochistan. Similarly, Baloch autonomist interests have been voiced by the Balochistan National Movement; Sindhi separatist sentiments by the Jiye Sindh; and expatriate Punjab and Pakhtun community interests in Sindh and Balochistan by the Pakhtun Khwa Milli Awami Party. The ANP, under the leadership of Asfandyar Wali Khan (b. 1949), did very well in the 2008 elections and was able to form the provincial government in the NWFP.

The most significant ethnoregionalist party to emerge since 1988 has been the Muhajir Qaumi Mahaz (Muhajir National Movement), since 1997 called the Muttahida Qaumi Mahaz. The MQM represents the interests of Pakistan's muhajir community. In the 1988 National Assembly elections, the MQM won thirteen seats; in 1990, it won fifteen seats; it refused to contest the 1993 election but returned in 1997 to win twelve seats; in the 2002 and 2008 elections, it won thirteen seats. Far more important than its role in national politics, however, is the authority the MQM holds in Pakistan's largest city, Karachi. The MQM dominates street politics in the city and has been deeply involved in numerous incidents of ethnonational violence over the years. The founder and leader of the MQM is Altaf Hussain (b. 1953).

Leaders

It is beyond the scope of this section to present a detailed treatment of the political careers of Pakistan's leaders. It is useful, however, to look briefly at the political backgrounds of ten of Pakistan's most significant leaders: Muhammad Ali Jinnah, Liaquat Ali Khan, Ayub Khan, Yahya Khan, Zulfiqar Ali Bhutto, Muhammad Zia-ul-Haq, Benazir Bhutto, Mian Nawaz Sharif, Parvez Musharraf, and Asif Ali Zardari. Table 10.5 presents a list of Pakistan's heads of state and government since partition.

TABLE 10.5 Heads of State and Government Since Independence

Leader	Position	Duties
Muhammad Ali Jinnah	Governor-general	August 1947–September 1948
Liaquat Ali Kahn	Prime minister	August 1947–October 1951
Khwaja Nazimuddin	Governor-general	September 1948–October 1951
Ghulam Muhammad	Governor-general	October 1951–August 1955
Khwaja Nazimuddin	Prime minister	October 1951–April 1953
Muhammad Ali Bogra	Prime minister	April 1953–August 1955
Iskander Mirza	Governor-general/president	August 1955–October 1958
Chaudury Muhammad Ali	Prime minister	August 1955–September 1956
H. S. Suhrawardy	Prime minister	September 1956–October 1957
I. I. Chundrigar	Prime minister	October 1957–December 1957
Firoz Khan Noon	Prime minister	December 1957–October 1958
Muhammad Ayub Khan	CMLA/president	October 1958–March 1969
Muhammad Yahya Khan	President	March 1969–December 1971
Zulfiqar Ali Bhutto	President	December 1971–August 1973
Zulfiqar Ali Bhutto	Prime minister	August 1973–July 1977
Fazl Illahi Chaudhry	President	August 1973–September 1978
Muhammad Zia-ul-Haq	CMLA/president	July 1977–August 1988
Muhammad Khan Junejo	Prime minister	March 1985–May 1988
Ghulam Ishaq Khan	President	August 1988–July 1993
Benazir Bhutto	Prime minister	December 1988–August 1990
Ghulam Mustapha Jatoi	Prime minister (caretaker)	August 1990–December 1990
Mian Nawaz Sharif	Prime minister	December 1990–April 1993
Balkh Sher Mazari	Prime minister (caretaker)	April 1993–May 1993
Mian Nawaz Sharif	Prime minister	May 1993–July 1993
Moeen Qureshi	Prime minister (caretaker)	July 1993–October 1993
Wasim Sajjad	President (caretaker)	July 1993–November 1993
Benazir Bhutto	Prime minister	October 1993–November 1996
Farooq Leghari	President	November 1993–December 1997
Meraj Khalid	Prime minister (caretaker)	November 1996–February 1997
Wasim Sajjad	President (caretaker)	December 1997
Mian Nawaz Sharif	Prime minister	February 1997–October 1999
Rafiq Ahmed Tarar	President	December 1997–June 2001
Parvez Musharraf	Chief executive	October 1999–June 2001
	President	June 2001–August 2008
Zafarullah Khan Jamali	Prime minister	November 2002–June 2004
Chaudhury Shujaat Hussain	Prime minister (caretaker)	June 2004–August 2004
Shaukat Aziz	Prime minister	August 2004–November 2007
Muhammad Mian Soomro	Prime minister (caretaker)	November 2007–March 2008
Yousaf Raza Gilani	Prime minister	March 2008–April 2012
Asif Ali Zardari	President	September 2008–June 2012
Muhammad Mian Soomro	Prime minister (caretaker)	June 2012–present
Raja Parvaiz Ashraf	Prime minister	June 2012–March 2013

Muhammad Ali Jinnah: The Father of Pakistan

Muhammad Ali Jinnah (1876–1948) was the son of a wealthy Khoja Ishmaili Shia merchant. His father, who expected the young Jinnah to take over the family business, sent him to London to study commerce. Jinnah found the study of law more congenial, however, and in 1895 was admitted to the bar at Lincoln's Inn. Already a member of the Congress Party, Jinnah in 1913 also joined the Muslim League with the intention of merging it with the programs of the larger and longer-established Indian National Congress. His efforts helped to pave the way toward the Lucknow Pact (1916), a cooperative agreement between the Muslim League and the Congress Party, which later led to the Government of India Act of 1919. But Muslim League–Congress Party unity proved short-lived, and Jinnah resigned his Congress Party membership in 1920 after disagreeing with Mahatma Gandhi's tactics of *satyagraha* (truth force/nonviolent resistance) and direct action. Between 1920 and 1937, Jinnah waged an uphill battle against the forces of Hindu-Muslim disunity, but his political strategy changed after the Muslim League's humiliating defeat in the provincial elections of 1937. Accordingly, Jinnah came to espouse the Two Nation Theory and eventually sponsored the Lahore Resolution of 1940. His argument was twofold: (1) in a united India, the majority community Hindus would dominate Muslim interests, and (2) such an outcome threatened to subvert the prospects of an Islamic state. Under this plank, the Muslim League came to dominate Muslim politics on the subcontinent, and Jinnah, as president of the party (1934–1948), emerged as its unchallenged leader.

Jinnah was an unlikely figure to assume such a role. He was an aloof, haughty, elitist intellectual. He never learned Urdu or Bengali, and his personal life was quite secular. However, Jinnah was brilliant and tireless, and his ability to deal with the British as well as with the legal complexities engendered by the prospect of partition made him an indispensable vehicle of Muslim nationalism.

The Quaid-i-Azam (great leader) died on September 11, 1948, within thirteen months of becoming governor-general of Pakistan. Although he accomplished much during his lifetime, his legacy is mixed. His dominance in the Muslim League and his assumption of the governor-generalship, perhaps necessary for pursuing the goal of Pakistan and preserving unity after independence, nevertheless retarded the growth of representative democracy in the state by providing a precedent for one-man rule. Similarly, Jinnah's Muslim League, crafted to secure its nationalist demands, proved ineffective as a political party after independence.

Liaquat Ali Khan: The Lieutenant

Liaquat Ali Khan's political career was mainly undertaken in the shadow of Jinnah. Liaquat (1895–1951) was born in Karnal, Punjab, a son of an important landlord. Like Jinnah, he was liberally educated, at Aligarh, Allahabad, and finally Oxford; also like Jinnah, he was a lawyer. Unlike Jinnah, however, Liaquat lacked personal charisma, and his political constituency was small. A younger son, he pursued his political career in the United Provinces (now Uttar Pradesh) rather than in Punjab.

The basis of Liaquat's power was his close relationship to Jinnah, who had selected the young, inexperienced lawyer to be general secretary of the Muslim League in 1936. The choice was propitious, as Liaquat proved an astute organizer who was able to hold the disparate factions of the party together. In 1947 Liaquat became Pakistan's first prime minister, although he remained in the background while Jinnah effectively ran the government from the post of governor-general.

After Jinnah's death, Liaquat became the dominant personality in the government, but most analysts agree that his performance in office was ineffectual. First, his leadership was challenged by the Bengali Khwaja Nazimuddin (1894–1964), who served as governor-general from 1948 to 1951 and later as prime minister. Second, the unresolved issues of political representation and the status of Islam, muted as long as Jinnah lived, were joined during Liaquat's tenure. Finally, Liaquat could not accomplish the critical task of drafting a constitution. Perhaps such issues would have been resolved if Liaquat had lived, but the Quaid-i-Millat (leader of the nation) was felled by an assassin's bullet in Rawalpindi on October 16, 1951.

Muhammad Ayub Khan: Soldier-Statesman

Muhammad Ayub Khan (1907–1970) was the quintessential British-generation military officer. Ayub was born in the village of Rehana, fifty miles north of Rawalpindi; his father was a *subedar major* (noncommissioned officer) in the British Indian army. Ayub was never a good student (admitting in his autobiography that he failed the sixth grade), but he worked hard and was eventually admitted to the Mohammadan Anglo-Oriental College at Aligarh. Impressed by his "sporting ability" and family background, Ayub's teachers encouraged him to undertake studies at Sandhurst (the British military academy), where he graduated with a commission in 1929. Ayub fought with British forces in Burma during World War II. After the war, as one of a handful of Muslim Sandhurst-trained graduates, his rise was meteoric. In 1951 he was selected by

Liaquat as Pakistan's first Pakistani army commander in chief (a post previously held by British officers under contract).

From his background and training, Ayub internalized two characteristics that would greatly influence the course of Pakistan's history. First, Ayub was firmly wedded to the integrity of the Pakistani army. Second, he distrusted the loyalties and vacillations of Pakistan's politicians. Therefore, when (according to Ayub) he was offered control of the government in 1954 (by Governor-General Ghulam Muhammad), he turned the job down because to take it would damage the prestige of the armed forces. But four years later, in the midst of the civil unrest caused by "self-serving politicians, wrangling over portfolios" and Iskander Mirza's abrogation of the 1956 constitution, Ayub moved.[9] On October 5, 1958, through the strategic repositioning of two brigades of troops, and without a single shot being fired, Ayub became chief martial law administrator (CMLA). He remained head of state and head of government (after February 1960 as a civilian president) until his forced resignation on March 25, 1969.

Agha Muhammad Yahya Khan: The Unwitting Architect of Pakistan's Dismemberment

Agha Muhammad Yahya Khan (1917–1980) was born in Chakwal, a town in the Jhelum district of the Punjab. He was the son of a police superintendent, and after his education at Punjab University, he was commissioned in 1938. He underwent military training at the Indian Military Academy in Dehra Dun. After partition he rose rapidly through the ranks, becoming chief of the army general staff in 1957 and commander in chief in 1966. When Ayub resigned, Yahya replaced him as president, a post he held until December 1971.

Yahya's presidency was brief but eventful. Following the disturbances that led to Ayub's resignation, Yahya was perceived as a caretaker until a civilian regime was established. Accordingly, Yahya dissolved the One Unit Plan in 1970 and oversaw Pakistan's first national election including universal adult suffrage. However well meaning, the 1970 election proved a disaster for unified Pakistan. Sheikh Mujibur Rahman (1920–1975), leader of the Awami League, won an overwhelming victory in East Pakistan and, as a consequence, a commanding majority of National Assembly seats. Zulfiqar Ali Bhutto, head of the PPP, came in a distant second, winning all of his seats in West Pakistan. Yahya attempted to forge a compromise between Bhutto and Mujib, ostensibly for some form of power sharing between East and West Pakistan.[10] But his efforts were thwarted by Mujib's demand to be prime minister of an undivided state and Bhutto's unwillingness merely to head up the opposition. On March 25, 1971 (the second anniversary of Ayub's resignation), Yahya ordered the catastrophic military crackdown on East Pakistani nationalists that led in turn to the horrors of the civil war, the capture of Dhaka by the invading (liberating?) Indian army, and the unconditional surrender of the Pakistan army. It also led to the secession of East Pakistan and the formation of Bangladesh. Yahya resigned from office and served five years under house arrest for his role in the debacle.

Zulfiqar Ali Bhutto: Islamic Socialist

Zulfiqar Ali Bhutto (1927–1979) was perhaps the most enigmatic of all of Pakistan's leaders. He was the son of Sir Shahnawaz Bhutto (1888–1957), a wealthy, well-known landlord from central Sindh. Sir Shahnawaz was very active in politics, and he bequeathed to his son the task of looking after the landed interests of his family as well as those of other landed aristocrats in the province. This influence contrasted with Bhutto's earned status as a member of the urban intelligentsia. Bhutto attended Oxford University and the University of California, Berkeley. The tensions between these interests were to shape his political career.[11]

At the age of thirty-one Bhutto was made minister of fuel and natural resources in Ayub's first cabinet; later he became foreign minister. Bhutto used these positions as a base for developing his own political constituency, increasingly espousing a leftist position in the process. Accordingly, as minister of fuel and natural resources, he worked out an oil-exploration agreement with the Soviet Union, and as foreign minister he worked toward strengthening Pakistan-China relations. After the 1965 war with India, and perhaps sensing that Ayub's hold on the government was slipping, Bhutto broke with Ayub and became openly critical of Ayub's foreign policy. He was dismissed from the cabinet in 1967 and set about building a national following through extensive travel, public speaking, and the publication of several books. Bhutto's support for third world causes, his socialist rhetoric, and his outspoken criticism of the unpopular Ayub regime won him many followers, particularly among students and intellectuals in West Pakistan's urban areas. He also organized the Pakistan People's Party.

After the 1970 election and the civil war, Bhutto emerged in the anomalous position of civilian head of a military regime; his official title on assuming office was president and chief martial law administrator. The termination of martial law and promulgation of the 1973 constitution redefined his position as prime minister.

Bhutto's leadership style was greatly influenced by his feudal background. Although he espoused a populist, egalitarian domestic program and a liberal, nonaligned foreign policy, Bhutto's approach to politics was autocratic. He perceived opposition to his policies as a personal affront, and the history of his rule is replete with the political repression of his rivals. Ironically perhaps, Bhutto fell victim to a comparatively minor gaffe (i.e., minor relative to the enormity of other alleged crimes): complicity in the bungled assassination of a former member of the PPP turned political opponent.[12] Bhutto was eventually convicted of murder, and his appeal was rejected by a 4–3 decision of the Supreme Court; he was hanged on April 4, 1979.

Muhammad Zia-ul-Haq: "Reluctant" Leader and Martial Islamist

Like Ayub, Muhammad Zia-ul-Haq (1924–1988) was a career military officer who served with British Indian forces during World War II. He received his commission in 1945 from the Indian Military Academy at Dehra Dun. Zia was born in Jullundur, East Punjab (India). After twenty years in the lower ranks of Pakistan's officer corps, he was promoted to colonel in 1968, brigadier in 1969, and major general in 1972; in 1975 he was appointed lieutenant general and corps commander. Up to this point, his military career had been unexceptional. He had a deserved reputation as a devout Muslim, he avoided political intrigue, and on many occasions he had proven his loyalty to the state and to the chain of command. These characteristics attracted Bhutto (who since assuming office had feared another military coup), and he appointed Zia chief of army staff (COAS) over the heads of several more senior generals in 1976.

Thus the military coup of 1977 headed by General Zia came as a surprise to Bhutto. Perhaps Zia was a reluctant participant in the coup, his hand forced by the military's long-standing grievances with the Bhutto regime and by the deteriorating law-and-order situation after the 1977 election. Regardless of motive, Zia maintained power for over eleven years as chief martial law administrator (1977–1985) and as president (1979–1988).

Zia is perhaps best remembered for shaping Pakistan's foreign policy during the Soviet-Afghan War and for initiating the Islamization process. His role in both proved controversial, and his legacy consequently remains mixed.[13]

Within months of dismissing the government of Muhammad Khan Junejo, Zia, along with several senior military officers and the US ambassador to Pakistan, Arnold Raphel (1943–1988), died when their military plane was targeted by unknown assassins on August 17, 1988.

Benazir Bhutto: Daughter of Destiny and Martyr

Benazir Bhutto's (1953–2007) life was shaped by her role as the daughter of Zulfiqar Ali Bhutto. At his insistence, Benazir was educated abroad (Radcliffe

College and Oxford University). He had entertained hopes that his daughter would undertake a career in the foreign service. His plans were derailed, however, after Zia's military coup in 1977 and his own execution in 1979. To Benazir, the military's actions were illegal, and the execution of her father murder. In her eyes his wrongful death made him a martyr (*shaheed*). Accordingly, she became obsessed with avenging her father's death, restoring the PPP to power, and reestablishing her father's 1973 constitution.[14]

Through a series of propitious circumstances, including Zia's dissolution of the National Assembly in May 1988 and the sudden death of Zia and several senior military officers before a new National Assembly could be elected, she managed partially to accomplish her goals in December 1988. At that time Benazir led the PPP to a narrow victory in the National Assembly elections and became prime minister. Subsequently Benazir was at the center of national politics in Pakistan either as prime minister (1988–1990, 1993–1996) or as opposition leader (1990–1993, 1997–2007).

Unfortunately, her performance as prime minister is generally acknowledged as disappointing. In 1990 her first government was dismissed by Ghulam Ishaq Khan. Her second government was dismissed by fellow PPP member Farooq Leghari in 1996. In both instances the Supreme Court upheld charges of corruption and mismanagement by her governments. Ironically, the vehicle for the restoration of the 1973 constitution (Zulfiqar's constitution), a longtime PPP demand, was the humiliating defeat of the PPP in the 1997 general election, which gave the PML(N) the requisite two-thirds majority to amend the constitution. After that defeat, Benazir's fortunes waned. She was convicted in absentia on charges of corruption in 1998 and lived in self-imposed exile until October 2007, when she was encouraged to return to Pakistan by the promulgation of Musharraf's National Reconciliation Ordinance. As tragic and senseless as her December 27, 2007, assassination was, it is somehow fitting that she died while campaigning for her party in Rawalpindi at Liaquat Bagh, a site named to honor the memory of another martyr of Pakistan who, like Benazir, was felled by an assassin's bullet.

Mian Nawaz Sharif: Industrialist Turned Politician and Statesman

Mian Nawaz Sharif was born near Lahore in 1949, the eldest son of a prominent industrialist family that owned Ittefaq Foundry, the largest steel mill in the Punjab. The young Nawaz Sharif was groomed by his parents to take over the family business, and unlike his forebears, who were self-educated, he received his bachelor's degree from Government College, Lahore, and his bachelor of law degree from Punjab University. In 1973 Zulfiqar Ali Bhutto nationalized the bulk of the Sharif family's holdings, but in 1978 Zia-ul-Haq restored the Ittefaq group of industries to their original owners. Under the able and dynamic leadership of Nawaz Sharif and his brother, Shahbaz Sharif (b. 1950), and with the help of numerous lucrative government contracts, the Ittefaq group rapidly became one of Pakistan's largest and most successful industrial houses. Nawaz first entered politics in 1981 as finance and sports minister in General Ghulam Jilani's Punjab provincial cabinet. In 1985 Zia appointed Nawaz chief minister of the province, a position he held until his election as prime minister in 1990. He remained in the latter position until 1993 and returned to power in the February 1997 general election. During his two tenures as prime minister, he boldly launched several policy initiatives, including privatization of public enterprises, the "yellow taxi scheme," and construction of the Pakistan motorway. But his boldest stroke was the passage of the Thirteenth and Fourteenth Amendments in 1997, which led to the dismantling of the controlled democratic system of 1988 to 1997 and the full restoration of the 1973 constitution. Subsequently he attempted to restrict the authority of Pakistan's military, which proved his undoing.

On October 12, 1999, his government was toppled by a military coup led by the Nawaz-appointed COAS, Parvez Musharraf. In a fate like that which befell Zulfiqar Ali Bhutto following Zia's coup in 1977, Nawaz was arrested and charged with a capital crime; also like Bhutto, Nawaz was convicted. But instead of being executed, he was sentenced to life imprisonment. In December 2000, Nawaz and his family were allowed to leave Pakistan to avoid that punishment. In August 2007 the Supreme Court, led by restored Chief Justice Iftikhar Chaudhry, showing its defiance and activism, accepted Nawaz Sharif's long-standing petition to allow him to end his exile and return to Pakistan. However, his triumphant return on September 10 was aborted when he was met at the Karachi airport by Pakistani security officials and put on a commercial flight back to Saudi Arabia.

In the fullness of time, most likely at the urging of the Saudi government, Nawaz was allowed to return to Pakistan on November 21, 2007. At first he called for a boycott of the elections, but later, bowing to pragmatic considerations (the PPP was not boycotting the elections), he announced that the PML(N) would contest. Despite many handicaps, the PML(N) did well in the 2008 elections, and a PML(N) government was formed in Punjab province with Nawaz's younger brother, Shahbaz Sharif, serving as chief minister. Nawaz Sharif was instrumental in supporting the Movement for the Restoration of the

Judges, which ultimately led to the resignation of President Musharraf. When Asif Ali Zardari delayed in restoring the Chaudhry Court, the PML(N) broke its alliance with the PPP and pressed Zardari to relent. During this time Nawaz and Shahbaz were the targets of the Dogar Court and were barred from holding public office in 2009[15]; the Chaudhry Court reversed the Dogar finding later that year after the restoration of the bench.[16] Since this time Nawaz Sharif and the PML(N) have remained the most potent political opposition to the PPP-led government.

Parvez Musharraf: Enlightened Moderate or Military Dictator?

Parvez Musharraf was born in New Delhi in 1943. His family was originally from Allahabad and moved to Pakistan after partition, making him a muhajir. As a child, Musharraf spent six years in Turkey, where his father was posted as Pakistan's ambassador. Back in Pakistan, Musharraf completed his intermediate from St. Patrick's College, Karachi, and after spending a year at Forman Christian College, Lahore, he entered the Pakistan Military Academy in 1962. He was commissioned into the artillery in 1964. Soon thereafter he joined the elite commando unit of the Pakistan army, the Special Services Group. In his thirty-five-year career with the army, Musharraf held several important posts, including director-general of military operations and corps commander, Mangla. He also taught at the Staff College in Quetta and attended the Royal College of Defence Studies in the United Kingdom. In 1998 Nawaz Sharif appointed him COAS, and following a military coup in 1999, he assumed the role of Pakistan's head of state, defining himself as the chief executive.

Musharraf's long tenure was dominated by three main policy concerns: accountability and good governance, devolution and the development of institutions of local government, and maintenance of security in light of the global threats from terrorism and extremism. In pursuing these goals, Musharraf styled himself as an "enlightened moderate" dedicated to the cause of restoring democracy in Pakistan and combating religious obscurantism.[17] Over the years his domestic enemies proliferated, and his carefully crafted image, always easier to accept in the West, became irreparably tarnished. Indeed, in the aftermath of his orchestrated reelection as president, the accompanying emasculation of the superior judiciary, the fallout from the untimely death of Benazir Bhutto, and the PML(Q)'s debacle in the 2008 election, Musharraf found himself weak and vulnerable. On August 18, 2008, he was obliged to resign after the long and embarrassing campaign of the Movement for the Restoration of the Judges, led by the PPP, the PML(N), lawyers and civil society groups, and the defrocked Chief Justice Iftikhar Chaudhry (see Chapter 9).

Asif Ali Zardari: Heir to the Bhuttos

Asif Ali Zardari was born in 1955, the only son of Hakim Ali Zardari (1930–2011), a prominent landlord and chief of the Sindhi–Baloch Zardari *biradari* (kinship group). He went to Karachi Grammar School, and his official biography indicates that he graduated from Cadet College, Petaro (near Hyderabad), in 1972.[18] He never completed university studies. In 1987 Zardari married Benazir Bhutto in an arranged marriage; a few months later, following Zia's plane crash, she became prime minister. Zardari's role in Benazir's first administration was peripheral; during the second administration, he served in several capacities as a federal minister and advisor. Through a series of unexpected events—Benazir's assassination in 2007, his resultant inheritance of the role of PPP cochairmanship, and the impeachment and eventual resignation of Musharraf—he was elected president in 2008.

Throughout his political career, Zardari has been saddled with numerous allegations of corruption, influence peddling, bank fraud, money laundering, extortion, kidnapping, and even responsibility for arranging the murder of his brother-in-law, Murtaza Bhutto, in 1996. His reputation as corrupt resulted in his infamous sobriquet, "Mr. 10 Percent," for his alleged requirement of a 10 percent gratuity for granting a government contract during Benazir's terms of office. Some of the criminal charges stuck. He was in and out of jail between 1990 and 1993, fighting various charges brought against him, including kidnapping and extortion. In July 1998 he was indicted in Pakistan on various charges of corruption; in April 1999 he and Benazir were convicted and sentenced to five years' imprisonment. In August 2003 he was convicted on charges of money laundering in a Swiss court. Such charges were motivated, at least in part, by political considerations. And political considerations certainly motivated Musharraf to allow Zardari to leave Pakistan and join his wife in political exile in 2005, then to issue the NRO that granted them immunity from prosecution in 2007. Charges of criminality and corruption have continued to follow Zardari since he became president. (See Chapters 9 and 12.)

SUGGESTED READINGS

Bhutto, Benazir. *Daughter of Destiny.* New York: Simon & Schuster, 1989.

Bhutto, Zulfikar Ali. *If I Am Assassinated.* Delhi: Vikas, 1979.

Kennedy, Charles H. *Bureaucracy in Pakistan.* Karachi: Oxford University Press, 1987.

Musharraf, Parvez. *In the Line of Fire: A Memoir.* New York: Free Press, 2006.

Nasr, Seyyed Vali Reza. *Mawdudi and the Making of Islamic Revivalism.* New York: Oxford University Press, 1996.

Rais, Rasul B, ed. *State, Society, and Democratic Change in Pakistan.* Karachi: Oxford University Press, 1996.

Syed, Anwar H. *The Discourse and Politics of Zulfikar Ali Bhutto.* New York: St. Martin's, 1991.

Talbot, Ian. *Pakistan: A Modern History.* London: Hurst, 1998.

Waseem, Mohammad. *Democratization in Pakistan: A Study of the 2002 Elections.* Karachi: Oxford University Press, 2006.

———. *Politics and the State in Pakistan.* Lahore: Progressive, 1989.

Wilder, Andrew R. *The Pakistani Voter: Electoral Politics and Voting Behaviour in the Punjab.* Karachi: Oxford University Press, 1999.

Wirsing, Robert. *Pakistan's Security Under Zia, 1977–1988: The Policy Imperatives of a Peripheral Asian State.* New York: St. Martin's, 1991.

Wolpert, Stanley. *Jinnah of Pakistan.* New York: Oxford University Press, 1984.

———. *Zulfi Bhutto of Pakistan.* New York: Oxford University Press, 1993.

Ziring, Lawrence. *The Ayub Khan Era.* Syracuse, NY: Syracuse University Press, 1971.

NOTES

1. The results of all previous general elections can be found in Craig Baxter et al., *Government and Politics in South Asia,* 5th ed. (Boulder, CO: Westview Press, 2002), 196–199.

2. K. K. Aziz, *Party Politics in Pakistan, 1947–1958* (Islamabad: National Commission on Historical and Cultural Research, 1976), 105–110.

3. *Mian Nawaz Sharif v. President of Pakistan, PLD* SC 473. For details see Charles H. Kennedy, "Presidential–Prime Ministerial Relations: The Role of the Superior Courts," in *Pakistan: 1995,* ed. Charles H. Kennedy and Rasul B. Rais (Boulder, CO: Westview Press, 1995), 17–30.

4. Murtaza Bhutto, politically estranged from his sister, had formed a rival faction of the PPP, the PPP (Shaheed Bhutto), in alliance with his and Benazir's mother, Nusrat Bhutto. The PPP(SB) fielded candidates in the 1997 election.

5. For details, see Seyyed Vali Reza Nasr, *The Vanguard of the Islamic Revolution: The Jama'at-i-Islami of Pakistan* (Berkeley: University of California Press, 1994).

6. The six parties that joined the alliance were the Jamaat-i-Islami, Jamiat Ulema Islam (Fazl Rahman) (JUI[F]), Jamiat Ulema Islam (Sami-ul-Haq) (JUI[S]), Jamaat Ulema-i-Pakistan (JUP), Tehrik Jafaria Pakistan (TJP), and Jamiatahl-i-Hadith. Only candidates of the first three parties won seats in the 2002 National Assembly election.

7. For discussion, see Cynthia Botteron, "Validating Educational Qualifications as a Prerequisite to Hold Elective Office," in *Pakistan: 2005,* ed. Charles H. Kennedy and Cynthia Botteron (Karachi: Oxford University Press, 2006), 158–197.

8. For more details, see International Crisis Group, "Islamic Parties in Pakistan," Asia Report no. 216, December 12, 2011, http://www.crisisgroup.org/en/regions/asia/south-asia/pakistan/216-islamic-parties-in-pakistan.aspx.

9. Mohammed Ayub Khan, *Friends, Not Masters: A Political Autobiography* (Karachi: Oxford University Press, 1967), 4, 52, 70–76. Also see Altaf Gauhar, *Ayub Khan: Pakistan's First Military Ruler* (Lahore: Sang-e-Meel, 1993).

10. See G. W. Choudhury, *The Last Days of United Pakistan* (Bloomington: Indiana University Press, 1974).

11. See Shahid Javed Burki, *Pakistan Under Bhutto 1971–1977* (New York: St. Martin's, 1980); Anwar H. Syed, *The Discourse and Politics of Zulfiqar Ali Bhutto* (New York: St. Martin's, 1990); Stanley Wolpert, *Zulfi Bhutto of Pakistan* (New York: Oxford University Press, 1993).

12. After Bhutto was removed from office, the Zia regime published a three-volume *White Paper* exposing in great detail Bhutto's alleged excesses.

13. Robert Wirsing, *Pakistan's Security Under Zia, 1977–1988: The Policy Imperatives of a Peripheral Asian State* (New York: St. Martin's, 1991).

14. See Benazir Bhutto, *Daughter of Destiny* (New York: Simon & Schuster, 1989).

15. *Federation of Pakistan v. Muhammad Shahbaz Sharif,* PLD 2009 SC 237; *Federation of Pakistan v. Mian Muhammad Nawaz Sharif,* PLD 2009 SC 284; *PLD* 2009 SC 531.

16. *Federation of Pakistan v. Mian Muhammad Nawaz Sharif,* PLD 2009 SC 644.

17. See Parvez Musharraf, *In the Line of Fire: A Memoir* (New York: Free Press, 2006).

18. The President of the Islamic Republic of Pakistan, "His Excellency Mr. Asif Ali Zardari," http://presidentofpakistan.gov.pk/index.php?lang=en&opc=2&sel=2 (accessed on November 2, 2012).

11

Conflict and Mediation

Since independence Pakistan has suffered from internal conflict stemming from ethnonationalism and sectarianism. The former characterized the dismemberment of the state in 1971 and has helped define competing nationalisms in the truncated state ever since. The latter encompasses conflict within Islam (Sunni-Shia conflict) and in defining who is a Muslim (Muslim-Ahmadi conflict). This chapter details such conflicts.

Ethnonationalism

As we have seen, the homeland for the Muslims of South Asia was formed with little concern for the ethnic homogeneity of its people. Today, Pakistan encompasses five major politically significant ethnic groups, and eight major languages are spoken by its population. Ethnonational identifications roughly correspond with provincial domiciles, but the fit is imperfect owing to the effects of partition and internal migration. Of course, of more importance than the linguistic differences (the mother languages) of Pakistan's peoples is the politicization of their perceptions of ethnonational differences. Indeed, the perception of ethnic discrimination against Bengalis that resulted in the eventual secession of Bangladesh was spawned within the contentious ethnonational environment of Pakistan.[1]

Punjabi Dominance

At the core of ethnoregional sentiment in Pakistan is the perception by Punjabis and non-Punjabis alike that the Punjabi community dominates the politics and society of the state. There is considerable objective support for this perception. First, Punjabis constitute a majority of the population when one includes closely affiliated Siraiki speakers in the nation (see Table 8.1).[2] Second,

Punjabis have long dominated membership in the civil and military bureaucracies.[3] Third, Punjab is by far the wealthiest and most developed province in the state. Indicators of such advantage include differentials in per capita income, life expectancy, levels of industrialization and urbanization, and literacy rates. In the face of such facts, nationals of the smaller provinces perceive themselves as underrepresented or even dominated by the larger ethnoregional group.

Sindhi Regionalism

Sindh, to a greater extent than any other province in Pakistan, has experienced an extensive influx of outsiders, first from India (the muhajirs) and, after partition, from the other provinces of Pakistan. More often than not, these non-Sindhis have continued to cling to their original cultures and languages, ignoring local traditions and often failing to learn the Sindhi language. In addition, such newcomers are often better educated, wealthier, more cosmopolitan, and better able to compete in a modernizing state than the Sindhi sons of the soil.[4] Particularly galling to the indigenous Sindhis has been the rapid commercial growth of Karachi, fueled by refugees and later by Punjabi money and talent, with relatively little corresponding benefit to the indigenous Sindhis. Indeed, the rural areas of Sindh have remained largely unaffected by the rapid growth of Karachi, and the social patterns that have prevailed in Sindh for centuries have remained largely unchanged. Rural Sindh is still largely dominated by a semifeudal system in which rich landlords, who often hold hereditary religious or tribal offices as well, dominate nearly powerless peasants. Government policies that have awarded tracts of reclaimed agricultural land in Sindh to retired civil and military officers, the majority of whom are Punjabi or Pakhtun, have exacerbated the perception of Sindhi subordination in the rural areas.

Originally the demand for Sindhudesh (Sindhi homeland) was directed primarily at the muhajir community, which controlled the commercial and industrial life of Karachi. Aggravating such sentiments in the early years of Pakistan's statehood were attempts by Muhammad Ali Jinnah and Liaquat Ali Khan (both muhajirs) to make Urdu the sole national language of Pakistan.[5] Also aggravating Sindhi grievances was the One Unit Plan (1955–1970), which integrated Pakistan's four western provinces into one administrative unit with its capital in Punjab at Lahore. Sindh was further isolated when the federal capital was moved from Karachi to Islamabad.

But the greatest impetus for Sindhi regionalism is inextricably linked to the career and demise of the late prime minister Zulfiqar Ali Bhutto. Bhutto was the scion of a prominent landholding family based in Larkana, Sindh. During his regime he encouraged Sindhi sentiments by empathizing with Sindhi grievances and promising to rectify past injustices. Among the policies pursued by his government were land reforms intended to weaken the power of the land-lords in Sindh and end non-Sindhi ownership of Sindhi agricultural land. Bhutto also nationalized heavy industry, banks, and insurance. Each of these actions was perceived in Sindh as a challenge to the interests of the muhajirs and the Punjabis; similarly, Bhutto's civil and military reforms were perceived as detrimental to non-Sindhi interests. In the aftermath of Bhutto's overthrow by a military coup and eventual execution, Sindhi regionalism gained a focal point, perhaps even a martyr, and has correspondingly proliferated.[6]

During President Muhammad Zia-ul-Haq's regime (1977–1988), Sindh be-came the most disaffected of Pakistan's provinces. Many Sindhis perceived Zia's government as Punjabi inspired—at best oblivious to the grievances of Sindhis, at worst conspiring to further strengthen Punjabis at the expense of Sindhis. Perhaps the most serious challenge to Zia's rule was the Movement for the Restoration of Democracy, which inspired the disturbances of 1983 that originated in, and for the most part remained confined to, rural Sindh. During the heyday of the 1983 disturbances, Sindhi separatists voiced grievances remi-niscent of Bengali leader Mujibur Rahman's Six Points (see Chapter 14). These dissidents called for increased provincial autonomy; insisted on reducing dis-parities in economic development; charged the federal government with inade-quate allocation of federal government funds; claimed underrepresentation in the military, bureaucratic, entrepreneurial, and political elites of the state; and charged that Sindhis were treated as second-class citizens, even in their own province. The assassination of President Zia in August 1988 and the subse-quent election of Benazir Bhutto to the prime ministership dramatically changed such perceptions. Sindhi grievances remained, but there was wide-spread confidence that Benazir's regime, led by the daughter of Zulfiqar, would be more accommodating of Sindhi interests.

As the daughter of the late prime minister, Benazir inherited the mantle of Sindhi leadership. Partially as a consequence, competing nationalisms (Sindhi, Punjabi, and muhajir) have largely come to define the Pakistani political arena since 1988. Benazir Bhutto, Asif Ali Zardari, and the Pakistan People's Party (PPP) have become increasingly associated with Sindhi interests, Nawaz Sharif and his faction of the Pakistan Muslim League (PML) with Punjabi interests, Parvez Musharraf with the interests of the military, and the Pakistan Muslim League (Quaid-i-Azam) [PML(Q)] with Punjabi and muhajir interests. Such ethnonational considerations have come to dominate electoral outcomes in the state (see Chapter 10).[7]

The strength of Sindhi regionalism and discontent was demonstrated force-fully subsequent to the assassination of Benazir on December 27, 2007. Mas-sive crowds expressed their collective grief through chaotic riots that targeted government institutions and Muttahida Qaumi Mahaz (MQM) and PML(Q) workers throughout the Sindh. Such riots claimed over one hundred lives. The legacy of the Bhutto's representation has been passed to her widower, Asif Ali Zardari, president since 2008, and her son, Bilawal Bhutto Zardari, party chairperson of the PPP.

Muhajir Nationalism

The recent emergence of muhajirs (Urdu-speaking immigrants from India) as a full-fledged ethnic group constitutes a pure case of what could be described as the creation of an acquired as opposed to a primordial ethnic identity. For most of Pakistan's history, muhajirs were a residual category, in effect newcomers to the country who had abandoned their respective primordial ethnicities when they opted to emigrate. It is true that nonmuhajir communities, particularly Sindhis, defined muhajirs as a group that took unfair advantage of state policies. But the overwhelming majority of so-called muhajirs rejected such definitions, preferring rather to be called Pakistanis. Such self-definition underwent rapid transformation following the communal riots in Karachi in late 1986.

During the riots, muhajirs organized by the fledgling muhajir national movement, the Muhajir (later Muttahida) Qaumi Mahaz, and its leader, Altaf Hussain, participated on the side of "indigenous Sindhis" (defined in 1986 to include both muhajirs and Sindhis) against "outsiders" (Pakhtuns, Punjabis, and Afghans). Muhajir militancy continued after the riots and resulted in the forceful expression of several MQM demands of the central government, four of which are salient. The first was a call for the repeal or significant revision of Pakistan's ethnic quota system for government employment. According to the MQM, the size of the "urban Sindh" quota (7.6 percent) unfairly restricted muhajir entry into Pakistan's elites. Second, the MQM demanded the repatriation of the approximately 300,000 Urdu-speaking Biharis and their descendents, many of whom continue to languish today as stateless people in refugee camps in Bangladesh. Third, Altaf Hussain also advocated the idea that muhajirs should be treated as a fifth nationality, a status commensurate with that of the Punjabis, Sindhis, Pakhtuns, and Baloch. Fourth, the MQM insisted on holding a fair national census, as earlier censuses had underreported the muhajir population. Each of these demands was clearly anathema to Sindhi nationalist interests.[8]

Despite such obvious conflicts of interest, the MQM joined the PPP's coalition government following the national elections of 1988. The PPP had promised to pursue the MQM's demands in exchange for its support. Benazir's government, however, proved unable or unwilling to keep its promises. As an immediate consequence, the MQM left the coalition government and joined the opposition Islami Jamhoori Ittehad (IJI) led by Nawaz Sharif. The IJI-MQM accord held firm throughout the 1990 elections, MQM candidates swept the polls in both Karachi and Hyderabad, and the MQM helped to form the government both at the center and in the Sindh Provincial Assembly. Following a military crackdown in Sindh province in 1992, which targeted the illegal activities of MQM activists, the MQM severed ties with the IJI.

Subsequently MQM-Sindhi and MQM-Punjabi relations continued to deteriorate and became major contributors to the ethnonational violence that plagued urban Sindh during the 1990s. Ethnic violence reached its peak between 1994 and 1996, claiming over 5,000 lives according to official figures. During Musharraf's regime, muhajir-related violence quieted. This trend was related to the MQM's joining the PML(Q)-led governing coalition in 2002, as well as to Musharraf's local government system, which empowered the MQM in Karachi's metropolitan districts. The return of the PPP to power and the passage of the Eighteenth Amendment to the constitution in 2010 have significantly upset this calm. The latter devolved significant power to the provinces (i.e., Sindh), largely at the expense of local government institutions that had empowered the muhajir community in Karachi.

Pakhtun Provincialism

Before partition, the demand for a separate Muslim state was weaker in the frontier regions of Pakistan than in the more settled areas. Undoubtedly, one reason for this was the fact that few Hindus lived in the frontier regions. Hence Pakhtun grievances at that time were with the British and not with the confluence of British and Hindu domination, as in Sindh or Punjab. Consequently, the prepartition sentiments of the Pakhtun leaders found a natural ally in the policies of the Indian National Congress, and few took part in the Pakistan movement. Indeed, Khan Abdul Ghaffar Khan (1890–1988), the most prominent prepartition Pakhtun leader, has often been referred to as the "frontier Gandhi" for espousing an undivided India and supporting nonviolent civil disobedience.

After partition, development in the North-West Frontier Province (NWFP) was slow and uneven. Khan Abdul Ghaffar Khan built on a similar foundation of grievances engendered by the status of a minority backward province that eventually resulted in Mujibur Rahman's Six Points and the secession of Bangladesh (see Chapter 14). He founded the West Pakistan portion of what, in 1957, became the National Awami Party (NAP). This party never amounted to much in Sindh or Punjab, but it took firm root in the NWFP and Balochistan. Indeed, in the 1970 election the NAP emerged as the most significant party in the NWFP, and with the cooperation of the Jamiat Ulema Islam (JUI), it was able to form the provincial government. Khan Abdul Wali Khan (1917–2006), leader of the NAP and son of Khan Abdul Ghaffar Khan, and Zulfiqar Ali Bhutto were natural rivals; both were ambitious politicians who saw their rivalry in zero-sum terms. Between 1971 and 1974, relations between the two became increasingly acrimonious, and after the assassination in early 1975 of NWFP minister and PPP member H. M. Sherpao, allegedly perpetrated by NAP sympathizers, Bhutto arrested Wali Khan, dissolved the provincial government, and banned the NAP. Wali Khan was subsequently tried for murder. Bhutto was ousted before a verdict could be reached, however, and the charges against Wali Khan were dropped.[9]

The Soviet-Afghan War and its aftermath complicated issues connected with Pakhtun provincialism. First, it created millions of refugees—at its peak, perhaps as many as 5 million—who took up residence in the NWFP and Balochistan. The majority of refugees were Pushto speakers. Second, resistance to the Soviet occupation through the creation of, and international support for, the mujahedeen focused on the Pakistan-based refugee community. Many became armed and militant, eventually providing the basis for the creation of numerous paramilitary warlord-led groups. Third, sectarian clashes between Shias and Sunnis were exacerbated by the influx of the refugees, further politicizing and radicalizing the Pakhtuns, particularly in the border regions of the Federally Administered Tribal Areas (FATA) and the Provincially Administered Tribal Areas (PATA). Following the Soviet withdrawal in 1989, such issues became still further complicated by the consequent inconclusive but brutal Afghan ethnonational war fought between contending warlords and leading to the eventual rise of the Taliban as a by-product of the chaos created by the wars.

The US-Afghan War linked to the tragic events of 9/11 has further problematized the border areas. The initial US target, the Taliban regime, was primarily made up of and supported by Pushto-speaking Afghans, close ethnic affiliates of the Pakhtuns on the Pakistan side of the border. The defeat of the Taliban, coupled with President Musharraf's support for US actions, created the impression that Pakistan, in league with the United States, "was fighting against Pakhtun nationals." But such considerations, albeit serious, paled to insignificance following the US decision to invade Iraq in 2003.

Since that time Pakistan has been obliged to be a more active participant in the global US war against terrorism; as a consequence Pakistani military and paramilitary units have come into direct conflict with local insurgents in the FATA and PATA and been targeted by terrorist attacks in the settled areas of the state. At first (in 2003–2004) such operations were limited to the two Waziristan Agencies (North and South), and the goal was clearly to allay international concerns that Pakistan was not doing enough to combat global terror. However, the scale of the insurgency eventually widened to other FATA agencies and, more alarmingly, to the PATA. During October and November 2007, insurgents under the titular leadership of Maulana Fazlullah (b. 1979), son of Sufi Muhammad, established a self-styled "parallel government" in the Swat Valley. After the Frontier Corps suffered humiliating loses and defections, Pakistan's regular military was forced to subject the area to shelling and bombardment. Many civilians died and thousands more became IDPs (internally displaced persons). Fazlullah's forces fled to the surrounding mountains, where they have continued to wage a guerrilla war against the government. It is important to note that much of the insurgency is driven by a jihadist sentiment, designed to establish Islamic law (Sharia) in the province. It is also important to note that Pakhtun identity among the insurgents, particularly in the FATA and the rural areas of the frontier, is inextricably linked to, if not indistinguishable from, such Islamist sentiments. Musharraf's regime, as well as its successor PPP-led government, have been ideal targets for jihad, as Musharraf and the PPP both espouse a secular approach to politics, and both governments are perceived as doing the bidding of the United States and condoning, if not supporting, the United States' use of drones in the FATA.[10]

As part of the Eighteenth Amendment package, the North-West Frontier Province was renamed Khyber-Pakhtunkhwa in 2010.[11]

Baloch Marginalism

Balochistan is Pakistan's largest, poorest, and most sparsely settled province. It constitutes roughly 40 percent of Pakistan's area but less than 5 percent of its population. Furthermore, a majority of Balochistan's population is non-Baloch. Balochi speakers are a minority in eight of Balochistan's twenty-two districts. Pashto speakers predominate in six of these, and Brohi speakers in the other two districts. In Quetta, Balochistan's capital and largest city, Balochi speakers constitute only around 5 percent of the population. These figures do not include the 750,000 or more Afghan refugees (mostly Pushto speakers) who live in the province, their camps clustered near Quetta.[12]

At the time of partition, Balochistan was only partially incorporated into Pakistan. British policy before independence had treated Balochistan as a large buffer zone and granted local Baloch leaders wide autonomy within their traditional sphere of influence. In 1955 Pakistan moved to incorporate the territories as part of the One Unit Plan, and the tribal leaders, in "merger agreements," ceded their territories to Pakistan. In practice, however, the Baloch tribal leaders maintained considerable autonomy over their former domains.[13] But the merger sparked demands by the masses for major social change. Such incipient politicization found expression in the 1970 elections, and Balochistan, like the NWFP, elected the NAP to power.

Tensions between the Baloch NAP government and the federal government came to a head on February 12, 1973, when a cache of arms allegedly destined for Baloch separatists was discovered in the residence of the Iraqi military attaché in Islamabad. The government reacted by confiscating the arms, dismissing the Baloch government, and arresting its leaders. As a result of such "provocations," Baloch guerrillas began to ambush army convoys. The war rapidly escalated; at its peak, between 80,000 and 100,000 Pakistani military personnel were in Balochistan. Despite considerable loss of life, the results of the conflict were inconclusive. Fighting continued intermittently until Bhutto was removed from government in 1977. Upon assuming power, General Zia released between 6,000 and 11,000 Baloch from jails and declared amnesty for the guerrillas who had taken refuge in Afghanistan or Iran.[14]

Since the civil war, most Baloch nationalists have tempered their demands for separation from the state but continued to stress the need for greater provincial autonomy. Such autonomist demands were countered with increasing fervor during the 1990s by Balochistan-domiciled Pakhtuns calling for the partition of Balochistan along ethnic lines. Small-scale violence between the two communities has become endemic since the late 1990s and been exacerbated by ethnic pressures related to the US-Afghan War and the continuing flow of refugees and insurgents (mostly Pushto speakers) into the province. Baloch nationalists increasingly see their interests being neglected by ethnic outsiders who are ignoring the needs of the indigenous people to favor their own developmental agenda, most notably the exploitation of oil and gas reserves in the province and the development of Gwadur as a major commercial port. Such dangerous perceptions were brought to a boiling point following the assassination of prominent Baloch leader Nawab Akbar Khan Bugti (1927–2006) in August 2006, allegedly by the Pakistani military. Since that time the Pakistani military and intelligence agencies have adopted harsh measures to quiet the ensuing uprising. Such measures have included the arrests and disappearances of hundreds of Baloch insurgents. Such "missing persons" (as the detainees were dubbed in the Pakistani press) became the object of a highly publicized Supreme Court decision, which may in turn have played a significant role in the subsequent suspension of Chief Justice Iftikhar Chaudhry and the ensuing constitutional crisis (see Chapter 9). Also, it is widely rumored that the directive body of the Afghan Taliban (in some versions, including Mullah Omar) is based in Quetta, hence the moniker "Quetta Shura." In any case, significant violence (nationalist, sectarian, and US-Afghan War related) continues to plague Balochistan.[15]

Azad Kashmir: Disputed Partition and Conflict Unending

Technically, Azad Kashmir (Free Kashmir) is not part of Pakistan.[16] Azad Kashmir has its own political institutions: its own constitution, its own court system, and its own legislature. However, in a de facto sense, the "state" is hardly sovereign with respect to Pakistan, though its independence is a logical consequence of the long-standing Pakistani claim that Kashmir is disputed territory. This dispute can only be settled, according to Pakistan, when a United Nations–sponsored referendum is held in the "whole of Kashmir," including the Indian state of Jammu and Kashmir, to determine the status of the entire territory. In lieu of such a referendum, which was sanctioned by the United Nations in 1949 and has little chance of ever being implemented over sixty years later, Kashmir will remain the focal point of the Pakistani-Indian conflict.

At first the conflict was seen in its original terms, as wholly between India and Pakistan. Kashmir could become part of either India or Pakistan, with the outcome to be decided by the aforementioned referendum, rather than be partitioned between the two countries. Since the mid-1980s, however, the issue has become far more complicated as the third option of Kashmiri independence has gained increasing salience. What such independence would entail remains problematic. The minimal boundaries of such an independent state could be confined to Srinagar and the Vale of Kashmir (wholly within India); the maximal boundaries could encompass the whole of Jammu and Kashmir (including Ladakh), Azad Kashmir, and Gilgit-Baltistan (formerly known as the Northern Areas).

Nevertheless, the conflict in Kashmir has been sporadically violent during the last twenty-five years owing in part to the Indian government's repressive (episodically brutal) policies, as well as Pakistan's complicity in supporting Kashmiri "nationalist" (India would use the term "terrorist") activities in the Vale of Kashmir. Conservatively, more than 50,000 people have died in the conflict since 1988, the overwhelming majority of them Muslims. In 1999, Pakistan and India participated in a brief war related to Pakistan's incursion into and occupation of an area across the Line of Control. The Kargil Incident, as it is most often called, was resolved when the Pakistani troops were obliged to retreat from their positions.[17]

The long-standing Indian contention that the conflict is at heart a terrorist uprising led by Pakistan has been given theoretical support by actions of the United States and its coalition partners during the ongoing war against terrorism. That is, if the justification for regime change in Afghanistan and later Iraq is that such regimes harbored terrorists, it follows that Pakistan should be obliged to crack down on those supporting the Kashmiri uprising. If Pakistan fails to follow through, the Indian government argues, its government should suffer the same fate as the Taliban. Pakistan rejects such a comparison, claiming that the Kashmiri uprising is a legitimate indigenous national movement and not akin to the Taliban's relation with external terrorists. Such Indian claims and Pakistani counterclaims led to the mass mobilization of troops along the India-Pakistan border following the December 13, 2001, attempted attack on the Indian parliament, which India blamed on Pakistani-supported Kashmiri insurgents. The November 26, 2008 (in India, "26/11"), Mumbai terrorist attack was allegedly masterminded by the Pakistan-based Lashkar-i-Taiba, a group internationally designated as a terrorist organization due to its earlier support of the Kashmiri jihad. Since that time both India and Pakistan have stepped back from the precipice of war: Pakistan has taken steps to ban Kashmiri jihadist groups, India has taken steps to reduce repression in the Vale, and the international community has been supportive of their efforts. But the Kashmir conflict remains endemic and far from resolution.

Sectarianism

Conflict within Islam: Sunni and Shia

Sectarian differences within Islam have widened the gulf between Islamists and nationalists in Pakistan. Most Muslims in Pakistan are Sunni followers of the Hanafi (*fiqh*) legal system, but there are significant numbers of Shias as well—both Ithna Asharis (the Twelvers, the branch of Shiism dominant in Iran) and Ismailis (followers of the Agha Khan). Census data do not exist on the size of each group, although it is generally acknowledged that Ithna Asharis constitute 10 to 15 percent and Ismailis 2 to 3 percent of the population.

The potential for Sunni-Shia violence is endemic to Pakistan, as it is in many Muslim-majority states, but for the most part Pakistan was spared such conflict until 1979. At that time the confluence of two factors exacerbated the Sunni-Shia rift—the rise of a militant and expansionist Shia regime in Iran and the promulgation of President Zia's Islamization program. The former was perceived as a threat to Sunni interests throughout the Muslim world; the latter was generally viewed, at least among the Shia community in Pakistan, as an attempt to enforce Sunni orthodoxy in the state. Such developments, international and domestic, alarmed both the Shia and Sunni communities.[18]

In 1980 the Shias formed the Tehrik-e-Nifaz-e-Fiqh-e-Jafariya (TNFJ, Movement for the Enforcement of the Jafariya Fiqh) to counter the effects of Zia's Islamization program and to defend their community. Sunni activists countered by forming the Sipah-e-Sahaba-e-Pakistan (SSP, Pakistan Army of the

Prophet's Companions). Militant factions of both soon developed, and violence has proliferated, with around 75 percent of the casualties Shia. The carnage has been centered on the districts of southern Punjab (particularly the Jhang district), the FATA (particularly the Kurram Agency), the Northern Areas (particularly near Gilgit), and Karachi. This conflict has almost certainly been exacerbated by the actions of two neighboring states, Iran and Saudi Arabia. It is also generally believed in Pakistan that India supports militants in both groups.

The ongoing US-Afghan War (2002–2012) has exacerbated sectarian conflict in the state. From the war's inception through February 2013, there had been 1,035 separate incidents of sectarian violence in which 3,091 individuals had been killed.[19]

The Ahmadiyya: Who Is a Muslim?

The Ahmadiyya are members of a religious sect that follows the teachings of the late-nineteenth-century religious leader and self-proclaimed prophet Mirza Ghulam Ahmad (c. 1840–1908). Ghulam Ahmad was a prolific polemicist and author of hundreds of pamphlets and religious tracts. His writing targeted primarily Christian missionaries, but he often ran afoul of orthodox Islamic groups as well. Between 1892 and 1906 Ghulam Ahmad made a confusing and contradictory set of claims that orthodox Islamic groups considered heretical but his followers interpreted as proof of his prophetic status. Such claims, contended orthodox Muslims, violated a central tenet of Islam that Muhammad was the final prophet.[20]

Consequently, clashes between the Ahmadi community and the politico-religious groups of ulema have been frequent. The most violent confrontation occurred in 1953.[21] One outcome of these disturbances was the discrediting of the ulema (whom the resultant inquiry commission blamed for instigating the violence) and, by implication, their demands for an Islamic constitution. Indeed, with many of the ulemas' leaders in jail, opposition to the secular nature of the proposed 1956 constitution evaporated. In 1973 the issue was resurrected, and in the aftermath of the resultant bloodbath, an amendment was made to the 1973 constitution that designated the Ahmadiyya as a non-Muslim minority community.[22] Similarly, President Zia, reacting in 1984 to threats of potential violence against the Ahmadiyya by disaffected ulema, placed further legal restrictions on the community that have resulted in widespread discrimination against the Ahmadi community.[23] It is likely that the Ahmadi question will continue to haunt decision makers in Pakistan for the foreseeable future. In an Islamic state the question of who is a Muslim is of crucial importance—and, as Pakistan's experience has demonstrated, the determination of that fact is very contentious.

Conclusion

In sum, Pakistan, like India and Sri Lanka, was formed through the amalgamation of several nations, groups with distinctive languages, cultures, and ethnicities. For the states of South Asia, such an outcome was partially a consequence of British colonial policy, which paid only slight attention to the ethnic homogeneity of its administrative units. But in Pakistan it was also the consequence of the ideological demand for an Islamic state. The ideal of Pakistan envisioned the creation of a state that would transcend the national particularisms of its population. Pakistan was to form a community of Muslims. Unfortunately, the integrative effects of Islam proved too weak to prevent the dismemberment of the state in 1971. Consequently, Pakistan has the dubious distinction of being the first state in the twentieth century to succumb to a successful violent separatist movement. Therefore, unlike its neighbors (although they too must contend with the deleterious effects of competing nationalisms and religions), Pakistan carries the double burden of precedent: it has been the victim of a successful secessionist movement, and would-be opponents of the continued integrity of Pakistan are encouraged by their predecessors' success.

SUGGESTED READINGS

Ahmed, Feroz. *Ethnicity and Politics in Pakistan.* Karachi: Oxford University Press, 1998.

Amin, Tahir. *Ethno-national Movements of Pakistan: Domestic and International Factors.* Islamabad: Institute of Policy Sciences, 1988.

Ayres, Alyssa. *Speaking like a State: Language and Nationalism in Pakistan.* New York: Cambridge University Press, 2009.

Iqbal, Muhammed. *The Reconstruction of Religious Thought in Islam.* Lahore: Ashraf, 1962.

Kennedy, Charles H. *Islamization of Laws and Economy: Case Studies on Pakistan.* Islamabad: Institute of Policy Studies, 1997.

————. "The Politics of Ethnicity in Sindh." *Asian Survey* (October 1991): 938–955.

Kennedy, Charles H., and Cynthia Botteron, eds. *Pakistan: 2005.* Karachi: Oxford University Press, 2006.

Nasr, Seyyed Vali Reza. *The Vanguard of the Islamic Revolution: The Jama'at-i Islami of Pakistan.* Berkeley: University of California Press, 1994.

Shafqat, Saeed, ed. *New Perspectives on Pakistan.* Karachi: Oxford University Press, 2007.

Wirsing, Robert. *Kashmir in the Shadow of War: Regional Rivalries in a Nuclear Age.* New York: Sharpe, 2003.

NOTES

1. Among the best-known and most useful works are Rounaq Jahan, *Pakistan: Failure in National Integration* (New York: Columbia University Press, 1972); Leo Rose and Richard Sisson, *War and Secession: Pakistan, India, and the Creation of Bangladesh* (Berkeley: University of California Press, 1991); Feroz Ahmed, *Ethnicity and Politics in Pakistan* (Karachi: Oxford University Press, 1998).

2. There exists a long-standing demand for the creation of a Siraiki province (a fifth province) in contiguous districts of "southern" Punjab. There is a strong demographic case supporting such a policy as ten of Punjab's thirty-six districts (1998 census) have a majority of Siraiki-speaking inhabitants (17.4 percent of the total population of Punjab). This demand has gained new life since the passage in 2010 of the Eighteenth Amendment to the constitution, which devolved significant authority to the provinces (see chapter 9). Also see Nukhbah Taj Langah, *Poetry as Resistance: Ethnicity in Postcolonial Pakistan* (New York: Routledge, 2011).

3. Charles H. Kennedy, "Pakistan: Ethnic Diversity and Colonial Legacy," in *The Territorial Management of Ethnic Conflict,* ed. John Coakley, 2nd ed. (London: Frank Cass, 2003), 143–172. The approximate numbers of senior officers in the Secretariat Group (core of the civil bureaucracy) in 2001 broke down as follows: Punjab, 67.4 percent; North-West Frontier Province, 11.4 percent; rural Sindh, 7.6 percent; urban Sindh, 6.0 percent; Balochistan, 3.3 percent; Federally Administered Tribal Areas, 2.2 percent; and Azad Kashmir, 2.2 percent. Similarly, over 75 percent of all ex-servicemen come from only three districts in Punjab (Rawalpindi, Jhelum, and Campbellpur Attock) and from two adjoining districts in the Khyber-Pakhtunkwha (Kohat and Mardan). Stephen P. Cohen, *The Pakistan Army* (Berkeley: University of California Press, 1984), 45.

4. For details of Sindhi-muhajir communal relations, see Theodore P. Wright, "Center-Periphery Relations in Pakistan: Sindhis, Muhajirs, and Punjabis," *Comparative Politics* (April 1991); 299–312; Charles H. Kennedy, "The Politics of Ethnicity in Sindh," *Asian Survey* (October 1991): 938–955; Ahmed, *Ethnicity and Politics in Pakistan,* 41–158.

5. See Alyssa Ayres, *Speaking like a State: Language and Nationalism in Pakistan* (New York: Cambridge University Press, 2009).

6. For the most complete treatment of Bhutto's term in office, see Shahid Javed Burki, *Pakistan Under Bhutto, 1971–1977* (New York: St. Martin's, 1980); for the most comprehensive treatment of the land reforms, see Ronald J. Herring, *Land to the Tiller: The Political Economy of Agrarian Reform in South Asia* (New Haven, CT: Yale University Press, 1983).

7. Mohammad Waseem, "Pakistan Elections 1997: One Step Forward," in Charles H. Kennedy and Craig Baxter, eds., *Pakistan: 1997* (Boulder, CO: Westview Press, 1998). Also see Mohammad Waseem, *Democratization in Pakistan: A Study of the 2002 Elections* (Karachi: Oxford University Press, 2006).

8. Indeed, a major reason for the delay in holding a national census in Pakistan was concern over prospective Sindhi/muhajir enumeration. Accordingly, the census originally scheduled for 1991 was delayed until 1998, and then was held only under pressure from the international community and administered by the military. Similarly, the census scheduled for 1998 was delayed until 2011, the results of which will not be released until fall 2013 if then.

9. Lawrence Ziring, *Pakistan: The Enigma of Political Development* (London: Dawson, 1980), 148–159; Tahir Amin, *Ethno-national Movements of Pakistan: Domestic and International Factors* (Islamabad: Institute of Policy Sciences, 1988), 88–92.

10. According to the India-based *South Asia Intelligence Report,* a total of 42,813 people were killed in terrorism-related violence in Pakistan from 2007 to February 3, 2013: 14,022 "civilians"; 4,289 "security or military personnel"; and 24,502 "terrorists/insurgents"; around 50 percent of these were in the FATA, and around 25 percent in Khyber-Pakhtunkwha, including PATA. Calculated by the author from the South Asia Terrorism Portal (www.satp.org, accessed February 14, 2013).

11. The name change was a compromise of sorts. The Parliamentary Devolution Commission considered several names, including "Pakhtunkhwa" and "Hazara-Pakhtunkhwa," as well as keeping NWFP, before settling on Khyber-Pakhtunkhwa.

12. Figures are derived from 1998 district census reports issued by the Pakistan Population Census Organization (various dates). These are the most recent census reports.

13. Ziring, *Pakistan,* 160. Privy purses were granted to rulers (as in the princely states of India and Pakistan) and to tribal leaders as compensation for their loss of revenue when the territories were incorporated into India or Pakistan.

14. For a more complete description of the war, see Selig Harrison, *In Afghanistan's Shadow: Baluch Nationalism and Soviet Temptations* (New York: Carnegie Endowment for International Peace, 1981), 35–40; Tariq Ali, *Can Pakistan Survive? The Death of a State* (London: Penguin, 1983), 115–123.

15. International Crisis Group, "Pakistan: The Forgotten Conflict in Balochistan," Asia Briefing no. 69, October 22, 2007, http://www.crisisgroup.org/en/regions/asia/south-asia/pakistan /B069-pakistan-the-forgotten-conflict-in-balochistan.aspx.

16. Robert Wirsing, *India, Pakistan, and the Kashmir Dispute: On Regional Conflict Resolution* (New York: St. Martin's, 1994); Ainslee Embree et al., *The Kashmir Dispute at Fifty: Charting Paths to Peace* (New York: Kashmir Study Group, 1997); Robert Wirsing, *Kashmir in the Shadow of War: Regional Rivalries in a Nuclear Age* (New York: Sharpe, 2003).

17. See Peter Lavoy, ed., *Asymmetric Warfare in South Asia: The Causes of the Kargil Conflict* (New York: Cambridge University Press, 2009); Shuja Nawaz, *Crossed Swords: Pakistan, Its Army and the Wars Within* (Karachi: Oxford University Press, 2009).

18. For context, see Afak Haydar, "The Politicization of the Shias and the Development of the *Tehrik-e-Nifaz-e-Fiqh-e-Jafaria* in Pakistan," in *Pakistan: 1992,* ed. Charles H. Kennedy (Boulder, CO: Westview Press, 1993), 75–94.

19. Calculated by the author from data found at the South Asia Terrorism Portal (www.satp .org, accessed February 14, 2013).

20. Yohanan Friedmann, *Prophecy Continuous: Aspects of Ahmadi Religious Thought and Its Medieval Background* (Berkeley: University of California Press, 1989); Spencer Lavan, *The Ahmadiyya Movement: A History and Perspective* (Delhi: Manohar, 1974); Charles H. Kennedy, "Towards the Definition of a Muslim in an Islamic State: The Case of the Ahmadiyya in Pakistan," in *Religious and Ethnic Minorities in South Asia,* eds. Dhirendra Vajpeyi and Yogendra Malik (Riverdale, MD: Riverdale, 1989), 71–108.

21. Government of Punjab, *Report of the Court of Inquiry Constituted Under Punjab Act II of 1954 to Enquire into the Punjab Disturbances of 1953* (Lahore: Superintendent Government Printing, 1954).

22. Articles 106(3) and 260.

23. Anti-Islamic Activities of the Qadiani Group, Lahori Group, and Ahmadis (Prohibition and Punishment) Ordinance, 1984, *PLD* 1984, Central Statutes, 102.

12

Policy Issues

The policies pursued by Pakistan's leaders are as important as the various constitutional forms of government the country has had. This chapter traces the policies of six of Pakistan's most important leaders (from 1958) and the effects of these policies on state institutions.

Ayub's Regime (1958–1969): The Military as Praetorians

Muhammad Ayub Khan believed in centralized, authoritarian government. He was convinced that the people of Pakistan were too uneducated, divided, impoverished, and unsophisticated to form democratic institutions. He was also convinced that Pakistan's politicians were self-serving parasites on the body politic. The institutions established and the policies pursued by Ayub reflected these biases.

The system of government established by Ayub relied greatly on Pakistan's civilian bureaucrats. To Ayub, bureaucrats were the ideal ruling elite. They were intelligent, well educated, loyal to the state, and experienced in administration. Therefore, the majority of Ayub's advisers and cabinet ministers were civilians with administrative, legal, financial, or agricultural experience. The most prominent group of such bureaucrats was the Civil Service of Pakistan (CSP), the lineal descendent of the Indian Civil Service (ICS). During Ayub's regime, the four-hundred-odd members of the CSP came to dominate virtually every locus of authority in government.[1]

Despite his military background, Ayub chose relatively few military officers to staff political or administrative posts.[2] The military served in Ayub's government (especially after 1962) as loyal praetorians (the emperor's loyal personal guards during the Roman Empire). Their role was to support the regime from the barracks. Accordingly, Ayub consciously downplayed his military origins.

Given Ayub's distrust of politicians, it should come as no surprise that his regime limited the importance of the legislature, political parties, and elections. There was no National Assembly during the period of martial law, and the 1962 constitution established a very weak legislature. Although Ayub reluctantly allowed the operation of political parties, he placed restraints on the political activities of many politicians and restrictions on the freedom of the press. Ayub's own party, the Convention Muslim League, was a creation of its leader and never amounted to more than a label for Ayub's colleagues in government. Ayub held four national elections, but every one of them had a severely restricted franchise. In each case, the electors were the 80,000 Basic Democrats. During the first election, a referendum in 1960, the following question was asked: "Do you have confidence in the President, Field Marshal Ayub Khan?" Of the total electorate, 96 percent answered yes.[3] During the second, in 1962, members of the National Assembly and the provincial assemblies were elected by the Basic Democrats. The third, the 1965 presidential election, followed a new election for Basic Democrats and involved a contest between Ayub and the Combined Opposition Party's candidate, Fatima Jinnah (1893–1967), Muhammad Ali Jinnah's sister. Given the nature of the franchise, Jinnah did surprisingly well, winning 34 percent of the total vote and 47 percent of the vote in East Pakistan.[4] The fourth, also in 1965, elected new assemblies at the national and provincial levels.

Ayub believed that Pakistan was not ready for democracy.[5] Therefore, in 1959 he established the Basic Democracies (BD), a program designed to teach democracy from the grass roots. Under the BD program, local councils were constituted at the union, subdistrict (tehsil), and district levels. Such councils were partially constituted by direct election, but above the union level, a majority of each council's membership was appointed. Functionally, the BD program was dominated by civilian bureaucrats. The functions performed by the councils were also severely constrained. As noted above, the Basic Democrats also served as an electoral college for members of the provincial and national assemblies and the president. Under Ayub, therefore, local government became increasingly dominated by bureaucrats, especially by the CSP. Ayub's government also introduced land reforms touted as reducing the power of landlords. The reforms placed ceilings on individual holdings of agricultural land, but most analysts agree that the reforms were ineffective.[6]

Ayub believed that capitalism would be the most direct path to economic development in Pakistan. Accordingly, he pursued industrial policies that favored business and capital-intensive investment. Indeed, Pakistan's gross domestic product grew rapidly (approximately 6 percent per year) during Ayub's regime. However, Ayub's policies also resulted in increased economic inequalities between East and West Pakistan, as most foreign aid and industrial investment were channeled to West Pakistan. His policies also increased the inequalities of income distribution within the population—the rich got richer, but the poor remained poor.

The two most important accomplishments of Ayub's foreign policy were the settlement in 1962 of the boundary dispute with the People's Republic of China, which paved the way for a lasting Sino-Pakistani friendship, and the Indus Basin Treaty of 1960, which provided for the division of waters with India. Ayub's greatest failure was the 1965 war with India. At least before 1965, Ayub had cultivated the image of the most trusted ally of the United States. However, during the 1965 war the United States (Pakistan's only major arms supplier), in an effort to appear neutral, cut off military supplies to both Pakistan and India. This action, viewed as a betrayal of trust by Ayub, gravely damaged US-Pakistani relations. In addition, the cutoff of arms forced Pakistan to the peace table. The Tashkent Agreement of 1966, negotiated by Ayub, ended the war, but many in Pakistan (including Foreign Minister Zulfiqar Ali Bhutto, a member of the negotiating party) viewed it as a sellout to India.

Many factors led to Ayub's resignation in March 1969. Among them were his deteriorating health (he had suffered a pulmonary embolism in 1968); the alleged corruption of his son, Captain Gohar Ayub (b. 1937); his increasing unpopularity in East Pakistan; and growing internal military disenchantment with his regime after the 1965 war. Pakistan's economy also suffered a downturn in the late 1960s. In addition, West Pakistan's urban masses took to the streets in 1968 and 1969, calling for the breakup of Ayub's system. The disturbances were spearheaded in West Pakistan by the gifted orator and politician Zulfiqar Ali Bhutto. After some delay, East Pakistan joined the protests.

Bhutto and Reforms (1971–1977)

Bhutto had agitated since 1968 for the end of Ayub's system of government. As a consequence, his task upon assuming office was to restructure institutions while increasing his personal authority.

One of the main targets of Bhutto's restructuring was the civil bureaucracy. In 1973 he purged 1,303 civil bureaucrats from the government and announced his administrative reforms. The reforms abolished all service cadres (semifunctional groups that had represented bureaucratic interests), including the CSP; modified the pay structure to weaken the advantage enjoyed by CSP officers; enlarged the Civil Service Academy by forming the Academy for Administrative Training; eliminated reservation of administrative posts (a practice that favored CSP officers); and began a program of lateral recruitment (political appointment of administrators).[7] One consequence of the reforms was the dilution of the power of civil bureaucrats and their replacement with members of Bhutto's Pakistan People's Party (PPP) and those personally loyal to Bhutto.

Like all other leaders of Pakistan, Bhutto ruled with the consent of the military. The civil war had left the military establishment weak and unpopular. In this context, Bhutto took the opportunity to dismiss some senior military officers and to promote others who were personally loyal to him. He also abolished the position of commander in chief, replacing it with that of chief of staff (General Zia was appointed to this position in 1976). Ultimate authority, therefore, was transferred to the prime minister. In addition, a clause was inserted into the 1973 constitution stating that any abrogation of the constitution, as had happened in the 1958 coup, would constitute an act of high treason against the state.

Bhutto, as an elected civilian and leader of the PPP, personally favored increasing the importance of the legislature and political parties. However, his authoritarian leadership style and his image of party politics allowed for little dissent from his positions. Accordingly, Bhutto placed restrictions on, and later banned, the principal opposition party, the National Awami Party (NAP), and periodically purged his own party of members who did not agree with his policies. Bhutto had hundreds of political opponents arrested during his regime and, like Ayub, restricted freedom of the press.

General Agha Muhammad Yahya Khan, Bhutto's immediate predecessor, had abolished the electoral college aspect of the Basic Democracies upon assuming office in 1969. Bhutto introduced a modified form of local government, the People's Works Program, which called for the establishment of four tiers of elected officials; like the BD program, however, such councils were functionally dominated by civil bureaucrats. The only significant change was that Bhutto had replaced some of the career bureaucrats with personally loyal party faithful.

More important than Bhutto's local government institutions were his land reforms. Bhutto, the self-styled champion of Pakistan's peasant masses, dubbed himself the "Quaid-i-Awam" (leader of the masses). He also campaigned on the platform of *kapra, makaan,* and *roti* (clothing, housing, and food) for the rural and urban masses. Bhutto introduced two land-reform policies (1972 and 1977). Both, like Ayub's policy, placed ceilings on the ownership of agricultural land, although Bhutto's ceilings were lower than Ayub's. In practice, however, Bhutto's land reforms were no more successful than Ayub's in curbing the power of the landlords or in distributing land to the landless.[8]

Whereas Ayub believed in capitalism, Bhutto espoused Islamic socialism. Thus, in 1972 he nationalized insurance, banking, and a number of heavy industries. During Bhutto's regime the economy performed poorly; analysts disagree as to whether this was the result of Bhutto's economic policies or a combination of unfortunate circumstances (e.g., the increased price of oil after 1973, disastrous harvests, and floods).

Perhaps Bhutto's greatest achievements were in foreign policy. When Bhutto assumed office, Pakistan was a virtual international pariah because of the highly publicized atrocities of the Pakistan army during the civil war. In this context, Bhutto's achievements are remarkable. Bhutto successfully negotiated for the return of Pakistan's prisoners of war from India and Bangladesh through the 1972 Simla Agreement with India; greatly strengthened relations with China; established stable détente with Pakistan's historical foes, India and the Soviet Union; improved relations with the United States (the latter reestablished military aid agreements with Pakistan during Bhutto's regime); and in 1974 convened the Islamic Summit, a meeting of the heads of the Islamic world.

But Bhutto's regime collapsed because his reforms made many enemies, especially among the military and the opposition politicians. As already noted, Bhutto introduced several reforms that affected the military. The most important motives underlying the coup of 1977 were the establishment of the Federal Security Force (FSF) and the Balochistan War. The FSF, a paramilitary security organization, preempted the authority of the military. The undeclared civil war in Balochistan also proved very unpopular among Pakistan's military officers, particularly as it occurred on the heels of the debacle in East Pakistan.

After the 1977 election, in which the PPP was returned in a landslide but tainted victory, the Pakistan National Alliance took its grievances to the streets. The military, led by General Zia-ul-Haq, intervened—ostensibly to maintain order.

Back to the Military with Zia (1977–1988)

General Zia promised to relinquish power and hold a general election within ninety days of the military coup that brought him to power. However, Zia held office for over eleven years, and only his death prevented him from continuing in power longer. Zia's was a military regime and demonstrated much in common with Pakistan's other military regimes (those of Ayub and Yahya), but there were important differences as well.

Like Ayub, Zia believed in centralized, authoritarian government. But whereas Ayub came to this conclusion reluctantly, aware as he was of the weakness of the state and its institutions, Zia justified his continued role as a matter of accommodating the necessities of Islam. Zia increasingly viewed his role as that of an Islamic head of state who legitimately holds power and deserves the loyalty and support of his subjects as long as he governs the state according to the precepts of Islam.[9] Central to the ideology of his regime, therefore, was the establishment of a *nizam-i-Mustafa* (rule of the Prophet).

The Zia regime took a position somewhere between those of Ayub and Bhutto on the question of the significance and importance of the civilian bureaucracy. As one of his first acts after assuming office, Zia abolished the lateral recruitment program of his predecessor and subjected Bhutto's bureaucratic appointees to review by the Federal Public Service Commission. In addition, Zia reappointed several former CSP officers and other senior bureaucrats whom Bhutto had dismissed. Zia also appointed many civilian bureaucrats as close personal advisers. He did not reestablish the CSP, however; nor was the civilian bureaucracy as central to the policy-making process as it had been under Ayub.[10]

Unlike Ayub or Bhutto, Zia relied greatly on the military to fill administrative posts, since Pakistan remained under martial law between 1977 and 1985. Under Zia's system of martial law, Pakistan was divided into several zones, each governed by a deputy chief martial law administrator drawn from the military and carrying the rank of lieutenant general. Further, Zia established martial law tribunals, which possessed jurisdiction parallel to Pakistan's civil courts and were staffed by senior military officers. Finally, Zia established a 10 percent quota for retired military officers at all officer-level ranks in the civilian bureaucracy. As a consequence, many important posts in the bureaucracy were held by active and retired military officers.[11]

Zia's distrust of politicians exceeded that of other Pakistani leaders, and his regime placed severe restraints on political activity. In 1979 a martial law regulation banned all political parties and prohibited the future electoral activity of any party that failed to register with the Election Commission. Most of Pakistan's parties failed to register. In addition, specially constituted Disqualification Tribunals (1970) barred hundreds of politicians from contesting future elections on a case-by-case basis. Finally, amendments in 1979 and 1984 to the Political Parties Act (1962) barred former national and provincial office bearers and former federal ministers who had held office during the Bhutto years (1971–1977) from contesting elections. Such restrictions were lifted shortly before the 1985 elections, although most of those barred chose not to participate. Most remaining restrictions on political party activity were lifted in 1986. Zia failed to hold national elections in Pakistan until December 1984. At that time, he held a referendum (reminiscent of Ayub's) asking the people of Pakistan whether they supported his policies of Islamization and the ideology of Pakistan, with a yes vote interpreted as giving Zia an additional five-year term as president (March 1985 to March 1990). Zia is said to have received a 98 percent affirmative vote. In February 1985 partyless elections for the national and provincial assemblies were held. Although many of the political restrictions were partially lifted for the election, few prominent politicians took part in the poll. However, campaigning for the elections was brisk, and the turnout at the polls was surprisingly high (53 percent). Moreover, the polls themselves may have been among the fairest in Pakistan's history. Nevertheless, the national and provincial assemblies elected remained weak and were dissolved by presidential fiat in May 1988.

Zia revived many aspects of Ayub's Basic Democracies through the establishment of local-bodies programs in each province. Elections to local bodies (a four-tiered system of subprovincial government) were held in 1979, 1983, and 1987. Unlike the Basic Democracies, however, Zia's system did not use the local-body representatives as an electoral college; nor were civilian bureaucrats as dominant in the system as in the BD or Bhutto's system. The elections were nonpartisan, and the local bodies were dominated by rural notables (members of the landholding elite). Whatever their shortcomings, the local-bodies institutions constituted the most representative and effective form of local government ever implemented in Pakistan up until that time. Although Zia did not abolish the land-reform legislation of his predecessors, he also took no steps to implement it.

Zia followed a capitalist line in economic policy, although he was reluctant to denationalize the industries that had been nationalized by Bhutto. In fact, the number of "autonomous corporations" and "public enterprises" actually increased during the Zia regime. The performance of Pakistan's economy under Zia was impressive, although it must also be stressed that the Pakistani economy benefited greatly from remittances from Pakistanis working abroad.

Zia's foreign policy centered on the Soviet presence in Afghanistan, and Zia's crowning achievement was the Soviet withdrawal in February 1989. Indeed, Pakistan's foreign policy was influenced by Afghanistan in several regards. First, the Soviet-Afghan War created many refugees who took sanctuary in Pakistan. The presence of the Afghan refugees and their sympathizers precipitated several Soviet-Afghan reprisals, including bombings, directed at refugee camps within Pakistan's borders. Second, the Soviet presence in Afghanistan prompted the resumption of US aid to Pakistan. In 1981 the United States signed a six-year, $3.2 billion military aid and economic credits package with Pakistan. In addition, the United States sold Pakistan forty F-16s. Third, the combination of the foregoing factors moved Pakistan toward a de facto alignment with the United States. It also affected relations with India, although, on balance, these relations improved under Zia.[12]

PPP Part Two: Benazir Bhutto (1988–1990)

Those who anticipated rapid change under Pakistan's first democratically elected government since 1977 were disappointed by Benazir's initial term in office. First, Benazir's government was unable to restore the 1973 constitution; nor did it rescind the Eighth Amendment. Second, the PPP-led National Assembly passed no new legislative bills during its tenure; in fact, only ten bills, all minor amendments to existing legislation, passed the assembly. Third, center-provincial relations deteriorated markedly during Benazir's tenure, as evidenced by the widening rift between the PPP and the Islami Jamhoori Ittehad (IJI) in Punjab and by the proliferation of ethnic violence in Sindh. Fourth, the Afghan civil war remained unresolved.

Of course, Benazir's government operated under severe disadvantages from the start. The PPP gained a very narrow plurality in the 1988 election and consequently was forced to enter into a shaky coalition with the Muttahida Qaumi Mahaz (MQM) and several independent members of the National Assembly in order to form the government. As a result, PPP leaders expended great energy in efforts to maintain power. Such efforts were complicated when the MQM decided to withdraw from the government in October 1989. Moreover, Benazir's government, like all civilian regimes in Pakistan, served at the sufferance of the military.

Despite such disappointments and inherent weaknesses, the accomplishments of Benazir's government were not inconsiderable. Benazir's greatest accomplishment was to further democratize the society. Also, Benazir improved Pakistan's relations with the United States, the Commonwealth nations, and India, at least until the Kashmir dispute was rekindled in February 1990.

Capitalist Caretaker: Nawaz Sharif (1990–1993)

Nawaz Sharif's first administration entered into power with decided advantages over his predecessor's regime. First, the IJI enjoyed a comfortable majority in the National Assembly and was able to form governments in each of Pakistan's four provinces. Second, Nawaz and his party were the obvious favorites of both the military and President Ghulam Ishaq Khan. Nawaz was thus able to act decisively during his first few months in office by implementing significant economic reforms, including the privatization of many of the firms that had been nationalized during Zulfiqar Ali Bhutto's regime. He also shepherded a Shariat bill through the National Assembly and sponsored the Twelfth Amendment to the constitution, which was designed to address the deteriorating law-and-order situation in Sindh province.

Unfortunately, his administration's effectiveness proved short-lived. Alleged involvement in financial misdeeds, including the Bank of Commerce and Credit International scandal and the collapse of several Punjab-based cooperative societies, plagued his regime during 1991 and 1992. The United States applied additional pressure to the government by withdrawing economic and military assistance to Pakistan, an action linked to the alleged continuation of Pakistan's nuclear weapons program. Communal unrest in Sindh was quieted somewhat, but at the cost of massive repression under the tenure of Chief Minister Jam Sadiq Ali and later by recourse to direct military involvement. Moreover, political support for Nawaz Sharif and the IJI quickly evaporated. In 1992 the MQM and the Jamaat-i-Islami (JI) deserted the IJI coalition, further weakening the government.

In April 1993 President Ghulam Ishaq Khan dismissed Nawaz Sharif's government. Sharif challenged the dismissal in the Supreme Court and was reinstated in May. But his reprieve was short-lived. Under pressure from the military and in the shadow of continuing civil unrest in Karachi, Sharif resigned in July, and soon Benazir Bhutto was returned to power.

PPP Part Three: Benazir Bhutto (1993–1996)

Benazir's second term in office was even more disappointing than her first. The policy accomplishments of her government were modest by any standard. She did establish a women's police force, designed in part to improve women's conditions in Pakistan's legal system; she also continued the privatization policy of her predecessor. In foreign policy her greatest accomplishment was a partial relaxation of the rigors of the US Pressler amendment, thus allowing some arms shipments from the United States already in the pipeline to be delivered to Pakistan.

As in her first administration, Benazir's government was hampered by the effects of a narrow mandate (the PPP had won by a razor-thin margin in 1993), and she was unable to dismantle Zia's constitutional system. Partially as a consequence, her administration was often consumed by petty political disputes with the opposition. For instance, during her second tenure Benazir's government brought hundreds of charges (mostly groundless) against members of the Sharif family. Of course, from the perspective of the PPP, these were retaliation for the actions that the Sharif regime had taken against the Bhutto family during the 1990–1993 period. Also, her administration spent an inordinate amount of time trying to prevent the Pakistan Muslim League (Nawaz), or PML(N), from gaining control over the Punjab provincial government.

Benazir ran afoul of the superior judiciary, too. Her government attempted to put pressure on the superior judiciary by manipulating the appointments, promotions, and assignments of judges. Benazir's administration also employed transfers or the threat of transfers to intimidate recalcitrant jurists. The Supreme Court eventually fought back, in the so-called judges case, in which the Court severely limited the power of the prime minister to make judicial appointments.[13] The publicity generated by this case, in which Benazir's government was portrayed as having attempted to usurp the judiciary, further weakened the government.

Unprecedented levels of ethnonational conflict raged in Karachi during Benazir's second term. Operation Clean-Up, which called in the Pakistani army to quiet the violence, was a signal failure. Several thousand casualties resulted from the three-sided conflict between the army, muhajir nationalists, and Sindhis. The Sunni-Shia conflict, largely dormant during most of Pakistan's history, raged during the mid-1990s as well.

Underscoring her government's difficulties was the growing perception that her administration was the most corrupt in Pakistan's history. The flamboyant lifestyle and enormous wealth of Asif Ali Zardari, Bhutto's husband, was generally believed to be the fruit of widespread kickbacks and influence peddling.

But the last straw came after Murtaza Bhutto's death in a police encounter in September 1996. Benazir's first reaction was to claim that President Farooq Leghari was behind the "murder." The president, perhaps encouraged by the military establishment, dissolved her government; the Supreme Court, still smarting from the effects of her judicial policies, quickly legitimized his action.[14]

The Triumphant Return and
Devastating Fall of Nawaz (1997–1999)

Nawaz entered his second administration with an overwhelming majority in the National Assembly and moved quickly to consolidate his position. In April, he orchestrated the passage of the Thirteenth Amendment, which eliminated the power of the president to dissolve elected governments. In May, he pushed through the Fourteenth Amendment, which prohibited party defection, ensuring his unchallenged control of the parliament without the threat of a no-confidence vote. For the remainder of the year, he fended off challenges to his actions by the Supreme Court and the presidency, ultimately securing the resignation of President Farooq Leghari and Chief Justice Sajjad Ali Shah. (See Chapter 9.)

He also targeted his enemies. Building on the accountability process initiated by the caretaker regime of interim prime minister Meraj Khalid (1916–2003), Nawaz revised the 1996 Ehtesab (Accountability) Ordinance by introducing the 1997 Ehtesab Act.[15] The latter act had the effect of stopping legal procedures filed during Nawaz's absence from power against corrupt practices that allegedly took place during his first regime, and it strengthened and streamlined procedures to target Benazir's administrations. The fruit of his exercise was the April 15, 1999, conviction of Benazir and Asif Ali Zardari for corruption and corrupt practices, resulting in a five-year jail term and a fine of $8.6 million. This conviction disqualified Benazir from holding future elected office.[16]

In the context of increasing Shia-Sunni sectarian violence, Nawaz also introduced an Anti-Terrorism Act in 1997 that established antiterrorism courts to dispense speedy justice.[17] The newly introduced courts bypassed the normal judicial system. In 1998, Nawaz went even further by establishing military courts in Sindh province that had jurisdiction to try civilians for acts of terrorism. In 1999 the Supreme Court ruled that the establishment of military courts with civilian jurisdiction was extra-constitutional; earlier they had limited the authority of the antiterrorism courts by making their convictions subject to direct High Court appeal.[18]

Nawaz also used his overwhelming mandate to attempt to downsize government by offering attractive buyouts to government servants—the so-called golden handshake scheme. He also dismissed hundreds of Benazir's political appointees. Against great odds, Nawaz completed the first section of the Pakistan motorway—the link between Lahore and Islamabad—a project he had initiated during his first administration.

But his boldest policy shifts came with respect to foreign policy. In 1997, the Nawaz government sought to diffuse the Kashmir issue and improve, if not normalize, relations with India. Nawaz met with Indian prime minister H. D. Deve Gowda in February and with his successor, Inder Kumar Gujral, in June. But India's United Front government was in no position to take bold steps on the Indian side, and the talks were put on hold when the hard-line Bharatiya Janata Party assumed power in January 1998. In May, fulfilling a campaign pledge, the new Indian prime minister, Atal Bihari Vajpayee, ordered the testing of nuclear weapons. The effect was chilling in Pakistan, and Nawaz Sharif, particularly in the light of jingoistic statements made by prominent Indian politicians, was compelled to order a similar round of nuclear tests in June.[19] Despite such setbacks, or perhaps because of the perceived danger of allowing relations between India and Pakistan to deteriorate, Nawaz continued to pursue a peaceful dialog with India. Surprisingly, when Nawaz extended an invitation to Prime Minister Vajpayee for a state visit, the latter not only accepted but decided to travel by bus on the inaugural run of a new bus service between Lahore and Delhi. Vajpayee's highly publicized visit, the first by an Indian prime minister to Pakistan since 1951, was a remarkable success and the resultant policy statement—the so-called Lahore Declaration—promised that the two sides "shall intensify their efforts to resolve all issues, including the issue of Jammu and Kashmir; shall refrain from intervention and interference in each other's internal affairs . . . shall take immediate steps for reducing the risk of accidental or unauthorized use of nuclear weapons and discuss concepts and doctrines with a view to elaborating measures for confidence building in the nuclear and conventional fields, aimed at prevention of conflict."[20]

As pleasantries were being exchanged, however, plans were being perfected for the Pakistani military's incursion into Indian-occupied Kashmir, known as the Kargil Operation. Pakistani forces along with Kashmiri nationalists crossed the Line of Control, entering Indian territory in April and May and occupying the strategic heights north of Kargil. From such heights Pakistani forces threatened to cut the main road from Srinagar to Leh. The Kargil Operation was a carefully planned attempt to seize the advantage offered Pakistan in light of nuclear parity. Unlike in the 1965 Pakistani incursion, which had been repulsed by a massive Indian conventional response, Pakistani military strategists assumed India would not risk nuclear war over such a provocation. They were also counting on the reluctance of the international community to intervene. Pakistani defense strategists miscalculated on both scores. India soon proved willing to take significant casualties to regain the heights, and the international community was appalled by what it interpreted as Pakistani aggression. Facing insuperable international pressure, Nawaz ordered the forces to leave on July 4 as a prelude to his visit to the United States. The retreating Pakistani forces suffered severe losses.

It remains uncertain who originally ordered the Kargil Operation. It is certain, however, that the operation proved a humiliating defeat for Pakistan. It is also certain that the fallout from Kargil poisoned the already unhealthy relations between the military and Nawaz. Whether or not the military originally sanctioned the operation, the precipitate withdrawal of Pakistani forces was clearly a disaster and openly opposed by the Pakistani chief of army staff (COAS), General Parvez Musharraf.[21]

The consequent military coup hardly came as a surprise. Nawaz had made his government impervious to change from civilian sources, and his actions had angered and humiliated the military. The last straw came when Nawaz attempted to sack General Musharraf. When Musharraf refused to be dismissed, the military chose to follow the deposed COAS rather than their civilian commander in chief.

Musharraf's Enlightened Moderation (1999–2008)

Musharraf's first and most important task after seizing power was to build a modicum of domestic and international confidence in his regime and to restore confidence in Pakistan. During the sixteen months before he seized power, Pakistan had tested nuclear weapons, breaking the long-standing strictures of the nonproliferation regime. It had also prompted a dangerous war with India, threatening, in the worst case, a nuclear war. And its much heralded democratic transition had been interrupted by Musharraf's coup.

Accordingly, his first act was to issue a Provisional Constitution Order (PCO), which hedged on the issue of whether Musharraf's regime was really a martial law regime. He insisted on taking the title chief executive and not chief martial law administrator (as had been the title of his military predecessors Ayub, Yahya, and Zia) (Chapter 9).

He also moved quickly to clean up the corruption left by his civilian predecessors. In November he established the National Accountability Bureau (NAB), an extension of Nawaz's Ehtesab Bureau. The NAB was granted extensive powers to seize assets and detain individuals suspected of corruption. The NAB initiated hundreds of cases against loan defaulters and others who had engaged in corrupt practices since 1988, although it avoided implicating judicial or military officials. This had the immediate effect of weakening his political rivals, especially Nawaz Sharif, who eventually had to leave Pakistan to avoid imprisonment. But it is generally acknowledged that Musharraf's anticorruption policies, introduced with such fanfare and fervor, ultimately proved at best partially successful and were selectively implemented. Indeed, in 2007, as part of a political arrangement with Benazir Bhutto, Musharraf promulgated the National Reconciliation Ordinance (NRO), which vacated all pending proceedings initiated by Nawaz Sharif's Ehtesab Ordinance. This had the effect of allowing Benazir Bhutto and her husband, Asif Ali Zardari, both convicted in absentia, to return to Pakistan.

Also, Musharraf attempted to convey the message to his domestic and international critics that his government was eager to restore democracy in Pakistan—not the "sham democracy" of his civilian predecessors but rather a "true democracy" based on the establishment of meaningful elected local government institutions. The vehicle for this transformation was the Local Government Plan (LGP), the brainchild of the National Reconstruction Bureau. Reminiscent of Zia's Local Bodies and Ayub's Basic Democracies, it called for the reestablishment of a three-tiered system of elected councils established at the union, subdistrict (*tehsil*), and district (*zila*) levels. But unlike its predecessors, the LGP provided that such councils would be given extensive authority and comparable budgetary resources to address such additional responsibilities. Even more revolutionary, the LGP called for the elected *nazims* (mayors; chairs of *zila* councils) to be accorded authority to transfer or dismiss deputy commissioners (senior civil servants in the district); this provision was later weakened. Therefore, the

LGP envisaged the reversal of the relationship between civil bureaucrats and elected politicians, a relationship that had been a dominant feature of local government in South Asia since the mid-nineteenth century. The LGP also called for a wholesale revision of the local government departments, creating new departments and eliminating or merging others. It also called for the reservation of one-half (later revised to one-third) of all seats in the union councils for women. Some of the more radical features of the original LGP were worn away as the program was implemented. But the thrust of the reform remained intact during Musharraf's tenure. *Nazims* maintained formal authority over civilian bureaucrats; district councils were provided significant funds to enable them to meet, at least partially, their expanded functions; district-level departments were significantly restructured; and women were elected in unprecedented numbers to the union, *tehsil*, and *zila* councils.[22] The first series of elections to local government councils were held in 2001; the second in 2005.[23]

Like his military predecessors, Musharraf was obliged to legitimize his extra-constitutional seizure of power. Accordingly, following the well-established traditions of his forebears, he held a referendum to get himself elected as a civilian president, intimidated the judiciary into legitimizing his election, rewrote the constitution in order to hold elections and reconvene national and provincial assemblies, and convinced the newly elected assembly members to pass a constitutional amendment (the Seventeenth Amendment) to complete the transformation from martial law to a restored constitutional order.[24] But, as chronicled in Chapter 9, Musharraf's carefully crafted system broke down, a victim of his attempt to dismiss an unsympathetic chief justice and a recalcitrant Supreme Court. Following the unsuccessful attempt to remove Chief Justice Chaudhry, Musharraf had to depart from Pakistan's military-governance paradigm by taking the unprecedented action of staging what, in effect, was a second military coup against his own government—forcing the resignations of noncompliant members of Pakistan's superior judiciary through the promulgation of a second Provisional Constitution Order in December 2007. In the ensuing months Musharraf's government fell prey to the increasingly insistent demands of the Movement for the Restoration of the Judges led by both major political parties and the legal community. He was impeached on August 7 and resigned on August 18, 2008.

Musharraf's regime was deeply affected by international events and foreign policy concerns. This proved both a blessing and a curse. Following the US decision to respond to the horrors of September 11 with regime change in Afghanistan, Musharraf quickly abandoned Pakistan's support for the Taliban and became a frontline participant in the US-led global war against terrorism. Pakistan's new role had several immediate benefits, including begrudging international acceptance of the 1999 military coup and Musharraf's authoritarian domestic policies. It also provided Pakistan space with India, blunting the latter's claims that Pakistan had provoked the Kargil Incident and was responsible for cross-border terrorism with respect to Kashmir. Pakistan's participation in the coalition also ended the halfhearted sanctions imposed following its nuclear weapons testing. In other words, Musharraf's government was able to extricate itself from the international disabilities that faced it in the months immediately following the coup.

But the war in Afghanistan was deeply unpopular in Pakistan. Indeed, since joining the global war against terrorism, the Musharraf government had walked a tightrope between meeting US and international expectations while maintaining at least the semblance of an independent foreign policy. This task became even more difficult when the George W. Bush administration decided to invade Iraq in 2003. President Musharraf proved incredibly adept at walking this tightrope, and in 2005 he coined, perhaps facetiously, a term that characterized his foreign policy strategy: "enlightened moderation." The core of such a strategy was to adopt policies that responded to international perceptions and pressure but were implemented or crafted in a way that provided only minimal challenges to domestic interests. For instance, bowing to international pressure, Musharraf outlawed several Kashmiri jihadi organizations that the international community deemed "terrorist" but later allowed them to continue operating in Pakistan under different names.[25] Musharraf adopted a similar strategy with respect to Waziristan in 2003–2004. Responding to international criticism that Pakistan had been less than attentive to cross-border violations of the Afghan-Pakistani border, he authorized raids by paramilitary units into the Waziristan Agencies that resulted in highly publicized successes, as defined by numbers of militants killed. But such operations were limited and prudent, and when the occasion arose, he negotiated cease-fire agreements with the insurgent leadership.[26] The Waziristan policy was designed to demonstrate that Pakistan was being proactive with respect to pursuing the goals of the global war against terrorism; at the same time, it was designed to be limited in scope and confined to the remote and largely inaccessible Federally Administered Tribal Areas. As long as military action was confined to Wana and Miramshah, as opposed to Peshawar and Lahore, few would notice or care. But enlightened moderation was a fragile and dangerous policy, ultimately falling victim to the United States' growing public perception that Pakistan and its army were a less-than-enthusiastic, if not unreliable, ally, as well as to the sharp rise in domestic terrorism and violence associated with Pakistan's participation in what increasingly became known in Pakistan as the United States' war in Afghanistan.

Zardari: The Politics of Survival (2008–Present)

Following Musharraf's resignation, Asif Ali Zardari was elected as per the constitution through a weighted vote of the national and provincial assemblies (281 of 420 votes) on September 6, 2008. His elevation to the presidency was owing to his role as PPP cochairperson, an office bequeathed to him by the late Benazir Bhutto in her "political will." Zardari, an unlikely candidate to assume this role, not only inherited Musharraf's carefully crafted presidential-dominant system but also the monumental problems, both domestic and foreign, that had led to his resignation. His most pressing challenge was to finesse the PPP's support for the Movement for the Restoration of the Judges. It was a foregone conclusion that, if reinstated, the Iftikhar Chaudhry–led Supreme Court would invalidate the NRO, which in turn could revoke Zardari's amnesty from his criminal convictions. His first tactic was delay; he did not act on the issue until his hand was forced by the threat of the "Long March" on Islamabad organized by the PML(N) in support of the defrocked justices. On March 16, 2009, Zardari relented, restoring the superior court judges, adding them to the ranks of those who had taken their oaths under Musharraf's December 2007 PCO. This occasioned further delay as the reinstated Chaudhry Court had to clear the detritus of the interim Hamid Dogar–led Court's rulings before eventually nullifying the PCO in July 2009 and upholding the resultant dismissal of the rogue justices on October 13, 2009. It took the Court two more months to nullify the NRO (see Chapter 9).

On another front Zardari and the PPP had to mollify the political opposition, which was unrelenting in its demands for the restoration of the 1973 constitution. Substantively this meant that the presidential-dominant system inherited by Zardari should be replaced by a parliamentary system of government that would rein in the extensive powers of the presidency. Here, Zardari's approach was a grand compromise that ultimately resulted in the passage of the Eighteenth Amendment (Chapter 9). The main features of the amendment were (1) elimination of the president's effective authority to dissolve the national and provincial assemblies; (2) empowerment of the office of the prime minister; (3) reduction of the role of the president to head of state; (4) a significant increase in the power of the four provincial governments at the expense of the federal government; and (5) placement of Musharraf's local government system under the control of the provincial governments, where district and local councils would languish and die. It is very important to note that the Eighteenth Amendment did not revise one of the more important pillars of Musharraf's presidential system, Article 248(2), which reads, "No criminal proceedings whatsoever shall be instituted or continued against the President or the Governor in any court during his term of office."

Although the Eighteenth Amendment stripped the presidency of its formal power, Zardari had escaped with his authority largely intact; as the PPP cochairperson and heir to the Bhutto legacy, he continued to exercise informal control over Prime Minister Syed Yousaf Raza Gilani, and the Court could not touch him as he remained immune from prosecution. The Court tried nonetheless by insisting that Gilani reopen the criminal cases against Zardari that had been suspended by the NRO. Prime Minister Gilani delayed creatively but was eventually held in contempt of court on April 12, 2012, and forced to leave office on June 19, 2012. One of Zardari's handpicked candidates, Raja Parvaiz Ashraf, was selected by the PPP-dominated National Assembly to replace him.[27]

Zardari also inherited Pakistan's very complicated and troublesome foreign policy dilemmas as well. His approach has been to deflect criticism of his government's shortcomings by attributing them to the legacy of Pakistan's military regimes (e.g., Zia's Islamist policies; Musharraf's reliance on nonstate paramilitaries to counter India) and to the continuing interference of the military since 2008, as the army and the all-powerful Inter-Services Intelligence (ISI) do not allow his well-meaning civilian government to control foreign policy. This has proven a convincing argument with both domestic and international audiences. Zardari's government remained relatively unscathed by the fallout from the Mumbai attacks in November 2008, which were attributed to terrorist groups that had enjoyed the support of the ISI since the 1980s. In September 2009 the Zardari government was the beneficiary of the US Congress's Enhanced Partnership with Pakistan Act (Kerry-Lugar Bill), an economic aid package (Chapters 13 and 30) that conditioned the distribution of US aid on the continuation of civilian rule in the state. Zardari's government has also been able to survive the greatest level of civil violence (terrorism, sectarian and ethnonational conflict) in Pakistan since the 1971 war.

It is possible, however unlikely the prospect may have been when he assumed power in 2008, that Zardari will someday be considered the most successful civilian political leader in Pakistan's sixty-five–year history. If the transition to another civilian government through a fair, democratic, and timely process (the National Assembly completes its term in March 2013) transpires as scheduled, Zardari will have presided over the first Pakistani government to have reached its term limit without an extra-constitutional interruption. He will also have presided over the transition from a presidential to a parliamentary constitution, a true restoration of the 1973 constitution. Of course, if this happy outcome transpires, it will have come despite Zardari's best efforts to derail this process, efforts thwarted at every turn so far by the activist machinations of the Iftikhar Chaudhry–led Supreme Court. But at the time of this writing (February 2013), Zardari's legacy is far from assured. His current term of office as president expires in September 2013. For him to continue in office past that date, the newly elected national and provincial assemblies would have to reelect him, and the Chaudhry-led Supreme Court (Iftikhar Chaudhry does not reach retirement age until December 2013) would have to allow that to happen.

SUGGESTED READINGS

Kennedy, Charles H. *Bureaucracy in Pakistan*. Karachi: Oxford University Press, 1987.

Kennedy, Charles H., and Cynthia Botteron, eds. *Pakistan: 2005*. Karachi: Oxford University Press, 2006.

Khan, Hamid. *Constitutional and Political History of Pakistan*. 2nd ed. Karachi: Oxford University Press, 2009.

Siddiqa, Ayesha. *Military Inc.: Inside Pakistan's Military*. New York: Pluto, 2007.

Talbot, Ian. *Pakistan: A Modern History*. London: Hurst, 1998.

Waseem, Mohammad. *Democratization in Pakistan: A Study of the 2002 Elections*. Karachi: Oxford University Press, 2006.

Ziring, Lawrence. *Pakistan in the Twentieth Century: A Political History*. Karachi: Oxford University Press, 1997.

NOTES

1. For details, see Charles H. Kennedy, *Bureaucracy in Pakistan* (Karachi: Oxford University Press, 1987), esp. 213–214.

2. Lawrence Ziring, *Pakistan: The Enigma of Political Development* (London: Dawson, 1980), 88.

3. Altaf Gauhar, "Pakistan: Ayub Khan's Abdication," *Third World Quarterly* (January 1985): 108.

4. Asaf Hussain, *Elite Politics in an Ideological State: The Case of Pakistan* (London: Dawson, 1979), 137.

5. See, for instance, Mohammad Ayub Khan, *Friends, Not Masters: A Political Autobiography* (Karachi: Oxford University Press, 1967).

6. For details, see Ronald J. Herring, *Land to the Tiller: The Political Economy of Agrarian Reform in South Asia* (New Haven, CT: Yale University Press, 1983).

7. For details, see Kennedy, *Bureaucracy in Pakistan,* 129–152.

8. Herring, *Land to the Tiller,* 100–103, 117–125.

9. See Government of Pakistan, Cabinet Division, *Ansari Commission's Report on Form of Government 4th August 1983* (Islamabad: Printing Corporation of Pakistan Press, 1984).

10. Kennedy, *Bureaucracy in Pakistan,* 122–125, 145–150.

11. Kennedy, *Bureaucracy in Pakistan,* 122–125.

12. For details of the Zia years, see Robert Wirsing, *Pakistan's Security Under Zia, 1977–1988: The Policy Imperatives of a Peripheral Asian State* (New York: St. Martin's, 1991); Shahid Javed Burki and Craig Baxter, *Pakistan Under the Military: Eleven Years of Zia ul-Haq* (Boulder, CO: Westview Press, 1991).

13. *Al-Jehad Trust v. Federation of Pakistan and Others, PLD* 1996 SC 324. For a discussion, see Nasim Hasan Shah, "Judiciary in Pakistan: A Quest for Independence," in *Pakistan: 1997,* ed. Craig Baxter and Charles H. Kennedy (Boulder, CO: Westview Press, 1998).

14. *Benazir Bhutto v. President of Pakistan, PLD* 1998 SC 388.

15. Respectively, Ehtesab Ordinance no. CXI of 1996 (November 18, 1996) and Ehtesab Act (Act IX) of 1997 (May 31, 1997). See discussion in S. M. Zafar, "Constitutional Developments in Pakistan, 1997–99," in *Pakistan: 2000,* ed. Charles H. Kennedy and Craig Baxter (Lanham, MD: Lexington, 2000), 1–23.

16. *State v. Benazir Bhutto, PLD* 1999 SC 535.

17. Anti-Terrorism Act (XXVI) of 1997 (August 20, 1997).

18. Respectively, *Liaquat Hussain v. Federation of Pakistan, PLD* 1999 SC 504, and *Mehram Ali v. Federation of Pakistan, PLD* 1998 SC 1445.

19. See Devin T. Hagerty, "Kashmir and Nuclear Question Revisited"; Thomas P. Thornton, "Long Way to Lahore: Pakistan and India Negotiate," in Kennedy and Baxter, *Pakistan: 2000,* 45–62, 81–106.

20. The complete text of the Lahore Declaration and its attendant memorandum of understanding is found in Thornton, "Long Way to Lahore," 58–60.

21. See Peter Lavoy, ed., *Asymmetric Warfare in South Asia: The Causes of the Kargil Conflict* (New York: Cambridge University Press, 2009). V. P. Malik, *Kargil* (Delhi: Harper, 2006); Parvez Musharraf, *In the Line of Fire: A Memoir* (New York: Free Press, 2006).

22. In the 2005 local government elections, 6,132 union councils were selected (each council has thirteen members). Therefore, 79,716 union councilors were elected, and one-third of these seats (26,306) were reserved for women.

23. For an analysis of the first local government election, see Farzana Bari, *Local Government Elections December 2000 (Phase One)* (Islamabad: Pattan Development Corporation, 2001); Mohammad Waseem, *Democratization in Pakistan: A Study of the 2002 Elections* (Karachi: Oxford University Press, 2006).

24. See Charles H. Kennedy, "A User's Guide to Guided Democracy: Musharraf and the Pakistani Military Governance Paradigm," in *Pakistan: 2005,* ed. Charles H. Kennedy and Cynthia Botteron (Karachi: Oxford University Press, 2006), 120–157.

25. Charles H. Kennedy, "The Creation and Development of Pakistan's Anti-terrorism Regime, 1997–2002," in *Religious Radicalism and Security in South Asia,* ed. Robert Wirsing and Mohan Malik (Honolulu: Asia-Pacific Centre for Security Studies, 2004), 387–411.

26. See International Crisis Group (ICG), "Pakistan's Tribal Areas: Appeasing the Militants," Asia Report no. 125, December 11, 2006, http://www.crisisgroup.org/en/regions/asia/south-asia/pakistan/125-pakistans-tribal-areas-appeasing-the-militants.aspx; ICG, "Pakistan: Countering Militancy in FATA," Asia Report no. 178, October 21, 2009, http://www.crisisgroup.org/en/regions/asia/south-asia/pakistan/178-pakistan-countering-militancy-in-fata.aspx.

27. Raja Ashraf is also a target of the Court for alleged corrupt practices committed during his tenure as the federal minister for water and power. His "rental power project," designed to increase electricity production, was a dismal failure, generating little electricity but a lot of cash. The Supreme Court directed that he resign this position, which he did in 2011. During this time his detractors in the media dubbed him "Raja Rental." His alleged corruption has dogged him since he assumed the position of prime minister; the Court has urged him to resign from this position as well.

13

Problems and Prospects

Pakistan faces an uncertain future. More than six decades after independence, it still confronts profound challenges to its integrity as an independent nation-state, stemming from numerous domestic shortcomings as well as its hazardous international-security environment. This chapter presents a brief discussion of the three most intractable challenges currently facing the state.

Institution Building

Pakistan's greatest shortcoming since partition has been its inability to establish stable, effective political institutions. The litany of its failures is long: numerous constitutions, dormant legislatures, ineffective political parties, and persistent military rule. From the perspective of political development, Pakistan is a signal failure. Unfortunately, such difficulties are likely to continue into the foreseeable future.

First, there is the question of national unity. For a state to build effective political institutions, a broad agreement on the fundamentals of the state is required. As demonstrated numerous times in Pakistan's history, however, no such agreement exists. Pakistan is torn by ethnonationalism. Even the potentially unifying effects of a shared religion, Islam, have at times constituted an additional source of ideological or sectarian disunity throughout Pakistan's troubled history.

Second, Pakistan's failures of institution building have been both a cause and a consequence of additional failures. Pakistan's policy makers have often sought the quick-fix solution to problems of institution building, scuttling existing programs or institutions when they encountered resistance. Pakistan's checkered history of local government is a case in point. Not one of the numerous local government programs established over the decades since partition has survived a change of regime; many have not lasted long enough for that. The most recent local government system, introduced by Parvez Musharraf in 2001, was the most carefully articulated and most fully implemented of such programs. Nonetheless it suffered the same fate as its predecessors, savaged by the passage of the Eighteenth Amendment in 2010, which placed local government in the unsympathetic hands of provincial governments.

Third, the stakes of politics in Pakistan are extremely high. The groups in control share the considerable perquisites of office; those out of power are often consigned to prison or exile. In such a setting, the emphasis is not on creating enduring institutions but rather on gaining and maintaining power. Also, at regime change the winners tend to adopt policies that discredit and disestablish the accomplishments of their predecessors.

Finally, like many new states, Pakistan faces the problem of chronic military rule. It has become an axiom of political science that once the threshold of military involvement in civilian politics has been crossed, crossing it again becomes increasingly easy. Indeed, Pakistani politics has been dominated by the military for fifty years, since 1958. The country has been under martial law for fourteen years, and military leaders or former military leaders have been the heads of government for thirty-two years. Military regimes are notoriously inept at creating representative political institutions, as Pakistan's experience with military regimes has clearly demonstrated.

External Threats

Pakistan faces one of the most difficult security environments in the world. On the east is India; on the west is war-torn Afghanistan. India is Pakistan's oldest and most troublesome opponent. Pakistan has fought three major wars with India (1948, 1965, and 1971) and came perilously close to a fourth in 1999 owing to the Pakistan-inspired Kargil Operation. The Kashmiri nationalist struggle, the source of much Indo-Pakistani conflict, continues to defy solution. Accordingly, many Pakistanis view Indians as implacable foes and vice versa. And since the summer of 1998, both states have had nuclear weapons arsenals. During winter 2001–2002, in the aftermath of the December 13 attack on the Lok Sabha in Delhi by militants whom India claimed were Pakistani-inspired Kashmiri jihadists, tensions nearly reached the breaking point between the two states. War was averted only by skillful diplomatic intervention by the international community and statesmanlike prudence on the part of Indian and Pakistani decision makers. In November 2008 India and Pakistan came close to war again following the Mumbai attacks attributed to Pakistanis. Since that time, the atmospherics of the India-Pakistan relationship have improved. Nonetheless, considerable tension remains between the two states, fueled by the unresolved issue of Kashmir, chronic Indian claims that Pakistan continues to inspire cross-border terrorism, and the firm belief among many Pakistanis, particularly in the establishment, that India still has hegemonic designs on its western neighbor.

Pakistan's difficulties with Afghanistan, also not of recent origin, were exacerbated by the Soviet occupation of that country (1979–1989). The Soviet invasion of Afghanistan caused millions of Afghans to flee to Pakistan as refugees. Their presence placed severe demands on Pakistan's economy and significantly increased underemployment, particularly in the North-West Frontier Province (now Khyber-Pakhtunwha) and Balochistan. Their presence also encouraged continuing Pakistani involvement in the Afghan civil war (1989–2001). Segments of the Pakistani military, particularly the Inter-Services Intelligence (ISI), became deeply involved in Afghan politics. The ISI is generally acknowledged to have been crucial to the organization, training, and arming of the Taliban, the Islam-oriented Afghan military regime that eventually controlled most of the state from the late 1990s until its ouster in 2001. Moreover, thousands of Pakistani young men and boys, joined by Afghan youth from the refugee camps, mostly Pakhtuns, fought with mujahedeen groups contesting the Soviet occupation and later with the Taliban after the Soviet withdrawal. Since the events of 9/11, Pakistan has been obliged to join the United States' global war against terrorism.

Pakistan's policy makers, understandably, have been very concerned with the security of the state. One indicator of such concern is military spending. Pakistan (2011) has a standing army of 1.5 million and spends nearly $5.7 billion per year on defense. Yet Pakistan's military is dwarfed by India's, which has 3.7 million soldiers. India spends $48.9 billion per year on its military.[1]

A second consequence of uncertain security has been Pakistan's nuclear weapons program. After India exploded a nuclear device in 1974, Prime Minister Zulfiqar Ali Bhutto launched a heavily publicized nuclear-development program in Pakistan. However, the international community, particularly the United States, disapproved of Pakistan's attempt at nuclear proliferation, and the United States subsequently applied pressure on France (which had agreed in 1976 to sell a nuclear reprocessing plant to Pakistan) to withdraw from nuclear agreements with Pakistan. When Pakistan continued clandestinely to seek nuclear capability, the United States invoked provisions of the Symington amendment to the Foreign Assistance Act in 1977 and cut all assistance except food aid to Pakistan, although this amendment was interpreted in 1981 as permitting the provision of new economic and military assistance. For the next seventeen years, the question of whether Pakistan possessed nuclear weapons capability generated much speculation. Successive governments consistently stated that Pakistan did not have the bomb but was seeking nuclear capability solely for peaceful purposes. Despite these assurances, the George H. W. Bush administration, invoking the Pressler amendment, failed to certify that Pakistan was not seeking to develop nuclear weapons capability and in October 1990 suspended military and economic aid to Pakistan. The effects of the Pressler amendment were relaxed in September 1995 by the passage of the Brown amendment to the Foreign Assistance Act. Uncertainty with respect to Pakistan's nuclear weapons capability was dispelled when Pakistan tested five nuclear devices in June 1998, following similar tests by India. This action violated the main tenet of the nuclear nonproliferation regime. A host of international economic and military sanctions on the state attended the violation and were eventually lifted fully subsequent to Pakistan's joining the international coalition targeting the Taliban in 2001. In 2004 there was considerable international perturbation associated with the confession by Dr. Abdul Qadeer Khan (b. 1935), the architect of Pakistan's nuclear program, that he had sold nuclear secrets to Libya, Iran, and North Korea. Musharraf contained the fallout from this crisis by placing Khan under house arrest, though pardoning him from prosecution by Pakistani courts.[2]

Pakistani-US Relations and the Global War Against Terrorism

Pakistan's most important ally is the United States. But the relationship has had many twists and turns. Pakistan's initial foreign policy called for nonalignment, but that stance began to change in the mid-1950s as the United States sought allies to combat the spread of communism. The United States found its most ardent South Asian support in the person of Muhammad Ayub Khan, and until 1965 Pakistan was its "most allied ally." But this arrangement ended when the United States stopped arms shipments to Pakistan during the 1965 Pakistani-Indian war. Until such aid was discontinued, the United States had been Pakistan's primary arms supplier, providing $1.2 billion in military aid from 1954 to 1965. The United States viewed the stoppage of arms as conducive to peace in South Asia; Pakistan viewed it as a betrayal by an ally. Between 1965 and 1979, relations between the two states remained cordial, and the United States periodically resumed limited arms sales to Pakistan, but never at or near pre-1965 levels. Indeed, during the 1971 war the United States provided little material assistance to Pakistan despite its well-publicized "tilt toward Pakistan."

US-Pakistani relations reached their nadir in 1979, when the US embassy in Islamabad was burned by an angry mob instigated by alleged US involvement in a plot to occupy the Kaaba in Mecca. However, this trend of events was reversed when the Soviet Union launched its invasion of Afghanistan in December 1979. After a change of administration in Washington and a year of negotiations, Pakistan emerged with a six-year, $3.2 billion arms-sale and economic-assistance package in 1981. This agreement was renewed for a three-year period in 1988 at $600 million per year. These agreements made Pakistan the third-largest recipient of US security aid in the world (after Israel and Egypt). In October 1990 the United States suspended economic and military aid to Pakistan, charging that Pakistan was continuing attempts to acquire nuclear weapons. This aid was partially restored in 1995, but it was halted again following Pakistan's 1998 nuclear testing.[3]

But again events in Afghanistan reversed this trend. Pakistan, after assuming the role of frontline state in the war against terrorism, once again became the recipient of significant US military and economic aid, which rose from (USD 2010) $3 million in 2001 to over $1.6 billion in 2002, and over the next five years, total US assistance to Pakistan exceeded $10 billion. Around 60 percent of the total was distributed under the Coalition Support Fund designed to aid countries associated with the global war against terrorism. Pakistan paid dearly for this financial assistance: it allowed the United States to use its airbases in antiterrorism operations, facilitated the flow of supplies through its territory to sustain the coalition forces in Afghanistan, shared intelligence, and captured, detained, and in many instances transported to US authorities hundreds of suspects implicated in terrorist activities. Nonetheless, there remained considerable US sentiment that supporting Pakistan, particularly Musharraf's military regime, was a mistake. In 2005, prompted by the Abdul Qadeer Khan affair, Congress passed the Ackerman amendment, reminiscent of the Pressler amendment, which required the CIA to make annual reports to Congress about Pakistan's nuclear activities, democratic development, and counterterrorism efforts.

The changes of government in the respective states—the election of Barack Obama in the United States and the establishment of Asif Ali Zardari's civilian regime—led to a change in US policy toward Afghanistan, the so-called Af-Pak strategy. As part of this strategy, the United States presented Pakistan with both a carrot and a stick: the carrot—the Enhanced Partnership with Pakistan Act of 2009 (Kerry-Lugar Bill), which called for the continuation of military and very significantly increased nonmilitary assistance to Pakistan ($1.5 billion per year for five years); the stick—a rapid increase in the use of unmanned aircraft (drones) to target "insurgent safe havens" in the Federally Administered Tribal Areas.

Both the incentives and the disincentives have proven problematic to Pakistani-US relations. The Kerry-Lugar Bill required that the disbursement of funds be conditioned upon the certification that Pakistan met counterterrorism requirements as established by the US Congress. As of 2013, only a small fraction of the nonmilitary aid funds authorized by the Kerry-Lugar Bill have actually been disbursed, and military assistance under the Coalition Support Fund has been interrupted or delayed on several occasions. Even more problematic than promises unfulfilled have been the effects of the US droning campaign on Pakistani-US relations. Before the start of the Obama administration, the United States had undertaken a total of forty-two droning strikes on targets within Pakistani territory (twenty-eight in the last six months of 2008); since the start of 2009, there have been 345.[4] In Pakistan the attacks are almost universally condemned as a violation of Pakistani sovereignty and as evidence of the impotence of Pakistan's government and military in protecting its borders from the designs of the United States, ostensibly its closest ally. The droning campaign has become the driving force behind the wholesale deterioration of the Pakistani public's perception of the United States and has contributed significantly to the virulent rise of anti-Americanism in the state. In the United States the droning campaign is thought to provide evidence that Pakistan is unwilling or unable to fulfill its part of the strategic partnership with the United States and demonstrates that Pakistan is an unreliable and disingenuous ally. The unilateral raid by US Navy Seals on Osama bin Laden's house in Abbottabad on May 2, 2011, conveyed similar messages. Indeed, in the aftermath of the raid, US officials repeatedly asserted that Pakistani officials were not provided with prior warning as the United States feared that such information would be leaked and foil the mission.

There has been a horrific rise in violence within Pakistan that seems to be associated with Pakistan's role in the Afghanistan War as well. The incidences of suicide bombing, in which the primary targets have been governmental institutions and personnel, have grown exponentially in recent years: prior to 2002 a suicide bombing had never been reported in Pakistan; from 2002 to 2007, 21 were reported; since 2007, 322 have been reported. Similarly, the total number of fatalities owing to terrorist violence in Pakistan has risen from an average annual total of 620 (2002–2006) to an average annual total of 6,994 (2007–2011).[5] It is also telling to note that around two times as many Pakistanis as Afghans died as victims of violence (2007–2011): 35,750 Pakistanis to 17,924 Afghans.[6]

Conclusion

Today Pakistan continues to grapple with many of the same problems it faced in 1947. First, Pakistan remains a relatively poor country. Although its economy has expanded rapidly since independence, the population has grown at an almost equal rate. Furthermore, the inequalities in distribution of resources have remained largely unaffected by such economic growth. Second, Pakistan still struggles to choose a structure of government acceptable to its people and to form stable and effective institutions. Third, Pakistan faces an insecure international environment. Finally, Pakistan is still searching for a distinctive national identity.

Pakistan's survival will require a combination of luck, dynamic and skillful leadership, an acceptable settlement of its long-standing constitutional and representational disabilities, and the cooperation of its diverse population.

SUGGESTED READINGS

Kux, Dennis. *The United States and Pakistan, 1947–2000: Disenchanted Allies.* Baltimore: Johns Hopkins University Press, 2001.

Rais, Rasul B. *Recovering the Frontier State: War, Ethnicity, and State in Afghanistan.* New York: Longmans, 2008.

Rizvi, Hassan Askari. *Military, State, and Security in Pakistan.* New York: St. Martin's, 2000.

Schaffer, Howard B., and Teresita C. Schaffer. *How Pakistan Negotiates with the United States: Riding the Roller Coaster.* Washington, DC: United States Institute of Peace, 2011.

NOTES

1. Stockholm International Peace Research Initiative (SIPRI) (www.sipri.org, accessed November 1, 2012).

2. Devin T. Hagerty, *The Consequences of Nuclear Proliferation: Lessons from South Asia* (Cambridge, MA: MIT Press, 1998).

3. Dennis Kux, *The United States and Pakistan, 1947–2000: Disenchanted Allies* (Baltimore: Johns Hopkins University Press, 2001).

4. Calculated by author from the New America Foundation, "The Year of the Drone," Counterterrorism Strategy Initiative, http://counterterrorism.newamerica.net/drones (accessed February 14, 2013). Also see International Human Rights and Conflict Resolution Clinic, Stanford Law School and Global Justice Clinic, NYU School of Law, "Living under Drones: Death, Injury and Trauma to Civilians from US Drone Practices in Pakistan," September 2012, http://livingunderdrones.org/report.

5. Derived from the South Asia Terrorism Portal (www.satp.org, accessed February 14, 2013).

6. Pakistan data derived from the South Asia Terrorism Portal (www.satp.org, accessed February 14, 2013]); Afghanistan data are derived from Susan G. Chesser, "Afghanistan Casualties: Military Forces and Civilians," Congressional Research Service, September 6, 2012, http://www.fas.org/sgp/crs/natsec/R41084.pdf. The Afghanistan number does not include US and NATO casualties.

PART III

BANGLADESH

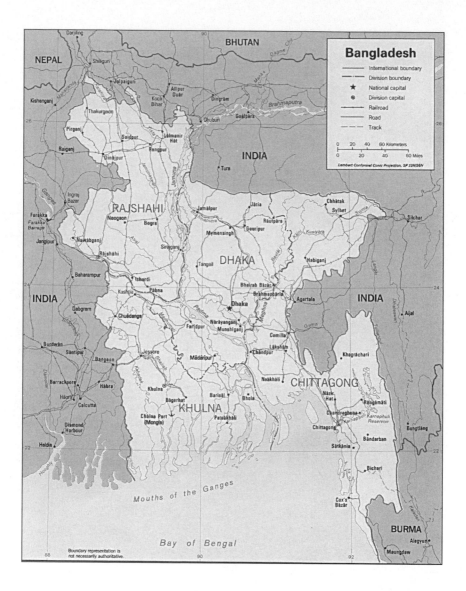

14

Political Culture and Heritage

After an intense and bloody *muktijuddho* (war of liberation), Bangladesh earned its independence in December 1971. Western countries, pursuing their own geopolitical agendas, viewed the conflict in Bangladesh from March 24 through December 16, 1971, as a civil war, thereby absolving themselves of any complicity in the mass killings that took place there. Radical scholars interpret what happened in Bangladesh in those nine months in 1971 as something close to genocide, to which Bangladeshis responded with courage, tenacity, and considerable self-sacrifice. Bangladesh is usually represented as a country prone to natural disaster where poverty is rampant. A Muslim-majority country with one of the highest population densities in the world and a political system that is continually embroiled in street politicking, Bangladesh is sometimes viewed as a country teetering on the precipice of internal implosion. Others view the country as heading toward radicalism, fundamentalism, and terrorism, both national and global.

Bangladesh in the first decade of the twenty-first century is one of the largest contributors to United Nations peacekeeping operations, and the country is transforming itself through the use of appropriate technology and novel organizational arrangements at grassroots levels. Its microcredit enterprise initiative is recognized as having a global impact and constituting a major new instrument in the fight to eradicate poverty throughout the world. Bangladesh has made such progress toward its millennium goals that many predict it will become a medium-income country within twenty years. In this chapter we examine the emergence of Bangladesh, its historical evolution and challenges, and the nature of its society and culture.

The Bangladesh Heritage

Bangladesh is bordered on the west, north, and east by India. On the east it is also bordered by Myanmar and on the south by the Bay of Bengal. Ancient Bengal primarily comprised several political and administrative units, which, at times, could be kingdoms such as Varendra, Vanga, Samatata, Harikela, Radha, Gauda, Anga, Vardhamana, Suhma, and Videha. Today it is composed of Varendra, Gauda, Radha, a part of Vardhamana, Vanga, Samatata, and Harikela.

Two major rivers, the Ganges and Brahmaputra, originate in the Himalayas and traverse Bangladesh. A third major river is the Meghna, originating in the Assam province of India. These three rivers are the life source of the country, converging to deposit tons of silt in the rich agricultural soil of the Bengal Delta. The implications of this phenomenon for the social, economic, and political life of Bangladesh are immense.

The combined catchment basin of the Ganges, Brahmaputra, and Meghna measures 1.758 million square kilometers—more than twelve times the size of Bangladesh. The amount of rainfall in the catchment basin of the Bengal rivers is more than four times the rainfall in the Mississippi River Basin, although in terms of area the former is less than half the latter.

The rivers of the Bengal Delta carry about 2 billion tons of sediment annually—far more than any other river system anywhere in the world. Under average conditions, from June to September, 775 billion cubic meters of water flow into Bangladesh through the main rivers, and an additional 184 billion cubic meters of stream flow are generated by rainfall in Bangladesh. This may be compared with the annual flow of only 12 billion cubic meters of the Colorado River at Yuma, Arizona. The combined channel of the Ganges, Brahmaputra, and Meghna is about three times the size of the Mississippi channel.[1]

Ancient Heritage

The Bangladeshi cultural and political heritage is drawn from a wide variety of sources. (See Table 14.1 for a list of historical studies on Bangladesh.) Religiously, Buddhism, Hinduism, and Islam have helped define its identity. Culturally, Dravidian, Mongol, Aryan, Persian, and Arab influences have been important. Not much is known about prehistoric Bangladesh. Information can be gleaned from copper and stone inscriptions and *prasastis* (eulogies). There is a general agreement among scholars that a tribe inhabited the Mahasthan area in Bogra district as early as the third century BC. Archeological and numismatic evidence from Mahasthangarh reveals the remains of one of the oldest cities of Bangladesh, known in the pre-Muslim period as Pundranagara ("the city of the Pundra," a tribe mentioned in the Veda). In the modern period (thirteenth to fifteenth centuries), the name changed to Mahasthan ("great or sacred place"). In 2007, a 1,500-year-old temple was discovered in Bogra about four kilometers west of Mahasthangarh.

By the fifth century BC tribes from the west had moved into Bengal. The interaction between the western tribes speaking an Indo-European language and the traditional people of Bengal is central to understanding the heritage of Bangladesh. Over many centuries the culture of the Ganges River became dominant in the delta as the traditional peoples moved to the periphery of the Bengal Delta. During this period the Bengali language and literature were Sanskritized. Prior to that the people used the Buddhist-Sanskrit Magadh-Prakrit family of languages. The descendants of the Gangetic people speak modern Bengali. However, modern Bengali has incorporated many non-Indo-European language groups, such as Austroasiatic, Dravidian, and Sino-Tibetan.[2]

Hindu and Buddhist Period

The earliest written records of the Bangladesh region can be traced to the tenth century AD. The earliest existing work is *Ramacharitam*, by Sandhyâkaranandi. It provides the genealogy of the Pala dynasty of Bengal and references the Raghu people of Bengal. Other scholarly works mention the Radha and Suhma peoples living in western and southwestern Bengal and the Vanga people living in central and eastern Bengal. Two dynasties, the Palas and the Senas, have played an important role in the sociocultural development of Bangladesh. While the Palas were Buddhists, the Senas were primarily Hindus. The Pala dynasty lasted from AD 750 to 1155. The Sena dynasty began around AD 1095 and collapsed in AD 1202, when the Sena capital, Nadia, fell to the Ghurid dynasty of the Delhi sultanate.

Prior to AD 750, parts of the land that later became Bangladesh were ruled by the Gupta dynasty. During the more than four centuries of Pala rule, there were eighteen rulers. The Pala dynasty began with Gopala and ended when Govindapala lost the Indian province of Bihar to the Delhi sultanate. The much shorter rule of the Senas, which lasted only 128 years, began with the rule of Vijayasena. Four other rulers followed. The last dynastic ruler was Kesavasena, who governed for only three years. The Pala rulers were ardent Buddhists, and their seat of power was located near modern-day Vikrampur, which is not far from Dhaka. The Senas were a Hindu dynasty that revived Brahmanism in Bengal. Records are sparse, but two anthologies, *Subhâsitaratnakosa*, consisting of verses from 275 authors from the seventh to the eleventh centuries, and *Saduktikarnâmtra,* also a compilation of verses in Sanskrit, provide a representation of the society, culture, religion, and economics of ancient Bangladesh. Many of the authors of the two anthologies are Bengalis. Two

TABLE 14.1 Authoritative Works on Bengal

Text	Author	Period Covered
(AD)		
ANCIENT PERIOD		
Râmacharitam	Sandhyâkaranandi	1075–1062
Pan Sam Zon Zang	Sumpa Mkhanpo	1747
Aryâsapkasati	Govardhanâchârya	c. 1200
ANTHOLOGIES		
Subhâsitaratnakosa	Vidyakara	1178–1206
Saduktikarnâmtra	Shridharadasa	1205
MEDIEVAL PERIOD		
Tabaqat-I-Nasiri	Minhaj-I-Siraj	1246–1266
Tarikh-I-Firuz Shahi	Ziauddin Barawi	1266–1357
Tarikh-I-Firuz Shahi	Shams-I-Siraj Afif	1351–1388
Futuh-Us-Salatin	Khwaja Abdul Malik Isami	1349
Tarikh-I-Mubarak Shahi	Yahya bin Ahmed bin Abdullah Sarhindi	1421–1434
Qiran-Us-Sadain	Amir Khausraus	1280–1325
Rehlâ	Ibn Batuta	1346–1347
Yin Yai Sheng Lan	Mahuan	1390–1411
Tarikh-I-Sher Shahi	Abbas Khan Sherwani	1538–1576
Tarikh-I-Khan Jahani	Khwaja Niamatullah	1538–1576
Makhjan-I-Aghani	Khwaja Niamatullah	
Tarikh-I-Shahi	Ahmed Yadgar	1538–1576
Tarikh-I-Daudi	Abdullah	1572–1576
Tabaqat-I-Akbari	Nizamuddin Ahmed Bakhshi	1592–1593
Tarikh-I-Frishta	Abul Qasim Firishta	1570–1623
Baharistan-I-Ghaybi	Mirza Nathan	1632
Sabh-I-Sadiq	Muhammad Sadiq	1628–1660
Ajiba-I-Ghariba	Shihabuddin Talish	1660–1688
Tarikh-I-Mulk Assam	Shihabuddin Talish	1660–1688
AFTER THE FALL OF THE EMPEROR AURANGZEB		
Naubahar-I-Murshid Guli Khan	Azad Husain	1707+
Ahwal-I-Mahabat Jang	Yusuk Ali	1740–1752
Muzaffar Namah	Karam Ali	1722–1772
Tarikh-I-Bangala	Salimullah	1760–1764
Wariat-I-Fath Bangala	Muhammad Wafa	
Siyar-Ul-Mutakhkherin	Ghulam Husain Tabatabai	
Riaz-Us-Salatin	Ghulam Husain Salim Zaidpuri	1788

Source: "Historiography," in *Banglapedia* (Dhaka: Asiatic Society of Bangladesh 2003), 5:93–104.

poems, one by Yogesvara about life and another by Vasukalpa in praise of rulers, provide a portrait of ancient Bangladesh.[3]

Verse 291
The days are sweet with ripening of sugar cane;
The autumn rice is high;
And Brahmins, being overfed at feasts
To which the leading families invite them,
Find the heat grows hard to bear.

Verse 1381
O King Kamboja, when your victorious army marches forth,
From the flood of dust raised by the hoofs of afghan steeds
And spreading to kiss the sky
The horses of the sun seem decked with rouge
And the lotuses that grow in heaven's stream
Anticipate the closing of their sunset sleep.

The Muslim Period

If the ancient culture of modern Bangladesh was more Buddhist than Hindu, the advent of Islam in the thirteenth century further transformed the country and posed the challenge of how to merge the social customs of the region with the religious practices of Islam.[4] Although Islam is generally thought to have been introduced in the thirteenth century, there is some evidence that Arab merchants visited the coastal areas of Bangladesh, especially Chittagong, as early as the eighth century. A silver coin found at an archeological site at the Paharpur monastery identified as issued by Abbasid caliph Harun al-Rashid dates to AD 788 and serves as evidence of such interaction. However, these interactions were neither systematic nor sustained.

How Islam spread in the area of Bangladesh is highly debatable. It arrived in Bengal in 1204 as a Muslim force conquered the area and maintained its grasp on the leadership for over four hundred years. While the rulers fought for supremacy over the domain, Islam spread among the people of modern Bangladesh. Prior to the advent of Islam, the people of the region were primarily Buddhist; then, when the tantric practices of the Hindu Sena became dominant, lower-caste Hindus and the Buddhist ruling nobility were relegated to the background. The British typically understood the subsequent spread of Islam in Bengal as a simple process of people converting to the Islamic faith because of its message of equality and fraternity and the escape it offered from the stratified and unequal structures within which most had become embedded.

Whatever the social conditions of people of the region may have been, other factors must be considered in relation to the spread of Islam in Bengal. First, the role of the expatriates who came to the region has to be considered. In AD 1204 Ikhtiyaruddin Muhammad Khalji, a son of Bakhtiyar, a general of the Delhi sultan Qutuddin Aibak, forced the Sena king to flee and took over Bengal. This rule lasted until 1227, when Prince Nasiruddin, son of the Delhi sultan Iltutmish, defeated Bengal ruler Sultan Ghiyasuddin Iwaz Khalji. The new rule lasted for sixty years, and fifteen Mamluk sultans occupied the governorship of Bengal, ten of whom were originally slaves in the imperial court of Delhi. The last governor of Bengal of this period was named Tughral. When he declared his independence from Delhi, Sultan Balban of Delhi defeated him and partitioned Bengal into four political divisions, one of which was eastern Bengal with its capital at Sonargoan. An armor bearer of the governor of Sonargoan took over the region, rebelled against the Delhi sultan, and assumed the title Sultan Fakhruddin Mubarak Shah in 1388. In 1342, Haji Shamsuddin Ilyas Shah set up an independent dynasty in Bengal. For the next two centuries, three independent dynasties—the Ilyas Shahis (1342–1487), the Sayyid dynasty of Alauddin Hussain Shah (1493–1538), and the Afghan Karranis (1564–1575)—ruled Bengal with some Hindu kings and Abbyssinian Habshi eunuchs. Not until the reign of the Mughal king Akbar did Bengal once again come under the rule of Delhi in 1575. In 1612 Bengal was finally consolidated into the Mughal Empire during the reign of the Jahangir. Further consolidation of Bengal into the Mughal Empire took place during the reign of Emperor Aurangzeb. However, upon his death in 1707, Bengal once again moved away from Delhi and established its independence under Murshid Quli Khan in 1717. This rule lasted until 1757, when the British East India Company defeated Bengali nawab Sirajuddaula at the Battle of Plassey. Since the rulers were all Muslims, they played a major role in promoting Islam. Actual evidence of forced conversion is rather rare, but the advantages of belonging to the faith and community of the ruling groups must have been substantial and seductive.

As the different regimes were established, different groups, like soldiers, traders, fortune seekers, and administrators, came to populate the area. The first Muslim immigrants to Bengal were Turkish. The Arab immigrants came after the Sayad Alauddin Hussain Shah dynasty (1493–1519) was established. The Abbyssinian Habshi came to Bengal during the Ilyas Shahi reign. Sufficient evidence is available to establish that people from Arabia, Herat, Samarkhand, Tabriz, Bukhara, Balkh, and Abyssinia systematically came to and settled in Bengal. Additional evidence suggests that prior to the systematic immigration of Muslims, sporadic contact and individual settlement took place in Bengal prior to the Turkish invasion. As settlers arrived and integrated into the community, they also helped transform the region into a Muslim society. Muslim holy men who settled in the different parts of Bengal, in effect covering all of the critical regions of what would become Bangladesh, constituted another group that helped spread Islam. Many of these sojourners were revered for their personal piety, special spiritual knowledge, and, at times, imputed magical powers. Shrines and *dargas* (mausoleums) dedicated to them routinely became associated with the sacred and remain popular sites for congregation, worship, and devotional rituals. Most of these saints had obvious orientations toward Sufi (mystical) traditions and practices and, hence, were largely instrumental in generating an environment in which a nondogmatic, inclusive, and tolerant Islam became the prevailing norm, an aspect of Bangladesh's political culture still evident today.

Most assertions about the spread of Islam in Bengal focus on personal conversion. However, for a society to become immersed in a new religion, as was the case in Bangladesh, an institutional structure is needed. During the sixteenth century, the first institutional structure was the land grant (*jagir*), which allowed for the permanent settlement of people associated with those in power. A second institutional structure was the rulers' patronage of their religion, Islam. Many of the rulers built beautiful mosques and other structures that blended Islamic and Bengali architecture, producing the distinctive Bengal *tughra* architectural calligraphy. Surface decoration, curvilinear roofs, and covered domes are other architectural aspects of the merger of the two cultures, which helped Islam permeate Bengali society.

The third institutional structure was the development of literary works on Islam. The early leaders of Muslim Bengal were known for their scholarship. Mawlana Sharfuddin Abu Tawwammah compiled a work on Islamic mysticism titled *Maqamat*. Makhdum Sharfuddin Yahya Maneri composed many works on Islamic theology and mysticism, among which *Ajiba, Fawaid-i-Rukmi,* is noteworthy. Haji Gharib Yamani wrote a book of Islamic knowledge titled *Lataif-i-Ashraf.* The Islamization of Bangladesh also corresponded with the enrichment of Bengali art and literature with the steady injection of Arabic and Persian into Bengali songs, folklore, poetry, and works of fiction. Islamic thought and practices were written not only in Arabic or Persian but also in Bengali, which demonstrates that people in Muslim Bengal not only had control over the vernacular language but also had mastered the religious language as well as the language of the conquering forces. Such works as Shaikh Jalal Mujarrad's *Shar Nuzhat-i-Arwah,* Afdal Ali's *Nasihat Nama,* a manual of instruction to Muslims in religious matters written during the reign of Sultan Nusrat Shah (1519–1532), and Zainuddin's *Rasul-Vijaya,* another book centering on the life of the Prophet of Islam written during the reign of Sultan Yusuf Shah

(1474–1481) all suggest that the local population also contributed heavily to the spread of Islam in modern Bangladesh.

The name Bengal came into existence during the beginning of the Muslim period.[5] Prior to the twelfth century AD, the area was known as Vanga, Gauda, Samatata, and Harikela, among other names.

Clearly during the Muslim period, from the thirteenth century to the middle of the eighteenth century, the rulers of Bengal were not indigenous people, usually came from other areas, and while mostly Muslim, at times maintained their independence from Delhi. The culture of Bangladesh was a mixture of Hinduism, Buddhism, and Islam, with Islam gradually becoming more popular and more dominant. There were undertones of societal tension as the new and the old regimes merged, but also evidence of internal harmony and understanding between different groups that lived in the region.

The British Period

It is generally accepted that the British rule of India started with the defeat of Nawab Sirajuddullah of Bengal in June 1757. However, the British formally entered India when the nawabs of Murshidabad gave the British East India Company permission to establish a trading post in Calcutta in 1690. One hundred years after the defeat of the nawab of Bengal, a conflict known as the Sepoy Mutiny of 1857, organized by the Bengal Regiment, shook the foundations of British authority in India. While the main battleground was in the Uttar Pradesh province of India, the mutiny impacted the Dhaka and Chittagong areas of Bangladesh. The British sent the last Mughal ruler of India to present-day Myanmar (Burma). As a result of the Sepoy Mutiny, power in India was transferred from the British East India Company to the British government, and the seat of British imperial authority was moved from Calcutta to New Delhi.

An 1872 census finding continues to have a major impact on the psyche of the people of Bangladesh. The census found a large Muslim population in Bengal, which could not be explained by the British. Baffling the British further was the fact the Muslims were not concentrated in the urban centers but mostly located in the rural areas of eastern Bengal, suggesting a mass conversion of lower-caste Hindus. An alternative explanation offered by some Muslim Bengalis was that the Muslims of Bengal were descendants of foreign soldiers who had settled in Bengal. The British point of view, however, prevailed. After Pakistan became independent, the conversion theory became a major source of ill will between the peoples of East and West Pakistan, since it had major social and political implications. The elites of West Pakistan, who considered themselves to be "original" Muslims, occasionally looked down on the Muslims from East Pakistan as inauthentic because they were considered to be lower-caste Hindus who had opportunistically turned to Islam and because they displayed various "un-Islamic" traditions and practices rooted in their culture.

During the British rule in India, three other events prior to the 1947 partition impacted modern-day Bangladesh. The first was passage of the Permanent Settlement Act of 1793, which sought to stabilize the land-revenue administration of the province granted to the East India Company in 1765. In trying to enhance revenue collection, this act helped to formalize the institution of private property in land (to replace the ambiguous notions of land ownership under the Mughals), fixed the amount of revenues to be provided to the British overlords (hence the phrase "permanent settlement"), and created a landed aristocracy of new owners, who contracted with the British to deliver the annual revenue assessments on the land and were left free to extract whatever they could from the peasants. The new arrangements privileged the more enterprising and better-educated *bhadralok* (vernacular elite classes, many of whom became absentee landlords centered in Calcutta), increased revenue demands through cruel and arbitrary taxes and levies imposed on the peasants, and sporadically provoked various forms of peasant unrest and resistance. Moreover, the new landlords (*zamindars*) were generally Hindu and the peasants largely Muslim, adding a religious dimension to this conflict between the poor peasants and the rich landlords that affected the subsequent political dynamic of the province. The second event was the partition of Bengal into East and West Bengal in 1905, essentially as an administrative restructuring, with Calcutta and Dacca being the two parts' principal cities and capital centers. Unfortunately, because of the religious divide, Calcutta solidified as the center of Hindu culture and society, and Dacca emerged as the cultural center for the Muslims. Continued opposition from mostly Hindu protestors made implementing the partition plan difficult, and the British subsequently had to merge the two divisions back into one in 1912. The third event was the great famine of 1943, the two most common explanations for which are a shortage of food and the scorched-earth policy of the Allied forces in India during World War II. Amartya Sen, in *Poverty and Famine: An Essay on Entitlement and Poverty,* challenges the food-shortage rationale. The scorched-earth policy remains a potent explanation particularly because the British felt that securing the future food supply for the troops during the war was much more important than feeding the obviously hungry population in the province. While the cause is debated, it is estimated that approximately 5 million people died in the great famine of Bengal, which resulted in severe socioeconomic devastation in the region with consequences felt even today in Bangladesh.

Politically, the last five decades of British rule in India witnessed the emergence of the Muslim League, founded in 1906 in Dhaka as a counterweight to the Indian National Congress, which had been formed in 1885. The role of the Muslim League became progressively more important as the British firmed up their plans to leave India. The formation of the Muslim League and the two provincial elections, one in 1937 and the other in 1945–1946, changed the dynamics of political negotiations between the Muslims, the dominant Hindus, and the British rulers of India. The 1937 election in the Indian provinces resulted in the Muslims winning the most delegates in Bengal. In the other Muslim-majority provinces, the Muslims did not win as many delegates. Nor were they able to form any provincial governments. Muslim members representing Bengal played a special role in the negotiations between the British, the Indian National Congress, and the Muslim League toward the partition of India. In the 1945–1946 election, the nature of representation changed dramatically. In Bengal and Sindh, the Muslim League won a majority to form a government. In other Muslim-dominated provinces, it won the largest number of seats but did not form the government, which a coalition of other parties formed. While in 1937 the Muslim League won only 109 out of 492 reserved seats allocated to the Muslims of India, in 1945–1946, the Muslim League won 445 out of 490 Muslim seats.

Embedded in the Muslim representation of Bengal was a major social phenomenon that was at the heart of differences between the two wings of Pakistan. The Muslim members representing Bengal derived primarily from the nonvernacular elites of the province, who can be traced to the Mughal period, when Mughal officials were posted in Bengal and given landholdings. While the vernacular Muslims were more interested in social issues impacting the Muslims of Bengal, the nonvernacular elites were more interested in nation building. Another issue of the British period that was at the heart of the differences between the two wings of Pakistan was the Lahore Resolution of 1940, which formally proposed separate Muslim homelands. The declaration, presented on March 23, 1940, by Maulvi Abul Kasim Fazlul Haq, a Muslim leader from Bengal, wanted the Muslim-majority areas of India, those of Northwest India and East India, to be grouped into independent states. However, the Delhi Declaration of 1946, made prior to a visit by an official British negotiation team known as the Cabinet Mission, changed the phrase "independent states" to "independent state," through which India was divided into two countries—India and Pakistan.

The Pakistan Period

Prior to the Pakistan period, Bengal was an ethnically separate region of India, and the ebb and flow of its independence depended on Bengal's ability to ward off the central authority of those in power in India (the Mughals and the

British). With the amalgamation of East Bengal as a part of Pakistan, modern-day Bangladesh became, for the first time, part of a nation-state based on religion and not ethnicity or regional identity. This dual identity of religion and ethnicity came to the forefront of the political development of Pakistan soon after the partition of India in 1947. Pakistan comprised a western part composed of four provinces: North-West Frontier Province, Sindh, Balochistan, and Punjab. Together they became known as West Pakistan. East Bengal, renamed East Pakistan, became the fifth province of Pakistan and was separated from West Pakistan by approximately 1,000 miles of Indian territory.

The euphoria of achieving a separate homeland for the Muslims of India did not last long, as the social and cultural differences between the two wings of Pakistan started to emerge. Ethnically the peoples of the two wings were different, but the immediate principal irritant was the issue of national language. The relationship between West and East Pakistan took a negative turn when the Pakistani leadership decided to make Urdu, at that time spoken by 7 percent of the population, the sole national language of Pakistan (English being the official language). East Pakistan's demand that Bengali, a majority language, be declared a national language was denied. This led to major protests in East Pakistan. The leadership of the protest movement came from the students enrolled in higher education institutions in East Pakistan, especially the University of Dhaka. On February 21, 1952, several students from the University of Dhaka were killed by police trying to disperse a crowd demanding that Bengali be made a national language. February 21 became known as National Language Movement Day and was celebrated each year to remember those who gave their lives for the cause of making Bengali a national language. Due to a global effort facilitated by Bangladesh, in 1999 the United Nations Educational and Cultural Organization declared February 21 International Mother Language Day. The discord over the national language played a major role in the separation of the two wings of Pakistan and the flowering of a cultural/linguistic nationalism in the East that ultimately led to the formation of independent Bangladesh.

Disputes over power sharing between the two wings and the five provinces of Pakistan emerged soon after independence. In the first Pakistani cabinet, East Pakistan found itself represented by a Scheduled Caste Hindu and an Urdu-speaking representative of the national elite. None of the Bengalis who were instrumental in the Muslim electoral victories of 1937 and 1946 were included. Representation thus became a major issue during the constitution-making process. East Pakistan had 7 percent of the total area of Pakistan but 54 percent of the population. The three major issues that needed to be addressed in formulating the constitution were (1) the structure of governance and composition of the national assembly, (2) the division of powers between the central and provincial governments, and (3) the national language. There was general agreement that both Bengali and Urdu should be accepted as national languages, although the bitterness of 1952 was to remain in the hearts of the Bengalis. The representation issue was to be resolved by providing East Pakistan with a majority in the lower house, whereas, in the upper house, representation would be based on area. In the end, the total number of combined seats would be equally distributed between East and West Pakistan. The debate over power sharing between the central and provincial governments was very intense. Although the general consensus supported a federal list of powers, a provincial list, and a concurrent list, the operational modalities were difficult to formulate. Just as the three issues were generally resolved, the constitution-making process was abruptly stopped in favor of a new process, which established the first constitution of Pakistan in 1956. Many of the earlier consensus provisions, such as a bicameral legislature and representation based on both population size and land mass size, were removed. However, the 1956 constitution did not last long as a military coup in 1958 abruptly ended Pakistan's experiment with democratic rule.

East Pakistan had a major economic grievance with West Pakistan. Economically, East Pakistan was the major foreign exchange earner from independence until the 1960s. However, only a small percentage of the foreign exchange was being reinvested in East Pakistan. In addition, international assistance was being directed toward West Pakistan. An inability to resolve these economic disparities led to a further separation of interest between the wings of Pakistan. Increasingly the economic disparity, coupled with the political disparity of not being provided majority representation in the parliament, started to generate discontent and added to the importance of East Pakistan's demand for greater political autonomy. Along with the political and economic issues, other structural disparities raised tensions between the two wings, principally representation in the civil service and in the armed forces. In both sectors, East Pakistan's representation was negligible, and the weakness, also in both sectors, of efforts to increase it further strengthened the sense among Bengalis in East Pakistan that independence had not brought the benefits expected and that those it had brought were disproportionately allocated in favor of West Pakistan.

Within East Pakistan major political changes also took place. The Muslim League, which had provided leadership during the prepartition phase, started to lose its base. Bengali nationalism and social issues came to the forefront of East Pakistan's political culture. Issues such as the role of landlords in society, poverty, and minority relationships, along with the demand for political autonomy, led leaders of the Muslim League like Hussain Shaheed Suhrawardy to leave and to join up with A. K. Fazlul Haq, a prominent Bengali political leader, to form the United Front, which defeated the Muslim League in the 1954 provincial parliamentary election. Suhrawardy, together with prominent Bengali leaders in East Pakistan (such as Maulana Bhasani, Shamsul Huq, Abul Mansur Ahmed, Sheikh Mujibur Rahman, and others) formed the Awami Muslim League, which later became the Awami League.

A decade of military rule started to unravel in the aftermath of the Indo-Pakistani War of 1965. Although no war was fought on the eastern front, East Pakistan felt vulnerable. Politically, the war pointed out the inherent weakness of military rule, and opposition to it began to grow and expand. In a 1966 meeting of the opposition in Lahore, West Pakistan, the Awami League, one of the principal grass roots–based political parties in East Pakistan, floated a power-sharing scheme known as the Six Point Program. The six points were as follows: (1) The constitution should provide for a Pakistani federation, in the true sense, on the basis of the Lahore Resolution and for a parliamentary form of government with a supreme legislature elected directly on the basis of universal adult franchise. (2) The federal government would deal with only two issues: defense and foreign affairs. All residual subjects would be vested in the federating states. (3) There should be either two separate, freely convertible currencies for the two wings or one currency with two separate reserve banks to prevent inter-wing flight of capital. (4) The power of taxation and revenue collection should be vested in the federating units, with the federal government to receive a share to meet its financial obligations. (5) Economic disparities between the two wings would be addressed through a series of economic, fiscal, and legal reforms. (6) A militia or paramilitary force would be created in East Pakistan, which then had no defense of its own. To Mujibur Rahman (Mujib), the Awami League, and East Pakistan, the six points constituted a political correction to underlying issues of the Lahore Resolution of 1940, whereby two Muslim states were to be created. They characterized the six points as issues of provincial autonomy and not separation, although effectively they would have brought about major schism between the two wings. The ruling class of Pakistan, however, mainly led by the political leaders of West Pakistan and the military leaders, saw the six points as a covert attempt by East Pakistan and the Bengalis to go their separate way. As a consequence, charges were brought against Sheikh Mujibur Rahman in 1968 for sedition and treason with the aim of declaring East Pakistan as an independent state; this became known as the Agartala Conspiracy Case. Eventually, the case collapsed, and Mujib was released in 1969.

Popular agitation against military rule resulted in the 1969 fall of General Ayub Khan, who was replaced with General Agha Muhammad Yahya Khan. Yahya described himself as a caretaker whose primary task, after restoring law and order, was to hold elections to determine the wishes of the people of Pakistan. He also set out his requirements regarding the nature of a new constitution and, in doing so, paid lip service to the principle of provincial autonomy. Of Mujib's six points, he particularly opposed the fourth, which would deny the power of taxation to the central government. To determine the return of civilian rule in Pakistan, elections were held in December 1970 after nearly a year of open campaigning by all political parties. Yahya had decided that elections should be held on a system of joint electorates and on the basis of population rather than parity. In a 300-member house (313 with the addition of 7 indirectly elected women members from the east and 6 from the west), the east wing would directly elect 162 members and the west wing 138 from single-member constituencies. In the east wing, the Awami League won 160 of the 162 seats, with more than three-quarters of the vote. Yahya reverted the west wing from one unit into the four original provinces of Punjab, Sindh, the North-West Frontier Province, and Balochistan. The Pakistan People's Party, led by Zulfiqar Ali Bhutto, won a majority in West Pakistan as a whole, with 81 seats of the 138, but a majority in only two provinces, Punjab and Sindh. Similar results were recorded for the provincial assemblies; the Awami League won 288 of 300 seats in East Pakistan.[6]

Mujibur Rahman claimed victory as well as the right to frame a new constitution on the basis of the six points and the right to form a government for Pakistan. At one point Yahya hailed Mujib as the "future prime minister of Pakistan." But the military was not pleased with the outcome, seeing, if nothing else, a diminution of its power and its budget. Bhutto, too, was dissatisfied, inasmuch as he saw himself playing second fiddle to a Bengali. Negotiations on a constitution and the transfer of power from the military to the civilians continued through January, February, and early March 1971, with greater opposition from Bhutto and steadfast commitment to its position by the Awami League. Bhutto claimed that there were two majorities in Pakistan, one of which he led, and that he would have to be accommodated in any arrangements made. Mujib came under increasing pressure to separate from Pakistan and allow Bangladesh (the name then being used) to declare independence in the context of the ethno-linguistic identity that the people of East Pakistan were clearly and assertively demonstrating. Meanwhile, Yahya had sworn to uphold the unity of Pakistan. It was clear that Yahya's troops, consisting mostly of Punjabis and Pathans, would prefer to repress Mujib and the Bengalis before they attempted to put down Bhutto and the Punjabis, if force became necessary. In the early part of March, a civil disobedience movement began on a wide and unprecedented scale in East Pakistan, and clashes between the Pakistani army and Awami Leaguers escalated.[7]

The Birth of a New State

On the night of March 25, 1971, the Pakistani army, strengthened by 80,000 troops flown in from West Pakistan, struck at Awami Leaguers and others in Bangladesh (especially Dhaka) in an effort to end the resistance the military had met. In the past, police and military measures had broken the Bengali opposition, but this brutal attack stiffened its resolve to achieve independent statehood. While the actual person who declared independence is disputed, most people in Bangladesh heard Major Ziaur Rahman's voice, broadcast over a radio transmitter in Chittagong, issuing the proclamation of independence in the name of Sheikh Mujibur on March 27, 1971. Ziaur Rahman would become a hero of the ensuing war and eventually president of independent Bangladesh later.[8] While precise figures are not available, Pakistani armed forces inflicted massive casualties (the official Bangladeshi figure is 3 million killed); hundreds of thousands of women were raped, and more than 10 million were forced to flee to safety in neighboring India during the nine months of the conflict.

It must be pointed out that India graciously helped to take care of the refugees, initially assisted Bangladesh's Mukti Bahini (Freedom Fighters), and eventually intervened militarily in the war against Pakistan in November and December 1971. Pakistani army units surrendered to a Joint Bangladeshi-Indian command on December 16, 1971, and Bangladesh became an independent, sovereign nation. Mujibur Rahman, who had been arrested on the night of the Pakistani army crackdown, taken to West Pakistan, and charged with treason, was released by the new Pakistani government headed by Bhutto, who succeeded Yahya after the latter resigned in disgrace following the surrender. Mujib returned to Bangladesh in January and assumed the reins of government as prime minister. The fall of united Pakistan seems to many observers to have been the final act in a play that began in 1947. There was little hope for an ending that would be anything but tragic for Pakistan and triumphant (even in tragic circumstances) for Bangladesh. Who should be placed in the dock? Many would say that Bhutto was responsible for the final act, but others would maintain that Muhammad Ali Jinnah played the key role in the first act. Ultimately, rather than the actions of a single individual, a failure of leadership, a lack of vision, and insensitivity to the economic, political, and cultural grievances of East Pakistan probably created this situation. The concept of Pakistan—a country based on religious commonality but with its two "wings" separated by culture, language, ethnicity, and a thousand miles of Indian territory—was problematic to begin with, and the "experiment" never had the benefit of wise statesmen who might have been able to sustain it and make it work.

In sum, the political culture of Bangladesh cannot be understood apart from the events of the periods beginning with the Mughals, followed by the British and finally the Pakistanis. A number of factors are paramount. A constant desire for independence brought about by people's struggle, be it the Sepoy Mutiny of 1857, the language movement of 1948, or the war of liberation of 1971, shows that Bangladeshis have always seen themselves as a separate entity. For a while the Muslims coalesced to form a larger community, but in the long run autonomy and independence overrode cooperation with the Muslim community in West Pakistan. Built into the idea of what some call "Bengalness" is the importance of language, arts and literature, social rituals, and religion, where none is superior and all are practiced in accordance with the needs of the individual rather than as dictated by the state. Bangladeshis tend not to accept their relative poverty as a result of an inherent lack of economic resources but prefer to believe that different peoples over the ages have plundered their national wealth and created the difficult economic circumstances they face today. This idea of external exploitation and oppression that has systematically destroyed the nation's economic advancements is part of the Bangladeshi popular imagination. Also embedded in the political culture is a concept of negotiation in which the rulers trade their rights and privileges in response to a set of demands. This has led to a socialization process, aided by the cultural-ethnic homogeneity of the population and its linguistic pride, that is more conducive to the establishment of liberal democracy and has resulted in democratic institution building that has been more successful than in Pakistan.

SUGGESTED READINGS

Ahmed, Kamruddin. *A Socio-political History of Bangladesh.* Dhaka: Zahuruddin Ahmed, 1975.

Ahmed, Moudud. *Bangladesh: Constitutional Quest for Autonomy.* Dhaka: University Press, 1979.

Ahmed, Rafiuddin. *The Bengal Muslims, 1871–1906: A Quest for Identity.* New York: Oxford University Press, 1981.

Ahmed, Sufia. *Muslim Community in Bengal, 1884–1912.* Dhaka: University Press, 1974.

Baxter, Craig. *Bangladesh: From a Nation to a State.* Boulder, CO: Westview Press, 1997.

Baxter, Craig, and Syedur Rahman. *Historical Dictionary of Bangladesh.* 2nd ed. Lanham, MD: Scarecrow, 1996.

Bhuiyan, Muhammad Abdul Wadud. *Emergence of Bangladesh and the Role of the Awami League.* New Delhi: Vikas, 1982.

Choudhury, G. W. *The Last Days of United Pakistan.* 2nd ed. Dhaka: University Press, 1993.

Jahan, Rounaq. *Pakistan: Failure in National Integration.* New York: Columbia University Press, 1972.

Karim, A. K. Nazmul. *The Dynamics of Bangladesh Society.* New Delhi: Vikas, 1980.

Maniruzzaman, Talukder. *The Politics of Development: The Case of Pakistan, 1947–1958.* Dhaka: Green Book House, 1971.

Muhith, A. M. A. *Bangladesh: Emergence of a Nation.* Dhaka: Bangladesh Books International, 1978.

O'Donnell, Charles Peter. *Bangladesh: Biography of a Muslim Nation.* Boulder, CO: Westview Press, 1984.

Rizvi, Hasan Askari. *Internal Strife and External Intervention: India's Role in Civil War in East Pakistan Bangladesh.* Lahore: Progressive Publishers, 1981.

Shelley, Mizanur Rahman. *Emergence of a New Nation in a Multi-polar World: Bangladesh.* Dhaka: University Press, 1979.

Zaheer, Hasan. *The Separation of East Pakistan.* Karachi: Oxford University Press, 1994.

NOTES

1. Nazrul Islam, "Let the Delta Be a Delta: An Essay in Dissent on the Flood Problem in Bangladesh," *Journal of Social Studies* 48 (1990)

2. Craig Baxter and Syedur Rahman, *Historical Dictionary of Bangladesh,* 3rd ed. (Lanham, MD: Scarecrow, 2003); Mohammed Anisuzzaman, *Bangladesh Public Administration and Society* (Dhaka: Bangladesh Books International, 1979).

3. The poems are taken from two works of translation by Daniel H. H. Ingalls: *Sanskrit Poetry from Vidyakara's Treasury* (Cambridge, MA: Harvard University Press, 1968), and *An Anthology of Sanskrit Court Poetry: Vidyakara's "Subhasitaratnakosa"* (Cambridge, MA: Harvard University Press, 1965).

4. The primary sources consulted for the section on the Muslim period are Richard M. Eaton, *The Rise of Islam and the Bengal Frontier, 1204–1860* (Berkeley: University of California Press, 1993); Rafiuddin Ahmed, ed., *Understanding the Bengal Muslim: Interpretive Essays* (New York: Oxford University Press, 2001); Nizamuddin Ahmed, *Islamic Heritage of Bangladesh* (Dhaka: Ministry of Information & Broadcasting, Government of the People's Republic of Bangladesh, 1980); Nazimuddin Ahmed, *Discover the Monuments of Bangladesh* (Dhaka: University of Dhaka Press, 1984); "Masjids Madrasah, Khanqah and Bridge: Reflections on Some Islamic Inscriptions of Bengal," *Journal of the Asiatic Society of Bangladesh* 42, no. 2 (1998): 231–286.

5. Muhammad A. Rahim, *Muslim Society and Politics in Bengal, A.D. 1757–1947,* Vol. 1, 2nd ed. (Dhaka: University of Dhaka Press, 1978), and *Muslim Society and Politics in Bengal, 1576–1757,* Vol. 2 (Lahore: Pakistan Publishing House, 1967); Anisuzzaman, *Bangladesh Public Administration and Society.*

6. For more detailed results, see Craig Baxter, "Pakistan Votes, 1970," *Asian Survey* (March 1971): 197–218.

7. For more information, see David Dunbar, "Pakistan, the Failure of Political Negotiations," *Asian Survey* (May 1972): 444–461; Craig Baxter, "Pakistan and Bangladesh," in *Ethnic Separatism and World Politics,* ed. Frederick L. Shiels (Lanham, MD: University Press of America, 1984), 209–262.

8. For a discussion of the war, see Baxter, "Pakistan and Bangladesh," in Shiels, *Ethnic Separatism,* 209–262; A. M. A. Muhith, *Bangladesh: Emergence of a Nation* (Dhaka: Bangladesh Books International, 1978); Mizanur Rahman Shelley, *Emergence of a New Nation in a Multi-polar World: Bangladesh* (Dhaka: University Press, 1979). For the diplomacy of the period, see Richard Sisson and Leo E. Rose, *War and Secession: Pakistan, India, and the Creation of Bangladesh* (Berkeley: University of California Press, 1990). On December 31, 2000, the government of Pakistan released the report of the Hamoodur Rahman Commission, which was set up in 1972 to review the causes and conduct of the war. See *Dawn* (Karachi), January 1–6, 2001, for reportage and analysis. The report had been released earlier and was published in 2000 by *India Today.*

15

Government Institutions

B angladesh has undergone a variety of regime changes since it became independent in 1971. Amendments to the constitution of 1972 have changed
the form of government from the original parliamentary system to a presidential
system in 1975 and back to a parliamentary system in 1991. The goal of the
newly independent state was to establish a socialist, secular democratic regime,
but Mujibur Rahman (Mujib) became increasingly authoritarian, and the experiment ended in a one-party, single-leader government under him. His assassination in 1975 brought a weak government to power for a brief period, followed by
a military government that gradually liberalized the political system under Ziaur
Rahman (Zia). Following Zia's assassination in 1981, a nearly decade-long period
of weak government and further military rule was unable to transform itself into
something resembling an open democratic system. The collapse of that government in 1990 was followed by free and fair elections and the return to a parliamentary system in 1991, although there has been much turmoil since. The
president of Bangladesh declared a state of emergency on January 11, 2007, and
a reconstituted caretaker government backed by the armed forces of Bangladesh
was formed with a stated goal of holding a free and fair election by the end of
2008. These elections were finally held in December of that year. Table 15.1 presents a list of heads of government in Bangladesh along with their respective titles.

The Progress of Government

The Democratic Regime of Mujibur Rahman
On December 16, 1971, the Pakistani armed forces in East Pakistan surren-
dered to a joint Bangladeshi-Indian armed force, leading to the creation of
Bangladesh as a state. Absent from Bangladesh during the initial weeks of inde-

TABLE 15.1 Heads of Government of Bangladesh

Date	Name	Title
April 1971–January 1972	Tajuddin Ahmed	Acting prime minister
January 1972–January 1975	Sheikh Mujibur Rahman	Prime minister
January 1975–August 1975	Sheikh Mujibur Rahman	President
August 1975–November 1975	Khondakar Mushtaq Ahmed	President
November 1975–April 1977	Abu Sadat Muhammad Sayem	President and CMLA*
April 1977–May 1981	Ziaur Rahman	President and CMLA
May 1981–March 1982	Abdus Sattar	Acting president, president
March 1982–December 1990	Husain Muhammad Ershad	CMLA and president
December 1990–March 1991	Shahabuddin Ahmed	Acting president
March 1991–February 1996	Begum Khaleda Zia	Prime minister
February 1996–June 1996	Habibur Rahman	Chief adviser
June 1996–July 2001	Sheikh Hasina Wajed	Prime minister
July 2001–October 2001	Latifur Rahman	Chief adviser
October 2001–October 2006	Begum Khaleda Zia	Prime minister
October 2006–January 2007	Iajuddin Ahmed	President, chief adviser
January 2007–January 2007	Fazlul Haq	Acting chief adviser
January 2007–January 2009	Fakhruddin Ahmed	Chief adviser
January 2009–present	Sheikh Hasina Wajed	Prime minister

* Chief martial law administrator.

pendence was Mujibur Rahman, who was a prisoner of the Pakistanis. Under international pressure Pakistan released Mujib, who arrived in Dhaka on January 10, 1972. Mujib immediately stepped down from the post of president, which had been assigned to him by the government in exile, to become prime minister of the new state. Mujib piloted the constitution of 1972 through the parliament, a body comprising members of the provincial assembly elected in 1970 along with those members of the National Assembly who had been elected in what was then East Pakistan.[1] The new constitution followed a parliamentary model, provided for the basic rights of the people, and contained directive principles that did not have the force of law but would, if followed, set the tone for the new regime. These basic principles were often described as Mujibism, or in Bengali, Mujibbad. This political philosophy had four components: nationalism, democracy, socialism, and secularism. Mujib's Bangladesh would not Islamize its polity.

Problems of Reconstruction, Authoritarian Leadership, and Development Failures

The new government was soon overwhelmed by the enormous reconstruction and rehabilitation challenges facing it after the immensely destructive conflict for independence. The social and economic fabric of the nation was mostly destroyed.

Aid arrived in the form of food and medicine, as well as assistance in reconstructing the severely damaged infrastructure. In the international arena, the Soviets made themselves too conspicuous, and the Indians stayed on long enough that many Bangladeshis suspected their intentions. The Americans, accused of being pro-Pakistani during the liberation war, provided much of the assistance, along with other Western nations, even though the Americans (and the Chinese) delayed full recognition of the new government longer than seemed necessary.

Few members of the new government had experience in governing. Mujib had been a minister briefly, and a rather unsuccessful one at that. His leadership is almost universally judged to have been ineffective. Like many other leaders of independence movements who are catapulted to power through their personal charisma and ability to mobilize the masses, he was unable to adapt to the role of decision maker. Mujib failed to use the talents of many senior politicians and civil servants, who, he thought, had opposed the freedom movement. Consequently many otherwise poorly qualified persons who had the right political connections and persuasions were appointed to key positions, adding to both inefficiency and corruption. Rehabilitation had to take precedence over development. Bangladesh faced critical food shortages and suffered famines during Mujib's administration, despite assistance from the developed world. Much of the industrial sector was nationalized.

Still basking in his glow as liberation hero, Mujib and the Awami League went to the polls in 1973 to elect a new parliament. The party won almost all of the seats (307 of 315), and it appeared that, despite some grumbling, Mujib's government would be firmly in office for the ensuing five-year term of parliament. Parties opposed to the creation of Bangladesh, such as the Muslim League and the Jamaat-i-Islami, were barred from contesting. The challenge came mainly from the left, and it was weak.

Challenges intensified, however, as the law-and-order situation deteriorated, the economy failed to return to pre-independence levels, and corruption became rampant. Liberation of the nation also meant liberation of public opinion. The press began to attack the policies and methods of the government. Members of the opposition and even some members of the Awami League in parliament began to join the press in voicing criticism. The famine of 1974, in which millions suffered, exposed the ineptness and callousness of the regime and intensified mass disenchantment with the government. Mujib declared a state of emergency in December 1974 and suspended fundamental rights. A month later the constitution was amended to a presidential system with Mujib as president. In June 1975, he made Bangladesh a single-party state and, for all practical purposes, gave himself absolute power. These steps did not alter the situation. The demands on the political system continued to be far greater than Mujib, his system, or the resources of the country could meet. On August 15, 1975, Mujib and much of his family were assassinated in a plot led by a group of Bangladeshi army officers. His system collapsed with his death.

The First Interregnum

With the death of Mujib and the arrest of several of his associates, the presidency was assumed by the next senior person in the cabinet, Khondakar Mushtaq Ahmad, a politician thought to be among the most conservative of the Awami Leaguers. He is also viewed as having betrayed Mujib and, in effect, the liberation movement. Mushtaq promised elections and a return to a parliamentary system. He disbanded the single party and promised to allow other parties to resume activities as elections approached. However, he did not take steps to prosecute Mujib's assassins. Nor did he seek to investigate those responsible for the brutal murder of four stalwarts of the Awami League while they were in prison. These four included the past president, prime minister, and leaders with important cabinet portfolios, all of whom had been actively involved in the core leadership of the Mujibnagar government (formed during the Liberation War).

In November 1975 a series of coups and attempted coups dislodged Mushtaq but did not permit pro-Mujib forces to regain power. Mushtaq yielded the office of president to the chief justice, A. S. M. Sayem, who also became chief martial law administrator (CMLA). The key person, however, was one of the deputy CMLAs, Major General Ziaur Rahman.

The Regime of Ziaur Rahman: Gradual Liberalization

Ziaur Rahman, the chief of the army staff, quickly emerged as the leading member of the ruling group. On November 30, 1976, he replaced Sayem as CMLA, and on April 21, 1977, he assumed the presidency when Sayem resigned on grounds of ill health. He was confirmed as president in May 1977, when a referendum approved his holding the office. The referendum, however, did not confer legitimacy on him or his system, if for no other reason than that no alternatives had been presented. In June 1978 Zia was elected president for a five-year term in a contested election.

Beyond these steps toward power, Zia developed a program that might be called the politics of hope. The nineteen points of this program called for a revitalization of Bangladesh, both economically and socially. Zia emphasized such measures as family planning and proposed expanding agricultural production, with the goal of reaching self-sufficiency in the production of food grains as soon as possible. Considerable progress was made during his tenure. Zia also had a vision of a subcontinent that worked as a unit to find solutions to economic, social, and technological problems affecting the entire region. Zia, a war hero, soon became a charismatic figure and a leader revered by many.

As he prepared to campaign in 1978 for the elected presidency, Zia sanctioned the formation of a political party dedicated to his program and candidacy. After the election, the party was reformed into the Bangladesh Nationalist Party (BNP), which became Zia's vehicle for obtaining a majority in the parliamentary election held in February 1979. The BNP won 207 of the 300 directly elected seats; the Awami League came in a distant second with 39 seats.

Zia was not without opponents. The Awami League opposed his military rule, his failure to punish Mujib's assassins (there were charges that he had actually helped to protect a few of them and facilitated their move to other countries), and his more market-oriented economic policies. Its members believed that the principles of Mujibism were being sacrificed, even though Zia's program represented for others a pragmatic stance toward the many problems of Bangladesh. Zia restored to office the civil servants Mujib had discarded. He also rehabilitated the military officers who had been forced to remain in Pakistan in 1971. A split in the army took place between the groups roughly termed "freedom fighters" and "returnees."

Considerable economic progress was made during the Zia regime. A series of appropriate economic policy directives and some curtailment of corruption and corrupt practices, coupled with relatively good weather conditions and extensive foreign assistance, led to an economic upturn. Zia's career was terminated on May 30, 1981, when he was assassinated in Chittagong by conspirators led by a disgruntled freedom fighter.

The Second Interregnum

Vice President Abdus Sattar became the acting president when Zia was killed. The constitution stated that a new election for president must be held within 180 days. The election was held in November 1981, and Sattar was elected president. The chief of the army staff, Lieutenant General Husain Muhammad Ershad, demanded a constitutional role for the military in the governance of the country; Sattar refused to comply. On March 24, 1982, Ershad led a coup and dismissed Sattar and his government.

Authoritarianism Returns: Husain Muhammad Ershad

With Ershad's assumption of power, the state returned to the political point it had left with the gradual liberalization under Zia. Parties were banned, the press controlled, channels of access closed or narrowed, and martial law reimposed. Ershad, following the pattern of many military leaders, said that conditions required the only organized force in the nation to assume power, temporarily, to set the government in order.

He further declared that elections would be held to restore representative government. In March 1985 Ershad asked for approval of his policies through a referendum. Although the government reported that he had won overwhelming support, it was widely believed that the count had been rigged and the turnout vastly overstated. Thus, the alleged approval did not add legitimacy to the Ershad regime. An election was finally held for parliament in May 1986, but the results were inconclusive, and there were reports of polling irregularities. The Jatiya Party, which had been organized to support Ershad, won a slim majority of the three hundred seats contested, whereas the opposition Awami League, now led by Mujib's daughter, Sheikh Hasina Wajed, and its allies won just under one hundred seats. The other major opposition group, the BNP, led by Begum Khaleda Zia, refused to participate in the election.

In the fall of 1987, widespread demonstrations against the Ershad regime, led by the BNP and the Awami League, caused Ershad to dissolve parliament and call for a new election, which was held in March 1988. The Jatiya Party won almost all the seats, as both the BNP and the Awami League boycotted the election. The undercurrent of opposition to Ershad reached its peak in November 1990 when the BNP and the Awami League joined forces again to demand Ershad's resignation and a free and fair election. Ershad resigned, and a caretaker government was established.[2]

The Caretaker Government and Elections

A temporary government was established without any constitutional premise to assist Bangladesh in transitioning from an authoritarian system to a democratic one. Ruling power was transferred to the chief justice of Bangladesh, Shahabuddin Ahmed, who became the head of government and conducted the election of 1991 to elect a new government. In order to legitimize the process, the elected members of the national assembly (Fifth Jatiya Sangsad) ratified all measures taken by the caretaker government.

The caretaker government was the subject of intense negotiations between the opposition political parties, and the government as Bangladesh was completing the first full term of a democratically elected government. In 1996 enactment of the Thirteenth Amendment to the constitution allowed for a constitutional caretaker government to be formed to conduct a national election at the conclusion of any five-year term of office. Specific modalities were enacted to ensure the neutrality of the caretaker government. In June 1996 a caretaker government headed by former chief justice Habibur Rahman conducted the election, which returned the Awami League to power after two decades in opposition.

In 2001 a third caretaker government was led by former chief justice Latifur Rahman. The BNP was returned to power. Continuing mistrust among the major political parties, attempts to manipulate the administrative structure responsible for conducting elections, questioning of the process of choosing the chief adviser, and intense desire to hold onto power severely stressed the concept of a caretaker government. When the time came for the establishment of the fourth caretaker government in October 2006, it essentially imploded.

A caretaker government was formed under President Iajuddin Ahmed when the political parties could not agree on a chief adviser. And when four of the advisers under President Ahmed resigned due to lack of transparency, Bangladesh was on the point of state failure. With the assistance of the armed forces, a state of emergency was declared in January 2007, and in place of the free and fair elections specified by the constitution, a principled caretaker government was established. This government, headed by Dr. Fakhruddin Ahmed, an economist who had gained both international exposure and administrative experience while serving in the World Bank and who was fully supported by the military under General Muin Uddin Ahmed tried to stem the rising tide of violence and lawlessness in the country, attempted to reduce the pervasive levels of corruption, and promised to hold free and fair elections by the end of 2008. While there were some questions about its efficiency and its commitments, and some skepticism about its intentions (given the fact that it remained in power for almost two years), this government did provide logistical support to the Election Commission not only to prepare updated voter registration rolls but also to arrange photo identifications for all registered voters in the land. The elections were finally held on December 29, 2008.

However, despite the caretaker government's success in organizing elections that most observers found credible, and although the Awami League won that election very convincingly, the party began to express its opposition to the idea of a caretaker government. In a rather unprecedented development, the Supreme Court of Bangladesh ruled that provisions of the Thirteenth Amendment, through which the institution of the caretaker government had been formalized, were unconstitutional (even though it advised that at least two more elections could be organized under those arrangements and the more detailed opinion of the Court had not yet been delivered). Inspired by this decision, the Bangladeshi parliament, dominated by the Awami League, passed the Fifteenth Amendment in June 2011, repealed relevant parts of the earlier amendment, and eliminated the need for such temporary and interim institutions altogether. This provoked an immediate and fierce backlash from the BNP-led opposition parties and evolved into a confrontational impasse. On the one hand, the Awami League maintained that the institution of the caretaker government would, under no circumstance, be considered valid or necessary in the future, while, on the other, the BNP-led opposition parties insisted that they would not participate in any election, or even allow one to be held, unless it was organized under such a nonpartisan, neutral authority. There is considerable irony in this turn of events. In the 1990s, when the BNP was in office, the Awami League had spearheaded the movement for a caretaker government to ensure that fraud and electoral manipulation by ruling regimes could not take place; and it was the BNP that resisted the practice. The tables were now completely turned. Given the usual rhetorical excess and street agitation that followed, the fate of future national elections, the next scheduled for late 2013 or early 2014, remained a bit unclear.

BNP and Prime Minister Khaleda Zia (1991–1996)

Outside observers declared the February 1991 election free and fair. The BNP won a plurality of seats in parliament and, by joining hands with the Jamaat-i-Islami (JI) in the indirect election for the seats reserved for women, achieved a majority.[3] Khaleda Zia, Ziaur Rahman's widow, became prime minister. The BNP, which had wanted to continue the presidential system, reversed its stand on this issue and joined with the Awami League to pass a constitutional amendment restoring the parliamentary system of the 1972 constitution.[4] During its tenure, the BNP, with support from the Awami League, democratized the office of the mayor in four principal cities by ensuring that the position became an elected one.

Two events led to increased political tensions during the BNP regime. First, the JI's 1993 election of Gholam Azam as its party chair propelled a political debate on national identity, which reignited the sensitive issue of the role of religion in the governance of the state and the role of parties opposed to the formation of Bangladesh.[5] Second, in 1994, a by-election resulted in the BNP candidate winning what was considered to be a safe Awami League seat, leading to widespread allegations of massive election rigging and fraud.

The two main parties have not cooperated since the national election. Consequently the government has been stormy since 1991 and was further polarized as the by-election result only confirmed in the minds of Awami Leaguers that they could not trust the BNP government. The Awami League, joined by the Jatiya Party and the Jamaat-i-Islami, began a series of strikes and demonstrations against the government, demanding that for each general election the government resign and a caretaker government be appointed by the president to conduct the poll. Members of parliament from the three parties resigned in December 1994, ending the possibility that some compromise might be reached, as the resignations deprived the parliament of more than one-third of its members, making the passage of a constitutional amendment impossible. The opposition strikes harmed the economy, but the BNP government remained in office until November 1995. An election in February 1996 was boycotted by the opposition alliance, but the new parliament, overwhelmingly dominated by the BNP, passed an amendment that fully met the opposition's demands. Having done so, that parliament was dissolved and another election was held in June 1996.

The Return of the Awami League: Prime Minister Sheikh Hasina Wajed (1996–2001)

The electorate decided to give the Awami League an opportunity to lead due to the policy failures and programmatic dishonesty of the BNP. The Awami League won nearly 49 percent of the vote and was the majority party in the parliament, having won 146 out of 300 seats. An informal coalition among the Awami League, the Jatiya Party of Ershad (which won thirty-three seats although Ershad was in prison), and the Jatiyo Samajtantrik Dal (with one seat) formed the government. In early 1997 Ershad was released from prison, suggesting that a tacit agreement was worked out between the Awami League and Jatiya Party for gaining his support and subsequently releasing him from jail.

The election of 1996 was considered relatively free and fair. The Awami League regime was targeted by the same types of strategies and tactics it had used against the BNP. The opposition joined the parliament but left it at the end of 1996, rejoined in early 1997, left in fall 1997, and returned again in March 1998. A year later the opposition left again. This back-and-forth strategy in parliament was accompanied by street agitation and strikes that debilitated the economy. The primary rationale was the opposition's inability to present its views and act as a partner in the governance of the country, particularly its inability to ensure that local and municipal elections were held in a free and fair environment. Violence of all types became endemic during the Awami League's tenure, as was the perception of corruption. A caretaker government took over in July 2001 and held the parliamentary election in a timely manner.

Back to BNP: Khaleda Zia Prime Minister for a Third Time (2001–2006)

An interesting development during this period of transitional government was the visit by former president Jimmy Carter. He got the principal political parties, the Awami League and BNP, to renounce violent street agitation and strikes, thus facilitating the work of governance. The electorate viewed the political rancor with trepidation but, as in the earlier election of 1996, was also alert to the policy and programmatic dishonesty of the government. It also noted the glaring rise of corruption in society. The election was determined to be free and fair, although the Awami League, having lost the election, charged that it was rigged in favor of the BNP.

The BNP won a two-thirds majority in the parliament, much to its own surprise and that of the Awami League. The results showed the maturity of the Bangladeshi electorate and its ability to punish the government for wrongdoing and reward the opposition for exposing it. It also showed that the Bangladeshi electorate is looking for ways to facilitate good governance practices. The BNP regime began with high expectations, but within two years, it started to show signs of internal dissension that resulted in a power struggle between the old guards of the BNP and the younger generation led by the son of the prime minister. As internal strife became more intense, the work of governance became less important, and corrupt practices once again became the hallmark of the reigning political party. The depth and intensity of the corruption only became evident when the state of emergency was promulgated in January 2007.

Back to the Awami League: Hasina Again

Given the perception of lawlessness, corruption, and internal strife associated with the BNP regime, the Awami League won a resounding victory in the election held under the caretaker government in December 2008. It won 230 seats (with its major coalition partners winning a further 32 seats) in the 300-seat parliament, while the main opposition party, the BNP, won only 30 (with other parties in its alliance winning another 3). A new government was duly installed in January 2009 with Hasina as prime minister for a five-year term. While some progress was apparent in areas such as education, agricultural production, garment exports, external remittances, the prosecution of war criminals, and discussion in various international forums of Bangladesh's vulnerabilities to the processes of climate change, the government struggled with problems relating to maintaining law and order and establishing a fair and equitable system of justice, providing adequate energy for both industrial development and private consumption, arresting the increase in prices for essential commodities, and controlling pervasive, and at times dramatic, levels of corruption and nepotism. The issue of human rights and civil liberties was frequently brought up in the foreign press, in the reports of various international rights organizations, and in the cautionary advice given by most foreign dignitaries, including Hillary Clinton, who visited Bangladesh in 2012.

Parliamentary Government

Bangladesh has an emotional attachment to instituting a parliamentary form of governance. But its experiment with parliamentary government resulted in massive official stagnation, at times teetering on failure. Parliamentary government, which requires the party in power to work closely with the opposition and to have functioning committees in which opposition parties are also included, has not been institutionalized in Bangladesh.

The first experiment (1972–1975) ended when the major proponent of parliamentary government, Mujib, converted the political system to a presidential one in 1975. The second experiment (1991–2006) was unable to develop any sound practices, as the opposition hardly participated in the operations of the parliament.

When they formed their governments, neither the Awami League nor the BNP actively sought to integrate the opposition into the committee system of operation. The opposition actually disrupted government operation by a combination of street violence and boycotts of the parliament.

In 2007, questions were once again raised as to whether the parliamentary system of government is the most suitable one for Bangladesh, which seems to be heading toward a system in which the head of state (president) and the head of government (prime minister) have shared power, rather than the presidency being ceremonial and the prime minister possessing real power and authority. While shared power has its challenges, this mixed parliamentary and presidential form may have to be in place for a period during which trust in critical institutions of governance (judicial independence, free and fair elections, an impartial public bureaucracy, regularized process of leadership change, and equitable sharing of power between the different levels of state authority) becomes institutionalized. However, while the determined boycott of the parliament by the opposition and the occasional use of unparliamentary behavior and language in the floor of the House have served to erode public respect for that institution, the commitment to parliamentary supremacy (buttressed by the British legacy and the Indian example) remains strong in Bangladesh today.

The Institutions of Government

The Central Government

The constitution of Bangladesh provides for a president elected by parliament but lacking executive powers, although some presidents have exercised them. The Speaker of Parliament serves as a temporary successor until a new president is elected within 180 days of the President resigning or otherwise being unable to fulfill his responsibilities.

The head of government is the prime minister, who is commissioned by the president, but the president must in practice select the leader of the majority party or of a coalition if no party has a majority. Mujib, Khaleda Zia, and Hasina Wajed were elected prime ministers. The prime minister must win a vote of confidence from the parliament to be confirmed in office. The prime minister selects the members of the cabinet, no more than 5 percent of whom may be chosen from outside the members of parliament. The three hundred directly elected members of parliament are elected in single-member constituencies; the first-past-the-post voting system is used—that is, the candidate with the most votes is elected, and a majority is not required. An additional thirty seats for women are filled by election by the directly elected members as soon as the newly elected parliament meets (although women can and do contest the directly elected seats as well: witness the present prime minister and her predecessor). Laws are passed by the parliament and approved by the president. Should the president not approve a law, a further passage by the parliament overrides what is, in effect, a suspensory veto.

The government at the center is organized into a number of ministries and departments. At the head of each is a political minister who is a member of the cabinet and may have authority over more than one department. Some ministries and departments have junior political persons with the title of state minister. The nonpolitical head of a department or ministry, the secretary, is usually drawn from the civil service, although occasionally secretaries are drawn from the police service or, during military rule, even from the military. Although the secretary is responsible, under the minister, for the operation of the department as a whole, he or she is assisted by a range of subordinate officers with lower-level responsibility for segments of the department's work.

The members of the higher civil service (i.e., those who enter at a level that will allow them to aspire to the rank of secretary) are selected through examination, and there is a prescribed course of training at entrance and during service. The unified Bangladesh Civil Service, established in 1980, features fourteen cadres designed to bring together a number of separate services inherited from Pakistan (and British India). The foreign service operates as a semiautonomous cadre, although the examination procedures are the same as those for the civil service. The police constitute a service separate from the civil service. Senior police officers also enter by examination; the highest level for a police officer is inspector general. A number of boards, commissions, and corporations on an all-Bangladesh level draw a great many of their senior officers from the civil service.

The Supreme Court of Bangladesh has two divisions. The Appellate Division, as its name indicates, has only appellate jurisdiction and is the final court of appeal. The High Court Division has both appellate jurisdiction and some original jurisdiction. However, the point of original jurisdiction in most cases is the district court. The Fourth Amendment of the 1972 constitution placed the judiciary under the president of the country, and therefore Bangladesh did not initially have full separation of the executive and judicial branches.

In June 2007, the caretaker government took relevant measures to separate the judiciary from the executive. Critical to effective separation are the rules that place the judicial services under the direct supervision of the Supreme Court. Even more important is the fact that in case of a dispute between the Supreme Court and the presidency, the opinion of the Court will take precedence. District officers are also magistrates; they serve as hearing officers in many cases and perform the role of judge in lesser matters. The separation of the judiciary from the executive at the national level will correspondingly change the role of the district officers as magistrates of the courts. The appropriate modalities have yet to be worked out to the satisfaction of the courts and the civil service from which the magistrates are appointed.

Local Government

Administratively, Bangladesh is partitioned into six divisions (Dhaka, Chittagong, Khulna, Rajshahi, Barisal, and Sylhet), each headed by a commissioner. Below the divisions are sixty-four districts subdivided into 460 subdistricts (a subdistrict is alternately know as a *thana* or *upazila*). Below the Thana level are the 4,451 unions and 80,000 villages. Tinkering with the form of local government has been a pastime of each regime, as it had been before independence among the regimes of Pakistan. Although both the BNP and the Awami League have stated their intention to change the local government system instituted by Ershad, neither has yet done so. Ershad's goal was to move decision-making power closer to the people. Thus his local government system focused on the *upazila* level rather than the district level. The four-tier system is the foundation of the local government system. Hasina's government wanted to make the village the most operational level of the local government system. The third Khaleda government was thinking about moving away from the village and back to the *thana* or *upazila* level. The caretaker government of Fakhruddin Ahmed, based on a local government study report, expected to hold local-body elections prior to or in tandem with the national parliamentary election but was unable to do so. The salient features are direct election to the district council, direct revenue under the control of the local government, and reserved seats for women increased from 30 to 40 percent for the next three elections. The current government under Hasina Wajed has held elections to many of these bodies, but they have been marred by inconsistencies and boycotts by the opposition.

Each district is headed administratively by a deputy commissioner drawn from the civil service. He or she also has the titles of district collector (of revenue) and district magistrate (responsible for law and order and some judicial functions). In a minicabinet, the deputy commissioner has representatives of most of the central government departments (e.g., a superintendent of police, a district judge, a district public health officer). He or she is charged with the overall administration and development of the district. The task is not an easy one, as the other government representatives have a dual loyalty: to the deputy commissioner and, more importantly, to the head of the central government department in Dhaka, where assignments and promotions are controlled. Coordination can be difficult.

Below the district is the *upazila* (literally, subdistrict), of which there are 460. Elections are held to the *upazila* councils, which are intended to be the voice of the people at this level, depending on the government of the day. (There are also indirectly elected district councils, the electors being the members of the *upazila* councils.) The *upazila* is meant to be the focal point of administration and development. Below the *upazila* are unions that comprise one or more villages and also have elected councils. The executive at the *upazila* is the *upazila nirbahi* officer.

Urban coordinating bodies cover entire cities. In the largest urban areas (Dhaka, Chittagong, Khulna, and Rajshahi) there are municipal corporations with mayors and elected councils. Each also has a government-appointed administrator, roughly the equivalent of a city manager. Smaller urban areas have city or town councils. There are twenty such urban areas, also known as Pourashavas.

Police administration is headed by the inspector general of police, who serves nominally under the authority of the Home Ministry. At the district level there is a superintendent of police, and at the *upazila* level, an inspector of police. Commissioners of police direct the work in major urban areas and report directly to the inspector general.

Conclusion

In sum, Bangladesh is developing a structure of government for the long term. The place of a freely elected parliament in the governmental system has perhaps been ensured by the success of free and fair elections in June 1996, October 2001, and December 2008. Local government is weak, primarily because the system is viewed as the power base of the political party forming the government. The evolving system of government also appears to lessen the specter of direct military intervention. But as Bangladesh marches toward democratic governance, the problems of economic inequality, viability of local bodies, endemic corruption, and intolerant politics (particularly the personal animosity between the two women leaders, who apparently have a visceral dislike for each other, evident in their policies, in the shrillness of their rhetoric, and even in their body language), remain as challenges to be faced in the future.

SUGGESTED READINGS

Ahamed, Emajuddin. *Military Rule and the Myth of Democracy*. 2nd ed. Dhaka: Gatidhara Press, 2003.

Ahmed, Moudud. *Democracy and the Challenge of Development: A Study of Politics and Military Interventions in Bangladesh*. Dhaka: University Press, 1995.

Ali, Shawakat A. M. M. *Bangladesh Civil Service: A Political-Administrative Perspective*. Dhaka: University Press, 2004.

Anisuzzaman, Muhammad. *Bangladesh Public Administration and Society*. Dhaka: Bangladesh Books International, 1979.

Chakravarty, S. R., ed. *Bangladesh Under Mujib, Zia, and Ershad*. New Delhi: Har-Anand, 1995.

Choudhury, Dilara. *Constitutional Development in Bangladesh*. Karachi: Oxford, 1994.

Franda, Marcus. *Bangladesh: The First Decade*. New Delhi: South Asian Publishers, 1982.

Islam, Mahmudul. *Constitutional Law of Bangladesh*. Dhaka: Bangladesh Institute of Law and International Affairs, 1995.

Khan, Zillur Rahman. *Leadership in the Least Developed Nation: Bangladesh*. Syracuse, NY: Maxwell School, Syracuse University, 1983.

Maniruzzaman, Talukder. *The Bangladesh Revolution and Its Aftermath*. Dhaka: Bangladesh Books International, 1980.

Rahman, M. Shamsur. *Administrative Elite in Bangladesh*. New Delhi: Manka, 1991.

Rahman, Rafiqur A. T. *Reforming the Civil Service for Government Performance*. Dhaka: University Press 2001.

Zafarullah, H. *Government and Politics in Bangladesh*. Dhaka: Centre for Administrative Studies, 1981.

NOTES

1. Two members of the National Assembly chose to remain in Pakistan.

2. Craig Baxter, "Bangladesh in 1990: Another New Beginning," *Asian Survey* (February 1991): 146–152.

3. Craig Baxter and Syedur Rahman, "Bangladesh Votes—1991: Building Democratic Institutions," *Asian Survey* (August 1991): 683–693.

4. Craig Baxter, "Bangladesh in 1991: A Parliamentary System," *Asian Survey* (February 1992): 162–167.

5. Zillur Rahman Khan, "Bangladesh in 1993: Values, Identity, and Development," *Asian Survey* (February 1992): 160–167.

16

Elections, Parties, and Interest Groups

The 1991, 1996, 2001, and 2008 elections in Bangladesh may indicate a marginal change, but the earlier tendency of the electorate in Bengal, since the beginning of mass politics in about 1905, was to support a single leader and a single issue. This tendency has been a major factor in Bangladeshi politics, as the review of elections below shows.

Elections

Two elections during the British India period impacted Bangladesh. The first was held in 1936–1937 for Bengal's legislative council and legislative assembly. Much of the electorate in the eastern part of the Bengal gave its support to Maulvi Abul Kasim Fazlul Haq and his Krishak Praja Party (KPP, Farmer People's Party). The KPP supported the cause of the smaller farmers, who were primarily Muslims, against zamindars (landlords), who were generally Hindus.[1] In the second election, held in 1945–1946, the issue was a national one: the separation of Muslim-majority areas of undivided India from the Hindu-majority territories. The Muslim voters in Bengal gave their support to the Muslim League, which won overwhelmingly, gaining all six seats in the Central Legislative Assembly of India, with 94.01 percent of the vote, and winning 112 of the 119 Muslim seats in the provincial assembly, with 82.04 percent of the vote.[2] The outcome, however, was slightly ambiguous at the national level, for at the time that the poll was held, the concept of a Muslim homeland in India was based on the plural phrase "independent states" in the Lahore Resolution of 1940.

The first election of the Pakistan period was held in 1954. The national positions taken by the ruling Muslim League had alienated most Bengalis. The Muslim League was routed by the United Front, which consisted principally of Fazlul Haq's party, renamed the Krishak Sramik Party (KSP, Peasants' and Workers' Party), and the Awami League of Husain Shaheed Suhrawardy.[3] In this election two regional elite leaders combined forces and had the cooperation of a third, Maulana Abdul Hamid Khan Bhashani. The single issue in 1954 was greater participation in the governance of the state, then dominated by West Pakistan. Demands, embodied in twenty-one points, included the designation of Bengali as one of the official languages of Pakistan, along with other concessions that would give Bengalis, in the eyes of the East Pakistanis, greater participation in governing the state. Direct elections were suspended during the rule of Muhammad Ayub Khan (1958–1969), but direct elections, with open and free campaigning, were restored by the decrees of General Agha Muhammad Yahya Khan, and elections were held in 1970.[4] Sheikh Mujibur Rahman (Mujib) led the Awami League, and the issue was provincial autonomy as demanded in his Six Points. Again, the issue and the leader combined to produce a large-scale victory.

The first election in Bangladesh was held in 1973. The issue at the forefront, which once more resulted in Mujib's victory, was a request for confirmation that the people desired the four pillars of Mujibism. After the elections there

TABLE 16.1 Bangladesh Parliamentary Election Results

Party	1991		1996		2001		2008	
	Seats	Percentage of Vote	Seats	Percentage of Vote	Seats	Percentage of Vote	Seats	Percentage of Vote
Awami League	88	30.6	146	37.4	62	40.97	230	49
Bangladesh Nationalist Party	140	31	116	33.6	193	40.13	30	33.2
Jamaat-i-Islami	18	12.1	3	8.6	17	4.28	2	4.6
Jatiya Party	35	11.8	32	16.4	14	7.25	27	7
Independents and others*	19	14.4	3	3.9	15	6.03	11	6.1

* Independents and Others:

1991: Bangladesh Communist Party, 5; Bangladesh Awami Krishak Sramik League, 5; National Awami Party (Muzzafar), 1; Workers Party, 1; Jatiya Samajtantrik Party (Seraj), 1; Islamic Unity Group, 1; National Democratic Party, 1; Ganotantrik Dal, 1; independents, 3.

1996: Jatiyo Samajtantrik Dal, 1; Ganotantrik Dal, 1; independents, 1.

2001: Jatiya Party (Naziur), 1; Jatiya Party (Monju), 1; Islamic Unity Group, 2; Krishak Sramik Janata Party, 2; independents, 6.

2008: Jatiyo Samajtantrik Dal, 3; Workers Party, 2; Bangladesh Jatiya Party, 1; Liberal Democratic Party, 1; independents, 4.

TABLE 16.2 Parliamentary Elections and Votes Cast

Years	Number of Parties and Alliances Contesting Election	Total Voters and Percentage of Votes Cast
1973	14	35,205,642 (55.61)
1979	29	38,363,858 (51.29)
1986	28	47,876,979 (66.31)
1988	8	49,863,829 (51.81)
1991	96	62,181,743 (55.45)
1996	41	56,149,182 (26.54)
1996	81	56,716,935 (74.96)
2001	54	75,000,656 (75.59)
2008	38	81,087,003 (87.13)

Source: Bangladesh Election Commission Secretariat.

was no doubt, despite a measure of tinkering with the results, that the people supported Mujib. The Awami League won 291 seats of the 300 contested and took 73.18 percent of the popular vote (see Tables 16.1 and 16.2).

Elections were not held again until 1978, under the regime headed by Major General Ziaur Rahman (Zia). Zia won the presidential election that year with 76.63 percent of the vote, whereas his nearest rival, General M. A. G. Osmany, who had the support of the major faction of the Awami League, won only 21.70 percent.[5] Zia followed this outcome with a major victory in the parliamentary elections held in 1979 when his party, the Bangladesh Nationalist Party (BNP), won 207 of 300 seats. The percentage of the popular vote (41.16 percent), however, was lower than that going to the winners in previous elections because of the extraordinarily large number of candidates running.[6] The leader was clearly the charismatic Zia, and the issue was economic stabilization and advancement. Like Mujib, Zia wanted a confirmation of his nineteen-point program for Bangladesh. In 1981 Zia was assassinated, and the BNP successfully elected a successor, Abdus Sattar, but his feeble and inconsequential term ended when Husain Muhammad Ershad led a military coup in March 1982. Parliamentary elections held by Ershad's regime in 1987 and 1988 were also one-sided, largely because the BNP boycotted the election in 1986, and both the BNP and the Awami League boycotted in 1988.

Free and fair elections were not held again until February 27, 1991, after the fall of Ershad. The principal contestants were the BNP, now led by Khaleda Zia (Ziaur Rahman's widow), and the Awami League, led by Sheikh Hasina Wajed (daughter of Mujibur Rahman). A close contest ensued when the two parties, which had joined hands in the demonstrations leading to Ershad's removal in December 1990, resumed their rivalry. The BNP stood for a presidential system, private enterprise, recognition of the place of Islam, and a sense of Bangladeshi nationalism. The Awami League favored a parliamentary system, some continuation of the socialist policies of Mujib, secularism, and a vaguely defined concept of Bengali nationalism, which was sometimes interpreted to mean a pro-India stance. For the first time, there were clearly defined issues. In the end, the BNP won 140 of 300 seats, short of a majority, but increased this to 168 of 330 by winning 28 of the 30 women's seats in alliance with the Jamaat-i-Islami. The Awami League and its allies, with 99 seats, formed the principal opposition. The Jatiya Party of Ershad won thirty-five seats, despite the fact that its leader was in jail, and the Jamaat-i-Islami, because of its seat-sharing arrangements with its BNP ally, won eighteen. Nonetheless, perhaps demonstrating the lack of a dominant leader and the presence of multiple issues, the popular vote gave the BNP 31.0 percent and the Awami League a close 30.6 percent (see Table 16.1).[7]

When the Khaleda Zia government's five-year term ended, an election was held in February 1996. The opposition parties, mainly the Awami League, the Jatiya Party, and the JI, boycotted the election because they did not feel that the election authority would conduct a free and fair election. The Zia government again resigned but passed a constitutional amendment requiring elections to be held under a neutral caretaker government. With this in place, the opposition contested the June 1996 election. The Awami League won 146 seats; the BNP, 116; the Jatiya Party, 32; and the Jamaat, 3. In terms of votes received, the Awami League garnered 37.4 percent; the BNP, 33.6 percent; the Jatiya Party, 16.4 percent; and the Jamaat, 8.6 percent. The remaining 4.0 percent went to independents and candidates of other parties. After the Awami League completed its five-year term of office, the transitional system of the caretaker government conducted the election of 2001. The single defining issue—the abuse and misuse of power and authority—put the BNP back in power with an overwhelming majority. BNP won 193 seats, with 40.97 percent of the votes. The Awami League won only 62 seats but received 40.13 percent of the votes. Jamaat won 17 seats, and the Jatiya Party, 4 seats.[8]

Elections were scheduled for January 2007, but before they could be held, a state of emergency was declared on January 11, 2007, postponing them. Clashes within the BNP during its 2001–2006 tenure, extreme politicization of the major institutions of governance (bureaucracy, caretaker government, judiciary), continued mismanagement and abuse of power and authority, and the BNP's blatant attempt to hold onto power by manipulating the election agencies produced chaos in Bangladesh. The Awami League during this period was able to systematically disrupt and stymie the normal operations of government and governance. The tipping point that started the chaos during the

2001–2006 period and during the caretaker period between October 2006 and January 2007 was the Twelfth Amendment, which changed the retirement age for judges on the Supreme Court of Bangladesh and correspondingly impacted who would head the caretaker government. The opposition parties led by the Awami League coalesced and countered the BNP's hold-onto-power strategy with street politics and demonstrations, mass strikes, work stoppages, and economic disruptions, bringing Bangladesh close to collapse. Like other events with a monumental impact on the political development of Bangladesh—like Bangladesh's becoming independent in 1971, or Sheikh Mujibur Rahman's 1975 assassination, or the 1990 overthrow of Ershad—the January 11, 2007, declaration of a state of emergency would unquestionably bring a sea change in the evolution of Bangladesh as a democratic state.

Charismatic personalities, factionalism, and ineffective leadership tend to define the political party system of Bangladesh. Their leaders are generally not known for their zealous commitment to democratic ideals. Mujib, Zia, and Ershad were leaders by their own capacities. Hasina became a leader as representative of her father and Khaleda of her husband. All five leaders have failed to develop and nurture alternate leaders within the party and show an inability to withdraw from an active party position. Almost like sheep, party members and officials follow, and are unable to see beyond, the leader. Moreover, the cult of personality that is usually fostered creates inevitable tendencies toward sycophancy, rewards the display of frequent and elaborate demonstration of personal loyalty to the leader, discourages internal debate and discussion, and leads to party structures and procedures that remain essentially undemocratic, arbitrary, and intrigue ridden. Another aspect of Bangladeshi politics is factionalism, which is mostly driven by individuals with their own ambitions and agendas rather than by policy or ideological differences. It caused the victorious Muslim League in 1946 to reject Nazimuddin and replace him with the urbane emerging regional elitist Suhrawardy, although Muhammad Ali Jinnah's intervention reversed this decision once independence had been won. After the 1954 election, the United Front was unable to remain united, and from then until 1958, when Ayub took over, there was a constant tussle between Fazlul Haq's KSP and Suhrawardy's Awami League for control of the provincial government. Bhashani's defection from the Awami League also hurt the party. Through the imposition of emergency rule, Mujib kept most, but not all, of the Awami League together after 1973. But he was merely sweeping factionalism under the rug, and it reemerged after Mujib was assassinated in 1975. Zia's party was also factionalized, but this became evident only after his assassination in 1981. Ershad's Jatiya Party split into rival factions in 1996. To curtail factionalism, especially during Ershad's authoritarian rule, both the BNP and the Awami

League selected leaders, Khaleda Zia and Hasina Wajed, respectively, who were considered neutral and were related to the fallen leaders. The crisis of 2007 and the elections of 2008 may be having some impact in terms of encouraging transparency and accountability, but such hopes are probably overly ambitious and not likely to be fulfilled soon. While the two leaders remain supreme, and dissent is barely tolerated, some Awami League parliamentarians have found the confidence to question some ministers and public policies on the floor of the House, and some BNP leaders have resigned, or sought alternative affiliations, to indicate a subtle, but clear, need for a more internally tolerant party system.

Though effective in bringing his people together to rise in anger against injustice, Mujib was ineffective in the day-to-day management of the country. Zia proved more capable in getting diverse and often countervailing forces within Bangladesh to work together but was unable to institutionalize the process so that these forces would continue to cooperate. Ershad decentralized part of the government structure to make it more accessible to the people but could not bring together sufficient forces to transform his regime into a democratic one.

Ineffective leadership by both Hasina and Khaleda led to mismanagement in government, abuse of power and authority, fear of dynastic leadership, politicization of major institutions of government, and a culture of corruption that in two decades completely permeated Bangladeshi society.

Political Leaders

Some of the Bengali Muslim political leaders mentioned in this discussion began their careers during the British period and some in the Pakistani period; Ziaur Rahman and Husain Muhammad Ershad began their careers in the postindependence period. Only Mujibur Rahman's spanned all three periods. It is useful to look briefly at some of these key figures and analyze their political skills.

Maulvi Abul Kasim Fazlul Haq: The Regional Elite

Maulvi Abul Kasim Fazlul Haq (1873–1962) came from the coastal district of Barisal (then called Bakerganj) in eastern Bengal.[9] He was truly a vernacular Bengali in that he had neither the landed aristocratic background of Nazimuddin nor the urbane Muslim intellectual background of Suhrawardy. He completed his education in college and law school in Calcutta, where he qualified to become a *vakil* (local lawyer) and was called *maulvi* (learned person) by his contemporaries. He set out to serve people and thereby built up his political reputation. He entered elective politics in 1913, when he was elected to the

Bengal Legislative Council, serving until the council ended in 1937. He was a member of the Indian National Congress and the Muslim League (serving also as president) and formed his own party, the Krishak Praja Party, in 1927 (renamed the Krishak Sramik Party in 1947), leading it to victory in the United Front alliance with the Awami League in the 1954 election. He was the first prime minister of Bengal.[10] After independence, he served briefly as chief minister of East Bengal in 1954, as a central minister in 1955 and 1956, and as governor of East Pakistan from 1956 to 1958. He was the prime mover behind the 1940 Lahore Resolution calling for separate states for the Muslims of India. He worked at the national and regional levels with equal diligence. He knew the problems of his fellow Bengalis and worked assiduously to solve them. He supported land-reform legislation and greater expenditures on education and health. His legacy of the KSP as a party has all but disappeared, but its policies oriented toward rural development have been incorporated into the platforms of the Awami League and Zia's and Ershad's parties. Given his distinguished and active career, his oratorical skills, and his occasional defiance of the British and the Muslim League, Fazlul Haq clearly earned the title Sher-i-Bangla (Lion of Bengal), by which he is still known.

Khwaja Sir Nazimuddin: The National Elite

Throughout much of his career, Khwaja Sir Nazimuddin (1894–1964) was the principal rival of Fazlul Haq. Nazimuddin, a member of the wealthy landed family of the nawab of Dhaka, belonged to the national elite. He attended Aligarh Muslim University and then continued his studies at Cambridge University. Nazimuddin too was elected to the Bengal Legislative Council and served as a minister (1929–1934). He was home minister (1937–1941) and became opposition leader (1941–1943) before being chosen as prime minister (1943–1945).[11] Nazimuddin, after the independence of Pakistan, was named chief minister of East Bengal in 1947. He succeeded as governor-general of Pakistan on Jinnah's death in 1948 and then stepped down from that position to succeed Liaquat Ali Khan as prime minister when Liaquat was assassinated in 1951. He was dismissed from office in 1953. Under Ayub Khan, Nazimuddin reorganized the Muslim League (council faction) and headed the combined opposition against Ayub until his (Nazimuddin's) death in 1964.

Despite Nazimuddin's long service in high positions, Bengali Muslims never viewed him as representing them and their interests. He was a member of the national elite and spoke for all-India and later all-Pakistan interests. Although Nazimuddin did not represent the aspirations of the regional elite and the mass of Bengali Muslims, his skills were recognized in Dhaka. He, Fazlul Haq, and Suhrawardy are buried in adjacent graves in a Dhaka park.

Husain Shaheed Suhrawardy: The National Elite

Husain Shaheed Suhrawardy (1893–1963) came from a Muslim Bengali family of exceptional intellectual and artistic talents. Suhrawardy was educated at Calcutta and Oxford and entered the bar from Gray's Inn in London. He achieved prominence as deputy mayor of Calcutta in the 1920s, for his presumed support of Muslims in the Great Calcutta Killing in 1946, and for his close work with Mohandas Gandhi to calm communal disturbances in 1947. In 1937 he was elected to the Bengal assembly and served as a minister during the coalition with Fazlul Haq and during the premiership of Nazimuddin, with whom he developed a rivalry. He moved the resolution that amended the Lahore Resolution to provide for a single Muslim state. Shortly afterward, he proposed a united Bengal as a third dominion in India.

Suhrawardy was a member of the Pakistan Constituent Assembly. He opposed the Muslim League policy of exclusive Muslim membership and proposed the establishment of a new party open to all Pakistanis. He subsequently broke with the Muslim League to form what became the Awami League, a party primarily based in East Pakistan that became the voice of Bengali interests. Suhrawardy canvassed the entire province and led the party, in alliance with the KSP, to victory in 1954.

Suhrawardy agreed with Fazlul Haq that the KSP would govern in East Pakistan while Suhrawardy went to West Pakistan to represent Bengali interests there. He served as prime minister of Pakistan in 1956 and 1957, and in the eyes of many, he was the most skilled prime minister in the pre-Ayub period.

Suhrawardy was a convert to regional elitism. Although his own skills were best used at the national level, he chose a group of locally skilled political figures who built the Awami League into the best-organized party in Pakistan (albeit only in the east). His political lieutenant in Dhaka was Ataur Rahman Khan (1907–1991), who was several times chief minister of East Pakistan before Ayub and prime minister of Bangladesh (1984–1985). His organizational lieutenant was Sheikh Mujibur Rahman. At Suhrawardy's death in 1963, the party leadership fell to Mujib, who represented the regional elite to an even greater extent.

Sheikh Mujibur Rahman

Sheikh Mujibur Rahman (1920–1975) was born far from the centers of power, in Tungipara in Faridpur district. He attended but did not graduate from a college in Calcutta, having become involved in politics through the All-India Muslim Students Federation in 1940. He was a member of the Muslim League but joined Suhrawardy and others in what became the Awami League in 1949. He became general secretary in 1952 after gaining experience at lower levels of the organization and was elected to the East Bengal Legislative Assembly in 1954. He did brief stints in the cabinet at Dhaka and Karachi, but his skills were more appropriate to party organization and campaigning. Having become the de facto successor to Suhrawardy in 1963, Mujib was jailed on several occasions during the Ayub period. After he stated his six points in Lahore in 1966 (see Chapter 14), he was accused of collaborating with India to set East Pakistan free in what was known as the Agartala Conspiracy Case.[12] During the agitation against Ayub in 1968 and 1969, demands were made for his release. He was freed in 1969, and the case was never completed.

After leading the Awami League to victory in 1970, he was arrested in March 1971, as the military brutally cracked down on Bengali nationalists, and taken to prison in West Pakistan, but he returned to lead Bangladesh in 1972—first as prime minister and then as president. He was assassinated on August 15, 1975, under circumstances that are described in Chapter 17. Mujib's skills were clearly those of an organizer at the party level who gained fame for his considerable resourcefulness and flair in mobilizing large crowds at public meetings and became inextricably associated with the ethnocultural nationalism that he espoused and personified. His roots were in the countryside, and in this respect he was more the successor of Fazlul Haq than the urbane Suhrawardy. The traditions of both the Awami League and the KSP seemed to merge in Mujib, but the KSP strand was probably stronger. At the beginning of the independent era in Bangladesh, he was adored by the masses and given the title Bangabandhu (Friend of Bengal). His skills, however, could not be transferred to the running of an independent government—hence his failure in that realm. His charismatic ability to lead was adaptable only to a movement, and in this regard, he had few equals.

Maulana Abdul Hamid Khan Bhashani

Maulana Abdul Hamid Khan Bhashani (1885–1976) is an enigma in Bangladeshi politics. Born in a small village in Tangail district, he was a Bengali by birth and first achieved political fame when he wandered as a barely trained Islamic leader (hence the title *maulana*) to Assam and there took up the cause of tenant farmers against landlords. His views were often considered radical within the Assam Muslim League inasmuch as he espoused the needs of the downtrodden, at least as he defined them. After independence he moved back to East Bengal and continued to support those causes. He joined Suhrawardy in founding the Awami League. Party discipline and Bhashani were strangers. He stood well to the left of the conservative Suhrawardy and worked poorly with the populist Mujib. Bhashani broke with the Awami League to form what became the National Awami Party in 1957, and under that umbrella he associated with groups ranging from the remnants of the banned Communist Party of Pakistan, to moderates who fought for the restoration of democracy, to others whose principal demands were the undoing of the single province of West Pakistan. Bhashani supported Ayub to the extent of endorsing Ayub's policy of closer relations with China, but in the end he was an outspoken opponent of Ayub, as he would later be of Mujib. Bhashani represented another element in the regional elite, often a group to whom the word "elite" can barely be applied. He and his party never gained significant electoral support, but he was expected to take up the cause of the less fortunate—whether it was against the West Pakistanis, or the Awami League in Bangladesh, or even India on the Farakka water question (see Chapter 26). No one has ever replaced him, as all potential claimants have lacked his charisma and his instinctive grasp of populist sentiments and demands.

Ziaur Rahman

Major General Ziaur Rahman (1936–1981) was the principal leader of Bangladesh from 1975 until his death. He was born in Bogra district and attended the Pakistan Military Academy. His military career was uneventful until he found himself in control of Chittagong on March 27, 1971, and broadcast a Bangladeshi declaration of independence. He was a hero of the liberation war but not a favorite of Mujib and had risen only to the position of deputy chief of the army staff by the time Mujib was assassinated. The sepoys (soldiers) claimed him as their leader in the series of attempted revolutions in November 1975, and he emerged then as the army leader in the martial law government. He subsequently became chief martial law administrator (CMLA) and then assumed the presidency in 1977, a post to which he was elected in 1978.

Despite his war record, Zia seemed an unlikely person to achieve a high degree of popularity. He was quietly efficient but propelled himself into the public image by a seemingly unending whirl of tours throughout Bangladesh. He exhorted the Bangladeshis to work together—a key demand in a factionalized nation—to develop the resources of the country, limited though they were. Indeed, he preached the politics of hope, winning his position of leadership by this means and through his ability to make quick decisions. Moreover, he had remained personally honest, overseen the popular food-for-work program, and tirelessly exhorted the people to adopt family-planning practices. There was no reconciliation between Zia and the Awami League, but his nineteen-point program drew on the demands of the regional elite and advocated rural-development ideas that could be traced to Fazlul Haq. From his start as a shy, almost retiring person, Ziaur Rahman grew to be one of the most success-ful of the postindependence Bangladeshi leaders.

Like the Awami League, the Bangladesh Nationalist Party founded by Zia, factionalized after the loss of its leader. The aged vice president, Abdus Sattar, was chosen as the party's candidate to succeed Zia in order to avoid rivalries among other contenders. However, the ultimate result was the choice of Zia's widow, Khaleda Zia, to lead the party. As noted earlier, she campaigned suc-cessfully in the 1991 and 2001 elections and became prime minister.

Husain Muhammad Ershad

Lieutenant General Husain Muhammad Ershad (b. 1930) led a military coup on March 24, 1982, against the regime headed by Abdus Sattar, who had been elected to succeed Ziaur Rahman. Ershad, like Zia, was a career military man. As he was in Pakistan during the civil war, he was unable to participate in the liber-ation campaign. Upon his repatriation to Bangladesh in 1973, he was appointed adjutant general, and in 1975, after a year at the Indian National Defence College in New Delhi, he was named deputy chief of staff of the army. When Zia relin-quished his post as chief of staff in 1978, Ershad replaced him and thereby became the principal military person on active duty. After Zia's assassination and Sattar's election, Ershad stated that the military should have a defined role in the governance of Bangladesh, a position that the civilian Sattar opposed.

As a leader (first as CMLA and then combining that position with the pres-idency), Ershad was unable to develop the charisma that characterized Zia. Er-shad did not hold elections until 1986, first for parliament and then for the presidency. His party, Jatiya, won the first and he the second, in both cases without the BNP's participation and in the second with no significant orga-nized opposition. The withdrawal of the Awami League from parliament trig-gered another election for that body in 1988, and the Jatiya Party won overwhelmingly against little opposition.

While Ershad continued the foreign policy set out by Zia and built on Zia's program of economic and social development, he never gained the popular sup-port that the preceding military president had achieved. His authoritarian rule often curtailed the freedoms provided by the constitution of 1972. He faced a serious uprising in the fall of 1987 but was able to put it down. Unsuccessful in repressing renewed demonstrations against him in the fall of 1990, he was forced to resign in December of that year. However, his party, as noted earlier, did win seats in the 1991, 1996, and 2001 elections. Although he was jailed during the Khaleda Zia regime, he was permitted bail and the right to take his parliamentary seat during the Sheikh Hasina government. He even supported the Awami League to the extent that one of his party's leaders joined the cabinet. He was convicted of corruption and returned to jail in November 2000. In 2007 he announced his retirement from active politics, but he continues to remain politically involved as a wily tactician with a solid vote bank in the northern district from which he comes.

Begum Khaleda Zia

Born in 1945, Begum Khaleda Zia, widow of Ziaur Rahman, became the leader of the BNP in 1984. She worked to keep the factionalized party together and firmly opposed Ershad. Under her leadership, the BNP refused to contest either of the two elections held during Ershad's presidency. After the February 1991 election, she became prime minister and, despite her previously expressed views, agreed to a return to a parliamentary system. She and her party were defeated in the June 1996 election, and she became leader of the opposition. In 2001 she returned to power, but within two years acceded to sharing the reigns of public authority with her son, who was perceived as excessively ambitious and cocky.

The caretaker government that came to power in 2007 charged her with corruption and graft, and many of those charges are currently being pursued by the Awami League government, which is intent upon punishing her two sons, who had apparently amassed huge assets and demonstrated a very cavalier attitude toward ethical principles or legal norms. She was even evicted from her residence, which the Awami League claimed had been improperly given to her. As leader of the opposition, she is challenging the government of Hasina by leading mass protests, meetings, and strikes; yet she is ignoring her obligations as an elected representative of the people by not joining the parliament.

Sheikh Hasina Wajed

The daughter of Sheikh Mujibur Rahman, Hasina Wajed was out of Bangladesh when her father was assassinated. With competition for leadership in the Awami League, she was called back to Bangladesh in 1981 to head the party. She led a change in the party's platform by dropping Mujib's professed commitment to socialism. She led the opposition after the 1986 election but withdrew her party from the parliament and did not contest the resulting 1988 election. In 1991 she again became leader of the opposition, and in June 1996, prime minister. Her domestic and foreign policy successes during this period were overshadowed by her inability to overcome the family tragedy of 1975 and the single-minded pursuit of her father's assassins. In July 2007 the caretaker government arrested her, alleging corruption and extortion. Voted back into power as prime minister with a comfortable majority in 2008, she has been able, as expected, to throw out most of the cases brought against her or powerful party members, executed the people found guilty of killing her father, started the International Crimes Tribunals of 1971 to try war criminals, scrapped the institution of the caretaker government, and tried to present a more secular image of Bangladesh to the world.

Political Parties

The Awami League

Having observed the sharp division between the all-Pakistan goals of the Muslim League and the aspirations of the East Pakistanis, two prominent pre-independence political figures returned to politics in the early 1950s. One of them was Fazlul Haq and the other was Husain Shaheed Suhrawardy, who strongly held the view that the Muslim League had accomplished its goal with the partition of India and should be dissolved in favor of a new national party that would include non-Muslims. In 1951 Suhrawardy and some others from East Pakistan formed the Awami (People's) Muslim League as an opposition group. This was renamed simply the Awami League, and membership was open to all Pakistani citizens. The new Awami League was unable to make serious inroads into the west wing of Pakistan, although it formed alliances with short-lived opposition groups in the west.

Suhrawardy's intellectual leadership was a major asset to the new party. He was joined by a large number of vernacular elite Muslim League members but by only a few members of the highest echelons of the East Pakistan Muslim League. Among the former were Ataur Rahman Khan and Sheikh Mujibur Rahman, who eventually succeeded Suhrawardy in the leadership of the party.[13] Still another was the religious and political leader Maulana Abdul Hamid Khan Bhashani. The Awami League's first venture into electoral politics came in 1954 when it joined hands with the KPP and other smaller parties to form the United Front, which defeated the Muslim League in the East Pakistan provincial election. The United Front government was dissolved within three months of its formation. The key election issue was the status of the Bengali language. During the Ayub period, the Awami League consistently opposed military rule and sought to pursue issues relating to provincial autonomy and ethnolinguistic impulses among the Bengalis in East Pakistan.

The Awami League remained the focus of opposition to Ayub and contested the indirect elections of the president's Basic Democracies Scheme. Several of the leaders, especially Mujibur Rahman, were jailed for significant periods. The quiet work of strengthening the organization continued. When

Ayub was dismissed and replaced by Yahya Khan, who promised free politicking and direct elections, the Awami League was ready to resume full and open activity. In the December 1970 election for the National Assembly, the Awami League swept the polls in East Pakistan by winning 160 of the 162 seats at stake and garnering about three-quarters of the popular vote. In the election for the provincial assembly, it all but duplicated this feat, winning 288 of the 300 directly elected seats.

The Awami League leaders who were able to escape arrest by Pakistani authorities in March 1971 set up a government in exile in Calcutta. Syed Nazrul Islam was designated acting president in the absence of Mujibur Rahman, who was in jail in West Pakistan. The Awami League coordinated the resistance to the Pakistani army, joined by several small leftist parties, although it remained a party of the center. It took over the reins of government after the Pakistani surrender in December 1971.

Mujib's one-party decree in 1975 led to the formation of the Bangladesh Krishak Sramik Awami League (BAKSAL), an amalgamation of the names of the two principal parties in the United Front of 1954. With the assassination of Mujib, BAKSAL was ordered dissolved. The Awami League was revived when parties were permitted to function again in 1976. It contested the presidential election of 1978 but lost. A split in the Awami League did not hurt the party in the parliamentary election of 1979, in which it finished a distant second to the Bangladesh Nationalist Party. In the presidential election of 1981 the Awami League ran Kamal Hussain, a former foreign minister, against the incumbent acting president, Abdus Sattar, and again was soundly defeated.

The party is now under the leadership of Sheikh Hasina Wajed, the daughter of Sheikh Mujibur Rahman. The party opposed elections under Ershad's martial law regime but reversed that position and participated in the May 1986 election, winning about seventy seats. Sheikh Hasina Wajed became leader of the opposition in parliament. However, in the fall of 1987, the party left the parliament, causing that body's dissolution, and did not participate in the 1988 election. It had returned to the "no vote under Ershad" stance. In the 1991 election, it finished behind the BNP and was formally designated the opposition; it won the 1996 election, lost the 2001 election, then won again in 2008.

The Awami League in 1972 strongly supported the four pillars of Mujibism: democracy, nationalism, socialism, and secularism. Despite the deviation to authoritarianism in the latter Mujib period, the party campaigned in 1991 for a return to a parliamentary system with regular free and fair elections. It has abandoned the socialism pillar of Mujibism, however, and its present economic platform differs little from that of the BNP and the Jatiya Party. It opposes the steps taken by Zia and Ershad away from what the party might describe as pure secularism. Some feel that the party takes a more favorable attitude toward India, a stance many consider controversial, if not questionable.

In 2006 the Awami League effectively counteracted the BNP's attempt to ensure electoral successes but also damaged its own most sacred pillar of secularism by signing a coalition agreement with a fringe religious party, the Bangladesh Khelafat Majlish. The memorandum of agreement dealt with who can issue a fatwa (religious edict) ban on laws that go against Quranic values, recognition of degrees awarded by Madrasas, and a ban on criticism of the Prophet Muhammad. Under the state of emergency in 2007 and following its victory in 2008, the Awami League undertook a self-analysis of its organizational structure and administrative and managerial procedures. Given its grassroots permeation in Bangladesh, and its fairly long history as a political party at the forefront in demanding, and later creating, the state of Bangladesh, the Awami League enjoys some emotional support and organizational stability. It is less likely to split into factions, although there is every likelihood that its leadership identification and selection process may undergo some changes.

Bangladesh Nationalist Party

Formed in 1978 in support of President Ziaur Rahman, the Bangladesh Nationalist Party was built partly on the basis of its predecessor, the National Democratic Party, which used the acronym JAGODAL. To the JAGODAL were added splinter groups from a wide variety of parties, ranging from a portion of the conservative Muslim League to several leftist fragments; collectively these now form the BNP. Abdus Sattar was appointed head of the BNP, although Zia was the real leader. The party supported the nineteen-point program for the reconstruction and development of Bangladesh (see Chapter 15). As the JAGODAL, the party was behind Zia's successful election to the presidency; as the BNP, it won about two-thirds of the seats in the parliamentary election of 1979. After Zia's assassination, the BNP successfully supported Abdus Sattar in his election to the presidency in 1981.

Following Zia's assassination, and even before the Sattar campaign, there were signs of factionalism in the party. Some younger members thought that a younger candidate for the presidency than Sattar should be chosen, but the party was unable to agree on an alternate. After Ershad took over, the party further factionalized. It co-opted as party leader Zia's widow, Khaleda Zia, who was very much in the background during her husband's term of office. Like the Awami League, the BNP opposed the holding of elections under Ershad's martial law. Unlike the Awami League, the BNP boycotted the election of May 1986 and also that of March 1988, a course that placed its future in question. But its position was consolidated when it joined the Awami League in demonstrations that resulted in Ershad's fall. In the 1991 election after the fall of Ershad, the BNP won a small majority of the seats and formed the government, but it lost the June 1996 elections, won in 2001, lost again in 2008, and now forms the leading opposition party.

The policies of the BNP were a moderate reversal of those of the Awami League. It supported a freer economy, maintained the present formulation of "absolute trust and faith in Almighty Allah," and stood for a presidential form of government. This position changed after the 1991 election, when the BNP agreed to a reversion to the parliamentary form. In foreign policy, the Zia government built close relations with the United States, China, and the Arab states—relations it wishes to maintain. It also prefers to carry out subcontinental politics in the context of the South Asian Association for Regional Cooperation (see Chapter 30), which was formed largely through his initiative and holds a more reserved position toward India than the Awami League.

In 2001, the BNP returned to form the government with an absolute majority but soon lost its traction because of internal dissension. Khaleda Zia allowed her son Tarique Zia to become increasingly the real power broker in the government. In effect, under the BNP rule of 2001 to 2006, the formal government was headed by Khaleda Zia and a parallel government was led by Tarique Rahman Zia. He initially held the post of joint secretary-general and, leading up to the expected January 2007 parliamentary election, became the senior secretary-general of the BNP. He was instrumental in the somewhat systematic removal of BNP old guards like former president of Bangladesh Dr. Badruddoza Chowdhury, who went on to form a political forum and later a political party, the Liberal Democratic Party. Since January 2007, and after its debacle in the 2008 elections, the BNP has been challenged to democratize its internal operations and is trying to quell the bickering and faction fighting that have inevitably resulted. However, the call for mass action and its successful demonization of the Awami League have helped it to withstand any major divisions within the party for the time being.

Jatiya Party

The party formed in 1983 to support the program and person of Ershad, which at that time used the acronym JANODAL (People's Party), is now known as the Jatiya Party (also meaning People's Party). It largely comprises defectors from the BNP, a few former Awami Leaguers, and certain others from smaller parties as well as some who were previously inactive in politics. Ershad was unable to generate the enthusiasm for himself or his program that Zia had been able to mobilize. But Ershad, having won confirmation in office in the March 1985 referendum, proceeded to a parliamentary poll in May 1986. The Jatiya

Party did not achieve a large majority; rather, it squeaked by with a bare majority of 152 of 300 seats. It won a large majority in the almost uncontested 1988 election. In 1991 it won thirty-five seats and 11.8 percent of the vote despite the fact that much of its leadership, including Ershad, was in jail. After the June 1996 election in which it won thirty-two seats and 16.4 percent of the vote, Ershad was permitted bail and took his seat in parliament. One member of the Jatiya Party took a seat in the Awami League cabinet, but Ershad maintains that his party's support is subject to review on each issue. As mentioned above, Ershad later broke with the Awami League and joined forces with the BNP and the Jamaat as the opposition. However, a faction of the Jatiya Party led by a minister remains supportive of the Awami League. In the 2001 election, the Jatiya Party won only fourteen seats. Internal dissension caused the party to split into two, and with Ershad's announcement in 2007 that he is retiring from politics, the Jatiya Party is likely to become insignificant, although for the time being it will remain active in the northern areas of Bangladesh, especially Rangpur, Ershad's birthplace. It contested the elections of 2008 as two different parties belonging to two competing electoral alliances, together received about 7 percent of the vote, and won about twenty-seven seats in parliament.

The Islamic Right

Islamic fundamentalism is a noisy—but not important—factor in Bangladeshi politics. The only party of any size is the Jamaat-i-Islami, an offshoot of the party by the same name in Pakistan. It stands for the adoption of an Islamic state in Bangladesh. The party polled 12.1 percent of the vote and won twenty seats in the 1991 election. Its support for the BNP in voting for the women's seats permitted the BNP to gain a majority in the parliament. It was embroiled in 1992 in a controversy over its leader, Golam Azam, who opponents claim is not a Bangladeshi citizen and who was allegedly responsible for the deaths of Bangladeshi nationalists while working with the Pakistani army in 1971. He has since retired from his position as amir, or the supreme leader of the party, and has been replaced by Matiur Rahman Nizami, who is also accused of anti-Bangladesh actions during 1971. The party's performance in the June 1996 election was poorer than in 1991; it won only three seats and 8.6 percent of the vote. In the 2001 election Jamaat won seventeen seats and could garner only 4.28 percent of the vote. The Jamaat was part of the 2001–2006 BNP-led government that also included the Islamic Oikyo Jote, which won two seats. Another Islamic party, the Islamic Jatiya Party, which won fourteen seats, did not participate in the BNP government. The Jamaat received about 4.6 percent of the vote in 2008 but could win only two seats in the legislature. The Islamic

Oikyo Jote also contested the elections, but its support base was negligible, and it won no contests. Other minor Islamic parties also exist; some have localized bases of support in some enclaves, and some may even employ extremist rhetoric and claim relationship with external jihadi (militant) forces operating at the global level, but they are, at best, fringe entities and have little resonance or legitimacy in Bangladeshi politics.

The Left

Nowhere is the Bengali penchant for factionalism more evident than in the fragmentation of the already small left wing of politics. There is a veritable multitude of such parties, often local groups gathered around a single leader. Although these parties can occasionally win a single seat in the parliament, they cannot seriously affect the outcomes of elections.

Other than the East Pakistan offshoot of the pre-independence Communist Party of India, the organized Left can best be traced to the 1955 split in the Awami League. Bhashani and certain others withdrew, combined with groups in West Pakistan, and formed the National Awami Party (NAP). The power of the new party in East Pakistan was attributed to the fact that it held the balance between the contending Krishak Sramik Party and Awami League in the provincial assembly after the breakup of the United Front.[14]

Like the other parties, the NAP was unable to work in a free environment during the Ayub period, although Bhashani strongly supported Pakistan's opening to China. The party began to fragment; indeed, the major division occurred in the mid-1960s, when a Bhashani faction competed in East Pakistan with one led by Muzaffar Ahmad. The former was often described as "pro-Peking" and the latter as "pro-Moscow," the designation of the Bhashani group having been highly exaggerated. The tiny Muzaffar group continues to exist, as it has for some time, as a leftist hanger-on of the Awami League. The Bhashani group has experienced continued and repeated fragmentation, to the extent that Bhashani's son was briefly in Ershad's cabinet. Many of the leftist leaders of the past have been incorporated into the Awami League, and after the 2008 elections, several of them have been given important ministerial positions in the Hasina cabinet.

Bureaucrats

The highly selective nature of recruitment for the upper levels of the civilian and military services makes them an elite with interests they are sure to pursue. The civilian bureaucracy was merit based but became increasingly politicized, first in 1970 and later in 1990, such that its performance was severely downgraded while its political activities became unethical and went against all norms of public service rules and regulations. However, the mystique of the civil services continues to impress many Bangladeshis, and many senior service holders are frequently given ambassadorial posts, advisory roles in the cabinet, or important administrative assignments. They may have lost their previous swagger, but given their experience and expertise, they generally retain their importance. It may also be mentioned that joining the government bureaucracy has been a coveted dream for many people in Bangladesh because of the promise of security, authority, and respect. The military bureaucracy was more professionalized, but in 1970 it became increasingly politicized, and it became part of several military-ruled administrations in the 1980s and early 1990s. In the latter part of the twentieth century it was less prone to participating in the direct political process unless there was an emergency of the kind that emerged in 2007. The military bureaucracy increasingly views itself as an international peacekeeping force, and its strategic interest lies outside Bangladesh today.

Students and Universities

The university community has long been a political force. Many Muslim League and Awami League leaders gained their first political experience at Calcutta or Dhaka before 1947. After 1947, students and some professors were at the forefront of the movements for recognition of the Bengali language, parity for East Pakistan, and eventually autonomy and freedom for the east wing of Pakistan. The most vicious attack by the Pakistani army in March 1971 was made against Dhaka University, and another round of killings of intellectuals took place just before the army surrendered in December 1971.

Student groups today are generally aligned with one or another of the political parties.[15] Students have become radicalized, and the polarization between the Left/secular and the Islamic/fundamentalist forces is clearly evident. Nonetheless, the fact that most student groups are located in key urban areas, Dhaka, Chittagong, and Rajshahi, causes concern to whatever government is in power. The students are capable of demonstrations, some of which are violent and can tie up the city, and they often support general strikes (*hartals*). Allegations against various student leaders of interfering in student dorm administrations, pursuing profitable business transactions, and engaging in threats and violence on campus have significantly eroded the high respect that student politics, or student leaders, used to enjoy in the country. Consequently, even though university students have a rich and proud legacy of standing in the forefront of many nationalist and progressive movements, their current activities have become questionable and unpopular with many.

Trade Unions

In nations with surplus labor, trade unions are unlikely to have a major impact on politics. Although Bangladesh has large numbers of potential laborers, many of them are unskilled; hence, there have been examples in the country of skilled and specialized groups of workers being able to exercise some influence on political and economic policies. Furthermore, the migration of some specialized groups for employment in the Middle East has created shortages in some areas. Unions are often closely tied to political parties, although there are also some factory unions. Strikes are generally discouraged by the government. Workers will, however, join other groups in demonstrations, especially when economic matters, such as changes in the subsidized price of food grains, are at issue. If and when significant industrial growth takes place, more trade union activity can be expected. It must be borne in mind, however, that the basic advantage that Bangladesh enjoys over other countries in terms of economic competitiveness is the low wages for the workers. Consequently, owners of various manufacturing plants, such as the flourishing garments industry, discourage and restrict the formation of trade unions. The frequent unrest and clashes seen in the manufacturing sector may be partly explained by the weak bargaining skills and resources of the workers who, after a period of accumulating grievances, react in desperate anger and lawlessness because negotiating mechanisms, or procedures to understand and respond to their demands, are either not in place or not accorded much significance (notwithstanding the government's support for relevant International Labour Organization conventions and owners' frequent promises to be more sensitive to worker demands). The murder of labor leader Aminul Islam in 2012 generated strong protests from human rights organizations, US garment importers, and even the US Senate.

Rural Elites: Secular and Religious

In a land-poor country such as Bangladesh, the holder of as little as five acres of land can be influential in his village area. Those with the land ceiling of thirty acres are very influential. Landlordism in the traditional sense of large estates disappeared in several stages, beginning with the Fazlul Haq ministry in united Bengal and culminating in land reforms during the early years after Pakistan's independence. Nonetheless, traditional elite families are accorded respect, and their members can draw on vote banks, though to a much more limited degree than earlier. Such elites are likely to oppose further land reform, support government programs that provide agricultural assistance, and look for higher government purchase prices for commodities. Until the landless and very small landholders and tenant farmers become better organized, these elites are likely to continue to exercise a high degree of domination in the rural areas.

Bangladesh has not yet followed the path of many Islamic-majority countries in demanding the establishment of an Islamic state. The constitution was amended by Zia to give recognition to the Muslim-majority by amending the secularist fundamental principle of state policy to read that the Bangladeshis had "absolute trust and faith in Almighty Allah" and that Muslims could order their lives according to the Sunnah. However, he also made it clear that the rights of minorities to practice and preach their faiths would not be inhibited. The reason behind the Zia move seems to have been an attempt to assuage Middle Eastern states' complaint that Bangladesh was not sufficiently Islamic to warrant large assistance packages from the oil-rich nations. During his regime, Ershad declared Bangladesh an Islamic state, but this seems not to have affected the role of non-Muslims.

The religious leaders, or *pirs*, have not played an important role in either East Pakistani or Bangladeshi politics. Although many are respected by their followers, a demarcation seems to have occurred between religion (viewed generally as a private matter) and politics—a demarcation that has become increasingly atypical of Muslim-majority nations. Early in his rule, Ershad had the constitution amended to declare Islam the state religion, but no further steps have been taken. An emerging fundamentalism in Bangladesh is supported indirectly by the Islamic right. Jama'atul Mujahedeen Bangladesh (JMB), an insignificant fringe party, was able to provide a distorted leadership to radicalism in Bangladesh. The party's public face was Bangla Bhai, who was involved in religious vigilantism with an intent to propel Bangladesh toward fundamentalism. In the waning hours of the 2001–2006 BNP rule, the extent of the JMB's plans to radicalize Bangladesh became known, and effective steps were taken to reduce this threat. Bangladesh under the caretaker government of Fakhruddin Ahmed executed Bangla Bhai and JMB's leading members after an open and fair trial. The poor showing of the Islamist parties in the 2008 elections and the self-consciously secular orientations of the Awami League government, which won a massive victory in that year, indicate the weaknesses of Islamist radicalism in the country.

SUGGESTED READINGS

Ahamed, Emajuddin. *Military Rule and the Myth of Democracy.* 2nd ed. Dhaka: Gatidhara Press, 2003.

Ahmed, Moudud. *Bangladesh: Era of Sheikh Mujibur Rahman.* Dhaka: University Press, 1983.

Ahmed, Rafiuddin, ed. *Religion, Nationalism, and Politics in Bangladesh.* New Delhi: South Asia Publications, 1990.

Banu, U. A. B. Razia Akhter. *Islam in Bangladesh.* Leiden: E. J. Brill, 1991.

Bhuiyan, Muhammad Abdul Wadud. *Emergence of Bangladesh and the Role of the Awami League.* New Delhi: Vikas, 1982.

Chakravarty, S. R. *Bangladesh: The Nineteen Seventy-Nine Elections.* New Delhi: South Asian Publishers, 1988.

Ghosh, Shyamali, *The Awami League, 1949–1971.* Dhaka: Academic, 1990.

Hossain, Golam. *General Ziaur Rahman and the BNP.* Dhaka: University Press, 1988.

Kochanek, Stanley A. *Patron-Client Politics and Business in Bangladesh.* Thousand Oaks, CA: Sage, 1993.

NOTES

1. For more detailed results, see Craig Baxter, *Bangladesh: From a Nation to a State* (Boulder, CO: Westview Press, 1997), 51.

2. Baxter, *Bangladesh*, 54.

3. Baxter, *Bangladesh*, 74–75.

4. Baxter, *Bangladesh*, 79.

5. Baxter, *Bangladesh*, 99–100, also presents the detailed results of the 1981 presidential election.

6. Baxter, *Bangladesh*, 101–102.

7. Baxter, *Bangladesh*, 113.

8. Baxter, *Bangladesh*, 118–120, and Eighth Parliamentary Election, *Statistical Report,* Bangladesh Election Commission, April 2002.

9. Baxter, *Bangladesh*, 128–129.

10. Biographies in English of Bengali leaders are scarce. See A. S. M. Abdur Rab, *A. K. Fazlul Haq: His Life and Achievements* (Lahore: Firozsons, 1966). Kazi Ahmed Kamal, *Politics and Inside Stories* (Dhaka: Kazi Giasuddin Ahmed, 1970), discusses Fazlul Haq, Suhrawardy, and Bhashani.

11. Under the Government of India Act of 1935, and until independence in 1947, the heads of government in the provinces were designated prime ministers (premiers). After independence the title in both India and Pakistan was changed to chief minister; the title of prime minister was reserved for the head of the central government.

12. So named from Agartala, the capital of the Indian state of Tripura, where the plot was allegedly hatched.

13. The actual head of the All-Pakistan Awami League was a West Pakistani, but Mujib controlled the bulk of the party through his leadership of the East Pakistan party.

14. The West Pakistan NAP held a similar balancing position in that wing between the Muslim League and the Republican Party.

15. These allowances are not formal but obvious, and student politics in the state universities tend to reflect the hyper-partisanship expressed at the national level.

17

Conflicts and Resolution

Bangladesh has seen a number of conflicts, some of which have already been discussed, such as the dispute between the parliamentary and presidential forms of government. This chapter focuses on four conflicts in particular. First, the military has played an extra-constitutional role, has at times been politicized, and at one time demanded a permanent role in the operation of the government. Second, Bangladesh has been involved in a lasting struggle with the tribes in the Chittagong Hill Tracts (CHT) that may be coming to an end. Third, there has been a lack of cooperation between the government party and the opposition, for which Bangladesh has at times incurred significant political and economic costs. Finally, as an aftermath of September 11, 2001, extremism and terrorism are emerging issues.

The Military

The roots of Bangladesh's military history can be traced back to the Sepoy Mutiny of 1857 (also known as India's First War of Independence), when the Bengal Army of British India rebelled against British rule. The Bengal Army was defeated and then disbanded. The upshot was that, even though most of the action of the "mutiny" unfolded in the north and west (Lucknow and Delhi) rather than in Bengal and the leadership was hardly ever in Bengali hands, the British decided not to recruit Bengalis into the Indian army. Moreover, the British tended to identify the Punjabis and Sikhs as "martial races" that could be recruited and be relied on to serve the cause of empire. Thus, at the time of Pakistan's independence, Bangladesh, then East Pakistan, did not have a large representation in the Pakistani armed force. Between 1947 and

1972, no systematic attempt was made to significantly increase the representation of Bengalis in the Pakistani armed forces. Thus, when the war of liberation began, Bengalis made up approximately 6 percent of the total armed forces of Pakistan. In March 1971 the Pakistani military took brutal and aggressive actions against civilians in East Pakistan and required all Bengali members of the armed forces to surrender their arms. The small force of trained Bengalis defected from the Pakistani military, joined the Mukti Bahini (Freedom Fighters), and became the core of the organized resistance against the Pakistani occupation and oppression. They were joined by the civilian police and Ansar brigades (a paramilitary force of Bengalis), border guards, and thousands of young men and women who took up arms in the defense of their country.[1] With their gallantry, determination, and guerrilla tactics, sustained by the continued and active support they received from the vast majority of the population, they were able to neutralize the well-equipped armed forces of Pakistan. When India interceded directly in the war in late November 1971, the Pakistani forces were defeated, and Bangladesh became independent in December of that year. Trained Bengali military personnel who were in West Pakistan at the beginning of the war of liberation were relieved of their duties and detained and isolated in camps in West Pakistan. Those who fought the war are known as the freedom fighters, and those who were in West Pakistan and came back to a free Bangladesh became known as the returnees.

The immediate problem facing the Mujibur Rahman (Mujib) era (1972–1975) was how to integrate regular army personnel with the civilians who had fought during the war of liberation and the regular military forces that returned from Pakistan. Mujib was understandably more comfortable with the soldiers who had fought in the war of liberation than with those who returned from Pakistan.

Mujib did not want the Bangladeshi military to be involved in the political process and consequently kept it isolated and ill equipped. At the same time, he was keenly aware that he needed a praetorian guard loyal to him first and then to the country. He built up such a force, known as the Jatiya Rakhi Bahini (National Security Force), composed of trusted regular military personnel and civilian fighters. He provided them with modern facilities, equipment, and advanced training. This force rivaled the regular military force and hence was looked upon as either threatening to or divisive of the position and morale of the regular forces. This action, followed by an attempt to concentrate all political power in himself, cost Mujib popular support. Eventually the military engineered a coup and assassinated him and most of his family.

Ziaur Rahman (Zia), who replaced him, disbanded the Jatiya Rakhi Bahini and quickly integrated the returnees into the higher-level military posts previously denied them, causing a split between the freedom fighters and the returnees. Up until the late 1980s, this split in the military led to several coups and countercoups. But as military officers and other personnel are starting to be recruited and trained solely in Bangladesh, the negative impact of the split is fading rapidly. A more serious internal conflict was the radicalization of soldiers who firmly believed in the concept of a people's army, patterned after the People's Liberation Army of China.[2] Such groups, led by the leftist Jatiyo Samajtantrik Dal (JSD, National Socialist Party), were behind serious mutinies at Bogra and Dhaka in 1977. Careful selection, retention, and programs for increasing professionalism seem to have reduced the danger of mutiny, and the increasing role of the Bangladeshi military in United Nations peacekeeping operations has further discouraged radical breakdown.

A Praetorian Army?

Reviewing the period between the assassinations of Mujib and Zia (August 1975–May 1981) and the period of Husain Muhammad Ershad's rule (March 1982–December 1990), we find that Bangladesh has been under military rule or domination for much of its early existence. Zia, of course, liberalized his regime and ended martial law, but the people never forgot that he came to power through the military and that the military would remain his ultimate support base. Although Ershad also took steps toward liberalization and ended martial law, the people did not overlook his military connection either. When demonstrations led to his downfall in December 1990, however, the military did not come to his assistance.

Clearly the military has been a major force in Bangladeshi politics. In order to meet Ershad's desire that the armed forces remain a part of the governance process, the military would have needed the constitutional status to play that role. Before he assumed power, Ershad demanded a role for the military through a national security council, invoking what is often called the Turkish model.

When in 1990 the government returned to civilian rule, in which the military was constitutionally subordinated to the government and a national security council had not been created, the potential for military intervention remained. Indeed, as history has shown, military establishments that have taken power demonstrate a high propensity for repeating the exercise.[3]

In 2007, this tendency to intercede in the political process was again demonstrated as Bangladesh stood on the brink of political and social disaster and the armed forces once again stepped in, although, given the context of the twenty-first century, the military did not directly assume power. The major contextual differences stemmed from a transformation of the Bangladeshi armed forces into a principal international peacekeeping force. This history began in 1988 with Bangladesh contributing fifteen members to the United Nations Iran-Iraq Military Observer Group. Since then, more than 100,000 personnel (mostly military but also some police contingents) have served in fifty-two UN peacekeeping missions, almost 100 have died (91 from the army, 1 from the navy, and 4 from the air force), and in 2012, with more than 10,000 volunteers serving in different theaters, Bangladesh stood as the single largest contributor to UN peacekeeping forces in the world. These peacekeepers have not only gained international prestige for the country but also, through wages, fees, and ancillary payments, earned millions of dollars in foreign exchange for Bangladesh (typically varying between $250 and $400 million annually over the ten years between 2001 and 2011), which has helped the country and benefitted them personally as well. Another factor is the primacy of its role as a disaster-management force, particularly relevant in a country vulnerable to periodic natural catastrophes. These two factors, when added to its informal role as a supporting element to the caretaker government in the conduct of free and fair elections in Bangladesh, provide the Bangladeshi military sufficient responsibilities in the functioning of the state without the need to take formal charge of the country. Moreover, the comfortable pay and privileges of military officers, the government's willingness to procure relevant defense materials from abroad according to their expressed needs, and the generally high respect they command among the population have all helped to placate the military establishment and encouraged it to remain within the bounds of professional responsibility.

However, one incident in February 2009 jolted the picture of stability and cohesion that the armed forces have traditionally presented. In one gruesome event, *jawans* (regular soldiers) of the Bangladesh Rifles (BDR) went on a rampage, killed fifty-seven officers (and seventeen of their family members) in the headquarters of the organization in the heart of the capital city. For thirty-three hours they held the headquarters and negotiated with political authorities before eventually agreeing to surrender. The abruptness of this uprising, its brutality (some of the people were killed in barbaric ways), and the huge number of fatalities confused and traumatized the entire nation. It became apparent that there were issues of command and control, that many BDR *jawans* had various grievances against their officers, particularly those drawn from other services (who, it was alleged, had looked down upon them), and that the BDR personnel felt they were not getting their due share in terms of rations, privileges, and promotions or had been shortchanged in the distribution of specific government programs meant for their benefit. Eventually the BDR was disbanded, and a new border security force, called the Bangladesh Border Guards, was established with a changed focus, leadership, and structure. Several thousand *jawans* were arrested for complicity in the uprising; some were tried in special courts in the military headquarters, several died in custody, and many were found guilty and duly punished. No one was executed. The trials of many others are continuing. Human rights organizations were critical of the mass trials being held and raised questions about the fairness of the proceedings. Still, the crisis seemed to be over.

Rebellion in the Chittagong Hill Tracts

Chapter 14 noted that the Bangladesh population includes several indigenous groups that are sometimes, perhaps misleadingly, called "tribal" populations. The tribes living in the plains have settled into the general population, but those in the Chittagong Hill Tracts have rebelled against the established governments in Dhaka, be they Pakistani or Bangladeshi. The CHT tribals have usually demanded autonomy, although some leaders have demanded independence, however impractical that might be. Autonomy usually means local self-government and restoration of land rights usurped by Bengalis migrating from the plains. An agreement (sometimes referred to as a treaty) signed in December 1997, if actually accepted by the tribals and the government, may herald a new era of peace and cooperation.

In the eighteenth century, the lands of the Chakmas (the largest tribe) formed an independent kingdom, although it paid revenue to the Mughal and later to the British rulers. Various measures passed by the British in the nineteenth century recognized the separateness of the Hill Tracts and its people from the territory directly administered by the British. By 1900 it was described as an "excluded area," meaning that it was excluded not only from direct British rule but also from settlement by nontribals. Although there was some question about the fate of the Hill Tracts at the time of Pakistani independence in 1947, the area was eventually assigned to Pakistan. In response, some tribals, mainly Chakmas, crossed into Indian territories.

The Pakistani government, uncertain that the tribals would give full allegiance to Pakistan, withdrew an 1881 regulation permitting them to police themselves and assigned regular Pakistani police to the task. By 1950 the government had allowed the settlement of several hundred Muslim families in the Hill Tracts, a direct violation of the 1900 regulation, although the regulation would be confirmed later in the 1956 constitution of Pakistan. The building of the Kaptai hydroelectric station on the Karnaphuli River displaced a large number of tribals whose land was submerged by the reservoir. This project was carried out without much warning, preparation, compensation, or alternative settlement options for the affected people.

With Bangladeshi independence in 1971, Mujibur Rahman assured the tribals that agreements limiting land acquisition by nontribals would be enforced, but enforcement over the years was lax, and tribal leaders formally demanded autonomy. Mujib, however, on a tour of the Hill Tracts on February 13, 1973, proclaimed, "From today, there are no more tribal subgroups in Bangladesh; everyone is a Bengalee." This declaration generated some disappointment among these groups because they felt their own cultural identity was being devalued and folded into the larger mainstream. In the election that year, the Solidarity Party of the tribals won two seats in the parliament. After Mujib's assassination in 1975, the Solidarity Party created an armed wing, the Shanti Bahini.

In 1976, under Ziaur Rahman, a plan was made to resettle poor Bangladeshis from the Chittagong district in the Hill Tracts. The tribals reacted with alarm and anxiety, and conflicts with the new settlers became routine. The government in turn responded with military action against the tribals, many of whom fled to India as refugees and set up a government in absentia. Throughout the Abdus Sattar, Ershad, and Khaleda Zia periods, armed conflicts alternated with meetings between the tribals and government officials. No settlement could be reached, and the problem seemed intractable.[4]

Nonetheless, the government and the tribals continued their negotiations. Finally, on December 2, 1997, a treaty was signed between the government and the political wing of the Shanti Bahini. The agreement envisages a high level of autonomy for each of the three districts that comprise the Hill Tracts, which includes taxing authority and the maintenance of law and order. Nontribal residents, who compose almost half the population, have objected to the agreement, as their representatives will compose only one-third of the membership of the new regional council. Some nontribals who have improperly obtained land will presumably be expelled. In short, most of the demands of the tribals have been met. Some have concluded that the treaty is unconstitutional, as it creates a level of autonomy that does not exist elsewhere in Bangladesh and is not subject to ratification by parliament.

If implemented in full, the treaty will be a major step toward the settlement of a long-standing sore in civil relations in Bangladesh. However, even in 2013 the treaty, according to most scholars and practitioners, remained only partially implemented. In terms of the implementation of local autonomy, in the regional council and the three districts, the head is a tribal person. However, tribal demands for the removal of Bengali settlers and redeployment of the military in a limited number of bases have yet to be implemented. The region, on the other hand, continues to be of great strategic and economic importance to Bangladesh. The CHT is the primary source of hydroelectric power for the country and also supplies the country with timber. Some of the rivers flow into the port of Chittagong and are a breeding ground for the local fish population. For all practical purposes, the CHT will continue to witness low-level violence, sometimes between the tribals, settlers, and government forces, unless changes in the Indian eastern provinces spill over and trigger more violence or the steady influx of Rohingya refugees from Burma (almost 300,000 of these Muslims from the Arakan, or Rakhine, province now live in Bangladesh, some in refugee camps but most in undocumented enclaves) creates other social and military disruptions. Moreover, there are questions of definition and identity. The Fifteenth Amendment, with its insistence that all people in Bangladesh be known as Bangalees, muddied the waters and alienated the tribals (they prefer the term "indigenous peoples"). They argued that while they are Bangladeshis because of their loyalty to the country, calling them Bangalees ignores their ethnic, cultural, and linguistic distinctiveness. The area remains highly militarized, allegations of exploitation and shabby treatment by Bangalee settlers are common, and the people of the Hill Tracts continue to demand that the government fulfill its promises, give back their land, respect their culture, and provide them with the fruits of independence and progress they deserve.

Government versus Opposition and Vice Versa

Until the fall of Husain Muhammad Ershad in December 1990 and the free and fair election that followed in February 1991, governments, including Mujib's parliamentary and presidential regimes and the military-dominated regimes of Zia and Ershad, had overwhelming power. There was opposition, but rules inherited from the British, the Special Powers Act enacted by Mujib, and martial law ordinances allowed the government to detain dissidents. Statements of dissent and demonstrations were thus dealt with harshly.

The election of February 1991 brought about a large opposition in parliament capable of hindering the operation of the government and the parliament. However, there was an early period of cooperation. The Bangladesh Nationalist Party (BNP) preferred to retain a presidential system for Bangladesh, whereas the Awami League wished to revert to the parliamentary system prescribed in Bangladesh's original constitution. (The Awami League held this view despite the fact that the presidential system had been instituted by the Awami League and its leader, Mujibur Rahman.) After the election the BNP modified its stance and was willing to revert to a parliamentary system. The BNP won fewer votes than the Awami League and its allies, and this brought into question Khaleda Zia's election as president by direct vote. A joint committee was set up, agreement was reached on changing the system, and it was confirmed by a constitutional amendment.[5]

The major event leading up to the opposition boycott of parliament was a by-election held in Magura district on March 20, 1994. The seat had been considered safe by the Awami League, but the BNP candidate was declared the winner. The Awami League immediately called foul and demanded a repolling. It is not clear that there was any electoral rigging; in fact, the Election Commission declared there was not. On May 5, the opposition, including the Awami League, the Jatiya Party, and the Jamaat-i-Islami, began a boycott of parliament, which grew into regular demonstrations and general strikes. The opposition demanded a change in the constitution to provide that future elections would be held under a "neutral caretaker government," a body to be appointed by the president. The BNP refused to accept this demand on the basis that parliamentary systems do not work this way.

Nonetheless, Prime Minister Khaleda Zia said she would resign thirty days before the election. This did not suit the opposition, as her resignation would not set a precedent that must be followed in the future—only a constitutional amendment would be binding—and the demonstrations and general strikes continued. A prominent commentator wrote, "The lack of a worldwide civil society . . . is why people of struggling Bangladesh are caged by 72- and 96-hour *hartals* [general strikes] that [have] virtually closed down the impoverished country. The reason for their predicament is the impractical stubbornness of their leaders as to how a civil society should resolve its problems in a civilized manner."[6] A "civilized manner" was not found. On December 28, 1994, the opposition resigned from parliament. The Speaker found a technicality that allowed him to reject the resignations, but on June 20, 1995, the seats were declared vacant under the constitutional rule that a member's absence from parliament (without excuse) for ninety days would result in the loss of his or her seat. Consequently it would be impossible to pass a constitutional amendment, as far more than one-third of the parliamentary seats had been vacated. The Khaleda government held on for a while but resigned on November 24.

A new election was held on February 15, 1996, with the opposition boycotting. The BNP won almost all seats and immediately passed a constitutional amendment incorporating exactly what the opposition had demanded. It thereupon resigned and turned the government over to a neutral caretaker government. The Awami League won a plurality in the June election and made an agreement with the Jatiya Party that permitted the Awami League under Sheikh Hasina Wajed to form a government.

The BNP soon found issues it could use to begin strikes and demonstrations. Among these was the treaty with India on the sharing of water from the Ganges. The BNP said the treaty was biased toward India, which demonstrated the pro-India tilt of the Awami League. To this allegation of the Awami League's overly obliging approach to India was added the alleged desire of the Awami League to export natural gas ("our birthright") to India and grant transit rights to India for crossing Bangladesh territory to reach the northeastern areas of India. Protests and demonstrations ensued, and a number of BNP members were arrested. The BNP and its allies, the Ershad faction of the Jatiya Party and the Jamaat, also boycotted parliament, and thus the legislature operated without a sitting opposition. The first attorney general has commented on this pattern of behavior: "Even if one party cannot show respect to the convictions of the other party, mutual tolerance is essential."[7]

At the end of the Hasina government, a duly constituted caretaker government took over the governance of Bangladesh and conducted a relatively free and fair election on October 1, 2001. A BNP government came to power, and the opposition Awami League soon found issues on which to boycott the parliament and take to the street to demand a fair share of participation in executive and legislative decision making. The tipping point for opposition distrust was the constitutional amendment to raise the retirement age of judges from sixty-five to sixty-seven. This change gave the elements of the opposition common ground and raised suspicion about the intentions of the BNP government regarding a smooth transition of power. Events associated with the formation of the caretaker government in October 2006 for the next election confirmed their suspicions. The system broke down to such an extent that a state of emergency was declared, and a military-backed caretaker government was established in January 2007.

The culture of material greed and violence that had permeated Bangladeshi politics since 1971 was so debilitating that the caretaker government was unable to conduct its constitutionally mandated role of supporting the Election Commission and conducting the parliamentary election within the stated ninety-day period. The caretaker government of 2007 provided itself the extra-constitutional role of transforming the fundamental institutions of governance, which it expected to complete by holding a free and fair election by December 2008.

The conflict between government and opposition is by no means over. With institutional changes such as an autonomous election commission, an independent anticorruption commission, and the separation of the judiciary from the executive, the conflict may have been reduced. One of the prerequisites of a functioning parliamentary democracy is a high level of cooperation between the government and the opposition. In Bangladesh neither side has practiced cooperation. One would have thought that the relatively successful elections organized under the auspices of the caretaker government and the Election Commission in December 2008 would finally usher in a new period of parliamentary effectiveness and democratic decision making. But political developments quickly nipped that promise in the bud.

The tone of noncooperation was set early when the BNP party leadership did not attend the swearing-in ceremony of the prime minister on January 7, 2009 (and sent in a token delegation of four individuals), walked out of the legislature on the very first day it convened (citing opposition to the president's remarks at the opening ceremonies), and walked out again on the first official working day of the parliament on January 29 (protesting seat allocations for their members and the fact that the victorious party had not lived up to its promise to appoint a Deputy Speaker from the opposition). Since that time, the BNP's participation in the parliament has been sporadic. Since parliamentary rules dictate that its members will lose their seats if absent from the parliament for more than ninety consecutive days, most BNP lawmakers register their presence once in a while to preserve their parliamentary privileges. They argue that the Speaker is not neutral in his role, the majority party makes them feel unwelcome and disrespected, and the coarseness and ad hominem nature of some of the speeches in parliament violate acceptable norms of parliamentary decency. The Awami League routinely mocks the BNP members' absence as a dereliction of their duties to their constituents, as ensuring the devaluation of the parliament, and as contributing to the environment of confrontation that feeds the agitation in the streets. The two parties' intense mutual dislike (particularly between the two leaders) and their insistence on playing a zero-sum game demonstrate the immaturity of the political leadership, foreshadow a rocky future, and present the highly awkward situation of a country seemingly taking pride in its parliamentary democracy, when the parliament itself becomes largely one-sided and dysfunctional. Tensions between the political parties further intensified when the Awami League, through its overwhelming majority in the parliament, passed the Fifteenth Amendment in 2011, through which the institution of the caretaker government was abolished. As discussed in Chapter 16, the BNP protested, the Awami League remained inflexible, and the stage was set for confrontation, inflammatory rhetoric, and agitational politics, which made the prospect of future elections a bit uncertain.

The Rise and Fall of Extremism and Terrorism

The fundamental question facing Bangladesh in regard to extremism and terrorism is whether either is internal to the system or is linked to global terrorism. In Bangladesh there are three types of extremism. The first is linked to the rise of Islamic fundamentalism and the second, to left-wing extremism. The third, on the eastern border of Bangladesh, is an evolving extremism linked to events in India and Burma. Islam has always played a role in the politics of East Bengal, East Pakistan, and Bangladesh. In the early nineteenth century, political

Islam supported the unity of the Muslims of India and the foundation of a separate Muslim nation. In the 1950s, Islam in East Pakistan stood for social justice and equity. In the 1970s, Islam became much more problematic as Pakistan tended to use Islam as an excuse to systematically kill Bangladeshis during the liberation war of 1971. During that war, two types of people collaborated with the Pakistani regime to try to fend off an independent Bangladesh, though these groups were not mutually exclusive. The first group comprised the political and social elites who defended the actions of the Pakistani army in international, national, and regional forums. The political party primarily associated with the Pakistani effort to deny the independence of Bangladesh was Jamaat-i-Islami.

The second group associated with collaboration included members of the Al-Badr and Al-Shams, which were religious groups, and of the Razakar and peace committees that were formed in each neighborhood of Bangladesh to act as informers, facilitators, and associates of the Pakistani regime and that became complicit in many criminal acts against the Bangladeshis. In the mid 1970s there was a return to Islam principally through the Eighth Amendment, which declared Islam the state religion of Bangladesh. Over time Islamic religious-based political parties like the Jamaat-i-Islami, Islamic Oikyo Party, and others were permitted to become a regular part of the political process. While the Islamic parties never received a significant popular vote, in the 2001–2006 political government, the Islamic parties had almost twenty seats in a three-hundred-member parliament and two ministers in the national government. During the Soviet-Afghan War of the 1980s, some Bangladeshi Muslims participated in the conflict in support of Islam. Though very few in number, the returned Bangladeshis had a role in radicalizing small, isolated segments of society. Three groups—the Jama'atul Mujahedeen Bangladesh, Harkat-ul-Jihad-i-Islami Bangladesh (Huji[B]), and Jagrata Muslim Janata Bangladesh (JMJB)—are principal proponents of Islamic radicalism in Bangladesh. After the Russian defeat in Afghanistan, the First Gulf War, September 11, and the Iraq War, these groups took on a more visible and violent role in Bangladeshi society, culminating in the explosion of over 450 small bombs in a coordinated attack on sixty-three of the sixty-four districts of Bangladesh on August 17, 2005. Many have opined that the Bangladeshi government of Khaleda Zia, because of its electoral alliance with Islamic parties, ignored growing Islamic extremism. With mounting international pressure to control extremism, the government of Khaleda Zia took steps to ban the radical parties and by May 2006 had arrested the principals, who were accused of specific crimes, put on trial, and sentenced to death. The caretaker government carried out the death sentences in April 2007 and gradually neutralized the radical elements. But it is too early to know whether sleeper groups are awaiting their turn.[8] Smaller radical groups like the Huji(B), Hizbut Tahrir (Party of Liberation), Shahadat al Hikma (Power Through Martyrdom), and Allahr Dal (God's Party) have also been cornered and isolated.

One spillover effect of extremism, especially since January 2007, is the underlying conflict within the Bangladeshi political culture over the role of collaborators during the war of liberation. Since the mid-1970s, the Islamic parties, especially Jamaat, have supported the BNP. To counter their growing influence, the Awami League in late 2006 formed an unfortunate alliance with the Khelafat Andolon Party, another Islamic political party, in preparation for the national election supposed to be held in January 2007, losing its well-earned reputation as a secular party. The caretaker government formed on January 12, 2007, undertook major reforms to transform the fundamental institutions in Bangladesh to propel the country toward democracy. In doing so, however, it unwittingly opened up the sensitive issue of collaborators, their identities, and their future role in the political development of Bangladesh.[9]

One way that Bangladeshi society in general and those who fought for the liberation of the country in particular are attempting to curb the rising role of Islam in the Bangladeshi political system is to have individuals and parties declared unfit for political participation. Following the liberation war Bangladesh was unable to bring to trial Pakistani war criminals and their Bengali and Bihari collaborators. International pressure and a weak Bangladesh declined to try the leadership of the Pakistani armed forces, who had committed not just criminal but genocidal acts. In the process Bengali collaborators also escaped trial and over a period of years were slowly reintegrated into and reinstated in the political structure of Bangladesh. With systemic reform in Bangladesh today, the divisive question of collaborators has once again resurfaced. Although the Bangladesh Collaborators (Special Tribunal) Act of 1972 was repealed in 1975, the International Crimes Act of 1972, which remains on the books, is being considered as the legal framework for trying the collaborators. The International Crimes Tribunal (ICT) was constituted in 2010 with the purpose of prosecuting those people against whom there is clear and legally admissible evidence of active engagement in "crimes against humanity." There is no question that collaborators must be tried and, if found guilty, duly punished. Young activists expressed these sentiments through spontaneous, passionate, and unprecedented nonpartisan rallies in various public spaces in early 2013. However, transparency, independence, and international judicial standards must be maintained so that the integrity of the process and the credibility of the judgments issued by the ICT are accepted as impartial and legitimate. Obviously, the Jamaat-i-Islami (JI) and BNP have questioned the fairness of the process, impugned the political motivations behind the exercise, and vowed to challenge adverse verdicts against their leaders (almost all of the twelve people initially facing trial in 2012–2013 were current or past stalwarts of the JI and BNP). The supporters and opponents of the trials have engaged in boisterous protests, intense confrontations, and sporadic violence (in which more than one hundred people on both sides, including some policemen, were killed in the early months of 2013). All of these developments, which clearly indicate a gradual fraying of the political fabric, have troubling implications for the future of democracy in Bangladesh.

An even weaker form of radicalism and extremism is often linked to the Gono Mukti Fouz, the Purbo Banglar Communist Party, and the New Biplobi Communist Party. Located in the western districts of Bangladesh, they sometimes want to establish a Hindu enclave within the country but are primarily involved in power plays with other factions loyal to establishing communist rule in Bangladesh. As mentioned earlier in this chapter, the Chittagong Hill Tracts continue to have a low-level insurgency movement seeking autonomy for tribal people. Because of the CHT's proximity to some eastern provinces of India and also Burma, extremists from these two countries have found refuge there. Two identified groups from India are the National Liberation Front of Tripura and the United Liberation Front of Assam. These two organizations undertake terrorist actions in India, stressing the relationship between Bangladesh and India. Burmese groups taking refuge in CHT include the National United Party of Arakan, the Arakan Rohingya National Organization, and the Rohingya Solidarity Organization. While all these organizations oppose the military junta of Burma, some are linked to the wider Islamic extremism of Southeast Asia.

The current global strategic scenario nourishes the development of terrorism, especially in a country like Bangladesh. If regional political machinations are factored out and national political positioning for power is held in check, the likelihood of radicalism and extremism in Bangladesh is limited. However, restraining such positioning will require constant vigilance. Bangladeshi organizations such as the National Security Intelligence and the Armed Forces Intelligence, as well as the intelligence-gathering capacities of the Home Ministry, police, and other security forces, must be constantly upgraded. Presently, while these agencies have performed credibly, significant modernization must take place in order for them to stop the rise of radicalism, extremism, and terrorism in Bangladesh.

The current government elected in 2008 has, by tradition and reputation, promoted more secular tendencies in its orientations and policies. After aggressively pursuing radical Islamist enclaves, it arrested and is in the process of trying war criminals usually associated with these groups' leadership; it has

charged several leaders of banned organizations, such as the Jama'atul Mujahedeen Bangladesh, Lashkar-et-Taiba, Hizbut Tahrir, and others, with arms
smuggling and currency racketeering; it has tried to regulate some aspects of
madrasa education (which has traditionally served as a vehicle for recruiting and
grooming radical Islamist leadership); and it has resolutely fostered the notion
of *Mukti-juddherchetona* (consciousness of the Liberation War), which is short-
hand for the idealized vision of Bangladesh as a secular and democratic state.
While it takes great pains to point out its own Islamic commitments, and its
leaders go to extraordinary lengths to demonstrate deference to Islamic values
of conduct and comportment as well as participation in Islamic rites and rituals (going on the hajj pilgrimage amid much fanfare and media attention, visiting the Biswa Ijtema in Dhaka, which is the second-largest gathering of
Muslims in the world after the hajj, paying due respect at holy shrines and religious centers), it professes a multifaith approach in its conduct of official business. It is true that Islam remains inextricably interwoven into the history and
culture of Bangladesh, and there is no doubt that the vast majority of the people of Bangladesh clearly identify themselves as devout Muslims. However, the
political use of religion has not been very successful (Islamic parties have never
received more than 10 to 15 percent of the vote in any election in Bangladesh,
and in the last election, they received less than 5 percent), there have been no
terrorist attacks in the country for several years, and the leadership of most of
these fringe groups is in disarray. Even though its existence or capacity for mis-
chief cannot be ruled out, it is abundantly clear that radical Islam faces a most
inhospitable environment in Bangladesh today.

Suggested Readings

Ahamed, Emajuddin. *Military Rule and the Myth of Democracy.* 2nd ed. Dhaka: Gatidhara
Press, 2003.

Ahmed, A. F. Salahuddin. *Bengali Nationalism and the Emergence of Bangladesh.* Dhaka: University Press, 2001.

Baxter, Craig. *Bangladesh: From a Nation to a State.* Boulder, CO: Westview Press, 1997.

Bleie, Tone. *Tribal Peoples, Nationalism, and the Human Rights Challenge: The Advance of
Bangladesh.* Dhaka: University Press, 2005.

Cohen, Stephen P. *The Indian Army.* Berkeley: University of California Press, 1971.

———. *The Pakistan Army.* Berkeley: University of California Press, 1984.

The *Dhaka Courier*, November 10, 2000, supplement, "Rule of Law and Democratic Accountability," contains a number of articles by Bangladeshi scholars and commentators on the subject.

Hossain, Golam. *General Ziaur Rahman and the BNP.* Dhaka: University Press, 1988.

Kabir, Bhuian Md. Monoar. *The Politics and Development of the Jamaat-e-Islami Bangladesh.*
Dhaka: A. H. Development Publishers, 2006.

Kennedy, Charles H., and David J. Louscher, eds. *Civil and Military Interaction in Asia and
Africa.* Leiden: E. J. Brill, 1991. Includes chapters on Bangladesh by Craig Baxter and Syedur
Rahman and on Pakistan by Hasan-Askari Rizvi.

Khan, Zillur Rahman. *Leadership in the Least Developed Nation: Bangladesh*. Syracuse, NY: Maxwell School, Syracuse University, 1983.

Maniruzzaman, Talukder. *Military Withdrawal from Politics: A Comparative Study*. Cambridge, MA: Ballinger, 1987.

———. *The Bangladesh Revolution and Its Aftermath*. Dhaka: Bangladesh Books International, 1980.

Mason, Philip. *A Matter of Honour: An Account of the Indian Army, Its Officers, and Men*. London: Jonathan Cape, 1974.

Olsen, Edward A., and Stephen Jurika Jr., eds. *The Armed Forces in Contemporary Asian Societies*. Boulder, CO: Westview Press, 1985. Includes chapters by G. L. Wood on India, S. P. Cohen on Pakistan, and J. Lundstead on Bangladesh.

Shelley, Mizanur Rahman. *The Chittagong Hill Tracts of Bangladesh: The Untold Story*. Dhaka: Centre for Development Research, 1992.

NOTES

1. For an interesting account by the mother of a civilian volunteer, see Jahanara Imam, *Of Blood and Fire* (Dhaka: Academic Publishers, 1990), translated from Bengali by Mustafizur Rahman.

2. For the text of a statement purportedly made by Taher, see Lawrence Lifschultz, *Bangladesh: The Unfinished Revolution* (London: Zed, 1979).

3. See Talukder Maniruzzaman, *Military Withdrawal from Politics: A Comparative Study* (Cambridge, MA: Ballinger, 1987).

4. The source for much of the material in this section is Naeem Mohaiemen, "A History of the Chittagong Hill Tracts," *Daily Star* (Dhaka), November 26, 1997; Naeem Mohaimen, "Chittagong Hills Tracts: Development Without Peace," *Daily Star,* February 25, 2010, www.thedailystar.net/suppliments/2010/02/ds19/segment3/peace/html (accessed on March 7, 2013); and Naeem Mohaimen, ed., *Between Ashes and Hope: Chittagong Hill Tracts in the Blind Spot of Bangladeshi Nationalism* (Dhaka: Drishtipat Writer's Collective, supported by Manusher Jonno Foundation, 2008).

5. For more detail, see Craig Baxter, "Bangladesh: Can Democracy Survive?" *Current History* (April 1996): 182–186. See also Golam Hossain, "Bangladesh in 1995: Politics of Intransigence," *Asian Survey* 36, no. 2 (1996): 196–203; Stanley A. Kochanek, "Bangladesh in 1996: The 25th Year of Independence," *Asian Survey* 37, no. 2 (1997): 136–142.

6. Mizanur Rahman Shelley, *Independent* (Dhaka), October 24, 1995.

7. Syed Ishtiaq Ahmed, *Dhaka Courier*, November 24, 2000, 19.

8. See also an assessment of Islamic radicalism by Rohan Gunaratna, director of the International Center for Political Violence and Terrorism, Nanyang Technological University, Singapore, in the *Daily Star*, January 19, 2008; Hiranmay Karlekar, "The Terrorism That Stalks Bangladesh," *Global Asia* 3, no. 1 (spring 2008), www.globalasia.org (accessed March 7, 2013). For excellent information and analysis of the phenomena of Islamic extremism in Bangladesh, see Ali Riaz, *Islamic Militancy in Bangladesh: A Complex Web* (London/New York: Routledge, 2008), and Ali Riaz and Christina Fair, eds. *Political Islam and Governance in Bangladesh* (London/New York: Routledge, 2011).

9. The South Asia Terrorism Portal has a weekly assessment of terrorism in South Asia. It did an assessment of terrorism in Bangladesh in 2006.

18

Modernization and Development: Prospects and Problems

Bangladesh is often described as the "largest poorest" nation in the world, and the title of one book on Bangladeshi political development refers to the country as "the least developed nation."[1] The dominant image of Bangladesh abroad is of a country racked by poverty, instability, and natural disasters. Comparative data may help to moderate that image in some ways but does not eliminate it completely.

The Human Development Index (HDI) published by the United Nations Development Programme (UNDP) in 2011, which ranked countries according to a composite index covering issues relating to health, education, and income, ranked Bangladesh 146 out of 187 countries (better than Nepal and Afghanistan but worse than Sri Lanka, India, and Pakistan). While its development dynamic was progressively inching upwards (its scores moved from 0.3 in 1980 to 0.5 in 2010), and its improvement was better than the countries with low HDI scores (which collectively moved up from 0.31 to 0.45), it did not do as well as the world (from 0.55 to 0.68) or South Asian countries combined (from 0.31 to 0.54) during the same period.[2] In current prices, the gross national income (previously computed as gross national product) per capita has more than doubled from $351 in 1992 to $770 in 2011. So, while some progress has been made, Bangladesh clearly has a fairly long journey ahead in terms of its efforts toward development.[3]

In terms of political development, it has fared only slightly better. According to the rankings of the Failed State Index, developed by the Fund for Peace and published in the magazine *Foreign Policy* in 2012, which uses various indicators consisting of pressures on a state ranging from refugee flows and poverty to public services and security threats, the position of Bangladesh improved from 12 (the bottom) in 2008 to 29 in 2012, which placed it above Afghanistan but below Nepal and Sri Lanka.[4] Freedom House's 2012 annual report identified Bangladesh as an electoral democracy but adjudged it to be only "partly free" because of corruption, weak rule of law, ethnic and religious strife, and single-party dominance despite some degrees of pluralism.[5]

In the context of the economic and political challenges it faces, Bangladesh has to be careful in terms of policies and directions it chooses so that it may build a prosperous and stable future. In this chapter we look at the problems and prospects of Bangladesh as it charts its difficult course forward.

The World's Largest Poorest Nation: Economic Challenges

The two principal goals of Bangladesh, as propounded by Ziaur Rahman, Husain Muhammad Ershad, and the parliamentary governments of Hasina Wajed and Khaleda Zia, have been attaining self-sufficiency in food grains and reducing the rate of population growth. The two are intimately related. The amount of land available for cultivation is basically constant. Hence, as the population increases, the amount of land per capita decreases. The challenge is to increase production per unit of land at a faster rate than population growth. Bangladesh has tried to meet that challenge.

First, the rate of growth of the population has been substantially reduced. In the 1960s, when Bangladesh was part of Pakistan, the population growth rate was around 3 percent annually; between 1970 and 1990, it was brought down to 2.3 percent, and from 1990 to 2010, to 1.7 percent. Government census reports suggest that the growth rate had fallen to 1.37 percent in 2011.[6] A combination of integrated and sustained government policy (widespread advertisement, mass education, availability of contraceptive methods, emphasis on women's health, and so on), the support of international donor communities, and the work of various nongovernmental agencies operating at the grassroots level all helped this process.

Second, Bangladesh also tried to increase food production in the country. In this regard its challenges were even more daunting. Land ownership is highly unequal, small farms (2.49 acres or less) compose 80 percent of landholdings, and a large percentage of farmers are landless. Also, much of Bangladesh's agriculture was rooted in fairly traditional habits and practices that, typically, yielded low yields.

Bangladeshi farmers responded to these problems with innovation and industry. First, the scarcity of land led to double and triple cropping efforts.

Winter rice production, which was traditionally limited, is now helped by the availability of engine-driven pumps, deep tube wells, and irrigation improvements and contributes almost half of all rice produced in the country. Moreover, expanded use of high-yielding grain varieties, increased application of chemical fertilizers, insecticides, and pesticides, enhanced access of farmers to information and credit from private and public sources, and intensification of their labor in the production process (what Willem Van Schendel calls "agrarian involution") have all helped to enhance agricultural productivity in the country. Thus, while Bangladesh used to produce only about 10 million metric tons (MMT) of rice in the 1970s, its estimated production for 2010–2011 was more than 30 MMTs. Moreover, between 1980 and 2010, egg production increased from 1.2 to 5.7 billion, and meat production increased from 0.2 to 1.3 MMTs, milk from 1.2 to 2.4 MMTs, and fish from 0.7 to 2.9 MMTs in the same period.[7]

However, despite the fact that rice production has tripled while the population has only doubled over the last forty years, Bangladesh continues to rely on some imported food. In 1974–1975 it imported 2.5 MMTs of food grain; in 2008–2009, it imported 3 MMTs. Fish and meat imports increased from negligible amounts in 1981, to 5,240 metric tons (MT) of fish and 9,710 MTs of meat in 2010. Total production of meat and fish has increased on an aggregate but not a per capita basis (some better-quality fish is actually exported). Imports of pulses, or lentils (a major source of protein for the poor), increased from 2,500 MT in the 1980s to about 0.5 MMT in 2010. Import of edible oils increased more than tenfold during the same period.[8]

Moreover, Bangladesh is always subject to natural disaster (floods tend to destroy approximately 10 percent of total crop production), and food stocks are depleted rapidly, requiring international assistance. Moreover, farmers are caught in a price trap because they sell their harvests when the market is glutted, which forces down the price of rice, but when they buy later for their own consumption (because they lack storage facilities), they have to buy at higher prices. Consequently, ensuring food and nutrition security for the people has been difficult and depends on seasonal challenges and fluctuations.

In the manufacturing field, Bangladesh benefitted from the globalization phenomena, which led to a shifting of the production of some commodities (such as ready-made garments and knitwear) to less developed countries, providing competitive and strategic advantages. In 1980–1981, Bangladesh earned only $1.3 million through export of these products, which increased to $1.1 billion in 1991–1992, $4.7 billion in 2000–2001, and over $12 billion in 2009–2010. The garment sector now constitutes almost 75 percent of its exports, employs more than 3.5 million people (most of them women), and has generated both backward and forward linkages in terms of creating other economic opportunities.[9] However, it must also be pointed out that the workers in this sector are poorly paid, have few rights, and toil in shabby, often hazardous environments. Fires and other accidents are frequent (almost seven hundred workers have died over the last six years), International Labor Organization standards are routinely flouted, and worker protests are dealt with rather harshly.

Bangladesh also demonstrated some degree of entrepreneurial success in the ship-breaking industry and in farming shrimp for export. It was apparent in the 1990s that dismantling large and no longer serviceable ships for salvage and other uses was profitable. Bangladesh's ship-breaking industry is now the third largest in the world, employing about 200,000 people and generating more than $114 million annually.[10] The shrimp industry also began to flourish in the 1990s and, together with frozen fish, has become the third-largest component of Bangladesh's exports, earning about $437 million in 2009–2010.[11] At the same time, both growth sectors have generated concerns about human and environmental costs that are bound to worsen in an unregulated environment.

The other unexpected economic opportunity occurred due to the unprecedented accumulation of wealth in many Middle Eastern countries following the oil-price increases, starting in the 1970s. Millions of professional and semiskilled workers from around the world, including Bangladesh, flocked to these oil-rich destinations, saved most of what they earned, and remitted huge amounts back to their home countries. In 1977–1978 Bangladeshi expatriates remitted $101 million; in 1997–1998 it was $1.5 billion; it reached almost $11 billion in 2009–2010.[12] Approximately 80 percent of this money came from countries in the Middle East, though there were gradual increases in remittances from the United States, United Kingdom, and Malaysia as well. These figures capture remittances through official channels only. Nonofficial remittances through various private networks and arrangements make the total contribution larger.

Despite some of these achievements, Bangladesh continues to face daunting problems. Its external debt increased from $501 million in 1973–1974 to more than $10.6 billion in 1989–1990 and more than $21 billion in 2009–2010. It had to pay approximately $876 million in debt-servicing payments in 2009–2010 (though as a percentage of its exports, these payments have come down quite strikingly). Its trade imbalance increased from approximately $2 billion in 2000–2001 to more than $5.1 billion in 2009–2010.[13] Poverty remains rampant and crushing. The 2011 UNDP Human Development Report estimates that, based on some measure of deprivations, almost 57.8 percent of the people live in poverty.[14] Similarly, the Department for International Development of the United Kingdom (2008) suggests that 36 percent of the population lives on less than $1 a day and 82.8 percent on less than $2 a day.[15] While there is spirited debate about measurement criteria and definitional clarity, and while some progress in reducing poverty has been noted (e.g., according to some estimates, the incidence of "extreme poverty" decreased from 28 to 19.5 percent between 1990 and 1991 to 2011, and "moderate poverty" fell from 56.7 percent in 1992 to 31.5 percent in 2011),[16] millions of Bangladeshis undeniably face grim realities.

Limitations on Resources, Human and Natural

Bangladesh is a nation with few natural resources beyond its fertile soil and abundant natural gas. Much of the soil is replenished each year with silt deposited by rivers during annual floods. The delta on which most of the country is situated serves as an interconnected outlet for much of the flow of the Ganges river system. It is the only outlet for the Brahmaputra and the Meghna. Other rivers include the Teesta, which feeds into the Ganges in northwestern Bangladesh, and the Karnaphuli in the southeast. The Karnaphuli has been harnessed for use with Bangladesh's only hydroelectric station.

A major source of power for Bangladesh is the abundant natural gas found in much of the country. Currently Bangladesh has 24.75 trillion cubic feet of gas reserves, of which about two-thirds are recoverable. With Jumuna River bridge construction completed, the entire country can be served by gas and electrical power but is dependent on foreign oil for power generation. In fact, Bangladesh has one of the lowest per capita electricity consumption rates in Asia (at less than two hundred kilowatt hours). While the country needs more than 5,000 to 6,000 megawatts (MW) of electricity (and demand is growing at the rate of about 10 percent annually), it has the current capability to produce only 4,500 MW and actually produces less than that. Moreover, distributional and administrative inefficiencies, large and unacceptable levels of system loss (which include various leakages and corrupt practices), and a dilapidated national grid result in frequent power outages, load shedding, and unreliable access to energy, which has a severe impact on agricultural and industrial productivity as well. Bangladesh has leased out different blocks for oil exploration to international companies, but few of them have generated hopeful results. The possibility of finding other exploitable mineral deposits is not very strong.

The rivers of Bangladesh are essential for the water supply and serve as an intricate transportation system. But they also divide the country and sometimes are so wide that they create hazards for travelers in storms; moreover, river flooding can be devastating, as was seen especially in 1988, 1998, and 2004. In

1988, 61 percent of Bangladesh was inundated. In 1998 the figure was 68 percent, and in 2004 it was 38 percent. Approximately 48 million people were impacted by the floods in 1988, 31 million in 1998, and 30 million in 2004. In 2007, although floods inundated only 7 percent of the land, 16 million people were affected. Although significant improvements have been made in flood control in Bangladesh, until India and Bangladesh resolve questions regarding the division of waters from the Ganges and establish regional flood-control strategies, Bangladesh will continue to be subject to flood disaster. Moreover, its geographic location makes it vulnerable to serious tropical weather turbulence, which may have devastating effects. The cyclones of 1970 and 1991 had huge economic and political consequences, but even smaller cyclones, such as Sidr in 2007 and Aila in 2009, killed thousands, affected millions, and cost billions of dollars in damages. Not only do these natural disasters cause immediate death and destruction, but their aftereffects in terms of loss of homes and livelihoods, water-borne diseases, nonavailability of food, and disrupted communications all take their toll later, and their impact can linger for years.

In terms of the infrastructural weaknesses in Bangladesh, obviously its communications networks, roads and highways, railways and shipping, ports and air connections, and prevalence of modern technologies and resources (availability of broadband, reliable Internet connections, telegraphs and telephones) all present logistical problems. However, one of its greatest challenges has been educating the people.

There is no doubt that significant advances have been made in this field. In 1971, when the country became independent, the literacy rate was only 16.8 percent, but it exceeded 50 percent by 2010. After primary education was mandated by a law passed in 1992, the average literacy rate between 2005 and 2010 for those between the ages of fifteen and twenty-four was 74 percent; quite remarkably, it was 77 percent for females. Net enrollment in primary education between 2007 and 2010 was 93 percent for males and 97 percent for females.[17] Bangladesh has earned international recognition for its progress in education, particularly in the gender parity it has achieved at the lower levels.

However, there are problems of resource constraints, the limitations of following a traditional curriculum, and, most importantly, retention (only 67 percent complete grade five, and only half of those continue beyond the primary level). There is also a dearth of technical and vocational schools. Public university education, traditionally the bulwark of higher education in the country, has lost some of its previous luster because of political unrest, which is both frequent and damaging. Many talented professors have also left the country. A relatively recent development has been the establishment of more than twenty private universities in Bangladesh, mostly in and around Dhaka. But while they have ample resources, there are questions about the quality of education some of them impart, as well as the high tuition and fees most charge

Bangladesh is host to a wide range of endemic and potentially epidemic tropical diseases. Malaria, cholera, and other intestinal illnesses are chief among them. Coupled with malnutrition, these diseases seriously debilitate much of the population, which in turn lowers the level of human resources. Fortunately, international groups have provided aid in the form of health-care delivery systems and drinking water. Dhaka itself is the site of the world's largest laboratory studying cholera and other intestinal diseases. Rapid urbanization has also caused both economic and political problems. With good reason, governments in Bangladesh, as elsewhere, are concerned about the potential for urban unrest. Accordingly, political leaders and economic planners pay greater attention to urban areas than to rural ones.

Political Uncertainty

The frequent changes of government in Bangladesh and the swings in economic policy have acted as disincentives to investors, both domestic and foreign. The Zia and Ershad regimes moved far from the doctrinaire socialism espoused (even if not fully implemented) by Mujibur Rahman's government. The divestiture of some government-held enterprises during the Ershad period encouraged local entrepreneurs. The Awami League government under Sheikh Hasina Wajed and the Bangladesh Nationalist Party under Khaleda Zia followed rather similar economic policies, but much-needed divestiture of state-owned enterprises has been painfully slow. The Hasina government in office since 2009 has pursued the move toward privatization of the economy and building what has been termed "private-public partnerships."

It is not just the frequent changes in government and the two-and-a-half martial law regimes that the country has endured (1975, 1981, and a military-backed caretaker government in 2007) that have created problems of political stability. Even when there is elected government, awkward questions arise about the quality of governance and the eventual prospect for democracy in the country.

Bangladeshis are justly proud that theirs is one of the very few Muslim-majority countries that has struggled for and established democratic forms of governance. Four parliamentary elections in 1991, 1996, 2001, and 2008 have been held with relative success, allowing peaceful transfers of power. The people are eager participants in the political process, and between 60 and 80 percent of the population has voted in various elections. There is a vibrant media environment in Bangladesh, with over 19 private TV channels and approximately

300 dailies and 1,500 periodicals published regularly (about 13 in English). There is high respect for the constitution, and the judiciary was separated from the executive in 2007. Appropriate institutions have been formed (e.g., the Election Commission, the Anti-Corruption Commission, and the National Human Rights Commission) to buttress democratic rule (though some may question their autonomy and effectiveness), and the Right to Information Act was passed in 2010 to ensure greater transparency in administration.

While many of the trappings and institutions of democracy appear to be present, worrisome problems do exist. First, troubling concerns about the rule of law in the country include increasing levels of crime and violence, as well as examples of people taking the law in their own hands and dispensing vigilante justice or of village adjudication councils issuing rulings that are usually detrimental to the interests of women and minorities. Moreover, the exercise of governmental power may at times be perceived as unfair and arbitrary. A culture of impunity suggests that some people with the right connections can flout the laws without fear. International human rights groups (e.g., Amnesty International and Human Rights Watch) also raise allegations of law enforcement entities engaging in extrajudicial killings, forced disappearances of individuals, inhumane treatment of prisoners, and random brutality. And, finally, the judicial system plods along in the traditional colonial style, with overfull dockets and long, ponderous, and draining procedures. All of this indicates that some ideas fundamental to the concept of democracy, such as the equal protection of the law and even the essentiality of human rights and civil liberties, may at times be jeopardized in Bangladesh.[18]

Second, corruption is pervasive. Bangladesh has the dubious distinction of being considered the most corrupt country in the world for five consecutive years (2001–2005) according to a ranking system (considered by some to be controversial) developed by Transparency International based in Germany. Its position has improved slightly (in 2006 it was ranked third, in 2007 seventh, and in 2011 thirteenth among 182 countries), but it still struggles with a profoundly sullied image.[19] All of this affects the amount of foreign assistance and investments in the country (both Western countries and multilateral bodies, such as the World Bank, become wary and skittish) and feeds cynicism and alienation among the public. It must be pointed out that in 2012 the World Bank decided to pull out of its commitment to provide more than $1.2 billion (out of a total cost of about $3 billion) for the construction of the vital bridge over the river Padma, because of charges of corruption in the procurement and tender process. Other donor partners of the project followed suit. This embarrassed the nation and forced the government to explore alternative financing arrangements.

Third, there is intense polarization in the polity. As noted earlier, the two major political parties and their respective leaders demonstrate a pathological dislike for each other that is reflected in an aggressive zero-sum game that is both confrontational and relentless. This has several unhappy consequences. For example, they refuse to cooperate with each other in the parliament. There are frequent walkouts, and legislators often display an indifference to parliamentary procedures and courtesies and engage in boycotts for long periods. The opposition has boycotted 43 percent of the sessions of the seventh parliament (1996–2001), 60 percent of the eighth (2001–2006), and 74 percent of the ongoing ninth (beginning in 2009).[20] The parliament has almost been relegated to relative irrelevance.

Unfortunately, instead of engaging in discussion and debate in parliament, the parties take their disagreements to the streets and mobilize their constituents to demonstrate their strength and resolve. There are protests, marches, strikes, work stoppages, threats, and ultimatums. Some of the strikes (*hartals*) may last for hours, even days; the economy grinds to a costly halt, all civic life is disrupted, and there are vehement, often bloody, encounters between supporters of the rival parties.

And finally, a partisan prism is forced on all issues. There is little continuity in public policies or stability in institutional leadership. There are allegations about the politicization of the judiciary, bureaucracy, and administrations of public institutions. Moreover, the party in power will often use the instruments of the state to hound members of the opposition. There is some degree of what Rehman Sobhan calls the "criminalization of politics," with leaders courting thugs and mafia-type elements to intimidate the opposition, extort funds for political purposes, and provide personal protection.[21] Even the naming (and renaming) of public buildings becomes part of this partisan drama.

The External Environment

Like most small and poor states, Bangladesh has to be very careful in its conduct of foreign policy in order to protect and promote its national interest. Its journey began with a lot of international goodwill and sympathy as Bangladesh emerged from a bloody struggle to achieve its independence. Many countries were generous with aid and assistance, and though grant components began to decline and loans to increase, Bangladesh has received annually, on average, about $734 million in the 1970s, $1.4 billion in the 1980s, and over $1.5 billion since then.[22]

However, its initial relationship with the United States was rocky and tentative. The United States had supported Pakistan during Bangladesh's liberation movement in 1971 and had been annoyed that Bangladesh had courted the Soviet Union (which had helped in the struggle) and sold jute bags to Cuba in 1974 against US advice. However, as the Soviet influence abated, US generosity became more manifest. Between 1973 and 1995 the United States contributed more than $1.6 billion in food aid and another $3 billion in loans and grants.[23] The aid amounts tapered off in the twenty-first century, but other relationships developed. The United States is one of the largest foreign investors in Bangladesh (though the total figure is quite modest) and one of the biggest importers of its products (in 2009–2010 the United States imported garments worth almost $4 billion and exported products worth $469 million, giving Bangladesh a hefty trade surplus).[24] Bangladesh joined Operation Desert Shield against Iraq in 1991 (suffering forty-three casualties) and has supported the United States in most global initiatives, particularly in combatting Islamic extremism; both countries have explored more substantial security and strategic partnerships.

Its relationship trajectory with India has tended to move in the opposite direction. The relationship began in a spirit of warmth and cooperation. India actively aided the liberation movement, sheltered almost 10 million refugees in 1971, was the first country to recognize Bangladesh, and provided critical assistance in the early years. However, several issues complicated this relationship and generated misunderstandings later. The most important was the problem of sharing water resources. Both countries have legitimate claims on the water from rivers that flow through them, but some Indian projects (e.g., the Farakka Barrage) have allegedly affected the lower riparian country in adverse ways, and several more ambitious plans (e.g., the Tipaimukh Dam, the Indian government's river-linking projects, and so on), while understandable from India's perspective, have caused serious concern in Bangladesh. Other issues between the two countries include the huge trade surplus enjoyed by India (climbing from $774 million in 2000 to about $2.9 billion in 2010), the demarcation of land and maritime boundaries, and the terms and conditions for the transit of Indian goods through Bangladesh. There are also Indian allegations of smuggling and illegal migration from Bangladesh and Bangladeshi complaints about the brutal behavior and trigger happiness of Indian Border Security Forces. The issues are not unresolvable, but they demand patience and vision from both parties.

Bangladesh has also tried to nurture its relationship with the Islamic world not only to bolster its identity as one of the largest Muslim countries but also to pursue economic interests in terms of trade relations and manpower exports that are vital to its economy. It has also tried to provide some regional leadership; it was instrumental in the formation of the South Asian Association for

Regional Cooperation, which was launched in Dhaka in 1985, and pushed for the South Asian Free Trade Area, which began in 2006 to be implemented in stages, and the Bay of Bengal Initiative for Multi-Sectoral and Technical Co-operation in 1997, which is still evolving. Given its vulnerabilities to the impact of climate change in the world, it has also taken a prominent role in promoting environmental concerns and achieved some international recognition in that regard. As noted already, Bangladesh is also the largest contributor to UN peace-keeping missions in the world today.

Conclusion: The Future

The problems Bangladesh must address are formidable but not insurmountable. It has already reduced population-growth rates, increased food production, made appreciable advances in education, and taken advantage of several opportunities to promote industrialization at home and ensure remittances from abroad. Between 2000 and 2011 its economy grew at a brisk rate of from 4.4 to 6.7 percent annually. It has also attempted to establish the habits and institutions of democracy and has a vibrant press, regular elections, a relatively independent judiciary, and a boisterous civil society that champions populist and human rights causes. It has conducted itself with relative ability in the international arena and has shown leadership in some areas. It has pioneered the microcredit program through Grameen Bank (for which the bank and its founder, Dr. Muhammad Yunus, received the Nobel Peace Prize in 2006), and today, relative to its population, Bangladesh has the largest number, of any country in the world, of nongovernmental organizations dedicated to alleviating poverty, empowering people, protecting rights, and delivering services, which have collectively affected the socioeconomic landscape of the country in positive and lasting ways.

Several areas will demand urgent attention, however:

- Large numbers of Bangladeshis live in grinding poverty, and the economic inequalities in the country are glaring and inhumane.
- Even though Islamic militancy has not reared its ugly head in the land, pockets of extremism, and their international contacts, warrant some vigilance.
- Despite the fact that the prime minister and the leader of the opposition are both women and gender parity in primary education has been established, women remain vulnerable in very stark and fundamental ways.
- A huge advantage that Bangladesh has enjoyed, the homogeneity of its

people, should not make it arrogant and insensitive to minorities (such as indigenous peoples, non-Bengali Biharis who were left stateless in Bangladesh in 1971, Rohingya refugees from Burma who have fled persecution, and Ahmadias who follow a nonmainstream version of Islam), many of whom have expressed legitimate anxieties about their identity and security.

- While Bangladesh has become vocal on environmental issues globally, it must not neglect the salinity and desertification in its own homeland, the urban dystopias that unregulated growth has created, or the disappearance of much unique and distinctive flora, fauna, and animal habitat, which fall victim to profit-driven recklessness.
- Bangladesh must resolve its problems with its neighbors and promote its objectives internationally with some degree of foresight and ability.
- It must pursue efficiency, proper recruitment and training, and professionalism in the bureaucracy.
- And finally, it must try even further to establish the rule of law, combat corruption, inculcate participatory values, strengthen democratic institutions, ensure some level of cooperation among political parties, and make democracy truly and substantively meaningful for citizens.

Bangladesh's greatest asset is its people. They are generally resilient, clever, industrious, culturally proud, and tolerant. Despite capricious weather patterns, poor material resources, leadership failures, infrastructural inadequacies, and "compassion fatigue" among international donors and well-wishers, Bangladeshis have managed to survive and, in some ways, to prevail. Bangladesh must nurture this spirit, more than anything else, as it ventures to the next level of modernization and development.

SUGGESTED READINGS

Ahsan, Abul, and Ahmad. S. Abbasi. *Education in a Rapidly Changing World: Focus on Bangladesh*. Dhaka: Independent University Bangladesh, 2005.

Andaleeb, Syed Saad. *Political Culture of Bangladesh: Perspectives and Analyses*. Dhaka: University Press, 2007.

Baxter, Craig. *Bangladesh: A New Nation in an Old Setting*. Boulder, CO: Westview Press, 1984.

Faaland, Just, and J. R. Parkinson. *Bangladesh: The Test Case of Development*. London: Hurst, 1976.

Franda, Marcus. *Bangladesh: The First Decade*. New Delhi: South Asian Publishers, 1982. See especially Part 3, "Population and Resources."

Heitzman, James, and Robert L. Worden, eds. *Bangladesh: A Country Study*. Washington, DC: Superintendent of Publications, 1989.

Hossain, Hameeda, ed. *Human Rights in Bangladesh 2005*. Dhaka: Ain o Salish, 2006.

Jannuzi, F. Thomasson, and James T. Peach. *The Agrarian Structure of Bangladesh: An Impediment to Development*. Boulder, CO: Westview Press, 1980.

Khan, Zillur Rahman. *Leadership in the Least Developed Nation: Bangladesh*. Syracuse, NY: Maxwell School, Syracuse University, 1983.

Kochanek, Stanley A. "Governance, Patronage Politics, and Democratic Transition in Bangladesh." *Asian Survey* (May–June 2000): 530–550.

Rahman, Latifur. *The Caretaker Days and My Story*. Dhaka: Mullick, 2002.

Rashid, Haroun er. *Economic Geography of Bangladesh*. Dhaka: University Press, 2005.

Rehman, Sobhan. *Privatization in Bangladesh: An Agenda in Search of a Policy*. Dhaka: University Press, 2005.

Notes

1. Zillur Rahman Khan, *Leadership in the Least Developed Country: Bangladesh* (Syracuse, NY: Maxwell School, Syracuse University, 1983).

2. See UNDP, "Bangladesh," International Human Development Indicators, hdrstats.undp.org/en/countries/profiles/BGD.html.

3. See World Bank data at World Bank, "Bangladesh," data.worldbank.org/country /Bangladesh.

4. See *Foreign Policy,* "Failed States," www.foreignpolicy.com/failed_states_index_2012_interactive.

5. See Freedom House, "Bangladesh," www.freedomhouse.org/country/bangladesh.

6. See UNICEF, "Bangladesh," www.unicef.org/infobycountry/bangladesh_bangladesh_statistics.html. Please also see Nurun Nabi, "Population Challenges for Bangladesh," *Forum: A Monthly Publication of the Daily Star* 6, no. 7 (2012), http://www.thedailystar.net/forum /2012/July/population.htm, and *Population and Housing Census: Preliminary Results, July 2011* (Dhaka: Bangladesh Bureau of Statistics, Ministry of Planning, Government of Bangladesh, July 2011), 4, table B, http://www.bbs.gov.bd/webtestapplication/userfiles/image/BBS/PHC2011 Preliminary%20Result.pdf.

7. See Willem Van Schendel, *A History of Bangladesh* (Cambridge: Cambridge University Press, 2009), 233–235. Also see Dr. Mahbub Ullah, "Forty Years of Bangladesh Economy," *New Age*, December 16, 2011, http://newagebd.com/newspaper1/archive_details.php?date=2011–12 –15&nid=43644; Dr. Aminul Islam Akanda, "Agricultural Growth versus Food Security and Safe-food Security," *New Age*, June 24, 2012, http://newagebd.com/detail.php?date=2012 –06–24&nid=14766.

8. See Bangladesh Bureau of Statistics, Statistics Division, Ministry of Planning, Government of Bangladesh, *Yearbook 2010,* bbs.gov.bd/WebTestApplication/userfiles/Image342010 (accessed May and June 2012). See especially appendix 281, 286–287.

9. See BBS, *Yearbook 2010,* Appendix 49, 311, and David Lewis, *Bangladesh: Politics, Economy and Society* (Cambridge: Cambridge University Press, 2011), 148–149.

10. Lewis, *Bangladesh*, 142.

11. BBS, *Yearbook 2010,* Appendix 49, 311, and Lewis, *Bangladesh*, 151.

12. BBS, *Yearbook 2010,* Appendix 53, 314.

13. For external debt, see BBS, *Yearbook 2010,* Appendix 59, 319; for debt servicing payment, see Appendix 58, 318; for trade imbalance, see Appendix 59, 316.

14. See UNDP, "MPI: Headcount (k Greater Than or Equal to 3), Percentage Population in Poverty (% of Population)," International Human Development Indicators, hdrstats.undp.org /en/indicators/38606.html.

15. See Aloysius Milon Khan, "DFID Bangladesh: Country Fact Sheet," India Pakistan Trade Unit, February 2008, www.iptu.co.uk/content/trade_cluster_info/bangladesh/factsheet_feb08.pdf.

16. See A. S. M. Juel, "Addressing Extreme Poverty: Are We on the Right Track?" *Daily Star*, July 1, 2012. See also US Global Health Initiative Report, 2010, which reports that 49 percent of children under five and 46 percent of women suffer from anemia. See US Global Health Initiative, "Global Health Initiative: Bangladesh Strategy," http://www.ghi.gov/country /bangladesh/documents/159681.htm.

17. See UNICEF, "Bangladesh," and Ullah, "Forty Years of Bangladesh Economy."

18. Bangladeshi rights organizations, such as Ain o Salish Kendra and Odhikar, publish very helpful annual reports that provide disaggregate data on various forms of crime, police abuses, and human rights violations. For example, Odhikar's 2011 annual report stated that 209 ethnic minorities were killed, raped, or abducted; 135 people were killed through political violence; 84 people were killed by law enforcement agencies; 30 people disappeared; and 711 women were raped. See Odhikar, "Human Rights Report 2009: Odhikar Report on Bangladesh," January 1, 2010, http://www.odhikar.org/documents/2009/English_report/HRR_2009.pdf and also the Ain o Salish Kendra website (www.askbd.org/web).

19. See Bangladesh Transparency International's Bangladesh annual reports at http://www.ti-bangladesh.org/index.php/2011–05–22–04–14–36/annualreport; also see Iftekharuzzaman, "Combating Corruption: People Are Watching," *Daily Star* special supplement: "40 Years of Independence," March 14, 2011, http://www.thedailystar.net/suppliments/2011/anniversary /part1/pg12.htm.

20. See Rounaq Jahan and Inge Amundsen, *The Parliament of Bangladesh: Representation and Accountability*, CPD-CMI Working Paper 2 (Dhaka: Centre for Policy Dialogue, 2012), 16.

21. See Rehman Sobhan, "Structural Dimensions of Malgovernance in Bangladesh," *Economic and Political Weekly*, September 4, 2004, http://www.epw.in/special-articles/structural -dimensions-malgovernance-bangladesh.html.

22. See BBS, *Yearbook 2010*, Appendix 57, 317.

23. See Ahrar Ahmad, "Bangladesh," in *International Security and the United States*, ed. Karl de Rouen and Paul Bellamy, Vol. 1 (Westport, CT: Praeger Security International, 2008), 99.

24. BBS, *Yearbook 2010*, Appendix 50, 312, and 52, 313.

PART IV

SRI LANKA

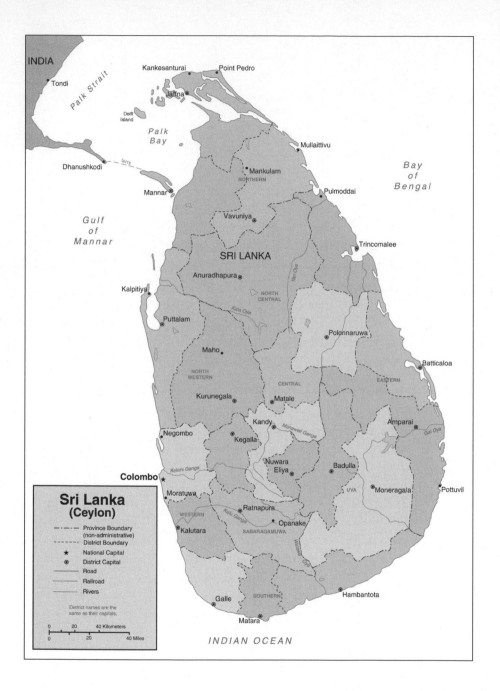

INDIA

Tondi

Palk Strait

Kankesanturai

Point Pedro

Jaffna

Delft
Island

Palk
Bay

Dhanushkodi

ferry

Mannar

Gulf
of
Mannar

Mullaittivu

Mankulam

NORTHERN

Pulmoddai

Bay
of
Bengal

Vavuniya

SRI LANKA

Trincomalee

Anuradhapura

NORTH
CENTRAL

Kalpitiya

Kala Oya

Puttalam

Maho

NORTH
WESTERN

Polonnaruwa

CENTRAL

Batticaloa

EASTERN

Kurunegala

Matale

Negombo

Kegalla

Kandy

Mahaweli Ganga

Amparai

Gal Oya

Kelani Ganga

Nuwara
Eliya

Badulla

Colombo

Moratuwa

WESTERN

Ratnapura

Kalu Ganga

Opanake

Kalutara

SABARAGAMUWA

UVA

Moneragala

Pottuvil

Walawe Ganga

SOUTHERN

Hambantota

Galle

Matara

INDIAN OCEAN

Sri Lanka
(Ceylon)

Province Boundary
(non-administrative)

District Boundary

★ National Capital

◎ District Capital

Road

Railroad

Rivers

District names are the
same as their capitals.

0   20   40 Kilometers

0   20   40 Miles

19

Political Culture and Heritage

The political systems of the third world are marked by violent upheaval, revolution, and military intervention. Only a few nations among the developing countries have been able to maintain a system of stable and representative government. From 1948 until the 1980s, Sri Lanka was one of these countries, and even during the civil war that threatened the unity of the country from 1983 until 2009, Sri Lanka maintained its democratic institutions. As a poor nation with a gross national product of $2,836 per capita (2012)[1] and a wide gap between the rich and the poor, how has Sri Lanka maintained this record of political stability and representative democracy? An examination of Sri Lanka reveals many factors that have led to political stability as well as other factors that would be expected to lead to instability and violence. The chapters in Part IV explore why Sri Lanka has been successful thus far in establishing stable political institutions and the diffusing threats to that stability. Specifically, they examine the cultural and historical heritage of Sri Lanka, the nature of its political institutions, the style of leadership exhibited by its leaders, and the ethnic problems and social divisions that threaten to destabilize it. The present chapter describes some of the basic features of the country, its historical heritage, and the social structure of its society.

Geography

The island now called Sri Lanka has long been known for its natural beauty and lush vegetation. Located at the foot of the South Asian subcontinent, it is a teardrop-shaped island about the size of West Virginia (25,300 square miles). In mid-2010, its population was estimated to be 20.9 million people, making it one of the most densely populated countries in the world, with over 809 people per square mile.[2] The population density is intensified by concentration of the population in the southwest corner of the island.

Despite its small size, Sri Lanka exhibits great geographic and climatic diversity. The southwest corner of the island, known as the wet zone, normally receives one to two hundred inches of rain annually. The rest of the island—the north and east—has an arid climate, with fifty to seventy inches of rainfall concentrated into a three-month period (October through December) when the northeastern monsoons blow rain clouds ashore. The southwest is affected by the monsoon in June and July and receives significant amounts of rainfall throughout the rest of the year.

The island also exhibits sharp topographical differences between regions. The south-central part of the island is marked by mountains and high plateaus, with cities and villages located above the 5,000-foot level. This region is known for its tea plantations; most of the mountains have been stripped of their natural vegetation and their soil replanted with tea. The rest of the island is a relatively level coastal plain with rolling hills and a landmass that rises sharply toward the center of the island.

Cultural and Social History

Amid this environment of geographic diversity and tropical climate, a strong cultural heritage developed. Ancient traders coming to Sri Lanka marveled at the natural beauty and friendly natives of the island they called Taprobane or Serendib, which stood at the crossroads of the Indian Ocean. Over 2,000 years ago a highly developed civilization emerged in the north-central part of the island, an area from which spices and other products were made available to the traders coming from the Orient and the Middle East. The arrival of the first Europeans in 1505 marked a change in the nature of life on the island. The Sri Lankans lost their independence, first to the Portuguese in 1505, then to the Dutch in 1656, and finally to the British in 1795, but they did not lose their strong sense of national identity and pride. This national pride, coupled with the political institutions left by the British, helped to create the stable and competitive political system mentioned earlier.

The strong sense of national identity and pride among Sri Lankans today stems from their deep cultural and historical heritage, which the island's inhabitants claim to trace back more than 2,000 years.[3] Most modern-day Sri Lankans are descended from one of two cultural-linguistic groups and are defined by the language they speak: Sinhalese or Tamil. The Sinhalese are descended from migrants from North India, believed to have arrived in around

500 BC, whereas the first Tamil speakers are believed to have come across from South India at about the same time.[4] The early Sri Lankans settled in the north-central regions of the country in the area now called the dry zone. The original inhabitants of the area, called Veddahs, were an aboriginal people who inter-married with the migrants and largely disappeared from the island as a distinct cultural group. Today, small groups of Veddahs still live in the eastern jungles of Sri Lanka.

The aridity of the dry zone spawned the growth of a major irrigation system to support the agriculture of the area. Great civilizations flourished from the third century BC until the twelfth century AD. Two of the major civilizations were centered on the present-day cities of Anuradhapura and Polonnaruwa. In the thirteenth and fourteenth centuries, these civilizations began to decline for unknown reasons. Theories suggest such causes as increased prevalence of malaria in the region, caused by the many irrigation tanks that fostered the breeding of mosquitoes; inability of the society to maintain the thousands of miles of irrigation canals and reservoirs; and decline in the groundwater levels as a result of overpopulation of the region.[5]

Buddhism and Hinduism were introduced to the island from India at the time of the development of the great civilizations of the north-central parts of Sri Lanka. Buddhism, it is believed, was introduced during the reign of King Devanampiya Tissa (307–267 BC)[6]; Hinduism appears to have been estab-lished even earlier.[7] Hinduism and Buddhism were readily accepted by many of the people, and many Sri Lankan Buddhists today consider themselves the pro-tectors of the faith.

These early civilizations thrived in the harsh climate by developing a system of irrigation tanks and canals to support the growing population of the region. With the success of the civilizations came a series of invasions from the Indian empires to the north, and by the thirteenth century, the Sri Lankan civilization of the dry zone was crumbling. While the civilization declined, a Tamil king-dom on the Jaffna Peninsula in the north continued to thrive. At the same time, the Sinhalese were abandoning the dry areas of the north-central island and moving into the forested southwestern section of the island and the hills of the south-central region.

Socioeconomic Changes with Colonization

When the Portuguese arrived in 1505, they found the island divided into three kingdoms. Two were Sinhalese, with their capitals at Kotte, near present-day Colombo, and at Kandy, in the central hill country. The third was a Tamil kingdom located on the northern Jaffna Peninsula. The Portuguese arrival marked the beginning of a three-hundred-year period of colonialism on the island. The Portuguese came with a desire to establish trade and spread the Roman Catholic religion. They became embroiled in Sri Lankan politics and were ultimately deeded the Kotte kingdom upon the death of the king in 1597. In 1697 the Portuguese conquered the Jaffna kingdom and ruled the entire island, except for the Kandyan kingdom in the central hills, which repelled all efforts to conquer it.[8]

A desire to control the cinnamon trade of South Asia led the Dutch to challenge the Portuguese for control of the island. Initially the Dutch set up a trading post in Batticaloa on the east coast of the island in 1602. A series of battles followed in which the Dutch allied themselves with the king of Kandy to attack the Portuguese forts on the island. The last fort was overrun in 1658, and the Portuguese were forced off the island. The Dutch turned the administration of the island over to the Dutch East India Company, which continued to transform the island into a Christian nation by spreading the faith of the Dutch Reformed Church and to transform the economy by establishing cinnamon plantations and cultivating coffee, cotton, tobacco, and sugar for export.[9]

The British arrived in Sri Lanka to head off French influence in South Asia. In particular, the British were concerned that the port of Trincomalee on the east coast would fall under French control. As a result, the British began negotiating with the Dutch in the late eighteenth century over the status of the port. Finally the Dutch were forced from the island in 1795. The British turned the administration of Sri Lanka (known as Ceylon before 1972) over to the British East India Company, which ran the country until it became a Crown colony in 1802. The British administration soon sought to unify the island by bringing the Kandyan kingdom under British control. The armies of the Dutch and Portuguese had tried to conquer the Kandyan kingdom, but the Kandyan armies, commanding the higher points in the rugged hill country of central Sri Lanka, were able to turn back armed attacks. Due to the isolation of the landlocked Kandyan kingdom, the people of the region developed a distinct culture and set of traditions that persist today.[10] The British brought the Kandyan kingdom under their control in 1815 and consolidated their rule over the whole island. From this time until their voluntary departure in 1948, the British ruled the island with only two serious challenges to their rule, the armed revolts of 1818 and 1848.

The British era was marked by further attempts to transform Sri Lanka into an export-oriented economy and to establish British customs and beliefs in the country. English became the language of both the government and the Sri Lankan elite, and Christianity, this time that of the Anglican Church, was fostered. It became customary for upper-class Sri Lankans to adopt the Christian religion and to speak the English language in their homes.

The British made several major changes in the economic life of the country. They used the hill country to establish first a coffee industry and then, after disease destroyed the coffee plants, a tea industry. At the same time, they established rubber and coconut plantations in the lower elevations of the hill country and in the coastal areas. Development and ownership of the plantations led to the growth of a landed aristocracy. This aristocracy included British settlers and Sri Lankans who were given land for their loyalty or service to the British. The development of the plantation economy transformed peasant agriculture by denying peasants use of land on which they had once cultivated vegetables.[11]

During the period of British rule, Sri Lankan cultural traditions and beliefs were neglected. The British ignored the Buddhist and Hindu religions, which were damaged when traditional temple lands were taken over by the British as Crown, or government, lands. The English language was used as the language of government and commerce, and the languages spoken by most of the population—Tamil and Sinhala—were associated with a backward and primitive peasantry. In addition, the government operated with British traditions in mind. Sunday replaced the Buddhist day of prayer (*Poya Day*) as the weekly day of rest, and Christian religious holidays were celebrated as national holidays.

After independence, attempts were made to reassert Sri Lankan Buddhist control over the society. These attempts reflected the influence of the dominant ethnic group in the society: the Sinhalese. In the mid-1950s there was a movement among the rural peasantry to restore the traditional values of the society and to remove the influence of the alien British culture. In 1956 the Official Language Act made Sinhala the national language, replacing English as the official language of government. Buddhism was later given special status by a series of laws passed in the 1960s and by the constitution of 1972. These attempts to restore Sinhala and Buddhism to a position of social dominance were accompanied by actions intended to return the traditional culture to a position of respect in the society. The wearing of traditional forms of dress, as well as the use of Sinhala in commerce and government, soon became popular among politicians.

However, these actions to restore the cultural heritage of Sri Lanka proved disruptive to the political system. As discussed in more detail in Chapter 22, Sri Lankans do not agree about what constitutes the traditional Sri Lankan cultural, linguistic, and religious heritage.

Socioeconomic Development

The social and economic environment in which a political system operates can have a great impact on how well the government performs and on how politically stable it is. In Sri Lanka several features of the socioeconomic environment have influenced the conduct of government and politics.

The quality of life in Sri Lanka is quite high, despite the fact that the country is one of the poorest in the world on the basis of per capita gross national product. It also has one of the best educational systems in Asia. The literacy rate in 2008 was estimated to be 90.6 percent, and a very high percentage of school-age children attend school, including over 98 percent of primary school–age children.[12] Education through the university level is free, and the average Sri Lankan is well aware of the value of education. The university system in the country is well developed, and competition to get into the institutions of higher learning is very stiff; only a small percentage of those taking the entrance examinations actually gain admission.[13]

Health standards in Sri Lanka are quite high. Life expectancy at birth is 74.7 years—less than four years lower than that in the United States and seven years higher than the average for other low- and middle-income countries.[14] This high life expectancy reflects the quality of medical services in the country. Medical care is free, and most Sri Lankans have easy access to doctors and hospitals. In addition, the government provides a system of nutritional care. Before 1979, every Sri Lankan was given a free measure of rice each week as well as reduced prices on other commodities. The size of the free measure of rice varied over time but was generally two kilograms. Since 1979, however, the free measure of rice has been replaced with a system of food stamps for the needy. Today only about 8 percent of the population receives food stamps.[15]

Accompanying these high levels of education and health has been a more equitable distribution of income and wealth than is found in other third world countries. The gap between the rich and the poor in Sri Lanka is wide, but not as wide as that in other developing nations.[16] Moreover, the gap decreased throughout much of the 1960s and 1970s. A strong sense of egalitarianism runs through the political culture of Sri Lanka and is reflected in the political behavior of the population.

In addition to this apparent sense of egalitarianism, the Sri Lankan people exhibit strong support for participatory democracy. As discussed in Chapter 21, Sri Lankans frequently contact their elected representatives for resolution of political problems. They also demonstrate widespread interest and involvement in the open and free elections held since independence. Voter turnout in Sri Lanka has been among the highest in South Asia, rising from a low of 55.8 per-

TABLE 19.1   Voter Turnout Rates in National Elections

Year	Percentage of Electorate Voting	Year	Percentage of Electorate Voting
1947	55.8	1989	63.6
1952	70.7	1994	76.2
1956	69.0	1994 (presidential)	70.5
1960 (March)	77.6	1999 (presidential)	73.3
1960 (July)	75.9	2000	75.6
1965	82.1	2001	80.1
1970	85.2	2004	76.0
1977	86.7	2005 (presidential)	73.7
1982 (presidential)	80.1	2009	61.3
1982 (referendum)	70.8	2010 (presidential)	74.5
1988 (presidential)	55.4		

All elections are parliamentary unless otherwise noted.

Sources: H. B. W. Abeynaike, *Parliament of Sri Lanka* (Colombo: Lake House); *Island*, December 19, 1988, February 18, 1989; W. G. Goonerathne and R. S. Karunaratne, eds , *Tenth Parliament of Sri Lanka* (Colombo: Associated Newspapers of Ceylon, 1996); and Sri Lankan Department of Elections (www.slelections.gov.lk).

cent in the first parliamentary elections shortly before independence in 1947 to a high of 86.7 percent in the 1977 parliamentary elections (see Table 19.1). The turnout rates in the national elections since 1977 have been lower than that year's peak, but they remain relatively high. However, the 2010 parliamentary elections resulted in a 61.3 percent turnout rate, the lowest level since 1947 and even lower than the turnout rates during periods of high violence in 1988 and 1989.

The Sri Lankan people exhibit strong support for open and free elections. In 1981 the country celebrated the fiftieth anniversary of universal adult suffrage. Even more impressive is the fact that Sri Lanka held its first election permitting universal adult suffrage in 1931, just two years after Great Britain held its first election with universal adult suffrage.

Ethnicity

Despite its small size, the island of Sri Lanka is marked by a relatively wide diversity of ethnic groups. Two thousand years of invasion and foreign interference have resulted in a highly diverse ethnic structure in which individual Sri Lankans display a strong ethnic identity. The result of this is a great deal of competition and conflict among the groups, which affects the conduct of politics in Sri Lanka. The society is divided by language, culture, religion, and caste. The first three cleavages in particular tend to reinforce each other, as

TABLE 19.2 Ethnic Population of Sri Lanka
(1981 Census)

Ethnic Group	Percentage of Population
Sinhalese	73.9
Sri Lanka Tamils	12.7
Muslims	7.1
Indian Tamils	5.5
Burghers	0.3
Malays	0.3

NOTE: Because of the conflict in the north and east, only one
census has been completed since 1981 (in 2011), and the
results have not been released.

Source: Department of Census and Statistics—Sri Lanka,
Statistical Abstract of the Democratic Socialist Republic of
Sri Lanka—1989, http://www.statistics.gov.lk/abstract2010
/chapters/Chap2/AB2-12.pdf.

the members of each major linguistic group tend to share the same culture
and religion.

The largest ethnic group on the island is the Sinhalese, who compose almost
three-fourths of the population (see Table 19.2). They trace their origins to
North India, claiming to be the earliest civilized inhabitants of the island and
to have been responsible for the dry-zone civilizations of Anuradhapura and
Polonnaruwa. The Sinhalese speak an Indo-European language similar to
Hindi that is not spoken anywhere else in the world. Most Sinhalese practice
Buddhism and consider themselves the protectors of the faith. Over two-thirds
of the population of the island practice Buddhism (see Table 19.3), which
was brought to Sri Lanka in the third century BC and subsequently spread
quickly through the dry-zone civilization. It persisted in Sri Lanka even after
Buddhism had lost much of its influence in India. On their arrival the Europeans challenged Buddhism, and a significant minority of the Sinhalese
adopted Christianity as their faith. Some of their descendants continue to
practice Christianity today, and there are significant numbers of both Roman
Catholics and Protestants.

The next largest ethnic community is the Sri Lankan Tamils, who trace their
ancestry to the same period as that of the Sinhalese arrival and challenge the
Sinhalese version of the historical origins of Sri Lanka. They are religiously and
culturally related to the Tamil community of South India and speak the same
Dravidian language, Tamil. Most of the Tamils practice Hinduism, although
significant numbers converted to Christianity after the arrival of the Europeans.
Thus the religion and the language of the Tamils are distinct from those of the

TABLE 19.3 Religious Composition of the Sri
Lankan Population (1981 Census)

Religion	Percentage of Population
Buddhism	69.3
Hinduism	15.5
Islam	7.6
Christianity	7.5
Others	0.1

Source: Department of Census and Statistics—Sri Lanka,
Statistical Abstract of the Democratic Socialist Republic
of Sri Lanka—2010, http://www.statistics.gov.lk
/abstract2010/chapters/Chap2/AB2-16.pdf.

Sinhalese. Although there is a significant population of Sri Lankan Tamils in the capital city of Colombo, most are found in the northern and eastern regions of the island. The northern Jaffna Peninsula and the land areas immediately to its south are populated almost exclusively by Sri Lankan Tamils.

The Indian (or Estate) Tamils in Sri Lanka consider themselves to be culturally distinct from the Sri Lankan Tamils, even though most speak the same language, practice the same religion, and trace their cultural origins to South India. The Indian Tamils arrived in Sri Lanka at a much later date than the Sri Lankan Tamils. The Indian Tamils trace their origins to the coffee and tea estate workers brought from India by the British in the nineteenth and early twentieth centuries. They are found in the estate areas of the Kandyan hill country in central Sri Lanka, where they make up an overwhelming majority of the tea estate workers on the island.

Shortly after independence, the government passed legislation that made it very difficult for Indian Tamils to be Sri Lankan citizens. The rationale behind this act was that even though many of the Indian Tamils had been born in Sri Lanka, they were only temporary residents of the island and did not have any long-term ties to the country. The government then sought to deport most of the Indian Tamils and other noncitizens to India and Pakistan. The governments of both of these countries initially resisted this move, and the Indian Tamils remained in Sri Lanka as stateless people. An agreement between Sri Lankan prime minister Sirimavo Bandaranaike and Indian prime minister Lal Bahadur Shastri in 1964 arranged for the granting of citizenship to approximately 300,000 of the 975,000 Indian Tamils in the country and the deportation to India of 525,000 of them. The status of the remaining 150,000 was to be the subject of further negotiations. This agreement was implemented very slowly and resulted in a new agreement in 1974 and, finally, in an effort to

avoid Indian intervention in Sri Lanka, the granting of citizenship to all remaining stateless Indian Tamils in 1985.

An additional ethnic community of importance is the Muslims (also called
Moors), who are descended from early Arab traders to the island. The Muslims
practice Islam and, for the most part, speak Tamil. They are found along the
east coast of Sri Lanka and in the larger cities. The Moors of the east coast have
traditionally constituted a backward community with low levels of income and
literacy, while those found in the trading centers tend to be wealthy and often
literate in several languages. However, in recent years, there have been large increases in the level of education and income among the east coast Moors.

Several smaller ethnic communities also inhabit Sri Lanka, including the
Burghers and the Malays. The Burghers are of mixed European and Sri Lankan
descent. Their native tongue is usually English, and most are Christians. The
majority of Burghers are found in the capital city of Colombo and make up
part of the economic elite of the island. The Malays are descended from the
Malay traders and guards brought to the island during the colonial era. They
are largely found in Colombo and practice Islam.

Both the geographic diversity of the island and its colonial history have contributed to the development of subcultures within the two major ethnic
groups, the Sinhalese and the Tamils. The Sinhalese are divided between the
low-country Sinhalese and the Kandyan Sinhalese. During the two hundred
years of colonial rule in which the Kandyan kingdom resisted the European
powers, the people in the hill country developed a culture that differs widely
from that of the people living in the lowland areas. In recent years, however,
the distinction between the two groups of Sinhalese has decreased as contact
between them has increased.

The Sri Lankan Tamil community is divided between those living on the
Jaffna Peninsula and those living along the east coast of the island. The east
coast Tamils tend to be poorer and less educated than the Jaffna Tamils and are
often thought to be more traditional in their outlook.

The Caste System

In recent years the Sri Lankan caste system has been declining in importance. It
is similar to that in India (see Chapter 2) in its general structure; however, it is
different in two very important respects. In Sri Lanka, unlike in India, the various caste groups are generally concentrated geographically such that an overwhelming majority of the people in any area are members of the same caste. In
addition, among both the Tamils and the Sinhalese, who have different caste
structures, the highest-status caste is also the largest in size.

Since no census of Sri Lankan castes has been taken since the nineteenth century, the size of the caste groups can only be estimated. It is generally agreed that the Sinhalese caste structure is dominated hierarchically and numerically by the Goyigama (cultivator) caste, which is estimated to comprise about one-half of the Sinhalese population. Beneath the Goyigamas are three castes of lesser status: the Karawa (fisherman) caste, the Salagama (cinnamon peeler) caste, and the Durawa (toddy tapper) caste. These three castes are found along the southwest coast of the island and generally constitute a majority in the regions where they are found. Untouchability is rare among the Sinhalese, although several important castes of very low status do exist. Among these are the Wahumpara (jaggery/palm sugar maker) and the Batgam (of uncertain occupational origin) castes. These castes, too, are geographically concentrated. Both are found in inland regions in the transition zones between the lowlands and the Kandyan hill country.[17]

Each of the Tamil groups (Jaffna Tamils, east coast Tamils, and Indian Tamils) has a separate caste structure. The Sri Lankan Tamil caste structure in the northern Jaffna Peninsula is also dominated by the cultivator (Vellala) caste, believed to comprise about one-half the Sri Lankan Tamil population in that region.[18] Beneath the Vellala are several other important castes, including the Koviyar (domestic servant) caste and two castes associated with fishing—the Karayars, whose members generally live along the northern coast, and the Mukkuvars, whose members generally live along the east coast. Untouchability is much more common among the Tamils than it is among the Sinhalese; an estimated one-fourth of the population of the Jaffna Peninsula is composed of members of the untouchable castes. These include the Palla (agricultural laborer), Ambattar (barber), Valava (toddy tapper), and Paraya (scavenger) castes. With the exception of the Indian Tamils, the Muslims and the other small ethnic groups—like the Muslims in Pakistan, India, and Bangladesh—do not recognize caste distinctions.

The consequence of the ethnic divisions in Sri Lanka has been communal strife. Since independence, the conflict between the Sinhalese and the Tamils has escalated, and smaller conflicts have been waged between the Roman Catholics and the Buddhists, as well as among the various caste groups. The most serious conflict is the Sinhalese-Tamil dispute. Each ethnic group fears the intentions of the other. The Tamils, as a minority in Sri Lanka, feel that they have not received fair treatment from the Sinhalese, who they believe are trying to turn the country into a Sinhala-speaking Buddhist state. The Sinhalese, on the other hand, despite their majority status in the population, also feel threatened. The Sinhalese culture and language are found only on Sri Lanka and hence are much smaller than the Tamil-speaking culture and society to the north of the island in the Indian state of Tamil Nadu. Fear has led the Sinhalese to be suspicious of the actions of the Tamil community in Sri Lanka. Some Sinhalese worry that their culture and nation may be absorbed by the Tamils.

This conflict became more violent after 1977 and upset the political stability of the country when it erupted into open civil war in 1984. Until the military defeat of the main Tamil rebel group, the Liberation Tigers of Tamil Eelam (LTTE), the Sri Lankan Tamil regions of the country, especially the Jaffna Peninsula, were in a state of open revolt against the government. Violence and bloodshed increased rapidly in the 1980s and continued until a ceasefire in February 2002. However, the violence increased sharply after the election of President Mahinda Rajapaksa in November 2005 (see Chapter 22). Since the defeat of the LTTE in May 2009, violence has ended, but ethnic tensions remain high.

For twenty-five years, Sri Lankan leaders focused on resolving the ethnic conflict. The defeat of the LTTE has allowed them to focus on economic development; however, the government has struggled to heal the wounds left by the war and its very bloody end.

NOTES

1. World Bank, "GDP per Capita (Current US$)," http://data.worldbank.org/indicator /NY.GDP.PCAP.CD (accessed February 25, 2013). When GNI is computed using purchasing power parity (PPP), Sri Lanka has a GNI per capita of $5,520. Also, World Bank, "GNI per Capita PPP (Current International $)," http://data.worldbank.org/indicator/NY.GNP.PCAP .PP.CD/countries (accessed February 25, 2013).

2. World Bank, "Data Bank."

3. K. M. De Silva, *A History of Sri Lanka* (Berkeley: University of California Press, 1981), ch. 1.

4. Some scholars have argued that the Sinhalese classification as Indo-Aryan was the result of nineteenth-century British politics rather than linguistic research. See Marissa Angel, "Understanding the Aryan Theory: Orientalist Scholarship in Colonial Ceylon and the Structure of Empire" (paper presented at the annual conference of the International Centre for Ethnic Studies, Colombo, March 1997).

5. De Silva, *History of Sri Lanka,* ch. 7.

6. K. M. De Silva, "Historical Survey," in *Sri Lanka: A Survey* (Honolulu: University Press of Hawaii, 1977), 33.

7. C. S. Navaratnam, *A Short History of Hinduism in Ceylon* (Jaffna: Sri Sanmuganatha Press, 1964). The question of which religion was the first on the island is highly controversial and an important part of the debate concerning the Tamil-Sinhala conflict.

8. See George Davison Winius, *The Fatal History of Portuguese Ceylon: Transition to Dutch Rule* (Cambridge, MA: Harvard University Press, 1971).

9. De Silva, *History of Sri Lanka,* chs. 10–14.

10. For a description of the Kandyan kingdom, see Robert Knox, "An Historical Relation of Ceylon," special issue, *Ceylon Historical Journal* 6 (July 1956–April 1957).

11. Asoka Bandarage, *Colonialism in Sri Lanka* (New York: Mouton, 1983).

12. World Bank, "Data Bank."

13. Swarna Jayaweera, "Education," in *Modern Sri Lanka: A Society in Transition,* ed. Robert N. Kearney and Tissa Fernando (Syracuse, NY: Maxwell School, Syracuse University, 1979), 147–148; Sunil Bastian, "University Admission and the National Question," in *Ethnicity and Social Change in Sri Lanka,* ed. Social Scientists Association (Colombo: Social Scientists Association, 1984), 174.

14. World Bank, "Data Bank."

15. *Lanka Business Online,* "Stamped Out," January 13, 2012, http://www.lankabusinessonline.com/fullstory.php?nid=82850245 (accessed June 15, 2012).

16. UNDP, "International Human Development Indicators," http://hdr.undp.org/en/data/map.

17. Bryce Ryan, *Caste in Modern Ceylon* (New Brunswick, NJ: Rutgers University Press, 1953).

18. Bryan Pfaffenberger, *Caste in Tamil Culture: The Religious Foundations of Sudra Domination in Tamil Sri Lanka* (Syracuse, NY: Maxwell School, Syracuse University, 1983).

20

Government Structure

Sri Lanka has struggled to create a viable political system that is sensitive to the culture of the country and maintains democratic institutions. There have been three constitutions since 1947, and a fourth has been debated since 1994. Each time a different party has come to power in the past twenty-five years, its members have tried to change the constitution. The last constitutional change in 1978 concentrated power in the presidency and is thus a source of danger today to the democratic institutions of the government.

Constitutional Development

In its efforts to find a suitable constitutional arrangement, Sri Lanka has gone from a political system modeled on the British Westminster form of government (1947–1972), to a similar unicameral government (1972–1978), to a French system of government (1978–present). The unpopularity of the French system has led to calls for a return to a Westminster form of government with significant changes to reflect Sri Lankan society and culture. To date, no significant changes have been made.

The most drastic change to the constitution came in 1978, when Junius Richard Jayawardene, who was first elected to parliament during the colonial era, became prime minister. He incorporated many of his personal views into the constitution, creating a quasi-presidential arrangement modeled on the French system of government.[1] He, of course, became the first executive president of Sri Lanka. The overall impact of the new constitution was to concentrate power in the hands of the executive and make the president the dominant figure in the government.[2]

Once Jayawardene left office in 1988, pressure to change the system began to mount. This pressure led to proposals to change the government in the

1990s under the leadership of President Chandrika Kumaratunga, née Bandaranaike (1994–2006). She entered office vowing to abolish the executive presidency. However, she was unable to obtain a consensus on constitutional change, and no action was taken. The current president, Mahinda Rajapaksa, has so far taken no action to change the quasi-presidential system.

During the colonial era Sri Lankans were given limited influence in their government. Although there have been many arguments concerning the contribution of the colonial experience, most writers agree that two elements of British rule left a major impression on today's Sri Lanka: the structure of government established by the British and the educational system created during the colonial period.[3] During the colonial era, the British created political institutions modeled on their own. They set up a parliamentary system and gave the Sri Lankans a limited degree of self-rule before granting independence. Sri Lanka, along with India, became one of the first British colonies to be allowed elected representatives from the local population in a colonial legislature. In 1912 Sri Lankans were permitted to elect three members of a twenty-one-member legislative council. The number of elected members was increased to four in 1917 and to twenty-three of thirty-seven members in 1920. (These proportions roughly parallel the development of indigenous representation in India.) This experience with self-rule during the colonial era provided Sri Lankans limited experience with self-government.

Just before independence a three-man commission of Englishmen headed by Lord Soulbury wrote a constitution modeled on the British Westminster system of government and very similar to India's constitution, though without the federal provisions (see Chapter 3). The Sri Lankans adopted and governed with the Soulbury constitution until they replaced it in 1972. This original constitution provided for a parliamentary system with a bicameral legislature.[4] The lower house, or House of Representatives, became the dominant chamber of government. Its members were elected directly by the people in a combination of single- and multimember electoral districts. The number of multimember districts was limited, never exceeding five districts with either two or three members elected. The House of Representatives was given the responsibility of selecting the prime minister and approving the cabinet. The upper house, or Senate, consisted of thirty members, fifteen nominated by the governor-general on the recommendation of the cabinet and fifteen elected by the lower house by proportional representation. The Senate's power was quite limited, and its main function was to provide the means for political parties to reward their supporters. In addition, the Senate's members could be named to the cabinet of ministers.

The Soulbury constitution generated many criticisms because of its similarity to the governmental structure of Sri Lanka's former colonial ruler, Great Britain. The United Front government led by the Sri Lanka Freedom Party (SLFP) and elected in 1970 was dedicated to changing the structure of government to fit the Sri Lankan society more effectively than the "alien" Soulbury government had done. In 1972 a new constitution, written by a constitutional convention consisting of the members of parliament (MPs) elected in 1970, was promulgated. The fact that the United Front had won the majority of seats gave the coalition a free hand in determining the changes the constitution introduced, which included the abolition of the Senate and provisions that not only accorded Buddhism a special place in the society but also affirmed the role of Sinhala in governmental actions.[5]

The 1972 constitution was very unpopular with the two major opposition parties, the United National Party (UNP) and the leading party of the Tamil ethnic group, the Federal Party (FP). The FP opposed the constitution because it designated Sinhala as the official language and bestowed special status on Buddhism. In addition, it did not provide the Tamil language with any special status. The UNP opposed the 1972 constitution because of fears that it would lead to an authoritarian government.

The UNP's 1977 election manifesto promised a new constitution and the creation of a presidential form of government. The new constitution unveiled in 1978 drastically altered the nature of Sri Lankan government.[6] The Westminster-styled parliamentary system was replaced by a government modeled on that of France. Its main features were as follows:

1. The executive presidency, unlike India's presidency, carries a great deal of power. The position commands many more powers than did the prime ministerships under the two previous constitutions. The president is elected by a direct vote of the people for a fixed term of six years. (The Third Amendment to the constitution, passed in 1982, allows the president to call a new presidential election at any time after serving four years of his or her term.) The parliament also has a term of six years, but the president is permitted to dissolve it and call new elections at any time.

2. The president appoints the prime minister and the cabinet, subject to parliamentary approval. In addition, the president rather than the prime minister presides over the cabinet when it meets.

3. Since the 1989 parliamentary elections, a system of proportional representation has replaced the single-member system of electoral constituencies.

4. All vacancies in parliament are filled by the party of the member who vacated the seat and not through by-elections, as they had been in the past. In addition, the party has the right to expel any of its members from parliament and to replace them with another member of the party. (The Second Amendment to the constitution, passed in 1979, allows the whole parliament to decide whether a member of parliament can be expelled by his or her party or change party allegiance.)

5. Finally, the constitution provides for national referenda on issues of importance.

The unique feature of the 1978 constitution is the power placed in the office of the president.[7] On paper, it divides governmental authority among the executive, legislature, and judiciary (see Figure 20.1). The executive presidency created by the constitution exercises a great deal of power. The president may declare war and peace, grant pardons, and carry out any actions approved by the legislature or ordered by the Supreme Court. In 2010, the Rajapaksa government passed the Eighteenth Amendment, which made several controversial additions to the constitution, all of which increased the power of the presidency.

FIGURE 20.1 Structure of Sri Lanka's Government

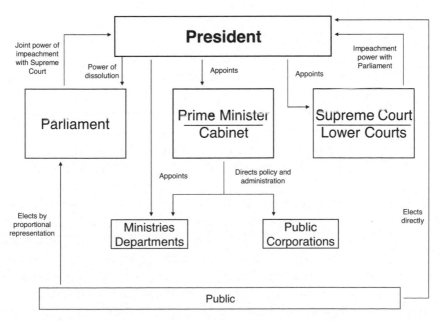

1. It removed presidential term limits, allowing the president to run for the office as many times as he or she wants.
2. The nonpartisan ten-member Constitutional Council was replaced by a Parliamentary Council consisting of a majority from the governing party. The council oversaw the nonpartisan commissions listed in the next point.
3. Independent commissions such as the Police Commission, Election Commission, Public Service Commission, Judicial Services Commission, Delimitation Commission, and Bribery Commission were placed under the authority of the president. The members of these commissions are appointed by the president with advice from the Parliamentary Council.

Under the Eighteenth Amendment, the president now holds the power to appoint the members of both the Supreme Court and the Judicial Services Commission, which appoints judges. This power, along with control of the Election and Delimitation (Reapportionment) Commissions, gives the president power over the judiciary and elections.

The constitution states that the president is responsible to parliament and that parliament may impeach the president with Supreme Court approval. However, presidential power over the membership of the Supreme Court makes impeachment highly unlikely. In addition, as a party leader, the president is in a position to remove from parliament any party members he or she does not like or disagrees with. As a result, the parliament may be reduced to little more than a rubber stamp if the president is in a position to control both the cabinet and the party.

Several other provisions of the constitution help maintain stability and keep one party in power. Before 1978, the governing party had lost each of the previous six elections. The new constitution created a system of proportional representation that contains an unusual provision. The leading party in each of the electoral districts receives a bonus seat before the seats are distributed on the basis of proportional representation. In addition, 160 seats are distributed on the basis of electoral constituencies, while 29 are distributed proportionally on the basis of the national vote. Since Jayawardene's party, the UNP, had been the leading vote getter in almost every election since independence, it forced the SLFP to form electoral alliances or likely face defeat. The successful elections of the SLFP have always involved electoral agreements with smaller parties in which the parties have decided not to contest each other in the same constituencies. Thus it was believed that the provision would aid the UNP.[8] In reality, both leaders of the SLFP since Jayawardene's era, Chandrika Kumaratunga and Mahinda Rajapaksa, have arranged alliances with smaller parties that have successfully defeated the UNP in four of the five parliamentary elections since the early 1990s.

The system of proportional representation also includes provisions for the electoral list of candidates to be determined by the voters. At the ballot box, voters select a party and a candidate from that party. The votes for the party determine how many seats are allotted to it, and candidate preferences determine who within that party wins those seats. Thus, if the SLFP wins eight seats in an electoral district, the top eight vote getters of the SLFP will be elected to parliament. This has created election campaigns in which the parties compete against each other while individual candidates run against members of their own party. The result has been the generation of ill will between party members.

The most serious area of discussion regarding alterations to the constitution dealt with those intended to resolve the civil war. These changes have involved proposals to devolve power to the north and the east. Even though President Rajapaksa announced his support of changes after the defeat of the Liberation Tigers of Tamil Eelam in 2009, no changes have been made. However, a number of recurring debates about the constitution have included the following:

1. Abolition of the executive presidency and its replacement with a ceremonial presidency with limited power and the return of executive power to the prime ministership.
2. Election of members of parliament by single-member electoral constituencies or a mixed system with some elected by proportional representation and some by single-member districts.
3. Devolution of power from the central government to regional governments. The most controversial of the discussions, these proposals have been intended to accommodate the Tamils and the Muslims, who feel that their needs are not being met by the highly centralized Sri Lankan political system. There is no consensus about the form that the devolution will take.

In 2006, President Rajapaksa created an All-Party Representative Committee (APRC) to find a political solution to Tamil demands for devolution of the government. The body quickly became deadlocked and was forced to present an interim report to President Rajapaksa in January 2008. The interim report called for implementation of the Thirteenth Amendment to the constitution. This amendment was passed as part of the Indo-Lanka accords and created a system of provincial councils. It was condemned by all important Tamil groups as inadequate when proposed in 1987. Immediately after the defeat of the LTTE, the government continued to propose the Thirteenth Amendment as a basis of devolution. However, by 2012, the government appeared to have abandoned the Thirteenth Amendment without proposing any alternative plan for devolution.

The Sri Lankan parliament, like that of Great Britain, maintains a rigorous separation between government supporters and the opposition. As in most parliamentary systems, the government and opposition benches face each other from opposite sides of the floor of parliament. Constitutional provisions barring crossovers from one party to another have limited what was once common behavior under the provisions of the earlier constitutions. Each side of the parliament chooses a leader: the majority selects the prime minister, and the opposition selects the leader of the opposition. A strict code of party loyalty ensures that members will vote as the party leaders want them to, unless they are released by the party leadership to vote their consciences— an alternative that does not happen very often. Thus most votes in parliament are highly predictable. Members who do not do as the party leaders wish are often expelled from the party and can be expelled from parliament as well under the provisions of the current constitution. The party leaders hold group meetings of their party's parliamentary members, thus providing the backbenchers—who are otherwise not allowed to express negative opinions about government policy—an opportunity to complain; at the same time, the party leaders are given the chance to determine the sentiments of their members on legislative proposals.[9]

The MPs represent the privileged elite of the country. Many speak fluent English (especially the more powerful members), and cabinet meetings are often held in English. Most come from the upper economic classes, hence the overrepresentation of the professional occupations and the landowning elite among MPs. The ethnic minorities are fairly well represented as well, although the Indian Tamils had no elected representation from 1952 until 1977, when they elected one representative to parliament. The Indian Tamils had elected six members to the first parliament in 1947, but soon afterward their ethnic group was denied citizenship (see Chapter 19).[10]

The proposal for the elimination of the presidential system in Sri Lanka stemmed largely from abuse of the power placed in the hands of the president. In the first presidential election, held in October 1982, the incumbent, Jayawardene, won reelection to office.[11] After his election triumph, Jayawardene decided to use the constitutional provision for referenda to ensure for his party the kind of dominance it had exercised from 1977 to 1982. It was generally believed that a parliamentary election might result in a UNP defeat but definitely would not result in the five-sixths majority that the 1977 elections had given the UNP. An election victory with a reduced UNP majority would have taken away the UNP's power to amend the constitution at will, as it had been able to do since the 1977 elections. Hence the first—and thus far only—national referendum in Sri Lankan history was held in December 1982, shortly after the presidential election. The question presented to the voters was whether the parliament elected in 1977 should be allowed to sit until 1989 without general elections.

More than 54 percent of the electorate supported the proposition, and the parliament was allowed to sit until 1989. However, the referendum was the first national election in Sri Lankan history to be marked by allegations of widespread election fraud.[12] Many voters opposed to the proposal had been intimidated into staying away from the polls. In addition, many poll watchers had been forcibly removed from the polling stations, after which irregularities had occurred.[13]

The referendum marked the beginning of a cycle of violence, election fraud, and intimidation, which increased during the other elections in the 1980s and returned in the local government elections of 1997 after a relatively free and fair national election in 1994.

In addition, the presidency of Ranasinghe Premadasa (1989–1993) was marked by a wide-ranging abuse of power. After being elected, Premadasa became quite ruthless with his opponents both inside and outside his party. Many also think he is responsible for unleashing the widespread violence and death squads that killed many supporters of the leftist Janatha Vimukthi Peramuna (JVP) as well as innocent bystanders in 1989 and 1990.

After his election in 1988, President Premadasa immediately arranged for parliamentary elections to be held in February 1989. This election was also marred by widespread violence and became the bloodiest election in Sri Lankan history. However, it was held, and 63.6 percent of the electorate turned out to vote. The UNP won 125 of the 225 seats contested (see Table 20.1).

The 1994 elections were marked by excessive violence and attacks on supporters of both parties. However, the violence level was considerably less than it had been in 1989. Chandrika Kumaratunga, elected in 1994 on a platform of reforming the system and bringing the violence to an end, was reelected as president in 1999, and her party was reelected to lead parliament in 2000. Both elections were marked by violence levels similar to those of the 1994 election.

Kumaratunga was unable to run for a third presidential term in 2005 and turned leadership of the party over to Mahinda Rajapaksa, a longtime SLFP MP from the southern district of Hambantota. Rajapaksa was opposed by the leader of the UNP and former prime minister Ranil Wickremasinghe. Ranil was expected to win, but the LTTE ordered all Tamils to abstain from the election.

TABLE 20.1 Results of Sri Lanka Parliamentary Elections

	1947		1952		1956		March 1960		July 1960		1965		1970	
	Seats Won	Percent Polled	Seats Won	Percent Polled	Seats Won	Percent Polled	Seats Won	Percent Polled	Seats Won	Percent Polled	Seats Won	Percent Polled	Seats Won	Percent Polled
UNP	42	39.8	54	44.1	8	27.9	50	29.4	30	37.6	66	38.9	17	37.9
SLFP	—	—	9	15.5	51	40.0[a]	46	20.9	75	33.6	41	30.2	90	36.6
LSSP	15	16.8[b]	9	13.1	14	10.5	10	10.5	12	7.4	10	7.4	19	8.8
CP	3	3.7[c]	4	5.8	3	4.6	3	4.8	4	3.0	4	2.7	6	3.4
MEP	—	—	—	—	—	—	10	10.6	3	3.4	1	2.7	—	—
TC	7	4.4	4	2.8	1	.3	1	1.2	1	1.5	3	2.4	—	—
FP	—	—	2	1.9	10	5.4	15	5.7	16	7.2	14	5.4	13	5.0
CIC	6	3.8	—	—	—	—	—	—	—	—	—	—	—	—
Others	22	31.4	13	16.9	8	11.4	16	16.7	10	6.4	7	7.0	5	7.4

(continues)

[a]Results for the MEP coalition of SWRD Bandaranaike and his SLEP.
[b]Includes two LSSP factions contesting the election separately.
[c]Includes the United Front of the CP and the VLSSP.

TABLE 20.1 (continued)

	1977		1989		1994		2000		2001		2004		2010	
	Seats Won	Percent Polled	Seats Won	Percent Polled	Seats Won	Percent Polled	Seats Won	Percent Polled	Seats Won	Percent Polled	Polled Won	Percent Polled	Polled Won	Percent Polled
UNP	140	50.9	125	50.7	94	44.0	89	40.2	109	47.6	82	37.8	60	29.4
SLFP/PA[d]	8	29.0	67	31.8	105	48.9	107	45.1	77	38.9	105	45.6	144	60.3
LSSP/USA[e]	0	3.6	3	2.9	—	—	—	—	—	—	—	—	—	—
CP[f]	0	1.9	—	—	—	—	—	—	—	—	—	—	—	—
JVP[g]	—	—	—	—	—	—	10	6.0	16	9.1	39	—	7	5.5
FP(TULF)	18	6.8	10	3.4	5	1.7	5	1.2	15	3.9	22	6.8	14	2.9
EPDP	—	—	—	—	9	0.1	4	0.6	2	0.8	1	0.3	—	—
EROS	—	—	13	2.7	—	—	—	—	—	—	—	—	—	—
SLMC/NUA[h]	—	—	4	3.6	7	1.8	4	2.3	5	1.2	5	2.0	—	—
JHU/SU	—	—	0	—	—	—	—	—	0	0.6	9	6.0	—	—
Others	2	6.6	—	1.7	5	2.6	6	4.6	1	.7	1	1.5	0	1.9

[d]The SLFP united with the USA to form the PA in 1994.

[e]The LSSP, CP, and SLMP united to form the USA in 1989.

[f]The SLMC ran as the NUA in 2000.

[g]The JVP with the SLFP; thirty-nine of their members were elected by preference votes.

[h]The Sinhala Urumaya renamed itself the Jathika Hela Urumaya and ran a slate of Buddhist monks.

The full names of the parties are UNP—United National Party; SLFP—Sri Lanka Freedom Party; LSSP—Lanka Sama Samaja Party; CP—Communist Party; MEP—Mahajana Eksath Peramuna; TC—Tamil Congress; FP—Federal Party; CIC—Ceylon Indian Congress; VLSSP—Viplavakari Lanka Sama Samaja Party; PA—People's Alliance; USA—United Socialist Alliance; JVP—Janatha Vimukthi Peramuna; DNA—Democratic National Alliance; TULF—Tamil United Liberation Front; TNA—Tamil National Alliance; EROS—Eelam Revolutionary Organization of Students; SLMC—Sri Lanka Muslim Congress; NUA—National Unity Alliance; EPDP—Eelam People's Democratic Party; SU—Sinhala Urumaya; JHU—Jathika Hela Urumaya; SLMP—Sri Lanka Mahajana Party.

Source: Sri Lanka Department of Elections.

TABLE 20.2. 2010 Presidential Election Results

Candidate	Party	Total Votes	Percentage Polled
Mahinda Rajapakse	SLFP	6,015,934	57.9
Sarath Fonseka	UNP	4,173,185	40.2
Eleven other candidates		204,494	2.0

Source: Sri Lanka Department of Elections, http://www.slelections.gov.lk/presidential2010/AIVOT.html.

Without Tamil votes, Ranil was unable to obtain a majority and lost the election by less than 200,000 votes (see Table 20.2).

President Rajapaksa's presidency (2005–present) has been marked by complaints and criticisms. Although he is widely supported for his defeat of the LTTE, his presidency has been marked by a sharp decline in media freedom, widespread attacks against political opponents, attacks against foreign and domestic nongovernmental organizations, and passage of the Eighteenth Amendment to the constitution, enacting a number of controversial proposals, all of which increased the president's power.

The Public Service and Administration

The national government oversees a large bureaucracy, which is in charge of carrying out the decisions of parliament and the executive. Unlike in the US system, employment as a bureaucrat in most of South Asia confers status, and government jobs are thus highly sought. The Sri Lankan administrative system, modeled on the British system of administration, has been severely criticized by some politicians who attribute Sri Lankan administrative problems to the introduction of an alien system into the country.[14] In particular, the bureaucracy is frequently accused of being partisan, lethargic, and insensitive to public needs.

The administrative system is overseen by cabinet ministries in which political appointees at the very top of the hierarchy make policy decisions. Beneath each of the sixty-five ministries[15] is a system of government departments that carry out functional activities such as irrigation projects, road construction and repair, and statistics gathering. These departments, which are highly centralized, have main offices in Colombo, where most decisions regarding the tasks of field officers are made.

The public service is hierarchical, with an elite corps at the top of the administrative structure. This upper elite is a highly professional and well-trained cadre that carries with it a great deal of social status. Beneath it are subordinate and minor employees who carry out most of the decisions made from above.

At the top of the administrative structure is the Sri Lanka Administrative Service (SLAS), which is similar to the Indian Administrative Service (described in Chapter 3). The SLAS, staffed according to the results of competitive examinations, has three levels of hierarchy. Promotion in the SLAS is handled by the secretaries of the ministry in charge of the SLAS position. The secretaries are the highest-ranking public officials in the ministry. Under the constitutions of 1972 and 1978, they have been political appointees rather than being drawn from the civil service, as had been the case from 1947 until 1972.[16]

In addition, a significant number of public corporations oversee government businesses and industries. The government of Sri Lanka has operated many corporations in such industries as tea, rubber, coconut, leather, and chemicals. Since the early 1980s the government has been selling the corporations to private investors as part of a vigorous privatization program.

Despite criticisms about the performance of the public service, few efforts have been made to change the system of administration since Sri Lanka became independent. The only major change has occurred in the administrative apparatus, which has been politicized: all of the governing parties have been guilty of trying to bring the civil service under their political control; as a result, promotion and hiring decisions are often handled on the basis of political criteria.

Local Government

Since Sri Lanka is a unitary state, its local government has been very weak. Government decisions are made in Colombo and sent to the rural areas of the country. In addition, the national government has control over most of the revenues generated by the government.

The country is divided into nine provinces, which were significant units of local governmental administration during the colonial era. Today, the system of local government is in a state of change. The district, which had been the main unit of local administration, has been partially replaced by provincial governments created in 1988. Each province has a popularly elected council with a chief minister and ministers approved by the council. The first elections to provincial councils were held in 1988.

The councils have not received adequate funding authority since their creation. Despite efforts by President Premadasa to strengthen them, they failed to meet the expectation that they would decentralize power to local governments. This led later governments to propose a more widespread transfer of power to regional governments.

The creation of the provincial councils has started the removal of the former system of local administration, the *kachcheri* system. Each province is divided into two or three administrative districts, which add up to a total of twenty-five on the island. Each district has a set of government offices called a *kachcheri,* which occupies the center of government administration in each district. Most government departments have district offices in the *kachcheri,* and the highest official in each *kachcheri* is the government agent (GA).[17] The GA is supposed to act as the chief coordinator of government activities in the district in addition to overseeing development projects.

Government agents were very important figures in the colonial administration of Great Britain. They were the most powerful officials in the provinces of their administration (during the colonial administration, the GAs oversaw the provinces rather than the districts). Although they were primarily revenue agents, they were soon given extensive powers to control almost all government activities in their regions. After independence, however, the influence of the GAs declined, as they now had to compete with the members of parliament and the main offices of the departments in Colombo for influence over the running of government activities in the district.[18] Because of the high degree of centralization in most government departments, the officials in the departments have been more likely to listen and respond to those who make the decisions about their promotions and transfers, namely, the department heads in the main offices in Colombo, rather than the GAs.

The members of parliament also eroded some of the power of the GAs. The development of a patronage system in which the members of parliament are the main distributors of benefits has focused citizen interest on the MPs and away from the GAs. The GAs no longer have the power and influence to resolve complaints. Rather, the MPs have sought this power in order to enhance their position with their electorates. In addition, the MPs have much more influence with the bureaucracy and are better able than the GAs to resolve citizen problems with government departments and agencies.[19] The future of the *kachcheri* system and the government agent is in doubt as the government tries to strengthen the provincial councils.

In addition to the *kachcheri* and the provincial councils, there are several elected local government councils in each district. Before 1981, local government revolved around a system of councils at the village, town, urban, and municipal levels. These governments carried out a relatively small number of functions. With limited tax revenues to work with, they were reduced to overseeing public works in the city or village under their jurisdiction.

In 1981 the government abolished the village and town councils and replaced them with district development councils (DDCs) with the intention of replacing the village and town council system with one council for every administrative district.[20] These councils were not very successful and were eventually replaced with a system of Pradeshiya Sabhas, which provided local councils for larger areas that comprised several of the former village council areas.

The creation of the 273 Pradeshiya Sabhas did not affect the urban and municipal councils. The twenty-three municipal councils function in most of the largest cities on the island, and the forty-one urban councils preside over the medium-size cities. Both types of councils are elected by proportional representation, and both select the mayor and deputy mayor of the city from among the council members.

The creation of the DDCs in 1981 and the provincial councils in 1988 was part of a broader attempt to decentralize the administrative process in Sri Lanka. Since Sri Lanka is a unitary state, most of its important decisions are made in the capital city of Colombo. In recent years the idea of decentralization has become quite popular among Sri Lankan and international experts of development and governmental administration.[21] Decentralization involves a transfer of decision-making authority from the central government machinery to local units of government or citizen groups. It is generally believed that the people who will be affected by administrative and development decisions should have more power to affect what happens to them. In other words, decentralization is conceptualized as a means of providing these people with the power to affect the decisions that directly affect their lives.

In sum, the Sri Lankan government has been structured in a way that provides the people with opportunities to become involved in government decisions. The highly partisan nature of politics (discussed in Chapter 21) has led to a strong patronage system in which the members of parliament try to please the people by meeting their demands. Both the high level of citizen input into the government and the open structure of the government have contributed to Sri Lanka's political stability.

NOTES

1. J. R. Jayawardene, "Parliamentary Democracy: The Role of the Opposition in a Developing Nation," *Parliamentarian* (July 1971): 191–194.

2. A. Jeyaratnam Wilson, *The Gaullist System in Asia: The Constitution of Sri Lanka (1978)* (London: Macmillan, 1980), 62.

3. James Jupp, *Sri Lanka: Third World Democracy* (London: Frank Cass, 1978), 28, 218.

4. See Jupp, *Sri Lanka*, 258–271, for a discussion of the constitution.

5. See K. M. De Silva, "The Constitution and Constitutional Reform Since 1948," in *Sri Lanka: A Survey,* ed. K. M. De Silva (Honolulu: University Press of Hawaii, 1977), 312–329.

6. See Wilson, *The Gaullist System in Asia,* for a thorough discussion of the constitution.

7. Wilson, *The Gaullist System in Asia,* 62.

8. Robert C. Oberst, "Proportional Representation and Electoral System Change in Sri Lanka," in *Sri Lanka in Change and Crisis,* ed. James Manor (London: Croon Helm, 1984), 118–134.

9. Robert C. Oberst, *Legislators and Representation in Sri Lanka: The Decentralization of Development Planning* (Boulder, CO: Westview Press, 1985), 77–81.

10. Under the Donoughmore Constitution of 1931, there were provisions for naming appointed members of parliament. During this time one Indian Tamil was appointed to parliament.

11. For a discussion of the 1982 election, see W. A. Wiswa Warnapala and L. Dias Hewagama, *Recent Politics in Sri Lanka: The Presidential Election and the Referendum of 1982* (New Delhi: Navrang, 1983); Manor, *Sri Lanka in Change and Crisis,* chs. 2–5; Robert C. Oberst and Amy Weilage, "Quantitative Tests of Electoral Fraud: The 1982 Sri Lankan Referendum," *Corruption and Reform* (spring 1990): 49–62.

12. Warnapala and Hewagama, *Recent Politics in Sri Lanka,* ch. 8; Priya Samarakone, "The Conduct of the Referendum," in Manor, *Sri Lanka in Change and Crisis,* 84–117.

13. Government of Sri Lanka, Sessional Paper No. II, *Report on the First Referendum in Sri Lanka* (Colombo: Department of Government Printing, 1987).

14. For the best description of the development of the administrative system, see W. A. Wiswa Warnapala, *Civil Service Administration in Ceylon: A Study in Bureaucratic Adaptation* (Colombo: Department of Cultural Affairs, 1974).

15. The number of ministries in the Rajapaksa era has increased sharply and has varied as Rajapaksa has needed to reward or win the support of members of parliament. Thus, the number of ministries may have changed.

16. Wilson, *The Gaullist System in Asia,* 138–139.

17. For a description of government agents, see G. R. Tressie Leitan, *Local Government and Decentralized Administration in Sri Lanka* (Colombo: Lake House, 1979), ch. 6.

18. Neil Fernando, *Regional Administration in Sri Lanka* (Colombo: Academy of Administrative Studies, 1973), 12–14; Robert C. Oberst, "Administrative Conflict and Decentralization: The Case of Sri Lanka," *Public Administration and Development* 5, no. 4 (1986): 163–174.

19. Oberst, *Legislators and Representation in Sri Lanka,* ch. 4.

20. Bruce Matthews, "District Development Councils in Sri Lanka," *Asian Survey* (November 1982): 1117–1134.

21. See Dennis Rondinelli, John R. Nellis, and G. Shabbir Cheema, *Decentralization in Developing Countries: A Review of Recent Experience* (Washington, DC: World Bank, 1983).

21

Political Parties and Interest Groups

Constituent demands in a political system are a way of linking the governed with the governors. In every successful democracy, there is a considerable amount of communication between the constituents, who bring their needs to their representatives, and the representatives, who, because of their accountability in elections, must respond to the demands.

Demands may be presented to the government by two broad categories of constituents: individuals and groups such as political parties and interest groups. As discussed later in this chapter, Sri Lankan members of parliament (MPs) receive a large number of individual requests from their constituents. In addition, government officials are approached by various groups in the society.

The Political Party Systems

National politics in Sri Lanka has been dominated by two parties, the United National Party (UNP) and the Sri Lanka Freedom Party (SLFP). In nine of the last twelve parliamentary elections, the parties have replaced each other as the governing party. Despite the national dominance of the UNP and the SLFP, Sri Lanka has had three party systems: one for the Tamil-speaking minority in the north and the east, one for the Muslims, and one for the rest of the Sinhalese. Neither the SLFP nor the UNP has won significant support from the Tamils of the north and east.

The Sinhalese Party System
The Sri Lanka Freedom Party. The Sri Lanka Freedom Party is the dominant party in the governing United People's Freedom Alliance. The party of the

TABLE 21.1 Heads of Government of Sri Lanka

	Party	Date of Birth	Date of Death	Term of Office	Caste
Don Stephen Senanayake	UNP	Oct. 20, 1884	Mar. 22, 1952	Sept. 1947–Mar. 1952	Goyigama
Dudley Senanayake	UNP	Jun. 19, 1911	Apr. 13, 1973	Mar. 1952–Sept. 1953	Goyigama
				Mar. 1960–Jul. 1960	
				Mar. 1965–May 1970	
John Kotelawala	UNP	Apr. 4, 1897	Oct. 2, 1980	Sept. 1953–Apr. 1956	Goyigama
S. W. R. D. Bandaranaike	SLFP	Jan. 8, 1899	Sept. 26, 1959	Apr. 1956–Sept. 1959	Goyigama
Wijayananda Dahanayake	SLFP	Oct. 22, 1902	Mar. 15, 1997	Sept. 1959–Mar. 1960	Goyigama
Sirimavo Bandaranaike	SLEP	Apr. 17, 1916	Oct. 10, 2000	Jul. 1960–Mar. 1965	Goyigama
				May 1970–Jul. 1977	
J. R. Jayawardene	UNP	Sept. 17, 1906	Nov. 1, 1996	Jul. 1977–Dec. 1988	Goyigama
Ranasinghe Premadasa	UNP	Jun. 23, 1924	May 1, 1993	Dec. 1988–May 1993	Hinna
D. B. Wijetunga	UNP	Feb. 15, 1922	Sept. 21, 2008	May 1993–Nov. 1994	Goyigama
Chandrika Kumaratunga	PA(SLFP)	Jun. 29, 1945	—	Nov. 1994–Nov. 2005	Goyigama
Mahinda Rajapaksa	PA(SLFP)	Nov. 18, 1945	—	Nov. 2005–present	Goyigama

NOTE: Through September 1978, the head of government was the prime minister; after 1978, the president.
UNP—United National Party; SLFP—Sri Lankan Freedom Party; PA—People's Alliance

Source: Author's notes.

moderate left, the SLFP has always had a difficult time holding its leftist sup-porters together. The party was damaged by factional infighting that led to its collapse after it governed from 1970 to 1977. However, its current leader, Mahinda Rajapaksa, has brought together a diverse collection of parties that have allowed it to control the government since 2004. He and his family have emerged as the dominant force in Sri Lankan politics.

The party was formed by S. W. R. D. Bandaranaike in 1951. Bandaranaike had been a popular minister in the UNP government formed in 1947 but chose to challenge the political dominance of the UNP. His first attempt was a fail-ure. The party received relatively limited support in 1952, when it elected only nine members to parliament. In 1956, however, Bandaranaike put together a strong coalition of leftist and anti-UNP parties and personalities. (For a list of Sri Lankan heads of government, see Table 21.1.) The party was swept over-whelmingly into power in the 1956 elections. It tapped a strong sense of dis-content among the rural Sinhalese, who felt that they had been discriminated against by the British and the first two governments of independent Sri Lanka. The party therefore committed itself to restoring the Sinhalese culture, lan-guage, and religion (Buddhism) to a position of dominance in the society. As a result, the government's first act was to make Sinhala the language of govern-ment, replacing English.

The coalition was held together until Bandaranaike was assassinated in 1959. After his death it fell apart, and the SLFP was unable to provide a cohesive force in the March 1960 elections. Many small parties emerged out of Ban-daranaike's 1956 coalition and split the party's support. By the July 1960 elec-tions, the SLFP had pulled its supporters together under the leadership of Bandaranaike's widow, Sirimavo Bandaranaike, who became the first woman ever elected as head of a democratic government. She was prime minister until 1965 and again from 1970 until 1977. In 1994 she was once again named prime minister and ruled in the executive presidency system under her daugh-ter, President Chandrika Kumaratunga, until her death on October 10, 2000.

After his election as president in 2005, Mahinda Rajapaksa consolidated power around his family and excluded Chandrika and the Bandaranaike family from influence in the SLFP. He placed his relatives in powerful positions in the government. As president he holds the position of minister of defense, finance and planning, ports and aviation, and highways. His brother Gotabaya is secre-tary to the Ministry of Defence (2004–current) and has controlled defense pol-icy since his appointment, as well as immigration and emigration, the Urban Development Authority, and the Land Reclamation and Development Corpo-ration. His brother Basil is minister of economic development. A fourth brother, Chamal, is Speaker of parliament. Mahinda's oldest son, Namal, is an

MP. Other family members hold such posts as the chief minister of the Uva Provincial Council, director and chairman of Sri Lankan Airlines, ambassador to the United States, and ambassador to Russia, to name a few.

The SLFP's success in elections has always been accompanied by electoral agreements with the major parties of the Left. This was the case in 1956, 1960, 1970, 1994, 2000, and 2004. President Rajapaksa has been highly adept at forming alliances with both parties and with individuals, persuading them to cross over to support the SLFP.

The United National Party. The United National Party is the party of the Right in Sri Lankan politics. It has generated such personalities as Don Stephen Senanayake, J. R. Jayawardene, and Ranasinghe Premadasa. Its emergence from the colonial era as an umbrella party was similar to the formation of the Indian National Congress of India (see Chapter 4) insofar as it represented a union of many different ideologies and personalities that arose out of the independence movement. The domination of the party by independence-movement politicians ended when President J. R. Jayawardene retired in 1988, precipitating a power struggle among party leaders.

Its first leader in the post-Jayawardene era, President Ranasinghe Premadasa, was killed in a bomb explosion in 1993. It is widely believed that the bomb was set by the guerrillas of the Liberation Tigers of Tamil Eelam (LTTE), but rumors persist that disgruntled members of his own party killed him.

After the UNP lost the 1994 elections, Ranil Wickremasinghe took control of the party and has dominated it since. His leadership has been challenged since 2004 as the party began losing elections. Many important personalities in the party have defected to the SLFP due to disagreement with Ranil. Despite criticism, no dominant leader has emerged to take over the leadership of the party. Among potential challengers is Ranjith Premadasa, son of the former president Ranasinghe Premadasa.

Until the 1994 elections, the UNP was the strongest vote getter in Sri Lankan elections. It dominated the first two elections after independence in 1947 and 1952 before losing the 1956 elections to the SLFP, and it returned to power for a brief period in 1960 after the elections in March of that year. Since those elections did not give the UNP a working parliamentary majority, it was unable to obtain a vote of confidence from parliament for its government. In the elections of July 1960, the UNP once again lost to the SLFP. It returned to power in 1965 and governed until 1970, when it lost the elections. In 1977 the UNP was returned to power with a commanding five-sixths majority in parliament. The scheduled 1983 elections were canceled after a referendum held in 1982 over the question of whether the present parliament, which had been elected in 1977, should be continued until 1989.

The 1989 parliamentary elections gave the UNP control over parliament but with a smaller majority (125 of 225 seats). In 1994 the party was in disarray under the leadership of Dingiri Banda Wijetunga, who replaced Premadasa as president in 1993. The elections resulted in a slim margin of victory for the People's Alliance, which obtained a majority by creating a wide coalition of leftist, Muslim, and Tamil parties. The UNP would gain a majority in the 2001 elections and ruled the country for two years before losing to the SLFP in the April 2004 elections.

The Other Parties

The Lanka Sama Samaja Party and the Communist Party. Sri Lanka has a long tradition of strong leftist parties based on two traditional Marxist parties. At one time, the Lanka Sama Samaja Party (LSSP) was billed as the world's only successful Trotskyite party. (Leon Trotsky was vanquished by Joseph Stalin in the power struggle that followed Lenin's death in 1924 in the Soviet Union.) Its support came from Marxists who objected to the close association of the Communist Party (CP) with the Soviet Union and thus preferred the independent Marxism of the LSSP. Moreover, it represents an independent Marxist doctrine adapted to the culture and needs of Sri Lanka rather than the Soviet-oriented Marxism of the Sri Lanka Communist Party.[1]

After the 1947 elections, the LSSP was the main opposition to the governing UNP. But the emergence of the SLFP provided many voters on the left wing of Sri Lankan politics with a moderate alternative to the Marxist LSSP and the Communist Party. The LSSP was an important element of the 1970 United Front coalition established by Sirimavo Bandaranaike. Three cabinet positions, including the important finance portfolio, were given to LSSP MPs in the government formed after the 1970 elections. Since that election, the party has lost influence but remains an ally of the SLFP.

The Communist Party. The Communist Party of Sri Lanka maintained close ideological ties with the Soviet Union. With the collapse of Soviet communism, the party has drawn closer to the LSSP. The CP has received strong support in the southern regions of the country, where it has been associated with the Durawa caste. Like the LSSP, its has experienced sharply declining influence, although it still holds several seats in parliament.

The Janatha Vimukthi Peramuna. Today, the most significant leftist party is the Janatha Vimukthi Peramuna (JVP, People's Liberation Front). Its founder and leader until his death in November 1989, Rohana Wijeweera, was responsible for youth-led insurrections against the government of Sirimavo Bandaranaike in 1971 and J. R. Jayawardene from 1987 to 1989. Formed in the late 1960s, the JVP came perilously close to overthrowing the government with a series of well-planned attacks against police stations and government positions in 1971.[2] Official estimates placed the death toll at around 1,200 people; unofficial reports placed it much higher. In addition, more than 16,000 suspected insurgents were taken into custody after the failed revolt.[3] As a result, many JVP leaders and followers were jailed. Wijeweera was sentenced to twenty years in prison; however, the UNP released him shortly after the 1977 elections.

The UNP legalized the JVP, which emerged as a leftist party dedicated to nonviolent means of social change. After its legalization, it contested local council elections, and Wijeweera ran for president. In the 1982 presidential elections, Wijeweera polled about 270,000 votes, or 4.2 percent of the total. After severe anti-Tamil riots in 1983, the party was accused of fomenting the violence and banned. After the July 1987 Indo-Lanka accords, which made concessions to the Tamil insurgents in the north of the island, the JVP began a campaign of assassinating government supporters. At the height of the violence (June to August 1989), over eight hundred people per month were being killed. Not all of the deaths were at the hands of the JVP, however. Death squads of government supporters and security forces are believed to have been responsible for many deaths as well.

In November 1989 the government captured Wijeweera and claimed that he was shot dead by his own supporters as he led government security forces to JVP hideouts. In any case, all of the JVP politburo and most of its district leaders were captured or killed in November 1989. Since that time, the JVP has rebuilt its organization and disavowed violence.[4] In the 1990s, it became the third-largest party in the country and elected thirty-nine MPs in the 2004 elections. The party also became more nationalist, adopting an anti-Tamil position and opposing efforts to resolve the civil war peacefully. After its 2004 alliance with the SLFP, the party began to strongly oppose the government, criticizing its economic policies, restriction of the media, and treatment of Tamils since the end of the civil war. Since 2004, the party has weakened, electing only five MPs in 2010. It has also experienced two serious splits. In 2008, a significant number of members joined the United People's Freedom Alliance as the JVP abandoned its support of the government. In 2010, a radical faction broke away claiming that the JVP had become too moderate.

The Tamil Party System

In Sri Lanka (as in India), some regional minority groups have formed their own political parties. The Sri Lankan Tamils, for example, have consistently supported their own parties and tried to win the support of the Sri Lankan Muslims. As a result, a separate party system operates in areas where the Sri Lankan Tamils are in the majority. The Sri Lankan Tamil party system has been redefining itself since the defeat of the LTTE and is currently in a state of transition.

The dominant political party of the Tamils for the last fifty years has been the Federal Party and its variations, the Tamil United Liberation Front (TULF) and the Tamil National Alliance (TNA). Immediately after independence, there was only one important Tamil party in Sri Lanka, the Tamil Congress (TC), led by G. G. Ponnambalam. The TC cooperated with the UNP in the first government after independence, when the Indian Tamils were denied citizenship and the right to vote. Several members of the TC deserted their party in opposition to its support of this action and formed the Federal Party. Under the leadership of S. J. V. Chelvanayagam, this new party demanded a federal system in Sri Lanka, with home rule for the Tamils in the eastern and northern parts of the island.

The Federal Party soon replaced the TC as the dominant party among the Sri Lankan Tamils. Shortly after the 1970 elections, the Tamil parties, comprising both the Indian and the Sri Lankan Tamils, came together in a coalition to form the TULF. A significant element of the TC opposed the union and reappeared as the Tamil Congress after the 1977 elections.

The TULF increased its demands for regional self-rule in 1976 and began demanding an independent state (Eelam) for the Tamil people. In the 1977 general elections, as well as in the local council and presidential elections in the early 1980s, the TULF received the overwhelming backing (70 to 80 percent) of the Sri Lankan Tamils in the north and along the east coast.

The call for Eelam, accompanied by increasing violence by Tamil youths in the north and east of the island, led the government to pass the Sixth Amendment to the constitution in 1983. This amendment specifically banned the advocacy of separatism. The sixteen TULF MPs were expelled from parliament for failing to recite a loyalty oath disavowing separatism as required by the amendment. The government then refused to hold by-elections in the areas represented by these opposition members because of the youth-led violence, and the Sri Lankan Tamils remained without representation in parliament until 1989. During their five-year absence from parliament, the radical LTTE replaced the TULF as the dominant political force among the Tamils.

The TULF originally included the largest Indian Tamil political organization, the Ceylon Workers' Congress (CWC). After the 1977 elections, however, the leader of the CWC was offered a cabinet post in the UNP government. As a result, the CWC disassociated itself from the TULF. In any case, the calls for Eelam were largely ignored by the Indian Tamils, who reside outside the territory that has been claimed for the state of Eelam.

As the tension between the Sinhalese and the Sri Lankan Tamils increased, Sri Lankan Tamil youths resorted to violence and joined several political groups commonly called "tigers." These organizations challenged the leadership position of the TULF in the Sri Lankan Tamil community and became the dominant force in Sri Lankan Tamil politics in the 1980s.

Despite the large number of tiger groups, only a few were important as political forces. The larger groups had sophisticated training camps in South India, and most were financed by the proceeds from bank robberies in Sri Lanka and drug sales in Europe, as well as by donations from wealthy Tamils living in the United States and Great Britain.

The political strength of the tigers became apparent after the July 1987 Indo-Lanka accords calling for a cease-fire between the tigers and the government, with the Indian army acting as a peacekeeping force. The accords also established a system of provincial councils. All but one of the major tiger groups went along with the treaty, turned over its arms, and became a legal political organization. The one exception was the group with the most powerful military, the Liberation Tigers of Tamil Eelam, which continued to fight against the Indian forces.

The other armed groups have formed into democratic political parties, joined by the Eelam People's Democratic Party (EPDP) and the Tamileelam Makkal Viduthalai Pulikal (TMVP), a breakaway faction of the LTTE. These other groups have not been able to win strong support among Tamil voters, and most elections have been dominated by the TULF.

The TULF split in 2004 when the largely ceremonial president of the party, V. Anandasangaree, refused to accept an electoral agreement with the LTTE. As a result, the rest of the party leadership formed the Tamil National Alliance and contested the 2004 elections with a mix of TULF leaders and Tamil candidates selected by the LTTE. They elected twenty-two MPs.

Since the end of the civil war, the TNA has continued to dominate Tamil politics. However, the EPDP has become a political force in the north, although many critics claim that it uses its armed militia and the support of the Sri Lankan security forces to intimidate voters and opponents. In the east the TMVP has become a political force and, like the EPDP, has allied itself with the SLFP. As with the EPDP, there are many allegations that the TMVP uses intimidation and kidnapping to win support.

The Muslim Party System

The Muslims have shifted their support between the UNP and the SLFP, and until recently, most voted for the UNP. In 1988, the Sri Lanka Muslim Congress (SLMC) was formed and almost immediately gained majority support among Muslim voters, especially in the Eastern Province. The SLMC was formed by the charismatic M. H. M. Ashroff, who died in a suspicious helicopter crash in 2002. The party then splintered into a number of factions. These factions have shifted, and their leaders have created alliances with other Muslim faction leaders. Currently, much of the party's organization has been absorbed by the SLFP.

Party Systems in Change

The many changes in the party system in Sri Lanka since 1977 have created a highly volatile situation that could pose a serious threat to the political system. Among the Tamil parties, a new generation of leadership has emerged. The TULF, representing the older generation of leadership, appears to have recovered from a near-fatal blow with the LTTE assassination of its leader, A. Amirthalingam, in July 1989. Since the defeat of the LTTE, the TNA has emerged as the strongest party. Although there are still LTTE sympathizers in the country and two factions of the post–civil war LTTE formed in the United States and Norway, the LTTE no longer plays a role in Tamil politics. The EPDP and TMVP appear to have limited followings, and Tamils, as in the past, have turned to the more conservative and traditional leadership offered by the TNA.

The Sinhalese party system has also been in a state of change, especially in regard to the apparent demise of the Sri Lankan "old Left," which consists of the Communist Party and the LSSP and its allies. Since the 1977 parliamentary elections, the parties of the old Left have not been able to run competitively with the UNP and the SLFP. The growth of the JVP, especially among young people, appears to reflect the inability of the LSSP and the Communist Party to win youth support as they did in the 1950s and 1960s. The JVP appeared to be in a position to challenge the SLFP as the dominant party of the Left in the mid-2000s, but its support declined in the 2010 parliamentary elections.

Change has not been confined to the parties of the Left. The SLFP and the UNP have both experienced pressure for change. The retirement of Chandrika Kumaratunga allowed a non-Bandaranaike to take over the leadership of the party. The new leader, Mahinda Rajapaksa, severed ties to Kumaratunga and placed his own loyalists in charge of the party. The Bandaranaike family no longer wields influence in the party. Instead, President Rajapaksa has placed family members in powerful positions in the government.

President Rajapaksa has also lured a number of prominent UNP MPs, most of whom were dissatisfied with the party leadership of Ranil Wickremasinghe, to cross over and support his government. They have formed a bloc in the Rajapaksa government, voting with his government but maintaining their identity as a UNP faction. The departure of these MPs has weakened the UNP, and the party's ability to win future national elections is in doubt.

Despite dissatisfaction with Ranil Wickremasinghe, he has remained in charge of the UNP. His power is questionable due to an unbroken string of election losses starting in 2004, including national, provincial, and local elections. A younger generation of UNP leaders is waiting to challenge Ranil's position but have so far failed to succeed in reducing his power.

A further question mark to the Sinhalese party system has been the emergence of Sarath Fonseka as a political figure. Fonseka was in charge of the military during the successful campaigns against the LTTE and emerged as a war hero until he challenged President Rajapaksa for the presidency in 2009. After losing in a close election, he was arrested and convicted on a wide series of sedition charges, many of them believed to be politically motivated and almost humorous. For instance he was charged with sedition, or saying bad things about the military, when he accused the president's brother and secretary to the Defence Ministry of ordering the execution of surrendered LTTE leaders. He spent nearly three years in prison before being pardoned by President Rajapaksa in May 2012. Although barred from seeking political office, he has begun to organize his supporters to challenge the government. Despite invitations from the JVP and the UNP, he has refused to join either party.

Because Muslims do not have a strong, charismatic leader, the Muslim vote has splintered based on dominant personalities who can command support. The once dominant SLMC is weakening.

The next few years will be very important to the future of democracy in Sri Lanka as the party system struggles with the forces that have been changing it. The nature of the changes is still not known, although their consequences will have a major impact on the structure of Sri Lankan politics in the future. The actions of President Rajapaksa to restrict media freedom and curtail opposition have posed a major threat to the future as the opposition parties try to find dominant leaders to challenge the Rajapaksa family.

Interest Groups

National Groups

Many have argued that the emergence of broad-based national interest groups is a part of the development process that third world democracies are undergoing.[5] Interest groups provide governmental representation for the various interests in the society. In Sri Lanka interest groups are unorganized and weak and do not exert significant pressure on lawmakers and bureaucrats. Their weakness can be attributed to several factors.

First, many interest groups do not find it worthwhile to approach the elected members of parliament with their demands. Hence they try to influence the administrative rather than the policy-making process. Public policy in Sri Lanka is the result of a party's election platform and its ideology. Many groups know in advance that the government's ideology is not favorable to their demands, and so they direct their demands to administrators, who may be more responsive and can circumvent the rules. But this practice is limited by a general sense of hostility among the governing Sri Lankan political parties toward what they call "sabotage by public officials" opposed to the governing party's policies.[6] Attempts are frequently made to transfer or suspend bureaucrats who may be sympathetic to the opposition party. Many politicians believe that bureaucrats work for one or the other of the major parties. As a result, elected politicians try to limit the amount of policy interpretation exercised by the bureaucrats. This limits the influence interest groups can exert over government decisions by approaching the bureaucracy.

A second factor is that the major parties establish interest groups they can control. In fact, most interest groups are closely connected with either the government or an opposition party and thus do not need access to politicians. This is especially the case among trade unions; the electoral triumph of the union's party is believed to lead to the achievement of the union's political objectives—hence the all-or-nothing view of the political process by the unions.[7] If the wrong party is in power, the unions do not expect to receive government cooperation and benefits. There is little bargaining and compromise between the government and the interest groups. The interest group either receives what it wants from its party when the party is in power, or it is denied its objectives.

A third factor is that policy-making power is concentrated in a few important ministries; therefore, the number of people who can influence policy is limited.[8] The domination of Sri Lanka by a few charismatic personalities has resulted in a small inner circle consisting of people who hold significant policy-making power.

A fourth factor is the nature of power and influence in Sri Lanka. Much pressure is exerted through family networks and friends. Sri Lankans tend to view power in personal terms; thus, when an individual, no matter how unimportant, goes to a person with power, he or she expects to be granted a personal meeting with that official.[9] No mere representative of that official will be acceptable. Access to power is indeed a personal affair.[10] Consequently a lobbyist in Sri Lanka is effective only if he or she establishes a set of personal contacts. At the same time, the highly partisan nature of politics in Sri Lanka makes it very difficult for an individual to maintain close personal contacts with powerful members of both parties.

A fifth factor is that interest groups tend to be ad hoc.[11] Groups may arise around an emotional issue, but once their initial objectives have been achieved or the issue loses its emotional appeal, the groups become inactive and disappear. This is especially the case with village-level interest groups. For instance, an important person in the village with a demand may gather some of his clients and go to the government official as a delegation representing the village. Many of the clients go with him because of the potential opportunity to present their own demands. Thus the important person's demand appears to reflect a broader segment of the village population than it actually does.

Nevertheless, people in positions of power do not generally feel pressured by these groups since they are usually led by friends.[12] This practice has been reinforced by the creation of ministries that cater to a specific clientele, such as the Ministry of Coconut Development and Janatha Estate Development, which was set up to deal with private and public coconut producers, and the Ministry of Civil Aviation, which regulates domestic aviation.

In short, the relationship between national interest groups and people in positions of power is not one of compromise and bargaining but rather one of cooperation and accommodation. These groups' ability to affect policy, although limited by poor organization, is enhanced by close ties to the political parties as well as by the personal relationships created by the leaders of the groups with people in positions of power.

These limitations, however, have not completely hindered the development of interest groups. Several Buddhist organizations have utilized their connections to powerful individuals in the government and mobilized mass support for their initiatives. In recent years they have been extremely active in trying to influence peace negotiations with the LTTE and to restrict the growth of Christian churches in the country.

Local Groups

Local interest groups function differently and are more influential than the national organizations. South Asian life revolves around the village. Nearly 85 percent of the Sri Lankan population lives in rural areas. The average villager is very active in village-level organizations, and a large number of village-level organizations have developed. These include development-oriented organizations such as rural development societies, religious societies, parent-teacher associations, cooperatives, and occupational groups, which are quite active and lobby vigorously for beneficial policies and government actions.

These organizations are dominated by a small elite of the village-level society and often revolve around one or two important people in the village. Villagers in Sri Lanka often look to people with high economic standing, good background, the right caste, educational attainment, and religious piety to lead them. Often the same people lead many village organizations, limiting the influence and input of the villagers themselves.[13]

In addition, these groups tend to be highly politicized, with their leadership allied to one of the major political parties. After elections, the leaders are often replaced by people acceptable to the newly elected national leaders or MPs. In some rural development societies, old leaders have refused to yield power after a national election, and the government has recognized a new organization led by government supporters. On the whole, however, village-level groups tend to deal with village-level concerns—new roads, electrification, bridges, development projects, and so on. The amount of influence they exert depends, once again, on how closely they are aligned with those who wield power.

Individual Demands

Most demands on the Sri Lankan political system are made by individuals. Many Sri Lankans expect government representatives to respond to their personal needs, and the benefits they receive are called particularized benefits. Sri Lankan members of parliament set aside time to meet personally with their constituents. As a result, they are inundated by constituents with highly personalized requests for such things as jobs for their children or themselves. The average member of parliament may meet with hundreds of constituents every week, and the ministers, who can fill a large number of patronage jobs, may see several thousand constituents each week.[14] The constituents begin lining up outside the meeting place before sunrise and wait for hours for their opportunity to speak to the MP, who will usually deal with each request quickly and move on to the next petitioner. Ministers are assisted by staff people who type letters of recommendation, call government servants who have refused to act on a government form, and take down information to follow up on requests.

The most frequent request received by MPs is for help with employment.[15] The petitioner may request help for him- or herself, a son or daughter, or another relative in finding a job, obtaining an employment transfer to a better location, or getting an improved appointment. Beyond this, the member of parliament may be faced with requests to resolve family feuds or even to speak to a husband who has been sleeping with other women. Rarely do the demands deal with national issues or questions of community development. Even then they often involve projects that personally benefit the petitioner, such as a paved road past his house or a new irrigation canal to his fields. Another important aspect of these demands is that both men and women make them, with women comprising more than 40 percent of the petitioners.[16]

The members of parliament have a limited number of jobs and other benefits to provide to their constituents. They base their decisions on patronage. Almost all government jobs are given on the basis of personal connections rather than merit. The patronage system has undergone considerable expansion since the 1960s, which has resulted in increased constituent demands and expectations as well as dissatisfaction from the supporters of the opposition parties.

The net consequence of this pressure for personalized treatment is overburdened legislators who spend most of their time dealing with petitioners' requests. In fact, the legislators are often left feeling that their time should be spent on more important activities, such as development work and national issues. Efforts to reduce the constituent pressure on legislators have not been successful. During the Jayawardene years, the creation of a computerized job bank to dispense government jobs turned into a fiasco as it rewarded those with access to the computer bank. The creation of proportional representation was intended to be a means of controlling job seekers. However, the preferential ballot requires that members of parliament be popular in their electoral districts. The main effect of the change was to enlarge the size of the electoral district to include a whole administrative district.

······

In sum, interest articulation and demands, like other aspects of Sri Lankan society, are highly personalized. Government representatives frequently respond to people's personal needs, and most people expect this. Yet, the most important part of this system of demands and government responses is its high level of institutionalization and effectiveness, especially where individual demands are concerned. Sri Lankans have access to their leaders, and they take advantage of it.

NOTES

1. For a thorough description of the early history of the party, see George Jan Lerski, *The Origins of Trotskyism in Ceylon* (Stanford, CA: Hoover Institution, 1968).

2. Robert N. Kearney and Janice Jiggins, "The Ceylon Insurrection of 1971," *Journal of Commonwealth and Comparative Politics* (March 1975): 40–65; A. C. Alles, *J.V.P.: 1969–1989* (Colombo: Lake House Investments, 1990).

3. Gananath Obeyesekere, "Some Comments on the Social Backgrounds of the April 1971 Insurgency in Sri Lanka (Ceylon)," *Journal of Asian Studies* 33 (1974): 367–384.

4. For an insider's description of the insurrection, see C. A. Chandraprema, *Sri Lanka, The Years of Terror: The JVP Insurrection, 1987–1989* (Colombo: Lake House Bookshop, 1991). For

a journalist's view from the outside of the movement, see Rohan Gunaratna, *Sri Lanka, A Lost Revolution: The Inside Story of the JVP* (Colombo: Institute of Fundamental Studies, 1990).

5. Gabriel A. Almond and G. Bingham Powell, *Comparative Politics: System, Process, and Policy,* 2nd ed. (Boston: Little, Brown, 1978), 196–197.

6. Robert N. Kearney, *Trade Unions and Politics in Ceylon* (Berkeley: University of California Press, 1971), 83–84.

7. Kearney, *Trade Unions,* 2.

8. Robert C. Oberst, "Democracy and the Persistence of Westernized Elite Dominance in Sri Lanka," *Asian Survey* (July 1985): 760–772.

9. Janice Jiggins, *Caste and Family in the Politics of the Sinhalese, 1947–1976* (New York: Cambridge University Press, 1979); James Jupp, *Sri Lanka: Third World Democracy* (London: Frank Cass, 1978), 174.

10. Robert C. Oberst, *Legislators and Representation in Sri Lanka: The Decentralization of Development Planning* (Boulder, CO: Westview Press, 1985), 34–35.

11. Urmila Phadnis, *Religion and Politics in Sri Lanka* (New Delhi: Manohar, 1976), 273.

12. Oberst, *Legislators and Representation,* 40–41.

13. Oberst, *Legislators and Representation,* 41–44.

14. Oberst, *Legislators and Representation,* 59.

15. Oberst, *Legislators and Representation,* 37.

16. Oberst, *Legislators and Representation,* ch. 3.

22

Conflict Mediation: Ethnic and Political Conflict

From the late 1970s until 2009, no issue dominated the debate in Sri Lankan society as much as the conflict between the Liberation Tigers of Tamil Eelam (LTTE) and the government. The government began an offensive in 2008 that gradually reduced the territory held by the LTTE until the government trapped the last remnants of the LTTE and about 250,000 civilians on a small strip of seaside land in Mullivaikal, Mullaitivu. The final victory resulted in the death of the total leadership of the LTTE and the capture of the last of its forces. While the defeat marked a new era in Sri Lanka, it did not end the conflict between the Tamils and the Sinhalese.

The conflict grew out of a long-standing sense of deprivation felt by the country's Tamil population. During the British era the Tamils adapted to the English language and British cultural mores more readily than the Sinhalese. As a result, the British rewarded them with important places in the colonial bureaucracy. After independence, however, the Sinhalese attempted to assert a dominant role in the society, and conflict resulted.

At first the Tamil leadership sought more power over Tamil affairs. The emergence of the Federal Party as the dominant party in the Sri Lankan Tamil areas was the result of its strong advocacy for federalism and regional autonomy for the Tamils. Its success in replacing the Tamil Congress as the dominant Sri Lankan Tamil party can be attributed to this advocacy. Until the 1970s the Federal Party demanded a federal system of government in Sri Lanka so that the Tamils could control their own affairs. In the mid-1970s, with the creation of the Tamil United Liberation Front (TULF), the Federal Party escalated its demands to include the creation of an independent state for the Tamils.

The Federal Party's demands for greater autonomy were fueled by several concerns. The first was the language issue. As long as the British ruled Sri Lanka, an alien language—English—was imposed on the people. As soon as the British left the island, the issue emerged as an important point of contention. When the Official Language Act of 1956 specified Sinhala as the sole official language of Sri Lanka, Tamils feared being denied employment in government jobs, which would now require proficiency in Sinhala; they also feared that they would be unable to understand government legal proceedings, also now to be held in Sinhala, and that they would be left out of the commercial life of the society, again, to be conducted in Sinhala. The government responded by passing a resolution allowing the use of Tamil in government transactions involving people who spoke Tamil. The resolution also provided government employees whose mother tongue was Tamil time to learn Sinhala. However, these requirements, which were passed in 1959, have not yet been fully implemented. Many government communications to Tamil-speaking people still appear in Sinhala. Moreover, although the constitution of 1978 gave the Tamil language special status in some government dealings, it maintained the superiority of Sinhala in the society; in addition, its designation of Tamil as a "national language," while Sinhala remained the only official language, failed to placate the Tamil leadership, and the problem remains a point of contention.

A second concern has been education: as noted in Chapter 19, Sri Lankans know its importance. Admissions to university are limited and coveted. After independence, admission was determined on the basis of examinations in the three languages used in the country: Sinhala, Tamil, and English. Only those receiving the highest scores were admitted. For many years the number of students admitted on the basis of the Tamil language exams exceeded Tamils' percentage of the population. Many Sinhalese felt that the Tamil examiners were inflating the scores so that more Tamil students would be admitted to the universities. In the 1970s the United Front government of Sirimavo Bandaranaike became concerned with the superior performance of the Tamil students. Quotas based on the size of each ethnic community were set, and university exams became a disputed issue. The United National Party (UNP) sought to defuse the issue by altering the system to one based on both quotas and merit, but this effort was slow to ease resentment.

A third concern pertains to employment. The government sector is the main source of high-status jobs. As Sinhala has become more important as the language of government, Tamil speakers have become more concerned about their community's access to government employment. But there has been a severe shortage of jobs for educated young people from all ethnic communities since the early 1960s. The lack of jobs has been cited as a cause of the youth insurrections led by the Janatha Vimukthi Peramuna (JVP) in the early 1970s and late 1980s. These uprisings involved many more Sinhalese than Tamil youths. The government's language and education policies helped to create a sense of deprivation among the Tamil youths, who now also had the Sinhalese and the government to blame for their plight. They also fueled the guerrilla warfare that engulfed the northern and eastern regions of the country.

A fourth concern has been the Sinhalese colonization of traditional Tamil areas. In Trincomalee, Vavuniya, Mullaitivu, and Batticaloa districts, recently irrigated lands have been opened for settlement. In many areas, especially Trincomalee, the lands have been given to Sinhalese. This has had the effect of reducing the Tamil percentage of the population in these areas. The problem has been amplified by the Mahaweli development project, which has opened up newly irrigated lands at a rapid pace. Most of the irrigated farmland created by the Mahaweli project has been distributed to Sinhalese settlers.

A fifth concern is the central government's neglect of the north and east. Both areas have been largely ignored in the government's development plans. The highly centralized Sri Lankan government has tended to focus its attention on the southwestern areas of the country. The rural areas of the north and east are much more traditional than other parts of Sri Lanka.

The sixth concern has been regional autonomy or control over significant policy decisions directly affecting the Tamils. One of these decisions has to do with the number and type of development projects in Tamil areas. The Tamils feel that they have not received their fair share of the projects available. This is especially the case with two major development initiatives of the J. R. Jayawardene government: the Mahaweli project, which, for the most part, affects Sinhalese areas, and the free trade zones, which are located in the Sinhalese areas. In short, the Tamils believe that they are not benefiting from the income and jobs generated by these projects.

A second issue raised by the question of regional autonomy is the maintenance of law and order. The majority of police and armed forces in the Tamil areas are Sinhalese. Many of the attacks carried out by the tiger groups were directed against Sinhalese police and soldiers. Since 1977, police and soldiers have sporadically rioted and attacked innocent bystanders or committed crimes against Tamil civilians. Several of these security force actions have resulted in over one hundred civilian deaths. These attacks became common during the 1980s and early 1990s. Since the end of the war, most of the actions have involved sexual harassment of women, burglary, and extortion.

Probably the most important issue related to regional autonomy is the question of which area the Tamil region should include. The Tamil National Alliance (TNA) and many Tamil leaders have supported the union of the Eastern and Northern provinces. This proposal has been criticized because of the large numbers of Sinhalese and Muslims in the Eastern Province. Most Muslims are concerned about a regional government controlled by the Tamils. They fear that their influence will be diluted in such an arrangement.

The Sinhalese population of the east poses another problem. Over the past fifty years, there has been a large influx of Sinhalese settlers into the Eastern Province. This growth was accelerated after 1977 when the Mahaweli project opened up land in Ampara, Batticaloa, and Trincomalee districts to Sinhalese settlers. These settlers fear a Tamil-dominated regional government.[1] Since the end of the war, there has been movement of Sinhalese into the Northern Province and statements from the president and other United Front leaders that no area of the country belongs to one ethnic group.

These six concerns led to the LTTE insurrection. The failure to resolve them has led to a continued threat of Tamil violence. Communications between the Sinhalese and Tamil leadership was poor before the war and continues to be nearly nonexistent.[2]

During the war, there were very few direct communications between the two sides. From 1984 until 1987, the two sides negotiated, with the Indian government acting as an intermediary. These negotiations met with little success. In July 1987 the Sri Lankan and Indian governments signed the Indo-Lanka accords, which brought Indian troops to Sri Lanka to enforce a cease-fire. The tigers were never involved in the negotiations, and the LTTE never agreed to the accords. Open warfare between the Indian peacekeeping forces and the LTTE erupted in October 1987 and continued until the Indian departure in March 1990.[3]

In 1989 President Ranasinghe Premadasa began the first direct negotiations between the Sri Lankan government and the LTTE; in June 1989 the LTTE agreed to lay down their arms, renounce separatism, and negotiate further on regional autonomy. The president then asked the Indian troops to leave the country by the second anniversary of their arrival. They refused and continued their war against the LTTE.

Indian troops finally left Sri Lanka in March 1990. Their departure was followed by a brief period of peace between the government and the LTTE. However, in June the LTTE began an offensive against police stations in the north and east. The civil war evolved into a bloodier conflict as the LTTE increased its attacks against Muslim and Sinhalese civilians and the government used air power to bomb targets in Tamil areas. By the end of August 1994, the government controlled the cities of the Eastern Province and some of the countryside but had failed to conquer the mainland of the Jaffna Peninsula in the north. The war had become a bloody stalemate.

President Chandrika Kumaratunga and her government were elected in 1994 on a platform of negotiating an end to the conflict. Kumaratunga took the courageous position of offering to grant regional autonomy to the Tamils. For the first time since independence, a Sri Lankan government acknowledged that the political system was not providing the Tamils with a fair role in the system.

President Kumaratunga began negotiations with the LTTE in January 1995. These talks became a comedy of errors: the LTTE was insulted by the limited power and stature of the government negotiators, and the government was angered by the LTTE's stipulation that before negotiations on substantive issues such as the devolution of power could begin, the problems and suffering of the Tamil people must first be alleviated.

After four months the negotiations had failed to achieve any progress. The LTTE finally gave the government a series of ultimatums and threatened to pull out of the negotiations. Finally, on April 19, 1995, the civil war resumed when the LTTE followed through with its threats.

The Kumaratunga government was stung by criticism for its trust in the LTTE and the concessions it had offered to them. Despite this, it promised to continue to propose and implement its devolution proposal to give the Tamils autonomy. In addition, it embarked on a massive military offensive against the LTTE.

The Sri Lankan military was expanded and the government sought to capture the LTTE capital, Jaffna. In December 1995 the Sri Lankan army raised the Sri Lankan flag over Jaffna and claimed to have reconquered the Jaffna Peninsula. For the first time in nearly ten years, Jaffna was largely under Sri Lankan government rule.

Although embarrassed by its loss of the Tamil heartland, the LTTE was not defeated militarily. Its members retreated to the dense jungles of the Vanni region to the south of Jaffna and set up a new capital in Kilinochchi.

In anger and frustration, the LTTE struck back at the government by blowing up the Central Bank building in Colombo on January 31, 1996. Nearly 100 people died, and over 1,400 were wounded, destroying the euphoria and celebration of the Sinhalese people over the fall of Jaffna. The bombing was a symbolic attack by the LTTE, but more significantly, it destroyed any realistic opportunity for the two sides to seek a negotiated settlement to the conflict. Sinhalese positions on the conflict hardened, and the government became resolute in its position that the LTTE must be militarily weakened before it would ever return to the negotiating table.

The war subsequently took new turns as the LTTE captured the Mullaitivu army base in July 1996, killing over 1,000 government troops and capturing tons of ammunition and supplies. The government responded by capturing Kilinochchi in September, which drove the LTTE into the jungles. The LTTE no longer controlled any major towns. In May 1997 the government began an operation to open a land route to Jaffna through the LTTE-controlled Vanni.[4] Success would have helped to normalize life in Jaffna and dealt a humiliating defeat to the LTTE. This maneuver resulted in another stalemate, however, as the government troops bogged down trying to consolidate their gains about halfway along the road to Jaffna.

In the spring of 2000, the LTTE launched a series of attacks on the Elephant Pass army camp at the entrance to the Jaffna Peninsula. The camp was captured in May as LTTE troops began pushing the government troops to the outskirts of Jaffna. With the imminent collapse of the government forces, the Sri Lankan government sought outside help. In response to their pleas, Israel provided massive supplies of armaments, including air power; as a result, the LTTE offensive was stopped. Once again the conflict entered a period of stalemate as the Sri Lankan army gradually recaptured small amounts of the seized territory at great cost to both sides.

In the late 1990s, the Sri Lankan government asked the Norwegian government to act as an intermediary between it and the LTTE. For the first time in over twenty years of conflict, the two sides communicated with each other on a regular basis. The Norwegian efforts resulted in a cease-fire agreement in February 2002, followed by a publicly announced willingness on the part of the LTTE to consider a solution that did not involve independence. In the December 2001 parliamentary elections, the UNP ran on a platform of accepting the LTTE's willingness to negotiate and cease hostilities. The LTTE stopped hostilities almost immediately after the election, and an official cease-fire agreement was signed in February 2002.

The agreement called for the two sides to control the territory they held at the time of the agreement and to normalize relations. For the first time in twenty years, the country was at peace. A massive effort was begun to rebuild the war-torn north and east.

However, the cease-fire agreement was not accepted by all within the government. The JVP and a significant segment of the Sri Lanka Freedom Party (SLFP) opposed it. In their view, the Norwegian-brokered negotiations between the two sides showed no progress, and in April 2004 the SLFP, with the support of the JVP, was able to form a minority government. Many of the government ministers appointed by the party had originally opposed negotiations with the LTTE. In November 2005, Mahinda Rajapaksa, the new leader of the SLFP, was elected president and immediately began to dismantle the peace accords. The party began a policy of localized offensives against the LTTE, attacking them at the extremities of their control and gradually reducing their area of control. This policy was coupled with an alliance with a breakaway faction of the LTTE in the Eastern Province. This faction, led by Colonel Karuna, began a program of attacking unarmed LTTE political operatives working in government-held areas and kidnapping Tamils in the east and elsewhere. In addition, the Eelam People's Democratic Party, an ally in the Rajapaksa cabinet, began a campaign of attacking the LTTE and other Tamils.

The program would reap success, with the LTTE effectively eliminated from the Eastern Province after a series of military victories in 2006 and 2007. In mid-2007, the government began to attack LTTE outposts in the Northern Province. In January 2008, the government officially announced that it was pulling out of the cease-fire agreement.

Accompanying the military policy was a series of severe human rights abuses as journalists, aid workers, and opposition members of parliament have been targeted by the government or its allies.

Beginning in 2008, the government forces began applying pressure from several different directions, gradually pushing the LTTE back toward their strongholds in Kilinochchi and Mullaitivu. Kilinochchi, the LTTE capital, would fall on January 2, 2009. The LTTE forces fled toward the remote seaside town of Mullaitivu to the southeast; 250,000 Tamil civilians fled with them. In the past, the LTTE had lost territory but had always recaptured it later. The choice for the civilians was to assume that the LTTE would recover and protect them or to surrender to the government forces and risk arrest of their children and sexual assault of their women.[5] The civilians chose to go with the tigers and ended up trapped on the Mullivaikal beach, an area about five miles long and one mile wide. For nearly three months, the LTTE held out against daily shelling and firing from the government forces. The government claimed that fewer than 50,000 civilians were present and allowed in only enough food for that many people. We will never know how many civilians died, for the government barred reporters and aid workers before and after the siege. While the government shelled civilian targets, the LTTE barred them from crossing over to the government side, creating a human shield as protection from the government security forces.

When it was over, the entire LTTE leadership was dead. The government claimed the tigers fought until the end, although eyewitnesses claim to have seen some surrendering and taken away alive by government security forces. Accounts of atrocities during the final siege have led to calls for war crimes charges against the Sri Lankan leadership. However, the United States and Great Britain have worked to protect the government from such charges.

The government placed the 250,000 civilians in locked camps while it investigated them. Most of the detainees were released within six months, and the government allowed detainees living in the camps to leave after January 2010.

The last camp was closed in 2012. The postwar period has been marked by many allegations against the government:

1. The government has been slow to resettle displaced Tamils. Tens of thousands have not been allowed to return to their homes or have been placed on land that they claim is not suitable.
2. The government has maintained a large security presence in the north. It has also been expanding its military camps and expropriating more land for the camps.
3. Sinhalese settlers have been allowed into parts of Mannar, Vavuniya, Trincomalee, Batticaloa, and Mullaitivu districts.
4. There have been numerous acts of violence against the Tamil population either by the security forces or by allied groups protected by them.
5. Law and order has declined to the point where burglaries and kidnappings are common.

The Tamil population is highly dissatisfied, which the government has acknowledged by publically claiming that the LTTE is reorganizing itself in the north and east.

NOTES

1. A strong discussion of the conflict is Neil DeVotta, *Blowback: Linguistic Nationalism, Institutional Decay, and Ethnic Conflict in Sri Lanka* (Stanford, CA: Stanford University, 2004). For a somewhat dated but still relevant analysis of the homeland issue, see Chelvadurai Manogaran, *Ethnic Conflict and Reconciliation in Sri Lanka* (Honolulu: University of Hawaii Press, 1987). S. L. Gunasekera, *Tigers, "Moderates," and Pandora's Package* (Colombo: S. L. Gunasekera, 1996), presents a Sinhalese nationalist position.

2. The government has given cabinet portfolios to the leaders of the Eelam People's Democratic Party and to the Karuna/Pilliyan factions. However, these parties do not have widespread support among the Tamil people and have been accused of using intimidation and violence to enlist support.

3. Ketheshwaran Loganathan, *Sri Lanka: Lost Opportunities* (Colombo: Centre for Policy Research and Analysis, 1996), presents a good description of the history of negotiations between the two sides.

4. A special summer 1996 issue of the *Harvard International Review* (18, no. 3), titled "Conflict and Cohesion: Identity and Politics in South Asia," carried two opinions about the conflict: Chandrika Kumaratunga, "A New Approach: The Democratic Path to Peace in Sri Lanka," and Robert C. Oberst, "Tigers and the Lion: The Evolution of Sri Lanka's Civil War."

5. This is a highly controversial statement. However, I have personally witnessed both the sexual assault and the extralegal detention of Tamil civilians. The placement of Tamil civilians in locked "protective camps" after the war is an indication of the choices facing the Tamil civilians. The postwar camps had few facilities and allowed the government security forces complete access to harass and abuse the inmates.

23

The Search for Prosperity

The defeat of the Liberation Tigers of Tamil Eelam (LTTE) led many to believe that Sri Lanka would finally be able to focus on economic development. The failure of the military victory to end ethnic conflict in the country and efforts by Mahinda Rajapaksa's government to restrict opposition activities have detracted from the real economic progress in the country since May 2009. Table 23.1 reports growth in gross domestic product (GDP) from the year before the end of hostilities until 2012. Despite the global economic slowdown, Sri Lankan economic growth has been strong.

Because of the civil war, Sri Lanka neglected its economic needs. Despite very strong economic growth over the last decade, Sri Lanka remains a low-income country. However, postwar economic growth is complemented by significant gains in the quality of life. Life expectancy is high and infant mortality, at 9.5 deaths per 1,000 births, nearly half the 2009 rate of 18.6, is the lowest in South Asia.[1] This standard of living is complemented by high standards of education.

It is important to note that while Sri Lankan socioeconomic-development indicators are impressive for a poor nation, the government has not published statistics on infant mortality or other measures of development from the Northern Province since before the war. Even after its end, no accurate statistics are available.

The search for economic development has been a difficult one for Sri Lanka. The high standard of living was produced through a series of programs, begun by S. W. R. D. Bandaranaike in the 1950s, that provided every Sri Lankan with a guaranteed measure of food and free health care. These programs were expensive and were ultimately discarded in favor of programs aimed at increasing

TABLE 23.1 GDP Growth Rates

Year	Percentage growth in GDP
2008	6.7
2009 (Jan.–Jun.)	2.9
2009 (Jul.–Dec.)	3.2
2010	7.4
2011	8.3
2012 (Jan.–Jun.)	7.2

Source: Trading Economics, "Sri Lanka—National Statistics," www.tradingeconomics.com/sri-lanka/indicators, based on Central Bank of Sri Lanka.

the productive capacity of the population rather than improving the quality of life of the citizens. The universal food ration was replaced by a needs-based program in the late 1970s. Since that time, benefits from the food-stamp program have not kept up with inflation in the country.

The conflict experienced in Sri Lanka since the 1970s is closely tied to the economic problems the country now faces. Economic stagnation in the Tamil areas fosters alienation and anger among Tamil youths, and the Janatha Vimukthi Peramuna (JVP) insurrections of 1971 and 1987 to 1990 reflect the discontent of Sinhalese youths. Both insurrections relied on the large number of educated youths produced by the Sri Lankan school system who failed to find jobs commensurate with their educations.

The two JVP insurrections reflected these problems. The 1987 Indo-Lanka accords and the 1989 Indian refusal to leave the country stirred Sinhalese nationalist emotions. The JVP, which had been organizing for armed struggle since 1983, emerged with a campaign of assassinations against supporters of the government and the accords. The JVP found a large number of potential followers among the ranks of the unemployed. This campaign was intensified in June, July, and August 1989 after the Indian refusal to leave the country. By 1989 the JVP insurrection had become bloodier than the Tamil conflict, with an estimated 20,000 to 50,000 people dying in the two-year period. In addition, pro-government death squads emerged and by July and August 1989 were responsible for most of the deaths that year. Thousands of low-caste youths and university students were murdered during the summer and fall of 1989 by the death squads, which consisted of off-duty security personnel and United National Party (UNP) supporters. In November the leader of the JVP, Rohana Wijeweera, and most of the JVP leaders were captured. Most were killed shortly after or during their capture, and the violence subsided.

Since that time, the JVP has become a legal political party and has been contesting elections and mobilizing its followers. The discontent that led to the two earlier insurrections has not disappeared, although it has subsided. The forces that led to the creation of the JVP remain. There is a strong sense of alienation among members of the younger generation in Sri Lanka. Today, unrest in the universities, led by pro-JVP student unions, has resulted in violent retribution by the security forces. Although the violence is not on a par with that of the 1980s, student leaders have been beaten by gangs of thugs, arrested, and sometimes tortured. These actions have led to continued unrest among university students and periodic closings of the universities.

The search for a solution to the country's economic problems has focused on three major efforts: a massive irrigation scheme to increase agricultural production, a liberalization policy to increase investment in the economy, and an effort to devolve power to regional governments.

The most aggressive effort to develop the agricultural sector has been the Mahaweli development project. The plan serves as an example of both the potential success of major development projects and the unintended problems they generate. The project seeks to irrigate the vast dry zone of northern and eastern Sri Lanka, recreating the massive irrigation systems of the Anuradhapura and Polonnaruwa eras. The scheme was first envisioned in the 1950s, but little work was done on it until the United Front government of the 1970s devised a thirty-year effort to implement the plan.

The UNP government that came to power in 1977 called for an accelerated Mahaweli project, scaling it down to four major dams and several irrigation zones, with the entire system to be finished in five years instead of thirty. As the reservoir projects were completed, water was diverted to the dry zone in the north and east. The government then planned the infrastructure to support the increased population drawn to these areas by the offer of free land. Unfortunately, the project required the diversion of large amounts of resources to its construction and created a large national debt in international loans used to fund it. However, the project has had a major impact on the economy of Sri Lanka. More than 168,000 families have been settled in the irrigated lands (see Map 23.1), including both farmers and nonfarm families that provide services to the farming community.[2]

The Mahaweli lands now produce 22 percent of Sri Lanka's rice crop, 13 percent of its chilies, 31 percent of its Bombay onions, and 17 percent of its electrical power.[3] Even more significantly, paddy rice yield per acre is 40 percent higher in the Mahaweli areas than in the rest of the country.

The settlers in the newly irrigated lands have been selected from the densely populated southwestern portion of Sri Lanka as well as from the Kandyan hill

MAP 23.1 Mahaweli project areas

country. The program has provided free land to settlers who can now earn a reasonable income. The settlement program has helped to relieve the overcrowding on farmlands in the hill country and southern Sri Lanka.

However, the project's success has been limited by the creation of social and economic problems that now require resources for resolution. The massive movement of families to new homes in the dry zone has created a host of social problems, including familial violence and alcoholism. These problems have been exacerbated by the logistical problems of setting up schools, shops, and other support facilities for the settlers. In addition, these areas have been breeding grounds for supporters of militant political movements.

Another problem is related to the ethnic composition of the settlers. Over 96 percent of the settled families are Sinhalese.[4] The Mahaweli areas are in the sparsely populated buffer region between the Tamil areas to the east and north of the Sinhalese settlements. The settlement of Sinhalese colonists has exacerbated Tamils' disillusionment. No other Mahaweli area reflects this disillusionment more than Area L, which straddles Mullaitivu and Vavuniya districts. It is situated at what were the front lines of the ethnic war and located in two districts that were almost exclusively populated by Tamils before the civil war. The settlements have created a line of heavily fortified farming communities, some located a few miles from important LTTE bases.

Despite the problems created by the Mahaweli project, agricultural production has increased and alleviated the population and job pressures of the densely populated southwestern sector of the country. The original Mahaweli plans envisioned the irrigation of lands in the Tamil-populated districts of Mullaitivu and Vavuniya. Now that the war is over, there is no indication that these plans will be implemented.

The cornerstone of J. R. Jayawardene's administration (1977–1989) was its effort to create a free market economy. In 1977 Sri Lanka embarked on an effort to reduce the government role in the economy through a number of programs, including creation of an "investment promotion zone," or free trade zone, sale of government-owned enterprises, reduction of economic regulations on doing business, and easier convertibility of currency. The creation of the first free trade zone at Katunayake and ten additional export promotion zones (EPZs) reflects the desire of the government to increase both domestic and foreign investment. The first EPZ was a 180-square-mile area north of the capital city of Colombo, adjacent to the city's international airport. In an effort to lure multinational corporations, it offered potential investors several benefits:

1. The right to import all equipment and inputs duty free
2. No taxes on all royalty payments
3. Exemption from taxes on the income of all foreign personnel attached to the project
4. Exemption from taxes on all dividends paid to all foreign and Sri Lankan investors in the project
5. A tax holiday for up to ten years, depending on the nature of the project
6. An additional period of reduced taxes after the ten-year tax holiday[5]

The program got off to a slow start, given the limited number of foreign corporations that took advantage of the tax holidays. The original export promotion zone near the Katunayake International Airport has grown to ten zones, most of which are near Colombo. The garment industry created by the zones has created more than 250,000 new jobs and now accounts for 42 percent of all exports and 56 percent of industrial exports.[6] Most of the exports are garments made for markets in Western Europe and North America.

The program also sought to privatize government-run corporations. This effort included the development of a private bus system, telephone companies, and television stations, as well as the sale of many government-run corporations. Chandrika Kumaratunga's government angered some of its leftist allies by adopting and continuing many of Jayawardene's free enterprise policies. Her successor, President Rajapaksa, has continued the policy.

As mentioned in Chapter 20, decentralization or devolution has been used to increase the power of local governments. It has also been used to enhance development projects. Serious attempts to decentralize development administration were begun in the 1970s, when a scheme later called the decentralized budget was created. This was a plan to provide each of the members of parliament with block grants for development projects in their electoral districts. The decentralized budget has undergone many changes in its forty-year history. Decentralized plans are now implemented at the provincial and divisional secretariat levels. The district secretariat is divided into divisional secretariats, which now play a major role in the implementation of local-level development projects.

The projects are coordinated by the District Development Committee, which draws all parties involved in development projects together to plan and implement projects in each administrative district. These projects offer Sri Lankan villagers hope for more realistic development projects and greater influence over the government actions that directly affect their lives.

The creation of provincial councils by the government has also helped to decentralize power. However, the future of the provincial councils and any decentralization efforts to reduce ethnic conflict depends on new constitutional solutions adopted by the Sri Lankan government.

The Boxing Day Tsunami

The 2002 cease-fire agreement gave the economic-development reforms an opportunity to foster economic growth in the economy. The GDP growth rate was −2.5 percent in 2001. It increased to 3 percent in 2002 and 5.1 percent in 2003.

On December 26, 2004, an earthquake, with a magnitude of 9.3 on the Richter scale, off the coast of Aceh province on the Indonesian island of Sumatra sent a shockwave across the Indian Ocean. A wall of water traveled nearly 1,600 miles beneath the Indian Ocean and smashed into the eastern and southern coasts of Sri Lanka. The hardest hit areas were along the east coast, especially in Ampara district. The World Bank estimated that 35,322 died.[7] This number does not include over 19,000 deaths claimed by the LTTE in its territory, which were not included in Sri Lankan government totals.

The tsunami destroyed or damaged all buildings within five kilometers of the sea and left 500,000 people without homes.[8] Roads and bridges were washed away. Although an outpouring of aid came from the rest of the world, the economic impact on those living near the sea or relying on the tens of thousands of boats that were washed away was massive. However, the Sri Lankan economy is largely based on garment exports and the economy of the Colombo area, which was largely untouched. In the end, the country did not experience a major economic downturn because of the tsunami. The inflow of aid and the fact that the main engines of the economy were left untouched resulted in economic growth (5.1 percent in 2005 and 6.3 percent in 2006).

While the economic damage inflicted by the tsunami appears to have been relatively limited, the coastal fishing communities were devastated by the destruction of their infrastructure. The main roads in coastal areas of Sri Lanka almost always travel along the seacoast. Most of the devastated areas were rebuilt over the five years following the tsunami, but the economic devastation caused by the wave is still depressing the economies of the east coast.

One exception to the depressed economics stemming from the tsunami is the southern town of Hambantota. President Rajapaksa's government has invested hundreds of millions of dollars into the development of his hometown. He has created a rebuilding and development plan to transform the town into a regional center. Sri Lanka's first superhighway was created in 2011, linking the south coast with Colombo. A seaport built with Chinese labor and financing was opened in 2010. Once completed, Hambantota will become the second-largest seaport in Sri Lanka. The first phase of the project, completed in 2010, cost about $440 million. The second phase, to be completed in 2014, is expected to cost $750 million. However, the port project has encountered difficulties, including large cost overruns and the discovery of bedrock at the bottom of the proposed port area, which has required more expensive and difficult blasting.[9] The government has also invested in a world-class cricket stadium, which hosted the 2012 T20 Cricket World Cup. The event was marred by a lack of hotel accommodations in the Hambantota area. The stadium and a failed attempt to host the 2018 Commonwealth Games cost Sri Lanka nearly $15 million.

Although reform and development efforts have helped create a good record of economic growth, poverty and malnutrition persist in Sri Lanka, and major changes must still be implemented. Despite peace in the north and east, poverty is a serious problem in the Tamil areas. Sri Lanka is still facing serious economic challenges.

NOTES

1. CIA, "Sri Lanka," CIA World Factbook, https://www.cia.gov/library/publications/the -world-factbook/geos/ce.html.

2. Mahaweli Authority of Sri Lanka, "Statistical Bulletin 2012," http://www.mahaweli.gov.lk /Other%20Links/SB_mahaweli/Statistical%20Hand%20Book%202012.pdf (accessed November 3, 2012). The 2012 bulletin has been replaced with *The Mahaweli Handbook, 2011–2012*, showing some different numbers, available at http://www.mahaweli.gov.lk/Other%20Pages/SB /Statistical%20Hand%20Book%202011%20Final.pdf.

3. Mahaweli Authority of Sri Lanka, "Statistical Bulletin 2012."

4. Mahaweli Authority of Sri Lanka, "Statistical Bulletin 2006," www.mahaweli.gov.lk /other%20pages/SB_mahaweli/2006%20SB/2005–46.htm (accessed November 3, 2012).

5. Government of Sri Lanka, *A Guide to the Foreign Investor* (Colombo: Ministry of Finance and Planning, n.d.), 2.

6. Board of Investment, "Key Sectors for Investment—Apparels," http://www.investsrilanka .com/key_sectors_for_investment/apparel_overview.html#.

7. Research Center for Disaster Reduction Systems (Kyoto), "The December 26, 2004 Earthquake Tsunami Disaster of the Indian Ocean," www.drs.dpri.kyoto-u.ac.jp/sumatra/index-e .html#lk.

8. Department of Census and Statistics, "Bulletin of Quarterly National Accounts, 3rd Quarter 2007," Table 1B, "Summary Indicators," January 8, 2008, www.statistics.gov.lk/national_accounts /Quarterly%20Bulletin%202007%20Q3.pdf.

9. Paneetha Ameresekere, "The White Elephant in Hambantota," *Sunday Leader*, April 15, 2011, http://www.thesundayleader.lk/2011/04/15/the-white-elephant-in-hambantota.

24

Modernization and Development: Prospects and Problems

This final chapter on Sri Lanka examines the effectiveness of the Sri Lankan government in resolving the problems it faces. Three serious problems stand out. The first is the search for economic development discussed in the preceding chapter. The second is the crisis of political development and the difficulty of maintaining a democratic system. The third is the need to resolve the deep ethnic differences that continue to divide the country, even after the end of the civil war. Each of these problems poses a serious threat to stable and representative government in Sri Lanka.

Maintaining Democracy

Most of the political systems of the third world are facing a political development crisis: trying to meet the needs of their societies with limited resources and government institutions that are incapable of achieving goals. The irony of Sri Lanka is that twenty years ago, the country appeared to have developed those institutions. Today, after twenty-five years of war, it is no longer certain that Sri Lanka can maintain its democratic institutions.

Chapter 22 discusses some of the human rights issues that have arisen during Mahinda Rajapaksa's presidency. While these issues pose a serious threat to democratic governance in the Tamil areas, the problems extend beyond the Tamil community.

The first issue has been the increasing levels of violence in Sri Lankan elections. Prior to 1988, Sri Lankan elections were remarkably peaceful, with only rare instances of violence. During the 1970s, violence began to appear after elections as supporters of the winning candidates attacked their political opponents. In the 1989 parliamentary elections, the Janatha Vimukthi Peramuna (JVP) threatened to kill anyone who voted. Consequently vigilante groups attacked suspected JVP supporters. Hundreds of people died during the electoral violence.

Since the 1989 election, it has become common for the supporters of the major parties to attack their opponents during the campaign and on election day. Hundreds of civilians have been killed in elections since the 1980s. In 2004, the government banned the pasting of election posters on public property, and the level of violence declined. Party supporters who put up election posters create an ideal opportunity for attack by their opponents. Banning the posters reduced the violence but did not end it.

Election violence is part of a broader decline of civility in Sri Lankan politics. Many politicians now have armed bodyguards. The seriousness of the threat has led some politicians to make deals with criminal groups to provide security for them in return for protection from the police. For example, Nalanda Ellawala, a Sri Lanka Freedom Party (SLFP) member of parliament (MP) from Ratnapura district, died on February 11, 1997, when his vehicle was stopped by a United National Party (UNP) MP, and a gunfight ensued. The UNP MP, Susantha Punchinilame, and UNP mayor of the city of Ratnapura, Mahinda Rathnatilake, were arrested for killing Ellawala and his police bodyguard and wounding SLFP MP Dilan Perera.

The murder charges against Punchinilame are still active. Despite the Ellawala murder charges and other murder charges in the deaths of three youths in 1989, the UNP nominated him for parliament. Ironically, he changed parties from the UNP to the SLFP in 2007 and became minister of fisheries in the Rajapaksa government. This led Minister of Justice and Law Reform Dilan Perera, the MP injured in the Ellawala shooting, to symbolically resign from the SLFP. Many expect that the Ellawala murder charges will eventually be dropped.

Electoral fraud is also growing as all major parties have resorted to using fake identification to vote. In the 2004 parliamentary election, one author of this book, Robert Oberst, was an election monitor in Ampara district in the Eastern Province. Men openly handed out electoral ID cards to a large crowd in front of a UNP office. In another area, a man flagged down the monitor's vehicle and asked for a ride to a polling station so that he could vote for a third time. The problem was so serious that even one of the drivers of the agency carrying out the election monitoring bragged about not needing to vote because he had given his electoral card to his wife to give to the SLFP to distribute to a voter who would impersonate him.

Beyond the electoral fraud, the Ampara election also included a government minister leading members of the police commando unit who fired gunshots into the air while masked men attacked homes in one neighborhood. In another incident, an independent candidate was assaulted as he left a polling station. As he stepped out onto the street, he was attacked by a man with a brick. Almost immediately, a police van came, and the assailant jumped into the van and left.

During the Rajapaksa presidency, there has been a growing intolerance for media outlets that criticize the government. While there have been many attacks against Tamil-language newspapers, journalists, and media men, the attacks have also targeted Sinhalese-language news media. Media that criticize the government commonly experience police raids on their offices, arrests or brief detentions of their employees, and in some cases violent attacks.

The most serious threat to democracy has been efforts to intimidate members of parliament. Members who vote against the government lose their security details. On January 1, 2008, UNP MP T. Maheshwaran, a Tamil, was shot in Colombo while praying in a Hindu temple. His security detail had been reduced from eighteen to two guards after he voted against the government budget in parliament on December 14. Shortly before the vote, Tamil National Alliance MPs were told that kidnapped relatives would be murdered if they voted on the budget. The relatives were released unharmed after the MPs failed to show up at parliament to vote.

For the first time in the postindependence period, rising violence and intimidation in Sri Lankan politics threaten the future of the democratic institutions of the country. While the reasons for the violence are complex, the violence of the civil war appears to be an important contributor. Twenty-five years of civil strife have desensitized the population to the violence in their society. In addition, large numbers of weapons used in the war and military deserters populate the country, resulting in the growth of crime by deserters and well-armed criminal types. Thus far, the government has been unable to stop the growth in crime.

The Search for a Solution to the Ethnic Problem

The defeat of the Liberation Tigers of Tamil Eelam (LTTE) and the end of fighting in the country in 2009 raised hope that Sri Lanka would return to the innocent, idyllic island of the past. Ending a war is relatively easy; building peace is a much more difficult process. The postwar experience of Sri Lanka has been troubled by the country's inability to heal the wounds of twenty-five years of war.

Peace building is the process by which countries that end their conflicts build a lasting peace in their societies. It involves restoration of security to the country, creation of a viable political solution to the problems that led to the conflict, rebuilding destroyed infrastructure and the economy, and healing of wounds.

As noted above, Sri Lanka has struggled to restore security in the country. This is especially the case in the north and east of the island. Burglaries and violent crimes against civilians are common in the Tamil-populated areas. Despite a large army and police presence, the security forces seem incapable of stopping the criminal activity. At least, in the first four years after the war, the government has failed to restore security, although the absence of warfare has made some areas more secure.

The Sri Lankan political system is majoritarian, meaning that it allows a simple majority to exert its will over the minority groups in the country. Majoritarianism is a common feature of British-modeled governmental systems in the former British colonies. Most successful multiethnic societies have found antimajoritarian ways to limit the power of the majority. Features such as federalism are common ways to reduce the majority's power. Ironically, Great Britain has dealt with its own ethnic problems with antimajoritarian measures. The regional councils in the United Kingdom have given Scotland, Wales, and Northern Ireland a certain degree of devolved power, which has helped reduce discontent in those areas.

The Thirteenth Amendment to the constitution sought to devolve power to provincial councils but failed to provide the power or revenue for the provincial governments to effectively operate. The Tamil United Liberation Front and the LTTE sought a federal solution or independence as a solution. Since the end of fighting, the government has failed to take any action to deal with the need to devolve power. In late 2012, the government leaked reports that it was going to get rid of the Thirteenth Amendment and create a new plan of devolution. That it took the government nearly four years to begin to address the problem is an ominous sign for the future success of the plan.

While the government has failed to resolve the political and security issues in postwar Sri Lanka, it has been much more successful rebuilding the infrastructure. The level of destruction was unimaginable. Large swaths of the north and east were without electricity, telephones, and safe water for decades. The remarkable Sri Lankan rail system was torn up by the fighting forces to build fortifications during the war. The roads were filled with potholes that could swallow cars. By the end of 2012, the road system had been largely rebuilt; the railroad was steadily moving north to the cities of Jaffna and Mannar, and the electrification of the north was nearing completion. The reconstruction of damaged irrigation systems was taking longer. Another problem hindering restoration of the economy of the north was the continued appropriation of large areas of land by the security forces, preventing farmers from returning to their land. This problem, coupled with the pollution of farmland by munitions, has reduced the north's ability to recover fully from the war.

Another problem in the economic recovery has been the continued neglect of the north and east by the central government. Before the war, development projects and infrastructure investment were focused on the southwest and the hill country. It appears that this pattern has not changed since the end of the war. The remarkable seaport in Trincomalee is grossly underutilized, while a new port has been built in Hambantota, President Rajapaksa's hometown. The northern Jaffna Peninsula has received very little foreign investment.

The final area of peace building is the psychosocial process. The trauma of war leaves unseen scars among the civilian and fighting populations. The need to address the psychological and physical problems of a war's survivors is immense. Despite the importance of dealing with the trauma of war, peace-building societies often fail to allocate adequate resources to alleviate the problems, and Sri Lanka has shown little interest in addressing them. The country had very few psychiatric workers before the war, and most of the psychiatrists in the country were utilized by the military. Many of the former fighters among both the government and the LTTE have displayed the signs of posttraumatic stress disorder. The extent of serious problems among the civilian population is still unknown.

In the four areas of peace building, Sri Lanka has achieved very little progress. The wounds of the war will take many years to heal. Unfortunately, the experience of other postwar societies shows that a country is at risk of returning to war when it fails to address peace building.

The Future of Democracy in Sri Lanka

The future of Sri Lanka is still clouded by the continuing political violence in the country and efforts by the Rajapaksa government to consolidate power in the presidency and to intimidate opponents.

President Rajapaksa has taken over many of the nonpartisan elements of Sri Lankan government, such as the Judicial Services Commission, which oversees the appointment of judges, the Sri Lankan police, the Bribery Commission, the Public Services Commission, and the Election Commission. All of these commissions oversee sensitive areas of the polity that require nonpartisan decisions.

Intimidation of the media and harassment of opponents of the government have also restricted the freedom of the political process. The Sri Lankan university system has become a battleground as students have both challenged the government and been attacked by thugs and arrested by the security forces.

Finally, the consolidation of power has been marked by the growing appointment of Rajapaksa family members to positions in the government. The president's brother Gotabaya is secretary to the Ministry of Defence, his brother Chamal is Speaker of parliament and a former minister of ports and aviation and irrigation and water management, and his brother Basil is minister of economic development. Other relatives have been appointed as ambassadors to Russia and the United States and as heads of banks and corporations. In the 2010 elections, his twenty-five-year-old son, Chamal, was elected to parliament. Increasingly, President Rajapaksa has relied on Gotabaya and Basil as his most trusted advisors.

For twenty-five years, the future of Sri Lanka was threatened by the LTTE insurrection. Today, its future is threatened by the consolidation of the power of the Rajapaksa government not just within its party but within the president's family. The unresolved problems left over from the war continue to threaten the stability of the country.

SUGGESTED READINGS

Bandarage, Asoka. *Colonialism in Sri Lanka*. New York: Mouton, 1983.

Chandraprema, C. A. *Sri Lanka: The Years of Terror: The JVP Insurrection, 1987–1989*. Colombo: Lake House Bookshop, 1991.

De Silva, C. R. *Sri Lanka: A History*. New Delhi: Vikas, 1987.

De Silva, Colvin R. *Ceylon Under the British Occupation, 1795–1833: Its Political, Administrative, and Economic Development*. 2 vols. Colombo: Colombo Apothecaries, 1962.

De Silva, K. M. *A History of Sri Lanka*. Berkeley: University of California Press, 1981.

———. *Managing Ethnic Tensions in Multi-ethnic Societies: Sri Lanka, 1880–1985*. Lanham, MD: University Press of America, 1986.

De Votta, Neil. *Blowback: Linguistic Nationalism, Institutional Decay and Ethnic Conflict in Sri Lanka*. Stanford, CA: Stanford University, 2004.

Dubey, Swaroop Rani. *One-Day Revolution in Sri Lanka: Anatomy of the 1971 Insurrection*. Jaipur: Aalekh, 1988.

Gunaratna, Rohan. *Sri Lanka: A Lost Revolution: The Inside Story of the JVP*. Colombo: Institute of Fundamental Studies, 1990.

Gunasekera, S. L. *Tigers, "Moderates," and Pandora's Package*. Colombo: S. L. Gunasekera, 1996.

Jiggins, Janice. *Caste and Family in the Politics of the Sinhalese, 1947–1976*. New York: Cambridge University Press, 1979.

Kearney, Robert N. *Communalism and Language in the Politics of Ceylon*. Durham, NC: Duke University Press, 1967.

———. "Territorial Elements of Tamil Separatism in Sri Lanka." *Pacific Affairs* (winter 1987): 561–577.

————. *Trade Unions and Politics in Ceylon*. Berkeley: University of California Press, 1971.

Kearney, Robert N., and Janice Jiggins. *Internal Migration in Sri Lanka and Its Social Consequences*. Boulder, CO: Westview Press, 1987.

————. "The Ceylon Insurrection of 1971." *Journal of Commonwealth and Comparative Politics* (March 1975): 40–65.

Knox, Robert. "An Historical Relation of Ceylon." Special issue, *Ceylon Historical Journal* 6 (July 1956–April 1957).

Loganathan, Ketheshwaran. *Sri Lanka: Lost Opportunities*. Colombo: Centre for Policy Research and Analysis, 1996.

Manogaran, Chelvadurai. *Ethnic Conflict and Reconciliation in Sri Lanka*. Honolulu: University of Hawaii Press, 1987.

Matthews, Bruce. "District Development Councils in Sri Lanka." *Asian Survey* (November 1982): 1117–1134.

Oberst, Robert C. "Democracy and the Persistence of Westernized Elite Dominance in Sri Lanka." *Asian Survey* (July 1985): 760–772.

————. "Federalism and Ethnic Conflict in Sri Lanka." *Publius* (summer 1988): 175–193.

————. *Legislators and Representation in Sri Lanka: The Decentralization of Development Planning*. Boulder, CO: Westview Press, 1985.

————. "Tigers and the Lion: The Evolution of Sri Lanka's Civil War." *Harvard International Review* 18, no. 3 (summer 1996): 32–35, 80.

Pfaffenberger, Bryan. *Caste in Tamil Culture: The Religious Foundations of Sudra Domination in Tamil Sri Lanka*. Syracuse, NY: Maxwell School, Syracuse University, 1983.

Rogers, John. "Social Mobility, Popular Ideology, and Collective Violence in Modern Sri Lanka." *Journal of Asian Studies* (August 1987): 583–602.

Ryan, Bryce. *Caste in Modern Ceylon*. New Brunswick, NJ: Rutgers University Press, 1953.

Sri Lanka, Government Human Rights Commission. *Report of the Commission of Inquiry on Lessons Learnt and Reconciliation*. Embassy of Sri Lanka, 2011, http://slembassyusa.org/downloads/LLRC-REPORT.pdf.

Tambiah, S. J. *Ethnic Fratricide and the Dismantling of Democracy*. Chicago: University of Chicago Press, 1986.

United Nations. *Report of the Secretary General's Panel of Experts on Accountability in Sri Lanka*. United Nations, 2011, http://www.un.org/News/dh/infocus/Sri_Lanka/POE_Report_Full.pdf.

Wilson, A. Jeyaratnam. *The Gaullist System in Asia: The Constitution of Sri Lanka (1978)*. London: Macmillan, 1980.

PART V

NEPAL

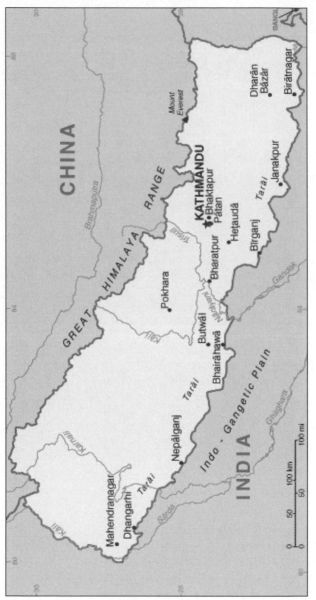

NEPAL

25

Political Heritage and Culture

Nepal is the oldest state in South Asia and one of the few developing countries that was never colonized. However, today it is still struggling to define its nationhood and establish a democratic state after nearly two and half centuries of existence. In fact, the spectacle of Nepal becoming a failed state was often mentioned in public and academic discourse when the Maoist movement expanded significantly in the late 1990s.[1] A peace settlement in 2006 ended the armed conflict, and a Constituent Assembly was elected in 2008, but Nepal's problems are not over yet. Despite being extended several times, the Constituent Assembly failed to promulgate a constitution even after four years, and it was dissolved in May 2012. The contestation over a federal model that pitted the traditional forces, which were against a federal model that would have provided autonomy to multiple identity groups, versus the Maoist, Madhesi, and indigenous nationalities, which demanded autonomy for multiple ethnic groups, could not be settled and contributed to the dissolution of the Constituent Assembly, despite its settling most other issues for a new constitution.

Nepal was territorially consolidated in the eighteenth century by Prithvi Narayan Shah (1722–1775), the dynamic king of a small princely state, Gorkha, in the western hills, and his descendants. The expansion came to a halt after Nepal's defeat in the 1814–1816 war with the British rulers of India. The resulting treaty gained British recognition of Nepal's sovereignty even though Nepal was rarely in a position to assert its complete independence. The Nepali rulers in the nineteenth and first half of the twentieth centuries safeguarded their despotic rule by maintaining a good relationship with the British.

After India became independent in 1947, Nepal freed itself from the century-long oligarchic, hereditary rule of the Rana premiers in 1951. However, India still has significant influence in social, economic, and political spheres in Nepal. A review of governance and politics in the country will shed light on the causes of Nepal's problems, the challenges it faces, and the opportunities it has.

Geography

Nepal is a landlocked country the size of the state of Illinois, with an estimated population of 26.6 million in 2011. Sandwiched between two giant neighbors, the People's Republic of China (Tibet autonomous region) in the north and India in the east, south, and west, Nepal today occupies a strategic position on the South Asian subcontinent. It has access to the sea only through Indian territories (see map on page 398) and has open borders with India, while the massive Himalaya massif makes travel to China difficult.[2]

Within a strip of land that ranges from 145 to 241 kilometers in width and 885 kilometers in length, Nepal contains a diverse topography. The snow-clad Himalayas in the north contain eight of the world's ten mountains higher than 8,000 meters (including Mount Everest, the highest in the world), the southern Tarai/Madhesh[3] is a tropical plain strip that rises from just a few hundred feet above sea level, and the Mahabharata mountain range, Siwalik hills, and Inner Tarai valleys lie between the Himalayas and the Tarai. This topographical variation produces diverse weather, flora, fauna, and culture. Monsoons from the Bay of Bengal generally bring more rain to southeastern Nepal, while clouds that come from the Arabian Sea bring rain to western Nepal.

Rivers flow south from the Himalayas, irrigating the land in the hills and the Tarai. The Kosi, Gandaki, and Karnali, the three major river systems in Nepal, form three distinct watershed regions from east to west. The rivers eventually flow to the Ganges in North India.

The northern Himalaya and the plains north of it receive little rain and are mostly infertile, rugged, and dry. They occupy around 25 percent of the country's landmass. The altitude ranges from 3,000 to 8,848 meters. People in the Himalayas are mostly pastoralists and traders, with some engaged in limited farming. The population density is sparse in the Himalayas. The intemperate weather also does not support agriculture. The culture and lifestyle of the residents of this region are similar to those of Tibetans. Many are Buddhist and nature worshipers and speak Tibeto-Burman languages.

The Mahabharata range south of the Himalayas and the Siwalik hills south of that form the heartland of the country. Heights range from 600 to 3,000 meters. The regions occupy around 50 percent of the landmass. The inhabitants of this region have ruled the country for its entire modern epoch. Large areas of the land are not fertile, but valleys, terraces, and river basins irrigated by the rivers produce ample amounts of food. Kathmandu Valley is very fertile and supports a rich, artistic civilization.

The fertile Tarai has become the breadbasket of the country. The dense forests have been cut down to make way for agricultural land. By the beginning of the twenty-first century, around half of the population lived in the Tarai. The region also boasts more infrastructure and industries than the mountain and hill regions. The latest immigrants to the Tarai are the hill people, who descended after malaria was eliminated in the 1950s. Tharus, Dhimals, Rajbansi, Santhal, and so forth, are the native peoples. Madhesis, who have a similar culture and lifestyle to inhabitants of North India, are believed to have migrated to the region before and after its conquest by the Gorkhalis.

The Inner Tarai consists of the valleys between the Mahabharata and Siwalik ranges. This region is fertile and subtropical. The Tarai and Inner Tarai occupy around 25 percent of the landmass. The region has been increasingly populated by migrants, mostly from the hills. Udayapur, Chitwan, and Dang are the largest and best-known Inner Tarai valleys.

Social and Political History

Before being conquered by the Shah dynasty, Nepal was divided into small principalities and autonomous indigenous republics.[4] The Karnali Basin had the Baise (twenty-two principalities), and the Gandaki region had the Chaubisi (twenty-four principalities) and a few other small kingdoms. The region east of Kathmandu and the Koshi region had autochthonous native communities. The Kathmandu Valley had three rich Malla principalities, which were supported by the fertile land as well as the India-Tibet trade route that passed through the dominion controlled by the Malla kings.

The Gopalas (cowherds) are believed to have been the first people to found a kingdom in Kathmandu, establishing their capital in Matatirtha in the western part of the Kathmandu Valley. They used primitive agricultural technology. Beyond that, not much is known about them, including the period of their reign.

The Kiratas ruled Kathmandu and the surrounding region after the Gopalas. The Kiratas are believed to have moved from the east and expanded their rule to the western hills. They introduced dry rice cultivation and a sedentary agricultural lifestyle. Yalamber, the Kirata king, is mentioned in the Mahabharata, the Hindu epic. The Kiratas established their capital in Gokarna in the eastern part of the Kathmandu Valley. Kirata rule is believed to have been established during the early first millennium BC, lasting for 1,000 years.

The Khasa established an empire in the Karnali Basin around AD 1100. The empire controlled around 142,000 square kilometers at its zenith and ruled parts of Kumaon in India and southwestern Tibet. The Khasa occasionally raided the Kathmandu Valley. They supposedly arrived in western Nepal in the first millennium BC and displaced the Kiratas. They were pastoralists and spoke an Indo-European language. The Khasa learned dry rice cultivation and a sedentary agricultural lifestyle from the Kiratas. The Khasa, initially Buddhists, were later Hinduized. Even though the latter Khasa adopted the title of Malla, they were not related to the Newar Malla of the Kathmandu Valley.

The Licchavis, who ruled the Kathmandu Valley after the Kiratas, left more documentation than others. From the first to the tenth centuries, the Licchavis ruled alternately with the Guptas. Both were of Indian background. A caste system was introduced to the valley during this period but was confined mostly to the rulers. Amsuvarma is one of the well-known Licchavi rulers. The Licchavis promoted urban culture, craftsmanship, and trade with Tibet and India. They observed Shaivism, Mahayana Buddhism, and Vaisnavism with equal respect. During the end of the Licchavi period, however, the Sanakaracharya, a Hindu spiritual leader from India, convinced Shiva Deva to destroy Buddhist culture and monasteries.

The Mallas began to dominate the Kathmandu Valley beginning in the fourteenth century. They promoted Hinduism and mistreated Buddhism and Buddhist monasteries. However, they were more tolerant than the Hindu rulers of the western hills, who conquered and ruled the valleys after them. Jayasthiti Malla (1295–1382) enforced a caste order among the Newars, the Kathmandu Valley inhabitants, and the society became rigid. The Mallas developed literature, fine arts, architecture, wood carving, and metal casting.

The Tarai also had several kingdoms during the ancient period. Lumbini, Kapilvastu, Devdah, Janakpur, and Simaraungarh were prominent sites in the Tarai. Kapilvastu emerged as a Buddhist center after Siddhartha Gautama established the religion around 400 BC. These kingdoms had connections with both the Gangetic Plain and the hills. Most of these kingdoms were decimated by disease, plundered by invading armies, and eventually reforested.

Modern Nepal's History

The history of present-day Nepal begins with the conquest of the Kathmandu Valley in 1768–1769. The period until 1951, when democracy was first introduced, can be divided into two periods: expansion and early consolidation and the Rana regime.

The Conquest and Early Consolidation Period, 1768–1846
After conquering the Kathmandu Valley, Prithvi Narayan Shah moved his capital to Kathmandu and began his expansion to the east. He extended the border of his kingdom to eastern Tarai and the Tista River, including some part of modern Sikkim.[5] He brought principalities and tribal chiefs under the Gorkhali realm through conquest or treaties, which gave some groups, like the Limbu, considerable autonomy over land, collection of taxes, and administration of justice. Prithvi Narayan Shah attracted a large number of land-hungry hill residents to the army by developing a land-military complex. Soldiers were given land in the conquered areas as compensation for their services.[6]

Prithvi Narayan died in 1775, but his descendants continued the mission of conquest. The Nepali court, however, witnessed increasing factionalism, conspiracies, murder of courtiers, and governmental instability. Once Pratap Singh, the eldest son of Prithvi Narayan, died in 1777, his wife, Queen Rajya Laxmi, and his brother, Bahadur Shah, vied for power. Bahadur Shah was expelled, and Rajya Laxmi (1777–1785) became the regent of the infant king, Rana Bahadur, until she died in 1785, at which point Bahadur Shah (1785–1794) became the regent. Nepal's conquest continued west to the Chaubisi, Karnali Basin, and Kumaon region under Rajya Laxmi and Bahadur Shah.

King Rana Bahadur dismissed regent Bahadur Shah and assumed full power in 1794 after coming of age. Palace infighting further intensified. A culture of eliminating court enemies developed during the period. The administration stabilized after Tripura Sundari became the regent and Bhimsen Thapa (1806–1837) became prime minister in 1806.

This phase witnessed the emergence of a feudalistic society in which the occupiers of key positions in the court, the army, and the administration began to amass landed property. The *bhardars* (courtiers) were drawn only from families from Gorkha that had helped Prithvi Narayan in the conquests. The administration began to become centralized, especially under Bhimsen Thapa. As the center increasingly penetrated the periphery, the administration became less tolerant of cultural differences in conquered territory. The spread of the ruling group's culture, language, and religion also contributed to its consolidation.

The British East India Company took an increasing interest in Nepal from the period of Rana Bahadur Shah. The Kirkpatrick mission to Kathmandu came in 1793, and Captain Knox became the first British resident in 1802. Nepal and the British East India Company finally fought a war from 1814 to 1816, which Nepal lost. Nepal's expansion was finally halted, and the resulting Sugauli treaty confined Nepal to roughly its present-day borders. The British returned Western Tarai to Nepal for helping repress the Sepoy Mutiny against the British in 1857.

The Oligarchic Rana Regime, 1846–1951

The Ranas emerged as the undisputed rulers for a century after Janga Bahadur Kunwar, aka Janga Bahadur Rana, and his seven brothers killed thirty influential courtiers and noblemen during the Kot massacre in 1846, expelled around six hundred family members of those killed, and effectively usurped political and military power. The culmination of a series of intrigues, conspiracies, and assassinations among the nobility and royal family members, the coup began with the junior queen's desire to crown her son king in place of the wayward Crown Prince Surendra, son of the late senior queen. The king was reduced to titular head of the state by Janga Bahadur, who later upgraded his family caste, Kunwar, to Rana.

Janga Bahadur made himself the maharaja (great king) of Lamjung and Kaski in 1856 and married his children into the royal family, further strengthening his position. Effective power passed into the hands of the Rana family, which provided the hereditary prime ministers of the country by agnate succession. Janga Bahadur's brothers were to succeed him, followed by his sons and nephews. The Rana family occupied all the key positions in the court, the administration, and the army. Efforts by the kings to break out of this order and to establish themselves as effective rulers of the country always ended in failure prior to 1951. The Ranas exercised despotic power and left no room for democratic reforms.

The Ranas discouraged education and did not attempt to develop the country and society. With the borders settled after the 1816 Sugauli treaty, additional agricultural lands were no longer available. This resulted in further exploitation of the peasants by the ruling elite, not only to maintain the government structure but also to sustain their lavish lifestyle.[7]

The Ranas, following the earlier established policy of discouraging interaction with foreigners, tried to keep Nepal isolated. However, a social and cultural revival in India and the rise of the nationalist movement under the Indian National Congress deeply influenced the emerging Nepali middle class and politically conscious Nepalis living in India. The Rana regime's suppression of the modernist aspirations of the educated classes gave birth to an anti-Rana movement. In 1936 the Praja Parishad, the first political party to be established in Nepal, began as an anti-Rana campaign. Several Praja Parishad leaders were killed and imprisoned in 1941, and the organization was brutally repressed.

Many educated young Nepalese living in India in the early 1940s were influenced by Indian socialist leaders like Jaya Prakash Narayan and Ram

Manohar Lohia. Close contact with the freedom movement in India encouraged young Nepali leaders, such as B. P. Koirala and D. R. Regmi, to organize political parties. The Nepali National Congress and the Nepali Democratic Congress were formed in 1947 and 1948, respectively. They merged in 1950 into the Nepali Congress, which spearheaded the anti-Rana movement demanding the democratization of Nepal.

The Ranas, unaware of the extent of middle-class alienation, responded with increased suppression. The break for the Nepali nationalists came in 1950 when King Tribhuvan and his family ran away from the closely guarded palace and sought asylum in India, depriving the Ranas of political legitimacy. Various anti-Rana organizations joined under the banner of the Nepali Congress and launched an armed struggle against the Rana regime. Faced with this popular upsurge and the tough attitude of the government of newly independent India, which was sympathetic to the aspirations of both the Nepali Congress and King Tribhuvan, the Ranas yielded, and the Rana regime came to an end in February 1951.

Hinduization in a Culturally Plural Society

Nepal is a multireligious, multilingual, multiethnic, and multiracial society. The 2011 census recorded 123 languages and dialects and 125 ethnic and caste groups.[8] Most of the languages belong to Indo-European and Tibeto-Burman families, but a few are Mundra and Dravidian as well. Followers of Hinduism, Buddhism, Islam, Kirat, Animism, Jainism, Sikhism, and Christianity live in the country. Hindus are the largest religious group, with 81.34 percent of the population, according to the 2001 census. The Hindu proportion declined in 1991 and 2001, after a steady increase since 1961, but it again saw a slight increase in 2011. The decline in 1991 and 2001 occurred because many ethnic groups began to reassert their identities and religions after the polity opened in 1990. The Buddhist, Muslim, Kirati, and Christian groups grew as a proportion of the population between 1991 and 2001 compared to the 1981 census, but Buddhists and Kiratis also witnessed a decline in the their proportion in 2011 (see Table 25.1).

The ethnic composition of Nepal and its cultural heritage have been deeply influenced by India and Tibet. The Nepali population is divided into two predominant racial groups, Caucasoid and Mongoloid. The Caucasoids possess predominantly North Indian traits. In the twelfth and thirteenth centuries, frequent Muslim invasions of India spurred Hindus to flee to Nepal. The ancestors of the people of Mongoloid origin in Nepal came mainly from the east and Tibet and the southern provinces of China before the arrival of the North Indians.

TABLE 25.1 Religious Diversity in Percentages, 1952/1954–2011

Religion	First Reported Census	1952/ 1954	1961	1971	1981	1991	2001	2011
Hindu	1952/54	88.9	87.7	89.4	89.5	86.5	80.6	81.34
Buddhist	1952/54	8.6	9.3	7.5	5.3	7.8	10.7	9.04
Muslim	1952/54	2.5	3.0	3.0	2.7	3.5	4.2	4.39
Christian	1961	-	-	-	-	0.2	0.5	1.42
Jain	1961	-	-	-	0.1	0.0	0.0	0.01
Kiranti	1991	-	-	-	-	1.7	3.6	3.05
Sikh	1991	-	-	-	-	-	0.0	0.00
Bahai	2001	-	-	-	-	-	0.0	0.00
Prakriti	2011	-	-	-	-	-	-	0.46
Bon	2011	-	-	-	-	-	-	0.05
Others or Unstated	-	-	0.1	-	2.4	0.2	0.4	0.23
All	-	100.0	100.1	100.0	100.0	100.0	100.0	99.99

Source: Mahendra Lawoti, Towards a Democratic Nepal: Inclusive Political Institutions for a Multicultural Society (New Delhi and Thousand Oaks: Sage Publications, 2005); Yogendra Gurung, "Adibasi Janajati Sawalma 2068 Rastriya Janaganana," presentation made at NEFIN, Kathmandu, January 6, 2013.

    Despite the multicultural composition of the society, Nepal was declared a Hindu kingdom until 2006, with the king recognized as the protector and promoter of the Hindu religion. The Hinduization process began early on. King Prithvi Narayan Shah, the conqueror of Nepal, also proclaimed Nepal as "asali [real] Hindustan." Bhimsen Thapa entrenched the Hindu caste system, and Janga Bahadur Rana introduced the Country Code in 1854, which formally imposed a caste system across Nepal, including for non-Hindus as well. The 1959, 1962, and 1990 constitutions declared Nepal a Hindu kingdom. The 1990 constitution stipulated that "the ruler must be an adherent of Aryan culture and a follower of Hindu religion."[9]

    As Hinduism spread in Nepal, the caste system became more entrenched. Despite its legal abolition, and even though it is slowly losing its grip in some arenas, it is still widely practiced in Nepal, including in the urban areas. Its prevalence can be ascertained from the fact that Dalits are denied access to public places like temples and face a tough time renting apartments even in urban areas. Preference for endogamous marriages even among modern high-caste groups and the practice of ritual purity in private and public functions and ceremonies have contributed to perpetuating the practice.

    The caste system practiced in Nepal varies slightly from that in India, and there are differences within Nepal as well. First, the caste system was imposed by the state in Nepal, whereas it was only practiced socially in India. Caste-

TABLE 25.2 Population of Major Ethnic/Caste Groups, 2001 and 2011

Group	2001		2011	
	Population	Percentage	Population	Percentage
CHHE (Bahun, Chhetri, Thakuri, and Sanyasi)	7,023,220	30.89	8,278,401	31.25
Indigenous nationalities	8,460,701	37.21	9,487,642	35.81
Hill	6,485,013	28.52	7,127,063	26.90
Tarai	1,975,688	8.69	2,360,579	8.91
Dalit	2,675,182	11.77	3,319,413	12.53
Hill	1,615,577	7.11	2,151,626	8.12
Madhesi	1,059,605	4.66	1,167,787	4.41
Madhesi (non-Dalit castes)*	3,312,341	14.57	3,929,942	14.83
Muslims/religious and linguistic minorities	1,033,849	4.55	1,198,013	4.52
Unidentified/others/foreigners	231,641	1.02	281,093	1.06
Total	22,736,934	100.00	26,494,504	100.00

*Madhesi becomes 32.67 percent (population: 8,656,321) if Madhesi Dalit, Muslim, and other religious and linguistic minorities and indigenous nationalities are added to it.

Source: Yogendra Gurung, "Adibasi Janajatiko Sawalma 2068 Janaganana," 2013.

based discrimination was practiced in Nepal with the backing of law until 1963. Lower-caste groups received more punishment for the same crimes compared to high-caste groups.[10] Second, the artisan castes, such as Biswakorma (blacksmiths) and Pariyar (tailors), were considered Dalit and a part of the fourfold Varnashram (Brahmin, Thakurs, Vaisya, and Sudra) in Nepal. In India and Nepali Tarai, Dalits are outside the Varnashram. Third, Thakuri, the hill ruling warrior caste, were put above non-Upadhyaya Brahmins in the Nepali caste system, backed by the Country Code. Madhesi Brahmins were put below hill Brahmins and Thakuri.[11] This clearly signified political manipulation of the caste system by the ruling families.

The caste system affected Nepal's political culture and society in myriad ways. By definition, a caste system privileges some groups while discriminating against others socially, economically, and politically. The caste system socializes people into respecting and obeying older people, upper-caste men, and authorities. Its value system may have contributed to undermining democracy by fostering a nonegalitarian political culture.

Prominent anthropologist Dor Bahadur Bista argued that the Hindu caste system and the rigid and fatalistic attitudes it introduced undermined development in Nepal. He labels the phenomenon as "Bahunism," the hill Hindu religious ideology propounded by the Bahun (hill Brahmin) religious advisers of rulers who forced the rest of the society to abide by the hierarchical caste system.

The phenomenon undermined physical work ethics and explained achievements and failures based on a fatalistic norm determined by one's prior life activities. The system of *afno manche* (one's circle), often determined by family, caste, and loyal friendship group, favored ascription-based mobility rather than an achievement-oriented system. Fatalistic culture contributed to undermining competence, hard work, and independence and impeded attempts to develop and democratize the country.[12]

The central place of Hinduism in Nepal's political setup has been increasingly challenged by different segments of the society in recent decades, especially indigenous nationalities and revolutionary groups. This challenge gained momentum after King Gyanendra dismissed the elected government in 2002 and usurped power directly in 2005.

The reinstated parliament after the Second People's Movement in 2006 declared the state secular, and Nepal ousted the Hindu king and declared itself a republic in the first sitting of the newly elected Constituent Assembly in 2008. Even though these formal declarations are a positive step toward reducing direct and excessive influence of the Hindu religion in the state and society, its influence is far from over. Many laws and public policies still promote the Hindu religion and its followers. The cow, a Hindu deity, is still the national animal, and killing it is punishable by up to twelve years' imprisonment. The majority of public holidays are on hill Hindu festivals. The prime minister and president regularly attended Hindu religious ceremonies in place of the king.

From the above discussion, it is clear that Nepali society is plural but unequal and exclusionary. The cleavages among groups in Nepal are based on religion, language, ethnicity/caste, race/physical differences, region, class, gender, historical memories, and norms against intergroup marriages. The many cleavages add complexity to identifying domination and exclusion. However, deeper analyses show the Caste Hill Hindu elite (CHHE), or the Bahun-Chhetri, to be the dominant group in almost all influential spheres, making ethnicity/caste the most salient and widespread basis for exclusion. Exclusion along ethnic/caste lines occurs within religious, linguistic, community, and gender groups.

It will be useful to identify various groups to understand the problems they face. The Nepali population of both racial stocks can be subdivided into four major categories. The sections below describe them, along with women and the problems they face. Intragroup differences exist among the groups, but groups are bound together by many common identity markers and issues.

The Dominant Group: Caste Hill Hindu Elite

The Caste Hill Hindu elite, or the upper-caste hill Hindus, made up of Bahun (hill Brahmin, 12.18 percent), Chhetri (hill Kshatriya, 16.60 percent), Thakuri

(1.61 percent), and Sanyasi (0.86 percent), form the dominant group.[13] The CHHE captured the state and defined Nepali nationalism and state institutions with its cultural and religious elements and imposed its values, lifestyles, dress, mother tongue (earlier known as Khaskura, now popularly called Nepali), and hill version of Hinduism on the rest of the society.

The CHHE is dominant in almost all spheres of the state, society, and market. Collectively, it constitutes around 31 percent of the population but its hold on different government branches and influential civil society sectors is overwhelming, ranging from 60 to 90 percent during the 1990s (Neupane 2000; Lawoti 2005). Within the group, Bahuns and Thakuri disproportionately dominate the various sectors. Many CHHE members are poor, but even they are advantaged culturally (language, religion, etc.) and often have an easier path out of poverty than poor members of other communities. The group's dominance began with the conquest of Nepal and was strengthened further with the consolidation of the Nepali state. Its domination has begun to erode politically since 2006 but remains pervasive in other sectors, like administration, the judiciary, and the media.[14]

The Indigenous Nationalities

Indigenous nationalities (*adibasi janajati*) are generally the Tibeto-Burman speaking groups. They are popularly believed to belong to the Mongoloid stock and are found in the mountains, hills, Inner Tarai, and Tarai. Around eighty such groups, varying in population from a few hundred to more than 1 million, exist. Collectively, they constituted around 36 percent of the population in 2011.[15] Some, like the Raute and the Kusunda, still live in relative isolation from the larger society, while a group like the Newar, with both Hindus and Buddhists in its ranks, is highly literate, internally caste stratified, urbane, and fairly well-off socioeconomically. The common thread that binds the indigenous nationalities is cultural discrimination, such as the linguistic and religious discrimination they face at the hands of the state and the dominant group. Most of the indigenous nationalities also generally face discrimination in accessing state and social resources.

Eleven of the indigenous groups had populations of more than 100,000 in 2011. The Magar, Gurung, Rai, and Limbu have produced Nepal's famed Gurkha soldiers. Some of these groups (Limbu, Rai, Yakha, Sunuwar) consider their religion to be Kirati and possess a distinct ethnic identity based on their language and religious affiliation. The Sherpas are Buddhists and are well known for their mountaineering skills. They often serve as guides on expeditions into the Himalayas. The Tamangs are a tribal group of Tibetan origin and follow Buddhism. The Tharus are the natives of the Tarai, speak multiple languages, and are nature worshipers.

Over the years many indigenous nationalities were Hinduized by assimilation policies of the state. Some of the groups gave up their customs and gradually embraced the dominant Nepali culture based on hill Hinduism. However, these groups have begun to reassert their non-Hindu identities, especially after 1990.[16] The Federation of Indigenous Nationalities (NEFIN), an umbrella organization of indigenous nationalities, defines the groups as non-Hindus.

The indigenous nationalities demanded the declaration of the state as secular, sociocultural equality among different ethnic/caste groups, equality among native languages (protection and promotion of native languages, schooling in native languages, and a three-language policy), proportional distribution of resources (proportional electoral method; reservation in education, administration, and political offices), cultural and political autonomy (federalism, House of Nationalities), the right to self-determination, an end to the assimilation policy of the state, rights over native land and natural resources, and recognition as indigenous peoples.

The Madhesi

The Madhesi, living in the Tarai, the fertile southern plains, are a regional community group. The Tarai is home to indigenous groups like the Tharus and Dhimals, "lower-caste" Hindu groups like the Dalits, "upper-caste" groups like Brahmins and Kshatriyas, "middle-caste" groups like the Yadav, and Muslims. Collectively, their population is slightly more than 32 percent. They speak various languages and dialects, including Maithali, Bhojpuri, Bajjika, and Avadi. Some of them, especially the caste groups and Muslims, bear close resemblance to and share culture and traditions with people of North India. The problems faced by indigenous nationalities and the Dalits of the Tarai overlap with those of the hill Dalits and indigenous nationalities. Thus some prefer to identify as Madhesi and others as indigenous nationalities or as Dalits; many identify both as Madhesi and as indigenous nationalities or Dalits, depending on context and issues. One must bear in mind this complex overlap of identity while counting the population of different marginalized groups as well as analyzing the problems faced by different groups. The Madhesi Dalits and indigenous nationalities face double discrimination: as Madhesis and as Dalits or indigenous nationalities.

The state of Nepal and the dominant hill society did not fully recognize the rights of Madhesi citizens for a long time. Millions of Madhesis were deprived of citizenship certificates until 2007, effectively hindering the citizenship-certificate-less Madhesi from enjoying the rights of citizens, such as purchasing land, getting government jobs, and standing for public offices. The hill community perceives them as immigrants from India and questions their loyalty toward the Nepali state. This perception is fueled by the acquisition of Nepali citizenship by many Indians over the years.[17] In reality, however, many Madhesis used to live in the Tarai before the Gorkha conquest. This racist attitude toward the entire community—whether to "upper-caste" Brahmins or other castes, Dalits, indigenous nationalities, and Muslims alike—has united the Madhesi people despite considerable intragroup differences. The Madhesi face linguistic, religious, and cultural domination, marginalization, and exclusion from the state, especially in the security forces.[18]

The Madhesi have been the most successful among the marginalized groups in political mobilization and electing representatives through ethnic parties. Madhesi demands include rightful citizenship, reservation in political offices, admission to educational institutions and administration (especially in security forces), cultural autonomy, regional federalism, linguistic equality, socioeconomic equality, an end to the neglect of the Tarai, and an end to mandatory *daurasuruwal* (Nepali dress) and racist prejudice and stereotyping.

The Dalit

Dalits are members of the "untouchable" castes, following orthodox Hindu tradition. In 2011, according to the census, Madhesi, hill, Himalayan, and Newar Dalits made up 13.12 percent of the population; 8.12 and 4.41 percent of Dalits lived in the hill and Tarai, respectively.[19] As with the indigenous nationalities, the Dalit proportion of the population in 2011 went down compared to 2010.

Dalits face severe social discrimination. They undergo the inhumane treatment of untouchability, such as denial of entry to the houses of upper-caste groups and some temples. Dalits rank lowest in the caste hierarchy, and all groups discriminate against them. The group has a low literacy rate and very limited access to economic resources. They are the most excluded group in accessing political, economic, and social resources. Social exclusion is more severe for the Madhesi Dalits because Tarai society is very conservative and the hill-dominated state is less informed and sensitive to their plight. Even though the hill Dalits do not face linguistic and religious discrimination, they do face severe discrimination based on religious traditions.

Dalits have organized as fraternal organizations of various political parties, as nongovernmental organizations, and more recently as political parties in the post-1990 multiparty Nepal. Dalits oppose Brahmanism,[20] untouchability, stereotyping of their group, and restriction from public places such as temples. Their demands included reservation in education, administration, and political offices; an end to untouchability; compensation for historical discrimination; social, economic, and political empowerment of the Dalit community; and secularism.

Muslims

Muslims are probably the least researched group in Nepal, and less is known about them than other groups. The 2011 census recorded the Muslims at 4.39 percent, a slight increase in proportion from 2001, when they comprised 4.29 percent of the population. Ninety-seven percent of Muslims live in the Tarai, and the remainder live in the Kathmandu Valley and mid-western hills. The majority of Muslims are Sunni, but the Nepali Muslims are divided by doctrinal orientation, such as Barelvi, Deobandi, Ahl-e Hadis, and Jamaat-i-Islami.[21]

Muslims face social, economic, and political inequality and exclusion, as well as cultural discrimination and extreme stereotyping and prejudice as a minority religious group in a largely Hindu country. Muslim organizations have demanded government assistance in raising the group's status, an end to discrimination against Muslims in recruitment for army, police, and government offices, public holidays during Muslim festivals, government funds to support madrasas for educating Muslims, recognition of madrasa education, a secular state, and an end to stereotyping.

Women

Women across almost all groups face domination, exclusion, and discrimination in Nepal. Patriarchal discrimination is stronger among the high-caste Hindus and Muslims and less prevalent among the indigenous nationalities. Dalit women face less gender discrimination compared to high-caste women because less significance is attached to the concept of purity among Dalits, who also lack the significant landholdings that sustain patriarchy.[22] While the indigenous nationalities, Madhesis, and women from religious minority groups face religious, linguistic, and cultural discrimination, the dominant-ethnicity/-caste women face discrimination mainly based on the cultural practices that emanate from their religion.

Women's socioeconomic status compared to men's is quite low. Their literacy and purchasing power are about half those of men. Women's participation in the state is very low. Their presence in the cabinet even after 1990 has been at a token level. Relatively more rapid changes occurred after 2006. Thirty-five percent of those elected to the Constituent Assembly in 2008 were women. Recent amendments to the Country Code have also lifted restrictions on women's inheritance rights, which had previously required that they be thirty-five years old. In 2009 Nepal passed its first law against domestic violence.

The women's movement has been generously supported by international nongovernmental organizations (INGOs). Compared to the social-justice movements of Dalit, indigenous nationalities, and Madhesi, women have produced the most impressive conference papers, reports, and documents in support of their demands. However, they have not been very effective politically. Their campaigns consist mostly of petitioning political leaders, government agencies, INGOs, and international agencies and forums. Nor has the mainstream women's movement been able to incorporate the issues of either Dalit and Madhesi women or women of indigenous nationalities. Because women have not threatened the electoral prospects of politicians by voting along gender issues, the male-dominated political leadership has been able to ignore them.

Suggested Readings

Bista, Dor Bahadur. *Fatalism and Development: Nepal's Struggle for Modernization*. Hyderabad: Orient Longman, 1991.

————. *Peoples of Nepal*. 7th ed. Kathmandu: Ratna Pustak Bhandar, 1996.

Cameron, Mary M. *On the Edge of the Auspicious: Gender and Caste in Nepal*. Urbana-Champaign: University of Illinois Press, 1998.

Dastider, Mollica. *Understanding Nepal: Muslims in a Plural Society*. New Delhi: Har-Anand Publications, 2007.

Gaige, Frederick. *Regionalism and National Unity in Nepal*. Berkeley: University of California Press, 1975.

Gurung, Harka. "Nepali Nationalism." In *Nepal Tomorrow: Voices and Visions*, edited by D. B. Gurung, 1–31. Kathmandu: Kosele Prakashan, 2003.

Hangen, Susan I. *The Rise of Ethnic Politics in Nepal: Democracy in the Margins*. London: Routledge, 2009.

Hofer, A. *The Caste Hierarchy and the State in Nepal: A Study of the Muluki Ain of 1854*. Innsbruck, Austria: University Press, Wagner, 1979.

Lawoti, Mahendra, ed. *Contentious Politics and Democratization in Nepal*. Los Angeles: Sage, 2007.

————. *Towards a Democratic Nepal: Inclusive Political Institutions for a Multicultural Society*. New Delhi: Sage, 2005.

Lawoti, Mahendra, and Susan Hangen. *Nationalism and Ethnic Conflict in Nepal: Identities and Mobilization after 1990*. London: Routledge, 2012.

Levine, Nancy E. "Caste, State, and Ethnic Boundaries in Nepal." *Journal of Asian Studies* 46, no. 1 (1987): 71–88.

Neupane, Govinda. *Nepalko Jatiya Prashna: Samajik Banot Ra Sajhedariko Sambhawana* [*Nepal's National Question: Social Composition and Possibilities of Accommodation*]. Kathmandu: Center for Development Studies, 2000.

Pradhan, Kumar. *The Gorkha Conquests: The Process and Consequences of the Unification of Nepal, with Particular Reference to Eastern Nepal*. Calcutta: Oxford, 1991.

Regmi, Mahesh C. *Thatched Huts and Stucco Palaces: Peasants and Landlords in 19th-Century Nepal*. New Delhi: Vikash, 1978.

Sijapati, Megan Adamson. *Islamic Revival in Nepal*. London: Routledge, 2012.

Stiller, L. F. *The Rise of the House of Gorkha*. Ranchi: Patna Jesuit Society, 1973.

Whelpton, John. *A History of Nepal*. Cambridge: Cambridge University Press, 2005.

Notes

1. Ali Riaz and Subho Basu, *Paradise Lost? State Failure in Nepal* (Lanham, MD: Lexington, 2007).

2. Nepalis and Indians do not need a passport to travel between the two countries.

3. The name of the region has become contested, with the Tharus claiming it to be Tarai and the Madhesh claiming it as Madhesh.

4. This section draws on Dor Bahadur Bista, *Fatalism and Development: Nepal's Struggle for Modernization* (Hyderabad: Orient Longman, 1991); John Whelpton, *A History of Nepal* (Cambridge: Cambridge University Press, 2005).

5. Kumar Pradhan, *The Gorkha Conquests: The Process and Consequences of the Unification of Nepal, with Particular Reference to Eastern Nepal* (Calcutta: Oxford, 1991).

6. L. F. Stiller, *The Rise of the House of Gorkha* (Ranchi: Patna Jesuit Society, 1973).

7. Mahesh C. Regmi, *Thatched Huts and Stucco Palaces: Peasants and Landlords in 19th-Century Nepal* (New Delhi: Vikash, 1978).

8. All the 2011 census data are from Yogendra Gurung, "Adibasi Janajatiko Sawalma 2068 Rastriya Janaganana" (PowerPoint presentation made at Nepal Federation of Indigenous Nationalities, Kathmandu, Nepal, January 6, 2013). I thank Yogendra Gurung for providing the PowerPoint presentation and data file, on which his analysis was based.

9. HMG Nepal, *Constitution of the Kingdom of Nepal* (Kathmandu: Ministry of Law and Justice, Law Books Management Board, 1990).

10. Nancy E. Levine, "Caste, State, and Ethnic Boundaries in Nepal," *Journal of Asian Studies* 46, no. 1 (1987): 71–88.

11. A. Hofer, *The Caste Hierarchy and the State in Nepal: A Study of the Muluki Ain of 1854* (Innsbruck, Austria: University Press, Wagner, 1979).

12. Bista, *Fatalism and Development*.

13. The population proportion is from the 2011 census.

14. Mahendra Lawoti, "Ethnic Politics and Building of an Inclusive State," in *Nepal in Transition: From People's War to Fragile Peace*, ed. Sebastian von Einsiedel, David M. Malone, and Suman Pradhan (Cambridge, MA: Cambridge University Press, 2012), 129–152.

15. See Dor Bahadur Bista, *Peoples of Nepal*, 7th ed. (Kathmandu: Ratna Pustak Bhandar, 1996), for coverage of major ethnic groups in Nepal.

16. Susan I. Hangen, *The Rise of Ethnic Politics in Nepal: Democracy in the Margins* (London: Routledge, 2009).

17. Harka Gurung, "Nepali Nationalism," in *Nepal Tomorrow: Voices and Visions*, ed. D. B. Gurung (Kathmandu: Kosele Prakashan, 2003).

18. Mahendra Lawoti, "Dynamics of Mobilization: Varied Trajectories of Dalit, Indigenous Nationalities and Madhesi Movements," 193–225; Bandita Sijpati, "In Pursuit of Recognition: Regionalism, Madhesi Identity, and the Madhes Andolan," 145–172; and Mollica Dastidar, "Refusing to Choose: The Muslim Madhesis and the Coexistence of Religious and Regional Identity in Nepal's Tarai," 173–189; all in *Ethnic Conflict and Nationalism in Nepal*, ed. Mahendra Lawoti and Susan Hangen (London: Routeldge, 2012).

19. Yogendra Gurung, "Adibasi Janajatiko Sawalma 2068 Rastriya Janagana."

20. Brahmanism incorporates the caste-based worldviews and values of both the hill and Tarai Brahmin, while Bahunism includes only those of the hill Bahuns.

21. Megan Adamson Sijapati, "The National Muslim Forum Nepal: Experiences of Conflict, Formation of Identity," in *Nationalism and Ethnic Conflict in Nepal*, ed. Mahendra Lawoti and Susan Hangen (London: Routledge, 2012), 102–120.

22. Mary M. Cameron, *On the Edge of the Auspicious: Gender and Caste in Nepal* (Urbana-Champaign: University of Illinois Press, 1998).

26

Political Institutions and Governmental Processes

Nepal's democratization attempts began in 1951 and continue today, with interruptions in between. The history of political transformation and institutional development after Nepal obtained freedom from the Ranas in 1951 can be divided into five phases: the first democratic period (1951–1960), the *panchayat* period (1960–1990), the second democratic period (1990–2002), the royal interregnum (2002–2006), and the post-2006 transitional phase.

The First Experimentation with Democracy: 1951–1960

The end of despotic Rana rule in 1951 and the return of King Tribhuvan as effective ruler of the country raised hopes for democracy. Attempts at the institutional development of Nepal started with the Interim Constitution of 1951, which was promulgated after the successful 1950–1951 rebellion against the Ranas.[1] The interim constitution promised free elections for a Constituent Assembly (CA) and set up a coalition government consisting of the representatives of the Nepali Congress and members of the Rana family, with the king to serve as the head of state. King Tribhuvan aroused hope that power would soon be transferred to the people's representatives. That hope evaporated, however, with the disintegration of the coalition between the Nepali Congress and the Ranas, the bickering among political leaders of different political parties, and the Royal Palace's slow but steady usurpation of power.

The Nepali Congress, the main reformist, modernist, and left-of-center party in the country, fractured into various factions and could not provide a united leadership. Amid the quarreling among politicians, political parties, and factions within political parties, political stability became elusive. The period witnessed several governments headed by Mohan Shamshere Rana, Matrika Prasad Koirala (twice), Tanka Prasad Acharya, Dr. K. I. Singh, Suvarna Sumshere, and B. P. Koirala, in addition to direct rule by the king with a council of advisers. Due to squabbling among the political leaders, the people viewed the monarch not only as a symbol of national unity but also as the savior of the country.[2] This allowed the monarch, especially King Mahendra, to consolidate power in the institution of the monarchy.

King Mahendra, who succeeded his father in March 1955, promulgated a modified form of parliamentary government through the 1959 constitution. This new constitution provided for a bicameral legislative body consisting of the Pritinidhi Sabha (Representative Assembly), with 109 members to be elected directly on the basis of universal suffrage, and the Maha Sabha (Great Assembly), the upper house, consisting of thirty-six members. The new constitution also provided for a cabinet responsible to both the parliament and the king.

In the first free elections to parliament, held in February 1959, the Nepali Congress won an absolute majority with 74 of 109 seats, and its leader, B. P. Koirala, became the prime minister. Gorkha Dal, the conservative party led by the Ranas, became the opposition party with nineteen seats. The Communist Party of Nepal (CPN) won four seats.

Nepal remained a basically feudal society during the period. Traditional ruling elites still occupied powerful positions in the army and the administration. The Nepali Congress leaders lacked not only solidarity but also an extensive organizational network to mobilize the masses against members of the landed aristocracy when they resisted governmental authority. The king sided with the traditional landowning segment of the society, which had held power for such a long time.

Nepal's experiment with parliamentary government did not last long. On December 15, 1960, King Mahendra dismissed the Koirala government on charges of failing to maintain law and order, being corrupt, and encouraging antinational elements; he then arrested the prime minister and the members of the cabinet. The king feared that a popular prime minister backed by a popularly elected parliament might impose severe restraints on his personal power and reduce him to a figurehead. The idea of a constitutional monarchy did not appeal to the king.

The Partyless *Panchayat* System: 1960–1990

Like many rulers in third world countries before the end of the Cold War, King Mahendra believed that a democratic system and parliamentary government were products of the Western cultural milieu and thus not suitable for societies such as Nepal. He needed some kind of popular association, however, to rule, and the *panchayat* (council) system, argued to have existed in Nepali society in the past, was considered more suited for its people than the representative institutions popular in Western societies. In 1962, the king introduced a new constitution with new popular institutions based on an indirect system of election. The *panchayats* were to be elected at the village, town, district, and national levels; only the lowest level, the village and municipal *panchayats*, were to be directly elected by the people. At the national level stood the Rashtriya Panchayat (national council or parliament), which was to be elected indirectly by the members of the lower *panchayats* as well as by the members of professional and class organizations. A council of ministers, to be selected from the members of the national parliament, was to serve as an advisory body to the king. The *panchayat* system was an attempt at a guided democracy, and the real power remained with the king, who had the authority not only to amend the constitution but also to suspend it by royal proclamation during emergencies. An important feature of the constitution was the abolition of all political parties.

King Mahendra introduced several socioeconomic reforms. The new country code in 1963 formally put an end to the caste system and untouchability. The Land Reform Act, passed in 1964, provided some rights to tenant farmers and landless peasants but took communal ownership of land (*kipat*) away from the Limbus and Rais, Kirati communities that had enjoyed these rights, and facilitated alienation of land from indigenous groups like the Tharus in the Tarai.

King Mahendra also attempted to modernize the country and foster development. Education was expanded throughout the country, the bureaucracy was expanded to steer development, and the communication system was strengthened. The period was also significant for promoting Khas hill as Nepali nationalism. The language, religion, dress code, and lifestyle of the CHHE were promoted over diverse languages, religions, and lifestyles in the name of modernization and development. This monoethnic policy had roots in the policies of the autocratic regimes of previous centuries and had been promoted since the mid-1950s as well, but it was launched more effectively during the *panchayat* period with the expansion of communication, bureaucracy, and education with instruction in Khas-Nepali.

King Mahendra's efforts, however, failed to satisfy the politicians, the intellectuals, or the students—the most articulate segments of Nepali society, especially during the second decade of the *panchayat* system. The demonstrations that ensued, often leading to considerable unrest, finally forced King Birendra, the successor to King Mahendra, to call in May 1979 for a nationwide referendum to determine the future form of Nepal's polity. The referendum gave the

people two choices: a partyless *panchayat* system with the prospect of future reform or a multiparty democratic system. The referendum was held on May 2,
1980, with 67 percent of eligible voters participating, and the reformed *panchayat* system won by a narrow majority with 54.7 percent of the vote.

Even though the new institutional system created after the 1980 referendum
failed to lift the ban on political parties, it nevertheless represented a significant
departure from the constitutional arrangements existing since 1962. Under the
new system, the 112 members of the Rashtriya Panchayat were elected directly
by the people on the basis of universal adult suffrage. Furthermore, the prime
minister was elected by the Rashtriya Panchayat, from which he selected the
council of ministers, and held office as long as the government enjoyed the parliament's confidence.[3] The constitutional reforms did not, however, alter the
status of the king, who still held sovereign power. At the societal level, more
pluralism came into existence, and the people's participation in the political
process also increased. More freedom of the press was tolerated than before
1980, and various social and cultural organizations, such as human rights organizations and ethnic associations and fronts, began to emerge.

Elections to the Rashtriya Panchayat were held in 1981 and 1986. In the absence of officially sanctioned parties, groups and factions organizing around
powerful members of the national parliament became common. Even though
the political parties could not contest the elections, their leaders were not restricted to seeking seats in the national legislature as independents. Some party
leaders were elected to the Rashtriya Panchayat on an individual basis, and
some of them began to demand more political rights inside the parliament.

Second Democratic Experience: 1990–2002

In February 1990 the Nepali Congress, joined by the Leftist United Front and
human rights activists, launched a movement to legalize political parties and restore a parliamentary system of government. Public pressure from the popular
movement finally forced the king to end the thirty-year-old *panchayat* system.
A new constitution promulgated in November 1990 provided fundamental political rights and civil liberties to the citizens and a parliamentary system of government based on universal suffrage. The constitution created a bicameral
parliament consisting of a lower house and an upper house, with 205 and 60
members, respectively. The lower house was directly elected by the people; the
upper house was partly nominated and partly elected indirectly by the lower
house and representatives of lower governments, and it was powerless. Executive power was vested in the prime minister and the cabinet, and the king
served as the constitutional head of state.

Despite the political transformation, the polity remained highly centralized and exclusionary. The state continued to be called a Hindu kingdom. The unitary structure continued despite a demand for federalism by different ethnic and regional groups. The first-past-the-post (FPTP) electoral method also helped centralize political power by creating artificial majorities.

The Central and Local Governments

Following the Westminster model of the winner-take-all parliamentary system, the cabinet held most of the state power in Nepal during the 1990s. Cabinets generally become powerful because the top leaders of the ruling party join the government, the government often introduces most of the legislation, and the parliament generally passes the government's bills in the traditional parliamentary system. Except for the Public Accounts Committee, other parliamentary committees rarely held the executive accountable. The parliament also did not enjoy the right to screen nominees to executive agencies and constitutional commissions.[4]

The FPTP electoral system also contributed to the centralization of power by generally awarding more seats to the largest political party and facilitating construction of an artificial parliamentary majority, which enabled political parties without majority popular support to enjoy centrally concentrated state power. Likewise, the political culture of centralizing power in political leaders and the electorate's preference for strong leaders also contributed to the centralization of power in the executive and top political leadership.

As with the judiciary and the monarchy, the executive, especially if abused, could have been checked or restrained by other branches of government and central agencies, like the judiciary or the monarchy. The king, even though designated a constitutional monarch, remained commander in chief of the army and enjoyed some power through it. He exercised that power by resisting deployment of the army against the emerging Maoist rebels. The possibility of a royal coup with the support of the army, as had happened in 1960, also bestowed the king with informal power and leverage during dealings with the political parties. Beyond that and nominating ten members to the Upper House and some ambassadors, the king, however, did not intervene in civil governance during the 1990s and gave the executive free rein.

The judiciary, composed of a Supreme Court, sixteen appellate courts, and seventy-five district courts, was powerful to some extent and challenged the executive in some cases. However, it was not immune from the influence of the executive, which authorized its budget and personnel. A cabinet minister also remained on the judicial council that recommended promotion of justices. Hence, despite the judiciary's exemplary role in protecting individual rights and press freedoms, it was sometimes accused of catering to the executive influence, especially during the mid-1990s. At the same time, as it was dominated by male Bahuns, the judiciary was also criticized for insensitivity to the issues of marginalized groups in ruling against citizenship-certificate distribution by mobile teams and adoption of multiple languages by local governments, which hurt the Madhesis and indigenous nationalities.

The executive was supported by the bureaucracy, which was recruited through merit-based examination in the Nepali language, which advantaged native speakers. In addition, the bureaucracy was politicized by the ruling political parties, eroding its competency and independence. Dominated by male Bahuns, it was ethnically biased and insensitive to diverse cultures and peoples. As the whole administration was directly controlled by the central government, the bureaucrats and police were more loyal to central authorities, less responsive and accountable to local people, and less sensitive to local needs and aspirations.

The centralized state and political culture meant that the local governments had inadequate power and funds to address the needs of local populations. The village development committees (VDCs) and municipalities were the lowest tier of local government. There were 3,913 VDCs and 58 municipalities during the 1990s; 41 new municipalities were added in 2011. The district development committees (DDCs) formed the middle tier; elected by members of the VDCs and municipalities, they were responsible for the development of the seventy-five districts. These local bodies were directly elected, but Nepal has not conducted local elections since 1997 due to the initial Maoist threat and obstruction and then failure to promulgate a new constitution after the peace settlement between the rebels and the state. Elected local governments have not existed since the terms of local bodies expired in 2002.

Decentralization in Nepal began in the 1960s, but minimal power was delegated since effective decentralization was not compatible with the centralized *panchayat* system. Local governments were provided with more power and resources after 1990. The minority Communist Party of Nepal (United Marxist Leninist) (CPN[UML]) government provided block grants to the VDCs in 1994. The funds increased the local governments' capacities as they conducted surveys of development activities, made plans, implemented projects, and kept accounts; mobilized communities to generate additional resources; built schools, roads, and bridges; constructed drinking water projects; managed trails; and initiated other development work. During the second local election in 1997, the CPN(UML)-dominated coalition government ensured 20 percent reservation for women in local bodies. This enabled thousands of women to be elected to the local bodies.[5]

The Local Self-Governance Act of 1999, although weak in political and fiscal decentralization, provided a legal framework for administrative decentralization (providing services). The local governments still did not control civil and police administration, however, which remained directly under the center.

If adopted in the new constitution, federalism, which the Interim Constitution of 2007 and major political parties are committed to, the power of regional and local governments is likely to increase as the center will have to shed substantial control. Activists associated with previous local governments have demanded more power for local government units, but the issue has been debated less than the power division between the central and provincial governments.

Governance Crises, 1990–2002 and Beyond

The attempt at democratization during the 1990s faced several challenges, such as abuse of power, corruption, governmental instability, and armed conflict. The Maoist rebellion, discussed in detail in Chapter 28, began during this period and expanded rapidly, due partly to these problems and to the inability of the state to address the aspirations of people. Eventually, the democratic regime was dismantled, albeit for a short period (2002–2006), and another popular street movement rose up to restore democracy and initiate major political reforms.

Abuse of Power, Corruption, and a Culture of Impunity

Abuse of power, corruption, and politicization of the bureaucracy and the police became widespread after 1990. The ruling parties often appointed, transferred, and promoted bureaucrats and police officers based on partisan, factional, and personal interests, in addition to often appointing political cadres to public corporations and other influential public offices. These activities undermined the autonomy and lowered the morale of the bureaucracy and the police, increased nepotism, eroded meritocracy, and effectively undermined the rule of law.

Corruption occurred both at the highest political level, involving millions of rupees, and in the everyday arenas that directly affected the common people. Payment of bribes became common for normal transactions in many public offices, including for obtaining driving licenses and passports. Corruption occurred in many sectors with the complicity of government officials: goods were smuggled into Nepal after customs officers were bribed, fraudulent medicines were openly sold in markets and distributed through public health agencies, vehicles stolen in India were sold in Nepal, mineral water companies sold regular bottled water, and so on. Media reports allege that the police abused their position in order to collect regular and irregular funds from businesses and small entrepreneurs.[6] A corruption scandal involving top police brass and tied to the purchase of armored personal carriers for a UN peacekeeping mission rocked the country in 2011–2012.

Corruption became institutionalized as the ruling political parties began to collect huge sums for running party organizations and funding elections by awarding lucrative government contracts and taking commissions from infrastructure and service-sector projects. Newspapers and opposition political leaders alleged that some cabinet ministers even permitted gold smuggling through the airport and took a cut during the late 1990s. After the end of the armed Maoist conflict, civil contracts were often monopolized or awarded with the involvement of armed gangs affiliated to political parties, even though the practice has declined from a peak reached a few years after the Maoist peace settlement.

Corruption occurred at the policy level as well during the 1990s. Cabinet decisions were beyond the purview of anticorruption agencies due to the protection of the confidentiality law. A law to declassify cabinet decisions was not legislated, resulting in all cabinet decisions remaining beyond public scrutiny. Some powerful ministers preferred to have the cabinet decide certain issues to avoid being questioned and investigated.[7]

As corrupt politicians went scot-free, others followed their lead and corruption became pervasive, fostering a culture of impunity.[8] People saw many political leaders go from paupers to millionaires overnight. The perception of increased corruption became widespread, perhaps even exaggerated. Many Nepalis viewed most politicians as corrupt, and this perception eroded the legitimacy of the democratic polity. According to Transparency International, the Corruption Perception Index declined in Nepal from 2.8 in 2004 to 2.2 in 2011.

After getting power to the people or their representatives, the challenge of democratization is to ensure that power does not get abused. "In framing a government . . . the great difficulty lies in this: you must first enable the government to control the governed; and in the next place oblige it to control itself."[9] Those who have power can abuse it, including elected leaders. Thus, in the event that they do, it is necessary to develop mechanisms to hold them accountable; failure to do this was a serious shortcoming in Nepal.

An important accountability mechanism is periodic elections, but power is abused between elections as well, even if they are held in a reasonably free and fair manner. Power holders must also be held accountable between elections. Guillermo O'Donnell argues that effective horizontal accountability mechanisms can achieve that.[10] Different central government branches and agencies, if empowered in their areas of jurisdiction and independent of the institutions they are supposed to supervise, can hold each other accountable. Independence can be ensured only if an agency that is supposed to hold another agency accountable is free from the latter's influence.

The constitutional commissions, such as the Commission for Investigation of Abuse of Authority (CIAA) and the Election Commission, were not empowered to question or restrain the abuses of the executive; nor were they independent of it during the 1990s. Due to an imbalance of power, the weak commissions were unable to hold the powerful executive accountable. Further, the executive directly and indirectly influenced the constitutional commissions. First, the ruling party could influence the constitutional council that nominated constitutional commissioners. The effectiveness of the constitutional commissions could also be undermined either by nomination of weak commissioners or by failure to nominate anyone for long periods, as happened in Nepal. Many constitutional commissions and the Supreme Court remained understaffed in 2012, as vacancies left by the retirement of constitutional commissioners and justices had not been filled, sometimes for more than a year. Second, the executive allocated the budget for the commissions, and it could reduce (or increase) or delay the budget transfer to the commissions. The commissions could perceive it as in their interest not to antagonize the cabinet to ensure a smooth flow of the allocated budget. Third, the cabinet also assigned personnel to the commissions, and it could understaff them, delay the hiring process, or transfer staff.

Only with empowerment in 2002 did the CIAA begin to investigate the powerful political leaders of the dominant parties. The Interim Constitution of 2007 further strengthened the mechanism by requiring the Constituent Assembly to vet cabinet appointees for commissioner and other high-ranking positions to screen out questionable people. The CIAA is still not independent, however, as the cabinet can influence nominations for its commissioners, its budget, and its personnel deputation. Despite accusations that the CIAA is politically motivated, in recent years several powerful former and serving ministers have been sent to jail on charges of amassing excessive wealth.

Other branches of government were also unable to check the executive's abuses of power because they were powerless or dependent on the executive. The parliament and its committees were weak and not in a position to hold the executive accountable, except perhaps through changing the government or threatening to do so. Similarly, even the powerful judiciary, which was less dependent, was constrained in holding the executive accountable. The Supreme Court protected the people from unlawful imprisonment and ruled in the mid-1990s that the CIAA could investigate and prosecute cabinet members, but the Supreme Court could not intervene in day-to-day administration, the location of frequent abuses of power, and corruption. The role of the judiciary

TABLE 26.1 Nineteen Prime Ministers in Twenty-Three Years, 1990–2013

	Prime Minister	Party of Prime Minister	Tenure	Caste/Ethnicity	Gender
1	Krishna Prasad Bhattarai	Nepali Congress	Apr. 1990–May 1991	Bahun/CHHE	Male
2	Girija Prasad Koirala	Nepali Congress	May 1991–Nov. 1994	Bahun/CHHE	Male
3	Man Mohan Adhikari	CPN(UML)	Nov. 1994–Sep. 1995	Bahun/CHHE	Male
4	Sher Bahadur Deuba	Nepali Congress	Sep. 1995–Mar. 1997	Thakuri/CHHE	Male
5	Lokendra Bahadur Chand	NDP-C	Mar. 1997–Oct. 1997	Thakuri/CHHE	Male
6	Surya Bahadur Thapa	NDP-T	Oct. 1997–Apr. 1998	Chhetri/CHHE	Male
7	Girija Prasad Koirala	Nepali Congress	Apr. 1998–May 1999	Bahun/CHHE	Male
8	Krishna Prasad Bhattarai	Nepali Congress	May 1999–Mar. 2000	Bahun/CHHE	Male
9	Girija Prasad Koirala	Nepali Congress	Mar. 2000–Jul. 2001	Bahun/CHHE	Male
10	Sher Bahadur Deuba	Nepali Congress	Jul. 2001–Oct. 2002	Thakuri/CHHE	Male
11	Lokendra Bahadur Chand	NDP	Oct. 2002–Jun. 2003	Thakuri/CHHE	Male
12	Surya Bahadur Thapa	NDP	Jun. 2003–Jun. 2004	Chhetri/CHHE	Male
13	Sher Bahadur Deuba	Nepali Congress (Democratic)	Jun. 2004–Feb. 2005	Thakuri/CHHE	Male
14	Gyanendra Bir Bikram Shan Dev	None	Feb. 2005–Apr. 2006	Thakuri/CHHE	Male
15	Girija Prasad Koirala	Nepali Congress	Apr. 2006–Aug. 2008	Bahun/CHHE	Male
16	Pushpa Kamal Dahal, aka Prachanda	CPN(M)	Aug. 2008–May 2009	Bahun/CHHE	Male
17	Madhav Kumar Nepal	CPN(UML)	May 2009–Feb. 2011	Bahun/CHHE	Male
18	Jhalanath Khanal	CPN(UML)	Feb. 2011–Aug. 2011	Bahun/CHHE	Male
19	Baburam Bhattarai	UCPN (Maoist)	Aug. 2011–Mar. 2013	Bahun/CHHE	Male
20	Khil Raj Regmi	None	Mar. 2013–	Bahun/CHHE	Male

CPN(M)—Communist Party of Nepal (Maoist); CPN(UML)—Communist Party of Nepal (United Marxist Leninist); NDP—National Democratic Party; NDP-C—National Democratic Party (Chand); NDP-T—National Democratic Party (Thapa); UCPN (Maoist)—Unified Communist Party of Nepal (Maoist)

NOTE: CPN(M) changed its name to UCPN (Maoist) in January 2009 after unifying with another communist party.

was limited in controlling power abuse and corruption in the administration except through empowerment of nonexecutive agencies when interpreting the constitutional articles. The power of interpretation, however, became limited because the 1990 constitution clearly made the executive powerful and other agencies weak and dependent on it.

The problems of power abuse and corruption may dog the country in the future as mechanisms to address them have not been seriously deliberated and proposed. The report of the thematic committee of the CA has largely provided constitutional commissions similar to those provisioned by the 1990 constitution, and they may continue to remain ineffective.

Governmental Instability

Nepal witnessed chronic governmental instability during its democratic and semidemocratic interregnums after 1951, and the problem persists today. Twelve governments were formed between 1990 and 2002, an average of one per year. During the royal interregnum from 2002 to 2006 (see below), four governments were formed. Since the 2008 election, another four governments have been formed, and discussions are underway to form a fifth government to hold the election to a new Constituent Assembly.

The frequent government changes occurred not only during the hung parliaments of 1994 to 1999 and 2008 to 2012 but also during majority-party parliaments formed in 1991 and 1999. Rapid government changes interrupted policy formulation, implementation, and the overall administration. The political elite, busy breaking and forming governments, devoted less time and energy on formulating new policies for the development and betterment of the people and the country. The frequent government changes fostered an unethical political culture and corrupt practices as legislators' votes were bought and sold to support or oppose governments during the 1990s.

Due to the high governmental instability under the parliamentary system and associated problems, many political parties (including the Maoists), commentators, and scholars have argued for a presidential system under the new constitution. They have argued that a fixed tenure of the presidential executive would ensure government stability. Such arguments have captured the popular imagination of people tired of the nonstop game of musical chairs in filling the prime ministership and cabinet portfolios. There appears to be lack of clarity among the proponents of the presidential system, however; some advocate it because it divides power, while others think it will strengthen the hand of the sole executive.

The proponents of the parliamentary system, the Nepali Congress, civil society leaders, and scholars point out that a presidential system could create an

authoritarian ruler and that the Nepali political culture of imposing *bandhs* at
the slightest pretext when another party is at the helm may result in sustained
street protests to change the executive, as has been the case in Latin America
and elsewhere, and hence create systemic instability. They also point out that
the presidential system has faced crisis in innumerable countries, while the rate
of democratic consolidation is higher in parliamentary systems.

Some parliamentary system advocates have proposed adopting a reformed
system in which the parliament is also vested with power through committees
led by the opposition and through promotion of private bills, unlike in the classical parliamentary system in which the ruling party enjoys most of the state
power. The debate remained hotly contested until the question was finally settled with a compromise on a mixed system, with a popularly elected president
sharing executive power with a cabinet elected by the parliament.

Culture of *Bandh*

Everyday life in Nepal is also affected by frequent *bandhs* (shutdowns), *dharnas*
(sit-ins), and *chhaka* jams (traffic blockades). The strikes are so frequent that
they have become part of the regular political repertoire. Three- and two-week
bandhs were called during the Madhesi movement in 2007 and 2008 and thereafter by indigenous Tharus and Limbus. In the month preceding the dissolution of the Constituent Assembly, a three-week-long *bandh* was called in the far
west by activists demanding a united far west, while the indigenous nationalities countered by shutting down Nepal for three days, demanding federalism
based on ethnic identity.

Protests are an inherent part of democratic practice, but the problem in
Nepal is that *bandhs* have often been enforced with coercion and threats and
employed by opposition political parties for trivial matters or to create obstacles
for the government. While some organizations resort to *bandhs* as a last resort
when the government has ignored peaceful petitions and demands, many of the
strikes, especially those called by the activists of political parties and their student and worker organizations, have taken place without warning and over trivial matters, such as when their cadres were taken into police custody on a
criminal matter.

Protesters have vandalized and destroyed public and private properties, such
as shops and government offices, vehicles, and roadside fences, while implementing their calls. Schools and colleges have been shut down for long periods,
including during centralized exams. Occasionally people have been murdered
during the *bandhs*. In the name of expressing dissent, many of these activities
have undermined the right of common people to go about their daily lives un-
obstructed.[11] They have crippled normal life, incurring huge losses for the

economy. Dhruba Kumar has estimated the economic costs of Maoist *bandhs* and similar actions during the armed conflict at 100 billion rupees.[12]

One major reason for *bandhs* is the unresponsiveness of governments, which know that the opposition cannot formally obstruct their policies or hold them accountable. Thus they often do not respond to the demands of the opposition and social-justice movements, which must therefore rely on coercive public protests to force the government to respond and to change policies. The opposition often perceives that it has no other option.

The *bandhs* are to some extent the legacy of the opposition's obstructionist politics during the end of the *panchayat* period. However, the higher frequency of *bandhs* after 1990 suggests that opposition powerlessness and government unresponsiveness have contributed more significantly. If the opposition had a role in governance, their priorities and energies would probably be spent on affecting policy changes through formal channels. Consider the *bandhs* called by Madhesi and indigenous organizations and parties before and after the 2008 Constituent Assembly election. The Madhesi, who elected significant numbers of Constituent Assembly members, have called far fewer *bandhs* after 2008 because they are in a position to make and unmake governments in the hung Constituent Assembly and to influence policies as well as constitution writing. On the other hand, the indigenous political parties elected very few members and hence cannot influence the policy- and constitution-making process through the system; they have called *bandhs* as frequently after 2008 as they did before.[13]

The Nondemocratic Interregnum— Royal Interventions: 2002–2006

Democracy was again dismantled on October 4, 2002, albeit for a shorter period, when King Gyanendra dismissed the elected government of Sher Bahadur Deuba on the pretext of its failing to settle the Maoist conflict and stem rising corruption. King Gyanendra had come to power after the massacre of his eldest brother, King Birendra, and the king's entire family, presumably by Crown Prince Dipendra, on the night of June 1, 2001. He formed four governments in four years after dismissing the elected government, the first two headed by *panchayat* stalwarts Lokendra Bahadur Chand and Surya Bahadur Thapa. As the movement against his takeover gained support among the people, the king reinstated Sher Bahadur Deuba and included the Communist Party of Nepal (United Marxist Leninist) in the government, among others. The king again dismissed the Deuba government on February 1, 2005, and formed a cabinet under his own chairpersonship.

The royal interregnum saw an increase in the militarization of politics in its attempts to repress both the Maoist rebels and the parliamentary political parties, pushing the two together. The Maoists and an alliance of seven parliamentary political parties that had launched a movement against the king reached an agreement in Delhi to join forces. The civil society also mobilized broader support. The king was finally forced to relinquish power after nineteen days of mass demonstrations in the Kathmandu Valley in April 2006.

The Second People's Movement, Transition, and Constitution Writing: 2006–Present

The endogenous peace process that became possible with the success of the Second People's Movement (SPM) generated a lot of hope within and outside the war-torn country, but these hopes turned into frustrations when the political leadership failed to promulgate a constitution after more than six years. The transition had begun when the Maoists and the interim government led by Girija Prasad Koirala, the leader of the SPM, signed a comprehensive peace treaty in November 2006. An interim constitution drafted by representatives of the seven political parties and the Maoists was promulgated in January 2007, paving the way for the Maoists to enter the interim legislature-parliament and subsequently to join the interim government in April 2007.

The monthlong Madhesi movement launched against the interim constitution, protesting its failure to include federalism, led to around fifty deaths. The indigenous nationalities and Dalits also launched protests and movements to exert pressure for incorporation of their demands into the constitution. Many armed organizations of Madhesis and indigenous nationalities (discussed in detail in Chapter 28) emerged during this period, demanding an end to inequality, exclusion, and discrimination. While the interim constitution eliminated some provisions discriminatory to the marginalized groups, others remained. Protests against some provisions of the interim constitution by the traditionally marginalized ethnic and caste groups indicated future problems for the constitution-writing process.

The election for the Constituent Assembly was finally held on April 10, 2008, after being postponed twice. A lot of people hoped that the considerably inclusive assembly would deliver a constitution acceptable to a wider cross section of Nepali citizens than the previous half dozen constitutions crafted by commissions and committees. As no party secured a majority in the Constituent Assembly, some thought the dynamic would facilitate consensus building. Unfortunately, the constitution was not delivered because, in the name of consensus building, forces seeking the status quo were able to derail the proposal for autonomy for indigenous and Madhesi groups, even though it enjoyed the backing of more than two-thirds of Constituent Assembly members.

The lengthy peace process—only to be expected in a war-torn society in which parties must develop trust and confidence in their former foes—delayed the constitution-writing process to some extent, but after half a decade and considerable confidence building among the previously warring sides, the failure to promulgate a constitution shows that identity has emerged as a new fault line in the country. Fundamental differences regarding ideology and government structures exist in all societies, however, and the failure to follow democratic processes was the proximate cause behind the Constituent Assembly's inability to promulgate a new constitution.

The undermining of the democratic process began when the top political leaders of the major political parties tried to resolve contested issues outside the Constituent Assembly. Even though they resolved some of them, sometimes by removing progressive elements from the reports of the CA thematic committees, such as more equitable gender provisions in marriages with non-Nepali citizens, settlements reached by a few old Bahun males in closed rooms undermined the democratic process in general and the Constituent Assembly in particular. The eventual reason behind the failure to finish writing a new constitution was the refusal of the top leadership to allow voting on the last remaining contested issue: federalism. If a vote had been taken, Nepal would have obtained a constitution because more than two-thirds of the CA members supported the identity-based federal model proposed by the CA thematic committee and the State Structuring Commission by a simple majority and a two-thirds majority, respectively. The refusal of top leaders to allow a vote on an issue for fear of losing their preferred federal model, which would have advantaged their ethnic group, set a dangerous precedent. Even if another Constituent Assembly is elected and the opponents of identity-based federalism obtain a two-thirds majority to pass their model, the advocates of identity-based federalism could cite the precedent as justification for not abiding by the new two-thirds majority.

Democratization Prospects

Democracy in Nepal continues to remain in flux, and there is no guarantee that it will consolidate in the coming days. Failure to adopt a constitution and dissolution of the Constituent Assembly have generated a sense of doom and gloom. A deeper analysis, however, of the country's political history, especially in the new global context of democracy being the only game in town, and of contemporary trends in Nepal from a broader perspective points to significant positive development that may foster democratization.

Successful Sectors Between 1990 and 2002 and Beyond

The post-1990 democratic years were not just plagued by problems; they also witnessed success in many arenas. A boom in print, radio, and electronic media occurred after the 1990 democratic change when the government removed media restrictions imposed by the previous regime and awarded licenses to FM radio and TV stations. Before 1990, Nepal only had government-owned English and Nepali broadsheet dailies. By the end of the 1990s, there were several Nepali and English broadsheet dailies. Hundreds of dailies, weeklies, and fortnightlies registered with the Press Council. Readership and circulation also rose sharply.[14] Despite the CHHE's overwhelming control of the mainstream media and use of it to deride and question issues, movements, and forces—such as the identity-based federalism demanded by Madhesi and indigenous nationalities—that challenge their group's hegemony, the growth of the media has been remarkable, even though much needs to done to make them more professional.

Community forestry efforts are regreening Nepal's hills and to some extent the plains. The process began when the government started to return forest management to the communities in 1978, but the trend gained momentum after 1990 with new legislation (the Forest Act 1993, forest regulations of 1995) giving community groups more rights. By 2008, 14,439 community user groups in Nepal were managing 1.2 million hectares, or 25 percent of forests.[15] New user groups were formed at the rate of nearly 2,000 a year in the 1990s. The gradual reversal of earlier deforestation sharply contrasts with the trend toward large-scale deforestation after 1957, when the government of Nepal nationalized the forests.[16] The government was unable to protect and manage the nationalized forests, whereas local communities no longer had the authority or desire to do so. Despite some remaining challenges, such as inequitable distribution and land transfer from indigenous people to others via nationalization of the forests, the Nepali experience shows that when governments transfer rights to communities, user groups can craft appropriate institutional arrangements to manage common-pool resources and reduce the threat of environmental degradation.

The civil society sector also witnessed remarkable growth after 1990. Over 11,000 nongovernmental organizations (NGOs) were registered by 2000 compared to only a few hundred in 1990.[17] Some NGOs focus on delivering services, whereas others work to protect the rights of citizens and advocate social justice. While the CHHE continue to dominate mainstream civil society organizations, like large human rights organizations, labor unions, and the professional associations of lawyers, journalists, and so on, marginalized groups have begun concerted efforts to challenge this domination by establishing alternate organizations or forging coalitions of marginalized groups in the election of professional associations.

Social-justice movements led by Dalits, indigenous nationalities, the Madhesi, and women exploded during the 1990s. Although they have not been able to root out discrimination and inequality, they have increased awareness, mobilized marginalized groups, sensitized the society and government to injustice and inequality, and contributed to reducing discrimination. They received important concessions from the state after the 2006 regime change as the movements became more politicized. Representation of Madhesis, Dalits, Muslims, and indigenous nationalities increased in the Constituent Assembly, the Nepali state was declared secular in 2006, the Hindu kingdom was made a republic in 2008, 2.5 million Nepalis received citizenship certificates in 2007, affirmative action policies introduced in 2003 were expanded after 2006 to cover more groups and sectors, women's rights have been extended (including in inheritance), and the interim constitution has committed to establishing federalism in the new constitution.

A common factor among all these successes is the withdrawal of the highly centralized state. For instance, the media grew because the government permitted the sector to operate more or less without restrictions. Forestry efforts grew when nationalized forests were returned to the communities. With more power and resources in the 1990s, local governments performed better. The financial sectors expanded and became more efficient after the state liberalized further. Likewise, the government encouraged NGOs and tolerated social-justice movements. When the state gave them space to operate, different actors used it to perform and deliver.[18] This suggests that if given opportunities, people will work to deliver in their arenas of interest, concern, and expertise.

The comparison between problematic and successful sectors makes it clear that the central state's excessive intervention created problems, whereas different sectors successfully functioned when the central state relinquished restrictive power. This does not mean that the state should withdraw completely. It can play a positive role as facilitator, regulator, and arbitrator. The state's role will continue to be essential in sectors where the market and community do not operate or are unwilling or unable to provide essential services and goods.

Institutional and Political Reforms

Even though the delay in promulgating a constitution has frustrated Nepali citizens and the country's other well-wishers, the long-term scenario is not all that gloomy in terms of democratization prospects. In fact, a number of indicators point to positive political transformations, even though there will still be bumps in the road ahead. First, the nondemocratic interregnum of 2002 to 2006 was much shorter than previous ones because the people ended it with sustained protests. This indicates that Nepal may have developed a critical mass of democracy activists and supporters who may struggle against any future attempts to impose autocracy. Second, growing political awareness among different segments of the society, such as Dalits, indigenous nationalities, Madhesis, Muslims, the third gender, and women, has motivated their activism to end the problems they face. This has extended democratic rights to a much wider base of Nepali people than before. These and other groups still face many problems, but major reforms have either ended or undermined discrimination toward them.

Third, as mentioned before, major institutional political reforms, which are rare in most countries, have been implemented. This becomes amply clear when the interim constitution is compared with previous constitutions. The major reforms, substantially and symbolically, include declaration of a republic and secular state, commitment to federalism, adoption of proportional electoral methods in the 2008 election, distribution of more than 2 million citizenships in 2007, extension of gender rights, affirmative action policies, adoption of an inclusive national anthem, declaration of public holidays during the festivals of minority ethnic and religious groups holidays, and so on.

Fourth, the participation of the Maoist rebels (see Chapter 28) in the 2008 election, their emergence as the largest party, and the complete integration of the Maoist army suggest that a powerful armed group may not challenge democracy. The radical faction of the Maoists that split from the mother party could take up arms, but even if it does, it may not gain wider support because the mainstream Maoist party has the support of a large number of former rebels. Some armed ethnic organizations could threaten democracy, but the political reforms that have taken place may provide political space to a large number of ethnic groups' members, especially if the state adopts identity-based federalism.

The road ahead may not be smooth, and Nepal may still encounter many problems, as new democracies do in their attempts at democratic consolidation. But one can say with some confidence that more Nepalis today are enjoying more political rights and civil liberties than ever before. Movements for social justice and equality in the future, although they might look messy, will probably be required to further extend equality, justice, and liberty and to put pressure on the government and ruling parties to address problems like corruption.

SUGGESTED READINGS

Adhikari, Damodar. *Towards Local Democracy in Nepal: Power and Participation in District Development Planning*. Spring Research Series 47. Dortmund, Germany: University of Dortmund, 2006.

Agrawal, Arun, and Elinor Ostrom. "Collective Action, Property Rights, and Decentralization in Resource Use in India and Nepal." *Politics and Society* 29, no. 4 (2001): 485–514.

Baral, Lok Raj, ed. *Election and Governance in Nepal*. New Delhi: Manohar, 2005.

———. *Oppositional Politics in Nepal*. New Delhi: Abhinab, 1977.

Brown, T. Louise. *The Challenge to Democracy in Nepal*. London: Routledge, 1996.

Chauhan, R. S. *Society and State Building in Nepal*. New Delhi: Sterling, 1989.

Kumar, Dhruba. *Electoral Violence and Volatility in Nepal*. Kathmandu: Vajra Publications, 2010.

———. *State, Leadership, and Politics in Nepal*. Kathmandu: CNAS, 1995.

Fisher, James F. *Living Martyrs: Individuals and Revolution in Nepal*. Delhi: Oxford University Press, 1998.

Gupta, Anirudha. *Politics in Nepal: 1950–1960*. Delhi: Kalinga Publications, 1993.

Joshi, Bhuwan Lal, and Leo E. Rose. *Democratic Innovations in Nepal: A Case Study of Political Acculturation*. Berkeley: University of California Press, 1966.

Khanal, Rabindra. *Local Governance in Nepal: Democracy at Grassroots*. Kathmandu: Smriti, 2006.

Lawoti, Mahendra, ed. *Contentious Politics and Democratization in Nepal*. Los Angeles: Sage, 2007.

———. *Looking Back, Looking Forward: Centralization, Multiple Conflicts, and Democratic State Building in Nepal*. Washington, DC: East-West Center, 2007.

Malla, K. P. *Nepal: Perspectives on Continuity and Change*. Kathmandu: CNAS, 1989.

Parajulee, Ramjee P. *The Democratic Transition in Nepal*. Lanham, MD: Rowman & Littlefield, 2000.

Shah, Rishikesh. *Nepali Politics: Retrospect and Prospect*. Delhi: Oxford University Press, 1975.

von Einsiedel, Sebastian, David M. Malone, and Suman Pradhan. *Nepal in Transition: From People's War to Fragile Peace*. New York: Cambridge University Press, 2012.

Uprety, Prem R. *Political Awakening in Nepal: The Search for a New Identity*. New Delhi: Commonwealth Publishers, 1992.

NOTES

1. It is the second constitution. The first was promulgated by Padma Sumshere Rana in 1948 to appease the rising movement for democracy.

2. Bhuwan Lal Joshi and Leo E. Rose, *Democratic Innovations in Nepal: A Case Study of Political Acculturation* (Berkeley: University of California Press, 1966).

3. The prime minister and ministers, however, in practice, could remain in office only if they continued to enjoy the confidence of the king and the Royal Palace secretariat.

4. Mahendra Lawoti, *Looking Back, Looking Forward: Centralization, Multiple Conflicts and Democratic State Building in Nepal* (Washington, DC: East-West Center, 2007).

5. Rabindra Khanal, *Local Governance in Nepal: Democracy at Grassroots* (Kathmandu: Smriti, 2006); Damodar Adhikari, *Towards Local Democracy in Nepal: Power and Participation in District Development Planning,* Spring Research Series 47 (Dortmund, Germany: University of Dortmund, 2006).

6. Basanta Thapa and Mohan Mainali, eds., *Dharap: Taskari, Hinsa Ra Arajakatako Katha* (Lalitpur: Khoj Patrakarita Kendra, 2001–2002); Basanta Thapa and Mohan Mainali, eds.,

Abyabastha Ra Aniyamata: Bhrastachar Sambandhi Khojmulak Lekhharu (Lalitpur: Khoj Patrakarita Kendra, 2003).

7. Binod Bhattarai, Jogendra Ghimire, and Mohan Mainali, *Excesses Unlimited: A Study on Impunity in Nepal* (Lalitpur: Himal, 2005).

8. Bhattarai, Ghimire, and Mainali, *Excesses Unlimited*.

9. Andreas Schedler, "Conceptualizing Accountability," in *The Self-Restraining State: Power and Accountability in New Democracies*, ed. Andreas Schedler, Larry Diamond, and Marc F. Plattner (Boulder, CO: Lynne Rienner, 1999).

10. Guillermo O'Donnell, "Horizontal Accountability in New Democracies," *Journal of Democracy* 9, no. 3 (1998): 112–126.

11. Genevieve Lakier, "Illiberal Democracy and the Problem of Law: Street Protest and Democratization in Multiparty Nepal," in *Contentious Politics and Democratization in Nepal*, ed. Mahendra Lawoti, 251–272 (New Delhi: Sage, 2007).

12. One US dollar was equal to 63.65 rupees in December 2007. Dhruba Kumar, "Consequences of the Militarized Conflict," *Contributions to Nepalese Studies* 30, no. 2: 167–216.

13. Mahendra Lawoti, "Dynamics of Mobilization: Varied Trajectories of Dalit, Indigenous Nationalities, and Madhesi Movements," in *Nationalism and Ethnic Conflict in Nepal*, eds. Mahendra Lawoti and Susan Hangen, 193–225 (London: Routledge, 2012).

14. Pratyoush Onta, "The Print Media in Nepal Since 1990: Impressive Growth and Institutional Challenge," *Studies in Nepali History and Society* 6, no. 2 (2001): 331–346.

15. Hemant Ojha, Lauren Persha, and Ashwini Chhatre, "Seeing the Forest Through the Trees," in *Millions Fed: Proven Successes in Agricultural Development*, ed. David J. Spielman and Rajul Pandya-Lorch (Washington, DC: International Food Policy Research Institute, 2009), 47–52.

16. Arun Agrawal and Elinor Ostrom, "Collective Action, Property Rights, and Decentralization in Resource Use in India and Nepal," *Politics and Society* 29, no. 4 (2001): 485–514.

17. Saubhagya Shah, "From Evil State to Civil Society," *State of Nepal*, ed. Kanak Mani Dixit and Shastri Ramachandaran (Lalitpur: Himal Books, 2002).

18. Lawoti, *Looking Back, Looking Forward*.

27

Political Parties, Elections, and Leaders

Political Parties

With the 1990 constitution and the periodic free elections it introduced, Nepal joined the growing number of new third world democracies. However, like other developing countries, Nepal also experienced problems in democratization. Even though political parties have played an important role in bringing about democracy, then restoring it when it has been taken away, they have struggled to provide good governance and consolidating democracy. Partly as a result of misgovernance by political parties, democracy has been derailed several times in Nepal.

Political parties are supposed to articulate and aggregate interests and to engage in electoral mobilization, candidate nomination, issue structuring, societal representation, and forming and sustaining governments.[1] The Nepali political parties have a mixed record in fulfilling their functions. This chapter evaluates the Nepali political parties based on the various functions they are expected to perform.

History of the Formation of Political Parties

The early political parties were established in Nepal with the aim of abolishing the despotic Rana regime (1846–1951). The Prachanda Gorkha, a political movement, began in 1931. The first political party, the Praja Parishad (People's Council), was formed in June 4, 1936, in Kathmandu and led by Tanka Prasad Acharya (president), Dasarath Chand (vice president), and Ram Hari Sharma, Dharma Bhakta Mathema, and Jeev Raj Sharma (founding members). Ganesh Man Singh and others joined the party soon afterward.[2] Praja Parishad distributed pamphlets and hatched conspiracies to overthrow the Ranas. It also contacted King Tribhuvan, who was under close surveillance, and gained his support. The Ranas discovered these activities and brutally repressed the party. Four non-Brahmin members of Praja Parishad were hanged by the Ranas in 1941; others were sentenced to life imprisonment.[3]

Several political parties were set up in India in the late 1940s by Nepali exiles and Indian-domiciled Nepalis. The All-India Nepali National Congress and the All-India Gorkha Congress, set up in Calcutta and Varanasi, respectively, were merged in 1947 to form the Nepali National Congress. The Nepali National Congress (B. P. Koirala) and the Nepal Democratic Congress (M. B. Shah) merged to become the Nepali Congress in 1950.[4] The Nepali Congress launched an armed movement against the Ranas in November 1950.

The Communist Party of Nepal (CPN), which espoused class struggle, was also formed in India in 1949. The CPN began splitting after 1960 between those who indirectly supported the king and those who opposed. The CPN (Marxist Leninist), a Maoist group that believed in violent revolution, emerged in early 1970s in East Nepal and became the largest faction by the 1980s, after it gave up its violent ideology, which facilitated its unification with other communist groups and factions.[5]

Rightist political parties were also established, often by those involved in the autocratic regimes. The Gorkha Parishad was established in the early 1950s by Ranas and their supporters. Likewise, leaders active during the *panchayat* period formed political parties, collectively called the National Democratic Party (NDP) in 1990. While the Gorkha Parishad merged with the Nepali Congress after the 1960 royal coup, the NDP factions have remained independent parties, even though their influence has diminished.

A major shortcoming of the party system in Nepal is that the dominant ethnic group dominates all of the major parties of the Left, Right, and Center, and the parties have largely ignored the substantive issues of the marginalized groups. This has resulted in the emergence of ethnically named parties to raise and push for issues related to marginalized groups. The Nepal Tarai Congress appeared in the early 1950s, and even though the Madhesi party, the Nepal Goodwill Party (NGP), only elected some members of parliament in the 1990s, Madhesi parties achieved considerable success in the 2008 election after many Madhesi leaders quit the Nepali Congress, the CPN (United Marxist Leninist) (CPN[UML]), and the National Democratic Party (NDP) to form Madhesi parties. Political parties of indigenous nationalities emerged in 1990 but elected only a few members of parliament only in 2008; while a Dalit party was established in the later half of the 1990s, another Dalit party elected only one member in 2008. The party-formation process continues as scores of indigenous nationalities quit the CPN(UML) and Nepali Congress in 2012 to form their own new national-level parties.

Ideological Orientation of Nepali Parties

Political parties in Nepal can be broadly categorized as leftist, centrist, rightist, and identity oriented. Some of the parties have engaged in violent movements as well.

The Communist Parties

An interesting feature of the Nepali party system is that despite the decline of the communist ideology after the collapse of the Soviet Union and the Warsaw Pact, the Nepali communist parties are still going very strong. The political parties that called themselves communist have in fact been increasing their vote share since the first general election in 1959. Table 27.1 shows that if the communist parties had formed a united front with common candidates, they probably would have defeated the Nepali Congress, the largest noncommunist

TABLE 27.1 Votes and Seats Received by Communist and Noncommunist Parties in the 1990s

Political Parties	1991		1994		1999	
	Vote Percentage	*Seats*	*Vote Percentage*	*Seats*	*Vote Percentage*	*Seats*
COMMUNIST PARTIES						
Communist Party of Nepal (United Marxist Leninist)	27.75	69	30.85	83	30.74	68
Nepal Workers Peasants Party	1.25	2	0.98	4	0.55	1
United People's Front Nepal	4.83	9	1.32	-	0.84	1
Communist Party of Nepal–D	2.43	2	-	-	-	-
National People's Front	-	-	-	-	1.37	5
Communist Party of Nepal (Marxist Leninist)	-	-	-	-	6.00	-
TOTAL	36.26	82	33.15	87	39.51	75
NONCOMMUNIST PARTIES						
Nepali Congress	37.75	110	33.38	83	36.14	113
National Democratic Party–C	6.56	3	-	-	3.33	-
National Democratic Party–T	5.38	1	-	-	-	-
National Democratic Party	-	-	17.93	20	10.14	12
Nepal Goodwill Party	4.10	6	3.49	3	3.13	5
TOTAL	53.79	120	54.8	106	52.74	128

NOTE: Only parties that secured seats in the parliament have been listed.

Source: Mahendra Lawoti, *Towards a Democratic Nepal: Inclusive Political Institutions for a Multicultural Society* (New Delhi and Thousand Oaks: Sage Publications, 2005).

party, in 1999 to form a government. In the 2008 Constituent Assembly election, the communist parties performed even better, collectively polling 57 percent of the popular vote and 61.4 percent (353 of 575) of elected seats.[6]

The Nepali communists called for a broad-based alliance of progressive forces to fight the Nepali Congress and an expansionist India, to establish a people's democracy, to relentlessly oppose the king (some factions, however, worked indirectly with the monarchy) and his feudalistic regime, and to advocate for radical social and economic reforms. Some of the communist parties are still critical of the parliamentary system and hope to launch a violent movement in the future, when the time is ripe, to establish communism. The CPN(UML), a party that became moderate, was the main opposition or ruling party during the 1990s. The Unified Communist Party of Nepal (Maoist) (UCPN [Maoist]),[7] a party that espoused a radical communist ideology, grew rapidly after it launched an insurgency in 1996. The growth of both the moderate and extremist communist parties during the 1990s demonstrates the contradictory tendencies within the communist movement, but the growth of the UCPN (Maoist) came at the cost of the CPN(UML).

The communist movement in Nepal has been deeply influenced by the Communist Party of India. Many young Nepali intellectuals residing in Bengal came under the influence of Indian Marxists, whose guidance in 1949 helped them found the Nepali Communist Party in Calcutta. The communist movement has undergone many ups and downs and splits and unifications in its history. The CPN was banned in January 1952 for supporting the rebellion led by Dr. K. I. Singh,[8] but the ban was lifted in April 1956 after the party agreed to engage in a "peaceful movement and accept constitutional monarchy when Tanka Prasad Acharya was prime minister."[9] During the *panchayat* period (1960–1990), it split numerous times but still expanded by operating underground (incognito). Not unlike the communist movement in India, the Nepali communist movement suffers from factional conflicts and ideological schisms. In addition to its various minor splinter groups, the Communist Party was divided into pro-Moscow and pro-Beijing factions until the end of the Cold War.[10] After the advent of the armed rebellion, the movement was divided between those who supported the armed conflict and those who supported the parliamentary process. After the end of the armed conflict and the participation of the Maoists in the Constituent Assembly election, it looked like most of the communist factions would remain in electoral politics, but the breakup of the Maoist party in June 2012 has generated some possibility, according to some news reports, that the radical breakaway faction could launch an armed outfit.

The Communist Party of Nepal (United Marxist Leninist)

The Communist Party of Nepal (United Marxist Leninist) emerged out of the merger of the CPN (Marxist Leninist) (CPN[ML]) and the CPN (Marxist) in January 1991. The former brought a mass-based organization and the younger generation of communist leaders, whereas the CPN(ML) provided well-known leaders from the communist movement.

The CPN(ML), whose leaders went on to control the united party, was formally launched through a convention on December 28, 1976. The organization was the culmination of the Jhapa Resistance, a movement inspired by the violent Naxalite (Maoist) movement in the bordering district of West Bengal, India, launched to physically eliminate class enemies in the Jhapa district in southeast Nepal in 1971.[11] The movement was brutally repressed by the government, but working underground, it was successful in expanding its organization and cadre base.

The CPN(UML) maintained a stable base in the country during the 1990s, with a strong hold on peasants, workers, and students, as well as large development and human rights nongovernmental organizations (NGOs), with an extensive network across the country. It projects a progressive image by raising issues of inequality but is largely dominated by male Bahun leadership. The party briefly ruled alone for nine months in 1994 as a minority government. It provided block grants to village development committees (VDCs) and ensured one female representative out of five members in the ward committees of the VDC.

The CPN(UML) moderated its ideological stance further during the 1990s, especially after 1993. It accepted a market economy and parliamentary democracy despite holding onto the communist name, formed various coalition governments with centrist, rightist, and ethnicity-oriented political parties, and accepted the constitutional monarchy, even joining the government formed by King Gyanendra under Prime Minister Sher Bahadur Deuba in 2004. This departure from core communist principles created ideological ambivalence within the party; as a result, the party often failed to produce coherent policy positions. This may have contributed to erosion of its support base, which was evident in the 2008 election when its voter base was reduced to 20.33 percent from an average of 30.78 percent during the 1990s. Many radical cadres and voters of the CPN(UML) shifted their allegiance toward the Maoists. The party suffered another blow when many senior leaders and cadres hailing from indigenous nationalities, as well as Madhesi and Muslim communities, quit the party in October 2012 to form an alternate party, accusing the mother party of going against the interests of the marginalized communities, which had been a strong vote bank of the party during contestation on the federal model.

The Communist Party of Nepal (Maoist)/Unified Communist Party of Nepal (Maoist)

The CPN (Maoist) was formed in 1995 by a more radical faction that split in 1994 from the CPN (Unity Center) headed by Prachanda, aka Pushpa Kamal Dahal. It expanded rapidly after launching an armed rebellion against the parliamentary democracy in 1996 to struggle for class and identity equality. With the peace accord in November 2006, the Maoists seemed to accept some form of multiparty democracy. They participated in the Constituent Assembly election and emerged as the largest party, winning 220 out of 575 contested seats, surprising numerous observers and commentators. The party has led the government twice since 2008. The party appeared to consolidate its hold in the polity by unifying with several small radical communist parties and expanding its organization in urban areas, but its split in June 2012 may have halted the trend and even eroded its support base.[12] We examine the Maoist movement in detail Chapter 28.

The Fringe Left Parties

There are several other small communist parties, such as the Nepal Workers Peasants Party, the CPN(ML), the National People's Front, and the CPN (Masal), with some having a few representatives in the Constituent Assembly. Most of these fringe parties lie between the UCPN (Maoist) and the CPN(UML) in their ideological orientations.

The Centrist Party: The Nepali Congress

The Nepali Congress, one of the oldest and best-known political parties in Nepal, often led the movements to introduce or restore democracy. As an umbrella organization founded in 1950 by the anti-Rana intellectuals residing in India, it sought to overthrow the Rana regime and democratize the society. After the 1950 revolution, the Nepali Congress became the ruling party for a short period. Under the leadership of the charismatic B. P. Koirala, it survived as a major political force in the country even after its government was dismissed and its leaders jailed in 1960.

Though the Nepali Congress emerged as a peaceful democratic party after the 1990s, it led several armed struggles before that. Its armed struggle against the Rana regime in 1950–1951 was successful, but those launched against the *panchayat* system in 1961–1962 and 1972 were unsuccessful. Shelving armed struggle, B. P. Koirala returned to the country in 1976 from exile in India with a policy of national reconciliation, which called for the restoration of democracy with an understanding with the king.

In the 1980 referendum, the Nepali Congress advocated the losing multi-party option in opposition to the reformed *panchayat* system. Although Koirala himself was ambivalent about the new postreferendum reformed *panchayat* institutional setup, his party decided to boycott the 1981 and 1986 Rashtriya Panchayat elections and adopted a rejectionist posture toward the new regime.

B. P. Koirala's death on July 22, 1982, created a void in the Nepali Congress, and in Nepali politics generally, because he had played a central role since 1950. He was also a moderating force within his party during his later years and consistently advocated for a policy of national reconciliation. Although his death left the Nepali Congress without a widely accepted leader, the party maintained its support among the different sections of the population in the country. Ganesh Man Singh, Krishna Prasad Bhattarai, and Girija Prasad Koirala, B. P.'s youngest brother, collectively led the Nepali Congress after B. P.'s death.

The Nepali Congress formed majority governments in 1991 and 1999 but could not maintain a stable government due to infighting. It frequently participated in the ever-changing coalition governments between 1994 and 1999. Despite still officially claiming democratic socialism as its ideology, the Nepali Congress introduced market-oriented reforms at the pressure of the World Bank and International Monetary Fund.

After 1990, the Koirala clan led by G. P. Koirala began to dominate the party. Senior leaders Ganesh Man Singh and K. P. Bhattarai were eased out of the party over the years. The party split into the Nepali Congress led by G. P. Koirala and the Nepali Congress (Democratic) led by Sher Bahadur Deuba in 2002 due to a power struggle between Koirala and the opposition faction led by Deuba. The two Congresses merged in 2007 in the run-up to the 2008 Constituent Assembly election but still suffered a huge loss, with its vote share reduced to 21.14 percent from an average of 35.76 percent during the 1990s. The desertion of the party by a host of Madhesi leaders, cadres, and voters in 2007 and 2008 severely eroded its electoral base, and further desertion in 2012 by indigenous leaders and cadres could further erode its base. Today the Nepali Congress is led by Sushil Koirala as the president, but ongoing infighting with the Deuba faction has inhibited it from developing and launching programs to recover its losses. On the other hand, increasing assertion and mobilization by the rightist NDP (Nepal) may also undercut the conservative votes the Nepali Congress received in 2008.

The party's moderately socialist and reform-oriented left-of-center platform of the 1950s, which sought to liberalize and reform Nepali society, had changed into a right-of-center platform by the 1990s. As the last party to come on board regarding secularism, republicanism, and federalism issues, it is increasingly

perceived as a status quo party leaning toward conservatism. During the constitution-writing process, the party, dominated by Bahuns and Thakuri, advocated for a parliamentary system, opposed identity-based federalism, and largely
stood for fewer sociopolitical reforms.

The Rightist Parties

Nondemocratic regimes in Nepal have fulfilled the interests of conservative
groups, and when democracy has been introduced or restored by dismantling
autocratic regimes, the political parties of the Right have borne the brunt of
people's bitterness in the elections. The Gorkha Dal emerged as the conservative party in the 1950s, representing the interests of the Ranas and their supporters. It became the major opposition party but received only around 17
percent of seats and votes. However, after King Mahendra dismissed the Nepali
Congress government in 1960 and ended the multiparty system, it merged with
the Nepali Congress. Thereafter, the ruling *panchayat* system carried the torch
of conservatives in Nepal.

Two conservative parties with the same name, the National Democratic
Party, were formed by the former *panchas* (politicians active during the *panchayat* period) in 1990 after the restoration of democracy. The parties have
merged and split several times since then. Close to the royal palace, a major
NDP faction supported King Gyanendra when he directly ruled the country
after 2005, while two other factions opposed the king's direct rule but supported constitutional monarchy.

As a combined outfit, the NDP received 17 percent of the vote in 1994 but
captured fewer seats and votes when it contested elections as separate parties.
The three conservative parties collectively received less than 5 percent of the
vote in 2008, showing their considerable and continuous decline in electoral
politics. The NDP (Nepal), which advocates for a Hindu state, reinstatement
of the constitutional monarchy, and a unitary state, is receiving some coverage
from the Kathmandu-based media and support from Far Right groups but may
not be able to expand considerably as the Nepali Congress, with its increasingly
status quo position, may continue to receive conservative votes.

The Parties with Explicit Ethnic Agendas

The failure of the Nepali party system, historically dominated by Bahuns and
Chhetris, to address the substantive issues and demands of the marginalized
groups has resulted in the emergence of political parties with explicit ethnic
agendas. Explicitly ethnicity-oriented political parties first emerged in the early
1950s. The Nepal Tarai Congress, whose major demand was autonomy for the

Tarai, received 2.1 percent of the popular vote but did not win any seats in 1959. More ethnic parties emerged after the restoration of democracy in 1990. Only the Nepal Goodwill Party of the Madhesi elected representatives to parliament in the 1990s. The NGP had been transformed into a political party from the Goodwill Forum established by Gajendra Narayan Singh, the champion of the Madhesi cause, during the mid-1980s. It raised the problems the Madhesi faced, such as the lack of citizenship certificates, domination by hill "upper-caste" people in the governance of country, and discrimination against Madhesi languages, dress codes, and values. Among its major demands were making Hindi a lingua franca in the Tarai, federalism, and inclusion of the Madhesi in governance.

Madhesi political parties emerged as kingmakers after the 2008 election. The Madhesi People's Right Forum (MPRF), which transformed into a political party after successfully leading a movement in 2007, emerged as the largest Madhesi party in the Constituent Assembly by winning fifty-two seats. The Tarai Madhesh Democratic Party (TMDP), a party primarily formed by Madhesi leaders who quit mainstream political parties to raise the Madhesi cause, emerged as the second-largest party with twenty seats. The Madhesi political parties have joined the government and split numerous times, and the Nepali media has delightedly covered the leaders' "corrupt" activities. Despite the splits and squabbles, the parties have come together to protect Madhesi interests, including during the debates on the restructuring of the state in the Constituent Assembly.

Among the indigenous nationalities parties, the National People's Liberation Party (NPLP), established in 1990, steadily increased its vote share after 1991 but was not able to elect a member to parliament under the first-past-the-post (FPTP) electoral system. Some parties with specific ethnic names, like the Mongol National Organization (MNO) and the National Nationalities Party, were denied registration by the Election Commission in 1990 based on a constitutional provision that bans ethnic parties.[13] The indigenous nationalities parties demanded federalism, declaration of a secular state, equality among native languages, and inclusion in governance, among other things. Even though the indigenous nationalities parties did not win any seats in the 2008 FPTP election, three parties elected five seats through the proportional representation method in the Constituent Assembly.

Dalits have been the last to establish an ethnically oriented party, and they have been the least successful in winning votes and seats. The Nepal Dalit Labor Front was established in 1996 and fielded candidates unsuccessfully in the 1999 election. Vishwendra Paswan became the first Dalit to be elected from a Dalit party, the Dalit Janajati Party, in 2008.

Problems in the Party System

Political Exclusion of Women and Marginalized Ethnic/Caste Groups

One major failure of the party system in Nepal, as indicated above, has been the excessive domination of the major political parties by male members of the Caste Hill Hindu elite (CHHE). For instance, CHHE dominated the central committee of the CPN(UML) in 1999 by 87 percent, despite the party's tireless progressive rhetoric. The same group dominated the Nepali Congress by 71 percent and the NDP factions by around 45 percent.[14] In the later part of the first decade of the twenty-first century, the central committees of the CPN(UML), Nepali Congress, and UCPN (Maoist) were dominated by CHHE at 59, 63, and 58 percent, respectively.[15] As before, all the top leaders of the three largest political parties continued to be male Bahuns in 2012.

The presence of women on the central committees of the political parties, including small and ethnically named ones, has also been negligible, with only a few at most during the late 1990s. The situation has slightly improved since then, but women are still heavily underrepresented. In 2009 the representation of women on the central committees of the CPN(UML), UCPN (Maoist), Nepali Congress, and MPRF was 17, 11, 9, and 14 percent, respectively, with none meeting the political parties' commitment to include 33 percent women in party organizations' memberships.[16] The Maoist party has emerged as the relatively more inclusive large party based on descriptive representation and advocacy of issues of marginalized groups, although its top leaders also hail from the dominant group.

Underrepresentation in the top political leadership of the major political parties has often resulted in the parties not taking the issues of marginalized groups seriously and sometimes even working against the interests of the marginalized groups. The political parties were largely not responsive to the major problems of the marginalized groups even when their movements took to the streets. In fact, the opposition of the top leaders of the Nepali Congress and CPN(UML) and the ambivalence of the Maoists were factors behind the failure to adopt identity-based federalism in the constitution. As the political parties and their top leaders controlled the political process in Nepal, the increased representation of marginalized groups in the Constituent Assembly did not result in decisions sympathetic to the marginalized groups unless the top party brass approved those issues.

Party Factionalism and Splits

The problem of regular factional politics and frequent splits has plagued parties of all ideological persuasion and sizes in Nepal. The frequency of splits has historically been much higher among the communist parties. During the Cold War, the communist parties fragmented along Russian and Chinese lines. When King Mahendra took power in 1960, they also split between those who sympathized with and those who opposed the king. They have also differed with regard to adopting violent revolution or peaceful strategies for societal transformation. At other times, the communists have tended to split over differences involving the interpretation of terms, concepts, and ideology. At any given time since the 1970s, there has been around a dozen communist parties in Nepal.[17]

The communist voters, however, tend not to be as divided and have generally favored one or two large parties. A large number of communist voters supported the CPN(UML), which integrated many factions of various communist parties, independent Marxist groups, and communist parties over the years during the 1980s and 1990s.[18] It always polled around 30 percent of the vote during elections in the 1990s. The party suffered a vertical split in 1998, but many leaders returned to the mother party in 2002. The rapid expansion of the more radical Maoists after 1996 divided the communist supporters as many radical ones quit the CPN(UML) to join or support the Maoists. The party was rocked again by the desertion of senior leaders and cadres from the marginalized groups in 2012. The Maoists united with several small radical communist parties after they joined open politics, but the split bug, which they had avoided for one and a half decades, eventually caught up with them in June 2012.

The Nepali Congress did not experience frequent splits after the party matured, but it was plagued by intense intraparty factionalism. Sometimes opposition factions worked to undermine party candidates in the elections. At other times, members of parliament opposed their own parties' government proposals. Founding senior leaders like Ganesh Man Singh and Krishna Prasad Bhattarai, dissatisfied with party operations, also stayed away from the party in their later years. As noted earlier, the Nepali Congress went through a major split in 2002, but the two factions merged again in 2007.

The conservative National Democratic Party and the Madhesi and indigenous nationalities parties have also frequently split. The NDP's factions generally merged after being routed in elections, but that has not prevented splits in the party from happening again. Other smaller political parties, including identity-based ones, have also split regularly. The political parties of the Madhesi (MPRF, TMDP, NGP) and indigenous nationalities (NPLP, MNO, Federal Democratic National Forum) have also split multiple times.

The splits in the parties, especially in the smaller ones, have often stemmed from personality clashes among the leaders as well as from fights for spoils when parties join government. The competition for ministerial berths is often very intense as they provide access to government resources for distribution among party, faction, and personal loyalists, allowing leaders to maintain the patronage system and enrich themselves. The lack of intraparty democracy has also contributed to splits in the parties.

Lack of Intraparty Democracy

Almost all the political parties in Nepal lack internal democracy, and most parties have been dominated by one leader for long periods, whether rightist, centrist, parliamentary, revolutionary communist, or fringe parties that have not been able to elect members to parliament. The Nepali Congress, CPN(UML), and UCPN (Maoist) and smaller parties like the Nepal Workers Peasants Party (NWPP) and the Nepal Goodwill Party have been governed by a dominant leader with unprecedented power for long periods.

Many of the top leaders demonstrate feudalistic characteristics, frequently ignore party rules and procedures, and govern based on factional interests and personal preferences and whims. They often run the parties like mini kings. They undermine intraparty democracy by not holding regular meetings and conventions, even when legitimately called by dissenting factions. In parties like the Nepali Congress and the NDP factions, major party decisions often have been made by the top leaders outside formal party forums. In the case of communist parties, except the Maoists, the dissenting factions, on the other hand, have often been hounded out or forced to split for questioning the establishment side's decisions.

Weak internal democracy is due to a monopoly of power held by the top leader, who often feels a strong need to concentrate power in the prevalent patronage-based politics. These leaders perceive that unless they distribute positions and other resources to loyal cadres, particularly their factional and personal loyalists, they may lose support and their position. The clients or supporters and loyalists also look upon and support strong leaders capable of nominating them to party organizations and as candidates during elections, appointing them to public offices when the party is in power, and distributing other resources to them. In addition, leaders feel that they must stay in power at any cost, even by flouting party rules, because once the opposing faction attains the prized leadership position, that faction may use and abuse power to retain it permanently. In some political parties, the dissenting factions' leaders could see no future in the party controlled by their nemeses because the establishment side could marginalize the dissenters further to reduce threats; hence some of the dissenting leaders and factions split their parties when they could muster enough support.

The patronage system operates beyond the party organization and extends to agencies like the media, trade unions, professional associations, human rights groups, and civic organizations, which are supposed to wield countervailing power to hold political forces accountable in democracies. For instance, many civil society organizations and NGOs, including human rights groups with independent facades, have a close affiliation with specific political leaders and political parties beyond ideological affinities. The few civil society organizations that are independent, on the other hand, find it challenging to be effective because political parties, through their cadres and supporters working in government agencies, NGOs, and donor organizations, influence distribution of resources and rewards to partisan civil society organizations and often ignore independent NGOs.[19] As political loyalty and affiliation seem to pay off more than being independent, many in the media, professions, and academia nurture their relationships with political leaders and political parties. This becomes a problem when the civil society is small and a large proportion of it has partisan affiliations.

The patronage system and weak internal democracy among political parties have made the parties less responsive and accountable to common citizens. As political leaders are often shielded from accountability within the party due to weak internal democracy and often win elections and party positions based on the support of their loyalists and cadres, there is less need for them to be responsive to citizens or members of the opposing faction, who might raise issues of concern to the general public.

Some differences exist among the political parties. Generally, the communist political parties tend to have more internal discussion and debate of various issues than the democratic parties, which are more often run on the whims of the political leadership. However, the communist parties are often intolerant of internal dissent and are less tolerant of other political parties. The democratic parties, like the Nepali Congress, on the other hand, are tolerant of factionalism and dissent within the party, even if the dissent goes public, but the establishment side hardly responds positively to address the issues.

The sociopolitical structure in Nepal has not been conducive to the development of a sound party system. With domination of political and administrative life by a few high-caste families, the prevalence of the caste system, patriarchy, a nonegalitarian culture, and power-aggrandizing attitudes among top leaders, the growth of a responsible, responsive, accountable, democratic, and competitive party system in the country has been slow. On the other hand, the public behavior of party leaders who regularly disregard public opinion and continual interparty conflicts have led to a poor image of party leaders in Nepali society.

Elections: Local and Central

Electoral History

Nepal's electoral history is shorter than India's and Sri Lanka's, even though Nepal existed long before them. Elections to a few village councils and municipalities were held during the latter part of the Rana regime, but the first democratic election in Nepal was organized to elect the Kathmandu municipality in 1953. The CPN won the most seats (six), followed by the Nepali Congress (four), Praja Parishad (four), Gorkha Parishad (one), and independents (four).[20] The first general elections were held in 1959 to elect a parliament. King Tribhuvan's pledge to hold an election for a Constituent Assembly after the Rana regime fell was never realized. The Nepali Congress won an overwhelming majority of seats in the first election with 37 percent of the votes. The Communist Party won only four seats, whereas the conservative Gorkha Parishad won nineteen.

The *panchayat* system (1960–1990) held direct and indirect elections based on partyless competitions. The king ruled directly, aided by different levels of government. Sovereignty rested with the king, who handpicked the prime minister and cabinet ministers. Political parties could not field candidates, and candidates competed individually against each other. Prior to 1980 *panchayat* elections were direct only at the local level. The people voted for village and municipal officials, and elected officials elected district-level officials, who in turn elected the zonal-level officials and Rashtriya Panchayat (central parliament) members. An important contribution of the *panchayat* period was the extension of village *panchayats,* or village units, across the country and the conduct of elections to elect office bearers. Less than 800 village units were established in 1956, whereas the *panchayat* period established 3,999 units.[21]

The referendum held in 1980 to choose between *panchayat* with reform and multiparty democracy mobilized people extensively. The referendum itself was the result of a student movement against the *panchayat* regime. The side for *panchayat* with reform narrowly won the referendum.

The elections held during the 1980s were based on universal adult franchise, but political parties were still banned, and candidates to the Rashtriya Panchayat had to compete in the elections as independents. The Nepali Congress boycotted both the 1981 and 1986 parliamentary elections but participated in the local elections. Some communist parties participated in the local and parliamentary elections. The CPN(ML) fielded candidates in thirty-two districts and elected six members to the parliament. CPN (Manadhar) and NWPP also elected one candidate each in 1986.[22]

TABLE 27.2 Local Election Results (Percentage of Seats)

| Parties | 1992 | | | 1997 | | |
	VDC	Municipalities	DDC	VDC	Municipalities	DDC
Nepali Congress	50.24	50.84	64.80	29.47	28.92	14.32
CPN(UML)	26.05	22.33	17.94	50.10	55.98	68.05
NDP	9.73	10.32	7.63	12.22	8.15	9.94
NGP	2.94	3.38	1.96	1.21	1.59	1.42
NPF	5.09	1.50	3.54	-	-	-
Independents and other parties	5.93	11.63	4.10	4.93	5.36	6.27

VDC—Village Development Committee, DDC—District Development Committee

Source: Adapted from Krishna Hacchethu, "Political Parties and Elections," in *Elections and Governance in Nepal*, ed. Lok Raj Baral (New Delhi: Manohar, 2005), 165.

Elections During the 1990s

The 1990s witnessed three general elections and two local elections. The centrist Nepali Congress and the leftist CPN(UML) emerged as the two major political parties (see Table 27.1). The Nepali Congress won a majority of seats in 1991 and 1999 but could not maintain stable governments. The CPN(UML) won the largest number of seats in the hung parliament of 1994. The Nepali Congress won a majority of seats in the 1992 local elections, while the CPN(UML) won a majority in 1997 (see Table 27.2). Both local elections saw massive mobilization of state agencies and resources by the parties that controlled the Home Ministry, the Nepali Congress in 1992, and the CPN(UML) in 1997.

The electoral trend shows that the communist parties grew significantly in the 1990s compared to the 1959 election, when they won only four seats and 7 percent of the vote. The communists expanded their organization during the *panchayat* period, remaining underground, while the Nepali Congress leaders were mostly in exile in India. The communists made a remarkable gain in 2008, winning a majority of the vote for the first time (see Table 27.3).

The electoral results show that conservative parties have not performed well, never receiving 20 percent of the vote during the country's entire electoral history. Associated with the previous autocratic regimes, they were unpopular during the democratic period. The political parties with explicit ethnic agendas have also appeared in the electoral fray but not fared well until the 2008 election. The explosive growth of identity politics since 1990 also suggests that parties formed explicitly to represent indigenous nationalities and Dalit issues may fare better in the future, like the Madhesi parties did in 2008.

TABLE 27.3 Seats Won in the Constituent Assembly, 2008

Name	FPTP	PR	Total	Name	FPTP	PR	Total
CPN(Maoist)	120	100	220	NPPP	0	3	3
Nepali Congress	37	73	110	NPLP	0	2	2
CPN(UML)	33	70	103	CPN (United)	0	2	2
MPRF	30	22	54	NGP-A	0	2	2
TMDP	9	11	20	Nepali People's Party	0	2	2
NGP	4	5	9	FDNF	0	2	2
NDP	0	8	8	SDPPN	0	1	1
CPN(ML)	0	8	8	Dalit Nationalist Party	0	1	1
PFN	2	5	7	Nepal Family Party	0	1	1
CPN(Joint)	0	5	5	Nepal National Party	0	1	1
NDP–N	0	4	4	NDSP	0	1	1
NPF	1	3	4	CBNUPN	0	1	1
NWPP	2	2	4	Independents	2	0	2

Source: Election Commission, "Constituent Assembly Election 2064—List of Winning Candidates," http://www.election.gov.np/reports/CAResults/reportBody.php.

CPN (ML)—Communist Party of Nepal–Marxist Leninist; PFN—People's Front Nepal; CPN (Joint)—Communist Party of Nepal–Joint; NDP-N—National Democratic Party–Nepal; NPF—National People's Front; NWPP—Nepal Workers Peasants Party; NPPP—Nepal People's Power Party; CPN (United)—Communist Party of Nepal–United; NGP-A—Nepal Goodwill Party–Anandidevi; FDNF—Federal Democratic National Forum; SDPPN—Socialist Democratic People's Party Nepal; NDSP—Nepal Democratic Socialist Party; CBNUPN—Chure Bhawar National Unity Party Nepal

Erosion of Electoral Institutions

Elections are supposed to be unpredictable. They become less meaningful if certain actors can increase the likelihood of winning through unlawful means. Nepal witnessed the erosion of the electoral process between 1990 and 2002, when most of the major parties attempted to influence the elections in whatever ways they could, including by unlawful means. The ruling party usually had more leverage because it exploited the coercive apparatus of the state as well as its vast resources, including the monopoly over state media.

State-owned Radio Nepal was very effective in spreading the ruling party's views, news, and propaganda during elections as it reached every nook and corner of the country, unlike other media. The ruling parties also collected a disproportionate amount of funds through government contracts and licenses. They transferred and deployed civil servants and police officials and distributed development projects and funds to influence electoral prospects.

In addition to looking at direct evidence of fraud, manipulation, and overt use of muscle and money,[23] we can use election results to assess the government's influence on elections. The two political parties that controlled the Home Ministry won the two local elections and two of the three parliamentary elections during the 1990s. The 1994 general election was an exception due to the high level of factional infighting in the ruling party, the Nepali Congress.

The stated desire of major parties to conduct elections when they are at the helm also implicitly acknowledges the advantages of being in the government during elections. This tendency became especially clear during the five-year hung parliament (1994–1999), when repeated governments faced with the threat of no-confidence votes attempted to dissolve the parliament in order to conduct fresh elections. The real or perceived ability of the ruling party to influence elections is also a reason for the parties to go to extreme lengths, including unethical ones, to retain power or topple the government.

The tendency to vote for the ruling party in exchange for patronage increases the incentive for political parties to conduct elections when in power. It underlines the importance of being in power so as to be able to distribute goods and benefits before and during elections. A candidate or his or her party being in government often makes promises appear more plausible.

The ruling party could influence elections partly because the horizontal accountability mechanism, the Election Commission, in this case, was not powerful or independent, despite being termed so, enough to restrain the government from abusing power to influence elections. As with other central constitutional commissions, the cabinet influenced the appointment of election commissioners, who were not publicly screened during the 1990s, and allocated budget and assigned staff to the commissions. This meant that the cabinet could often appoint party loyalists and restrain or facilitate the operation of the commission. Due to the weakness of the Election Commission, the ability of the common people to hold leaders accountable through the threat of not voting was undermined because the ruling parties' abuse of power diminished the unpredictability of the electoral process.

To the credit of the Election Commission, it held the twice-postponed 2008 election in the challenging environment of a postconflict society in a reasonably free, fair, and peaceful manner. Even though it was the most violent election in Nepal's history, it can be deemed to have been reasonably well executed under the circumstances, if viewed in comparison with other post–civil war societies.

The election produced some major surprises. The Maoists emerged as the largest party at the cost of established parties. Likewise, ethnic/nationalist parties, especially the Madhesi, also won a considerable number of seats. The results indicated that people voted for movement parties and were seeking change. The Constituent Assembly became the most inclusive legislature to date, partly because the large parties had to distribute seats proportionally along ethnic/caste and gender lines, ethnic/nationalist parties won considerable seats for the first time, and the Maoists fielded many marginalized groups' candidates under the FPTP electoral method.

Elections in Nepal have shown that they may not be sufficient to make political leaders responsive and accountable. Nevertheless, the ruling parties had to bear the consequences of their misgovernance in the 1990s with loss of their base in the 2008 election. When the ruling parties remained unresponsive, many people supported the rebel Maoists, which then spread rapidly and finally trounced the ruling parties in an election. This suggests that vertical accountability could operate indirectly as well as over a longer time frame. Likewise, even though the marginalized groups continued to be excluded during the three elections in the 1990s, the more mobilized group, the Madhesi, won substantial seats in 2008, suggesting that democracy could extend through elections, even though slowly, as others have demonstrated elsewhere.[24]

Political Leaders

This section discusses political leaders who have made significant contributions to Nepali politics and changed the direction of the polity.

The Conservative Leaders

Prithvi Narayan Shah

Prithvi Narayan Shah (1722–1775), who succeeded his father Narbhupal Shah in 1743 as the king of Gorkha, a small principality in the west-central hills, established the Shah dynasty by conquering Nepal. In his bid to conquer the Kathmandu Valley, which he finally succeeded in doing in 1768–1769 after a two-decade campaign, he first defeated small principalities surrounding the valley. Thereafter he expanded his conquest to the east, as far as Sikkim and the Tista River, through brilliance as well as trickery (attacks during festivals, which was against the war norms of the time), cruelty (blockades and inhumane punishments), and diplomacy (marriages, friendships, and treaties).

Prithvi Narayan was an ambitious king and a shrewd tactician. He conquered the valley kingdoms with greater resources than his small principality of Gorkha. He established a standing army, which did not exist in other Himalayan principalities during the period, and deployed it in his conquests. He devised a land-military complex; the land-hungry hill peasants who joined the army were given land from the conquered regions.[25]

He lived a frugal life and dictated *Dibya Upadesh,* his treatise on governance, before he died. The treatise protected local products, discouraged dependence on foreign goods, and discussed the challenge Nepal faced in trying to survive between two large countries, India and Tibet/China. However, the treatise also upheld and promoted the caste system and facilitated caste-based domination, despites the modern state's popular projection of him as a multiculturalist. He introduced the more intolerant version of Hinduism in the valley that went on to become state policy in subsequent centuries.

He became known as the father of the nation after 1951, when his descendants regained power, but that status was challenged after democracy was restored in 1990 and more so after the 2006 Second People's Movement.

Janga Bahadur Rana Kunwar

Janga Bahadur Rana Kunwar (1817–1877), an ambitious upstart courtier, eclipsed the kings by capturing effective political power. He was appointed prime minister in 1846 following the Kot massacre, in which he and his brothers' troops killed most other contenders for power. He exploited the extreme factionalism in the court, which stemmed from a weak king, a wayward crown prince, and a junior queen who wanted to install her son on the throne. Janga Bahadur engineered the replacement of King Rajendra with Crown Prince Surendra but kept real control in his own hands. He assumed the title of maharaja (great king) in 1856. He established a hereditary premiership based on a transfer of power to his brothers and their children thereafter. The family ruled autocratically over Nepal for a century, tightly controlling political, military, and administrative power within the Rana family and repressing political awareness and mobilization. They used and abused state and societal resources for personal and family enrichment at the cost of the peasants, who were heavily taxed to support rulers' luxurious lifestyles.

Janga Bahadur adopted the family name Rana to upgrade his caste to that of the ruling family. This allowed him to marry his children into the royal family, further consolidating his power. Janga Bahadur assisted the British in suppressing the Sepoy Mutiny in 1857. The British, as a reward, returned the western Tarai, which had been ceded to the East India Company in 1816 after defeat in the Anglo-Gorkha war. He introduced the Country Code in 1854, which formally stratified the society along caste lines and imposed Hinduism on the indigenous population and others.

King Mahendra Bir Bikram Shah

King Mahendra Bir Bikram Shah (1920–1972), who was ambitious and wanted a more active role for the monarchy in the governance of the country, succeeded his father, King Tribhuvan, in 1955. He began consolidating power by exploiting the infighting among the political parties during the 1950s. He removed the elected prime minister, B. P. Koirala, and his Nepali Congress government in December 1960 and introduced a *panchayat* constitution in

1962 that provided for an active monarchy. The *panchayat* system, an experiment with guided democracy, had a facade of representative democracy.

In 1963, he promulgated a new Country Code that dropped the caste system and attempted to modernize the kingdom through development programs, such as industrialization, administrative reforms, and infrastructure construction. The period also witnessed an active assimilation policy of the diverse ethnic and linguistic groups through the public education system, with instruction in the Khas-Nepali language, and promotion of hill Hindu nationalism (Nepali language, Hindu religion, Khas-Nepali *daurasuruwal*, etc.). The 1962 constitution declared the state as Hindu.

The Centrist Leaders
Bishweshwar Prasad Koirala
Bishweshwar Prasad Koirala (1915–1982), probably the best-known Nepali political leader as well as a highly regarded novelist, became the first elected prime minister of Nepal in 1959. He played a leading role in setting up the Nepali Congress in India to revolt against the Rana regime in the 1940s. After the 1950–1951 armed resistance, he became the home minister in the 1951 Rana-Congress coalition after India brokered a settlement in New Delhi between the Ranas, the king, and the Nepali Congress. He frequently bickered with his elder stepbrother, Matrika Prasad Koirala, who was made prime minister twice by King Tribhuvan.

B. P., who was the party's chief ideologue and a charismatic leader, briefly flirted with communist ideology in his youth but later became a democratic socialist and persuaded the Nepali Congress to adopt the ideology. He participated in the Indian independence movement and was close to Indian socialist leaders.

B. P.'s government was dismissed, and he was imprisoned by King Mahendra from 1960 until 1968. He went into exile in India after his release and organized an unsuccessful armed resistance; later he returned to Nepal to promote national reconciliation and opposed the *panchayat* system peacefully.

The Communist Leaders
Pushpa Lal Shrestha
Pushpa Lal Shrestha (1924–1978) was the founding father of the communist movement in Nepal. Brother of Ganga Lal Shrestha, one of the Praja Parishad martyrs executed in 1940 by the Ranas, he was the first general secretary of the Communist Party of Nepal (1947–1949). He remained on the radical wing of the party as it witnessed many splits and called for restoration of the parliament when King Mahendra dismissed it. In 1968 he split from the Tulsi Lal group. He advocated for a joint movement with the Nepali Congress against the

monarchy, but his colleagues and the Nepali Congress did not heed his call during his lifetime. When the Nepali Congress and a communist front finally came together and launched a joint movement, the king was forced to bow down and restore democracy in 1990.

Prachanda, aka Pushpa Kamal Dahal

Prachanda (1956–present) was the general secretary of the CPN (Maoist) party that launched a violent insurgency in 1996. A small extremist party, it spread its influence throughout the country within a decade. Prachanda kept the party united, even in the context of a Nepali communist culture of splitting over small disputes, until June 2012.

Prachanda, who became an underground communist activist in 1971, worked with Mohan Bikram Singh, a doyen of the communist movement, in the CPN (Fourth Convention) and CPN (Mashal) (different manifestations after splits). He broke away from Mohan Bikram in 1985 to set up the CPN (Masal) (different from Mashal). His new party merged with the Fourth Convention in 1990 to form the CPN (Unity Center), which was part of the United People's Front, a second communist front during the 1990s people's movement that did not align with the Nepali Congress. He established the CPN (Maoist) in 1995 and has been in firm control of it ever since.

The party in 2001 adopted the "Prachanda path" as its official ideology, which urged simultaneous armed mobilization in rural areas and urban mobilization and unrest. The Maoists reached an understanding with the seven parliamentary parties to fight against King Gyanendra after the monarch assumed direct absolute power in February 2005 and subsequently signed a comprehensive peace agreement with the government that was formed after the success of the movement in 2006. Prachanda became the prime minister in 2008 but resigned after nine months when the president reinstated an army chief Prachanda had fired.

Ethnic and Women Leaders

Gajendra Narayan Singh

Gajendra Narayan Singh (1930–2002) was a democrat and a champion of the Madhesi cause. He began his political career in the Nepali Congress but formed a Madhesi front and political party after the Nepali Congress failed to address the problems faced by the Madhesi, despite receiving significant votes from the Tarai.[26]

He participated in the 1950–1951 resistance against the Ranas and was imprisoned by King Mahendra in 1960–1961. He was again imprisoned briefly in 1985 for setting up the Nepal Sadbhawana Parishad (Nepal Goodwill Council) to fight against discrimination faced by the Madhesi. He was first elected to the parliament (Rashtriya Panchayat) in 1986. He launched the Nepal Goodwill Party in 1990, advocating for regional autonomy and inclusion of the Madhesi in the government. He headed the NGP until his death and served in various coalition governments from 1995 onward.

Shaileja Acharya

Shaileja Acharya (1944–2009), the niece of three prime ministers, rose to become deputy prime minister, the first woman to reach this political office ever in Nepal. She was initiated into politics when very young and was one of the few people who protested when King Mahendra dismissed B. P. Koirala's elected government in 1960. She spent many years in prison and in exile in India. She became a minister after 1990 and deputy prime minister in 1998. She was considered a noncorrupt leader but close to India and Indian leaders. During her tenure as agriculture and water resources minister, she favored small-scale projects following her democratic socialist background. Her role in the party hierarchy diminished in later years because she did not openly come out against royal rule after King Gyanendra took power in 2002.

SUGGESTED READINGS

Borre, Ole, Sushil Raj Panday, and Chitra Krishna Tiwari. *Nepalese Political Behavior*. New Delhi: Sterling, 1994.

Dhruba Kumar. *Electoral Violence and Volatility in Nepal*. Kathmandu: Vajra Publications, 2010.

Fisher, James F. *Living Martyrs: Individuals and Revolutions in Nepal*. Delhi: Oxford University Press, 1998.

Hachhethu, Krishna. *Party Building in Nepal: Organization, Leadership, and People*. Kathmandu: Mandala Book Point, 2002.

Hangen, Susan. "Between Political Party and Social Movement: The Mongol National Organization and Democratization in Rural Nepal." In *Contentious Politics and Democratization in Nepal*, edited by Mahendra Lawoti, 175–198. New Delhi: Sage, 2007.

Joshi, Bhuwan Lal, and Leo E. Rose. *Democratic Innovations in Nepal: A Case Study of Political Acculturation*. Berkeley: University of California Press, 1966.

Khanal, Rabindra. *Local Governance in Nepal: Democracy at Grassroots*. Kathmandu: Smriti, 2006.

Lawoti, Mahendra. "Exclusionary Democratization in Nepal, 1990–2002." *Democratization* 15, no. 2 (2008): 363–385.

————. "Political Exclusion and the Lack of Democratisation: Cross-national Evaluation of Nepali Institutions Using Majoritarian-Consensus Framework." *Commonwealth and Comparative Politics* 45, no. 1 (2007): 57–77.

Neupane, Govinda. *Nepalko Jatiya Prashna: Samajik Banot Ra Sajhedariko Sambhawana* [*Nepal's National Question: Social Composition and Possibilities of Accommodation*]. Kathmandu: Center for Development Studies, 2000.

Rawal, Bhim. *Nepalma Samyabadi Andolanko: Adbhav Ra Bikash* [*Communist Movement in Nepal: Rise and Development*]. Kathmandu: Pairavi Prakashan, 1991.

Shah, Rishikesh. *Modern Nepal: A Political History, 1769–1995*. Delhi: Manohar, 1996.

————. *Nepali Politics: Retrospect and Prospect.* Delhi: Oxford University Press, 1975.

Stiller, L. F. *The Rise of the House of Gorkha.* Ranchi: Patna Jesuit Society, 1973.

Surendra, K. C. *Nepalma Communist Andolanko Itihas* [*The History of Communist Movement in Nepal*]. Kathmandu: Vidhyarthi Pustak Bhandar, 1999.

Whelpton, John. *A History of Nepal.* Cambridge: Cambridge University Press, 2005.

NOTES

1. Richard Gunther and Larry Diamond, "Types and Functions of Parties," *Political Parties and Democracy*, ed. Larry Diamond and Richard Gunther (Baltimore: John Hopkins University Press, 2001).

2. James F. Fisher, *Living Martyrs: Individuals and Revolution in Nepal* (Delhi: Oxford University Press, 1998), 36.

3. Brahmin were exempt from capital punishment. Fisher, *Living Martyrs*; Krishna Hachhethu, *Party Building in Nepal: Organization, Leadership, and People* (Kathmandu: Mandala Book Point, 2002).

4. Rishikesh Shah, *Modern Nepal: A Political History, 1769–1995* (Delhi: Manohar, 1996).

5. Krishna Hachhethu, *Party Building in Nepal: Organization, Leadership and People* (Kathmandu: Mandala Book Point, 2002).

6. The major political parties nominated twenty-six members, largely their party cadres and supporters.

7. CPN (Maoist) changed its name to UCPN (Maoist) after it united with CPN (Unity Center–Masal) in January 2009.

8. Dr. K. I. Singh had been imprisoned for opposing the 1951 settlement between the king, Nepali Congress, and the Ranas brokered by India. He rebelled on January 21, 1952, from prison with the assistance of his supporters in the Rakshya Dal, the paramilitary police force formed from the military wing of the Nepali Congress during the rebellion against the Ranas. Bhuwan Lal Joshi and Leo E. Rose, *Democratic Innovations in Nepal: A Case Study of Political Acculturation* (Berkeley: University of California Press, 1966), 100–101.

9. Bhim Rawal, *Nepalma Samyabadi Andolanko: Adbhav Ra Bikash* [*Communist Movement in Nepal: Rise and Development*] (Kathmandu: Pairavi Prakashan, 1991), 36.

10. Narayan Khadka, "Factionalism in the Communist Movement in Nepal," *Pacific Affairs* 68, no. 1 (1995): 55–76; Rawal, *Nepalma Samyabadi Andolanko.*

11. In June 1975, it held a secret conference to establish the All-Nepal Revolutionary Coordination Committee (Marxist Leninist). It changed the name to CPN(ML) subsequently. Rawal, *Nepalma Samyabadi Andolanko.*

12. The party changed its name to Unified Communist Party of Nepal (Maoist) [UCPN (Maoist)] after it united with the Communist Party of Nepal (Unity Center–Masal) in January 2009. The radical faction that split in 2012, headed by Kiran, aka Mohan Baidya, has retained the old name of CPN (Maoist).

13. Susan Hangen, "Between Political Party and Social Movement: The Mongol National Organization and Democratization in Rural Nepal," *Contentious Politics and Democratization in Nepal*, ed. Mahendra Lawoti (New Delhi: Sage, 2007), 175–196.

14. Govinda Neupane, *Nepalko Jatiya Prashna: Samajik Banot Ra Sajhedariko Sambhawana* [*Nepal's National Question: Social Composition and Possibilities of Accommodation*] (Kathmandu: Center for Development Studies, 2000), 71.

15. Lynn Bennett, Bandita Sijapati, and Deepak Thapa, *Forging Equal Citizenship in a Multicultural Nepal*, unpublished manuscript, 2011, 276.

16. Dhruba Kumar, *Electoral Violence and Volatility in Nepal* (Kathmandu: Vajra Publications, 2010).

17. Rawal, *Nepalma Samyabadi Andolanko*; Khadka, "Factionalism in the Communist Movement in Nepal"; K. C. Surendra, *Nepalma Communist Andolanko Itihas* [*The History of Communist Movement in Nepal*] (Kathmandu: Vidhyarthi Pustak Bhandar, 1999).

18. Hachhethu, *Party Building in Nepal*, 50–51.

19. Krishna B. Bhattachan, "Manab Adhikar Ra Nepalko Pratibadhatta" (seminar organized by Nepal Foundation for Advanced Studies and Friedrich-Ebert Stiftung, Kathmandu, Nepal, 1999).

20. Rawal, *Nepalma Samyabadi Andolanko*, 37.

21. Rabindra Khanal, *Local Governance in Nepal: Democracy at Grassroots* (Kathmandu: Smriti, 2006).

22. Rawal, *Nepalma Samyabadi Andolanko*, 131.

23. See Mahendra Lawoti, "Bullets, Ballots and Bounty: Maoist Electoral Victory in Nepal," in *The Maoist Insurgency in Nepal: Revolution in the Twenty-First Century*, ed. Mahendra Lawoti and Anup Pahari (London: Routledge, 2010), 287–303; Kumar, *Electoral Violence and Volatility in Nepal*.

24. Staffan I. Lindberg, ed., *Democratization by Elections: A New Mode of Transition* (Baltimore: John Hopkins University Press, 2009).

25. L. F. Stiller, *The Rise of the House of Gorkha* (Ranchi: Patna Jesuit Society, 1973).

26. Vedananda Jha established the Nepal Tarai Party to raise the issues of the Madhesi in the early 1950s, but later he joined the Panchayat system, and the party was not revived.

Class and Identity Conflicts

Nepal recently settled the decade-long violent Maoist rebellion, but ethnic conflicts appear to be escalating. Episodic violent ethnic conflicts existed prior to the Maoist armed conflict but were largely ignored or were investigated superficially by the media, academia, and policy makers. Many ethnic, caste, and regional groups began mobilizing peacefully, demanding an end to discrimination and exclusion after the restoration of democracy in 1990, but since around the turn of the century, armed groups, some even demanding separatism, have sprouted in the south and east of Nepal.

The emergence of violent conflicts generated surprise for at least three reasons. First, Nepal had been portrayed as a peaceful Shangri-la where different ethnic groups and classes of people lived harmoniously. Second, the Maoist armed conflict expanded rapidly after the end of the Cold War, when communist governments and movements were in decline around the world. Third, democracy is supposed to manage conflicts and contestations peacefully through voting or peaceful lobbying and mobilization, but violent conflicts rose after democracy was restored in 1990. This chapter discusses the nature, causes, and consequences of the violent class and identity conflicts, beginning first with the Maoist rebellion.

The Maoist Rebellion[1]

The Maoist rebellion, launched by a small, extreme communist party in 1996, expanded rapidly. Almost all of the seventy-five districts in the country were affected within a decade.[2] During the armed conflict, around 15,000 people were killed, thousands were injured and displaced, and millions were affected psychologically, economically, and politically. Human rights groups accused both the Maoists and the security forces of gross human rights violations.

The Maoists initially attracted support by initiating popular activities like punishing moneylenders and local well-off people, whom they labeled as exploiters. Many opposing social and political activists also fell victim to their wrath. They increased their domination in many parts of the country by terrorizing people into submission with threats of dire consequences. The strategy worked because the state failed to provide the people with security.

The Maoists demanded a republic, an all-party government, a new Constituent Assembly election, and a new constitution. Other prominent issues they raised included class inequality, discrimination faced by marginalized ethnic/caste groups and women, and concerns about Nepal's sovereignty. The Maoists, however, strategically highlighted different demands during different periods, depending on context. Since the Maoists launched the rebellion when the parliamentary democracy was running, the overall objective of the Maoists was to form a Maoist communist state—a people's democracy. With the signing of a comprehensive peace accord, participation in an election in 2008, leadership of the government twice after 2008, and conclusion of the peace process in 2012, the Maoist establishment faction has at least formally given up on that objective. The important question is why and how a Maoist rebellion grew after 1990, defying the global trend of decline in the communist movement.

Economic Inequality and the Maoist Rebellion

If one surveys Nepal's national economic well-being and development indicators from the 1990s, more surprises await. The gross domestic product (GDP) in the mid-1990s increased compared to the mid-1980s, and the country's Human Development Index (HDI) ranking improved in 2001 compared to 1996.[3] Likewise, roads, schools, health facilities, banking, university, and other development sectors expanded in the 1990s.[4] If things appeared to be getting better in the 1990s and thereafter, why did a primarily class-based rebellion grow rapidly?

The literature on insurgency and civil strife identifies income inequality as a major cause of violent conflict.[5] Relative deprivation, or the gap between expected and achieved well-being, can increase alienation and push groups toward violent conflict. Despite some positive national indicators, the inequality dimension was relevant in Nepal, which was not only poor but had become a more unequal society in terms of material well-being. John Bray, Leiv Lunde, and S. Mansoob Murshed point out the relatively low-level HDI in the Maoist strongholds and significant inequality across districts in Nepal.[6]

In the 1990s, Nepal had become the most unequal country in South Asia. It had the highest Gini Index (0.426). Inequality, as measured by the Gini Index, was lower in the 1980s in Nepal (0.300) than in India (0.312), Sri Lanka (0.341), and Pakistan (0.326).[7] Growth in a few select areas and stagnation in others led to increases in inequality despite a rise in national HDI indicators.

Inequality in Nepal exists among different sectors—ethnic and caste groups, geographic regions, and rural and urban areas—as well as between genders. The stagnation of the rural regions during the 1970s was portrayed vividly in the book *Nepal in Crisis,* which shows the neglect of the rural regions, the increasing pressure on limited land in the hills, and the decline of traditional professions and sources of income.[8] Different economic and demographic indicators demonstrate the continuous neglect of the rural regions. Poverty levels were 33 percent in 1976–1977 but rose to 42 percent by 1995–1996. The "income share of the top 10 percent of the people increased from 21 percent in the mid-1980s to 35 percent by the mid-1990s, while the share of the bottom 40 percent shrank from 24 percent to 15 percent by the mid-1990s."[9]

Some regions in Nepal face greater inequality. Poverty levels are significantly higher in rural areas (44 percent) than in urban areas (20 percent). Poverty is also more widespread in the mountains, where the incidence is 56 percent, compared with around 40 percent in the hills and plains. The incidences of poverty in the rural central (67 percent) and mid- and far-western (72 percent) hills and mountains far outweigh those in eastern (28 percent) and western (40 percent) regions.[10]

The stagnation of agriculture had a more detrimental impact on rural residents (87 percent in 2001), who largely depend on it. Annual growth rates of agricultural output (major crops) declined from 1961–1962 to 1991–1993. The growth rate was –0.07 percent for all crops in Nepal during the period, whereas other South Asian countries witnessed an increase. The stagnation in agriculture was due to the government policy of import substitution industrialization, following which it attempted to industrialize urban areas at the cost of rural areas. This neglect occurred despite the importance of agriculture as a major source of employment and national income. According to Kishor Sharma, agriculture, in which more than 80 percent of the people are engaged, "has not received more than 26 percent of development expenditure in any development plan since the mid-1950s. . . . Nepal, which had the highest agriculture yield (per hectare) in South Asia in the early 1960s, fell significantly behind other countries by the early 1990s."[11]

Landownership patterns also contributed to poverty and inequality. Despite the relatively low levels of landownership, the inequality reflects the persistence of the feudal system: "44 percent of households in the country are marginal landowners [0–0.5 hectare], but this group only accounts for 14 percent of total privately owned agricultural land. In contrast, the 5 percent of agricultural households who own plots greater than 3 h[ectares] account for around 27 percent of total agricultural land."[12] Alan MacFarlane's ethnographic study also supports the pictures painted by the broad aggregate data. In a hill village in central Nepal, to which he has frequently returned for decades, a wage earner could buy a chicken with a day's wages in the late 1960s, whereas in the mid-1990s it took eight days' wages.[13]

The deregulation of the market since the mid-1980s led to an improvement in some economic indicators such as GDP, growth in output, and exports and international reserves. These were mainly brought about by an expansion of the urban-based modern sector and did not close the inequality gap. For instance, the nominal income of the people living in urban areas increased by 16 percent per annum (from US$126 to US$285) between 1988 and 1996, compared to only 4 percent for the rural population (from US$95 to US$125). Sharma argues that "when the average annual rate of inflation is taken into consideration, the growth in rural income is in fact negative. This not only increased poverty in the rural areas but also increased rural-urban inequality."[14] Large parts of the rural areas stagnated while the urban centers, especially the Kathmandu Valley, developed into centers of wealth. The growth in urban areas and stagnation in the rural areas may have further increased the perception of inequality among rural residents.[15]

The neglect of the rural regions and the poor by a centralized state is not news for a student of Nepali history. The Nepali state-building process involves extracting resources from the peasantry by the state and ruling groups.[16] The state gave land as *jagir* (compensation) and *birta* (tax-free land grants) to various central government and military functionaries as rewards or payment for their services. The peasantry had to turn in a large proportion of their products to these often distant landholders, who extracted as much as they could from the peasantry, often to build "stucco palaces." During wars the peasantry had to cough up extra taxes and provide free labor services for carrying weapons and war supplies.

State neglect of the peasants continued after the 1990 regime change, which, despite formally ushering in the fundamental rights of expression and organization, primarily ended up expanding the ruling group.[17] The state was still controlled by an elite caste that largely failed to represent the peasantry, the poor, and marginalized ethnic and caste groups. The needs and aspirations of the rural poor were rarely represented in the corridors of power and decision-making processes. Consequently deep economic inequality continued, as the elite monopolized economic resources through political domination.

The continued marginalization of the peasantry in the 1990s was ironic because one of the major political parties was communist (the Communist Party of Nepal [United Marxist Leninist], or CPN[UML]) and claimed to speak for the poor. However, which segments of the poor the CPN(UML) and other parliamentary communist parties represent is another question. In terms of other large mainstream parties, they represent the less well-off, but their core constituency is not the poorest of the poor. The trade unions, college students, and primary and high school teachers who form their core constituency belong to the relatively well-off strata in an impoverished country like Nepal. Only the village elite can send their children to college. The claim to represent the downtrodden is apparently not sufficient. The attraction of rural poor to the Maoist movement, which promised radical transformation and did take some actions to address the issues of poor and marginalized groups, shows that the parliamentary communist parties failed to retain the support of the poor. The inequalities in different sectors and regions and neglect of the periphery contributed to the dissatisfaction among the rural people, especially the youth, and created a fertile ground for the spread of the Maoist movement.

The Exclusionary Democratic Political Process

The majoritarian democracy Nepal adopted in 1990, ironically, contributed to the initiation and growth of the violent Maoist rebellion. The notion that the majority had the right to rule in whatever way it pleased, often abusing the state machinery and resources for partisan purposes, was prevalent in Nepal during the 1990s. Such a conceptualization and political culture reinforced a structure that provided little or no formal political power in governance to the opposition and encouraged the executive, on the other hand, to undermine other branches of state agencies and disregard other political actors. A consequence of power concentration in Nepal's patronage-based politics was that non-ruling-party politicians felt impotent due to their inability to influence policies and protect their turfs in a system in which the ruling party blatantly disbursed state resources for partisan purposes aimed at undermining their position.

While even the majoritarian democracy provided political space to opposition groups to dissent and mobilize, its winner-take-all nature denied the opposition a substantive role in governance. The ideological opposition groups and ethnic minorities utilized the political space to raise and create awareness about issues of concern to them, expand organizations, and mobilize to pressure governments to address problems. This raised the expectation of the poor and marginalized groups that their issues would be addressed. However, due to their lack of presence in governance, a majoritarian structure that denied a role to opposition and other branches and levels of government, and the partisan approach of the government, many demands were not addressed, and alienation among the groups increased.

The Maoists' predecessor, the Communist Party of Nepal (Unity Center) (CPN[UC]), participated in the first general elections in 1991 under its political front, the United People's Front Nepal, and won nine seats in the parliament. However, the Prachanda-led CPN(UC) faction boycotted the second parliamentary election in 1994 after it split from the Nirmal Lama–led faction and the Election Commission did not recognize its faction.[18] Events and activities between 1991 and 1996 contributed to pushing the Maoists toward a violent rebellion. First, as mentioned above, the winner-take-all political structure and culture did not give them a role in policy making and implementation. The Maoists began making demands of different governments beginning in the early 1990s and submitted a final forty-point list of demands to the Sher Bahadur Deuba government before they launched the insurgency. The different governments from 1991 to 1996 did not take the demands seriously. These experiences reinforced the Maoists sense of the uselessness of the parliamentary system.

Second, in local political tussles and conflicts in the Maoist stronghold of the western hills, the administration took the side of the party that controlled the center and persecuted the Maoist cadres, forcing them underground. These activities contributed to pushing the Maoists toward a violent movement.[19] Third, once the Maoists had decided to launch an insurgency, they were able to exploit the insensitivity of the state and other parties toward ethnic, caste, and gender issues to recruit members and expand the movement.

Significant numbers of people participated in the rebellion, showing their lack of faith in the ability or desire of the formal political process to address their needs and aspirations. This perception may have been fueled by the ruling political leaders and cadres' abuse of power, the growth of corruption at the local and central levels, and the insensitivity of those in power toward the weak, poor, and disadvantage groups, as well as the negative attitudes toward minorities demonstrated by the government and embedded in the constitution.

The Ethnic and Gender Dimensions of the Insurgency

As mentioned above, the exclusionary democratic process alienated marginalized groups, which subsequently participated in the armed conflict in significant numbers. The Maoist armed conflict saw much higher participation by indigenous nationalities, Dalits, and women (as well as the Madhesi in later years) than did mainstream political parties and the state.

The Maoist actively began to target, attract, and recruit members of the marginalized groups by recognizing and raising their problems and issues and taking action against untouchability, ethnic prejudice, and sexism. This generated a pull-push phenomenon: the ignorance of the state and other parties pushed the marginalized groups away, while the attention of the Maoists attracted the marginalized groups to the rebellion.

The Maoists incorporated into their demands those of marginalized groups, such as a secular state, the right to self-determination, ethnic autonomy, and an end to the imposition of Sanskrit in schools. The Maoists also formed ethnic/national fronts and declared autonomous provinces.

The mainstream political parties, ethnic political parties, and mainstream identity movements were not able to stop the flow of substantial marginalized groups to the Maoists. The mainstream political parties were largely ignorant and insensitive and did little to raise, address, or accommodate the marginalized groups' demands. The ethnic parties, on the other hand, despite raising the issues vociferously, were inexperienced, thus ineffective, and appeared unattractive and unviable as they had not been able to expand their organizations. The government largely ignored identity movements led by ethnic associations except to address less consequential demands. The failure of ethnic parties and identity movements to wrest substantive concessions from the state and dominant society alienated many marginalized groups from the democratic political process and pushed many toward the Maoists.

Weak, Divided, and Incapable State

The environment of a country can provide the conditions for a rebellion, but whether that rebellion grows and expands depends considerably on the strategies and actions of the actors pitted against each other—the state and the rebels. The state can repress civil strife using its coercive capability, even though successful repression may only postpone the conflict if the underlying causes are not addressed.[20] In Nepal, one could argue that the weak, divided, and incapable state also contributed to the growth of the Maoist rebellion.

Ironically, the Nepali state was ineffective due to the centralization of power in Kathmandu and within the executive at the center. Excessive concentration of power in the executive meant that its scope was wide, requiring it to stretch its time and resources over a wide range of sectors and activities, often making it difficult to focus on necessary, essential, and priority sectors and issues. At the same time, nonexecutive government branches and agencies had no effective power to formulate and execute public policies to address problems and ameliorate the conditions of the people. As a result the overall state was ineffective in fulfilling its tasks.

The presence of the Nepali state was weak in many rural areas, except in occasional schools, village development committee offices, agricultural-extension service centers, police posts, and banks. Local governments enjoyed very limited power despite the rhetoric of decentralization. The state did not provide significant services to the rural residents and hence probably did not command deep loyalty from the people. The weakness of the Nepali state can be shown by its initial reaction to the insurgency: when Maoists began attacking rural police posts and government offices, the state agencies were withdrawn to district centers and other safer areas, whereas the local governments collapsed with the Maoist threat. These withdrawals allowed the Maoists to consolidate their hold in rural regions with minimum effort. Even the people who opposed the Maoist ideology did not resist the rebels because the state could not guarantee their security.

The division of establishment political actors and institutions rendered the state further ineffective. The state initially did not deploy the army against the rebels as the king was reluctant to use it internally, despite the interest of the government in employing it. If the army had any chance of being effective against the rebels, it would have been in the initial stages of the rebellion, when the rebels had yet to develop their army. However, the ineffectiveness of the police—whose excesses may have in fact pushed some people into the Maoists' arms—suggests that the army, with less knowledge of the terrain and local networks, would have been effective. The political parties and the monarch did not develop a coherent policy toward the Maoists even after the rebels developed into a formidable force. The political parties, on the other hand, continued to use the rebellion as a partisan political tool to gain or remain in power. The cleavages within the establishment side further deepened when the king dismissed the elected government in 2002.

The incapability of the state can be demonstrated by describing the small Maoist army and its limited weaponry. According to security expert Ashok Mehta, the Maoists had few weapons, most of them looted from the police and the army. Including homemade guns, shotguns, and .22-caliber rifles, the Maoists had fewer than 3,000 weapons at the turn of the century. Magazine photos of Maoist army training show that not all combatants held arms. The arms submitted by the Maoists after the peace process approximate this number. This demonstrates that not every Maoist guerrilla had a weapon and raises the question of why an army of 90,000, along with additional police and armed forces, was not able to defeat the Maoists. Mehta argues that the Royal Nepal Army's ceremonial nature, lack of preparation for internal insurgencies, inexperience in war, and absence of motivation were some of the reasons for its failure to contain the Maoist rebellion.[21]

Violent Ideology, Agency, and Strategies of the Maoists

While the state demonstrated ineptitude, its enemy, the rebel Maoists, demonstrated a relatively higher level of capability and leadership in understanding national, international, and local conditions and developing appropriate strategies. The Maoists' call for an armed rebellion to address the problems of poverty, inequality, and discrimination attracted a large number of people. Why was the violent ideology so attractive to so many Nepalis? Historical analysis shows that all the major political forces had grown after engaging in armed movements. The CPN(UML) emerged as the largest communist party during the 1990s, after launching violent activities in the 1970s. Likewise, the Nepali Congress emerged as the largest party after it successfully led the armed anti-Rana movement in 1950–1951. The attraction to violent parties is probably due to some level of viability imparted to the organizations by extreme actions undertaken in furtherance of their promised goal of transformation in an extremely poor and unequal society.

The Maoist leaders contributed significantly to the growth of the rebellion as well through their commitment, farsightedness, and unity. They not only risked their lives but avoided party breakup for more than one and half decades, unlike most communist parties in Nepal and the Indian Maoists. Prachanda, the top leader, was skillful in balancing different factions and leaders and incorporating and co-opting issues raised by others into the official party line.

The Nepali Maoists formulated policies that brilliantly exploited the societal conditions and divisions among other political actors. At the societal level, in addition to class issues, they raised identity, cultural, and social issues to attract large numbers of indigenous nationalities, Dalits, and women. This turned out to be a brilliant strategy to fill their fighters' ranks. At the political level, the Maoists effectively exploited the fault lines and divisions among their enemies. Initially, the Maoists selectively attacked the cadres of the ruling Nepali Congress. The moderate communist factions and rightist groups did not care much about these attacks on their political opponents, who were abusing their political power. When the moderate Left formed the government, the Maoists began attacking their cadres. This turn of events pleased the Nepali Congress and the royalists. When the Maoists targeted the rightist cadres, the Nepali Congress and CPN(UML) seemed to be least bothered.

The competition and conflicts of interest within mainstream political forces kept the army from being mobilized until November 2001, after the Maoists attacked and looted substantial arms and ammunition in an attack on an army barracks. In the initial years of the rebellion, when the Maoists were much weaker, they avoided direct confrontation with the army.

The Maoists began to highlight their republican demands after King Gyanendra began intervening in politics. The mainstream political parties were allowed to operate more freely in rural areas by the Maoists after that. The political parties then moved closer to the Maoists. The Maoists expanded and grew due to their well-conceived plans and effective strategies; their strategies worked, however, because other actors played to their tune.

The Post-Peace-Settlement Maoists

The Maoist movement and the 2006 regime change brought significant transformations to Nepali society and politics: declaration of a republic and secular state, commitment to federalism, adoption of a proportional electoral method, election to the Constituent Assembly in 2008, increased representation of marginalized groups in the polity, and so on. Some of these transformations occurred due to direct Maoist mobilization; in other instances, they were assisted by Maoist support.

The Maoist movement has also brought about a degree of social transformation. The Maoists have contributed, to some extent, to undermining untouchability, ethnic prejudice, sexism, and political disempowerment of the poor and disadvantaged by challenging the status quo, traditional elite, patriarchy, and ethnic and caste domination. The Maoist impact on economic equality and welfare is less certain as the Maoists have not been able to push through their economic reform agendas, such as land redistribution.[22] The Unified Communist Party of Nepal (Maoist) adopted the line of peace and constitution in its seventh convention held in February 2013, leaving behind the people's revolt line and thus formally transforming into a nonviolent organization.

The Maoists are set to remain one of the major political parties, despite the hard-line faction's split. They have been less affected by the desertion of indigenous nationalities, as well as Muslims and Madhesi leaders and cadres, in 2012. The Maoists also benefit from the perception that they are the most sincere of the major political parties in terms of raising and addressing class- and identity-based problems.

National/Ethnic and Caste Conflict[23]

Nepal witnessed a rise in ethnic assertion, mobilization, and conflict after the armed Maoist conflict was settled. This has surprised many because Nepal was portrayed as a peaceful country where ethnic and caste groups lived harmoniously prior to the Maoist insurgency. Deeper analysis, however, reveals that ethnic conflicts, both peaceful and violent, have a long history in Nepal. As the conquering group began to impose its language, religion, culture, and dress nationally, assimilating some while portraying the rest as "other," the foundation for the conflict being witnessed today was laid.

The history of major violent ethnic resistance goes back to the last quarter of the eighteenth century, when the House of Gorkha was consolidating its domain. More than two dozen ethnic rebellions and violent conflicts occurred before 1990. The Limbu, Khambu, and Tamang rebelled violently, even though they were unsuccessful in reclaiming their territories.[24] Ethnic rebellions and protests lessened during the nineteenth century as the autocratic regime became consolidated and succeeded in repressing dissent and fostering assimilation. The decline in violent conflict as a state consolidates is typical of the state-building process. Interestingly, in Nepal many armed ethnic groups have appeared and grown in the last decade.

Incidences of violent ethnic and religious conflict increased after democracy was restored in 1990, but they were eclipsed by the Maoist rebellion, partly because they were less violent and did not directly threaten the state. The identity movements, which gained momentum and became more visible after 1990, fight for equal recognition of their language, religion, and culture, as well as for equal opportunities in the polity, economy, and society. The movements of the early 1990s were mostly peaceful in nature, but violent discourse and practice began increasing, partly due to frustration with the nonresponsive state and partly due to the demonstrated effects of the increasingly violent Maoist movement. Activists began to discuss taking up arms against the state if their demands went unmet. The initiation of violent discourse is significant because David Apter and colleagues argue that it legitimizes violence when it occurs.[25]

Two types of violent ethnic conflict have appeared in Nepal over the last six decades. One type, involving armed ethnic groups, is a new phenomenon that began to appear in the late 1990s and mushroomed after the turn of the century, with some of these groups even demanding separation from Nepal. The Ministry of Home Affairs, in August 2009, listed 109 armed organizations active in Nepal. Many of the names on the list, however, included criminal groups and even radical political parties represented in the Constituent Assembly. Nevertheless, a large number of armed groups were operating at the time, especially in the Tarai and eastern hills, demanding autonomy or separation. Several Hindu extremist and monarchy-supporting armed groups were also active. In June 2011, the government claimed that only twenty-six groups remained active, and by September 2012 the Home Ministry claimed that only ten armed groups were operating in the eastern hills and Tarai.

The second type of violent ethnic conflict is relatively more spontaneous in nature and involves different identity groups (religious, ethnic, regional). Table 28.1 shows that many violent ethnic riots and conflicts occurred after 1951, mostly during the democratic period (the list does not include the activities of armed rebel groups). We next discuss the violent conflicts associated with different groups.

TABLE 28.1 Nonarmed Groups' Violent (Ethnic, Religious, and Caste) Conflicts Since 1951

Year	Event	Locality/Region
1950–1951 (East)	Kiranti rebellion	Majh and Pallo Kirant
1956–1957	Movement against making Nepali the only language of instruction	Tarai
1958–1959	Desecration of mosque, arson, and looting against Muslims	Bhawarpur, Mahotari
1960	Hindu-Muslim riots—two burned to death, one hundred houses set on fire	Adhyanpur, Mahotari
1960–1961	Tamang rebellion	Nuwakot
1971	Hindu-Muslim riots due to the murder of a Muslim on cow-slaughter charge	Bara, Rautahat
Oct. 1992	Desecration of mosque, violence by Muslims, Hindu-Muslim riots during Deepawali	Tulsipur, Dang, Nepalganj
Nov. 3–4, 1994	Hindu-Muslim riots during parliamentary election	Nepalganj
Dec. 3–9, 1994	Hindu-Muslim riots during well renovation at a temple	Nepalganj
Oct. 25–28, 1995	Brawl between Muslim vegetable vendor and Hindu customer, which snowballed into Hindu-Muslim riots during Deepawali	Nepalganj
May 1997	Hindu-Muslim riots during local elections	Nepalganj
Dec. 26–27, 2000	Pahadi-Madhesi (Hritik Roshan) riots	Kathmandu, eastern and central Tarai
Sept. 1, 2004	Riots against Muslims (reactions against killings of Nepalis in Iraq)	Kathmandu
Dec. 2006	Madhesi-Pahadi riots after a bandh called by Nepal Goodwill Party	Nepalganj
Sept. 16, 2007	Madhesi-Pahadi riots after a Muslim civil defense leader Moid Khan	Kapilvastu
Sept. 21, 2007	Hindu-Muslim riots—spillover of September 16 incident with Muslim shops looted and houses vandalized	Tulsipur, Dang

Source: Lawoti (2012).

Group-Related Conflicts in the Modern Era

Indigenous Nationalities Rebellions

The indigenous nationalities began to engage in sporadic violent activities from 1950 to 1951. The Limbu in the far-eastern and Rai/Khambu in mid-eastern regions were involved in unorganized violent rebellion against exploitation by the high-caste Hindus during 1950–1951. Some of the groups demanded their own states. The Tamang of central Nepal engaged in violent activities against the high-caste group in 1960–1961 (see Table 28.1).

During the early 1990s, the indigenous nationalities mobilized peacefully, demanding a secular state, federalism, proportional representation, linguistic equality, and so on. When most of their demands were ignored, some began to engage in violent conflict. The Khambuwan National Front formed in the early 1990s and came to attention after it launched an ethnic rebellion demanding autonomy for the Khambuwan in 1997. It eventually merged with the Maoists but broke from them to form the Kirat Workers Party. The group's activities resulted in deaths, kidnappings, extortion, and the destruction of public property. The Mongol National Organization (MNO) threatened violent rebellion and announced the formation of an army after the turn of the century.

After the peace settlement with the Maoists, some indigenous groups, like the Tharus, Tamangs, and Khambus/Rais, have demonstrated "armies," or armed contingents, to the media; except for the Kirat Workers Party, other indigenous groups have not engaged in armed rebellion. After 2006 several Limbu political parties and factions maintained armies and army camps, but they no longer claim to have "armies," just a Limbu volunteer force that provides security during public meetings, enforces party-called *bandhs,* and so forth. Though most Limbu organizations seek autonomy, the Pallo Kirat Limbuwan Rashtriya Manch (Pallo Kirat Limbuwan National Forum) declared Limbuwan an independent state on March 23, 2008, arguing that the end of the monarchy voided the agreement the Limbus had made with King Prithvi Narayan Shah to remain under the House of Gorkha. The group is largely inactive and in decline after the Nepali state took security actions against its cadres and leaders, many of whom were imprisoned or fled into exile in Sikkim and other parts of India. Even though separatist organizations have not been able to get traction among the people, the autonomy movements of the indigenous groups have gained considerable momentum, with the movements stronger on the eastern side of the country. The support base is not confined to group members but even includes members of dominant groups in areas like Limbuwan.

Madhesi Violent Conflicts: Riots, Movement Violence, and Armed Groups

Madhesi-related violence and deaths have occurred in three ways. First, riots and violent confrontations have occurred when the Madhesi have launched movements for their rights. Second, relatively spontaneous riots have also affected the Madhesi. Third, armed Madhesi groups have launched rebellions that have resulted in killings, kidnappings, torture, and extortion.

The first recorded riots involving Madhesis occurred when they launched protests opposing the imposition of Khas-Nepali as a medium of instruction in public schools in the late 1950s. The yearlong movement resulted in occasional riots in 1957.[26] Around fifty people died during the three-week Madhesi movement launched in January 2007 against the interim constitution. In March 2007, conflict between the Madhesi People's Rights Forum (MPRF), a nonarmed Madhesi group, and the Maoists, who had convened a meeting at the same venue, resulted in the killing of more than two dozen Maoist activists.

The Madhesi fell victim to riots targeted against them in December 2000 in Kathmandu and a few other areas with predominantly hill-origin residents after rumors spread that an Indian actor had criticized Nepal. Hill-versus-Madhesi riots occurred in Nepalganj in December 2006 when the hill-origin administration turned a blind eye to attacks on the Madhesi and their property.

Armed Madhesi organizations began to appear in 2005 when Jay Krishna Goit, Nagendra Kumar Paswan, aka Jwala Singh, and Shambhu Prasad Yadav broke away from the Maoists and formed their own organization. The Janatantrik Tarai Mukti Morcha was formed by Goit, but it split into Paswan and a number of other factions. More than three dozen armed groups, such as the Madhesi Tigers and the Tarai Cobra, operated in 2008 and 2009 in much higher numbers than the indigenous nationalities. The Madhesi armed groups were engaged in higher numbers of violent activities as well. For example, the Madhesi groups killed 108 people in 2007, while the indigenous and Hindu armed groups killed only a few people. Some of the groups have demanded separation. The armed groups' numbers and activities appear to be on the decline, partly due to state security actions but also because the Madhesi have been able to influence the state from 2008 to 2012 as coalition partners.

Dalit and Minority Religious Groups: Victims of Violence

While the indigenous nationalities and the Madhesi, despite suffering state violence, have launched countermovements against the state dominated by the Caste Hill Hindu elite (CHHE), Dalits and minority religious groups have largely been victims of state discrimination and societal attacks. Hindu-Muslim conflicts have been recorded in modern Nepal since 1958–1959 when a mosque was desecrated and Muslims were attacked in Mahotari district. Mahotari district again witnessed Hindu-Muslim conflicts in 1960 when two persons were burned to death and more than one hundred houses were set on fire. The next Hindu-Muslim riots occurred in Bara, Rautahat, in 1971, when a Muslim was killed based on allegations of cow slaughter.

After that, there was a lull in Hindu-Muslim violent conflict, which began to occur again after the opening up of the polity in 1990. Several Hindu-Muslim conflicts, riots targeting the Muslim community, and riots involving the Muslims occurred after 1990. Nepalganj witnessed five violent conflicts between Hindus and Muslims from 1992 to 1997. In September 2004, violent mobs attacked Muslim places of worship, businesses, and properties in Kathmandu. A Madhesi hill conflict spilled over into an attack against the Muslims on September 21, 2007, in Dang and Butwal.

Christian priests and places of worship have been attacked after the 2006 regime change, even though no riots against Christians have occurred. A Christian priest was murdered in eastern Nepal in 2008, while a Catholic Church in Lalitpur was bombed by the Nepal Defense Army, an underground Hindu organization, in 2009. The Shiva Sena Nepal was active in inciting violence against Muslims in Nepalganj in the 1990s, while the Nepal Defense Army has been involved in some of the violent activities against Muslims and Christians in the last decade.

The Dalits, on the other hand, have fallen victim to everyday structural violence through the practice of untouchability, which is still pervasive though it has declined to some degree. Dalits have been beaten for touching the food of higher-caste Hindus, denied drinking water from taps and other public water sources used by high-caste group members, and even killed for allegedly not washing the cups they have drunk from in tea shops. Even in Kathmandu, Dalits often have to hide their identities to rent apartments. They have been punished and their businesses boycotted in Kathmandu when they have disobeyed the societal norms of not accessing water at the same time as high-caste members.[27]

To date, Dalits have not launched violent campaigns on their own initiative. Many Dalits supported the violent Maoist rebellion, and the Dalit Liberation Front sided with the hard-line group when the Maoists split in 2012. A Dalit organization announced the establishment of an armed group, but its activities are unknown.

Since the 1990s Dalits have engaged in many public protests and movements, demanding to be allowed to enter Hindu temples, sell milk to dairies, use water from public taps and wells, and refuse to engage in traditional work such as carcass disposal. Many of these activities led to conflict with members of local dominant groups.

Challenging Ethnic Domination

Ethnic conflicts have resulted in Nepal either due to protest against CHHE hegemony, especially after the polity opened up in 1990, or when the dominant group and the state it controlled attempted to repress minority groups. After the formation of the Nepali state, the CHHE consolidated its domination over the state and society, and that ethnic domination has been the major cause of violent ethnic conflicts.

The CHHE monopoly extends to almost all spheres, including the political, economic, social, and cultural, and a description of this domination will help to clarify why some groups rebel and others become victims of violence.[28] Govinda Neupane found that the CHHE overwhelmingly dominated twelve influential sectors he investigated in 1999: the executive, the judiciary, constitutional councils, the civil administration, the parliament, political party leaderships, local government leaderships, and the leaderships of industrial and commercial, academic, professional, cultural, science and technology, and civil society associations.[29] After a decade, the marginalized groups have achieved higher representation in political sectors like the Constituent Assembly (2008–2012) and the cabinet (which are, however, still led by CHHE), but the nonpolitical sectors, like the judiciary, show little progress, and the gap appears to be widening in the top positions of the bureaucracy.[30]

The domination extends beyond the state to even the mainstream civil society. The CHHE and Newars dominated around 90 percent of the top positions in prominent Nepali nongovernmental organizations and human rights groups in 1999.[31] Praytoush Onta and Shekhar Parajuli found that the CHHE made up 80 percent of media elite (editors, publishers, and columnists).[32] Despite challenges, CHHE domination in mainstream media and other civil society organs persists. For example, in 2008, not a single Dalit, Muslim, or non-Newar indigenous nationality was an editor of one of the top forty daily, weekly, and bimonthly print publications ranked by the Nepal Press Council.

In addition to political, social, and economic domination, marginalized groups also face discrimination in the cultural sphere, formally as well as informally. Even economically well-off groups, like the Newars and Thakalis, face cultural, religious, and linguistic discrimination. The Hindu state discriminated against religious minorities for a long time, and informal and formal Hindu domination continues even after the state has been declared secular. Khas-Nepali has been given special privileges, whereas other native languages have not received comparable support. Citizenship discrimination occurred based on racial markers and gender. More than 3 million adult Nepalis, mostly Madhesis but also Dalits, indigenous nationalities, and others, were denied citizenship prior to 2007.[33]

Cultural imperialism, or imposition of the dominant group's language, religion, and values on the rest of the society, is a consequence as well as a cause of ethnic domination. The CHHE perform better in schools taught in their native language, and their social standing is enhanced because their culture and values have been projected as superior by the state. Likewise, the poor CHHE receive opportunities for social mobility from central policies. For instance, a poor, hard-working Bahun boy can get free residential education in Sanskrit up to the PhD level fully supported by the state, while similar opportunities are not provided to members of other linguistic groups.

Even though representation for marginalized groups did not increase during the 1990s and their major problems and demands went unaddressed, they began to organize and mobilize using the political space obtained in 1990. They generated awareness among community members, expanded organization, and made demands of the state. By the end of the 1990s, however, the lack of positive response from the state had generated alienation among many members of the marginalized groups. Some of the marginalized groups began to support and participate in the violent Maoist rebellion, while other alienated members formed their own armed groups and launched armed struggle against the state.

Monoethnic State to Polyethnic Polity

Nepal is slowly moving from a monoethnic to a polyethnic polity, even though the dominant groups are resisting through the media, the bureaucracy, and the political parties they control. Whether the ethnic conflicts will be managed depends on whether the country fully transforms into a polyethnic polity. The declaration of the state as secular, its transformation from a Hindu kingdom into a republic, affirmative action policies, and adoption of proportional representation as the electoral method all point to that direction, but the all-important tool to make Nepal truly multicultural, identity-based federalism, has not materialized yet due to the resistance of the dominant groups. If autonomy is granted to various groups, they will have less reason to mobilize, and conflict will possibly lessen. But if autonomy is denied, they will have a strong reason to mobilize, which could increase the possibility of violent ethnic conflicts.

SUGGESTED READINGS

Bhattachan, Krishna B. "Ethnopolitics and Ethnodevelopment." In *State, Politics, and Leadership in Nepal,* edited by Dhruba Kumar, 127–147. Kathmandu: CNAS, 1995.

Bista, Dor Bahadur. *Fatalism and Development: Nepal's Struggle for Modernization.* Hyderabad: Orient Longman, 1991.

Blaikie, Piers, John Cameron, and David Seddon. *Nepal in Crisis: Growth and Stagnation at the Periphery.* Delhi: Oxford, 1980.

Brown, T. Louise. *The Challenge to Democracy in Nepal.* London: Routledge, 1996.

Caplan, Lionel. *Land and Social Change in East Nepal.* Rev. ed. Kathmandu: Himal, 2000.

Dastider, Mollica. "Muslim Mobilization and the State in Nepal." *European Bulletin of Himalayan Research* 18 (2000): 20–35.

Deraniyagala, Sonali. "The Political Economy of Civil Conflict in Nepal." *Oxford Development Studies* 33, no. 1 (2005): 47–62.

Gaige, Frederick H. *Regionalism and National Unity in Nepal.* Delhi: Vikas, 1975.

Gellner, David N. *Resistance and the State: Nepalese Experience.* New Delhi: Social Science Press, 2003.

Gellner, David N., Joanna Pfaff-Czarnecka, and John Whelpton, eds. *Nationalism and Ethnicity in a Hindu Kingdom: The Politics of Culture in Contemporary Nepal.* Amsterdam: Harwood Academic, 1997.

Hangen, Susan I. *The Rise of Ethnic Politics in Nepal: Democracy in the Margins.* London: Routledge, 2010.

Holmberg, David. "Violence, Non-violence, Sacrifice, Rebellion, and the State." *Studies in Nepali History and Society* 11, no. 1 (2006): 31–64.

Hutt, Michael, ed. *Himalayan People's War: Nepal's Maoist Rebellion.* Bloomington: Indiana University Press, 2004.

Kumar, Dhruba, ed. *Domestic Conflict and Crises of Governability in Nepal.* Kathmandu: CNAS, 2000.

———. "Proximate Causes of Conflict in Nepal." *Contributions to Nepalese Studies* 32, no. 1 (2003): 51–93.

Lawoti, Mahendra, ed. *Contentious Politics and Democratization in Nepal.* Los Angeles: Sage, 2007.

———. *Towards a Democratic Nepal: Inclusive Political Institutions for a Multicultural Society.* New Delhi: Sage, 2005.

Lawoti, Mahendra, and Susan Hangen, eds. *Nationalism and Ethnic Conflict in Nepal: Identities and Mobilization After 1990.* London: Routledge, 2012

Lawoti, Mahendra, and Anup Pahari, eds. *The Maoist Insurgency in Nepal: Revolution in the Twenty-First Century.* London: Routledge, 2010.

Lecomte-Tilouine, Marie, and Pascal Dolfus, eds. *Ethnic Revival and Religious Turmoil.* New Delhi: Oxford University Press, 2003.

Maddox, Bryan. "Language Policy, Modernist Ambivalence, and Social Exclusion: A Case Study of Rupendehi District in Nepal's Tarai." *Studies in Nepali History and Society* 8, no. 2 (2003): 205–224.

Mehta, Ashok K. *The Royal Nepal Army: Meeting the Maoist Challenge.* New Delhi: Rupa, 2005.

Mishra, Chaitanya. "Locating the 'Causes' of the Maoist Struggle." *Studies in Nepali History and Society* 9, no. 1 (2004): 3–56.

NESAC. *Nepal Human Development Report 1998.* Kathmandu: NESAC, 1998.

Neupane, Govinda. *Nepalko Jatiya Prashna: Samajik Banot Ra Sajhedariko Sambhawana* [*Nepal's National Question: Social Composition and Possibilities of Accommodation*]. Kathmandu: Center for Development Studies, 2000.

Onta, Praytoush, and Shekhar Parajuli, eds. *Nepali Mediama Dalit Ra Janajati.* Kathmandu: Ekta, 2001–2002.

Pradhan, Kumar. *The Gorkha Conquests: The Process and Consequences of the Unification of Nepal, with Particular Reference to Eastern Nepal.* Calcutta: Oxford, 1991.

Regmi, Mahesh C. *Kings and Political Leaders of the Gorkhali Empire, 1768–1814*. Hyderabad: Orient Longman, 1995.

———. *Thatched Huts and Stucco Palaces: Peasants and Landlords in 19th-Century Nepal*. New Delhi: Vikash, 1978.

———. *Land Tenure and Taxation in Nepal*. Vol. 3: *The Jagir, Rakam, and Kipat Tenure Systems*. Berkeley, CA: Institute of International Studies, 1965.

Sijapati, Megan Adamson. *Islamic Revival in Nepal: Religion and a New Nation*. London: Routledge, 2010.

Thapa, Deepak, and Bandita Sijapati. *A Kingdom Under Siege: Nepal's Maoist Insurgency, 1996 to 2003*. Kathmandu: Printhouse, 2003.

NOTES

1. This section draws on Mahendra Lawoti, "Evolution and the Growth of the Maoist Insurgency in Nepal," in *The Maoist Insurgency in Nepal: Revolution in the Twenty-First Century* (London: Routledge, 2010).

2. By 2004, only Mustang and Manang, two mountainous districts inhabited by indigenous nationalities, had no insurgency-related deaths.

3. Sharma, Kishor, "The Political Economy of Civil War in Nepal," *World Development* 34, no. 7 (2006): 1237–1253.

4. Ram Sharan Mahat, *In Defense of Democracy: Dynamics and Fault Lines of Nepal's Political Economy* (New Delhi: Adroit Publishers, 2005).

5. Edward N. Muller and Mitchell A. Seligson, "Inequality and Insurgency," *American Political Science Review* 81, no. 2 (1987), 425–451; Ted Robert Gurr, "A Causal Model of Civil Strife: A Comparative Analysis Using New Indices," *American Political Science Review* 62, no. 4 (1968): 1104–1124.

6. John Bray, Leiv Lunde, and S. Mansoob Murshed, "Economic Drivers in Nepal's Maoist Insurgency," in *Political Economy of Armed Conflict Beyond Greed and Grievance*, ed. Karen Ballentine and Kake Sherman (Boulder, CO: Lynne Rienner, 2003).

7. Udaya R. Wagle, *Inclusive Democracy and Economic Inequality in South Asia: Any Discernible Link?* (Kalamazoo: School of Public Affairs and Administration, Western Michigan University, 2006).

8. Piers Blaikie, John Cameron, and David Seddon, *Nepal in Crisis: Growth and Stagnation at the Periphery* (Delhi: Oxford, 1980).

9. Sharma Kishor, "The Political Economy of Civil War in Nepal," 1245.

10. Sonali Deraniyagala, "The Political Economy of Civil Conflict in Nepal," *Oxford Development Studies* 33, no. 1 (2005): 52.

11. Kishor Sharma, "The Political Economy of Civil War in Nepal," 1241–1242.

12. Land ownership, on the other hand, may hide poverty in the hills and mountains: "Over 40 percent of medium and large landowners in the hills were classified as 'poor' in 1996" (Deraniyagala, "Political Economy," 54–55).

13. Alan Macfarlane, "Sliding Down Hill: Some Reflections on Thirty Years of Change in a Himalayan Village," *European Bulletin of Himalayan Research* 20, no. 1 (2001): 105–123.

14. Sharma, "The Political Economy of Civil War in Nepal," 1242–1243.

15. Deraniyagala, "Political Economy."

16. Mahesh C. Regmi, *Land Tenure and Taxation in Nepal*, Vol. 3: *The Jagir, Rakam, and Kipat Tenure Systems* (Berkeley, CA: Institute of International Studies, 1965); Mahesh C. Regmi, *Thatched Huts and Stucco Palaces: Peasants and Landlords in 19th-Century Nepal* (New Delhi: Vikash, 1978).

17. T. Louise Brown, *The Challenge to Democracy in Nepal* (London: Routledge, 1996).

18. In contrast, another extremist communist group boycotted the 1991 elections but participated in the subsequent elections.

19. Deepak Thapa and Bandita Sijapati, *A Kingdom Under Siege: Nepal's Maoist Insurgency, 1996 to 2003* (Kathmandu: Printhouse, 2003); Mahendra Lawoti, *Towards a Democratic Nepal: Inclusive Political Institutions for a Multicultural Society* (New Delhi: Sage, 2005).

20. Ted Robert Gurr, *Minorities at Risk? A Global View of Ethnopolitical Conflicts* (Washington, DC: United States Institute of Peace Press, 1993).

21. Ashok K. Mehta, *The Royal Nepal Army: Meeting the Maoist Challenge* (New Delhi: Rupa, 2005).

22. Mahendra Lawoti and Anup Pahari, "Violent Conflict and Change: Costs and Benefits of the Maoist Rebellion in Nepal," in *The Maoist Insurgency in Nepal: Revolution in the Twenty-First Century*, ed. Mahendra Lawoti and Anup Pahari (London: Routledge, 2010), 304–326.

23. This section draws on Mahendra Lawoti, "Dynamics of Mobilization: Varied Trajectories of Dalit, Indigenous Nationalities and Madhesi Movements," and "Transforming Ethnic Politics, Transforming the Nepali Polity: From Peaceful Nationalist Mobilization to the Rise of Armed Separatist Groups," in *Nationalism and Ethnic Conflict in Nepal: Identities and Mobilization After 1990*, ed. Mahendra Lawoti and Susan Hangen (London: Routledge, 2012).

24. Kumar Pradhan, *The Gorkha Conquests: The Process and Consequences of the Unification of Nepal, with Particular Reference to Eastern Nepal* (Calcutta: Oxford, 1991); Mahesh C. Regmi, *Kings and Political Leaders of the Gorkhali Empire, 1768–1814* (Hyderabad: Orient Longman, 1995); Mahendra Lawoti, "Contentious Politics in Democratizing Nepal," in *Contentious Politics and Democratization in Nepal*, ed. Mahendra Lawoti (New Delhi: Sage, 2007), 17–47; Neupane Govinda Neupane, *Nepali Samajko Rupantaran [Transformation in Nepali Society]* (Kathmandu: Center for Development Studies, 2001), lists over a dozen peasant resistances and half a dozen student mobilizations between 1950 and 1990 that were often brutally repressed.

25. David Apter, ed., *The Legitimization of Violence* (New York: New York University Press, 1997).

26. Frederick H. Gaige, *Regionalism and National Unity in Nepal* (Delhi: Vikas, 1975).

27. Sambridhi Kharel, "The Struggle for Full Citizenship for Dalits in Nepal: Approaches and Strategies of Dalit Activists," *Himalaya* 27, no. 1–2 (2007): 55–69.

28. This section draws on Mahendra Lawoti, *Looking Back, Looking Forward: Centralization, Multiple Conflicts and Democratic State Building in Nepal* (Washington, DC: East-West Center, 2007).

29. Govinda Neupane, *Nepalko Jatiya Prashna: Samajik Banot Ra Sajhedariko Sambhawana [Nepal's National Question: Social Composition and Possibilities of Accommodation]* (Kathmandu: Center for Development Studies, 2000).

30. Mahendra Lawoti, "Ethnic Politics and Building of an Inclusive State," in *Nepal in Transition: From People's War to Fragile Peace*, ed. Sebastian von Einsiedel, David M. Malone, and Suman Pradhan (Cambridge, MA: Cambridge University Press, 2012).

31. Neupane, *Nepalko Jatiya Prashna*.

32. Praytoush Onta and Shekhar Parajuli, eds., *Nepali Mediama Dalit Ra Janajati* (Kathmandu: Ekta, 2001–2002).

33. Dhanpati Upadhaya, *Report of the High Level Citizenship Commission—2051* (Kathmandu: HMG Nepal, 1995).

29

Modernization and Development: Problems and Prospects

Although Nepal is making some progress on its economic and social fronts, it is still a poor county. According to the United Nations Development Programme, its gross national income per capita in purchasing power parity was US$1,160 in 2011.[1] Its Human Development Index ranking was 157 out of 187 countries in the world, life expectancy was 68.8 years, and the adult (ages fifteen and older) literacy rate was 59.1 percent in 2011. The infant (under one year) mortality rate was 41 per 1,000 in 2010, and the under-five mortality rate was 55 per 1,000 in 2007.[2] Much of the Nepali population suffers from serious malnutrition. According to the World Bank, about 47 percent of children under five are stunted, 15 percent are wasted, and 36 percent are underweight. Nepal, however, has been trying to overcome the problem of poverty through economic development and modernization.

Late Start in Modernization

Nepal began its modernization attempts late in the 1950s. At the time of independence from the Ranas in 1951, Nepal possessed no significant infrastructure for modernization. There was no drivable road linking Nepal to the outside world, only a few industries existed, literacy was at 5 percent between 1952 and 1954, and only twenty-five telephone lines existed in the country.

The dismal level of infrastructure and development at the time was due to the Rana regime's policy of not promoting economic development for fear of rebellion against its autocratic rule. It restricted establishment of schools for fear of raising awareness. The regime limited outside contact to maintain control over the population. It was a regime that did not care about the welfare of its subjects. It extracted resources from peasants to support its members' luxurious lifestyles and to build palaces but did not invest back in the country and its people. Ironically, a country that was not colonized did not build infrastructure before 1950, while the colonizing British built infrastructure, such as the railway and postal system and higher educational institutions, across the country in India.

Since 1956 Nepal has launched various economic-development plans. It has expanded its roads, airports, and postal services, enhanced its power-generation capacity, and increased irrigation facilities. Nepal has also built several higher educational institutions to develop technically skilled human resources and has improved its health-care facilities.

Nepal has received economic and development aid from its two giant neighbors, India and the People's Republic of China, which compete to woo the Himalayan kingdom. In addition, Nepal has benefited from development assistance provided by the United States, Japan, and the former Soviet Union. Despite these efforts, Nepal's economic growth remains dismal. According to the World Bank's *World Development Report* for 1987, "Nepal's economic growth on a per capita basis was only 0.1 percent per year during 1965–85, with a per capita income of $160 in 1985, the fifth lowest in the world." The 1995 per capita income was reported to be $200, whereas in 2006 it was $290. Nepal's growth in gross domestic product (GDP) per capita in 2005 was 0.7 percent. As a result of this dismal performance, Nepal's attempts have been termed "failed development."[3]

Recent economic indicators suggest that Nepal may have begun to perform better, especially with the settlement of the decade-long Maoist armed conflict. Its GDP growth rate was 3.8 percent in 2011 and projected to be almost 5 percent in 2012. Its Gini coefficient (based on expenditure), the measure of inequality, has declined from 41 to 35 between 2003–2004 and 2010–2011.[4]

Problems in Modernization and Development

Nepal's long-term economic-development prospects depend on democratic state building, political stability, agricultural development, modernization, and the cooperation of its neighbors. The path toward modernization and development has not been easy for Nepal. Various factors have hindered its attempts. Historical factors, mentioned above, played a role. The lack of infrastructure meant that Nepal had to start from the ground up. Absence of educational institutions and low literacy rates meant that Nepal lacked human resources and the institutions to produce them. Hence Nepal had to overcome a vicious circle of constraints.

Geographic factors also contributed to Nepal's underdevelopment. Three-fourths of the country is mountainous, and the northern mountains are very rugged and steep. Good agricultural land is limited, and irrigation is difficult. Further, due to the ruggedness of the territory, the development cost per unit of area is high. Population settlements are dispersed throughout the mountains and hills, also increasing the cost of providing services. Infrastructure-development costs increase because of the need for bridges and so on. The cost of imports and exports is high due to large transportation costs.

The landlocked condition of the country has also hampered development. Nepal is practically surrounded by India, and the massive Himalayan range and valleys that border China (Tibet Autonomous Region) make travel and trade with China difficult and limited. Sea access via China is distant and not feasible. Though the open border with India has facilitated movement, it has also promoted smuggling. And since it has to conduct trade with other countries via Indian roads and ports, Nepal has to rely on the goodwill of the Indian government. This condition has allowed India to negotiate favorably in its dealings with Nepal, often to the detriment of Nepali interests. As a result Nepal has been a backwater market for India. Nepal is flooded with Indian goods, but India often hampers the export of Nepali goods to its territories. Thus the Nepali manufacturing sector and industrialization policy have been affected negatively. In the words of some critics, Nepal was a semicolony of India during the British Empire, and it remains so.[5]

Sociologists have also pointed to the fatalistic attitude of the society as a cause of underdevelopment. Dor Bahadur Bista has argued that the caste system, which provides status and privilege to high-caste citizens and socializes people in caste-based norms, has eroded the work culture. People think that their current position is due to a past life.[6] The ascriptive caste system also denies a large segment of the people equal opportunities to develop and contribute to national economic growth. Fatalistic and deterministic caste-based attitudes mean that achievement and work-oriented values receive less importance, resulting in the inculcation of clerical, and not entrepreneurial, values among educated sections of the society.

Development Policies

Nepal adopted mixed development policies in the mid-1950s with the initiation of five-year plans. The state established large corporations to produce and distribute goods and monitored the private sector through the licensing of small-scale enterprises. The government established cement factories, agricultural-implement industries, a national airline, brick factories, and a national trading center. The private sector was allowed to operate small industries, but the mandatory licensing process was cumbersome. The industrialization policy was based on the principle of import substitution—producing goods and services in the country to become self-reliant.

The focus on industrialization led to neglect of the agricultural sector. No five-year plan spent more than 26 percent of the development budget on agriculture, which accounted for more than 80 percent of employment. Hence the agricultural growth rate did not meet the population growth rate. A net agricultural export country in the 1960s, Nepal had become a net importer of food products by the 1980s.[7]

The industrialization policies failed to make the country self-reliant in manufactured products. Due to the licensing system, free competition did not occur, inefficiency grew, and many corporations lost money. They had to be sustained by state subsidies, resulting in an increased national debt. In the mid-1980s the state had to borrow from the International Monetary Fund and the World Bank to address the deficit problem. The agencies attached a condition for structural adjustment on the loans they forwarded, and the country was forced to begin a liberalization process in the mid-1980s.[8]

Economic liberalization, initiated in 1985 and expanded in the early 1990s, increased the economy's efficiency in some sectors. Private domestic airlines, which went into operation after the promulgation of the open-air policy in the early 1990s, provide reliable services to more destinations, reversing the inadequacy and unreliability of previous years. Total passengers on domestic flights increased from 228,000 in 1989–1990 to 1.209 million in 2002–2003.[9] The banking sector also improved dramatically. The number of commercial banks, development banks, insurance providers, finance companies, and savings and credit cooperatives increased, and the economy grew. There were 148 financial institutions in 2004, compared to 73 in 2000 and 5 in 1990. With regard to commercial banks, 17 were operating in 2004 compared to 13 in 2000 and 5 in 1990.[10] By the end of 2008, over twenty-five banks, fifty-eight development banks, and seventy-nine finance companies had been established.[11] Liberalization also benefited the education sector. Educational opportunities expanded at all levels. Approximately thirty engineering colleges and a dozen medical colleges, most of them established through private initiatives after 1990, provided higher technical education.[12] Liberalization also resulted in the availability of affordable consumer goods. These varieties of goods would never be available under a state-controlled or mixed economy. Opportunities to engage in different entrepreneurial activities also expanded. The expanded economy resulted in more jobs.

The picture painted by market reforms and their impact on the economy, however, is not entirely rosy. Business in Nepal has historically relied on trade, and this has resulted in less focus on the industrial and service sectors. Nepal's private sector, historically closely tied to the aristocracy and the caste system, often lobbied to protect its market turf and frustrated reforms. This has prevented some businesses, like international travel companies, from operating in Nepal, hindering competition and growth in the tourism sector. The state still plays a significant role in the economy, and different regimes have favored different groups over the years. This has meant that the business class often engages in the politics of getting elected to business associations to access and influence the state for making a profit through getting quotas, licenses, or contracts rather than investing time and resources to professionalize industries and services. The business sector has missed plenty of opportunities to expand the economy as a result.[13]

Resources

Nepal does not have extensive mineral resources but is rich in water resources. Its hydropower potential is estimated to be the second highest in the world, after Brazil, at 83,290 megawatts.[14] The rivers that flow from the steep mountains have very high potential to generate electricity. Nepal has been trying to develop hydropower for export but has not succeeded. The only viable external market is India, but Nepal has not been able to reach an agreement with that country to rationalize building large hydropower projects. In such a context, the best chance for Nepal may be to develop smaller hydroelectric projects to meet its needs and to sell any surplus energy for profit.

Tourism is another sector with potential due to Nepal's diverse flora and fauna. The country is extremely beautiful, and the people are very hospitable. Tourism was developing steadily, but instability and law-and-order problems that emerged with the advent of the Maoist insurgency hindered its growth. As tourism declined, many hotels and tourism-related businesses went bankrupt. With the settlement of the Maoist insurgency, tourism has bounced back.

Since the 1980s, Nepal has developed a carpet industry, and since the 1990s it has expanded its garment industry. However, due to the lack of quality control and fickle international trends, both these sectors began to decline in the late 1990s. People with connections with the state benefitted by getting the export quotas in the sector, and such a policy meant that connections and networking mattered more than entrepreneurial ability.[15] This factor may have also contributed to the garment and carpet sector's decline.

A remittance economy has supported Nepal for a long time. Earlier, Nepalis working in the British and Indian armies and the Singapore police sent in remittances. People working in India also contributed. During the late 1990s, people increasingly began to go to East Asian countries like Malaysia and South Korea and the Middle Eastern countries for work. The trend increased as young people fled the villages to escape forced recruitment by the Maoists or perception as Maoist sympathizers by the security forces. The contribution of remittances to the economy has become so big that by 2009 they contributed 23 percent to GDP, and Nepal was the fifth remittance-receiving country in the world.[16]

Challenges

Nepal has witnessed success in various sectors. Literacy has risen. Infant mortality has decreased. Life expectancy has risen. More roads have been built, more telephone lines have been distributed, more people have access to drinking water, and so on. However, many challenges remain. As noted above, one-third of the people still live below the poverty line. Rural people, members of marginalized groups, and women face higher poverty and inequality. Many people have not accessed the benefits of development. Some regions, like Karnali, still occasionally witness hunger, famine, and starvation.

When the Maoists and the government settled their disagreements in 2006, a lot of hope was raised. A new constitution was to be drafted by representatives elected by the people, but the Constituent Assembly was dissolved in May 2012 without completing a new constitution. This state of not having a constitution has increased uncertainty, which is not good for the economy. The immediate challenge in Nepal is to complete a new constitution in a form and manner that is acceptable to the widest possible section of the people.

SUGGESTED READINGS

Acharya, Meena, Yubaraj Khatiwada, and Shankar Aryal. *Structural Adjustment Policies and Poverty Eradication*. Kathmandu: IIDS, 2003.

Bista, Dor Bahadur. *Fatalism and Development: Nepal's Struggle for Modernization*. Hyderabad: Orient Longman, 1991.

Blaikie, Piers, John Cameron, and David Seddon. *Nepal in Crisis: Growth and Stagnation at the Periphery*. Delhi: Oxford, 1980.

Deraniyagala, Sonali. "The Political Economy of Civil Conflict in Nepal." *Oxford Development Studies* 33, no. 1 (2005): 47–62.

Mahat, Ram Sharan. *In Defense of Democracy: Dynamics and Fault Lines of Nepal's Political Economy*. New Delhi: Adroit, 2005.

Panday, Devendra Raj. *Nepal's Failed Development: Reflections on the Mission and the Maladies*. Kathmandu: Nepal South Asia Center, 1999.

Seddon, David. *Nepal: A State of Poverty*. New Delhi: Vikash, 1987.

Shakya, Sujeec. *Unleashing Nepal: Past, Present and Future of the Economy*. New Delhi: Penguin Books, 2009.

Notes

1. UNDP, "Nepal," Human Development Indicators, http://hdrstats.undp.org/en/countries/profiles/NPL.html, and UNDP, "Select an Indicator," International Human Development Indicators, http://hdrstats.undp.org/en/indicators/default.html (accessed November 5, 2012).

2. UNICEF, "Nepal: Background," May 25, 2012, http://www.unicef.org/infobycountry/nepal_nepal_background.html.

3. Devendra Raj Panday, *Nepal's Failed Development: Reflections on the Mission and the Maladies* (Kathmandu: Nepal South Asia Center, 1999).

4. World Bank, "Nepal: Country at a Glance," http://www.worldbank.org/en/country/nepal (accessed November 5, 2012).

5. Piers Blaikie, John Cameron, and David Seddon, *Nepal in Crisis: Growth and Stagnation at the Periphery* (Delhi: Oxford, 1980).

6. Dor Bahadur Bista, *Fatalism and Development: Nepal's Struggle for Modernization* (Hyderabad: Orient Longman, 1991).

7. Kishor Sharma, "The Political Economy of Civil War in Nepal," *World Development* 34, no. 7 (2006): 1237–1253; Sonali Deraniyagala, "The Political Economy of Civil Conflict in Nepal," *Oxford Development Studies* 33, no. 1 (2005): 47–62.

8. Meena Acharya, Yubaraj Khatiwada, and Shankar Aryal, *Structural Adjustment Policies and Poverty Eradication* (Kathmandu: IIDS, 2003).

9. Ram Sharan Mahat, *In Defense of Democracy: Dynamics and Fault Lines of Nepal's Political Economy* (New Delhi: Adroit Publishers, 2005).

10. Mahat, *In Defense of Democracy*; Acharya, Khatiwada, and Aryal, *Structural Adjustment Policies*.

11. Sujeev Shakya, *Unleashing Nepal: Past, Present and Future of the Economy* (New Delhi: Penguin Books, 2009).

12. Mahat, *In Defense of Democracy*.

13. Shakya, *Unleashing Nepal*, and Mallika Shakya, "Nepali Economic History Through the Ethnic Lens: Changing State Alliances with Business Elite," in *Nationalism and Ethnic Conflict in Nepal*, ed. Mahendra Lawoti and Susan Hangen (London: Routledge, 2012), 58–82.

14. Vinod Prasad Shrestha, *A Concise Geography of Nepal* (Kathmandu: Mandala Book Point, 2007).

15. Shakya, "Nepali Economic History Through the Ethnic Lens."

16. World Bank, *Migration and Remittance Factbook 2011*, 2nd ed. (Washington, DC: World Bank, 2011), available at http://siteresources.worldbank.org/INTLAC/Resources/Factbook2011-Ebook.pdf (accessed November 5, 2012).

PART VI

SOUTH ASIA

0   1000 Miles

0   1000 Km

30

The Future: South Asia as a Region and a Player in the World System

The past twenty-nine chapters have examined each of the major nation-states of South Asia. In this final chapter we look at the region as a whole and discuss the major issues it faces. As South Asia emerges as an important actor in world affairs, the region must address the most serious issues that can harm its development and growth. The first and foremost of these is its relationship with the rest of the world, followed by two major conflicts between the countries of the region. After a discussion of these issues, the final sections of the chapter examine continuing efforts to create a national identity in the region and the rise of militant Islam.

Foreign Affairs

The strategic location of South Asia makes it an area of importance in the world system. Pakistan is almost as much a part of Southwest Asia as it is of South Asia, given its proximity to the Persian Gulf and its border with Iran. It is also a neighbor of Afghanistan and looks beyond that country toward a major role in central Asia and that region's newly independent states. India, as the second most populous nation in the world, is important not only in terms of its geographic location but also as a huge market, a destination for foreign direct investment, a rapidly growing technological power, a longtime leader among third world nations, and an active and effective participant in Asian economic, strategic, and cultural activities. Both India and Pakistan, as nuclear powers, are important players in the diplomacy of nuclear weapons and missile proliferation and nonproliferation. Sri Lanka, which extends south into the Indian Ocean, sits across some of the world's important shipping lanes. Bangladesh lies adjacent to the volatile eastern regions of India. Despite efforts to entangle the country in the rise of global Islamic militancy, barring sporadic incidents inside its borders, Bangladesh has been able to avoid becoming embroiled in it. At the same time, it has actively pursued an international peacekeeping role for itself.

The region sits astride Indian Ocean sea lanes that are critical for oil trade between Asia and the Middle East and for peaceful commerce in the Indian Ocean area that involves Africa and Australia as well as the interests of key US allies in the vast region. The Indian Ocean is a pathway for the military, air, and naval movement of the major global and regional powers during wars and crises (e.g., in Afghanistan and Iraq) and humanitarian disasters (e.g., the 2004 tsunami). Two major US military commands—the Pacific and Central commands—maintain access to the Indian Ocean, since the area is a part of their operational jurisdiction.

Growing interregional interactions between South Asia and its neighbors suggest that the political, economic, military, and cultural boundaries of the Cold War era no longer make sense. Then it made sense to place central Asia as a part of the Soviet Union, Iran as a part of the Middle East, and Afghanistan and Burma (now Myanmar) as parts of the Middle East and Southeast Asia, respectively, on the basis of the pattern and intensity of interactions among members of each region. In the twenty-first century, this pattern no longer prevails. Terrorism, illicit drug trade, and weapons proliferation, as well as changing patterns of intensity in interactions between South Asian states and those in central Asia, Southeast Asia, China, and the Indian Ocean area, indicate that territorial borders are no longer working as boundaries or limits of state and nonstate actions. For example, Chinese rail and road links in the Tibetan region are planned for extension into Nepal and Pakistan, while China and India plan to revive the World War II Stillwell Road through Myanmar that ferried Western supplies to fight Japan's military expansionism. The expansion of the North Atlantic Treaty Organization (NATO) into Afghanistan and the US military expansion into central Asia indicate that contemporary wars and crises will make interregionalism the basis of academic and policy analysis in the twenty-first century. We also see the increased presence of nontraditional players in the South Asian, Middle Eastern, and Indian Ocean scene—for example, the buildup of Israeli-Indian diplomatic and defense ties, Saudi Arabia's growing interest in checking extremist influence within the kingdom and its neighborhood in South Asia and the Persian Gulf, and Japan's buildup of its economic and strategic ties with India and its naval presence in the Indian Ocean. These changes appear irreversible and indicate a sea change in the politics and policies in the region, as well as a rapidly changing international environment.

India's Relations Outside the Region

It is interesting to note that India rejected dominion status within the British Commonwealth of Nations in its Lahore Resolution of 1930 but accepted a similar offer at independence in 1947. When India became a republic under the constitution of 1950, the pattern of the Commonwealth was altered. Previously, all members of the Commonwealth had accepted the British monarch as monarch of their newly independent states as well (as in Canada or Australia). But in India's case, it was agreed that India would remain a member of the Commonwealth as a republic but accept the British monarch as occupying a symbolic position as head of the Commonwealth. The pattern applied to India has been followed by many of the members of the Commonwealth that have become independent since World War II, including Pakistan, Bangladesh, and Sri Lanka.

India had already set another precedent for the colonies of Great Britain by organizing a political party that looked beyond the achievement of freedom to the creation of a polity, economy, and society following independence. Many of the parties in other colonies used the word "congress" to denote a party seeking freedom. Relations between the Indian National Congress and other freedom movements were often close—a situation India could build on after independence to assert its leadership in what was called the third world. Jawaharlal Nehru, who participated in the Bandung (Indonesia) Conference in 1955, is credited with being one of the three principal leaders involved in forming the Nonaligned Movement (the other two being Gamal Abdel Nasser of Egypt and Marshal Josef Broz Tito of Yugoslavia).

Nonalignment was a part of Nehru's creed. To him, it meant avoiding alignment with either of the two blocs led by the superpowers, the United States and the Soviet Union. It did not mean neutrality. Nehru maintained that India reserved the right to take whatever position on an issue best served India's interests. However, such interests often seemed to US governments to favor the Soviet view over the American. During the Cold War India tilted toward Moscow on a number of important diplomatic issues, such as the Korean War and the China question, appearing to blame the United States for the Cold War and to see the Soviet Union as inclined toward peace. Nehru was ambivalent about Soviet interventions in Eastern Europe (e.g., Hungary in 1956) and lost the moral high ground in Western eyes as a result. Soviet diplomatic and military support regarding Kashmir, Pakistan, and China, as well as Nehru's economic socialism and the military buildup after 1962, showed that despite Nehru's declarations about nonalignment, he tilted toward Moscow.

The stance on nonalignment that Nehru had advocated for India was further eroded after his death when his daughter, Indira Gandhi, signed a treaty of friendship with the Soviet Union in 1971. The agreement stated that the two countries would consult with each other when either was threatened by a third party. This treaty, an alliance in all but name, formalized the India–Soviet Union alignment. India under Nehru had protested strongly when Pakistan joined the Central Treaty Organization (CENTO) and Southeast Asia Treaty Organization (SEATO) alliances with the West in the 1950s on the grounds that the alliance arrangements would bring one of the superpowers into the subcontinent. This argument apparently did not concern Indira Gandhi in 1971. The treaty was renewed in 1991, and the Soviet Union collapsed shortly thereafter.

The Soviet Union was by far the largest supplier of military equipment to the Indian military as well as an important trading partner. It also provided both diplomatic and military support during India's conflict with China in 1962. India, however, maintained a somewhat more neutral stance during its leadership of the Nonaligned Movement beginning in 1983. For instance, India favored the Soviet withdrawal from Afghanistan but continued to support the Soviet puppet regime that was left behind in that country. After the Soviet Union collapsed, India found itself looking to the industrialized countries (especially the United States) for much-needed technology and investment in contrast to its earlier reliance on the Soviet Union for military and technical assistance. Indian relations with the United States improved during the presidency of Bill Clinton. When India conducted its nuclear tests in 1998, the Clinton approach was to engage in a nuclear dialogue, separating the nuclear issue from other issues, while building areas of convergence. President George W. Bush went even further. His agreements with India announced in 2005 and 2006 recognized the need to bring India into the global economic and strategic mainstream by recognizing its nuclear-energy needs and the value of international nuclear cooperation with India. President Barack Obama has continued the Bush policy of bringing India into the global mainstream.

India's relations with China appeared to be close after communist forces gained power in 1949. The slogan *Hindi-Chini bhai bhai* ("Indians and Chinese are brothers") was frequently heard. However, relations cooled when India discovered that China had built a road between Sinkiang and Tibet across the Aksai Chin in Ladakh, which India believed to be its territory. China also disputed the legitimacy of the border in the northeast, demarcated by the 1914

McMahon Line. Accordingly, China claimed much of Northeast India, all of Bhutan, and parts of Nepal, Kashmir, and Uttar Pradesh. In October 1962 war broke out between China and India, and Indian forces suffered a humiliating defeat, especially in the Northeast Frontier Agency (now Arunachal Pradesh). China withdrew unilaterally but made it clear to all that India had been given a black eye. Diplomatic and trade relations between the two states have since improved (e.g., ambassadors have once again been exchanged and visits at high levels have taken place). But until recently China treated India as a subregional power. Now, due to India's economic growth, its nuclear weapons status, and its strategic partnership with the United States, China has started to negotiate seriously with India on many important issues, such as the border and China's nuclear and missile aid to Pakistan. China no longer wholly champions Pakistan's position on Kashmir and urges a bilateral and peaceful settlement. However, mistrust remains. China opposes the US-Indian nuclear-energy supply deal and insists on India's denuclearization. India remains adamant in its demand that the territory occupied by China in the Aksai Chin be returned to India. China has proposed the application of the "watershed principle" in both the northeast (i.e., essentially the McMahon Line) and the Aksai Chin. Complicating the Indian-Chinese relationship has been the growth of ties between Sri Lanka and China. The Mahinda Rajapaksa government in Sri Lanka has utilized Chinese funding and workers to build a major seaport in southern Sri Lanka. The Chinese presence in Sri Lanka is a Chinese effort to isolate India in the region.

India and the United States have had a love-hate relationship. Historically, US investment in India has been modest. The opening up of the Indian economy in the 1990s, however, has greatly increased investment in India from the United States and other developed countries. India, as mentioned earlier, strongly opposed the US relationship with Pakistan, especially its provision of sophisticated military equipment to Pakistan. The United States still supplies arms to Pakistan, but now the context is different. Washington is sensitive to Indian fears of Pakistani military adventurism and misuse of US arms, and the United States has developed robust defense ties with India under the view that India should be built up as a major global power. Moreover, with growing military capacity, India no longer sees Pakistani military growth as changing the balance of power. With growing self-confidence and political maturity, India no longer brackets itself with Pakistan and sees itself as an emerging power in a changing global context.

Indeed US-Indian relations have improved markedly in recent years. Presidents Clinton and Bush visited India during their terms in office. President Obama visited India in November 2010 and expressed support for a permanent

Indian seat on the United Nations Security Council. US presidential interest in India reflects the growing importance of economic relations between the two countries. President George W. Bush stunned the world in 2005 by waiving economic sanctions that the United States had imposed on India following its testing of nuclear weapons in 1998. This exemption required major changes in US nonproliferation laws and international nuclear-trading regulations.

Pakistan's Foreign Relations

Faced with the disadvantage of being the new country following the partition of India and being in conflict with its larger coinheritor of the British Raj, Pakistan believed that it had to look outside the subcontinent for possible allies in defending itself against what it thought would eventually be an Indian bid to reunify South Asia.

Pakistan lobbied for and accepted Western offers to join the ring of security pacts built in the 1950s to close the gap between US commitments in Europe (through NATO) and those in East Asia (following the Korean War). Pakistan in 1955 joined SEATO, along with Thailand and the Philippines, and CENTO, along with Iraq (briefly, until 1958), Iran, and Turkey. Its negotiations with the United States also brought US military assistance through agreements initiated in 1954. This assistance met with strong objections from India, which perceived that the purposes of the United States and Pakistan were very different: Pakistan accepted the weapons as protection against India, whereas the United States provided them in an effort to build strength against possible Soviet or Chinese action. (For details of Pakistani-US relations, see Chapter 13.)

Pakistan's relations with the Soviet Union, never very close to begin with, were severely damaged by the Soviet invasion of Afghanistan in 1979. Since the breakup of the Soviet Union, however, Pakistan has looked toward the central Asian republics as an area for economic expansion, though for the time being this possibility is stymied by the continuing war in Afghanistan. By contrast, Pakistan has had close and valuable relations with China, owing in part to the chronic rift between India and China. The Chinese supported Pakistan diplomatically in 1965 and 1971, and China has provided important military aid. Moreover, Pakistan played a key role in facilitating the visit of Henry Kissinger to China in 1971, which led to the opening of Sino-American relations. China has been a staunch supporter of Pakistan, given their common enmity with India and Pakistan's utility as a pathway for China's influence in the Gulf and Middle Eastern Muslim world. But the convergence of interests between the two countries is not total. And as China has sought to rebuild its commercial, political, and strategic links with India, the triangularity of the China-Pakistan-India linkage has weakened. Since the 1960s Beijing had seen South Asia through Islamabad's eyes. Now its perspective has become more balanced and fluid.

Since 1971, Pakistan has expanded its ties with the Islamic countries of the Middle East. The religious ties are close, but the economic ties have been even more important. Trade has expanded greatly, and Pakistani migrant workers have found employment in the Gulf states. Remittances from workers abroad account for the largest single item in Pakistan's foreign exchange earnings. Pakistan has also had military relationships with several countries, including Saudi Arabia, Jordan, Oman, and the United Arab Emirates.

Bangladesh Emerges

At independence Bangladesh found itself in close association with India and the Soviet Union and was subject to delayed recognition by the United States and China. Relations with India are defined by the party in power in Bangladesh, with relationships becoming more friendly during Awami League governance and distant when the Bangladesh Nationalist Party is in power. Since January 2007 Bangladesh has pursued a steadier and more balanced relationship with India. Relations with Russia have generally remained correct, if not particularly cordial, throughout.

The United States recognized Bangladesh in early 1972, and the anger that resulted from the US tilt toward Pakistan in the liberation war has largely dissipated. US-Bangladeshi relations are now built on bilateral assistance, the US need to prevent China from becoming the dominant power in Bangladesh, and commercial preferential treatment sought by Bangladesh for its textile products.

China's recognition of Bangladesh followed that of Pakistan. The Chinese have provided some economic assistance as well as a small amount of military aid, primarily for the air force. In 2000, Bangladesh agreed to purchase MiG-29s from the Soviet Union. China has developed its defense ties because of its strategic location and as a line of pressure against India's northeastern areas, just as Pakistan has served as a line of pressure on India's western and Kashmiri fronts.

Bangladesh's location has prompted it to reach out to Southeast Asia, while its majority religion has drawn it close to the countries of the Middle East. Southeast Asia provides a limited market and is a source of open-market purchases of rice, whereas the Middle East has been a source of economic assistance and an outlet for migrant workers from Bangladesh. Bangladesh receives economic assistance from many other sources as well, Japan being the largest donor. The discovery of natural gas is a positive development for its economy, and its eastward economic orientation involving Myanmar and other Southeast Asian states is a promising channel for its development, pending settlement of controversies with India and in its internal political arrangements.

With India and Pakistan embroiled in regional and strategic positioning, Bangladesh carved out its own sphere of influence in two areas. It gained regional influence in the mid-1980s by pushing for regional cooperation and is currently seeking a global strategic role by becoming the critical country involved in international peacekeeping operations. The award of the Nobel Prize to a Bangladeshi citizen, Muhammad Yunus, for his innovative work with nongovernmental microlending points to the importance of civil society work in Bangladesh and further lends credence to the country's international role in this arena.

Nepal: From Isolated Kingdom to Major Player in the Region

Nepal's international affairs have largely focused on India and China. Many of its concerns have dealt with questions of trade, transit, and defense. Regarding the latter issue, India has had troops stationed in Nepal to monitor Chinese movements across the Himalayas in the Tibet region of China. This arrangement has ended, however, as Nepal (which tries to maintain equal relations with its two neighbors) objected. Also, there is a psychological dimension to the relationship. Nepal is a predominantly Hindu kingdom, but nationalism among the Nepalese centers on the fear of Indian domination and resentment of India's attitude. India, however, gives Nepal a special status by its policy of an open border with Nepal, recruitment of Nepalese Gorkhas into the Indian army, and commitment to Nepal's development. India's difficulties with China and the buildup of Chinese road and rail links in Tibet ensure that Nepal is of long-term geopolitical value in Indian security planning and diplomacy.

The trade and transit issues have created strains in Indo-Nepalese relations, particularly in the 1980s. India and Nepal assumed treaty obligations concerning trade and security, which are meant in part to ensure Nepal's buffer status vis-à-vis China. A key provision was that Nepalese defense requirements would be met by arms imports from India. In 1987 Nepal toyed with the idea of Chinese arms importation. India questioned the need and asked Nepal either to abandon its special links with India or to maintain India's special position regarding its defense ties with Nepal. India imposed a trade embargo on Nepal. A nasty spat followed, the Nepalese king and his advisers realized that China could not replace India in meeting Nepal's needs, and the treaty relationship was confirmed.

Nepal has emerged as a major player in the region and a center of action and change that involves the attention of Pakistan, China, India, and the West. Pakistan, China, and Bangladesh played on anti-Indian sentiments in Nepalese public opinion. India alleges that Pakistan's Inter-Services Intelligence has used Nepal as a base of insurgency against Indian targets. In addition, India played a role in the resolution of the Maoist insurrection in order to diminish the power of the palace, bring the Maoist guerrillas into the democratic political process, and strengthen the position of Nepal's weak party system. Despite the difficulties in Indo-Nepali relations, the open border remains a sign of a unique relationship as well as recognition of the importance of assured mutual dependency. It should also be noted that the border between China and Nepal is such that commerce is severely restricted by topographical factors.

Nepal does have leverage in one respect that is of importance to India and potentially to Bangladesh: the rising of many key tributaries of the Ganges in Nepal. Storage and hydroelectric dam sites in Nepal can regulate the flow of the Ganges and provide power for export from Nepal to India. They could also be part of a long-term solution to the Farakka Barrage problem between Bangladesh and India.

Sri Lanka: From Model Colony to Civil War

After independence, Sri Lanka, under the leadership of the United National Party of D. S. Senanayake and Sir John Kotelawala, generally maintained close ties with the West, especially with Great Britain, which provided the largest market for Sri Lankan goods and also maintained a naval base at Trincomalee. The somewhat leftist regimes of the two Bandaranaikes (S. W. R. D. and Sirimavo) ended the naval arrangement, and Sri Lanka began to associate more closely with the East, developing close trade ties with China. This was the view of many in the West, although Sri Lankans would aver that Sri Lanka was actually moving toward a stance of more balanced nonalignment. Sri Lanka annoyed India in 1962 by joining in a third world proposal to end the Sino-Indian War—calling for mediation rather than an acceptance of the Indian view. Sri Lanka also became the leader of the Nonaligned Movement in 1976 and gained greater recognition of its position in the world. Sri Lanka has greatly opened its economy and is using its highly educated labor force to serve as an offshore manufacturing base.

The civil war and postconflict issues in Sri Lanka have dominated its relations with the rest of the world. The Liberation Tigers of Tamil Eelam (LTTE) established an international fund-raising network with extensive activities in Great Britain, France, Canada, and the United States, where they raised money from the well-educated Tamil expatriate community. In response to the international reach of the LTTE, the Sri Lankan government established close military relations with potential military suppliers and established a strong propaganda network to counter LTTE lobbying in the West. During the war, the United States at times provided both armaments and training to the Sri Lankan military. The US State Department also placed the LTTE on its list of terrorist organizations.

Sri Lanka's postwar policies have focused on trying to prevent Tamil expatriate groups from bringing war crimes charges against the government. China, Russia, and Iran emerged as close allies of the Rajapaksa government during the last years of the war and continue to work closely with the government.

Interests of the Major Powers

US interests in South Asia fall into five categories. First, the United States would like to see the nations of South Asia settle disputes through negotiation rather than open conflict. Second, the United States supports democratic regimes responsive to the wishes of the people in each nation. Third, the United States supports economic development of each nation with the goal of reasonable standards of living for all. Fourth, the United States neither seeks a position of primacy in the area nor wishes to see any other outside power gain such a position. Finally, since 2001, the United States has added the importance of pursuing the global war on terror in the region.

China's interests have been seen as generally compatible with those of the United States. China feared an expanded Soviet presence in South Asia and accused both the Soviet Union and India of seeking hegemony in the region. China therefore worked closely with Pakistan and Bangladesh on many issues, such as Afghanistan. China maintained that it was prepared to negotiate its outstanding border problems with India, but negotiations produced only ritualistic declarations until recently. Indian-Chinese relations have improved significantly in recent years.

The Soviet Union anchored its policy toward South Asia on its close relationship with India. In return, it received diplomatic support from India on a wide variety of issues ranging from Afghanistan to Kampuchea. India found the alliance useful, as the Soviets not only constituted a good market for its exports but also, and more importantly, supplied military equipment. At the same time, many Indians believed that the former Soviet Union was far behind the West in industrial and military technology. Following the collapse of the Soviet Union, the South Asian states—especially India—are in the process of sorting out relationships with Russia and the other countries of the former Soviet

Union. Russia is reemerging as a major power in European, Middle Eastern, and Far Eastern affairs, and Indian strategists are aware of its growing importance and of the value of maintaining substantial military and economic links with Russia even as the world is eyeing the rapid rise of China.

Regional Affairs: South Asian Association for Regional Cooperation

In August 1983 the seven South Asian nations signed an agreement in New Delhi formally establishing the South Asian Regional Cooperation. The group was renamed when the 1983 agreement was ratified at a summit meeting in Dhaka in December 1985. It is now known as the South Asian Association for Regional Cooperation (SAARC).

SAARC was founded through the efforts of Bangladeshi president Ziaur Rahman, who was the first head of government to visit each of the other four major states of South Asia (India, Pakistan, Sri Lanka, and Nepal). Ziaur Rahman preached the importance, as he saw it, of the states coming together to work on economic, social, and technological matters as a prelude to political cooperation. India resisted at first, as it saw SAARC as a limitation on its strength; Pakistan also had misgivings as it feared that India would dominate the group. However, both were eventually persuaded that the formation of a regional group would be advantageous to all.

SAARC generally avoids political matters and shuns strictly bilateral issues, but it has agreed to explore a wide range of social, economic, environmental, and technological matters. Though a far cry from a common market, it has established a South Asian Preferential Trade Area under which each country, at its discretion, can lower tariffs on specific goods. This is thought by some to be a prelude to a South Asian Free Trade Agreement, but such an agreement appears to be at best a distant hope. Trade among the countries of South Asia (except between Nepal and India) is quite limited; each nation trades more with developed countries than with its neighbors. If trade within South Asia were to expand, however, India would surely benefit the most. Further, the annual summit meetings provide a means for private discussions between heads of government.

The formal establishment of SAARC raised the hope that disputes within the region would be moderated and solutions found—in short, that there would be no repetition of the three wars fought between India and Pakistan in 1948, 1965, and 1971. Arguably this goal has been achieved. However, the economic links between the member countries have remained minimal inasmuch as intraregional trade is infrequent (Indo-Nepali and Indo-Bhutanese trade being exceptions). Cultural links are also minimal, as the three largest states have been separated from each other for more than sixty years. Kolkata, for instance, is no longer the prime magnet for Bangladeshi Bengalis; nor is Lahore for Indian Punjabis. And although there are many Islamic pilgrimage sites in India and some Sikh shrines in Pakistan, they are important to only a small number of people. Still, SAARC plays a great potential role in such areas as technology, tourism, meteorology, and trade.

The twenty-first century is likely to see the growth of regionalism on a pan-Asian basis. Many Asian countries—from Japan to India, including China and the Southeast Asian nations—are involved in an interstate dialogue to develop economic and cultural links on a pan-Asian basis. Such a movement is likely to place subregional rivalries into a narrow box of manageable controversies. The challenge before South Asian leaders is to think outside the box and create new situations that produce paradigmatic changes.

Regional Conflicts

As South Asia emerges as an important actor in world affairs, it must resolve the major issues that prevent regional unity. While there are many issues, several are serious and have defied resolution. Most important are the conflicts between Pakistan and India and the chronic dispute between Bangladesh and India concerning water resources. While there are other important regional conflicts, space considerations limit us to a brief discussion of these two.

Conflict Between India and Pakistan

The issue of contention between India and Pakistan that has caused the greatest difficulty and drawn the most international attention is that involving Kashmir. In brief, at the time of independence in 1947, the ruling princes of the Indian states (see Chapter 1) were given a choice as to which of the two successor states, India or Pakistan, they wished to join. At this early stage joining meant cession of powers over defense, foreign affairs, and communications to one or the other state; as it turned out, it would eventually mean full integration into the state chosen. All but three of the more than five hundred princes decided quickly to accede to one state or the other, taking into consideration primarily the geographic location of the state and the religious majority of its people. Two of the states that delayed—Hyderabad (the most populous of the princely states, whose Muslim ruler desired independence even though Hyderabad was surrounded by Indian territory) and Junagadh (a small state with a Muslim prince who acceded to Pakistan despite its majority Hindu population)—were eventually merged with India by force.

The third state, Kashmir, remains a problem that has not been formally and finally settled. Had the princely states been subject to partition as the provinces were, Kashmir might have been divided as its minority Hindu population lived in a clearly defined area bordering India. Moreover, the majority-Muslim community and its also fairly well-defined area could have joined Pakistan, although that would have left a sparsely populated Buddhist area, Ladakh, on the Chinese border to be argued about. The maharaja, however, wished to retain control of the state and desired independence; the British were not willing to consider this an option. The maharaja then concluded "standstill" agreements with both India and Pakistan. These agreements stipulated that official services, such as post and transport, would continue unhindered. The maharaja also faced internal demands for constitutional rule from the multicommunal party known as the National Conference, led by Sheikh Muhammad Abdullah, a close friend of Nehru.

In October 1947, Muslim tribesmen from Pakistan began a series of raids into Kashmir and detached some of the northern and western areas of the state as governments independent of the ruler in the capital of Srinagar. The northern areas have since been, in a de facto sense, incorporated into Pakistan, and the western areas, including Muzaffarabad, have been designated as the independent state Azad Kashmir (Free Kashmir), an entity not recognized by any country except Pakistan. The threat to Srinagar caused the maharaja to appeal to India for assistance, which was given only after the maharaja acceded to India on October 26, 1947. The accession was accepted by the government of India the following day with the proviso that the will of the people would be ascertained after conditions in the state had returned to normal.[1] The maharaja subsequently installed a new government under Sheikh Muhammad Abdullah. Because Indian troops were involved, Pakistani troops also entered the war.

India brought the matter of what it called "Pakistani aggression" to the United Nations in January 1948. Resolutions of the Security Council in August 1948 and January 1949 made provisions for a Pakistani withdrawal and the withdrawal of the bulk of the Indian troops preparatory to the holding of a plebiscite under United Nations auspices. A cease-fire became effective on January 1, 1949. A United Nations peacekeeping force was set up in the area (and, though small, remains to this day). Several attempts were made by Security Council representatives to implement the plebiscite agreement, but all failed. In 1954 Prime Ministers Jawaharlal Nehru of India and Muhammad Ali Bogra of Pakistan met in an attempt to resolve the difficulties, but they too were unsuccessful. Earlier, in 1953, Abdullah had been removed as prime minister of Jammu and Kashmir and arrested on the charge that he opposed the integration of the state into the Indian union. Abdullah was released in 1964 and returned to the state as chief minister in 1975—a post he held until his death in 1982. In 1958 another meeting was held between Nehru and Pakistani prime minister Firoz Khan Noon, but this also failed to produce a mutually satisfactory settlement of the issue.

The question of Kashmir continues to plague Indo-Pakistani relations. Pakistan still demands that the plebiscite be held, as required by the Security Council resolutions. India in turn maintains that the regular elections in the state have returned parties favoring integration with India and that these elections have served as a surrogate for the plebiscite; in the view of many observers, however, the elections were far from free and fair. India has thus responded that the only issue still to be resolved is the "vacation" of the Pakistani "aggression" in the northern area and in Azad Kashmir. Neither country has yet publicly recognized that these nonnegotiable demands are unrealistic and that only a compromise agreement can ultimately resolve the issue.

In the summer of 1965, disturbances in Kashmir signified (falsely, as it turned out) to the Pakistanis that Muslim Kashmiris in the Srinagar area were prepared to rebel against Indian rule and that, with some help from Pakistan, they would be successful. Apparently at the urging of the foreign minister, Zulfiqar Ali Bhutto, President Muhammad Ayub Khan authorized Pakistani troops to cross the 1949 cease-fire line and to invade Indian-held Kashmir. The result was a disaster for Pakistan. The Pakistanis had initially caused the Indian military situation in the Vale of Kashmir to become difficult by threatening the key land communications line, but India responded by attacking Pakistani Punjab at Lahore and Sialkot in early September. Within two and a half weeks, a cease-fire was arranged. Ayub and Indian prime minister Lal Bahadur Shastri met under the auspices of Soviet prime minister Aleksey Kosygin at Tashkent in January 1966 and arranged for a mutual withdrawal both in Kashmir and along the international boundary.

Kashmir also played a limited role in late 1971 when India entered the Bangladeshi liberation war. The cease-fire in December covered both the eastern (Bangladesh) and western (Kashmir and Punjab) fronts. The 1949 cease-fire line was modified to a limited extent by the 1972 Line of Control that separates the territories administered by India and Pakistan (or Azad Kashmir). The issue continued to fester. No Pakistani politician could publicly accept the status quo in Kashmir and expect to survive politically, whereas India could perhaps accept the present Line of Control as an international boundary. In 1989 and 1990 dissident Muslims in the Indian part of Kashmir raised demands, often violently, that the government of Farooq Abdullah, the sheikh's son, be dismissed. Then Indian prime minister V. P. Singh dismissed Farooq, but this did not quiet the situation. Civil order unraveled rapidly, and the ensuing violence between the Indian military and Muslim Kashmiri militants (many of whom advocated secession from India and Kashmiri independence) claimed thousands of lives. There was clear "moral" and material support for the militants from Pakistan, with Pakistan officially claiming that such support was unofficial and, in any case, justified by the draconian repression by the "Indian occupation forces" of the "freedom-loving peoples" of Kashmir. India held a different view—that Pakistan was the main cause of the conflict and was sponsoring "cross-border terrorism" against the legitimate government of Jammu and Kashmir (see Chapter 11). Numerous attempts have been made by both Pakistan and India to quiet the Kashmir dispute subsequently. The most promising initiative to date was the unprecedented visit of Prime Minister Atal Bihari Vajpayee to Lahore in February 1999 that resulted in the Lahore Declaration, which, among other things, called for a just settlement of the Kashmir conflict. But such hopes were dashed when Pakistan decided to occupy parts of "Indian-occupied Kashmir" in the spring of 1999—the so-called Kargil Operation. India strenuously contested the occupation, and a bloody if limited war erupted between India and Pakistan. India, with the diplomatic support of the United States, eventually prevailed, and the Pakistani forces were obliged to leave their positions, suffering many casualties as a result. The debacle of Kargil weakened the civilian government of Nawaz Sharif and was a contributing factor to Musharraf's military coup in October (see Chapter 12). It also effectively ended, for the time being, diplomatic efforts to solve the Kashmir dispute.

The Kargil Operation furthered the decline of relations between India and Pakistan, which reached new lows in December 2001 and again in November 2008. The December 2001 attack on the Lok Sabha in Delhi by Islamic militants resulted in Indian claims that the attackers were officially sponsored by the Pakistani government. Pakistan denied such involvement, but in subsequent months both India and Pakistan conducted threatening military exercises on their common border. Many worried about the prospect of a fourth war between India and Pakistan—and the first war between two states possessing nuclear weapons. Cooler heads and skillful international diplomatic intervention prevailed, but the optimistic days of the Vajpayee–Nawaz Sharif accord on Kashmir have so far not returned. In late November 2008, Pakistani Islamicists carried out eleven attacks across Mumbai, striking at the heart of the city and killing 163 people. Once again, both sides made claims and counterclaims. Kashmir remains unsettled, episodic violence is still chronic in the state, and the unresolved dispute continues to poison Pakistan-India relations.[2]

Other unresolved issues also continue to plague Pakistani-Indian relations, including Hindu-Muslim relations (each state claims that the other mistreats its respective minorities), and perhaps the world's longest-lasting pointless international conflict—the Siachin Glacier dispute.

One major dispute was resolved successfully, however, through international intervention—the division of the waters of the Indus River system. Immediately after partition the rivers from which irrigation canals branched were those running through India (i.e., the Ravi, the Sutlej, and the Beas Rivers), but the areas using the water were principally in Pakistan. India naturally wished to use these waters to develop and expand its irrigation systems, but in doing so (beginning in the late 1940s) it would leave the Pakistan areas without water. In response, Pakistan threatened to go to war. The flow was restored, but the Indian desire to use the waters was clearly communicated. During the 1950s the World Bank became involved and offered the two countries several plans for solving the problem. A treaty was signed by Nehru and Ayub Khan in 1960 under which the waters would be divided and international donors, including the World Bank, India, and most Western nations, would finance the building of replacement works in Pakistan. These works included two large storage dams at Mangla on the Jhelum and Tarbela on the Indus, several barrages designed to divert the waters of those two rivers and the Chenab, and a series of link canals to carry the water from the western rivers into the irrigation system formerly supplied by the eastern Ravi, Beas, and Sutlej. In turn, India was permitted to use the waters of the three eastern rivers. The plan, which was completed by the end of the 1960s (except for the dam at Tarbela), has worked exceptionally well. It has also demonstrated that the application of engineering solutions to a problem not charged with communal issues (as is Kashmir) could lead to a settlement that would meet most of the interests of each party.[3]

India and Bangladesh: Water Problems and Other Issues

In its initial period of independence, Bangladesh expressed strong gratitude for India's aid in the civil war. But this feeling dissipated quickly, despite the twenty-five-year treaty signed in March 1972.[4] Bangladeshis felt that the Indians were staying on too long after the war, especially in the Chittagong Hill Tracts, to the extent that they had almost become an occupying army. India, the Bangladeshis claimed, had taken charge of the prisoners and removed almost all of the captured Pakistani military equipment. And the Indian building of the Farakka Barrage on the Ganges River, which was completed in 1975, aroused strong anger toward India as well as toward Mujibur Rahman, who seemed to some to be unable to do anything to protect Bangladeshi interests.

During most of any given year, the flow in the Ganges is sufficient that India's withdrawal of 90,000 cubic feet per second (cusecs) has no significant impact on the flow received downstream in Bangladesh. But during the low-flow period in April and May, such a withdrawal would all but dry up the Ganges below Farakka in Bangladesh. Clearly the needs of both India and Bangladesh could not be met during this low-flow period.

It might be thought that the upper-lower riparian conflict could be settled along the lines of the Indus settlement. The political differences involved made that unlikely, however. According to the terms of the Indus settlement, India and Pakistan have almost total control over the rivers that are assigned to them. But this solution could not be applied to the Ganges waters, even if the Brahmaputra waters were taken into account, because both rivers then would be subject to Indian control. The Indians proposed building a link canal that would run from the Brahmaputra at a point just inside India, then across about 150 miles of Bangladeshi territory, and then empty into the Ganges just above Farakka in India. Bangladesh objected on the grounds that this plan would give India control of the intake on the Brahmaputra as well as the outflow on the Ganges and would also displace a large number of Bangladeshis.

In turn, Bangladesh has proposed that the flow of the Ganges be controlled by means of storage dams in Nepal on tributaries of the river. But India has objected on the grounds that, as the matter is bilateral, a third party should not be introduced into the discussions. The issue was the subject of regular meetings of a Joint Rivers Commission, but not until 1997 was a long-term agreement signed that provides for division of the waters during the dry season, a division that each side has termed "equitable," despite opposition by the Bangladesh Nationalist Party, which sees the agreement as an Awami League sellout to India.

The polarized party politics of Bangladesh and its external policies reveal a rising trend toward Islamic militancy within Bangladesh and its effect in Islamizing India's northwest. Also, Bangladeshi poverty and a porous border with India have stimulated mass illegal migration into India's northeast, and the demographic changes have increased prospects of political, economic, and social instability in the region.

The Growth of Terror and Extremism

While South Asia has struggled to democratize, the rise of Islamic extremism has posed the newest threat to the growth of democracy in Pakistan, Bangladesh, and Nepal and threatened to destabilize the Muslim communities in India and Sri Lanka. This has been added to the problem of developing national identities in each of the states.

South Asia is home to a number of organizations that appear on the US terrorist list. These include al-Qaeda, the Liberation Tigers of Tamil Eelam, and the Communist Party of Nepal (Maoist) (CPN [Maoist]). Both the LTTE and CPN (Maoist) have focused their activities within their own countries, while al-Qaeda has sought to create an international network of Muslims.

The Soviet invasion of Afghanistan in 1979 led President Jimmy Carter's national security adviser, Zbigniew Brzezinski, to try to make Afghanistan into Moscow's Vietnam. The mujahedeen, or freedom fighters, opposed to the Soviet Union were trained in military tactics and were well funded by the United States, China, and others. The Carter administration identified Pakistan as a frontline state and provided economic and military assistance to Pakistan and military supplies to the Afghan mujahedeen. During the war more than 3 million Afghans fled to Pakistan and perhaps another million to Iran. Pakistan, despite international assistance, found the cost of supporting these refugees to be a great burden on its economy and its political and social systems. It worked through the United Nations in an effort to find a means by which Soviet troops could be removed from Afghanistan and a nonaligned government free of outside interference established in Kabul. The first of these goals was met, as the Soviets completed their withdrawal in 1989. But the fall of the Muhammad Najibullah government in 1992 led to another civil war in Afghanistan, in which the Taliban movement (literally, "students movement") gained ascendancy and sought to recreate Afghan society along lines they imagined the Quran countenanced.

Following September 11, 2001, the United States launched a massive military campaign against the Taliban regime after it refused to expel al-Qaeda (blamed for the 9/11 attacks) from the country. The US military action drove the Taliban from power, but both al-Qaeda and the Taliban regrouped in southern Afghanistan and along the tribal frontier with Pakistan. Also, since 2001 Pakistan has been obliged to join the United States in its global war against terrorism. Consequently Pakistani authorities have killed or captured thousands of "Muslim insurgents" (mostly Afghans, Arabs, Uzbeks, or Tajiks) and turned many of them over to US and coalition authorities. Furthermore, since 2005 Pakistan has engaged in increasingly large-scale military operations, which have targeted the Federally Administered Tribal Areas, especially North and South Waziristan. The blowback from such military operations has been associated with the alarming rise of civil disorder within the settled areas of state. In 2007, Pakistan suffered the effects of over fifty suicide bombings and the deaths of over 3,500 individuals associated with acts of terrorism. The negative reaction to Pakistan's cooperation in the war on terror has forced the current government to be highly critical of US drone attacks and military actions inside the country's borders. The May 2, 2011, US raid on Osama bin Laden's compound in Abbottabad ignited anger among many Pakistanis. As a result, the government was forced to condemn the raid and ultimately to arrest and sentence to thirty-three years in prison a Pakistani doctor who helped the United States locate bin Laden. Despite some support for the Taliban and al-Qaeda in Pakistan, the Islamicist movement still appears to comprise a small minority in the South Asian states.

SUGGESTED READINGS

Baxter, Craig. *Bangladesh: From a Nation to a State.* Boulder, CO: Westview Press, 1997.

Bhutto, Zulfikar Ali. *The Myth of Independence.* Lahore: Oxford University Press, 1969.

Carnegie Endowment for International Peace. *Nuclear Weapons and South Asian Security.* Washington, DC: Carnegie Endowment for International Peace, 1988.

Choudhury, Dilara. *Bangladesh and the South Asian International System.* Buckhurst, UK: Scorpion, 1992.

De Silva, K. M. *Regional Powers and Small State Security: India and Sri Lanka, 1977–90.* Washington, DC: Woodrow Wilson Center Press, 1995.

Dutt, V. P. *India's Foreign Policy.* New Delhi: Vikas, 1985.

Ganguly, Sumit. *The Origins of War in South Asia.* Boulder, CO: Westview Press, 1986.

Hagerty, Devin T. *The Consequences of Nuclear Proliferation: Lessons from South Asia.* Cambridge, MA: MIT Press, 1998.

Hardgrave, Robert L., Jr. *India Under Pressure: Prospects for Political Stability.* Boulder, CO: Westview Press, 1984.

Jalal, Ayesha. *Democracy and Authoritarianism in South Asia: A Comparative and Historical Perspective.* New York: Cambridge University Press, 1995.

———. *The State of Martial Rule: The Origins of Pakistan's Political Economy of Defense.* Cambridge: Cambridge University Press, 1991.

Kohli, Atul. *Democracy and Discontent: India's Growing Crisis of Governability.* Cambridge: Cambridge University Press, 1990.

Kux, Dennis, *Estranged Democracies: India and the United States.* Thousand Oaks, CA: Sage, 1993.

Lamb, Alastair. *Crisis in Kashmir, 1947–1966.* London: Routledge & Kegan Paul, 1966.

———. *Kashmir: A Disputed Legacy, 1846–1990.* New York: Oxford University Press, 1991.

Lu, Chih H. *The Sino-Indian Border Dispute.* Westport, CT: Greenwood, 1986.

Mansingh, Surjit. *India's Search for Power: Indira Gandhi's Foreign Policy, 1966–1982.* Beverly Hills, CA: Sage, 1984.

Maxwell, Neville. *India's China War.* London: Jonathan Cape, 1970.

Michel, Aloys A. *The Indus Rivers: A Study of the Effects of Partition.* New Haven, CT: Yale University Press, 1967.

Palmer, Norman D. *The United States and India: The Dimensions of Influence.* New York: Praeger, 1984.

Rizvi, Hasan Askari. *Internal Strife and External Intervention: India's Role in Civil War in East Pakistan Bangladesh.* Lahore: Progressive Publishers, 1981.

———. *The Military and Politics in Pakistan.* 3rd ed. Lahore: Progressive, 1986.

Rose, Leo E., and John T. Scholz. *Nepal: Profile of a Himalayan Kingdom.* Boulder, CO: Westview Press, 1980.

Talbot, Ian. *Pakistan: A Modern History.* London: Hurst, 1998.

Thomas, Raju G. C. *Indian Security Policy.* Princeton, NJ: Princeton University Press, 1986.

Vertzberger, Yaacov Y. I. *Misconceptions in Foreign Policy Making: The Sino-Indian Conflict, 1959–1962.* Boulder, CO: Westview Press, 1984.

————. *The Enduring Entente: Sino-Pakistan Relations, 1960–1980*. New York: Praeger, 1983.

Wirsing, Robert. *Kashmir in the Shadow of War: Regional Rivalries in a Nuclear Age*. New York: Sharpe, 2003.

————. *Pakistan's Security Under Zia, 1977–1988: The Policy Imperatives of a Peripheral Asian State*. New York: St. Martin's, 1991.

Ziring, Lawrence, ed. *The Sub-continent in World Affairs: India, Its Neighbors, and the Great Powers*. New York: Praeger, 1982.

NOTES

1. The text of the maharaja's letter of accession and Lord Mountbatten's reply on behalf of the government of India are contained in Josef Korbel, *Danger in Kashmir,* rev. ed. (Princeton, NJ: Princeton University Press, 1966), 80–83.

2. Robert Wirsing, *Kashmir in the Shadow of War: Regional Rivalries in a Nuclear Age* (New York: Sharpe, 2003). For a useful discussion of attitudes of Indians and Pakistanis toward the Kashmir dispute, see Kashmir Study Group, *The Kashmir Dispute at Fifty: Charting Paths to Peace* (Livingston, NY: Kashmir Study Group, 1997).

3. Aloys A. Michel, *The Indus Rivers: A Study of the Effects of Partition* (New Haven, CT: Yale University Press, 1967).

4. The treaty was not renewed when it expired in 1997.

STATISTICAL APPENDIX

	India	Pakistan	Bangladesh	Sri Lanka	Nepal
Population (millions)	1,241.49	173.6	148.7	20.7	30.0
Area (thousands of square miles)	1,269.3	310.4	55.6	25.3	56.8
GDP per capita (current $)	1,375	1,019	675	2,400	535
GDP per capita (purchasing power parity, US$)	3,373	2,676	1,652	5,106	1,198
Average annual GDP per capita growth (1990–2005)	4.2	1.3	2.9	3.7	2
Average annual growth rate GDP (2011)	6.9	2.4	6.7	8.3	3.9
Average annual growth rate of value added in agriculture	2.8	1.2	5.0	5.0	4.5
Average annual growth rate of value added in manufacturing	2.5	3.0	9.5	6.0	2.3
Total GDP (millions of current US$)		211,091	110,612	591	189
Distribution of GDP (2006)					
Agriculture	17.2	21.6	18.4	13.7	38.1
Manufacturing	13.9	14.5	18.2	17.2	6.4
Services	56.4	53.1	53.0	58.5	46.6
Percentage of population without electricity	33.7	37.6	59.0	23.4	56.4
Merchandise trade (percentage of 2006 GDP)	40.4	33.1	54.8	51.0	35.5
Exports	24.6	11.9	22.7	24.12	8.9
Imports	29.8	15.9	31.2	36.2	32.8
Official development assistance per capita (in US$)	2.30	17.36	9.52	28.02	27.32
Debt service ratio as percentage of GNI	1.2	2.4	0.9	3.0	1.2
Debt value as percentage of GNI	17.7	24.1	16.2	36.6	19.9

(continues)

STATISTICAL APPENDIX *(continued)*

	India	Pakistan	Bangladesh	Sri Lanka	Nepal
Foreign direct investment as percentage of GDP	1.4	1.1	0.9	1.0	0.6
Human Development Index	0.547	0.504	0.500	0.691	0.458
Gender Inequality Index	0.645	0.611	0.597	0.447	0.665
Population Growth, average percentage					
1975–2005	2	2.8	2.2	1.1	2.3
2011	1.4	1.8	1.2	1.0	1.7
Urbanization (2005)	31.2	36.2	28.4	15.1	17.0
Infant mortality (per 1,000 births)	48.6	60.4	38.6	10.8	40.6
Percentage of population with access to Births attended by a skilled					
health professional	52.7	31	26.5	96	11
Improved water source	92	92	81	91	89
Improved sanitation	34	48	56	92	31
Life expectancy	65.5	65.2	68.9	74.7	68.4
Male	63.9	64.3	68.2	71.7	67.9
Female	67.1	66.1	69.7	77.9	69.6
Adult literacy	74.0	55.5	55.9	90.6	59.1
Male	82.1	68.9	60.7	92.2	72.0
Female	65.5	40.1	51.0	89.1	46.9
Schooling, expected years	10.3	6.9	8.1	12.7	8.8
CO2 emissions per capita (tons)	1.46	0.97	0.32	0.58	0.12
Inequality measures, ratio of richest 10 percent to poorest 10 percent	8.6	6.0	6.8	11.1	7.3
Central government expenditures as percentage of GDP					
Defense	2.8	3.2	1.3	3.0	1.6
Education	3.1	2.4	2.2	2.1	4.7
Health	1.2	0.8	1.2	1.3	1.8
Women in parliament (%)	10.8	22.2	18.6	5.8	33.2
Women in ministerial positions (%)	10.2	3.6	8.3	5.7	20.0

Sources: World Bank, World Development Indicators, http://data.worldbank.org/data-catalog/world
-development-indicators, and United Nations Development Programme, "International Human Development
Indicators," Human Development Reports, http://hdrstats.undp.org/en/indicators/default.html.

INDEX